JAMES MORTON OMNIBUS

Gangland Volume 1
Gangland Volume 2

JAMES MORTON

CW00894228

timewarner
paperbacks

A *Time Warner* Paperback

This omnibus edition first published in Great Britain by
Time Warner Paperbacks in 2003
James Morton Omnibus Copyright © James Morton 2003

Previously published separately:
Gangland Volume 1 first published in Great Britain in 1992 by
Little, Brown and Company
Published by Warner Books in 1993
Reprinted 1993 (twice), 1994 (three times), 1995 (twice), 1996,
1997, 1998, 1999, 2000, 2001
Copyright © James Morton 1992

Gangland Volume 2 first published in Great Britain in 1994 by
Little, Brown and Company
Published by Warner Books in 1995
Reprinted 1996 (twice), 1998, 1999, 2000, 2001
Copyright © James Morton 1994

A CIP catalogue record for this book
is available from the British Library.

ISBN 0 7515 3515 X

Printed and bound in Great Britain by
Clays Ltd, St Ives plc

Time Warner Paperbacks
An imprint of
Time Warner Books UK
Brettenham House
Lancaster Place
London WC2E 7EN

www.TimeWarnerBooks.co.uk

Gangland Volume 1

Contents

Photograph Credits

For Dock Bateson with love

Introduction

On 8 March 1882 C. Vincent at Scotland Yard wrote in beautiful copperplate to the Clerk of Arraigns at the Old Bailey:

> I have to request that you will have the goodness to furnish me with copies of Mr Justice Hawkins' observations as to the prevalency of organized bands of roughs in the metropolis, as expressed by him at the trial of Galliers and Casey for manslaughter at the Central Criminal Court on the 4th inst and Kennedy and others for riot at Hackney.
>
> The Commander of the Metropolitan Police is particularly desirous of having that portion of the learned judge's remarks relating to the existence of 'gangs' on the streets and the alleged general lawlessness of the roughs. He would also like to have a copy of the evidence adduced in support of the statements that such bands do exist, and that on a certain occasion through the absence of police some roughs scoured the neighbourhood of Hoxton for three hours stabbing persons as they went.

The reply indicated that the Clerk of the Court had been present during the evidence and he confirmed the existence of two gangs, the Dover Road Fighting Gang and the Green Gate Gang. Thomas Galliers and James Casey together with some twenty others had encountered Frederick Williams and Arthur Thompson from the Dover Road boys and had asked where they came from. On being told, they said 'we pay [meaning hit] the Lambeth chaps' and 'trashed them with square brass-buckled belts'. Williams died from his injuries.

Nearly 110 years later, on 23 October 1991, the Kray twins' birthday, the Labour MP turned television presenter, Robert Kilroy-Silk, hosted a programme devoted to crime and posed the question whether things were better, for the public, when the so called gangs or firms of the 1960s ran various parts of London as their own small empires.

This book is an informal history of what happened between those two events. It is intended only as that and not as a sociological explanation of how gangs rise and fall, or of their effects on the community.

But were things better in the days of the gangs? The answer would be no so far as the Dover Road Gang was concerned. There is, however, some evidence that throughout the century, alongside their other less attractive habits, powerful families both north and south of the Thames have provided rudimentary community policing in their areas with the consensus of the public.

Anyway what is a gang? 'I don't act for gangs,' one North London solicitor told me recently, 'I act for families.' And if those families find they need the help of friends and acquaintances, does that make them a gang? Surely gangs are for little boys giving secret passwords and meeting in the same shed every Thursday? Gangs are for American television films, says Reggie Kray. They are not for London and the rest of the country.

I think that is a matter of semantics. A gang does not

necessarily maintain the paid-up subscription requirement and list of members that the Garrick does. It is nevertheless a clearly recognizable if floating body with the equivalent of a chairman, members of the board, officers of the club and ordinary members who come and go for a variety of reasons. Some are in prison, some die, some go to another club as Garrick members might move to the Savile. But for a period of time they are members in one form or another.

'Gangsters', from the turn-of-the-century East End villain Arthur Harding onwards, have been keen to paint the picture of a loose association of helpful friends rather than a gang. It may be that the word itself and its connotations of organization brought heavier punishment from the judge. Nearly half a century later Eddie Richardson supported that contention. The friends of the Haward brothers who fought with him one fateful night in Mr Smith's Club were not a gang. They were a 'group'. 'In the villain business they are not called gangs,' wrote Maurice O'Mahoney. On another occasion, 'Arrangements were made to meet a south London team.'[1]

In the first part of the book I have tried to present a more or less chronological history of the various families and their friends who have exerted both a benevolent and malevolent presence in their communities. Although some of the gangs have indulged in pimping and trafficking in women, this is more of a sideline than anything else. These activities have never been a British sport; it is said that we, as a nation, lack the temperament. Accordingly prostitution and pornography are dealt with as separate if integral subjects in a chapter on Soho. Armed robbers too earn a separate chapter: although they have generally drawn their teams from one

---

[1] O'Mahoney, M (1978) *King Squealer*, p. 27. London, W. H. Allen.

area of London or the country, since the mid-1960s they have been a more amorphous body and many have operated independently of the families. The helpers and hinderers, wives, friends, go-betweens, solicitors and, of course, the police who regularly play a most ambiguous role are all also given a separate chapter. At the end there is an account of the current state of play and of the players who are still left in the game, those who have been sent off the field and, in some cases, those who have been buried under the grandstands.

Some people, I suspect, and many, I certainly hope, will buy the book in the anticipation that their names will appear. Several, I am afraid, will be disappointed. I have not dealt in detail with the question of art robberies or forgeries, except for the fatal shooting in 1986 at the Sir John Soane's Museum in London.

Some things and some people have had to be left out. For example, I have not given a chapter to those perennial criminal sports of horse- and dog-doping. With few exceptions there has been no hard evidence that the dopers have been more than fringe members of the underworld, although one did have the distinction of being sentenced in a horse-doping trial before appearing in a dog-doping case two years later. Perhaps he was weaning himself from the heroin of horses by way of the methadone of greyhounds.

Over the years there have, of course, been great scandals, such as cutting the blower at Bath and ringing, doping and fixing cases. Eleven racehorse trainers were disqualified in the years 1948–50 and in 1955, and being stood down as a trainer at a dog track is even today an occupational hazard. Everyone has heard stories of dogs not exercised the night before the race or who have run with elastic bands round their paws, but these have been small-time operations.

Early in my career as a criminal lawyer I was involved in the defence of a greyhound trainer. His weekly earnings and outgoings were totted up and showed a horrible deficit. 'How do you survive?' he was asked. 'Well sir, once a fortnight, one of them dogs runs just for me,' he replied.

In the first of the major horse-doping cases of the 1960s, the police interviewed Bertie 'Bandy' Rogers at stables in Oxfordshire. He shot himself that night and so missed the trial at Gloucester Assizes when a former jockey was found guilty of attempting to dope a horse and, despite the pleas of Sir Gordon Richards, received an eighteen-month sentence.

Three years later in 1963, at Lewes Assizes, in what was perhaps the last of the great horse-doping trials, William Roper, as ringleader, received three years for conspiracy to dope horses. A pretty Swiss girl had toured stables on the pretext of buying a horse and of the twenty-one stables she had visited, twelve favourites had been got at. She received a sentence of twelve months' imprisonment but her punishment was doubtless more tolerable since she had taken the precaution of selling her story to a Sunday newspaper to be published on her conviction. Another defendant, Edward Smith, known as the Witch Doctor because of the potions he carried with him, had unfortunately fallen to his death from a landing in Lewes Prison on the eve of the trial and so missed the proceedings. Can his name have had any possible connection with the Catford club where the Richardsons had their shoot-out with the Haywards and Hennesseys, or is it sheer coincidence?

In more recent years a number of betting coups and ringers have been run, one of the more celebrated being when the three-year-old Flockton Grey had run in a two-year-old race at Stockton and, not unsurprisingly, won by a considerable margin. These enterprises, however, have in general been the work of individuals, such as the Irish gentlemen who on their arrest in a betting coup said, 'We were just out for some Saturday afternoon's crack.'

So far as dog-doping is concerned there has been a steady stream of cases, including one in 1954 when a Harley Street doctor received fifteen months for his part in a conspiracy. His mitigation was that he only functioned at flapping, or unlicensed, tracks rather than at the real thing. In 1965 Peter Hubbard was named by the *People* as King of the Dog Dopers – in fact over the years, depending on which newspaper printed the article, there have been several claimants holding that title concurrently. Hubbard later went into pirate videoing and pornography as a career, along with one of his co-defendants, although he always maintained his interest in racing. At the time of his death in the late 1980s he was a close friend of a prominent Newmarket trainer.

As for boxing, that arena beloved by the fraternity, again there is no evidence of systematic interference. There have been suggestions over the years that the Sabinis and Jack Spot took a particularly close and unhealthy interest in some contests, whilst Buller Ward recounts the sad tale of Tony Mella who was being groomed for stardom with the assistance of his opponents. He also tells of a couple of title fights in which Dai Dower and John L. Gardner faced men who, unbeknownst to the champions, had been paid to take an early shower. But certainly there have never been any underworld figures taking any kind of control of the sport.

An informal history of this nature is bound to be selective, particularly in the field of armed robbery and drug smuggling, where some former and current participants will, perhaps rightly, believe that their efforts were financially or technically superior to the ones I have recorded. I can only apologize to them. If they care to send me details of their exploits I will carefully consider them for any future edition. Nor have I tried to deal with crimes which went to finance politics in any shape or form. Therefore the accounts of money obtained through bank robberies and protection of bookmakers at dog tracks, to be channelled back to the IRA, go unrecorded. Profit and not politics has been the keyword.

Of course much of this book is oral history and the narrators of the tales may not be wholly reliable. Quite genuinely their memories will have faded but also there are axes to grind, scores to be settled, no longer with knives but in print, proving yet again that the pen is mightier than the sword. It has also to be said that some of the reporting in the old days, as since, was not aimed at a sociological study but at the number of copies of the newspapers or magazines to be sold. In their time Hill and Spot were just as much sought after for quotations, gossip pieces and their accounts of life as the Krays and, to a lesser extent, the Richardsons. One of the major causes of the break-up of the Spot–Hill partnership was their rivalry over the publication of their respective memoirs. Wearing one of his less attractive hats, the newspaper reporter Duncan Webb was used by Hill, whose autobiography he ghosted, to discredit and embarrass Spot. Nevertheless, I have tried to check one recollection against another before setting it down.

Many books have been written on specific cases, some of which are more accurate than others. Indeed most police officers who published their memoirs have been keen, no doubt at the insistence of their publishers, to emphasize their involvement in cases in which they had only a peripheral part. A good example appears in *Fabian of the Yard*, where Robert Fabian ends his account of the murder of Berthier with his return to his wife and the news that he had solved his first murder case. A perusal of the committal papers shows that his part was confined to producing a plan of the club where the murder took place.

I have relied in particular on some of the seminal accounts of the London gangs, such as Piers Paul Read's *The Train Robbers*, John Pearson's *The Profession of Violence* and Robert Parker's *Rough Justice*, for, respectively, aspects of the Great Train Robbery, the lives of the Kray twins and of the Richardson family and friends. I have, of course, consulted the memoirs of Charles Richardson and all those of the Kray brothers. In respect of the supergrass era, *Scotland Yard's Cocaine Connection* by Andrew Jennings, Paul Lashmar and Vyv Simpson, as well as *Lundy* by Martin Short, have been invaluable.

My thanks go in strictly alphabetical order to Michael Beckman, Dave Brady, Carl Chinn, for his introduction to the world of betting and the Sabini family, Peter Donnelly, Tony Edwards, Jeremy Fordham for allowing me to use his aunt Peta Fordham's papers, John Frost, Jeffrey Gordon, Dominique Harvie, Mrs G. Houghton-Jones, Bill Ilsley, Ralph Haeems, Frances Hegarty, Brian Hilliard, John Kay, Peter Kelly, Cal McCrystal, Bernard Perkoff, Sid Rae, Nipper and Pat Read, Robert Roscoe, Linda Silverman for the picture research, Harry Stevens, Etta Tasiemka for endless patience in letting me use her cuttings service, Richard Whittington-Egan, and the staff of the Lord Chancellor's department, Public Records Office, Hendon Public Library and the Law Society's library, plus the many others who have made a contribution but who, for various reasons, did not wish to be acknowledged personally. Obviously without them this book would have been even more imperfect. Such errors as there are are mine alone.

Finally, I could not possibly have written this book without the unfailing help and support of Dock Bateson.

1

The Early Years

Nowadays, the consensus of opinion among lawyers, police and those of the villains' friends who are still alive and able to think straight is that in the 1940s and 1950s Billy Hill and Jack Spot between them were the first to control the twentieth-century London underworld to any great extent. They were not. They were only following in the long, if not honourable, line of more disorganized protection men, minders, bully-boys and racketeers, thieves, hitmen and hardmen, who went before them in such districts of London as Clerkenwell, Elephant and Castle, Hoxton, the Angel and Notting Hill, and who eventually gravitated in the 1920s to Soho and Mayfair where the pickings were that much bigger. Nor seemingly were Spot and Hill any more violent than their predecessors.

In his autobiography *Detective Days*, published in 1931, Frederick Wensley, former Commander of Scotland Yard who arrested the Clapham Common murderer, Steinie Morrison, wrote:

Any reader of the daily papers these days might come to the conclusion that Chicago is the only place in which organized bands of desperate criminals ever existed. The public have a short

1

memory. It is not so very long ago that we, in the East End and some other districts of London, were engaged in stamping out groups of criminals, many of whom carried arms, and who waged a sort of warfare among themselves and against the public.

In the early part of the century there was one gang of this class who had established a real reign of terror among certain people in the East End.

The victims were those same people who are always the victims.

In the main, however, the victims were persons who for some reason or another were a little shy of bringing their troubles to the notice of the police. Keepers of shady restaurants, runners of gambling dens, landlords of houses of resort, street bookmakers and other people on the fringe of the underworld were among those peculiarly open to trouble.

And of the others:

Sometimes small tradesmen were offered 'protection' against other gangs at a price. If they did not take kindly to this blackmail all sorts of unpleasant things were liable to happen to them. . . . Persons who had resisted their extortions had been brutally assaulted, their premises wrecked – in one case an attempt to burn down a building had been made – and any portable property stolen.

The East End gang which operated around the turn of the century was the forty-strong pack, the Bessarabians, from the predominantly Russian–Jewish Whitechapel quarter.

The Russian Jews with their ingrained terror of the police would, in practically every case, rather put up with the gangs than risk the consequences of complaining to the police. . . . we were continually having to let cases drop through lack of evidence.

They levied a protection toll on timid alien shop-keepers, proprietors of coffee-stalls and so on. The faintest shadow of protest on their part at this blackmail and the gang descended on them in force armed with guns, knives and such weapons as broken bottles.[1]

In *Lost London* former Detective Sergeant B. Leeson gave another example of their methods:

Lists of people to be blackmailed were drawn up by the gangsters, and amongst these, prospective brides provided the happiest and most productive results. A few days before the wedding ceremony a gangster would approach the bride's parents and threaten to expose all sorts of imaginary indiscretions of which their daughter had been guilty if their silence was not bought. The victims, fearful of the scandal that might ensue, invariably paid up.[2]

The chief rivals of the Bessarabians were the Odessians, so called because the proprietor of a restaurant called the Odessa took the gang on. Weinstein, also known as Kikal, refused to pay protection money and according to Leeson fought them off with an iron bar when they came to demand their wages. The rival gang, which did not include Weinstein, took his restaurant's

[1] G.W. Cornish, *Cornish of the Yard*, p. 4.
[2] B. Leeson, *Lost London*, p. 147.

name as a tribute to his courage.

For the next year or so there were the usual gang skirmishes. The Odessians threatened to cut off the ears of a leading Bessarabian named Perkoff. He was lured into an alley and one ear was removed before the local police arrived. In return a coffee-stall under the protection of the Odessians was attacked.

The end of the Bessarabians came in October 1902 following an attack by them on a sing-song in the York Minster, a public house in Philpot Street off the Commercial Road where a number of Odessians were thought to be. The Bessarabians attacked indiscriminately, slashing and stabbing. One man, sometimes called Brodovich but also known as Kaufmann, was stabbed to death.

In the ensuing confusion the public was less discreet than usual and names were named. As a result a Bessarabian leader, Max Moses, who boxed as Kid McCoy and who had fought at the old Wonderland Arena in Whitechapel, was sentenced to ten years' penal servitude following a conviction for manslaughter. He had been thought to have had championship potential.

With the leaders in custody the local population began to name more names. Members of both gangs were arrested and convicted on a variety of charges, including another of the leaders, Samuel Oreman, who received five years' penal servitude. With their leaders in prison the gang disintegrated. Meanwhile the police chipped away at the Odessians. Many went to America, where they joined forces with the local crooks. One known as 'Tilly the burglar' is said to have become a Chicago policeman.[3] It is interesting to note that one of the current terrors of New York is the so-called Russian Mafia.

---

[3] According to Leeson, McCoy also went to America on his release and became a successful businessman.

After the convictions following the York Minster affray remnants of both the Odessians and the Bessarabians lingered on. Even before them, however, the Blind Beggar gang, a team of skilled pickpockets who were not averse to roughing up their victims if they complained, had flourished. They took their name from the Blind Beggar public house, later to become famous as the scene of the Cornell shooting by Ronnie Kray. One story about them concerns an attack on a travelling salesman by a man named Wallis who, acquitted of murder, is said to have been driven back from the Old Bailey in triumph in a phaeton drawn by a pair of bays. This whole story, like so many stories of the gangs, is probably apocryphal and seems based on the true story of Paul Vaughan, who went under the name of Ellis. He was charged with manslaughter following the death in 1891 of Frederick Klein, a perfectly respectable man who with his wife had been subjected to a series of racial taunts. There is no record of Vaughan's acquittal and the gang broke up.[4]

Another team, the Strutton Ground Mob from Westminster, which ran protection rackets there, endeavoured unsuccessfully to move on the stall-holders in Petticoat Lane, a manoeuvre regarded by local villains as requiring swift and violent reprisals. But it seems that after the rule of the Odessians and the Bessarabians, for a short time at any rate, properly organized crime in the East End died away.

An early trick was coining, regarded by the police as a particularly despicable crime because, once again, it was the small shopkeeper who suffered. A coiner would make dud coins from plaster of paris moulds filled with heavy metal, which was poured through a hole in the mould called a 'git'. They were then sold in loads to

---

[4] In some accounts the Wallis story is attributed to a Tottenham-based gang.

'smashers' – men and, more often, women who would make a purchase requiring change from a half crown in a small shop. There would be a back-up man to keep a look-out for emergencies and only one half crown would be carried at a time. The reason for this was simple. To be in possession of one coined half crown was a misfortune which could happen to anyone. To have two or more was almost inexplicable to even the doziest of police officers and magistrates. It is interesting to note that many of the stolen credit cards and cheques about in the country today are proffered by women.

The gangs of the early years of the century seem to have been informal associations, something which has continued throughout the century. One, led by the engagingly named One-Eyed Charlie, hung out around Clark's coffee-shop near a railway arch in Brick Lane. According to Arthur Harding, a major villain of the time and later a chronicler of the East End, they do not seem to have acted much in concert. The leader, Charlie Walker, had tuberculosis and, true to his name, had lost an eye. Another of the gang, Edward Spencer, seems to have been the only 'complete all round criminal'. A well-built man who took a great pride in his appearance and was known as 'the Count', he was a thief and robber. Most of the others were pickpockets and tappers (beggars), van draggers (those who stole from vans), watch-chain or handbag snatchers, or petty blackmailers. The Walker team flourished, if that is the right word, until about 1904, when Charlie Walker died in a prison hospital, and re-formed some years later with younger men, among them Arthur Harding who became the leader. Although he did not regard his loose 'connection of youngsters' as a gang, it was a much more cohesive organization: 'We were a collection of small-time thieves ripe for any mischief. . . . We were ready to steal anything. Sometimes we went in couples, sometimes alone – it was only when there was a big fight on that we went as a gang.'[5]

It was their activities as a gang that earned them the name the Vendetta Mob. Associations were formed and broken. For example, the 'top man of the Jews', Edward Emmanuel, at one time had a liaison with Harding, then broke with him and joined up in the 1920s with the Sabinis, broke with them and later in the 1920s worked almost as an independent, being regarded as a great fixer with the police.

A more organized gang which came from the very rough area of Nile Street, a market street off Shepherdess Walk near the City Road police station, was the Titanic Mob, so called (in tribute to the liner) because they were always well dressed. Their specialities were robbery and pickpocketing at race meetings, railway stations and at the theatre, although they do not seem to have been averse to burglary either. They were highly regarded in the trade, partly because they only robbed men. Harding recalls that in 1908 his gang fought the Titanics following an argument over the protection of a coffee-stall in Brick Lane. The Titanics seem to have been the smarter of the teams.

What they done was crafty. They set a trap for us. They was well in with the police and directly the fight started the police were there. They got hold of us – including Cooper who had a loaded gun on him. It wasn't an offence to carry a gun, but we got a week's remand for causing an affray. I always had it in for them afterwards. I thought, 'You twisters – you always have the bogies on your side.'

Guns were easy to come by. Harding bought his first

[5] R. Samuel, *East End Underworld*, quoting Arthur Harding, p. 148.

in about 1904. A Royal Irish Constabulary revolver cost half a crown in Brick Lane, others four or five shillings. Harding and the Vendettas made a speciality of holding up spielers (illegal gambling clubs) and stealing the cash-box.

The Titanics, whose operational strength totalled around fifty, received a severe set-back in January 1922 when they were swooped on by the Flying Squad after a football match. A further raid took place a few days later when other members were found to be working the underground at Baker Street. Although only short sentences were handed out to members, from then on it would seem the team splintered and broke up.[6]

A succession of gangs from around Hoxton Street, with the generic name of the Hoxton Mob, operated over some forty years. One of the early versions had its headquarters at the Spread Eagle public house and, amongst other interests, they were into the protection of the local clubs and spielers such as Sunshine's, a card and billiard club in an alley off Shoreditch High Street. Harding is dismissive of them: 'They weren't such good-class thieves as the Titanics. They were more hooligans than thieves. . . . They worked ten- or twelve-handed. . . . They all finished up on the poor law, or cadging. Their leader died a pauper, whereas the leader of the Titanics ended up owning a dog-track.'

Another local gang leader of the time was Isaac Bogard, known as Darky the Coon. Although he was Jewish he was so dark-skinned that some references to him are as a black man. His mob was accordingly known as the Coons. Although when giving evidence he described himself as an actor, Bogard had a long criminal record which included a sentence of flogging for living off immoral earnings. He was certainly functioning

---

[6] S. Felstead, *The Underworld of London*, p. 41.

from the early years of the century until the 1920s, when he was then what was euphemistically described as the 'governor' of the market stall-holders in Petticoat Lane and Wentworth Street.

On 10 September 1911 about 8.30 in the evening he was set upon by Harding and the Vendetta Mob in the Blue Coat Boy in Bishopsgate. Bogard and his team ran a string of prostitutes in Whitechapel High Street and the quarrel had been about their ownership and the protection of a stall in Walthamstow Street market. Harding describes the fight: 'We did a lot of damage. The Coon had a face like the map of England. He was knocked about terrible. I hit him with a broken glass, made a terrible mess of his face. I knew I'd hurt him a lot, but not anything that could be serious.'[7]

Bogard, who in evidence at the subsequent trial said his throat had been cut, was taken to the London Hospital where after he had been stitched he discharged himself. But the next weekend there was more of the same for him. He was attacked once again by Harding and friends on the Sunday evening.

The outcome was dramatic. The police arrived and arrested Bogard and a man called George King on charges of disorderly conduct, for which they were to appear at Old Street Magistrates' Court on the Monday. Meanwhile Harding – then known as Tresidern – and his Vendettas met at Clark's the coffee-shop in Brick Lane to rally support against the Coons, who were about to commit the one really unforgivable crime: ask for police protection.

Accounts vary as to exactly what happened, as they do to the exact lead up to the battle and the arrest of Bogard. This is not surprising. Wensley, the police officer in the case, did not write his memoirs for another

[7] R. Samuel, *East End Underworld*, p. 154.

twenty years and Harding did not give his oral account of his life for another forty. Sir Charles Biron, the magistrate that day, wrote:

One morning two men were charged before me with disorderly conduct. It was a confusing case. The only thing clear was that there had been a disturbance in the street in which they had been involved. In the end I bound them both over to keep the peace. One of them applied to me for police protection on the ground that there was an armed body of men waiting outside the court to murder them. I told the man to sit down and affected to doubt the story, which indeed seemed incredible, but I had a very shrewd suspicion there was something in it. If there were, I felt it would be a mistake to do anything that would put the gang on its guard; accordingly I gave instructions to the police not to let either of the men leave the building and then sent for the Inspector of Police and saw him in my private room.

'Is this true?' I asked.

'Yes,' he said, 'it is. These two men used to belong to the Tresidern [Harding] gang. They turned respectable and left them. The gang regarded them as deserters and attacked them this morning in the street, which led to them being arrested for their own safety.'

It was an amazing story and seemed incredible.

'Do you mean to tell me,' I said, 'that a mob armed with revolvers is waiting outside this court to murder these two men?'

'Yes,' he said, 'that is so.'

Then I saw a great opportunity.

'Telephone at once to Scotland Yard,' I said, 'mention my name and state the facts. Tell them on my authority to send down an overwhelming force of armed police as soon as possible to deal with the situation and,' I added, 'impress upon them above everything not to make the mistake of failing to send a sufficiently strong force.'

This was done and Scotland Yard adopted my suggestion. I finished my work for the day and sat in my room awaiting the result. Just after five o'clock my Inspector came to me and said 'It's alright sir.' The police force had arrived.

Leading from the Old Street Police Court there were two not very wide roads. These the police had blocked with two hooded vans, filled with a force armed with revolvers. 'Now,' I said, 'let the two men out.' In a second, firing began and the police surrounded the gang.

There were five, all armed, and they were five of the most desperate characters in Hoxton led by their chief, Tresidern. In a few minutes they were all arrested and that day's work was the beginning of the end of what is hardly an exaggeration to call a reign of terror. Tresidern conducted the defence, which he did with considerable spirit. After his arrest his rooms were searched and Stones' *Justices Manual* was found carefully underlined and noted up. They were all committed for trial and in due course sentenced. The result was salutary. The Tresidern gang was finished, and the rival gang was a very inferior combination; the ordinary police methods together with firm administration of the law soon put them out of action, and after a few months the police had the criminal element fairly in hand.[8]

[8] Sir Charles Biron, *Without Prejudice*, p. 267.

According to the depositions taken on committal Wensley arrived at Old Street Court early in the afternoon and kept observation from an unmarked horse-drawn van, turning the horse from time to time to avoid suspicion. Bogard and King were taken to the entrance of the court at infrequent intervals and each time the crowd, led by Harding, rushed the steps. Harding had a revolver which he displayed quite openly. Eventually Wensley made his move on the crowd.

Both Wensley and Harding agree there were more arrests. Harding was taken at the court but the police foraged down Brick Lane and arrested another three people. The defendants were on remand for fourteen weeks and the police had trouble keeping a hold on their witnesses. Bogard thought better of giving evidence and a witness summons had to be issued.

Money was found from somewhere because Harding and the others were defended privately; Harding by the well-known barrister Eustace Fulton. It did him little good. In December 1911 the team appeared at the Old Bailey in front of Mr Justice Avory, who when passing sentence gave this little homily:

This riot was one of the most serious riots which can be dealt with by law, for it was a riot in which some, at least, of the accused were armed with revolvers, and it took place within the precincts of a court of justice.

I wish to say that the condition of things disclosed by the evidence – that a portion of London should be infested by a number of criminal ruffians, armed with loaded revolvers – ought not to be tolerated further, and if the existing law is not strong enough to put a stop to it some remedial legislation is necessary.

Harding received twenty-one months' hard labour to
be followed by three years' penal servitude. His career
was sketched by Wensley when giving the antecedents
of the convicted men before sentence:

> When he was fourteen – he is now only twenty-five
> – he was bound over for disorderly conduct and
> being in possession of a revolver.
>   At the age of seventeen he became a terror to
> Bethnal Green, and captained a band of desper-
> adoes. In all he has been convicted fourteen times,
> yet he was one of the complaining witnesses before
> the Police Commission.
>   He has developed into a cunning and plausible
> criminal of a dangerous type. I have never known
> him do any work.[9]

Wensley records that after Harding's sentence, peace
returned to the East End – for a little while anyway.

But Harding and his Vendetta Boys were children
compared to the well-organized and long-lived Sabinis,
a gang which flourished for something like three
decades. There is a tendency nowadays to dismiss them
as 'only working the race-tracks' but there was very
much more to them than that. Horse racing was certainly
a major way into the protection business and organized
crime. The Sabini brothers, of whom Charles (known as
Darby, and said to be connected to the Mafia), Harryboy, Joseph, Fred and George can be counted as the
leaders of the London underworld from the 1920s, are
best remembered for that but they had other activities.
They came from the Clerkenwell area of London near
King's Cross, and they provided what was euphemistically called protection and what, in reality, was
demanding money with menaces from the bookmakers.

[9] *Illustrated Police News*, 23 December 1911.

Darby Sabini was born in 1889 in Saffron Hill, known as Little Italy. Although the leader of the Sabinis, he was one of the youngest of the six brothers. His Italian father died when he was two and the family was raised by their Irish mother. He left school at the age of thirteen and joined Dan Sullivan, a boxing promoter and bookmaker. At one time it was thought he could, in the words of Marlon Brando, 'have been a contender'. Whilst still in his teens he had knocked out the fancied middleweight Fred Sutton in the first round. Unfortunately he did not like the training required and instead became a strong-arm man for Sullivan's promotions at the Hoxton baths.

The race-track protection worked in a number of ways. First there was the question of the pitches themselves. The Sabinis and their rivals simply bullied the hapless bookmakers away from their spots and then sold or let them to their cronies. Much later, in 1947, Jack Spot took over the £2-a-day pitches provided at point-to-points and charged the bookmakers £7. One way of preventing a bookmaker attracting any business was to surround his stand with thugs so the punters could not get to it to place their bets.

Then there was the bucket drop. If a bookmaker wished to avoid this trouble he would drop half a crown in a bucket containing water and a sponge. The bucket was carried up and down the line between races and the sponge used to wipe out the odds next to the printed sheet of runners on the board. If the tribute was not paid then the odds would be wiped at inappropriate and totally inconvenient times. The sheets of runners had themselves to be purchased; costing about a farthing to produce, they were retailed by the Sabinis to the bookmakers for another half a crown. Chalk had to be purchased and a stool cost ten shillings to hire for the day. Other manoeuvres included starting fights near a bookmaker's pitch, claiming a non-existent winning bet, and having other pitches put so close to the non-paying bookmaker that he physically could not operate. Quite apart from that there was a straightforward demand for a non-repayable loan of £5 or £10.

The sums may seem small but, added up, came to big money. 'The race-course business was a profitable one. When a gang went to a race-course like Brighton they could clear £4000 or £5000 easy. At Epsom on Derby Day, it could be £15,000 to £20,000.'[10]

There was not much subtlety in their operations. 'Darby Sabini and his thugs used to stand sideways on to let the bookmakers see their hammers in their pockets,' wrote Detective Chief Superintendent Edward Greeno in his autobiography.[11]

The Sabinis cannot be given the credit for thinking up the idea of race-course protection. It was well established in the nineteenth century. In 1848, for example, there was considerable trouble with a Glasgow gang, known as the Redskins because of their scarred faces, at Paisley Races, and from the 1870s onwards the bookmakers themselves had protection – often in the form of active and retired prize-fighters – paying out only when they had done well and using bully-boys to dissuade punters from claiming their winning bets. After the First World War the bookmakers themselves became the victims.

There were, of course, a number of well-organized gangs outside the Smoke. One of the first originated in Birmingham. Run by bookmaker William Kimber, it was known as the Brummagen Boys despite the fact that most of the members came from the Elephant and Castle area of London. They had a fearsome reputation, being said to be willing and able to kill rats by biting them.

[10] R. Samuel, *East End Underworld*, p. 184.
[11] E. Greeno, *War on the Underworld*, p. 12.

Their organized race-course protection began in around
1910 and for a time Kimber's mob had control of the
race-courses down south such as Newbury, Epsom, Earls
Park and Kempton. There were also other gangs
operating from Leeds and Uttoxeter. Later Kimber's
men had a loose alliance with one of the metamorphoses
of the Hoxton mob known as the 'Lunies' (not to be
confused with a small independent marauding team, the
'Looneys'). The southern bookmakers accepted the
imposition fairly philosophically.

Around the same time the Sabini brothers, known as
the Italian Mob, began to put together their organization; it became a mixed Italian and Jewish alliance
which was said to import gangsters from Sicily. The fact
that 'there wasn't an Englishman among them'[12] did not
mean they spoke anything but English. Once when Mr
Justice Darling, who fancied himself as a linguist,
addressed one of them in Italian the man stared in
amazement.[13]

The Sabinis may have had no command of Italian but
they had command of the police:

> Darby Sabini got in with the Flying Squad which
> had been formed about 1908 or 1909; they got in
> with the race-course police, the special police, and
> so they had the police on their side protecting
> them. Directly there was any fighting it was always
> the Birmingham mob who got pinched. They was
> always getting time, five-year sentences and that.[14]

[12] R. Samuel, *East End Underworld*, p. 182.

[13] Apparently until this moment Darling had been taking a close
interest in the case. After that he confined his remarks to the jury to
the effect that the witness must be descended from the Sabines and
went on to tell the story of the Sabine women.

[14] R. Samuel, *East End Underworld*, p. 183.

With the arrival of the Sabinis and their superi
relationship with the police, Billy Kimber and his ga
retreated to the Midlands. For some time the factio
lived in an uneasy relationship. Kimber and Co. work
the Midlands and northern tracks; the Sabinis, alo
with a gang called the East End Jews, the London a
southern ones.[15]

The favourite weapons were razors but these we
subject to changing fashion and regional preference
Ex-Superintendent Fred Narborough recalls:

> The safety razors embedded in the peak of the pull-
> down cloth cap, which would gouge out a man's
> cheek with one swipe, originated in Glasgow.
>
> The same kind of blades, preferably rusty to set
> up infection, stuck into a big potato with only a
> quarter of an inch of metal showing, came from the
> Midlands. In the eyes of the owner this possessed
> the merit of leaving warning weals once the wounds
> had healed, without risking a murder charge.
>
> The flick knife was unknown at the time and
> even recently I have heard this backwardness on
> the part of the manufacturers deplored in certain
> circles.
>
> Coshes came in infinite variety, many weighted
> with lead to give the gangster the right 'feel' – like
> a golfer with his set of clubs. Then there were
> bayonets with serrated blades, the metal shavings
> from workshop lathes enclosed in old cotton
> stockings, jemmies, carefully chosen lead piping
> which would go down a trouser leg, tyre levers

[15] There were numerous tracks in the south many of which, such
as Gatwick, Lewes, Alexandra Park and Hurst Park, have now
closed down. In addition trotting was popular, with courses at
such places as Greenford and Hendon.

fitted with non-slip rubber grips, the hair-splitting stilettos of the Sabini gang from Clerkenwell bottles of vitriol and other acids.[16]

In some versions of the legend the meteoric rise of Darby Sabini can be traced back to a fight he had in 1920 with 'Monkey' Benneyworth, the enforcer for the Elephant Gang, when Benneyworth deliberately tore the dress of an Italian girl serving behind the bar of the Griffin public house in Saffron Hill. Benneyworth was knocked out and humiliated by Sabini and when his broken jaw had mended he returned with members of the Elephant Gang. They were driven out of Little Italy by Sabini with the help of young Italians who looked on him as their leader. Now, with them behind him, he saw the opportunity to muscle in on some of the smaller gangs who were operating protection around the race-tracks. Although the big gangs such as the Broad Mob from Camden Town, the mainly Jewish Aldgate Mob and the Hoxton Mob could boast a membership of up to sixty they could be spread thinly because they were obliged to operate several tracks a day. Darby and the rest of the Sabinis moved in in force.[17]

It is curious how throughout the history of organized crime the victims align themselves with their oppressors who, in turn, through that alliance somehow gain a quasi-respectability. After bookmakers at Salisbury races had been forced, at gun point, to pay a levy for the privilege of having a pitch, in 1921 they formed themselves into the Racecourse Bookmakers and Backers Protection Association, today a highly respected

---

[16] F. Narborough, *Murder on my Mind*, p. 36.
[17] For a full account of the early days of bookmaking and the involvement of the Sabinis, see Carl Chinn's *Better betting with a decent feller*.

organization. Eight stewards were appointed at a wage of £6 per week. The stewards were the Sabini family and their friends, including Philip Emmanuel, son of Edward. It is said that at the time Darby was earning £20,000 a year. This may be an exaggeration but taken at the lowest level sixty runners' sheets sold at 2s 6d amounted to a working man's wage for the week, and there is no doubt Darby did better than that.

Kimber's Birmingham or Brummagen Boys did not give in easily and the fighting continued throughout the year. A bookmaker under the Sabinis' protection was threatened at Sandown Park and was beaten up when he refused to pay a £25 pitch fee. Darby Sabini sent a retaliatory force to Hoxton. He himself was caught at Greenford trotting track on 25 March 1921 and seems to have escaped a bad beating by the Birmingham Mob by shooting his way out of trouble. It was one of the occasions when he was arrested but he was acquitted after arguing self-defence and bound over to keep the peace.

From time to time offers of reconciliation, genuine or not, were made and spurned. Kimber went to Darby Sabini's home at King's Cross. He was found two hours later shot in the side but was quite unable to identify his assailant. He was, after all, only obeying the underworld tradition of silence. A Jewish bookmaker, Solomons, from Sandown Park gave himself up to the police over the shooting but the case was stopped. 'If that's all the evidence you can produce it's useless to go on,' said the trial judge. Solomons remained a Sabini friend for the next fifteen years, eventually paying for that friendship at Lewes race-course.

Reprisals came quickly. On 4 April at the 'Ascot of North London', Alexandra Park, a small track known as Ally-Pally which closed in the 1960s, the police were informed of a showdown. By one o'clock all they had

found were two Birmingham bookmakers' touts who had
been beaten up. Later, however, two Jewish taxi-
drivers, chauffeurs to the Sabinis, were caught in the
silver ring by the Birmingham men. One was shot twice
as he lay on the ground. He too could not identify his
shooter. A further reprisal came at Bath when Billy
Kimber and his men attacked the East End Jews found
in the two-shilling ring.

Not all the attacks were well directed. A fight on
Derby Day 1921 appears to have been engineered by
Reuben Bigland, the Birmingham tycoon, following a
complaint by the publisher and later convicted swindler
Horatio Bottomley. He complained that it was wrong
that Italians such as the Sabinis should be depriving 'our
boys' of a living, particularly after their gallant fight in
the First World War. The outcome was a punitive
expedition by the Brummagen Boys, the Mancinis and
the Vendetta Boys. After the Derby itself, won by Steve
Donoghue on Humorist, the Birmingham Boys left the
course and blocked the road with their charabanc, lying
in wait for Sabini and his friends. Unfortunately for them
the Sabinis had already left the scene and the victims
were their allies.

Violence spread away from the race-courses. In April
1922 four 'racing men' were stabbed in and near
Coventry Street and another was beaten up in nearby
Jermyn Street.

The Derby meeting that year, when Captain Cuttle
won after spreading a plate on the way to the start,
passed off quietly but, two months later, the Sabinis
were back in the dock, charged after a fight in Camden
Town during which shots were fired. A Birmingham man
had been out walking with his wife and some friends
when he was ambushed. For once the Birmingham men
were able to give the names of their attackers to the
police but by the time the case was heard they had

forgotten them.

Things did not stop there and the Jockey Club seriously considered shutting down the courses on which there was trouble. A Sabini boy was stabbed to death in a club off the Strand, another was thrown on a fire. Cardiff bookmakers were beaten up in their offices, a man was killed in a Tottenham Court Road fight. The Sabinis and their rivals fought for supremacy on street corners, on trains, on the roads and at the race-courses.

At the Doncaster St Leger meeting the Brummagen team sent word that no bookmakers or their employees would be allowed to attend Town Moor. As a result, in open defiance, Sabini and his men 'protected' the London bookie Walter Beresford, putting him safely on the train to Doncaster where it was met by Kimber's men, who then allowed only him and his staff to go to the race-course.

The next trouble spot was at the autumn meeting in Yarmouth, a course claimed by the Sabinis as theirs. They arrived the day before to search the public houses in the town to see if the Brummagen men had arrived. They had not. Instead they were met by Tom Divall, an ex-Chief Inspector of the CID now working for the Jockey Club, and something of a supporter of the Midland team. He calmed things down.

Divall wrote of Kimber that he 'was one of the best' and of another incident: 'Just to show what generous and brave fellows the aforesaid Sage and Kimber were, they would not give any evidence or information against their antagonists, and stated that they would sooner die than send those men to prison.'[18]

It is difficult to comprehend Divall's attitude without alleging corruption. Describing another incident when the Leeds organization had tried to take control of

---

[18] T. Divall, *Scoundrels and Scallywags*, p. 200.

Hawthorn Hill in the south and Divall was attacked by them, he wrote:

> One of them swore with a terrible oath he would kill me. He made for me and was just about to carry out his intention, but Darby Sabini rushed up to my aid and knocked the other chap down with a heavy blow in the mouth. The others seeing 'the red light', got hold of the wounded warrior and hurried him away. I have often wondered what would have been my fate if such a good ally as Darby had not popped up at that critical moment.[19]

Whatever Divall's position, one explanation of the Sabinis' success and longevity comes from Billy Hill:

> There were more crooked policemen about than there are today. The Sabinis received protection from certain elements of the law. If a thief or pickpocket was seen on a course a Sabini man would whiten the palm of his hand with chalk and greet the thief with a supposed-to-be 'Hello'. In doing so he would slap the thief on the shoulder, just like a long lost friend. The whitened hand-mark would identify him to the law. Then they knew without doubt that this man was safe to be nicked for being a suspected person . . .[20]

According to Divall, however, it was Beresford who 'brought the two sides together, he is still continuing in the good work, and I am very pleased to see the two crews are associating together, and, in addition, to have their principals assuring me that no such troubles will ever occur again.'

[19] Ibid, p. 209.
[20] B. Hill, *Boss of Britain's Underworld*, p. 4.

Divall had it only partly correct. The Sabinis and Kimber did agree to divide the race-courses between them and certainly the race-course wars did die down, but not before the Jockey Club had threatened to close down courses such as Bath and Salisbury where the worst troubles were taking place. In 1925 the Jockey Club set up a team under Major Wymer to drive out the undesirable elements from the official enclosures. By 1929 the bookmakers' pitch committees were firmly in control and a strict pecking order amongst bookmakers had been established. The pitches were personal to the occupant. They could not be sold or leased out. When a bookmaker retired or died the next in seniority took his pitch and a vacancy occurred at the end of the line.

There were still, however, the independents and in 1927, when one Dai Lewis tried to muscle in on the Rowlands Gang who controlled Cardiff, his throat was cut.

But if by the 1930s Darby Sabini had made his peace with that fine fellow Billy Kimber, in the 1920s he had been under threat from other sources inside his own organization. Some of the troops decided to seek a higher percentage of the takings. The four Cortesi brothers, also known as the Frenchies (Augustus, George, Paul and Enrico), were deputed to act as shop stewards to put the case. Almost immediately afterwards part of the Jewish element in the gang, to become known as the Yiddishers, also formed a breakaway group. In true business fashion the Sabinis negotiated. The Cortesis would be given a greater percentage. The Yiddishers were given permission to lean on one, but only one, of the bookmakers under protection.[21]

Peace did not last long. The Yiddishers began to side with the Cortesis and defections amongst the troops to

---

[21] A. Tietjen, *Soho*.

the Frenchies substantially weakened the Sabini position. In the autumn of 1922 the new team effectively hijacked the Sabini protection money from the bookmakers at Kempton Park. Retribution was swift. As a result of the reprisals, Harry Sabini was convicted at Marylebone Magistrates' Court of an assault on George Cortesi. More seriously, one of the other leaders of the breakaway group was attacked, for which five of the Sabini troops were sentenced to terms of imprisonment for attempted murder.

On 19 November 1922, just before midnight, Darby and Harry Sabini were trapped in the Fratellanza Club in Great Bath Street, Clerkenwell. Darby was punched and hit with bottles whilst Harry was shot by Augustus and Enrico (Harry) Cortesi. Darby suffered a greater indignity. As he told the magistrates' court, his false teeth were broken as a result of the blows from the bottles. He was also able to confirm his respectability. 'I am a quiet peaceable man,' he asserted. 'I never begin a fight. I've only once been attacked. I've never attacked anyone. . . . I do a little bit of work as a commission agent sometimes for myself and sometimes for someone else. I'm always honest. The last day's work I did was two years ago. I live by my brains.' He had only once carried a revolver and that was when he was attacked at Greenford Park. Indeed he turned out his pockets in confirmation that he was not carrying a gun.

The Cortesi brothers, who lived only five doors away from the Fratellanza Club, had been arrested the same night and at the Old Bailey on 18 January 1923 each received a sentence of three years' penal servitude. A recommendation by the Grand Jury that the Cortesi brothers should be deported was not followed by Mr Justice Darling:

I look upon this as part of a faction fight which has

raged between you and other Italians in consequence of some difference which the police do not
entirely understand. You appear to be two lawless
bands – the Sabinis and the Cortesis. Sometimes
you are employed against the Birmingham people,
and sometimes you are employed against each
other. On this occasion you were carrying out a
feud between you and the Sabinis. . . . I have the
power to recommend an order for your deportation. I am not going to do it. I can see no reason
to suppose that you two men are worse than others
who have been convicted in these feuds and have
not been recommended for deportation. But the
whole Italian colony should know of the Grand
Jury's recommendation, and I wish to say to you
all if this kind of lawless conduct goes on, those
who get convicted in future will be turned out of
this country with their wives and children.

Without their leaders the Cortesi faction folded. The
rebellion had been short-lived and it was not until the
1930s, when the Sabinis had expanded their territory
into greyhound racing, that the Sabinis again came under
serious threat from another team. This time they came
from Islington and were the White family. They had
been getting stronger over the years and were now set
to challenge the Sabinis. There was also the small matter
of the pitches on the open courses at Epsom and
Brighton which were outside the control of the race-
course stewards, as well as bookmaking at point-to-
points, let alone the dog-tracks where 'they terrorized the
bookmakers' according to the son of a man who ran a pitch.
  On 1 September 1936 Massimino Monte Columbo was
stabbed to death at Wandsworth Greyhound Racing
Track, which had been opened some four years earlier.
A fight broke out in the 2s 6d ring, witnessed by Jim

Wicks, who thirty years later was to be a manager of boxers who included Henry Cooper. At the time Massimino, described as the idol of the girls in Little Italy, worked for Bert Marsh, the *nom de ring* of boxer Pasqualino Papa. Marsh, a popular bantamweight, had fought at Lime Grove Baths and Shepherd's Bush. He was described by the officer in the case as 'quick-tempered, excitable and easily provoked'. Once Marsh was appointed to a job at the stadium he got the Columbo brothers work there and at his request Wicks employed Camillo. The quarrel was allegedly over a bookmaker called Samuels employing Bert Wilkins rather than another Monte Columbo brother, Nestor, who along with Marsh and Wilkins came from Little Italy. The Columbo family objected. They were also looking for more money from Marsh. Fighting broke out and Massimino was stabbed in the neck.

Marsh had undoubtedly suffered kicks and punches in the fight and when he and Wilkins were surrendered by their solicitor, J.A. Davies, to the police, Marsh sensibly asked that the fingerprints on a 'life preserver' or cosh were checked. 'It'll show they weren't mine. I was nearly killed,' he told Divisional Detective Inspector John Henry.

At the Old Bailey Marsh and Wilkins were defended by eight barristers including three silks led by Norman Birkett KC. The funds for their defence were said to have been subscribed by racing men and the 'pretty young Mrs Marsh, mother of eight', who had pawned her jewellery and drawn out her savings to retain Birkett. It was money well spent. Newspapers noted that many bookmakers and even film stars were in court for the verdict.

Whilst on remand in Brixton Prison, on 28 October Marsh and Wilkins had assisted Prison Officer Payne during exercise when, according to reports, he had been attacked by a powerfully built man and bitten and kicked. It was something which stood them in good stead throughout the trial.

The murder charge was dismissed and Marsh, as the older man with a criminal record of assaults and unlawful wounding, received twelve months for manslaughter; Wilkins got three months less. The judge specially took into account the part they had played in assisting the prison warder, who 'might have been killed'. Later it was alleged that friends had organized the 'attack' so that Marsh could step in and obtain credit for his efforts. This sort of 'put up attack' was by no means new, nor was it the last time it was used. In a later incident Billy Hill 'pulled' Jackie Rosa, one of a number of brothers from the Elephant, off a screw, thereby gaining both kudos and a loyal member of his organization.

Both the Berts were to become major figures in Soho in the 1950s, Marsh as a street bookmaker, supporter of Albert Dimes and friend of George Dawson, the Cockney businessman later imprisoned following a commercial fraud. Bert Wilkins owned the Nightingale Club which was later to become Aspinalls.

Meanwhile, from the 1920s onwards, the Sabinis had been branching out, taking interests in the West End drinking and gambling clubs, and installing and running slot-machines. They were also extending their protection to criminals. If a burglary took place the Sabinis would send round for their share.

> Burglars and thieves had no chance. If they wandered up West they had to go mob-handed. And they had to be prepared to pay out if they were met by any of the Sabinis. If they went into a club it was drinks all round. The prices were usually especially doubled for their benefit. If they did go into a spieler they never won. They knew better than to try to leave while they were showing

even a margin of profit. If one word was spoken out of place, it was all off. The Sabinis, who could rustle up twenty or thirty tearaways at a moment's notice anywhere up West, stood for no liberties, although they were always taking them.[22]

But the Sabinis and the Whites were not without rivals. In 1937 the crime writer and novelist Peter Cheyney wrote in the *Sunday Dispatch* that there were five major London gang districts: Hackney, Hoxton, North-East London, North London and the West End, this last being 'worked over' by a loose alliance of the Hoxton Mob, the Elephant and Castle Boys and the Hackney Gang as well as the 'West End Boys'. Until 1927, wrote Cheyney, 'the Hackney Gang was supreme in the West End. Then came the battle of Ham Yard when the gang suffered a severe reversal in terms both of blood spilled and prestige lost.'

Apart from the gangs which ran their areas, splinter teams such as the squad of pickpockets from Aldgate worked the nearby City. Additionally there were teams of smash-and-grab raiders, one of which was led by the future self-styled 'Boss of the Underworld' Billy Hill. Also flexing his young muscles was his rival for the title, Jack Comer, known as Jack Spot. He had interests in the pitches on the open courses at Epsom and Brighton.

There are in the London District quite a number of shops and cafes which are either actually owned or controlled by gangs. The merchandise, provisions, cigarettes, hosiery or fancy goods sold at these places are invariably stolen property, the result of burglaries effected by crooks who work in

[22] B. Hill, *Boss of Britain's Underworld*, p. 5.

close co-operation with, or under definite orders from, gangs.[23]

Cheyney considered that the activities of the London gangs – excluding greyhound and race-course affairs – included working on the smaller and more subversive night clubs, arranging the pickpocketing of what he called 'Good time Charlies' – men looking for 'a bit of fun', organization and protection of street prostitutes, selling lines of stolen goods, organizing the beating (paying) of individuals who have upset members or friends, and protecting and organizing independent sneak thiefs whose work was now often contracted (laid-out) for them and from whom a cut was taken.

As for the race-courses, the last major pre-war fight took place at Lewes race-course on 8 June 1936 when the Hoxton Mob ran riot. In retaliation for an incident at Liverpool Street when a member of the Whites had had his throat cut, thirty members of that gang went to the races with the specific intention of injuring two of the Sabinis. They did not find them and instead set upon the bookmaker Arthur Solomons (who nearly two decades earlier had been acquitted of the attempted murder of Billy Kimber) and his clerk, Mark Frater, who were known to be friendly towards the Sabinis. After a running battle sixteen men were arrested. They were defended privately at Lewes Assizes by the very fashionable J. D. Cassels KC and G. L. Hardy. On pleas of guilty, the ringleaders drew five years' penal servitude from Mr Justice Hilbery, who imposed a total of fifty-three and a half years on the defendants.

After that an accommodation was reached. The Sabinis would have the West End, the Whites the King's

[23] P. Cheyney, *Making Crime Pay*, pp. 65–6.

Cross area. The latter became known as the King's Cross Gang and Alf White would hold court in the Bell public house or Hennekeys in the Pentonville Road, exercising strict discipline amongst his followers. 'No bad language was allowed,' says John Vaughan, a police officer from King's Cross. 'First time you were warned. The next time – out.' It had been the same with Darby Sabini: women were to be treated properly; Italian youths could not drink before they were twenty. It was a reasonably benevolent dictatorship.

Darby Sabini lost another battle when, following a series of unfavourable articles, he sued the offending newspaper for libel. On the day of the action he failed to appear and costs of £775 were awarded against him. He did not pay and bankruptcy proceedings were commenced. It was put to him by the counsel appearing for the petitioning creditor that he was the king of the Sabini gang.

'I do not admit that,' he replied.

'And that you make twenty- to thirty-thousand pounds a year?'

'No.'

Thirty years later his successor Jack Spot was to fare no better in the civil courts when he battled with the *People*.

The Sabini empire was effectively destroyed by the outbreak of the Second World War. Darby Sabini had moved to Brighton, where his daughters were educated locally – Saffron Hill legend said it was Roedean but there are no records of the girls there – and where he had a penthouse flat in the Grand Hotel. With the beginning of the war in 1939, they were regarded as enemy aliens and were interned on the Isle of Man. The one brother who escaped internment was sentenced in 1942 to nine months' imprisonment for attempting to prevent that fate. Their business empire was up for grabs. For a time their West End interests were shared by the Whites, 'Benny the Kid' from the East End (the *nom de guerre* of Jack Spot) and the Elephant Gang, with the Whites increasingly the dominant force.

Just what were Darby Sabini and his brothers like? A picture taken of the Cortesis and the Sabinis before the Fratellanza shooting shows Enrico Cortesi in a straw hat sitting in the centre of the group like the captain of a cricket team. To his left is Darby, less than middle height, wearing his customary flat cap and a shirt with no collar. His dark brown suit with a high buttoned waistcoat, black silk stock and light-checked cap was the outfit he had selected when he was twenty and he wore it for the rest of his life, indoors, outdoors and, so it is said, sometimes in bed. To Cortesi's right and in the background is handsome Harryboy Sabini, who wore highly polished spring-sided boots. Brother Joe liked cherry checks whilst George wore a grey fedora.

Over the years Darby became a folk hero to the Italians of Saffron Hill. Tradition there has it that he was one of the three people to whom to turn when the rent was due. A white five-pound note – no interest asked – would be produced and the debt repaid because the borrower knew he could ask again in times of trouble. He may not have had to pay interest but he incurred a debt of loyalty. Sabini, in turn, defended the locals against the depredations of the Hoxton Mob when in the late twenties they invaded the quarter demanding protection money. The Sabinis placed minders in the shops to repel boarders. The culmination was the battle of Ham Yard in 1927, which resulted in the defeat of the Hoxton boys and their allies, the Hackney Gang, and the emergence of Darby as the controller of the West End.

'I called him Uncle Bob,' says the son of one of the men who worked for Darby Sabini. 'Every time I saw him he gave me a shilling.'

After the war Harry joined his brother in Brighton, to which Darby had retired with, according to Saffron Hill legend, two sacks of gold. In the late 1940s Darby functioned as a small-time bookmaker with a pitch on the free course at Ascot. When he died in Hove in 1950 his family and friends were surprised that he apparently had little money. Yet the man who had been his clerk, Jimmy Napoletano, was stopped leaving the country on his way to Italy with £36,000. The racing tradition is kept up. A member of the family still runs a book in the silver ring at London race-courses. Another, outside the racing fraternity, had a newspaper pitch in Holborn.

But Darby and his brothers' names lived on in the courts as an example of gangster stardom. 'Don't go thinking you are the Sabini brothers,' said a judge, discharging the Krays through lack of evidence. Darby also lives on in fiction and film as the Brighton gang leader, Colleoni, in Graham Greene's *Brighton Rock*. One of the key scenes in both book and film is the meeting between him and Pinky in a Brighton hotel. The slashing of Pinky at the race meeting is based on the Lewes battle in 1936.

'Darby had a purist dislike of razor-slashing and though he was to send razor teams in pursuit of his enemies he always walked away when the cutting began,' recalled George Sewell, his one-time lieutenant. It resembles the story of the Bishop of Chicago who when the first snow fell each winter left for Miami because 'he couldn't bear to see the poor suffer in the cold'. But, on the greyer side, 'In company with most of his top men, he toted a gun, a loaded, flat black Webley and Scott automatic pistol in his back pocket. Like his cap, that gun stayed with him twenty-four hours a day.'

The family 'kept in touch'. One member, Johnny Sabini, 'though now an older man, comes to see me in Broadmoor,' wrote Ronnie Kray nostalgically.[24]

[24] R. and R. Kray, *Our Story*, p. 19.

2

After
the War

With the internment of the Sabinis, the Whites, according to both Jack Spot and Billy Hill, took over the West End (although Hill called them the Blacks).

They were a gang of hoodlums run by five brothers named Black. Some of them had been in their time thieves and burglars, but they had neither the guts nor the brains to do any good at it. They looked at the Sabinis and came to the conclusion that there was room for two at that game. They nearly got away with it. At least, they made room for one and a half. The war was a godsend to them.

They took over the horse-race tracks and the dog-tracks concessions. They continued the blackmail of club owners, cafe proprietors and publicans. They even ran some of the brasses on the streets and used them to steer the mugs into the spielers and drinking-clubs.

All through the war years they had it all their own way. No one could open a drinking-club or spieler in the West End without the Blacks' permission. And their permission usually meant the payment of a dollar-in-the-pound out of the takings.[1]

[1] B. Hill, *Boss of Britain's Underworld*, p. 6.

On the night of the declaration of war against Italy there had been rioting in Soho. Shop premises owned by Italians had been stoned and there had been fighting amongst the rival patriotic factions. The round-up of the Sabinis had left the area open to the Whites and to the Yiddishers, who now aligned themselves with the new masters. One of the Italian Gang, Antonio 'Baby Face' or 'Babe' Mancini, remained, however, to lead the group protecting the old order's interests.

Over the years protection of clubs has worked in a tried and tested way: a suggestion of a weekly payment, a refusal, the entry into the club by two or more men whilst the public is present, a fight, bottles and glasses smashed, a foot through the drummer's kit, furniture overturned, staff molested, and the next day a reminder that for a smallish weekly sum this sort of behaviour which frightens off the punters and costs very much more to repair can be prevented. But for a time, at the beginning of 1941, protection was a very different game. The rule seems to have been to inflict the maximum amount of damage so that the rival's club could be closed for good, leaving one less competitor.

On 20 April Eddie Fletcher, also known as Eddie Fleicher and Joseph Franks, became involved in a fight with Bert Connelly, the doorman at Palm Beach Bottle Parties, a club in the basement of 37 Wardour Street. The worse for drink, Fletcher not only received a beating but was banned from the club for his pains by Joe Leon, the manager. Two more clubs were housed at 37 Wardour Street, the Cosmo on the ground floor and the West End Bridge and Billiards Club on the first floor. On the night of 30 April a Sam Ledderman – who many years later would give evidence in the first of the Kray trials – came to the Palm Beach to tell Mancini, the catering manager and doorman for the night there, 'They're smashing up the [Bridge and Billiards] club.'

According to the statement made by Mancini to the police, he replied that it was no real business of his but a friend was upstairs. Leon told Mancini to go on the door of the Palm Beach and let no one in.

'I went and stood inside the door and then went and changed out of evening clothes,' he told Detective Inspector Arthur Thorp, adding, 'I went up to see the damage. As I was going upstairs I heard someone say, "There's Babe, let's knife him."' The voice resembled Fletcher's. Mancini sensed someone was behind him and went into the club. He was followed by Fletcher, Harry 'Little Hubby' or 'Scarface' Distleman, whom Mancini had known for some fifteen years, and another man. Distleman had managed the Nest Club in Kingly Street for four years until 1938. Since then he had not worked but, so his brother said, he had won a good deal of money on horses and greyhounds. His brother, 'Big Hubby', ran a string of small brothels in the West End. He died in the 1980s leaving £4 million in safety deposit boxes.

According to Mancini, Fletcher started fighting and came at him with a raised chair. Mancini saw a knife on the floor and picked it up to defend himself. Distleman, stabbed five inches deep in the chest, called out, 'Baby's stabbed me in the heart, I'm dying.' He was right. Half-carried out to the street by his friends, he fell down in the doorway of another club and died later in Charing Cross Hospital. Mancini then left the club and threw the dagger away. Later he changed his story to say that he had carried the dagger to protect himself from gangs from Hoxton and King's Cross.

At Mancini's trial for murder the evidence emerged that Eddie Fletcher and other members of the Yiddisher Gang had earlier been playing pool in the club when in walked part of the Italian Gang led by Albert Dimes. Fighting broke out and the unlucky Fletcher was badly beaten again. He went to hospital and returned an hour later 'to get his coat'. This was when Mancini, quite by chance, came up the stairs to survey the damage. According to such witnesses who were prepared to speak at the committal proceedings, Albert Dimes, along with Joseph Collette and Harry Capocci, were still there, with Albert being held back by his brother Victor. As usual in these matters the prosecution had difficulty in persuading any of the forty people present at the affray to give evidence. Few had seen anything happen at all.

Mancini was unlucky. At his trial it was argued that a death in a gang fight was at worst manslaughter. Indeed, the closing words in the brief to prosecuting counsel read that if Mancini was prepared to plead guilty to wounding Fletcher and to the manslaughter of Distleman, 'Counsel will no doubt consider it, as the witnesses of the assault on Distleman are vague and shaky.'

Despite a summing up to that effect by the trial judge, Mr Justice McNaughten, Mancini was convicted and sentenced to death. In September his appeal was rejected by the Court of Appeal. The summing up had been 'favourable to the defence, perhaps too favourable in some respects', said the Lord Chief Justice. And the House of Lords also found against him. On 31 October 1941 Mancini became the first London gangster to be hanged for over twenty years.

Afterwards Dimes, Collette and Capocci were arraigned for the unlawful wounding of Fletcher. One by one the witnesses declined to identify any of them and as the prosecution's case collapsed the Recorder of London, Sir Gerald Dodson, asked whether it was worth going on with the trial. Capocci was acquitted and Collette was bound over in the sum of £5 to come up for judgment if called on to do so within three years. 'You were probably expecting prison,' the Recorder told them, 'and no doubt you deserve it, but I am going to bind you over.'

Dimes was also convicted and he too was bound over to come up for sentence. A deserter from the RAF, he was returned to the force. Over the next thirty years he was to become a major figure in the control of the London underworld, best known for his 'fight which never was' with Jack Spot in Frith Street on 11 August 1955, an event which threw that control into turmoil.

'Italian' Albert Dimes was born of a Scots mother and Italian father who came from Scotland to Saffron Hill in the 1930s. His father first opened a fish shop and, when that failed, a cafe club, La Venezia. Nor did that succeed. In those days Little Italy was a square of four streets in which the whole community lived and worked cheek by jowl and Dimes, along with many others who knew the Sabinis and their friends, drifted into their company. Until the 1950s he operated as a bookmaker, strongman and owner of small spielers principally for the Italian community. Apart from his troubles with Babe Mancini he received only one further sentence, on a conviction for larceny in 1943 at Marlborough Street Magistrates' Court.

Jacob, sometimes John, Colmore, also known as Jacob Comacho, also known as Jack Comer and best known as Jack Spot, was around a long time – not as long as the Sabinis, but getting on for twenty years – as one of the kings of the underworld. In fact that title was a contributing factor which led to the violence which ended his reign.

One of four children, Spot – so called because he liked to say he was on it if help was needed (or more prosaically because he had a mole on his cheek) – was born on 12 April 1912 in Myrdle Street, Whitechapel, the son of Polish immigrants. His brother was a tailor, his sister a court dressmaker. At fifteen he became a bookie's runner and the next year joined forces with a leading figure of East End protection rackets. Strictly small-time, together they protected the Sunday morning stall-holders in Petticoat Lane. He fell out with the man and they fought, leaving Spot the winner. He then called himself the King of Aldgate.

After a short spell as a partner with Dutch Barney, an East End bookmaker, he joined forces with a house-breaker, acting as his look-out and minder. This ended with an appearance at Middlesex Quarter Sessions when amazingly, since he admitted to around forty offences, he was bound over. He returned to bookmaking and the race-courses.

For a time he ran a typical fairground scam called 'Take a Pick' at the major race meetings. The mug punters paid 6d to pull a straw with a winning number from a cup. If they were extremely fortunate they won a cheap prize whilst Spot cleared between £30 and £40 a day. Later the enterprise was extended to Petticoat Lane where 'Take a Pick' earned him another £50 a morning. He was also an active bookmaker on the free course. On a bad day he welshed, leaving before paying out on the last race. The old-time jockey Jack Leach may well have had Spot in mind when he advised racegoers, 'Never bet with a bookmaker if you see him knocking spikes in his shoes'.

In 1935 Spot became a local folk hero by leading a Jewish team against Oswald Mosley's Blackshirts when they marched down Cable Street in the East End. According to Spot he approached Mosley's leading bodyguard, a six-foot-six all-in wrestler, 'Roughneck', and felled him with a chair leg filled with lead. It was a story on which he traded for the remainder of his working life.

The rest of his pre-war career was not as heroic.

Certainly he protected the Jewish shopkeepers against Mosley's Blackshirts but they were obliged to pay up to £10 to ensure their premises were not damaged in the demonstrations. In 1937 he was sentenced to six months' imprisonment for causing grievous bodily harm to a Blackshirt during one of the marches through the East End. It was to be the only prison sentence he received in his career. When he was released from prison he became an enforcer, collecting subscriptions for an East End stall traders' fund run by Larry Sooper. 'This was a private association formed by stall owners who kept the depression at bay by refusing to let any other new trader break in and set up a stall.'[2]

During the war he served for a short time in the Royal Artillery stationed in Cornwall but was given a medical discharge in 1943. It is impossible to trace the accuracy of some of Spot's stories but, according to him, after his discharge he returned to London and gravitated to the West End where he became involved in a fight in a club in the Edgware Road. The man, Edgware Sam – in all Spot's stories the men are Manchester Mike, Newcastle Ned and so forth – ran out of the club, some said to get a gun. Whether Spot believed this or thought that Sam had gone to the police, he feared a prison sentence and fled north to a land where the black market and organized crime were rampant. Goods were being stolen from the ships at Hull docks and the cash had to be spent somewhere. Where illegal gaming and drinking clubs are established, protection is sure to follow. Spot helped a club owner, Milky, of the Regal Gaming Club in Chapeltown, Leeds, clear out a Polish protection racketeer from his club, became the owner's bodyguard and, as a reward, was given a pitch at the local greyhound-track.

He worked as what he described as a 'troubleshooter'

[2] H. Jansen, *Jack Spot, Man of a Thousand Cuts*.

for various northern clubs until he heard Edgware Sam had been gaoled for fraud. Perhaps fraud is too grand a word. It seems to have been for 'working the tweedle', a short-time con trick of taking a ring into a jewellers for valuation and then declining to sell it. At the last moment the grifter changes his or her mind and offers the ring once more. This time, however, the ring appraised by the jeweller has been switched and he is now offered a fake in the hope he will not bother to examine it a second time. In any event Spot returned to London, pleaded self-defence and was acquitted.

Now he was in great demand. He was called to help club owners in the major northern cities, which was when he earned his nickname. According to his accounts, which appeared not only in book form but in numerous articles in Sunday newspapers, he assisted in establishing the proper allocation of pitches at northern bookmaking tracks, having to deal with 'Fred, leader of a big mob in Newcastle' along the way.

> Newcastle Fred was not only a gangster but a race-course operator as well. He thought he had the say-so on flogging out bookmakers' pitches, but he made a mistake when he tried to get nasty with me and a few of my pals at Pontefract races. There was a battle . . . a proper free for all, and we had settled it before the police and race-course officials got wise to it. We'd settled Newcastle Fred's business too.[3]

There were other accounts of the story, including one from an eyewitness. One bookmaker recorded, 'What Spot doesn't tell is that old Fred celebrated his sixty-fifth birthday a few days before Spot bravely kicked him with

[3] *Daily Sketch*, 29 September 1958.

his pointed shoes into the race-course dirt covered in blood. That's how courageous Spot was.'[4] Again it is difficult to assess the accuracy of the story. It could be said the bookmaker, who had 'scars tearing across the top of his scalp – relics of the days when he had to fight the slashing gangs who terrorized Britain's race-tracks between the wars', was not wholly disinterested. The bookmaker was Harry White, the son of Alf White who had challenged the Sabinis during the 1930s.

Shortly after the end of the Second World War Spot ran the Botolph Club, a spieler in Aldgate, reputedly taking £3000 a week tax free from illegal gambling. The figure may be accurate; large sums of money changed hands there. A solicitor's elderly managing clerk remembers:

> There was a burglar known as Taters, best screwsman in London. He once went out and did a job, pulled in £7000 and then went and did it all in a night playing chemmy with a Jewish bookmaker in Spot's club in Aldgate. It was a straight game but mugs always want to beat the finest and they never succeed. Tragedy really.

'We didn't serve drinks,' said Spot, 'drinks interfere with business and they can lead to people taking liberties or starting a battle.' Spot saw himself as a Jewish Godfather in the East End. He left an account of how his version of protection worked:

> I didn't have to buy nothing. Every Jewish businessman in London made me clothes, give me money, food, drink, everything. Because I was a legend. I was what they call a legend to the Jews.

[4] *Daily Herald*, 8 October 1955.

Anywhere they had anti-semitic trouble – I was sent for: Manchester, Glasgow, anywhere. Some crook go into a Jewish shop, says gimme clothes and a few quid, the local rabbi says Go down London and find Jack Spot. Get Jack, he'll know what to do.

So they did and I'd go up and chin a few bastards. The Robin Hood of the East End, a couple of taxi drivers told me once. 'You helped everyone', they said.[5]

But Spot was still interested in race-course bookmaking. The White family had control of the pitches on the free courses at Ascot, Epsom and Brighton and at the point-to-point races not yet under the control of the Jockey Club and the National Hunt Committee. It was an arrangement which had been going for more than thirty years.

[H]arry White's father, Alfred, had been collecting about £2 from every bookmaker working at the Points meetings.

It all went as a voluntary contribution to the Hunt Committees which organized the meetings.

Harry himself eventually became responsible for organizing bookmakers' pitches; he kept off welshers and pickpockets.

Everybody – including County police forces – was pleased with the arrangements.

Now Spot took over. Exactly how it happened depends upon the version preferred. This is Harry White's account as related to Sidney Williams in the *Daily Herald*.

[5] *London Standard* (Michael Ewing), 6 January 1986.

His fear of Spot began in January 1947 in a club in Sackville Street, off Piccadilly. He was drinking with racehorse trainer Tim O'Sullivan and a third man.

Spot walked in with ten thugs, went straight up to Harry and said 'You're Yiddified' – meaning he was anti-Jewish.

White denied it. He said: 'I have Jewish people among my best friends.' Spot wouldn't listen, and hit him with a bottle.

As White collapsed in a pool of blood, the rest of Spot's men attacked O'Sullivan and the third man who was employed by White.

O'Sullivan was beaten unconscious and pushed into a fire in the corner of the club. The other man was slashed with razors and stabbed in the stomach.

It is not totally surprising that Spot's version of events is a different one. His account in the *Daily Sketch* reads:

But the biggest, toughest and most ruthless mob was the King's Cross gang, led by a bookmaker named Harry who had taken over the race-course protection racket from the Sabini Boys.

Their word was law, not only on the race-courses but in the clubs and pubs – even in the fashionable night clubs of the West End.

He goes on to record that in a 'Mayfair Club' a challenge was thrown down and the King's Cross Mob 'partly wrecked' the place. A few nights later the 'same crowd' returned and were told that Jack Spot was a friend of the Guv'nor.

'F— Jack Spot,' came the answer. 'He doesn't work for us – when we want him we'll call him.'

43

There were other encounters until 'We finally ran them down at a place in Sackville Street off Piccadilly.'

> Harry had seven of the toughest of his boys with him when I led my pals into the room. There wasn't any politeness this time. They knew what I'd come for. And I sailed right in.
>   At the first smack I took at them Harry scarpered. You couldn't see the seat of his trousers for dust.[6]

Clearly they are both talking about the same incident.

If one accepts White's version there was another fight, this time at the point-to-point races at Bletchley in February 1947. With little difficulty Spot cleared the decks: the £2 pitch fee became £7. For the next eight years he exercised such strict control over point-to-point bookmaking that, for example, at the Puckeridge Hunt meeting in 1955 he refused to let betting take place on the Grand National; the announcement was broadcast to the meeting over loudspeakers. Meanwhile Harry White paid him twenty-five per cent of his winnings.

According to both Hill and Spot (whom Hill calls Benny the Kid in his memoirs) the Whites were finally routed in the week of 9 July 1947 when Hill and Spot united to clear them out of their interests. There had been a previously scheduled meeting, the Baksi–Woodcock fight at Harringay Arena on 8 April that year, but the police had wind of this and had warned both sides to stay out of trouble. According to both Spot and Hill huge armies were summoned and searched for the Whites. In Spot's tale Harry simply vanished and the gang faded away. Hill has a rather more colourful version which included roasting one White over the fire.

[6] *Daily Herald*, 3 October 1955.

Each tells the story in almost identical terms with the emphasis placed on the teller's organizational qualities. This is not surprising; after all, each was writing for a different publication. It was this vanity which was to tell against Spot.

According to Hill it was he who was giving the orders. '"It's alright," I said to Benny the Kid, "we won't need shooters in this town anymore. Get 'em off the boys and get rid of them." They collected the shooters and the bombs and the machine gun and destroyed them. They were actually thrown down a manhole.'[7]

But according to Spot he had had a compulsory chat with Chief Superintendent Peter Beveridge, who had explained that the police were not going to have gang warfare in London:

> When I got back to Aldgate I called the heavy mob together at once.
>
> 'We've got to pack it up,' I said. 'Get rid of the ironmongery.'
>
> So we collected all the Stens, the grenades, revolvers, pistols and ammunition, loaded them into a lorry and dumped the whole lot into the Thames.[8]

Whoever was in charge, the West End had new owners for nearly a decade, each keen to emphasize how order and safety were restored to the streets. Both Hill and Spot were essentially businessmen. Accommodations could be reached with anyone and since neither had any real interest in vice it was easy to continue the *laissez-faire* arrangement with the prostitute-running Messina brothers.

[7] B. Hill, *Boss of Britain's Underworld*, p. 7.

[8] *Daily Sketch*, 3 October 1955.

They were peaceful and highly profitable years in 1950 and 1951. Visitors and strangers must have found the West End a rather dull place with no running gang-fights and feuds. . . . The truth was that we cleared all the cheap racketeers out. There was no longer any blacking of club owners and restaurant keepers. In fact so peaceful did it all become that there was no gravy left for the small timers.[9]

'Hill reigned almost with the blessing of the police,' says a solicitor's managing clerk from the period. 'He was a very likeable bloke, always paid his bills. If you overlooked his reputation you'd never have dreamed who he was. Whilst he was in control there was a peaceful scene. He kept discipline.'

Others believe the peaceful reign was simply that Spot and Hill paid off the police and an even less charitable view comes from one of Hill's friends. 'He kept control with the razor. People were paid a pound a stitch, so if you put twenty stitches in a man you got a score. You used to look in the evening papers next day to see how much you'd earned.'

Support for that opinion comes from a West End solicitor of the era. 'If no one tried to muscle in it was because they didn't dare to.'

One of those who did dare and who failed was Tommy Smithson, an ex-fairground boxer with a penchant for silk shirts and underwear, a man of immense courage and little stability or ability who was known as Mr Loser. Born in Liverpool in 1920 and brought to the East End two years later, he had served in the Merchant Navy until his discharge in the 1950s. Back in Shoreditch he found things to be different. The Maltese coming to

[9] B. Hill, *Boss of Britain's Underworld*, p. 155.

England on subsidized passages which had, in some cases, cost as little as three pounds, had moved in and had themselves established a network of their own gambling and drinking clubs and stables of prostitutes. Smithson decided to set up his own protection racket devoted to these Maltese businessmen, as well as working a spinner[10] with a Tony Mella around the dog-tracks.

Initially he worked as a croupier for George Caruana, whose gambling clubs included one in Batty Street, Stepney. At the time Caruana and the other Maltese were keen to avoid trouble and Smithson soon extended his interest to a share of the takings in the clubs. Smithson took a shilling in the pound from the dice games, earning up to £100 an evening. He also obtained backing and opened up a one-room club in Maidenhead Passage near Wardour Street.

But police raids followed and Smithson moved to nearby D'Arblay Street where he opened the Publishers' Club 'for authors'. Nobody was fooled and it was back to Berwick Street. Raided again, he could not raise the fine and in default of paying it went to Brixton, from which he was rescued with a whip-round by his friends. He moved to yet another address in Berwick Street and set up as a bookmaker. But now he had moved into competition with the Hill–Spot interests. He was involved in a fight with Frederick 'Slip' Sullivan and threw him out of French Henry's club, cutting his throat in the process. Sullivan, who was later stabbed to death by his girlfriend, was the brother of a member of the Hill–Spot firm and reprisals were swift.

A week later Smithson was betrayed by the Maltese he had been protecting. Told there was a peace offer on the table, he was asked to attend a meeting and was

---

[10] A crooked roulette wheel.

collected in a shooting-brake. On the dramatic signal of a cigar butt tossed on to the pavement Smithson was dragged from the car and slashed over his face, arms, legs and chest. He was then thrown over a wall in Regent's Park and left to die. The slashes on his face were in the form of the letter V, cut down each cheek to meet at his chin. Smithson had not been wholly naive; two loaded revolvers had been taken from him before his slashing. Somehow he survived and forty-seven stitches were put in his face.

His reward for honouring the code of silence was a party, the soubriquet 'Scarface' and £500, with which he bought a share in a club in Old Compton Street, and then another for illegal gaming. This too was closed down by the police and Smithson took up fencing as an occupation. For a time he was successful but then word began to spread that he was a police informer. This time he received twenty-seven stitches.

It signalled his retreat from what he had seen as the big time and he went back to the East End to provide protection for the Maltese. But yet again he miscalculated. The new generation of Maltese were becoming more powerful. They may not have wished to have trouble but they were themselves preparing for a move into the recently vacated Messina territory and were not prepared to tolerate the likes of Smithson.

Poor Tommy had other problems. At the time he was involved with a former prostitute, Fay Richardson, on remand in Holloway Prison on forged cheque allegations. Originally from Stockport where she had been a mill girl, she was what could be described both as a gangster's moll and a *femme fatale*. Three of her lovers were murdered and others suffered bad beatings. According to Commander Bert Wickstead she was

a blonde lady of many secrets, very preoccupied

and very hard . . . She couldn't have been described as a beautiful woman by any stretch of the
imagination. When she spoke there was no out-
ward sign of any great wit, warmth, intelligence or
charm. Yet she did have the most devastating
effect upon the men in her life – so there must have
been something special about the lady.[11]

Pictures of her at the time show a mousey-haired,
rather plain, thin-lipped woman. She had met Smithson
in an all-night cafe in Baker Street and it was something
approaching love at first sight. At least from the time she
met him her convictions for soliciting ceased, although
at the time of her arrest she was working as a prostitute's
maid. She said of the handsome Smithson, '[He was] a
dapper dresser, very fussy about having a clean shirt
every day. He was a big gambler. He could have £400
on the nose.'

On the cheque charges she was being defended at
Inner London Quarter Sessions by William Hemming, a
former detective who was one of the first police officers
to become a barrister and who modelled his speech
patterns on Winston Churchill whom he admired
greatly. Much of his work came from recommendations
by former officers and he was not known for accepting
legal aid work. Money had to be raised for Fay's
defence. Smithson collected £50 from his former
employer, George Caruana, and complained bitterly it
was not a hundred. On 13 June 1956 Smithson, together
with Walter Downs and Christopher Thomas, went to a
cafe in Berner Street, Stepney, and confronted Caruana
and Philip Ellul, a Maltese who ran a second or third
division string of prostitutes. Smithson said he wanted
more than £50 from Caruana and in the ensuing fight

Caruana's fingers were slashed as he protected his face from a flick knife. Other Maltese in the cafe were held off at gunpoint by Thomas. Thirty more pounds were produced. In accordance with standard gangland practice Ellul was told to start a collection for Fay and provided with a book to record the contributions.

On 25 June Smithson was found dying in the gutter outside Caruana's house in Carlton Vale. He had been shot in the arm and neck. His last words were said to be 'Good morning, I'm dying.' The full story of his death did not emerge for almost another twenty years. Its solution was to have considerable repercussions for the next generation of criminals and the police alike.

With Smithson's killing as her mitigation and given that she had no prior criminal convictions – for the purposes prostitution does not count – Fay Richardson was placed on probation with a condition she returned to Lancashire and did not visit London for three years. Whilst on remand, she had applied for leave to attend Smithson's funeral and had been refused. Instead a wreath was sent in her name: 'Till we meet again, Fay.' Other tributes at the funeral, attended not by the bosses but by almost everyone else from the milieu, included pairs of dice, an anchor in recognition of the fact he was a naval man and, from his mother, a chair. It was a classic example of a major gangland funeral with the cortege half a mile long.

Some time after that, Tommy's old mum, a wonderful old girl, had a life-size statue of an angel made to place over Tommy's grave. It's still there in St Patrick's Cemetery, Langthorne Road, Leytonstone. When she had it made, she showed me a photo of it, and out of respect I couldn't laugh at the time, but I had to have a good laugh as I walked away – a villain like Tommy Smithson to have an angel over his grave.[12]

Fay Richardson headed back north, pausing only to visit Tommy's grave in Leytonstone – an act of piety faithfully recorded by the press. Later she returned to London and took up with Jackie Rosa, Billy Hill's team mate and Elephant and Castle hardman. Some time later Rosa was killed in a car crash. He was disqualified from driving at the time and his last words to the police are said to have been, 'It wasn't me who was driving.'

'Her men never did have any luck,' said one of Rosa's friends cynically.

Of course from time to time there were other troubles to disturb the Hill–Spot-induced calm. One arose when Francis Fraser from the Elephant and Castle, who had had interests in the West End for over a decade and was to continue to do so for another, re-emerged. According to Hill, Fraser and his team quarrelled in Soho with the Carters from South London and Hill stepped in to quieten things down after a man was glassed. Alliances were formed and broken and as the relationship between Spot and Hill deteriorated so Fraser became a running mate of Hill.

Just how much control Spot did exercise is debatable. He claimed to have united the gangs from as far apart as Upton Park and Aldgate in the east, Forest Hill and the Elephant and Castle in the south, through to Islington, Shepherd's Bush and Clerkenwell. Possibly he never even aspired to 'running' Soho which was, at the time, synonymous with the 'underworld', although he had a club there and took a cut of £200 a week from another. He held court in the Galahad Club off the Tottenham Court Road. He was a family man living at Hyde Park Mansions in Bayswater with a beautiful wife,

[12] H. Ward, *Buller*.

Rita, whom he had met at Haydock Park races and who had stood by him for years through the troubles which came his way. Perhaps, as has been said, he was too happily married to be a proper gang leader. Yet at his peak he maintained a style reminiscent of the American gangsters of the 1930s.

The crime reporter Michael Jacobson thought little of him. 'I knew Spotty well and he was never more than just a thug. He had no initiative of his own. He was never a gang leader. Hill was.'

On the other hand, Leonard 'Nipper' Read, who as a young officer at Paddington knew Spot and later arrested the Krays, thought quite well of him.

By the 1950s he . . . was something of a grand old man. He had mellowed since his early days and was now well groomed with well tailored, usually brown suits, a brown fedora hat and hand-made shoes. He would leave his flat, walk across the road to his barbers and then down to the Cumberland Hotel where at a table in the corner of the Bear Garden he would hold court offering advice and wisdom to anyone who sought it. He looked like a successful businessman. He seemed to have modelled himself on the American mafioso, Frank Costello, but had neither that man's intellect, power or political connections.[13]

Read had not much time for Billy Hill, whom he described as 'short, slim, and with his hair greased and pasted back [and] looked every inch a spiv of the 1950s'.[14] Hill had been born in Seven Dials, near Leicester Square, in 1911. For years, indeed up until the gentrification

[13] L. Read and J. Morton, *Nipper*.
[14] Ibid.

of Covent Garden in the last twenty years, it was one of the rookeries of London crime. He was one of twenty-one children and his one-eyed sister, Maggie, was a famous shoplifter known in the trade as 'Baby Face, the Queen of Forty Elephants'. The nickname came from the shape she acquired after hiding the merchandise in her hoister's bloomers and coats.

According to his version of events, Hill did his first chivving (slashing or stabbing) at the age of fourteen. 'Suddenly he took a liberty with me. Without the slightest qualm I got hold of a pair of scissors and drove them into his back. And it came quite natural to me. It was as easy as that.'[15]

Even earlier he was a fully fledged burglar. According to Narborough, his arrest of Hill was to lead to his first gaol sentence. It was for being a suspected person and Hill seems to have been most co-operative. 'No one was quite sure where we were, so Billy Hill volunteered to direct us to the nearest police station.'[16] From there he continued a life of burglaries for which he received a string of prison sentences, at the same time moving ever upwards in the hierarchy of the underworld. He was popular with his lawyers. 'Send in a bill and it was paid on the nail,' says one managing clerk who acted for him.

The consensus is that despite their totally different personalities Hill and Spot got along well. For years they maintained a low profile and were always prepared to enter an accommodation with, say, the Maltese who ran prostitution. 'It was as if the police gave them a licence to keep things under control,' says a solicitor's managing clerk.

Spot's troubles when they came were mainly in the form of Duncan Webb, the crime writer for the *People*

[15] B. Hill, *Boss of Britain's Underworld*, p. 19.

[16] F. Narborough, *Murder on My Mind*, p. 38.

and ghost writer for the other boss of the underworld, Billy Hill. Spot became jealous at the publicity being handed out and which was not rubbing off on to him. Spot wrote in his book: 'Billy Hill was a friend of mine. But he had his own way of working. His own personal ambitions and his own ideas and plans; ambitions and ideas can sometimes clash.' And on another occasion: 'I made Billy Hill. He wrote to me when he was in gaol, wanted me to help him. . . . Then he got to be top over me. If it wasn't for me he'd never have got there. I should've shot Billy Hill. I really should.'[17]

Hill had this to say of the deterioration in their relationship: 'Jack was becoming insecure and a bit jealous of me. He was an older man, you see, and once he got this persecution complex he was impossible to work with anymore.'[18] 'The worst thing I ever did,' he told an acquaintance, 'was to give Jack £14,000 from the Eastcastle Street job.'

There is no doubt that by the summer of 1955 Spot's career as a gang leader was just about in ruins. Things had deteriorated so much that he feared for his pitches on the course at the Epsom spring meeting. Fraser and another hardman, Billy Blythe, were now more closely aligned with Hill than he was. They would be at the meeting. So he called on the Kray brothers in their billiard hall in the East End to seek help. The Krays were never keen on Spot, nor, it seems, he on them. They had their day at the races, their first outing into the upper echelons of underworld society. There was no trouble. At the end of the meeting they took their money and drove off.

It wasn't that we liked him. We despised him

[17] *Sunday Times* magazine, 8 August 1965.
[18] J. Pearson, *The Profession of Violence*, p. 85. (1977 Ed.).

really. We just turned out with Spotty to show everyone that *we* was the up-and-coming firm and didn't give a fuck for anyone. Old Spotty understood. Whatever else he may have been he wasn't stupid. He knew quite well that though we were there in theory as his friends, we meant to end up taking over from him.[19]

According to Pearson, after the spring meeting Fraser and Blythe wished to meet the Krays at a pub in Islington to sort things out. The Krays spent time arming themselves and assembling a team but Hill, having got word of the challenge issued by Fraser and Blythe, was strong enough to have the meeting called off. 'The last thing he wanted was to have bloodshed,' says Pearson. The Krays waited around the pub and then drove home, no doubt satisfied that Fraser did not dare to enter their manor.

As for Spot, he lamented:

At first little things went wrong. When a raid was carefully planned and schemed, something would go wrong at the last minute. The man detailed to steal the getaway car wouldn't be able to steal it or a bunch of skeleton keys that should have opened a door failed to do so at the crucial moment.

The men who'd been responsible for these slip-ups had been bawled out. But they hadn't cried. Instead they'd walked straight out on me and got themselves a job with another organization.[20]

Slowly he lost both his gang and his reputation. The word was out in the underworld that he was a grass. 'We'd had his sheet pulled from the Yard,' says one of

[19] Ibid, p. 87.
[20] H. Jansen, *Jack Spot*, pp. 117–18.

Hill's close friends, 'and there it was for all to see.'

On the other hand Hill's friends and allies remained staunch. They included the daredevil safe-breaker, Eddie Chapman, who had been released from prison during the war for work in German territory, and ex-boxer George Walker, brother of Billy, who was to go on to found the Brent Walker group of companies and whose daughter married into the aristocracy.

Spot was also being pursued by Duncan Webb and on 21 October 1954 he assaulted his tormentor, breaking his arm. On 18 November at Clerkenwell Magistrates' Court he was fined £50 for inflicting grievous bodily harm. More seriously, the incident led to a civil action in the High Court and to Spot's eventual bankruptcy.

Once splits occur in underworld factions even the slightest quarrel or perceived insult can trigger a string of repercussions. One such incident occurred in Manzi's restaurant off Leicester Square when one of Spot's men, Bill Diamond, gave Johnny Jackson, a man more aligned to Hill, a backhander. Such a public display caused both a loss of face and loss of patience.

The effective end of Spot's reign came on 11 August 1955 when he was told in the drinking club, the Galahad, that 'Big Albert' Dimes wanted to see him. This must have been the crowning insult. His temper up, he went to find Dimes and caught up with him on the corner of Frith Street in Soho, where they fought amongst the barrows with a large lady fruiterer trying to stop them by banging Spot with a brass weighing-pan.

'If she hadn't intervened Spot would have done him,' says a bystander who never gave evidence. 'Once she hit him Albert got the knife away and did him.' Both men were badly injured. Dimes got away in a taxi. Spot picked himself off the pavement, staggered into a nearby barber's shop, said 'Fix me up' and fainted. Both went to hospital and were arrested as they left their respective hospital beds. When questioned Spot had said, 'It is between me and Albert Dimes – between us, and nothing to do with you.' When asked who had attacked him Dimes replied, 'You know as well as I do. It was Jackie Spot. I'm not prossing.' When he was asked to make a formal statement he said he had been attacked by 'a tall man. . . . I don't know his name.' Another version of the story is that Spot went after Dimes because he was not paying his tribute. A third is that the Italian Mob led by Bert Marsh had put Dimes up to aggravate Spot because he was losing control and was ripe to be taken.

Spot had been stabbed over the left eye and in the left cheek as well as the neck and ear. He had four stab wounds in the left arm and two in the chest, one of which had penetrated the lung. Dimes had his forehead cut to the bone, requiring twenty stitches, a wound in the thigh and one in the stomach which, the prosecutor later said, 'mercifully just failed to penetrate the abdominal cavity'.

But, almost miraculously, their wounds had sufficiently healed eleven days later for their appearance before Marlborough Street Magistrates' Court charged with wounding with intent to commit grievous bodily harm and affray. Clearly the tradition of the underworld that one member should not give evidence against another did not apply to their defending lawyers. Counsel for Dimes said his client had acted completely in self-defence after being attacked by 'this other murderous, treacherous rascal'. Bert Marsh, who just happened to have been in Frith Street at the time and who could not now abide his former friend Spot, loyally gave evidence favouring Dimes and was roundly attacked for his pains. There was clearly a case to answer, said the magistrate. Spot and Dimes were committed for trial at the Old Bailey where they were prosecuted by Reggie Seaton, later to become chairman of the Inner London Quarter Sessions.

The way Seaton put the case for the Crown was that Spot had started the attack and that Dimes had at some time in the struggle wrested the knife from him and struck back, going far beyond the limits of self-defence.

The trials which followed were genuinely sensational. At first Mr Justice Glyn-Jones refused an application for separate trials. This, on the face of it, was reasonable. The defendants were charged with making an affray. Unfortunately he had what would be described, in the world of Spot and Dimes, as a touch of the seconds. The next day he asked the counsel for Spot, Rose Heilbron (who was later to become the second woman High Court judge), and that for Dimes, G. D. 'Khaki' Roberts, a doyen of the Bar, what they had to say about making an affray in a public place.

Roberts argued that the reactions of a man fighting for his life could never be described as making an affray. Reggie Seaton for the Crown, accepting that view, then tried to take the affray into the greengrocery shop itself where the fight had ended. If, he argued, it was a public place then Dimes' conduct after he had wrested the knife from Spot was capable of being an affray. It was not a view accepted by the judge, who withdrew the charge of affray against both Spot and Dimes from the jury and told the jury that, if they wished, they could acquit Dimes on the charge of wounding Spot.

'It is not for Dimes to prove that he was acting in self-defence. It is for the prosecution to prove that he was not.' The jury were not convinced and in the circumstances Glyn-Jones discharged them, saying that 'a joint trial without the first charge would not be lawful'. He then directed that Dimes be acquitted of possessing an offensive weapon, gave him bail and remanded Spot in custody. The separate trial of Spot was fixed to take place forty-eight hours later.

On 22 September Spot went into the witness box to say that he had gone to Frith Street to meet Dimes following a telephone call which warned him off racecourses. He told the jury that he paid £300 for the pitches and, keeping one for himself, let the rest out at a fee. Dimes had told him: 'This is your final warning! I don't want you to go racing any more'; adding that he had been going on long enough and it was time someone else had his pitches.

As for the fight, 'We started pushing each other. All of a sudden he pulls a knife out and makes stabs at me. I put my arm up, and it goes through my arm. I fight my way back to the door of the greengrocer's shop. He goes at me again and gets me in the face.' So far as he was concerned Dimes received his injuries in the struggle.

There was a witness to corroborate this version of events: Christopher Glinski, then an interpreter, who a decade later would feature in the Richardson torture trials and a number of other criminal cases both for and against the prosecution. Spot was right, he said. 'I saw Spot push the other man. Then the other man charged him. The other man took a knife out of his pocket. The man in the dock lifted his arms to defend himself. I saw the knife cut into his arm. Then I saw another blow cut his face.' Glinski had got in touch with Peters & Peters, Spot's solicitors, after reading the reports of the magistrates' court committal proceedings and realizing they did not tally with what he had seen.

But there was more, and better, to come. The Reverend Basil Claude Andrews, eighty-eight years old, came to court to say exactly the same thing. He was sure the darker man (Dimes) had attacked the fairer one (Spot). On the face of it here was an unimpeachable eyewitness. In scenes of triumph and jubilation Spot was acquitted. Immediately afterwards in a separate trial Dimes too was acquitted.

But retribution was to follow. The police were informed by disgruntled bookmakers and friends of Dimes that, far from being a saintly old man, the Reverend Basil was an old rascal who welshed on his bets. His only course of action was to go to a newspaper, the *Daily Sketch*, longtime supporters of Spot, to publish his side of the story.

I am fully aware that cowardly people who dare not come forward into the light of day are suggesting that I am a fraudulent witness and that I hood-winked Mr Comer's [Spot's] legal advisers.

I would recall to you that when I gave my evidence last week I gave it on my solemn oath, and I need not remind you that I am a Clerk in Holy Orders.

He went on to deny he had committed perjury, adding:

Any financial difficulties due to my changes of address and my harmless flutters in the sporting world are only temporary, due to my age and inexperience.

Those who are dunning me will soon be repaid if they have patience – some debts have been settled already.

My innocent walk in Frith Street, Soho, that day has made me finish up in a nest of trouble, with enemies in an underworld I never dreamed existed.

And for good measure, he finished: 'I would like to bring about a reconciliation between the parties in the strife who seem to have forgotten that, by what they have done, they are debasing the sacred Brotherhood of Man.'

By the end of the year the Reverend Basil was back in the Old Bailey giving evidence, this time on behalf of the prosecution. The police, unhappy about the collapse of the Spot–Dimes case, had been busying themselves and had now brought a prosecution for conspiracy to pervert the course of justice. Andrews admitted that he had given his evidence following a meeting with Bernard Schack, known as 'Sonny the Yank', and Morris Goldstein, 'Moisha Blue Boy', in the Cumberland Hotel at Marble Arch. His reward had been £25. The Reverend Basil was again believed. Goldstein was sent to prison for three years, Schack for two, whilst Rita Comer, Spot's wife, was fined £50. No one seems to have thought twice about Glinski.

After the trial Spot announced he was quitting Soho and the race-courses. He would, he said, open a small cafe. He would have been fortunate if he had done so. Soho was up for grabs once more. Dimes does not appear to have been too interested. He took over Spot's point-to-point interests. Newspapers reported that there were five major gangs each seeking to put their top man into the position vacated by Spot. Francis Fraser, along with Robert Warren, the elder cousin of boxing promoter Frank, was re-establishing his business of putting gaming machines into Soho clubs. Billy Hill now returned from Australia. He had decided to emigrate there but was refused entry when he turned up with a young woman who certainly was not Aggie, the lawful Mrs Hill. Curiously, however, the outbreak of gang violence, anticipated with some relish by the press, never quite reached all-out war.

There were, however, to be further reprisals against Spot, who knew from rumours in the underworld that he was due for punishment and repeatedly went to Paddington police station seeking protection. Read recalls:

He started by talking to Peter Beveridge, the Detective Chief Superintendent of the District, and worked his way down through the Detective Inspector and various sergeants until he ended up with me. He told me on numerous occasions that the other mob was going to do him and he often pleaded with me to do something about it but as I pointed out, unless there was more direct evidence there was nothing we could do. As a betting man Jack must have known that it was 6/4 on that he would become a victim eventually but it would have been impossible to offer him any sort of protection against a situation he had manufactured himself.

When the police could not help, Spot rented himself a personal bodyguard, Joe Cannon, the minder at the Miramar Club where he drank, paying him £50 a week.

Spot had thought seriously about buying a pub in Paddington and on 2 May 1956 he and Rita had been to look at the Little Weston off Praed Street when at about 9 p.m. they were attacked by a number of armed men. Spot was knocked to the ground with a shillelagh (recognized by his wife as one which, in happier days, he had given Billy Hill), kicked and slashed. At first he made a statement giving the names of his attackers but later retracted it. Rita was made of sterner stuff. She named Frank Fraser and Bobby Warren as leaders of the attack. Both Hill and Dimes were arrested and questioned but never charged.

But where was Spot's minder, Joe Cannon, a man who had been in Portland Borstal, although rather later in time than another former pupil, Billy Hill? Spot had told him that he was taking Rita out for a meal in the Edgware Road and to meet him back at the flat. Cannon had taken his girlfriend Ellen out for the night and had forgotten the time.

. . . when I looked at my watch it was one o'clock in the morning, long past the time when I was due to meet Jack and Rita. Still, there was no use crying over spilt milk, so I spent the rest of the night with Ellen.

In a way I was lucky. If I had been with Jack when he made his way home I would have been dead or, at best, seriously injured.[21]

After the attack, and once it was realized it was a police matter, there were the usual out of court negotiations. It was arranged that Cannon should go to Hill's office at Warren Street, just off Tottenham Court Road. According to his memoirs Cannon took the precaution of taking a .45 revolver with him to the rendezvous, where he met Hill and Albert Dimes. The message he was to convey was that Spot knew Rita was set on going to court but that he, Jack, would talk her out of it. The quid pro quo was that Hill should stop the escalating aggravation between them. Hill was not pleased, telling Cannon that Spot was a wrong 'un and that he would get the same treatment if he remained his man. Indeed, it was only the kindly intervention of Frankie Fraser, who had put in a good word for Cannon, which had kept him unmarked so far.

Dimes appears to have been the peacemaker. All that mattered now was that no one was nicked. Could Cannon fix it so that a couple of the Hill boys could get in to Spot's bedside so things could be agreed in person? One problem was the police sitting by the bedside. The negotiator, a man called Jimmy Woods, went with Cannon to the hospital and in whispers it was agreed that there was no point in nicking Fraser and the rest. Jack

[21] J. Cannon, *Tough Guys Don't Cry*.

said he would persuade Rita not to go ahead. So far as Spot knew it was a genuine settlement negotiated by interested but not involved parties. As he was leaving Woods was asked by the ever percipient Spot whether he had seen Hill recently. 'Haven't seen him for months,' was the reply. Unfortunately, instead of waiting for Cannon and Woods at the Fifty One club as arranged, Hill had come to the hospital, where he was photographed with Woods and Cannon. Cannon and Spot realized they had been set up.

Fraser went to Ireland until matters had, so he thought, died down. He was only lured back when the police let it be known the matter was closed and was arrested at London Airport on his return.

Nevertheless, once the trial began Spot tried to do his best for his attackers. 'I do not recognize these men,' he told the court. 'I know that these men did not attack me.'

But Rita was quite prepared to go through with it. She was cross-examined vigorously by Patrick Marrinan on behalf of Warren, who put to her that she was giving evidence to get rid of Hill, Dimes and friends to re-establish her husband as 'King of the Underworld'.

'I don't care about the other people. I just want to be left alone with my husband and children,' she replied, after earlier saying, 'I would be very happy if they let my husband and me alone. I'd like him to get just a small job.'

Marrinan asked her whether it was right that on the day after the attack she had telephoned a Mrs Harry White and said, 'I'm going to get your husband ten years. I saw him with a knife in his hand stab my husband last night.'

'No,' she replied, she had said, 'I suppose you and your husband are pleased now.'

Harry White certainly must have been.[22] After the Spot–Dimes fight he had given an interview to his old friend Sidney Williams, spitting on the floor as he said, 'That's how frightened we are of Jack Spot and his men now. He hasn't got five men he can rely on to stand at his back.'[23]

Frankie Fraser, who by then had fifteen convictions and had twice been certified 'insane', had, said his counsel John Ritchie, been made use of by other persons for a foul purpose. Warren, with no convictions for violence, received the same seven-year sentence as Fraser.

A week later the same judge, Mr Justice Donovan, sentenced two others, Richard 'Dicky Dido' Frett and David Rosa, for a separate attack. The victim, Johnny Carter of the Carter family and friend of Spot, was connected with the Elephant and Castle Boys who were now flexing their muscles to establish control over Soho and to clear out once and for all any remnants of the King's Cross gang who might be thinking of returning to the West End. An effort by Patrick Marrinan, appearing now for the defendants, to establish that Carter was a member of the Elephant Boys was ruled inadmissible.

'It sounds like the worst days of Prohibition in Chicago rather than London in 1956,' said the judge when imposing seven-year sentences.

On 11 July two more men, 'Billy Boy' Blythe and

[22] Harry White's actress daughter was killed while filming *Ocean's 11* with Frank Sinatra and the Ratpack in America. White had close links with Sinatra and provides an early connection with transatlantic interests. A devout Catholic, he discovered whilst providing the betting for a Church Donkey Derby that the animal a boy was riding was a heavy favourite. 'If it looks like fucking winning make sure you fall off,' he told the child, who duly obliged.

[23] *Daily Herald*, 8 October 1955.

Robert 'Battles' Rossi, were to appear to answer for the attack on Spot, and later another man, William Dennis, joined them at the Old Bailey. Blythe received five years and the others four apiece.

But by now Jack Spot was himself back in the dock at the Old Bailey. He was accused of attacking 'Big Tommy', Thomas Falco, a driver for Dimes – 'I work for Albert Dimes when we go to the races. . . . When he wins, I get wages' – outside the Astor Club on 20 June 1956. He had required forty-seven stitches as a result of this attack and maintained that as Spot had slashed him he had said, 'This is one for Albert . . .'

A witness, ex-boxer Johnny Rice, who gave his occupation as a steel merchant but who was photographed within a few days on a bookmaker's stand at Brighton races along with Tommy Falco and Harry White, remembered the words as 'This is one for Albert Dimes . . .'

At the committal proceedings, James Dunlop for Spot said of the allegation that 'it is a complete and utter fabrication from start to finish'. He would, he said, be calling a witness who had volunteered first-hand information.

The whole story came out at Spot's trial at the Central Criminal Court when that witness, Victor 'Scarface Jock' Russo, came to give evidence. He had, he said, been offered £500 by Albert Dimes to allow himself to be slashed so that Spot could be framed. The offer had come in a car in Frith Street. He had gone there and met Dimes, Hill, Frannie Daniels and Johnny Rice after a back-room meeting at Peter Mario's restaurant in Gerrard Street, Soho. There Hill had said to Duncan Webb, the crime reporter, 'I want you to have a go at Spot this week', and Webb had agreed to write something to Spot's detriment in the *People*. How would they know that Spot did not have a cast-iron aiibi? 'I will get Kye-Kye [Sid Kiki, a bookmaker] to find out,' said Hill. Russo had thought it over and then declined. Later he had heard of the slashing of Falco. When Spot had been arrested he had both gone to the police and telephoned Billy Hill telling him what he had done.

Hill gave evidence denying Russo's allegation. Almost all he would admit to was being boss of the underworld. Afterwards he held a press conference saying that Fraser and Warren were his boys and complaining that the police watched him day and night.

Would he make peace with Spot? 'I am a powerful man,' he said, 'and I don't have to make peace with anyone.'[24]

Billy Hill retired to his villa in Spain saying he had had enough. He had become a minor celebrity. The launch of his book had been attended by Lord and Lady Docker and he had organized the return of her Ladyship's jewels when they were stolen. A picture taken at the book launch shows Frankie Fraser draped artistically over the piano.

'His bottle went,' said one of his former friends, 'he'd lived by violence and now was afraid of getting it.'

Spot went downhill. On his bankruptcy examination he maintained that his memory had gone through too many bangs on the head. He had liabilities of £12,321 and assets of £125. He and Rita were evicted from their Hyde Park Mansions flat. He obtained his discharge from bankruptcy in January 1957 and later that year, with her earnings from newspapers – shortly after the attack she had been paid £300 by the *Daily Express* for posing with her husband – she opened the Highball Club in Bayswater. On 21 July it was wrecked by a gang. Whilst still under police guard it was set ablaze on 13

---

[24] There are numerous accounts of the series of trials. One of the more entertaining is by Laurence Wilkinson, *Behind the Face of Crime*.

August. It was not reopened.

According to Cannon he expected some reprisals from Hill but in turn he was offered the then enormous sum of £2000 to shoot him. He waited outside the Modernaires Club and shot at Hill and Dimes as they left in the early hours.

> I reckon Hill knew that I was the culprit. So did the Old Bill, but there was no reaction from either, maybe Billy felt that it was beneath his dignity to declare war on a nineteen-year-old. . . . It all came right in the end. Dimes contacted me and offered me a drink if I would have nothing more to do with Spotty. I took it, and there the whole thing finished.[25]

Spot drifted into employment as a meat packer and some years later was fined for stealing from his employer. He became estranged from Rita and changed his name to Comacho. Over the years he could be seen at small-hall boxing tournaments in London as perky and ebullient as in his prime.

[25] J. Cannon, *Tough Guys Don't Cry*, p. 45.

3

The Years
Between

By the late 1950s control of Soho and the West End was
seemingly wide open. Curiously enough none of the
likely candidates appeared either to want it or to be
capable of taking it. Although he retained interests in
the West End, Hill was living in Spain in semi-
retirement. Such families as the Carter brothers from
Peckham still remained loyal to Jack Spot, but he was
effectively disgraced and exiled to Notting Hill. Immediately after the Dimes–Spot fight in August 1955 there
had been reports of meetings to discuss the Soho scene
but nothing had really come of them. Frankie Fraser,
who had had interests in the Soho clubs for some time
and whom the newspapers considered a natural successor, was in prison serving seven years for the second Spot
stabbing. For the time being it seemed there was no one
with the necessary charisma and will to take over.

A number of small-timers popped their heads over the
parapet to see what was about, but no real hardman,
capable of dominating the scene, emerged. This was
probably for a number of reasons apart from the fact that
there was no one person or family about with the interest
or, if they had the interest, the strength and ability to
convert it into action. Although he does not seem to
have wanted Soho for himself, the now middle-aged 'Big

Albert' Dimes, as Hill's right-hand man, almost certainly exerted a calming influence. Questions of territory and ownership were referred to him for a solution.

But as for ownership, 'he couldn't fight for fuck,' says one contemporary. Albert Donaghue, later on with the Kray firm, puts it more diplomatically. 'He didn't have the backing necessary,' he says. 'What he was, though, was King of the Point-to-Points.'

Certainly Dimes was now in control of the best pitches at the tracks, and he remained so, granting the concessions and making sure that the odds chalked up suited him. 'If he had the favourite at say 7/4 and took a load on it then he would wipe it to 6/4 and Bobby Warren or one of his men would walk down the line telling us it was the same price for the rest of us,' says Donaghue.

It is a curious fact about the English gang leaders of the period that they never seemed to aspire to the trappings of wealth sported by their admittedly grander-scale American counterparts. True, Hill had a boat, but that was used for business purposes – for the smuggling of cigarettes. He lived in a modest flat in Moscow Road. Spot was a seemingly devoted family man living in Hyde Park Mansions. 'If they went to the Astor Club a couple of nights a week that was a big deal,' says Nipper Read.

Dimes seems to have been in that mould. Read says:

> Of course he never had to pay for a meal anywhere, never had to spend any real money. He held court in the Italian Cafe in Frith Street and would have his suits made for free, free haircuts, and tributes like chickens and meat brought to him. But he was never a man who, whilst he was always well dressed, ever threw money about.

At the time the earnings of a gang leader were in the five-figure mark annually. Lesser fry would receive £20 a week, said *The Times* in 1956.

Dimes remained the almost unseen Godfather, keeping out of the public eye and surfacing only on rare but sometimes quite spectacular occasions. In 1956 he was awarded £666 for a back injury sustained when the cab in which he was travelling was involved in an accident with a van. He was, he said, working as a commission agent, earning about £10 a week. He was fortunate enough not to have paid tax since 1951. A little later in a separate case he agreed to pay arrears of National Insurance Contributions of £135.

In 1956 he was named in the House of Commons by Anthony Greenwood, who called him a 'squalid, cowardly, small-time hoodlum'. He went to see Mr Greenwood for an explanation of the adjectives but the Conservative MP refused to see him. Dimes admitted to a short stretch in Borstal in 1931 and a four-month sentence 'years ago' but surely, he complained, that did not qualify him for Mr Greenwood's attack.

Then in November 1959 he fell out with the National Hunt Committee over the collection of bookmakers' voluntary contributions at the East Essex point-to-point. He had been the only one capable of collecting these illegal payments and had taken on the job out of the goodness of his heart when Harry White, showing even more public spiritedness, had refused to make the collections because 'they [the NHC] wanted too much. I thought it was a liberty asking £10 each for a pitch when they might not take that much from the punters. Albert took over just to keep the peace.'

A year later his name came up in the trial of a former apprentice jockey charged with conspiracy to dope racehorses. The jockey said he had made £1200 from bookmakers and backers when Faultless Speech won the William Hill Gold Cup at Redcar earlier that year. Dimes was alleged to have contributed £100 to the jockey's earnings.

In 1961 he was said to have received £8000 from the swindling of a Bradford chinchilla dealer who had been persuaded to part with £35,900 to finance the purchase of a fleet of ships. The con man, a Charles de Silva, received only £4100 from the deal, and later six years' imprisonment.[1] Dimes obtained the services of Dai Tudor Price, later a High Court judge, to make a statement in open court denying his involvement in the scam.

Two years later Brighton club owner Harvey Holford, accused of the murder of his wife Christine and convicted of her manslaughter, explained his possession of a gun by saying it was to protect himself against Hill, Dimes and their cohorts. Holford had been having difficulties over the installation of 'Legalite' gaming machines in his Blue Gardenia Club.

Dimes last swam into public view in early 1968 when he was at the Tavistock Hotel in Bloomsbury to discuss money owed by a Max Fine to a Mr Corallo, described in a subsequent libel hearing as an 'American gangster'. He also met Angelo Bruno of the Philadelphian family, of whom it was said he was the secret and trusted representative. Bruno came to London between 27 November and 3 December 1966 in a gambling junket organized by a New York gambling club. Another of the card players on that junket was the celebrated Meyer

[1] Ceylonese-born de Silva, described as looking like Omar Sharif, had been a long-time friend of Billy Hill. He was supposed to be the black sheep of a wealthy family and lived well off the art of the con man. He is one of the few examples of a Hill man who was linked with the Krays but at one time he was under their protection. He had been paying over a share of his profits to Charlie Mitchell. The sale of the fishing fleet was the last of his great scams. Later he took a drug overdose rather than face another substantial term of imprisonment.

Lansky, now accepted as one of the great Mafia financiers. Dimes visited Bruno in Philadelphia the next year to discuss the installation of gaming machines in various clubs.[2]

In November 1972 Dimes died of cancer. The Krays sent a wreath costing £20 with the inscription 'To a fine gentleman', a message destroyed by friends on the grounds that it brought shame to the family. The funeral in Kent was attended by over 200 mourners, among them Stanley Baker to whom he had given technical advice on films, including *Robbery*, based on the Great Train Robbery. On his deathbed Dimes is said to have ordered that the police be told the truth about the killing of 'Scotch Jack' Buggy at a gambling club in Mayfair. At his funeral the priest spoke of how proud Dimes had been that he could recite the Creed in Latin.

So ended an unbroken forty-year involvement with Soho, its clubs and frequenters.

But was Dimes the true Godfather or was there someone else standing behind, and over, him? The suggestion in some quarters is that there was. It was the redoubtable Pasqualino Papa – Bert Marsh, who had been acquitted of the murder of a Columbo brother at Wandsworth Greyhound Track. He seems to have been noted by the press only once, when at the Spot–Dimes trial he was accused by Spot's barrister of trying to provide false witnesses for Albert Dimes. But, even today, some major underworld figures speak very highly of him:

---

[2] On 21 March 1980 Angelo Bruno left the Cous restaurant in Philadelphia and was shot behind the right ear when in his car, along with his bodyguard John Stanfa. Bruno died instantly. It was advanced that the reason for his death was his refusal to enter into the lucrative narcotics trade.

Bert ran a betting shop in Frith Street and had an off-licence in Old Compton Street and an interest in at least six books. He was a quiet man, a very very dapper man. He was the Guv'nor all right. He died a very rich man.

Another says:

He was something of a mystery. I met him in the early sixties in Clerkenwell when I was going out with an Italian girl. He was a very pleasant man, very courteous. People respected him, something I didn't understand then. I was later told that he was the Mafia's top man in this country and a man to be friends with.

Meanwhile, fairly unobtrusively, the Maltese had strengthened their grip on the Soho entertainment industry into a stranglehold. Although from time to time the press did what it could to generate some interest in the Soho protection scene, there was little mention of the Maltese involvement until 1971.

On the domestic front, however, in August 1957, with little else going on in the journalists' silly season, the *Daily Sketch* reported that Robert Padgett from West Hartlepool had his sights on the big time. 'I reckon things are soft in London so I'm taking my Pink Domino Gang (named after the tattoos on his left hand) down there. . . . Jack Spot and all that don't frighten me. They don't know what street fighting is.' He was rapidly exposed as a fake a few days later by the same paper, which called in a psychiatrist to evaluate the lad's boasts.

Nearly two years later, in June 1959, a rather more genuine claimant, Joseph Francis Oliva, a Gibraltarian by birth but now from the Bourne Estate in Clerkenwell, London, emerged to give an interview also in the *Daily*

Sketch. He was known, he said, as King Oliva and ran protection rackets and could call up a gang of 400 men. He had been shot a couple of days previously in retaliation, so he claimed, for a fight in a dice spieler in a Camden Town club three weeks before when he and five others had cleaned up all the money, amounting to some £80.

I am going to be boss of the night clubs – and run the night clubs around the West End. I have got to shift one or two big gang leaders to do it. But I have got a man behind me financing me. I already work for him. We have got to have cars to get around in and 'clobber' to look the part.

We already get a nice little living from East End clubs and some in the West End. And we look after about twelve clubs. We see no one takes liberties with the juke-boxes and we make sure there is no trouble in the clubs. The club owners pay us for this and we give the money to the 'Governor'. He is a London businessman who owns property and lives in a big house on the outskirts of town.

I command about 400 people. I can get them all at twenty-four hours' notice just by fifteen to twenty phone calls to individual top men in each gang. Then I am the governor of them all. They are different gangs from all North and South London but mostly in the Theobalds Road area.

All the 400 do not get paid. They do it for kicks. They are all teenagers. They worship me – King Oliva.

We last called the 400 up six months ago for a big fight at the Memorial Hall, Camden Town. But the other side backed out.

I have two lieutenants. I split equally with them. I am drawing about £30 a week at the moment.

He stalwartly maintained that he was no menace to the general public. 'We don't want to have a go at the public. Only gang governors like us in the underworld. I am going to be boss because there are some rich pickings. All a fellow needs is guts and backing – and I've got both.'[3]

It was a statement he largely denied when five years later he was called to give evidence at an enquiry into the behaviour of Detective Sergeant Harold Gordon Challenor and how it was possible for that officer to continue on duty at a time when he appeared to have been affected by the onset of mental illness. Both James Fraser, a relation of the better known Frankie, and Oliva had received sentences following a brush with Challenor. Oliva had received six years' imprisonment for conspiracy to demand money with menaces in relation to the Geisha Club in Moor Street and the Phoenix in Old Compton Street, Soho, and related offences; Fraser had been given fifteen months for possessing an offensive weapon in a public place. Both convictions had been quashed by the Court of Appeal in July 1964.

In their turn some club owners became fairly blasé about violence, regarding it as part of life's rich tapestry. On 11 February 1961 a home-made cocoa-tin bomb was thrown into the Gardenia Club in Wardour Mews, blowing a hole in the door, after Harry Bidney, the manager, had refused admission. On the previous Friday the owner of a nearby club had been slashed when he refused admission. 'A gang of young men are trying to terrorize club owners, but I'm not afraid,' said Bidney.

By then one family had emerged as a force with which

---

[3] Report of Inquiry by Mr A. E. James QC, p. 127, Cmnd 2735. Whilst £30 a week now seems less than pocket money it should be remembered that in 1959 a newly qualified solicitor would be earning less than £20 a week.

to be reckoned. They were the Nash family from Islington, 'the wickedest brothers in England' said one newspaper happily.[4] There were six brothers, from Billy (the fixer and the eldest, in his late twenties) ranging through Johnny (five years younger), Jimmy, Ronnie and George to Roy, the youngest, who had been convicted of manslaughter at the age of sixteen following the knifing of a youth in a dance hall fight. They were friends of the Krays and also of the Richardsons, so establishing a loose cross-London alliance.

Starting out in the 1950s in the traditional way of minding Cypriot cafes at £2 a week, the enterprise had grown until in the early 1960s Johnny Nash, who liked to be called the Peacemaker, was believed to have twenty clubs, including the Embassy in the West End, under his protection. He was said to have escalated the art of the gang fight so that fist was fought with knife, knife with axe and axe with gun. He maintained he was now King of the Underworld. In an interview on 5 March 1961 Billy Nash, who blamed the Street Offences Act of 1959 for much of the troubles in the West End, said there were ten to a dozen families in the club game, running prostitutes, protection, gambling and one-armed-bandits.[5] 'A back-street club was taking £30 to £50 a week and then the birds came in and it became a goldmine.'

Operational methods hadn't changed much, nor had payments. One of the Nash minders reported that he and friends had broken up the Little Londoner Club on Christmas morning 1959. 'I was paid £10 for the smash-up and £5 expenses.' Life was more expensive in London

---

[4] *Sunday Pictorial*, 19 February 1961.

[5] Following the Wolfenden report, the Street Offences Act of 1959 had effectively eliminated street prostitution. The girls had moved into clubs or taken rooms in Soho from which to work.

than in Liverpool, from where it was reported that a slashing could be organized for eighteen shillings.

The Nashes had a considerable North London following. After the dance hall fight at Highbury Corner in December 1959, when Ronald Marwood stabbed a policeman to death, he was hidden out for nearly a month by Johnny Nash. 'I had Big Ronnie stashed away. I had him in a flat in Holloway. He never left the place except after dark and even then he did not go far.'

Underworld legend has it that when the police net was closing in Marwood gave himself up rather than cause trouble for his protector and in return Johnny and another brother tried to help Marwood escape from Pentonville. Later the brothers sent wreaths on the anniversary of his execution.[6]

Although the Nashes held sway for some years, their power was never really the same after a seemingly unimportant occurrence – a minor road accident – blew up into a major gangland incident.

Selwyn Keith Cooney, manager of the Billy Hill-owned New Cabinet Club in Gerrard Street, and no friend of the Nashes, was in a relatively minor car accident involving another car driven by prostitute Vicky James, known as Blonde Vicky, who was a friend of Ronnie Nash. Cooney, a huge personable man from a middle-class Leeds family, known both as Jimmy Neill and, despite his size, Little Jimmy, instead of doing the more sensible thing and forgetting about the matter, sent the bill for 54s 9d damages to Vicky James. She was not insured and the bill remained unpaid. Quite by chance Cooney met Ronnie Nash in a Notting Hill drinking club. Words were exchanged and each suffered a black

---

[6] The Krays also claim to have hidden Marwood. For a full account of the Marwood story and the Krays' version of their involvement see chapter 5.

eye in the subsequent fight. Reports were that Ronnie Nash came off the worse. Two days later Cooney went to the Pen Club in Duval Street near Spitalfields Market.

The Pen Club, said to have been bought with the proceeds from a robbery at the Parker Pen Company and named as an underworld joke, was managed by none other than Tommy Smithson's nemesis Fay Richardson, now renamed Fay Sadler after her marriage to a gambling man. At the time, however, the club was owned by former boxer Billy Ambrose and Jeremiah Callaghan, a member of another leading family from Walworth and a figure who was to reappear time and again over the next two decades. Both were serving ten-year prison sentences but came home on parole at the weekends. The club was frequently raided by the police and, almost as frequently, it changed hands.

Reports of the background to the incident on 7 February 1960 vary. One version is that Jimmy 'Trunky' Nash, who worked as a minder at the Astor Club in which the family had an interest, set out to avenge his brother's beating. Another is that Jimmy, the mildest of the brothers, was sucked into the incident. Bert Wickstead, later a Commander of the Flying Squad but then a Detective Sergeant, believed that, no matter what was on the surface, the real reason behind the incident was that it was part of the West End power struggle with the chance accident providing an opportunity to establish a new pecking order.

Jimmy Nash, together with his red-headed girlfriend, a hostess named Doreen Masters, and two other former professional boxers arrived at the Pen Club a little while after Cooney. According to witnesses Cooney was pointed out to Nash by Doreen Masters and, together with the boxers, he went straight over, broke Cooney's nose with one blow and proceeded to give him a severe beating. 'That will teach you to give little girls a spanking,' he said. Cooney, protesting he had done nothing of the kind, fought back and there was a cry, 'He's got a gun.' Two witnesses were adamant that Nash then shot Billy Ambrose in the stomach and Cooney in the head at point-blank range.

Others in the club attacked Nash and another man, who was hit over the head with a bottle. They ran out of the club and Nash was driven away. Billy Ambrose, although badly hurt, still managed with some help to carry Cooney's body from the club and put it on a pavement some distance away. He then drove himself to hospital, reporting that he had been shot outside a club in Paddington. He could not remember its name.

With a death on the pavement and the wounds Billy Ambrose had suffered it was clear the police would be notified by somebody sooner or later, and they were – by the hospitals which received the body of Cooney and the injured Ambrose. Jeremiah Callaghan couldn't resist going back to the club to find out what was happening and was seen in Duval Street by the police. The bloodstains on his clothing came from a brawl outside a pub in Walworth, he said. Fay Sadler was seen leaving the London Hospital. Giving her name as Mrs Patrick Callaghan, she said she had simply called to see her friend Billy Ambrose. Then two others in the club were brought in for questioning. The first was Cooney's girlfriend, a nineteen-year-old barmaid from the New Cabinet, Joan Bending. The second was Johnny Simons, who had hit the man over the head with a bottle. Both were to point the finger at Jimmy Nash and the boxers. Fay Sadler was brought in for questioning and she too confirmed the picture. Jimmy Nash's flat in the Charing Cross Road was searched and a mackintosh stained with blood of the same type as Cooney's was found. Of Nash himself there was no trace. Meanwhile Joan Bending had picked out both the boxers at an identification parade.

Two days later James Nash surrendered himself at City Road police station. He was accompanied by Manny Fryde, a solicitor's managing clerk from Sampson & Co. Fryde, said by some to have qualified as a solicitor in South Africa but never in England, was one of the doyens of criminal work in post-war London. In those days, well before the Police and Criminal Evidence Act of 1984 with its built-in safeguards for suspects, the arrangement for Nash's surrender had been negotiated on the basis that there would be no pressure on him to make a verbal or written statement.

Bert Wickstead recalls him as a negative person.

> He had a very quiet voice for such a violent man, but I don't recall him saying anything that seemed worth remembering. He was a man of negative values – a non-smoker, non-drinker, who ate a pound of boiled sweets every day. He would sit in his cell, chewing them endlessly. Judging by the expression on his face he could have been on another planet.[7]

He, the boxers and Doreen Masters were charged with the capital murder of Selwyn Cooney. What followed was one of the worst examples of post-war witness interference and jury intimidation.

It began on 16 March with a razor attack on Johnny Simons in a Paddington cafe. His face needed twenty-seven stitches to repair it. The assault was followed by two on his girlfriend, a twenty-three-year-old model, Barbara Ibbotson. On the first occasion she was snatched in broad daylight in Soho and thrown into a car

[7] B. Wickstead, *Gangbuster*.

where her face was slashed four times. Three weeks later she was the victim of another attack when three men broke into her flat whilst she was taking a bath, held her under water and slashed her again. This time she received wounds requiring twenty-seven stitches. Now Bending and Simons accepted the police protection offered them. Joan Bending went to the Edgwarebury Country Club at Elstree.

On 20 February the officers in the case had heard that Fay Sadler had disappeared and the police went to considerable efforts to persuade her to contact them. There was a report that she would come out of hiding if she was guaranteed protection for five years. 'Our message is – come forward at once . . . we will guarantee you full and complete protection at all times.' She did not.

The trial began on 21 April with the public gallery filled with 'faces', including members of the Billy Hill organization, the Callaghan family and the Kray twins as well as the Nash family in force. Now only Nash and the boxers stood trial. The charges against Doreen Masters had been dismissed.

Of the ten male jurors one who was later found to have a conviction for dishonesty as a juvenile had appeared to nod towards Billy Nash in the public gallery. The police overheard a remark that one of the jury was to be nobbled and a watch was kept on this particular juror. One day after court he was followed by officers who had seen a young man run away from his car. 'You won't catch me putting a foot wrong now,' he said with the emphasis on *now*. Meanwhile, it seems that one of the two women on the jury had a husband on remand in Brixton. He is alleged to have told Nash and the boxers that his wife had made up her mind that Nash was guilty of capital murder.

The facts were reported to the judge by both the

prosecution and defence and on 25 April Mr Justice Gorman discharged the first jury.

In the second trial both Simons and Bending stood up under considerable fire from the defending lawyers. This time the defence case was reached and a surprise witness, David Sammons, was called to say that at the time Cooney had been shot Johnny Simons had been drinking in another bar and that Joan Bending was so drunk she had had to be helped out of the bar before the fight. The boxers were acquitted on 2 May and the next day James Nash gave evidence that he had never had a gun but that he had hit Cooney 'twice on the nose with my fist because of the things he was saying'. He had hidden out at his brother William's flat in Old Street for four days before surrendering. 'I didn't want to get involved. I was waiting for the police to arrest the shooter.'

Wickstead believes the real turning point was Victor Durand QC's final address to the jury. '[It] surpassed anything I have ever heard before or since. It was brilliant, spell-binding stuff.' But there is little doubt that Durand's brilliance was helped by the forgetfulness of many of the witnesses.

The all-male jury took ninety-eight minutes to acquit Nash of Cooney's murder, but at a second trial which began an hour later he was found guilty of causing grievous bodily harm and was sentenced to five years' imprisonment. 'You have been found guilty on abundant evidence of a brutal assault upon a man who is now dead, in a drinking club frequented by crooks. . . . An example must be made of you and people like you,' said Mr Justice Diplock.

'My son's death won't go unavenged,' shouted Cooney's father from the public gallery. Cooney's body was taken back to Leeds for burial. 'I have read somewhere that a Mr Billy Hill was giving Selwyn a funeral, but this is not a circus. He will have a funeral with dignity,' said Cooney's mother.

Simons, under police protection, was put on an aeroplane for Majorca where he hoped to work for a Spanish bookmaker. Three months later he was back saying he was broke and he could not get a job. He went to stay with Cooney's parents in Leeds and three months later was attacked outside the city's bus station. He was cut three times on the face and once on his arm.[8]

Fay Sadler did turn up again on 12 May but only to allow herself to be photographed by a *Daily Express* reporter in the Anchor public house in Clink Street, Southwark, and to give a short interview.[9] The reporter, Victor Davis, paid a fee for the privilege to her minder, who gave his name as Ted. Fay had been ill and this had given her another chance to rethink her lifestyle.

'I was just being faithful to the code by which I have lived,' she said, adding, 'I am waving goodbye to the drinking clubs, the dog-tracks, the mad parties, and all the boloney that I thought was the essence of life when I was a kid.' Would she go somewhere ducky like Cheltenham? speculated the *Express*.

That was the effective end of the Nashes, but lurking in the background and gaining in strength were Ronnie and Reggie Kray, the twins. There were also small, independent and often not very successful teams operating. In May 1963 John Maguire of Kentish Town received four years and six other members of the firm lesser terms for operating a protection racket on the Chinese community in Soho. They had been convicted of demanding money with menaces and robbery and assault. Maguire had worked on the principle that the

---

[8] N. Lucas, *Britain's Gangland*.

[9] Clink Street had been the site of a prison in the nineteenth century, giving rise to the expression 'in the clink'.

Chinese had difficulty in distinguishing one European from another. They may have had but they did have clothes sense. He was caught after one Chinese business-man had identified a girl member of the team by the dress she wore when posing as a prostitute and working the Murphy game.[10]

Out of the immediate central London area the Mussies, from Muswell Hill in North London, led by Ronald Gordon Fletcher, enjoyed a reputation as tearaways. Their three-year reign of terror ended at the Old Bailey in July 1962 after a fight at a youth club dance in Finchley. Mr Justice Melford Stevenson gaoled Fletcher for five years.

Another singular influence in Soho at the time was the very odd Detective Sergeant Harold Challenor, feared by villains everywhere. He had spent several years in the Flying Squad when, in 1962, he was sent to West End Central police station (Savile Row) as a second-class sergeant. In the 1960s, when the time between arrest and trial by jury at the Old Bailey or the Inner London Sessions was only a matter of a few weeks, he soon made a great impact on the community and the courts.

> Soho sounded like Chicago when Challenor des-
> cribed it. The courts were obviously impressed,
> although magistrates, judges and members of
> juries all knew that perfectly respectable people –
> like magistrates, judges and members of juries –
> could spend a pleasant evening in Soho without
> indulging in crime or coming to any harm. Lon-
> don's West End has the best theatres, restaurants,
> cinemas, clubs and pubs in the country, and they

---

[10] The Murphy game is the robbing of a prostitute's client by her pimp. It is also a confidence trick and gets its name from the alleged simplicity of the Irish.

are frequented by regular customers and provincial visitors who never once catch a glimpse of a drug-orgy or a gun-fight. Yet the detective-sergeant was not only believed when he brought his conspiracy and offensive weapon charges; he was increasingly admired for his skill and courage in tackling the bandits.[11]

His finest hour came in September 1962 with his smashing of the protection racket being run by Riccardo Pedrini, Oliva, John Ford, Alan Cheeseman and James Fraser. That, at least, was the evidence of Wilfred Gardiner, a man with a conviction for living off immoral earnings, who ran the two strip-tease clubs, the Phoenix and the Geisha. Gardiner gave evidence of threats, damage to his car, demands to be 'looked after' and 'If you try nicking us I shall shoot you. You're a dead man anyway. You won't live the rest of the year.' He also spoke of another occasion when he saw Oliva cutting the hood of his car. 'That's how we're going to cut your face,' he was told.

On 21 September Riccardo Pedrini and Alan Cheeseman were arrested outside the Phoenix Club by two of Challenor's aides to CID. They were taken to Savile Row police station and told to put their belongings on a table. Cheeseman was slapped and, so he said at the trial, Pedrini was taken into a cell and beaten. Both he and Cheeseman had weapons planted on them. Ford, who had been involved in a longstanding quarrel with Gardiner, lived in the next block of flats to Pedrini. There is no doubt there had been trouble on a fairly regular basis between them. He was arrested on 22 September and charged with demanding money with menaces. On 24 September Joseph Oliva was arrested

[11] M. Grigg, *The Challenor Case*.

driving along Berwick Street. Challenor and two younger officers dragged him from his car. He was found to have a bottle of turpentine with a piece of torn-up towel in the neck and a knife in his pocket. At the trial Challenor said he had information that Oliva intended to attack the Phoenix Club and Oliva was said to have remarked, 'If I don't burn him someone else will.' Fraser was arrested on 26 September when he was pointed out to police officers by Gardiner. He was found to have a knife. It seems that the only connection between him and the others was that he had once been in a van with Oliva when there had been a near accident with Gardiner in his open car. On that occasion both had called the police.

On 6 December, charged with conspiracy to demand money with menaces, demanding money with menaces and possessing offensive weapons, they appeared at the Old Bailey. After a retirement of two and a half hours Fraser was acquitted of conspiracy and the others found guilty. Their convictions were quashed by the Court of Appeal in 1964.

By this time, Challenor, the former scourge of Soho, was in disgrace. His war on Soho characters had been perfectly successful whilst he stuck to the louche element who had a few convictions in their background, and even their associates with no convictions but on whom the tar would stick. They were not likely to be believed by a jury when they flatly contradicted the evidence of a detective sergeant who, in addition to being a rising star in the Met, was a deservedly well-decorated war hero from the Tank Corps. Unfortunately for Challenor and the police he lighted upon political demonstrators rather than underworld figures, which was to prove his undoing.

On 11 July 1963 a demonstration took place around Claridge's hotel to protest against a state visit by Queen

Frederika of Greece.[12] One of the demonstrators carrying a banner was Donald Rooum who, fortunately for him, happened to be a member of the National Council for Civil Liberties. He was arrested by four plainclothes policemen, one of whom was described by Rooum as 'a big, stocky, flat-nosed man with a dark suit, boots and a very short back and sides'.

'You're fucking nicked, my old beauty,' said the policeman. At West End Central police station Rooum was pushed upstairs to a detention room by Challenor who repeatedly hit him on the ear.

'Boo the Queen would you?' he asked.

'No, not at all,' replied Rooum and was rewarded with another blow.

'There you are, my old darling,' said Challenor, 'have that with me. And just to make sure we haven't forgotten it . . . there you are, my old beauty. Carrying an offensive weapon. You can get two years for that.' And with that, said Rooum, Challenor produced from his own pocket a piece of brick wrapped in paper. That evening six other men and a juvenile were arrested. Each was given a piece of brick by Challenor or his subordinates. Each refused to sign for their property, denying the bricks had been in their possession.

When it came to it Rooum was doubly fortunate. He had been refused bail by the police and he was represented by Stanley Clinton Davis, a well-known criminal lawyer. Rooum's case was adjourned for trial until 19 July. The basis of his defence was that he could not have been carrying a brick because there was no brickdust found in his pocket. An independent expert was found who confirmed this. Here was Rooum's good

---

[12] The origins of the protest, now almost forgotten, had arisen following the death of a Greek political activist, Lambrakis. A banner carried by Donald Rooum read 'Lambrakis RIP'.

fortune, for since he had been refused bail he had had no chance to change his clothes before handing them over to Clinton Davis after the initial remand hearing.

At the hearing Rooum was defended by Michael Sherrard, who would later defend Hanratty. A forensic scientist gave evidence that there could have been no brick because not only was there no dust but a broken brick, the size of the one produced, would inevitably have scratched the lining. Edward Robey, son of the comedian Sir George, was the magistrate sitting at Marlborough Street when the case was heard. After he had handled the brick and found how easily it crumbled he expressed his doubts and acquitted Rooum, refusing an application for his costs to cover his expenses.

Another of the defendants, John Apostolou, was not so fortunate. With the same solicitor, barrister, forensic scientist and the same story Robey found him guilty and fined him £10. Two juveniles, Ronald Ede and Gregory Hill, were due to appear at Chelsea Juvenile Court. The case was first adjourned because Challenor was ill and then on 9 October the prosecution offered no evidence. Apostolou appealed against his conviction and on 22 October the prosecution indicated they would not seek to support it. Later Rooum was awarded £500 and Apostolou £400. There had been a number of convictions of other defendants who had been fined £5 and in one case given a conditional discharge.

Challenor, who had had a distinguished war record winning the Military Medal, now found himself at the Old Bailey on 4 June 1964 on a charge of corruption. Defended by Manny Fryde, of Sampson & Co, solicitors for the Krays, he was committed to a mental hospital having been found unfit to plead. Three other officers were found guilty, receiving sentences of four and three years.

At the end of the trial Mr Justice Lawton called for John du Rose, known as Four Day Johnny because of the speed with which he solved his cases.

Chief Superintendent du Rose, I would be very grateful if you would bring to the attention of the Commissioner my grave disturbance at the fact that Detective Sergeant Challenor was on duty at all on 11th July 1963. On the evidence which I heard from the doctors when he was arraigned, it seems likely that he had been mentally unbalanced for some time, and the evidence which I heard from Superintendent Burdett in the case has worried me a great deal. It seems to me the matter ought to be looked into further.

At the enquiry which followed, Arthur James QC, later to preside over the Great Train Robbery trial, reported on the circumstances in which it was possible for Challenor to have continued on duty at a time when he appeared to have been affected by the onset of mental illness. The report was a whitewash. Mr James found that Challenor was allowed to continue because of the extreme difficulty in diagnosing paranoid schizophrenia and it was no fault of his fellow officers that they had failed to notice his unsocial behaviour. If there was a clash of evidence between witnesses to the enquiry and police officers, then the evidence of the latter was invariably preferred. Allegations that Challenor had taken bribes were dismissed almost out of hand. 'Such allegations form part of the armoury of the criminal and are directed at any target which it wished to destroy.'

In the Pedrini case, Fay Sadler's defender, William Hemming, along with his long-time companion Margaret Laville, a solicitor's clerk through whom he obtained much of his work, gave evidence. Not only was Hemming a member of the Bar, he was also a longtime member of a louche Soho drinking club, the Premier, as was Miss Laville. Evidence that Cheeseman had met Challenor in the club in her presence could not be accurate, she said, and Mr James unhesitatingly accepted it. Hemming gave evidence that he had held Challenor in high regard as an officer. The allegation that Challenor had received a £50 bribe was dismissed.[13]

Later Challenor found work as a solicitor's clerk, taking instructions in criminal cases. He was certainly not able to accept the acquittal of Rooum with good grace. In his own memoirs he wrote:

> . . . soon afterwards Rooum heard me repeating details of his arrest and stating that I had found the brick in his pocket.
>
> Whether Mr Rooum had prepared himself for such an eventuality I do not know, but he certainly had his wits about him for his mind went back to a book he had read entitled *Science in the Detection of Crime*, by a former Scotland Yard officer, and he realized that if he could prevent the brick being placed in his pocket he could prove his innocence because there would be no trace of dust in his pocket and no fingerprints on the brick. This would make nonsense of my evidence.
>
> To achieve this, however, it was essential for him to remain in custody over night in order to prove that he was wearing the same clothing when he was examined by an independent forensic expert. For that reason he did not seek bail, but refused to sign for his property which included the brick.[14]

[13] It was always said that the Bar never forgave Hemming over the evidence he gave at the Challenor enquiry and that it was a major reason he was never made a QC.

[14] H. Challenor with A. Draper, *Tanky Challenor*, pp. 13–14.

Whatever the truth behind the Challenor illness there is no doubt he presented a formidable figure to the Soho villains, and was undoubtedly feared by them. He knew the gang leaders and believed that 'fighting crime in Soho was like trying to swim against a tide of sewage; you made two strokes forward and were swept back three. For every villain you put behind bars there were always two more to take their place.'[15]

Once Challenor was out of the way there were reports that:

London's West End is bracing itself for an out-break of violence between rival gangs running the 'protection' rackets in strip clubs, gambling casinos and betting shops. The power struggle created largely by the recent release from prison of notorious mob leaders and by a more inhibited police approach to the job of tackling criminals is expected to lead to a vicious internecine gang war.

Recent petrol bomb attacks on betting shops in Shepherd's Bush are believed to be the work of a South London combination of five gangs determined to take over the territory of established gangsters. A Soho strip club set alight; a member of a powerful East End gang beaten up.

By securing the services of a dangerous psychopath who gained underworld prestige during the violent gang warfare in the fifties the South London family has managed to merge five small gangs, drawn from an area embracing Southwark, Camberwell, Balham and Tooting.

Already the new syndicate has installed its own fruit machines in some West End clubs and the leader is said to be collecting a modest £50 a week

[15] Ibid, p. 154.

for 'looking after' at least one gambling casino.

The new boys can't win. They don't have the money behind them and their stooges only get about £20 for a petrol bomb attack. The men behind the established mobs are rich and almost respectable. They have had it good in the West End for years and they are greedy. They won't give it up easily.[16]

Whilst it was right that Frankie Fraser was now out of prison, the petrol bomb attacks on betting shops in Shepherd's Bush were something of a red herring. They were nothing to do with Billy Hill or his successors. Rather they were the work of a small independent firm headed by Patrick Ball, who went under the name of the Professor because of his neat appearance. He had approached one of the leading bookmakers in the area, James Burge, asking for the princely sum of £5 a week. When Burge turned him down his shop was bombed a fortnight later. Nathan Mercado, who traded as Sid Kiki and who was a police informer, was also threatened and he turned to the police for help. Nipper Read, then a sergeant at Paddington, was sent to Kiki's shop to work as a clerk one Saturday afternoon in June and arrested Ball and his colleagues when they came into the shop after the last race to collect their share of the winnings.

In his autobiography Read tells both of the traumas of the afternoon when there were meetings all over the country and he pulled the ticker-tape from the machine and broke it, as well as those when Kiki, enraged at the approach by Ball, forgot the prepared script. It had been agreed he should ask such questions as 'How much will it cost?' and 'What will I have to do?' Instead he started shouting, 'You can fuck off, I'm not having any of this,'

[16] Cal McCrystal in the *Sunday Times*, 1964.

and Read had to step in to make something of a premature arrest. Ball received a six-year sentence and his companions three years each.

But by now the twins – 'It's unlucky to call them by their names' – were moving westwards.

4

The Richardson Brothers

Just as history at large is constantly in the process of being rewritten and revised, so is the history of the London underworld. In 1967 the Richardson brothers' empire was described in suitably shocked terms by Mr Justice Lawton and the press as 'built on fear', 'built on thuggery', 'terror', 'torture'. Now with the passage of time Charles Richardson at least is seen in more pastel colours. Was he really anything more than an over-enthusiastic businessman struggling to protect his companies against the ravages and predatory overtures of con men and crooks?

Until recently the East End villains have always had a much greater press coverage than their South London counterparts, but informed observers have always regarded the latter as the more dangerous, perhaps because they have displayed a greater ability to keep their heads below the parapet. One good example is Kimber's Brummagen boys, many of whom really came from the Elephant and Castle.

Sometimes, of course, things happened almost by accident and lives became more public. In May 1961 George Porritt killed his stepfather and was nearly hanged for it. Porritt had become involved with Florence 'Fluffy' Copeland, the former girlfriend of Edwin

Copley, also known as Cadillac Johnny, who had been killed when his car crashed at 75 mph in a chase over Tower Bridge. He had been given a traditional gangland funeral. Fluffy had subsequently defected to a rival family, the Porritts. It was not an arrangement which pleased the remainder of the Copleys and a quarrel broke out in the Manor House Club near Wrotham in Kent between Mrs Copley and Fluffy. Later that night six armed men came to the Porritt home and George, who had amassed a complete arsenal of guns, seeing two men attacking his stepfather, fired a shotgun, hardly damaging the men but killing his stepfather. He was charged with capital murder.

On 5 July 1961 the jury convicted him and recommended mercy. Porritt was sentenced to be hanged at Wandsworth Prison on 27 July. Now began a period of intense activity. George had to be saved and Fluffy began collecting signatures to present in a petition to the Home Secretary. The Copleys joined in. 'We think the dead man was the real villain in the piece, inciting Georgie to violence against us,' said one of the family.

His appeal was allowed on the day before he was due to hang. Even though the defence had not raised the question of manslaughter the judge should have done so on his own volition, said the Court of Appeal. A sentence of ten years' imprisonment was substituted. Although she told newspaper reporters she did not drink Fluffy celebrated with whisky and gin. 'We owe it to George.' As part of the triumph she had changed her platinum-coloured hair to gold.

It would be pleasant to record that things went well for George and Fluffy after this near miss but it would be inaccurate. Fluffy faded from the scene. On 17 February 1963, whilst he was in Dartmoor, George married a Manchester girl, Sheila, a former heroin addict ('H', as addicts call it, she told a newspaper on her wedding day). Nor was that marriage a conspicuous success. She was later convicted as the driver in a wages snatch back in her home town. She had apparently taken along her child from a former relationship because she could not find a child minder. Later she did find a minder for an evening and paid her £2 with some of the stolen money. She received five years whilst others in the team drew up to fifteen. One of them, Albert Reddans, collected ten years but this was made consecutive to another ten-year sentence he had received the previous month.

There were rumours and press stories of South London villainy, of course. The so called Elephant and Castle Gang of the immediate post-war years were said to have a language of their own – it turned out to be the usual Cockney and underworld backslang. Unusually for the period they were said to include women in their teams, behaviour unheard of at the time. Members were certainly involved in the shooting of Alec De Antiquis in Tottenham Court Road in 1947. Even so the history is littered with names – the Hawards, the Hennesseys, the Callaghans, the Copleys, the Porritts, and the Frenches, as well as those of two of the great South London families, the Brindles and the Frasers.

Tommy 'Tom Thumb' Brindle was originally a small-time crook who dealt in the black market during the war, disposing of cigarettes, stockings and razor blades. 'But he was a gentleman,' says one solicitor's managing clerk who remembers him.

After the war he decided crime was no fun and so he started as a street bookmaker taking about £50 a week. Later he formed the Street Bookmakers' Federation and when the Betting and Gaming Act came into force in 1960 he applied for a licence and was granted one. From then on he was totally respectable.

'Tommy didn't care for Frankie Fraser. He regarded him as you would an obnoxious neighbour,' says one long-time observer of the South London scene, whilst another comments, 'There wasn't much outside violence. The Brindles were too occupied feuding with the Frasers and the reverse.'

Tommy's brother Jimmy had married Frankie Fraser's sister Eva. It is Frankie Fraser, now in his late sixties and said to be partly of Red Indian blood, who, along with Albert Dimes half a generation before him, has provided one of the great continuing professional criminal links of the century. And it is Fraser, one of a number of brothers from South London, who was a stalwart of the Richardson family's empire.

Fraser is described by Charles Richardson as 'one of the most polite mild-mannered men I've met but he has a bad temper on him sometimes'.[1]

He was quite small – a stocky bloke of about five foot two – but he was game, he was hard to handle, he was not afraid to speak out for his rights, and he was more than capable of doing what he threatened. His word was his bond. People knew they should never say to Frank, 'I want to chin a screw,' unless they meant it because he would expect them to do it, and rightly so.[2]

Since the age of thirteen when he was sent to an approved school for stealing forty cigarettes, he has racked up thirty-two years in prison or detention sentences. Seemingly impervious to pain during his years inside, he was switched from prison to prison on over a hundred occasions as one governor after another found

[1] C. Richardson, *My Manor*, p. 62.
[2] T. Lambrianou, *Inside the Firm*, p. 148.

him almost impossible to control. In November 1959 he was sentenced to be birched for his attack on one prison governor. He was due to receive eighteen strokes. Jimmy Andrews, whom Georgie Cornell had visited shortly before his death, was due for fifteen, and Jack 'the Hat' McVitie a mere twelve. The Home Secretary remitted the punishment, much to the indignation of the Prison Officers' Association.

On two occasions he was certified insane, something of which his defence would make use. 'He had not been the willing tool that a man in full possession of his faculties would have been,' said John Ritchie ingenuously during the Fraser–Rossi trial for the slashing of Jack Spot.

Certainly during the 1970s and 1980s, after his involvement in the Parkhurst Prison riot of 1969 in which he was designated the leader, he was regularly tormented by prison officers.

Nothing ever got to Frankie. He was a rock. Once when he was in prison, he was in solitary for months – not unusual for Frank. Every day a group of screws would deliver his food but just before the plate was handed to him a screw would spit in it. Frank would throw the plate at him. There would be a fight, Frank would get a terrible beating and the screws would leave him to nurse his bruises for another day. This went on for months.[3]

One prison officer stole his medical records and sent threatening letters to Fraser's sister Eva Brindle. The warder slipped under the door of his cell the part of Fraser's record which said he would serve at least twenty years, to 'blow him up to kick up trouble so the

[3] C. Richardson, *My Manor*, p. 83.

authorities would have him moved'. On conviction the prison officer received a conditional discharge.

In June 1959 Fraser had brought an unsuccessful libel action against the now defunct Sunday newspaper the *Empire News*. He complained that the article implied that he knew about the false allegation that Spot had attacked Falco, but the judge would have none of it.[4]

After his release from prison, on 17 May 1985, when he was driven away in some style in a Rolls-Royce, Fraser found himself in more trouble. He was convicted of dishonestly handling coins amounting to £35,000. He was sentenced to three years' imprisonment, reduced in November 1987 to two years when Canon David Diamond told the Court of Appeal he believed Fraser had reformed and had been doing good work in the community. It was his twenty-sixth conviction.

Fraser goes back to the days of Spot and Hill. Apart from the picture of him draped on the piano at the launch of Billy Hill's book, another shows him with the actor Stanley Baker, the boxing promoter Burt McCarthy, and a train robber or two, as part of the Soho Rangers football side. In the front row is his friend and business partner Eddie Richardson.

Eddie Richardson and his more celebrated brother Charlie were born in 1936 and 1934 respectively, Charlie in Twickenham, Eddie in Camberwell. Four years later a third brother, Alan, was born.[5] The elder two boys

---

[4] After the beating he received following the Parkhurst Riot he brought an action for assault. Tickets for a benefit were sold at £4 a head to raise sufficient money to pay the lawyers as he had been refused legal aid. Later he was offered, and reportedly rejected, £750 for his injuries.

[5] Alan drowned in a motorboat accident near Waterloo Bridge. The boat driven by Charlie ran into the wash of a larger boat and overturned. Charlie and his girlfriend, Jean Goodman, survived. Alan did not.

were evacuated during the war and on their return went to Avenue Secondary Modern School in Camberwell. Their first excursions into crime were the so called jump-ups, thefts from the backs of lorries. It was then that Charlie began to acquire the nucleus of friends who would later stand trial with him. Brian Mottram, an expert fraudsman, said of the time: 'It marked Charlie out, even at this age, as an organizer. We all looked up to him.'

Run-ins with the police were common. After a spell on probation, the remand home, Stamford House, was followed shortly afterwards by three years in an approved school. It was not a success. Charlie escaped and was sent to another school where he finished his sentence.

Charles Richardson from the start was a businessman. Born in another world, in another generation, he might have ended up with a company quoted on the stock market. He began selling his mother's ice-cream and soon moved into the scrap metal business. Even from the start, however, he was not too worried if his sponsors got their money back. His first coup was the purchase of two aeroplanes as scrap. He and his Uncle Jim borrowed money from a local businessman and started cutting up the craft. Unfortunately they neglected to repay the investor, who called in the Fraud Squad. Here Richardson learned an early lesson. Many policemen had their price. For £150 they were prepared to drop the investigation and put a frightener into old Uncle Jim as a joke for Charlie.

At the age of nineteen he heard of a scrapyard for sale in Addington Square. His mother was persuaded to stop work and look after the books. Eddie was cajoled into joining the family firm. With a combination of hard work and an astute eye for bent goods, the scrapyard prospered. Then tragedy struck. He was accused and convicted of receiving stolen scrap. The two-year probation order was nothing compared to the revelation that he had not registered for National Service. Like the Krays he developed an instant allergy to military life. Like the Krays he engineered his own court martial. Like the Krays he ended up in the military prison at Shepton Mallet, where he met up with his future rivals as well as Johnny Nash. It took him all of eight months before he could return to South London.

Back in Peckham he began to consolidate his business. One of the first to join him was Roy Hall, whom he found stealing copper wire from his yard and then trying to resell it to him. Hall's father had been killed while working on the railway at Waterloo Station and his mother had been left with no pension. After bawling him out Richardson employed him. He could have asked for no more loyal helpmate.

By 1956 Richardson had some £20,000 saved up and a business of five scrapyards in and around South London. Hall was now allowed to run his own yard at Waterloo, at a wage of £25 a week. A year later Richardson reckoned that he personally was worth £250,000. Some of the money came from the purchase of stolen metal but much came from sheer hard work.

Richardson was not satisfied. Many of his enterprises were at least a percentage legitimate. He had, in his words,

to swim hard upstream and feel the current on my gills. Like any good entrepreneur I had to feel I was growing and diversifying all the time. I opened up yards and drinking clubs all over the place. The breweries had the pubs sewn up so I started clubs where drinking was twenty-four hours. They were a bit illegal, given the licensing laws, but the police were on the payroll. When a big raid was planned they gave us the nod and the target club would be closed when the vice squad turned up.[6]

But acceptance as the King of the Manor was what he craved and the opportunity came to establish his credentials once and for all when Jimmy Brindle, Frankie Fraser's brother-in-law, was involved in a fight with one of the Rosa brothers. They were of Turkish extraction and were a force to be reckoned with in the Elephant and Castle area. It was Jack Rosa who had had the fake fight in Borstal, which helped Billy Hill and who later became associated with the Black Widow, Fay Sadler. Now a Rosa-led gang had beaten up Jimmy Brindle and another friend, Reggie Jones, in the Good Intent. Despite his relationship with the Frasers, Brindle was not really a Richardson man. He was a street bookie carrying on his brother's business. At the time he believed the police fancied to pull him if they saw him driving in the neighbourhood. Rosa asked him for a lift to the West End. Jimmy Brindle, who saw himself at risk of a prison sentence if he was caught driving, declined and so earned himself a beating.

Jones escaped and went round to one of the Richardson clubs, the Casbah, for help. According to Richardson he and his friends went in search of the Rosa brother, finding him in the ineptly named Reform Club at the Elephant.

He was much taller than me so I got good momentum when I leaned up and nutted him on the bridge of his nose which I felt crumble under my head . . . Meanwhile Eddie and Roy and the others jumped on Rosa's friends. We worked together like a well-practised team until they lay unconscious at our feet in pools of blood and

[6] C. Richardson, *My Manor*, p. 106.

broken teeth. We sat and had a drink. Everybody else in the bar watched as we calmly stepped on the broken bodies on the way out. The deed was registered and guaranteed for entry in local folk-lore. It was not the first time we had sorted somebody out but Rosa was big PR and our soaring reputation would protect us from challenges from ambitious competitors.[7]

They were certainly not prepared to venture much across the river and into Kray territory. After a fight in an East End pub in which a man had his jaw broken, the Kray firm turned up at the New Church Road yard. It took considerable negotiating to calm things down. The Krays returned across the water, leaving Richardson 'heading the biggest firm on the manor and my manor was South-East London. To outsiders it might have looked like a gang, but gangs are what kids have – or big kids in American films. I was a businessman who had to protect his interests.'[8]

But in his own manor Richardson behaved like the Sabinis of old. There was help for those who needed it with turkeys at Christmas and a few quid here and there.

We reduced local crime to a dribble. I was pissed off with all the thefts from my yard and I would be enraged when local people would come to tell me of burglaries to their houses. While the police filed incident reports and complaints in their dusty drawers we would know within hours who had done the job, give them a smack and tell them to fuck off to the West End to steal from rich people who could afford an insurance policy. The sad

[7] C. Richardson, *My Manor*, p. 108.
[8] Ibid, p. 110.

battered radios and half crowns from the tin in the kitchen would be returned with our compliments.[9]

There was also a sinister side. Whilst the Sabinis and the Whites had held court in clubs and pubs, the Richardsons held trials of their acquaintances and former friends who had in some way offended or even cheated them. It did not seem to alter the relationship too much. John Bradbury, supplier of much of the stolen merchandise which was sold in Richardson's long firm markets, seemed to regard a beating he took over a £10 debt as an occupational hazard.[10]

And if there were difficulties with the police, witnesses were there to be straightened. A man had an argument with his wife, who took off with the family furniture and another man. The man was beaten and the furniture liberated. His wife went to live in Albany Road, Camberwell. Later she told police her husband and Eddie Richardson had hit her with the butt of a gun. At Tower Bridge Magistrates' Court she changed her story.

There had also been a shooting incident outside her house, following which Johnny Nash, Charlie Richardson and John Lawrence were charged. It was alleged they had been trying to persuade the Roff brothers, another local family, not to give evidence in an assault case. There were witnesses, including Mrs Lawrence, and the police were no doubt confident of a successful prosecution, but at the committal proceedings Mrs Lawrence, although she had been with the men when the shots were fired, could not identify anyone.

Charlie's luck was to run out soon. In 1959 he was charged with receiving sides of bacon. He was sentenced to six months' imprisonment. Almost immediately, in

[9] Ibid, p. 111.

[10] R. Parker, *Rough Justice*, p. 88.

May 1960, he was charged again, this time with receiving stolen metals. Now the matter was more serious and Charlie did not stay around to try to deal with witnesses. He left for Canada together with his mistress, Jean Goodman, whom he had met at the Astor Club. He left behind his wife Margaret and their five children. Two sureties forfeited £500 each but were repaid by Eddie, who now took control of the businesses.

In Canada he and Jean Goodman put together a scrap metal business but, tiring of Toronto, sold it and slipped back into England. It was inevitable he would be arrested but once more the witnesses went his way and he was acquitted.

Now it was time to restructure his empire. The Addington Club was burned in a fire which destroyed its contents but not the fabric of the building. With the insurance money it was completely refurbished as a wholesale business complete with a small menagerie. John Bradbury ran Richardson's Shirley Anne drinking club in Peckham and supplied goods for Richardson's East Lane market. Much of the merchandise sold there had been hijacked. It was through Bradbury and his friend Tommy Costello that Richardson learned how a long firm fraud could really be profitably operated.

Long firm frauds are simple swindles to run. A warehouse or shop is taken by a front man, preferably someone who has no previous convictions. Goods are bought on credit and then sold perfectly properly through the shop. The supplier receives his or her money. More business is done with more and more suppliers until there is one big bang, a massive amount of goods are obtained on credit, knocked out at prices often below the purchase price in a great 'liquidation sale', and the premises are closed. The scam is not a new one. In the 1920s it was estimated that several million pounds a year were being made through long firm frauds. In the 1960s a properly run small LF could expect to realize a profit of between £100,000 and £150,000.

One variant on the long firm was used for Richardson's initial foray into the art form. A warehouse in Mitre Street in Aldgate was filled with silk stockings. In the late autumn of 1962 the stock was taken out and sold before the premises were torched. The idea was for the front men in the LF to tell the manufacturers that there had been a fire and that unfortunately the stock was uninsured. There would, however, be a perfectly good insurance claim. In this way the profits would be doubled.

The torching was a greater success than anyone could have hoped for. Petrol was poured inside the building one Saturday afternoon and the arsonist, a friend of Charlie's, went to have dinner. When he came back there was a courting couple in the doorway so he had to wait until they left, by which time the fumes had spread. A Guy Fawkes' rocket in a milk bottle was aimed at the semi-basement window, the site of the petrol spillage, and because of the build-up of the fumes the blast was far greater than had been anticipated. Much of the street was effectively wrecked, including the building of a spice merchants opposite.

When the facts were reported and the dishevelled arsonist and his assistant returned to report, Richardson was initially furious. 'I was mad with them but the picture of Tommy and Mike trying to aim this rocket in a milk bottle at the window was too much for me and I exploded in a fit of laughter that had me doubled up with tears streaming down my face. The others joined in and after a change of clothes for Tommy and Mike we all went out to a club.'[11] Charlie made around £250,000 from the explosion.

[11] C. Richardson, *My Manor*, p. 128.

Gradually he learned how a simple long firm fraud could be turned into a complex structure with interlocking companies. His mentor was his old friend, Brian Mottram, who had had a share in the Mitre Street business and had counselled against the fire. Although he had known him from childhood, initially it was not a relationship without problems. Mottram, a man to be reckoned with, had taken some of the Richardson men from the Catford end of the business and opened up his own long firm near the Charlton Athletic football ground. Richardson believed one of Mottram's men had turned him over and he, Eddie and a third man arrived at Mottram's premises to give him a whack. They were told by Mottram, a hulking great man who ignored his longstanding heart condition, to go away. They disregarded the request and Mottram, defending his employee, had dealt satisfactorily with the third man and was giving Eddie a seeing to when he was hit over the head from behind by Charlie. When he recovered he threatened he would shoot Charlie.

Quite apart from being a physically huge and handsome man, Mottram was connected to a team from the Surrey Docks. Charlie deemed the best way to deal with things was to send down some tame policemen to speak with his by now wholly alienated friend. If Mottram did not co-operate he could expect a spot of prison. They in turn were given their marching orders and Mottram began to carry out a guerrilla war, putting canisters of gas up the exhaust pipes of Richardson cars. A meeting was arranged at the Army and Navy pub in South London. Richardson grudgingly apologized and paid Mottram £3000 as compensation, additionally giving him another long firm to run.

It was shortly after this that, through Tommy Costello, Richardson met his nemesis, Jack Duval, an extremely talented con man who had been operating untroubled on

Richardson territory for the past few years. A Russian-born Jew, Duval had in turn lived in France, joined the Foreign Legion, deserted from it, served in the RAF, owned a club in Great Marlborough Street, run an airline ticket fraud, and been involved with George Dawson in the great Orange Juice swindle which had ended the career of one of the earliest post-war tycoons. He also managed to acquire the ownership of the Bank of Valetta. He arranged to supply Richardson with yet more stockings.

It was when his empire began to fold in March 1963 that Duval slipped away to Milan. He had been declared bankrupt over a Camberwell car company, there was an enquiry into a fraud at the bank and the major airlines were just discovering how they had been swindled out of up to £500,000-worth of airline tickets. From Italy he sent over some of the stockings but when the supply dried it was discovered he had been using the age-old trick of paying off past debts with present monies. Nevertheless he sent over airline tickets and Eddie Richardson went to sort things out. The supply of stockings recommenced.

With Charlie trying to expand his horizons he began to encounter men who were much smarter than himself. Duval may not have had any muscle behind him but he was mega-smart as well as being mega-crooked.[12] Eddie, who was more old-fashioned in his thinking, began to worry about Duval and his equally astute and dishonest friends, such as Benny Wajcenburg and Lucien Harris who ran offices in Cannon Street. For a time the brothers split, with Eddie – disenchanted with life in general and Jean Goodman in particular – striking off

---

[12] Other deals of his at the time included trying to sell fake Old Masters to the Krays and the swindling of a Lugano jeweller to the tune of £50,000.

back to his roots and working the race-courses. In time he set up his own wholesale business, a large walk-around supermarket in Deptford High Street.

Gradually things improved between the brothers and Roy Hall returned to work with Charlie. John Bradbury was brought back to work Bradbury Trading in the Addington Square premises, running a scam involving the purchase tax on radios.[13] A company with its own purchase tax number was a valuable commodity in those days. The Krays too had been sniffing around Harris, whose Cannon Street company was wrongly believed to have such an item.

And then from Duval's friend and helpmate, Bunny Bridges, Richardson heard the con man was back, if not in town, at least in Brighton. He was summoned to talk about a bit of business. On his arrival Duval found that Charlie was too busy to see him immediately and was sent round to Bradbury Trading in Addington Square where he was set upon by Eddie Richardson and Bradbury. Afterwards he was taken to see Charlie, who appears to have behaved with kindliness. If Eddie might be PC Dirty, then Charlie was DS Clean. Duval was given a cup of tea and then sent off with Wajcenburg to buy a new shirt and to the local chemist to be patched up. On his return it was all sweetness and light again. He was given some money and sent away to consider new business propositions. Duval was back in the fold but now surely he knew who was the master and who the dog.

The business proposition was a major long firm

---

[13] If a company had a purchase tax number it did not need to pay the then twenty-five per cent tax to the manufacturers. It was supposed to, but did not, pay the tax itself. This allowed a crooked company to undercut its rivals – another variant on the long firm. For a full account of these and other deals see R. Parker, *Rough Justice*.

working out of the Cannon Street offices and called Common Market Merchants. Duval was to change his name to Longman and be the buyer in Germany. Wajcenburg was invited in. Apart from his own proven abilities he had that invaluable asset, his own purchase tax number. A local magistrate added respectability to the board of directors. But things did not go well. Shortly before Christmas 1963 Wajcenburg wanted commission on the old radio transactions. Charlie did not wish to pay him and said in reality it was he who was owed – £5000 to be exact. Wajcenburg did not agree. The books were checked by Duval and a local businessman, Ken Nicholson, who had been brought into work at Peckfords. Wajcenburg was right. No money was owing. Richardson, believing he was being taken by the smart boys, lost his temper and began to shake the Pole. Later that evening Wajcenburg borrowed £1000, sent it round to Richardson and fled the country. It was only after the intercession of Duval that, a year later, he agreed to return to Common Market Merchants.

On Christmas Day Richardson quarrelled with Tommy Costello, whom he visited along with his brother, Roy Hall and Johnny Longman at the Rabbit Club in Catford, over Tommy's refusal to have anything to do with Common Market Merchants. Perhaps it was Christmas, perhaps old friendship, but Costello escaped a beating, warning Richardson against the rapacious Duval.

Charlie didn't listen. Nor apparently did he see anything wrong when the magistrate resigned from Common Market Merchants early in January 1964, seeing it as a clash of temperament between the magistrate and Jack Duval, who was spinning the con man's web of greed. The loss of the magistrate did not matter, a man called Phil Wilson would take his place. Duval had found four or five others to make similar investments. In a few years' time there would be enough money to open a merchant bank. One company would lead to the next. Despite the advice of the doubting Thomas Costello, Wilson invested £1400, Charlie £4000, and Jimmy Bloor (or Blore) and Harry Waterman also became investors. One company which did lead to the next was Twelve Estates, which arose phoenix-like from the ashes of Bradbury Trading. Bradbury himself and Jimmy Bloor were in charge whilst Duval and a friend set up Exmosdale to provide the references essential for a successful long firm. At the same time the more or less legitimate scrap side of the Richardson business was going well, with contracts from the Ministry of Works.

The year 1964 was a turning point for the Richardsons. Back into the fold came George Cornell, aka Georgie Myers, a former member of the Watney Street mob on transfer, so to speak, from the Krays. He had fallen out with them after an association over the years and had teamed up with none other than Frankie Fraser, now released from prison for his part in the Spot slashing. Back also came Brian Mottram, everything forgiven and forgotten, to join in another long firm with Cornell and Charlie.

Poor Wilson lost all his investment in Common Market Merchants. Most of the time he was just dazzled by Duval's sleight of speech. Cheques were shoved at him 'for wages', 'for purchasing samples' and he signed them. He did, however, find out that the office manager, a Mr Wade, was an undischarged bankrupt. Duval was unrepentant and replaced him with a Len Rugg whose company was then facing charges of receiving stolen material. There was worse to come. Wilson answered the telephone and heard an irate bank manager demanding £2500 to meet cheques that afternoon. Other calls followed. Wilson went to see Richardson to complain that Duval had been emptying the kitty but, once more,

Duval talked his way out of trouble. Later a solicitous Duval went to see Wilson and offered to buy him out for £2500. Wilson completed the transfer of his shares; Duval did not complete the cheque.

There followed the first of the main incidents which were to lead to the Old Bailey. On 12 June 1964, along with Jimmy Bloor, Duval was summoned to Peckfords. Fat Jack Duval was knocked to the ground. When he came to he was sitting in a chair, his wallet and watch together with his wig on the desk in front of him. Bloor's problem was that he was inextricably linked in Richardson's mind with Duval. Richardson picked a knife from a canteen of cutlery and threw it at his arm. Then he did the same again. However angry Richardson was he had the sense to realize that with the collapse of Common Market Merchants there were serious problems. Wilson had already told the Fraud Squad in Holborn of his fears. In any event another English creditor had complained. The banks would certainly have followed. After all they could not be fobbed off in the medium term like German manufacturing companies. By his actions, Duval had jeopardized a number of people.

Once I defended a man charged with a long firm fraud. According to the evidence he had been taken to see a solicitor in North-West London whose first question was 'Is it too late to have a fire?' After Mitre Street another fire was out of the question for Common Market Merchants, but a robbery was the next best thing. Cornell and Bradbury were sent round to clear the premises. They did – of stock and paper work. Next they cleaned out Duval's flat off the Edgware Road. Cornell and Bradbury were seen at the Cannon Street offices and the police were called. It cost Richardson £1500 to shut down the police investigation.

While Bradbury and Cornell were office cleaning, Duval was explaining how the money could be recovered. Bloor was sent to be cleaned up at the chemists and on his return he and Duval were ordered to be back the next morning. Duval took the opportunity of cashing three cheques, one with Johnnie Longman and two with Charlie's friend Alfie Berman. All would be dishonoured but he had no intention of being there when that happened. He went to ground in a hotel in Russell Square, telling only Lucien Harris, another man and his girlfriend where he was. Next day he left for Brussels and on to Israel. There were to be no further beatings for him.

The relatively innocent Lucien Harris was not so fortunate. Johnnie Longman turned up at Inter City, Harris' firm in Great Portland Street. Where, Charlie wanted to know, was Jack Duval? Harris knew that Duval was by now abroad but he certainly was not going to say so. Next day Harris went to see Richardson. He wanted to collect some money owed. Richardson wanted to collect information. At first things were calm. Harris was, after all, not the toe-rag Duval was. He had a degree. It is also possible that he sneered at Richardson about his ill-fated dealings with Duval. Richardson kicked Harris in the hand and threatened him with a knife. 'Is this going to take long?' asked Eddie Richardson. 'There's something I want to watch on the telly.'

According to Harris' evidence, it was now that the infamous wooden box was brought out by Roy Hall. One of the men was sent out to buy scampi. On his return Charlie Richardson shoved some into Harris' eye. His shoes and socks were taken off and the box was fixed to his toes. Hall turned the handle. Harris crashed to the floor. He was stripped and the handle turned again. Nothing much happened and a bottle of orange squash was tipped over him to increase the conduction. Harris was now tied and gagged. One lead was attached to his penis, the other inserted into his anus. The handle was turned again and again.

And then suddenly it was all over. He was untied and ordered to put his clothes back on. While he was doing so Bradbury stabbed him in the foot. Then, according to Harris, Charlie changed again. Harris had done well and stood up to things bravely. Now, asked Charlie, how would you go about finding Jack? Harris replied he would use the phone and he did so. It did not really matter. Duval was long gone. A bottle of scotch was sent for and Harris had a couple of drinks. Charlie gave him £150 and sent him on his way.

The next to receive the treatment was Bunny Bridges, Jack's longtime friend. He was attacked from behind by Cornell and then kicked as he lay on the ground. The box was again produced, with little effect. Bridges did not know where Duval could be found except possibly with his ex-wife in Manchester. He was ordered to drive there to find out. In the meantime some papers he had with him regarding a heavy plant deal were confiscated.

Eddie Richardson was increasingly distancing himself from his brother. He had teamed up with Frankie Fraser in the fruit machine operation. Through Albert Dimes, Fraser had long had an entree into Soho, where some of the most profitable sites could be found. Sir Noel Dryden was recruited to be the respectable front man for Atlantic Machines, the Fraser–Richardson company.[14]

From the beginning Billy Nash, one of the most enterprising of the Nash brothers, had been one of the first to see the benefits of the machines and others were quick to follow him. A machine, costing £400, could, when placed in a good site, bring in £100 a week. The usual percentage split was 65–35 in favour of the

[14] On 29 March 1970 the *News of the World* reported the death of Sir Noel Dryden of an overdose of drugs and alcohol. It was said that people had traded on his naivety.

operator. As an inducement to take their machines Atlantic would offer club proprietors forty per cent. There were small problems. If their machine went into a club, someone else's had to go. But both Eddie and Frank were more than capable of dealing with a problem such as this. They employed good mechanics and good machines. In addition they were well connected. It did no harm to a club owner for them to be seen drinking in his premises.

But it was Atlantic Machines which was to provide another link in the chain which would lead to the downfall of the Richardsons. In the summer of 1964 Eddie and Frank were invited to Southport to the Horseshoe Club where the proprietor was having trouble with staff dishonesty. Late in the evening they told Peter Joannides, a Greek who was operating the gaming tables, that they were running the club from now on and invited him outside. Sensibly, he declined. The ensuing fight was stopped by the stewards and Joannides went to the bar. Eddie pushed a broken glass in his face and in turn was set upon by the locals. He and Frank were chased ignominiously from the club. The next day they were charged with grievous bodily harm.

Eddie was allowed bail of £15,000 and went to work. By the time the case was heard in July it was the familiar story. If anything, Joannides had been the aggressor. The Greek personally could not remember much about the incident. He had been drinking heavily. There was no case to answer. Atlantic Machines went into the club and some fifty other clubs countrywide. And then two years later the proprietor of the Horseshoe opened Mr Smith and the Witchdoctor Club in South London.

Charlie Richardson's businesses expanded independently of his brother's. Eddie was content to work primarily in London and certainly within England.

Charles had his eyes on wider horizons. He toyed with the idea of a coal tip in Wales, discarded that and then met Major Herbert Nicholson. The Major, an alderman in Bedford and well connected in the Conservative party, was to be to Charles what Sir Noel Dryden was to Eddie, but on a much greater scale. Through a Welsh contact Charles had heard of the opportunity to obtain the mining rights on four million acres in Namaqualand, South Africa. The group who had the rights needed finance. Nicholson was the man to help Charles along the road.

Once in South Africa, Richardson found a number of opportunities available, including the chance to smuggle diamonds in frozen fish.[15] He learned this from a business friend of Thomas Waldeck, the geologist involved in the Namaqualand mining rights scheme. Gradually Waldeck persuaded Richardson of the benefits of the mining rather than the illicit diamond smuggling. He would sell Richardson half his stake in Concordia. Richardson was hooked, not least because he had fallen in love with Jean La Grange, the stunningly good-looking wife of a South African journalist.

The South African venture deteriorated steadily. First Waldeck and Richardson agreed to turn over the remaining partners in the mining venture and stake a claim for themselves alone. Then over the months the relationship Waldeck had with Richardson cooled. Each came to believe the other was trying to swindle him. John Bradbury had come to South Africa and for a time soldiered as a mercenary. To complicate matters he let it be known that he was Charlie Wilson, one of the Great Train Robbers who had escaped from prison. On 29 June 1965 Waldeck was shot dead on the porch of his

---

[15] The idea was not really new. It formed the basis of an early Raymond Chandler story, 'Moors', when he was writing for the pulp magazines. It was none the worse for that.

home. Bradbury was picked up and questioned for a period of three weeks but the police investigation got nowhere.

There were still business matters to be attended to in England. Richardson had to raise money for the machines to work the mining rights. Berman, who had invested over £30,000, did not want to invest any more. He pleaded poverty, blaming a man called James Taggart for owing him money. Taggart received a major beating from Fraser and Charlie Clark, a new man on the firm.

Similar treatment was dished out to a man involved in a swindle being run by the National Car Park attendants at Heathrow Airport, well known as Fiddle City. The men were taking £1000 a week by altering time clocks to show that customers – who paid the full price – were staying for shorter periods. One of the attendants was kidnapped, stripped naked and beaten with a knotted wet towel. He had already agreed to pay the £500 and the beating was, said Richardson, to show who was the guv'nor.

Things finally fell apart almost by accident. Richardson had heard of a bank being opened in Wigmore Street. Frankie Fraser and Frank Prater were sent to check it out. Quite by chance they ran almost point-blank into Taggart. He tried to ignore them and was followed along Oxford Street. As he walked towards a policeman Richardson appeared in front of him. He managed to hail a passing cab and escaped. The next morning he went to see Gerald McArthur, then the Chief Constable of Hertfordshire.[16] Taggart, Harris and the others felt that they could not go to the Flying Squad

---

[16] McArthur had been the officer in charge of the investigations into the Great Train Robbery. He had never really been given the credit he deserved and had left the Met.

with their stories, fearing that it would only be a matter of time before a corrupt detective would pass the information back to Richardson. Prater was soon to defect as well.

Back in South Africa it looked as though all Charlie's efforts were going to come to a successful conclusion. He had interested yet another businessman in providing finance; he was buying out or dismissing staff and former partners who stood in his way. His affair with Jean La Grange was going well.

But John Bradbury had started to drink and he told his wife that he and another man had shot the Waldecks' dog, Rex. They left South Africa and crossed to Zambia to find work. He drank more, began to pick fights in hotels and was eventually deported back to South Africa. Sheila Bradbury decided to return to England while her husband stayed behind to try to earn some more money. Instead he drank more and began talking to one of his drinking companions about the killing. His chanced-on buddy was an investigator looking into the insurance aspects of Waldeck's death. On the second night of drinking the police were tipped off. Bradbury made a full confession, naming Charlie Richardson.

When the story of Bradbury's confession appeared in the *News of the World* Richardson had his solicitors send a letter before commencing a libel action. Undeterred, the newspaper began its own investigation. On the home front Frankie Fraser quarrelled with the old-time con man Christopher Glinski, a former witness in the Spot–Dimes case, beating him with an umbrella. Glinski joined the team telling all to McArthur.[17] The South

---

[17] Glinski was a perennial thorn in the side of both the police and the villains. On one occasion he was awarded £250 damages for wrongful arrest. He had been prosecuted for fraud but the trial judge stopped the case against him.

African proceedings rumbled on.

On the night of 7 March 1966 came the incident in Mr Smith's which finally broke the Richardsons' hold on South London. Richard Hart, a Kray associate, was killed, whilst Eddie Richardson and Frankie Fraser, described initially in newspaper reports as businessmen having a drink on their way home, were badly injured.[18]

The club was popular; it had a dance floor, gaming table, a bar and a decent restaurant. It also had minders. A South London team led by the Haward brothers, Billy and Flash Harry, described variously as 'a League Division Two team' and 'amateurs but reckless amateurs', had originally dealt with trouble in the club in exchange for free drinks. The Hawards themselves had clubs and were well known to the Richardsons. Indeed, in the previous few weeks, there had been what euphemistically could be called some discussions between Frank Fraser, on behalf of Charlie Richardson, and Billy Haward over a possible partnership in one of Haward's clubs. For the moment that had come to nothing.

But now there were signs that the Hawards were beginning to make Mr Smith's their unofficial headquarters, using it as an answering service, something which did not appeal at all to the management. Eddie Richardson was approached to see if he could help. It was something he was good at. In return for clearing out the Haward team he could expect to have his and Frankie Fraser's gaming machines installed in Mr Smith's.

In the first week of March 1966 Eddie and some

---

[18] Hart, a firm friend of the Krays, was not a run-of-the-mill gangster. He had attended a grammar school and had several 'O' levels. He had then left school and drifted into selling cars and bricklaying. A gambler by nature, he was gaoled for hijacking a lorry and later held a club licence.

friends had visited Mr Smith's. He and Frankie Fraser
returned on the Monday afternoon. Security was discussed. 'I wanted to get hold of some employees with
good local knowledge who would keep better order than
I thought was being kept,' said one of the witnesses in
the subsequent court case. Eddie now regarded himself
as having an unwritten contract to police the club. All
that remained was for the position to be explained to the
Hawards.

Richardson and Fraser stayed in the club the rest
of the evening. Eddie spoke with the barmaid, then
Billy Haward had a word with her. Seemingly the
Richardson team mixed sociably with the Hawards.
But as the evening progressed the staff noticed not
only signs of tension but also a .410 shotgun strapped
inside Billy Haward's jacket. 'We'll be alright, don't
worry,' he said as he took a telephone call. It was noticed
that Dickie Hart had a .45 automatic pistol.

As another friend of Eddie Richardson's, Jimmy
Moody, joined the party, the manager sent home as
many of the staff as possible and breathed a sigh of relief
when about 2 a.m. the men seemed to be chatting
happily, pulling tables together and drinking with each
other.

The trouble came an hour later.

'Right, drink up, that's your lot,' said Eddie. Haward
protested, saying he and his friends were just getting the
taste. 'No more,' replied Richardson. 'I'm running the
club.'

Dickie Hart told the barmaid to get into the kitchen.
'Let her stay here,' said Haward, 'there's nothing to
bother us.' It cannot be that he wanted a witness.
Perhaps he genuinely thought the situation was under
control. She sat down alone, well away from the men.
Peter Hennessey, one of the family, called out to
Richardson, 'Who do you fuckin' well think you are?'

Adding, 'I'll take you any day, you half-baked fuckin' ponce.'

Eddie said that from now on he was the only one who could order drinks. Hennessey was not best pleased. 'Ah, fuck you, you cunt, I'll help myself.' He grabbed at the bottle. Richardson smashed his glass on the table and dragged him to the dance floor. It was then, as the newspapers say, fighting broke out.

Hart fired his gun, Eddie continued to hammer Peter Hennessey and the remaining thirteen men started to fight. Harry Rawlins was shot in the left arm. Haward was hit on the head with a rod and collapsed. Then somehow, Hart lost his gun. He ran through the back entrance into Farley Road chased by Frank Fraser and some others. Ronnie Jeffrey, a Richardson man, seems to have tried to stop the fighting in Farley Road. He was right to. The neighbourhood was awake; 999 calls were being made. It was only a matter of time before the police arrived. 'Turn it up,' he screamed and started to walk away. His name was called. He turned and was shot in the groin.

Now Henry Botton, a Haward man, saw Fraser kicking the prostrate Hart on the pavement. 'You're fucking mad, Frank,' he yelled.

When the police arrived all that was left of the fight was the body of Dickie Hart lying under a lilac tree in the garden of Number 48. He had been shot in the face and his face was smashed in. Initially he was mistaken for a sack. Fraser had escaped; he had been shot and his thigh bone shattered. Haward was gone; he had taken himself off to a friend's where his head had been stitched. Jimmy Moody had scooped up Eddie Richardson, who had also been shot in the thigh and the backside, driving both him and the wounded Henry Rawlins off in his Jaguar. Rawlins was in a poor state and Moody, with Eddie, who was discomforted rather than badly injured, and another man laid him over a children's cot in the casualty department of Dulwich Hospital. Once done, Moody raced off into the dawn.

The hospital reported the gunshot wounds and Chief Superintendent John Cummins, head of the Catford police, went to see just who was there. Rawlins was unconscious and he spoke to Richardson, who had first given his name as Smith and then George Ward. 'Well,' said Cummins, when he saw who was in the cubicle, 'if it isn't Eddie Richardson. And how did you get this little lot?'

Two days later George Cornell went to visit Jimmy Andrews, who had been shot in the leg, in hospital across the water. Despite the fears of his friends, he stopped off in the Blind Beggar for a drink. He was shot at point-blank range by Ronnie Kray, incensed that an enemy should be found on his territory.

The next weekend the *Sunday Times* believed that 'crime syndicates hired gunmen to carry out killings'. They had been told that the men who had killed Richard Hart had received some £50 each, while the killer of George Cornell 'is thought to have received £1000'.

Eddie Richardson and Francis Fraser were arrested. Fraser was charged with the murder of Hart; the rest of those rounded up after the fight with an affray. On 28 June Greenwich Magistrates committed them all in custody for trial. There was solidarity amongst the Richardsons and their friends in prison but there were still enemies about. Ray Rosa was one of them. Somehow he had managed to obtain an iron bar to attack Richardson and avenge the battle at the Reform Club. A bystander reported, 'Ray's eyes are very bad. He hit Bobby Cannon as he came down the stairs.' Bobby Cannon was not a man to report such a mishap. He had, he said, fallen and hurt himself.

Charlie Richardson was now back in London and

doing what he could for his younger brother. Initially he tackled the witnesses and the management of Mr Smith's Club. He had some success with the witnesses, whose recollections of events became vague and imperfect, but the latter were fearful of losing the valuable drinks licence. He decided the best bet was the jury.

When the trial opened at the Old Bailey on 1 July 1966 Charlie, together with his friend Johnny Longman, was in the public gallery looking for likely helpers. A unanimous verdict was still required in 1966 and so it would only require one juror to obtain the necessary disagreement. A very strong bent juror might even sway the rest, as Henry Fonda had done in the film *Twelve Angry Men*, and so produce an acquittal.

By the fifth day of the trial the judge, Mervyn Griffiths Jones (who as Treasury Counsel had asked the jury in the Lady Chatterley case, 'Would you allow your wife or maid-servant to read this book?'), said he had been told that 'two attempts have been made since Thursday to "nobble" an Old Bailey juror hearing the trial of seven men accused of offences connected with a gang fight at Mr Smith's gambling club, Catford.' He went on: 'Unhappily there are often people who are ill intentioned or misguided enough to think they can help their friends or relatives by acting in this kind of way.'

Charlie's second effort had been to have a bottle thrown through the juror's window. The bottle contained a note, intended to confuse things, reading '. . . bring them in guilty or else. A lot more where this came from. You're not alone amongst twelve.'

After long deliberations the jury returned mixed verdicts. Frankie Fraser, tried separately, had been found not guilty of Hart's murder on the judge's direction. There was no evidence he had fired the fatal shots, but he was found guilty of affray and sentenced to five years' imprisonment. Now Billy Haward was convicted of an affray, as was Henry Botton,[19] but Ronnie Jeffrey and Harry Rawlins, two of the Richardson team, were found not guilty. The jury failed to agree on the cases of Eddie, Jimmy Moody and Billy Stayton. Next day Haward received a total of eight years and Botton five.

At the retrial Richardson gave evidence that he had been the victim of an unprovoked attack. He was found guilty and sentenced to five years' imprisonment. Stayton and Moody were found not guilty.

Charlie had already issued a writ against the *News of the World*, but his solicitors had lodged no statement of claim – the detailed account of just what is complained about. The action was struck out with costs.

When Bradbury's trial began he pinned his defence on long-range duress, saying he feared reprisals by the London gang against his family. In support of his story that he was the driver forced to go to the scene, he told the judge of the mock trials held in London by Charlie.

Along with Brian Mottram, Roy Hall, Tommy Clark, Alf Berman, Jean Goodman and some others, Richardson was arrested on 30 July 1966.[20] McArthur had conducted his enquiry with great secrecy, taking a

---

[19] In common with the others Botton received five years for his part in the affray. On 17 July 1983 he was shot dead on the doorstep of his house in Shooter's Hill Road, Greenwich. It was said he had been having troubles over 'some recent deals'. The recent deals turned out to be giving evidence against a powerful South London operator. On 16 October 1984 Billy Clarkson was convicted of Botton's murder. He had given nineteen-year-old Colin Burke a shotgun with which to kill the sixty-three-year-old Botton, saying 'Go out and shoot him for me.' Burke, dressed as a policeman, shot Botton as he opened his door. Burke, sentenced to life youth custody, had told the police, 'I wanted to refuse the favour, but it was like being under hypnosis.' Clarkson was recommended to serve a minimum of twenty-five years.

well publicized holiday in Austria shortly before the arrests.

Richardson was not to go down without a fight. Bunny Bridges was offered £3000 to tone down his evidence, and Frank Prater's wife was similarly approached. Frankie Fraser's loyal sister Eva Brindle, along with Albert Wood and Josephine Shaer, was later charged with attempting to bribe Benny Coulson. Today she still insists she had merely been trying to assist her brother. Miss Shaer, who was Charlie Richardson's secretary, had been to ten firms of solicitors and finally to the National Council for Civil Liberties to get an affidavit drawn up in which Coulson withdrew his allegations. All except the NCCL had thrown her out or threatened to call the police. Clifford Smythe from the NCCL came to court to confirm the evidence. One curious incident occurred in the trial. Much was made of the point that she had the exact amount of £2000 in her wardrobe, the specific sum Coulson said he had been promised. When the money was counted so that the defence solicitors could have their fees paid it came to several hundred pounds over the sum. All three were convicted.

Shortly after that, on 14 March, Mr Smith's Club lost its licence. With true advocate's rhetoric Richard Du Cann told the licensing committee that the club was a 'canker that has gone too deep'. The club was now called the Savoy Social Club but in a police raid the officers had found there were some 300 people present and the guest book in a poor state, full of scribbles and blanks. On 29 June 1967 at a creditors' meeting of Wellreed Ltd, the owners of Mr Smith's, creditors were told there was a deficiency of £38,450. The directors blamed the club's downfall on that single night of violence. One of them

[20] No evidence was offered against Jean Goodman and shortly before the trial she married Peter Colson, a window cleaner.

spoke of his dream smashed by London gangsters. 'We did not know about the gangsters. If we had, we would never have come.'

Brian Mottram never stood trial in the main case. He had a heart condition which, it was said, could be fatal under stress. Shortly before the remand hearings he would be found in his cell in a state of collapse. Eventually, the day before the Richardson case began, he was given bail and finally no evidence was offered. It was said informally and unkindly that he was able to produce his heart condition by masturbating. He lived another fourteen years with the help of a pacemaker. Part of the time was spent in custody for his part in a substantial long firm fraud which he worked with Jack Duval. Duval received nine years for his part and on his release ran a dress shop in North London. He had earlier been acquitted of stealing a car. The judge at the Inner London Sessions in July 1967 ruled he had no case to answer.

The 'Torture' trial, which lasted ten weeks, began on 4 April 1967 before Mr Justice Lawton. There were fifty challenges by the defence to potential jurors and a further thirty-five were stood by for the Crown, its equivalent of a challenge. The trial had only been going a short while when Frankie Fraser, through his counsel, objected to the trial judge on the basis of an incident at Victoria Station when he had abused the judge after he and Richardson had had a night out at the Astor. The application was rejected.

Charles Richardson received twenty-five years' imprisonment. Eddie got ten, as did Roy Hall and Frankie Fraser. Tommy Clark was sentenced to eight.

In December 1967 twelve men were convicted of the parking fraud at Heathrow. They were said to have netted £200,000 in four years.

Fraser did his time the hard way. He was given a

further five years as leader of the 1969 Parkhurst Prison riot. Losing nearly all his remission he served most of his total of twenty years. Charlie Richardson escaped from an open prison in May 1980 and spent some weeks on the run in London and Paris complaining bitterly that he had unjustifiably been refused parole. Whilst on the run he conducted part of his campaign from a porn shop near Earls Court station.[21] He became careless and was arrested after giving the name Roy Hall. Unfortunately for him the real Roy Hall, who had been chauffeuring him earlier in the day, had also been stopped and had given his correct name.

Eddie Richardson was released from prison in 1976 and returned to work at his scrap business. Charlie was finally released in 1984.

In October 1990 at Winchester Crown Court Eddie Richardson was sentenced to twenty-five years' imprisonment for his involvement in a drug smuggling operation. Along with Donald Fredwin from Crystal

---

[21] On 8 October 1984 Johnnie Maile, known as Johnny the Flower, who ran a flower-stall at Earls Court tube station, was found shot dead in a lock-up garage in Redfield Lane, Earls Court. He had been killed with two shots to the head from a small-calibre weapon. The killer had cut the garage's padlock with bolt cutters and then lain in wait. A substantial sum of money, thought to be the takings of his business, was found in Maile's pockets.

He had witnessed Richardson's arrest and had given a graphic account to the newspapers. At the inquest held the following March Detective Chief Inspector Michael Anderson was at pains to emphasize that Maile was not a police informer. He went on to say that 'Mr Richardson is fully aware of how he came to be arrested and he knows that it is not attributed to John Maile.' Anderson, who said, 'This was professional work, a contract killing', added after the inquest that the police had also investigated the possibility that Maile had been mistaken for another man who was having an affair with a prisoner's wife.

Palace he had been the central figure in the importation of cocaine from Ecuador. In March 1990 153 kg of cocaine, nearly one third of the total seized by Customs, plus two tonnes of cannabis had been confiscated at Portsmouth, hidden in a consignment of balsa wood on a ferry from Le Havre. Richardson had bought the cocaine from South America at between £12,000 and £13,000 a kilo, selling it on in the UK for £26,000 a kilo. By the time it had reached the streets suitably cut, the price was an astounding £240,000.

Richardson had been seen in his Peckham scrapyard with Fredwin and had been watched when he visited three South Americans in a Bayswater hotel. He was also seen with them at his daughter's home at the Surrey Docks. The drugs were shipped, addressed to Globe Overseas Ltd, from Ecuador on the appropriately named *Silver Happiness*, and then transferred on to the *Viking Valiant* where they were intercepted by customs officers.[22]

During his time in prison Eddie Richardson has developed into a considerable artist.

[22] *Daily Telegraph*, 21 July 1990.

5

The Rise and Fall of the Firm

Legend has it that Ronnie and Reggie, the Kray twins, had their first proper outing in polite society at the spring bank holiday meeting at Epsom Races in 1955. Spot and Hill were feuding – a quarrel which would come to a head in August of that year – and Spot was afraid that his now tenuous hold on the bookmakers' pitches on the Downs, the free course, would be taken from him. He had, according to his rank, the No 1 pitch and he collected rent from the others. But now Billy Hill had with him Frankie Fraser and another wildman, Billy Blythe. Spot needed help from somewhere and he went down to the twins' billiard hall, the Regal in Eric Street at Mile End. He found them a good bookmaker to mind. No hard work unless Fraser and the others made a move. All they had to do was to stand by his pitch and take their percentage at the end of the day.

According to John Pearson the Krays did not take their work that day too seriously. When one of the Saffron Hill Italian Mob offered them the advice that they were stark raving mad to show up as Spot's minders they laughed and offered him a drink.

For the rest of that day the twins kept up their show of insolent indifference against the best-known

gangsters in the country. They drank, they enter-
tained their friends, they roared with laughter, they
ignored the racing and the betting. Finally Ronnie
yawned and rolled off to sleep. When the day
ended they collected what was owed them, and without bothering to thank Spot drove off in their van.[1]

The day's exercise had gone well. They had seen and
been seen, although they were not to make any
substantial move on the West End for nearly another
decade. With the impetuosity of youth they dismissed
Spot and the others as tired old men. 'We never liked
Spotty. Never thought much of him,' said Ronnie.[2]
Years later Spot bemoaned the fact that the twins had
not listened to him and his advice. 'I could have taught
them everything,' he explained.

In fact legend is wrong about that Epsom outing being
a first. The twins had been out of their area and about
for some time, working as minders first for Jack Spot in
his spieler, the Aldgate Fruit Exchange, confusingly
located in Covent Garden, and then making a book with
Teddy Machin, at Marks Tey races. At that time
meetings about pitches and how they should be allocated
were run by Albert Dimes at the Central Club in
Clerkenwell. At one meeting a shot was fired at
bookmaker Tommy Falco and from then on the Krays
had five shillings in the pound from the pitch takings.
The twins also had a foothold in the West End, minding
the Stragglers Club at Cambridge Circus for a half share
with Billy Jones and a former boxer, Bobby Ramsey.

The Kray twins – Ronnie was the elder – were born in
1933 in Stean Street, London E8. They had an older and
loyal brother, Charles, a grandfather, Cannonball Lee,

[1] J. Pearson, *The Profession of Violence*, p. 96.
[2] Ibid, p. 93 et seq.

who was once a well-known flyweight boxer, and a father, Charles senior, who spent much of their early years either totting or ducking and diving his way out of the army. They also had a devoted mother, Violet.

Much has been made of the brothers' boxing abilities but their ring records, kept by the British Boxing Board of Control, show that of the three only Reggie, a lightweight, had much promise. Ronnie, as a welterweight, won four of his six bouts between July and December 1951, ending his career with a disqualification against Doug Sherlock at the National Sporting Club and finally a points defeat by Bill Sliney at the Royal Albert Hall on 11 December. It was a night when all three brothers boxed on the same bill. Reggie, who had one more bout, had boxed Sliney twice, beating him both times on points. He began and ended his career with a points win over Bobby Manito. Charlie Kray's sporadic career lasted nearly two years. He lost all three of his contests, finally being counted out in the third round that night at the Albert Hall, in a bout against the up and coming Lew Lazar.

The twins' much more successful career as club owners began with the Regal in Eric Street, which they simply commandeered. From there they acquired the Green Dragon and later Reggie opened their showpiece, the Double R Club, financed in part by their profits and in part by poncing from local villains. Poncing in this context takes the form of demanding a share of proceeds from a burglary or robbery in a given area. 'On an occasion when two youngsters did Attenboroughs the jewellers in Bethnal Green Road the twins copped £2000 from the proceeds of the job,' says one former colleague.

The twins had their ears to the ground. It was often not a complete secret when a good job was to take place, partly because others, not involved, wanted to be able to put up an alibi. The twins' information service put them in a position to know when good jobs such as major breakings, hijackings of lorries and sometimes, but not usually, bank raids were to take place. After a job members of the Firm, as the Krays' organization had become known, were sent to see the perpetrators and to invite them out for a drink. The twins would chat about the job and assess its overall value and then ask for a substantial part of the take. Even members of the Firm were not immune. If they conducted a piece of business out of hours, so to speak, they were still expected to pay up. For thefts, the going rate paid by a receiver was one third of the value of the goods. The Krays would ask for a third of a third.

But they were despised by the real heavy bank robbers.

There really is a load of shit talked about them. They ran the East End but they never ran the West End. If they'd come near us they'd have been seen to. Of course they protected clubs. There's a lot of weak people in this world. They never had the arsehole to rob for themselves. Are they nice people? Well, tell me if this is nice. You get a young boy come into the club with his girlfriend. He's got a load of cigarettes to sell. They take the cigarettes, never pay him and he ends up getting shagged.

'Is that nice?' asks a former bank robber.

The twins also knew villains who were stealing cheque books by office creeping and then flew kites[3] to get equipment to set up a gymnasium over the Regal club, itself just a drinker. It was at the Regal that the Firm

3 In criminal slang office creeping is burglary and to fly a kite is to proffer a stolen or forged cheque.

was born, helped by the loyalty of former prisoners whose families had been looked after by the Krays while they themselves were away.

The twins also had the controlling interest in the Regency, a Stoke Newington club run by the Barry brothers, one of whom, Tony, was to be instrumental in bringing down their empire. Once the brothers had opened up the club and paid the expenses the Krays started 'nipping' – demanding up to a pony (£25) or a few bottles of spirits at a time – until they simply moved in, took over a room for their private drinking and required a pension. On to the door went their helpmate and bouncer 'Big' Pat Donnelly, a twenty-stone ex-boxer.

But even had they wanted, they were not in a position to challenge their friends the Nashes for the title of Emperors of the Underworld. One of the reasons was that Ronnie was about to get three years' imprisonment.

The trouble arose from the twins' connection with Bobbie Ramsey, part-owner of the Stragglers, as well as from a long-running feud with a mainly Irish fighting gang, the Watney Streeters. The Watney Street Mob were mainly dockers who, apart from their fighting qualities, stole from the docks. They were led by Jimmy Fuller and many of them were related. The gang's decline in strength paralleled the decline of the London Docks. Other East London gangs of the time included the Trocksy Mob from Pitsea Street. 'They were all thieves and good drinkers, but as they grew up and got married the gang broke up in the 1950s and 1960s,' says a contemporary. Another team of the 1950s was the Butlers. 'A lot of these families had a brother who was a bit divvy, sort of backward, fearless and violent.'

One of the Streeters, Charlie, had a small scam going with local post office drivers, who would readdress parcels to places where he could collect them. Ronnie, hearing of the potential, demanded fifty per cent of the profits. Charlie was dilatory with payments and was listed by Ronnie as someone with whom he would soon have to deal severely. The opportunity came when Charlie had a fight with Billy Jones, another part-owner of the Stragglers. The next night Bobby Ramsey, as Jones' partner, sought out Charlie and beat him up. Two nights later Charlie, this time with a complement from the Watney Street Gang, beat Ramsey unconscious outside the Artichoke pub in the East End.

Although strictly not involved, Ronnie apparently wanted to make an example of Charlie and shoot him but both Ramsey and Jones argued against this. Instead it was agreed that a severe beating would be handed out to the Watney Streeters in the Britannia public house on Watney Street territory. Ramsey and Jones went with Ronnie, backed by a dozen others. They found the Britannia empty except for a boy, Terry Martin, who was playing gin rummy. The Watney Street Gang had escaped through the back entrance. Martin was made to suffer for their display of cowardliness. He was dragged out of the pub, slashed with a bayonet and kicked about the head.

Instead of going home Ronnie decided to look for the Watney Streeters. Driven by Ramsey, he was found with a revolver when the police stopped the car in Stepney around midnight. In the car there was a crowbar and a machete. Ronnie explained the bloodstains on his shirt by saying he had had a nose bleed. Efforts to buy off Terry Martin failed and Reggie was also charged, but was acquitted after the jury accepted that bloodstains on his jacket might have come from boxers in the gym.

On 5 November 1956 the Recorder of London sentenced Ronnie to three years' imprisonment. Ramsey received five years and Jones three. The Stragglers was shut down shortly afterwards. Reggie said, 'But it didn't really matter. . . . I bought an empty shop in the Bow Road and turned it into a club. I called it the Double R – a sort of tribute to Ron. Above the club we built a very snazzy gym and I got Henry Cooper to open it.'[4]

The Double R may have been the jewel in the crown but even then there were numerous other interests, each paying money – a drinking club in Stratford, second-hand car businesses, and the celebrated illegal drinking club next door to Bow Road police station.

Reggie claims that one of the great problems he had with the law was over police killer Ronnie Marwood, of whom he maintains, 'I owed Marwood nothing and I knew he was going to cause me nothing but trouble. But, despite what they say, there is some kind of honour among thieves, a sort of code of conduct. Right or wrong, I took Marwood in and hid him in a safe place until he was ready to make a run for it.'[5]

It is interesting how this story corresponds and contrasts with the Nash version. The run for it in Reggie's tale never took place in the Nash account, in which Marwood surrendered himself to a police station. On the whole the Nash version is the one to be preferred. There are, for example, no pictures of Reggie

---

[4] R. and R. Kray, *Our Story*, p. 34.
[5] R. and R. Kray, *Our Story*, p. 35. On 14 December 1958, his first wedding anniversary, Ronald Marwood went drinking in various pubs and ended up outside a dance hall in the Seven Sisters Road, involved in a fight between the Essex Road and the Angel gangs. A twenty-three-year-old police constable, Raymond Summers, tried to break up the fight and was fatally stabbed by Marwood, who, believing to the last that he would be reprieved, was hanged at Pentonville Prison on 8 May 1959. The jury had recommended mercy. A demonstration outside the prison had been broken up by the police and booing took place in cinemas when newsreels of the incident were shown. Marwood's was one of the executions on which abolitionists based their campaign.

sending wreaths; no interviews with the press. For a self-publicist it is unlikely he would pass up such a splendid opportunity. In its way the two versions run parallel to the Spot and Hill stories of the flushing out of the Whites. The most likely version is an amalgam. The Nashes were then in the ascendancy. Reggie was a friend who may well have helped out, just as Spot helped Hill clean out his rivals in the 1940s.

Whichever is the correct version, it did not take the police long to close down the Double R and Reggie now maintains that every club he and Ronnie owned after that was persecuted – 'And all because we tried to help someone out.'

By the early 1960s, although Reggie claims that he disliked the protection business, feeling it was none too glamorous, he was looking after the remainder of Billy Hill's interests. Any connection with Jack Spot had long since been severed and there is no mention of the Nashes. He was, he says, also looking after Peter Rachman's interests in Notting Hill. Rachman, who provided a new word for the English language with an empire built from prostitution and slum properties, used a collection of wrestlers and strongmen as minders. Reggie says, '[Rachman] was paying us for protection. He had to – it was either that or his rent collectors were set upon. They were big, but our boys were bigger.'

Albert Donaghue, one of the Firm, explains how protection may not really be as bad as it seems to the outsider:

The Krays would know the right guys who would open a club and approach them. Anyone opening a club would go to them. Young guys only respect someone who is a name, otherwise the doorman is a target. It makes sense. I worked the Green Dragon in Aldgate. I got paid and there was £40 to the twins over and above my wages. People who came to the club knew who I was and why I was there.

Then another time I was approached when I was working in an after-hours drinker opposite Stratford Place – the owner of a mini-cab firm down the East End was having scrub calls, you know, you get called out and then there's no one there. Now it can only be people you've interfered with yourself. The fellow asks me to be the manager. Sixty/forty per cent. I'd had a few drinks and I said 'my way' and he said 'yes'. I couldn't believe it. I made a few calls [to locate the people doing it] and said if it didn't stop I'd be round, and it did.

But according to the twins' cousin, Ronnie Hart, another who was to turn against them when the going became rough in 1967, from that percentage Donaghue had to pay a share from his interest in Advance Mini Cabs of £10 per week, rain or shine, to the twins.

The list of clubs in and around North and East London and the West End from which the twins, at one time or another during their reign, were 'on a pension' is staggering. Benny's in Commercial Road, a spieler run by a cab driver, paid £15 a week. The owner of Dodgers in Brick Lane paid £15 and a further £15 for a betting shop. A Club opposite the dog-track in Walthamstow was another. The Krays had invested around £200 to get it started and they took £30 a week plus the wages of the man they had there to mind both the premises and their interests. That £30 went straight to their mother Violet for her housekeeping. The Green Dragon in Whitechapel Road paid £40 protection and when another blackjack table went into the basement a further £10 a week was levied. It was later turned into a betting shop and the payment remained the same. The Little Dragon next door paid £25 a week, and they were not too proud to receive £10 from the Two Aces, a spieler in the Whitechapel Road. Terry O'Brien's club in Cambridge Circus was taken over by them.

In Soho the twins, through their collectors, tapped Bernie Silver for £60 a week from his clubs: the Gigi in Frith Street and the New Life and the New Mill off Shaftesbury Avenue. This pension went three ways, between the twins, Freddie Foreman and the Nashes. In return Johnny Nash gave the twins a share of his pension from the Olympic Club in Camden Town as well as from the celebrated haunts, the Astor and the Bagatelle off Regent Street, an arrangement which left the twins with the lion's share of the take.

In Chelsea there was the La Monde Club in the King's Road and out at Kingston the Cambridge Rooms over the top of the Earl of Cambridge public house on the Kingston bypass. It was here, in one of their well-publicized acts of charity, that a racehorse was auctioned and bought by the actor Ronald Fraser. Then there was a share of the monies Freddie Foreman received from the tables at the Starlight Rooms off Oxford Street. Run by two men named Boot and Barry, the club had been opened after they had quarrelled with the Richardsons. They had gone to the Krays for help and had been installed in the Starlight as managers.

Of the more famous clubs, the Colony in Berkeley Square paid £100 a week and the Casanova, off New Oxford Street, half that sum. But there were occasional reverses. When John Bloom, the Rolls Razor washing-machine king whose empire collapsed in the 1960s, opened the Phone Booth club in Baker Street, a fringe member of the Firm, Eric Mason, an old-time heavy – reputed to be the last man to receive a flogging in prison – was sent round to ask for a 'pension'. He was thrown out and barred from the club. Later Ronnie Hart was dispatched along with Mason to explain the position. Mason could not be barred but the pension would be scrubbed. If Bloom stepped out of line again he 'would go' and his club along with him. The owner of the Monmouth Club in Monmouth Street, Smithfield, was less successful in repelling boarders. He received a beating for his troubles and later paid over a percentage.

The money from all subscribers to the Firm was collected on a Friday by Donaghue, Ronnie Hart, Scotch Jack Dickson and Ian Barrie. It was known as the milk round and the collectors were treated just like the milkman making his weekly call. From time to time the collectors would be given a small gift such as drink or another £10 for themselves. Scotch Jack Dickson and Ian Barrie kept the money from Benny's and the Dodgers as their own wages.

Back in the suburbs there was £10 a week from a scrap metal merchant in Hackney, and the same from another in Poplar. The twins took £15 of the £30 collected by George Dixon from a pub in Leytonstone. A Greek-run casino in Stoke Newington provided a share of its profits and in Leicester, just before the arrest of the twins in May 1967, Rayners Club paid out over a half share of the takings in return for a £500 investment.

In 1960, in accordance with their increasing social status, the twins acquired Esmeralda's Barn in Wilton Place off Knightsbridge. A once smart and fashionable night club, it had declined into producing strip shows and, with gambling legalized by the Gaming Act of 1959, it had applied for and been granted a licence for gambling. The acquisition was brought about by the simple expedient of frightening the controlling share-holder, Stefan De Fay, into signing away his shares to the twins for £1000. They had heard of the vulnerability of De Fay from Peter Rachman and, their implied threats being heeded, the club was theirs within six hours. De Fay stayed on the board of directors for the next two years but drew no salary. In the heyday of the club the twins cleared £40,000 a year, and they had Lord Effingham on the board with the princely retainer of £10 a week or the sum taken from the Two Aces in Whitechapel Road. The day-to-day running of the club and the twins' financial affairs was now firmly in the hands of an adroit long-firm fraudsman, Leslie Payne.

All went well until Reggie was returned to prison, serving his sentence in Wandsworth. Ronnie, not the brighter of the brothers, became lonely and frustrated. As John Pearson says, it was not sufficient for him to sit in a smart dinner-jacket and watch his tables make him money. He started to take an active interest in the club. Indiscriminately he began to grant long lines of credit and, when a punter could not pay, Ronnie took to threatening him. The serious players began to drift away to find other clubs. A lesbian-orientated discotheque was started in the basement. The club continued its decline until 1963, when it collapsed.

De Fay and his co-owners may have been frightened into signing away Esmeralda's Barn but Hew McCowan was made of sterner stuff. His refusal to sell the Hideaway Club coincided with the first of the two major enquiries by the police into the activities of the Krays.

By 1964, as befitted top-class villains, the twins had racked up very little prison record. In the main, witnesses and victims had been straightened. The police, it seems, had been prepared to adopt a policy of live and let live, even to the extent of letting them operate their illegal drinking club next to Bow Road police station. But things could not remain this way. On 12 July the police were galvanized into action by news of a claim that a set of photographs existed of a peer and a gangster. The Commissioner of Police, Sir Joseph Simpson, issued a statement denying a witch-hunt against titled homosexuals. The owner of the photographs obtained an injunction in the High Court to prevent the pictures being printed by the Mirror Group of Newspapers.

On 13 July the *Daily Mirror* ran an editorial: 'This gang is so rich, powerful and ruthless that the police are unable to crack down on it. Victims are too terrified to go to the police. Witnesses are too scared to tell their story in court. The police, who know what is happening but cannot pin any evidence on the villains, are powerless.'

The next day Sir Joseph made a statement that he had asked senior officers for 'some enlightenment' on reports that enquiries were being made into allegations of a relationship between a homosexual peer and East End gangsters.

On 16 July the *Daily Mirror* led with the story 'The picture we dare not print' and described it as one of a 'well known member of the House of Lords seated on a sofa with a gangster who leads the biggest protection racket London has ever known.'

Rumours abounded: the picture showed the peer in a compromising position; there were stories of orgies at Mayfair parties; a coven of homosexual clergy in Brighton; blackmail; surveillance by Scotland Yard.

The picture, which appeared a week later in the German magazine *Stern*, turned out to be totally innocent. The peer was Lord Boothby, one-time darling of the Conservative Party and widely believed to be the true father of one of Prime Minister Harold Macmillan's children. The gangster was Ronnie Kray.

Boothby issued a statement:

I am not a homosexual. I have not been to a Mayfair party of any kind for more than twenty years. I have met the man alleged to be King of the

143

Underworld only three times, on business matters; and then by appointment in my flat, at his request, and in the company of other people.

He retained Arnold Goodman, of Goodman Derrick & Co, a prominent solicitor and later adviser and confidant to the powerful both in and out of government, to claim damages for libel. The Mirror Group settled for the then very considerable sum of £40,000. Ronnie, for whom Goodman did not act, sold a copy of the picture to the *Daily Express*, and obtained an apology from the *Mirror* but no damages. But, as John Pearson says, the apology kept the *Mirror* away from launching an investigation into him and Reggie.

Nevertheless, prodded by the Labour MP for Brixton, Marcus Lipton, who put down a question in the House of Commons concerning reports he had received about extortion from club owners and what action the Home Secretary was taking, the police began to make active enquiries into the Kray affairs. On 27 July, Area Chief Superintendent Fred Gerrard called on the up and coming young Detective Inspector Leonard 'Nipper' Read at Commercial Street police station and asked him if there was any reason why he should not conduct a detailed investigation into the twins' business and personal interests. Read, rightly taking this as an implication that he might be in their pockets, angrily denied it and a squad was formed.

In his autobiography Read discusses why the police had previously made no serious attempt to break the Krays' hold on the East End:

Over the previous years the Krays had been taken on by the police but not concentrated on. Before Gerrard formed my squad the CID had never taken their actions personally and I think they should have done. If ever there was a shooting and the overwhelming level of opinion amongst detectives was that it was down to the Krays, the attitude had been that you went along to see them first and they said 'No, we got an alibi'. Then you would go and look for the evidence. It should have been the other way round. This is what appalled me even before I started the first enquiry. You'd talk to CID officers and they'd say 'Oh this is down to the Krays', and you'd say 'Well what are you doing about it?' And the answer was they were doing nothing about it. They never sort of took up the cudgels. They never got keen enough or personally involved enough to want to have a go. That was the sort of thing that surprised me.[6]

Read's first move was to go and have a look at the Krays in one of their favourite haunts, the Grave Maurice, where he knew they were to meet a TV interviewer, Michael Barrett. He arrived before six o'clock, the time he had heard was fixed for the meeting, and settled down out of the way.

They came within half an hour, in a large American car. First a man named 'Duke' Osborne got out, his hand in his jacket pocket so it seemed he was carrying a gun. He looked up and down the road, came into the pub and gave the place a swift East to West – I was the only one who was there and he ignored me – checked out the lavatories, went back out on to the pavement, and gave a nod in the direction of the car. Through the open door I watched as Ronnie Kray unfolded himself from the back seat, straightened up, and hurried across the

---

[6] L. Read and J. Morton, *Nipper*, p. 89.

pavement flanked by minders.

For a moment I could not believe what I saw. His hair was smartly cut and gleaming and his gold-rimmed spectacles firmly in place. He was wearing a light camel coat which almost reached his ankles, the belt tied in a casual knot at the waist. For all the world he looked like something out of the Capone era. Once inside the Maurice the minders selected two booths and Ronnie sat in one whilst the minders collected two gins and a whisky from the bar. Ronnie remained in solitary splendour with his men in the next booth until Barrett arrived. He was wearing a neckbrace at the time and the minders did everything but frisk him. He was escorted by them to Ronnie's table before they went back to collect his drink. At the end of the interview Osborne and the others went out, 'swept' the street, and then Ronnie hurried to the car. I have no reason to think that this was anything other than for show. It was not a period in the life of the twins when they were facing a war with anyone.

In a way it was a joke but, at the same time, it was a bit unnerving. I'd heard all these stories about the Krays and here they were behaving exactly as their reputation suggested they would do. If it had been mocked up for a TV serial you'd have said 'Come on, this is a bit over the top.'

As the months went by little progress was made, although Read's squad contained a talented collection of officers, some of whom were to reach the top echelons of Scotland Yard. Read went to see Jack Spot, but he was now out of the scene; journalists to whom he spoke could add little to the articles they had written; and investigations into the story that an Italian restaurant near the British Museum was paying protection money were abandoned after lengthy observation failed to identify anyone remotely connected with the Firm going within yards of the premises.

Nor did the persistent stories of torture amount to anything. The Krays had been reputed to hold mock trials with the punishment of a razor slashing of the buttocks – known as striping the arsehole and a favourite sport amongst villains of the time – but a combing of the records of every hospital in the Greater London area produced nothing. Read also went to see a gambler whom Ronnie was said to have slashed when he was unable to pay a gaming debt at Esmeralda's Barn, but the man would not make a statement. Read and his men trawled the London night clubs but none of the owners and managers would admit to paying protection money. There was a blank, too, when enquiries were made of local bookmakers who were said to have had to pay into funds of the 'aways', those members of the Firm in prison.

The best that Read could come up with was the information that the main source of the Firm came from long firm frauds. The beauty of a well organized long firm fraud is that goods are bought over a telephone by a 'blower-man', so that identification of the purchaser is improbable, and managers fronting the warehouse or shop are changed weekly or fortnightly, making it difficult if not impossible for the investigations to establish a chain of command leading back to the true operators. Another thing in favour of the LF operator was the laborious way in which an investigation would be conducted. The company had to go bust, then creditors had actually to make a complaint, rather than just lick their wounds and write it off to tax and experience. After that it would go to the Board of Trade for an investigation, which could take a year or more and, if they found grounds for concern, the papers would be sent to the Fraud Squad. By then witnesses would have lost interest and the principals would be long gone.

Read bypassed the Board of Trade and the Fraud Squad, steaming straight into the LFs, which he found fairly easy to identify, and arresting the front operators for conspiracy. By doing this he hoped to find someone who might be persuaded to admit to the involvement of the Krays. But no one would admit anything. Although he mounted six prosecutions for fraud, by January 1965 Read was no nearer to the Krays than when he had started. Gerrard as his superior was under considerable pressure from Commander Ernie Millen to terminate the enquiry. While Gerrard was away on annual leave, Millen called Read to the Yard and asked for a report commenting unfavourably on the progress of the investigation and indicating that it would be shut down. When Gerrard returned Read told him of the conversation and an angry exchange took place with Millen.

Then, seemingly, Read had a piece of luck. He heard through an officer at Paddington that club owner Hew McCowan had been pressured to pay protection money for the Hideaway Club in Gerrard Street, which he had just opened in partnership with Gilbert France, who also owned the restaurant Chez Victor in Wardour Street.

The Hideaway had previously been the Bon Soir, owned by France in partnership with Frankie Fraser and Albert Dimes. There had been a dispute with France over the Bon Soir, which was managed by a young man called Sydney Vaughan, and the club had closed in early autumn 1965. At Vaughan's twenty-first birthday party an agreement had been signed giving Vaughan *carte blanche* to run the premises. For this he had to pay Gerrard Enterprises, France's company, £150 a week. McCowan employed Vaughan as his agent and manager, and spent some £4000 on refurbishing the club, which opened for business on 16 December.

McCowan had already met the twins through both a Johnny Francis and their financial adviser Leslie Payne when they had tried to interest McCowan in an investment in a housing project in Eastern Nigeria. This had been a scam run by the son of Manny Shinwell, the old Labour MP, and was the same project in which they had tried to interest Boothby. In turn this had led to the photographs getting into the hands of the *Mirror*.

McCowan had foolishly mentioned that he was thinking of opening a club and it was arranged he should meet the twins in the Grave Maurice public house. According to McCowan's statement Reggie had maintained it was essential that McCowan have two of his men installed in the club to prevent trouble. Initially a figure of twenty-five per cent was suggested, which was to rise to fifty per cent. A table for ten was reserved for the twins' party on the opening night but no one showed. Three days later a friend of the Krays, a writer called 'Mad' Teddy Smith, appeared, very drunk, caused trouble and did a minor amount of damage in the reception area before being bounced out by the waiters.[7] When McCowan next saw the Krays it was pointed out that this sort of thing would not have happened had their men been there to prevent it. An agreement was reached that now twenty per cent would be payable. McCowan asked for and was told he would receive a written agreement. He telephoned the police.

Once he had taken statements Read liked the way McCowan stuck to his version of events and, even more, he liked the way Vaughan gave his account. He would

---

[7] Smith, who had written a play for radio and who was a part-time driver for the twins, disappeared in the 1960s and was thought to have been killed in a quarrel over a boy in Steeple Bay, Kent. His body was never found and no charges were brought.

have liked to have had sight of the agreement but what he had was better than nothing. Read thought he had enough for arrests.

They took place at the Glenrae Hotel in Seven Sisters Road in North London, run by Phoebe Woods and her husband. There was a drinking club in the basement originally for commercial travellers but later taken over by the twins as one of their regular drinking haunts. The pattern of events had been remarkably similar to other takeovers. Mrs Woods had run the trouble-free hotel for some five years until in September 1964 her son was attacked by three men. She shut down the drinking club. Three weeks later men came into the hotel threatening that the club must be reopened. She reported the matter to the police. A fortnight later her husband was attacked in the basement kitchen.

Two weeks later matters were under control again with long-time Kray stalwart, the former boxer Billy Exley, in charge of the bar and the doorman none other than Bobby Ramsey. The Krays moved into rooms 1 and 2. It was there that Gerrard and Read arrested them along with Teddy Smith. Of Johnny Francis, who had made the initial introduction, there was no sign. But if Read thought that his troubles were over he was to find they were only just beginning.

The Krays remained in custody until their trial at the Old Bailey the next year, despite a question in the House of Lords from their old friend Lord Boothby, who wanted to know if it was the intention of the government to imprison the Krays without trial indefinitely. Meanwhile Read hoped that with the twins out of harm's way people would come forward. He was wrong but it was a mistake from which he learned two years later. His case now began to fall apart, starting with the defection of Sydney Vaughan, who went to the twins' home at Fort Vallance to retract his statement before a local vicar.

McCowan was offered money not to give evidence but refused.

The first trial came to an abrupt halt on the second day with McCowan still in the witness box. Manny Fryde, the solicitor's clerk who was handling the Krays' cases, said he had a witness who had overheard a juryman discussing the case with a police officer. The witness turned out to be a man who had been questioned about the sale of the shares in Esmeralda's Barn but the juryman was stood down and the case proceeded with eleven jurors. Vaughan maintained that the only reason he had made his original statement was because Mc-Cowan had threatened to withdraw his financial support. After three and a half hours the jury announced it was deadlocked. At the retrial things went worse for the Crown. Evidence was produced by the defence that McCowan had spent some time in a psychiatric hospital. Vaughan was called neither by the Crown nor by the defence. The jury took less than ten minutes to acquit.

The same day the Krays purchased the Hideaway Club from McCowan, renaming it the El Morocco. Read and his men went to watch the guests turning up for the celebratory party. Seen by George Devlin, a private detective hired by the Krays, he was invited into the party, an offer he could not refuse. Reggie accepted his presence with something approaching equanimity; Ronnie glowered. Read left after a few minutes. His squad disbanded, it was the last he was to see of the twins for four years. In effect the Krays now had a licence to behave as they wished in both the East and West End.

But possibly the Hideaway trial was the pinnacle of their careers. A month after the case, on 20 April 1965, Reggie married a young girl, Frances Shea; the wedding photographer was the fashionable David Bailey. At the wedding Ronnie believed that not sufficient enthusiasm was being shown by the guests. 'Sing, fuck you, sing,' he ordered them. Frances, increasingly unhappy with her husband, committed suicide just over two years later, on the night of 6 June 1967. At her funeral Albert Donaghue was ordered to make a list for future reference of those who had not sent flowers. Reggie was distraught. Worse, Ronnie was beginning to show increasing signs of mental instability. Another list was compiled, this time of those by whom Ronnie felt threatened. All his energies were being channelled into revenge and retribution.

One of those by whom he felt threatened was George Myers, who changed his name to Cornell. An East London tearaway and one of the old Watney Streeters, Cornell had run a long firm fraud which had been turned over by the twins and he resented it. Now he shifted his allegiance to Frankie Fraser and to the Richardsons. His name too went on the list.[8]

In theory there was no need for the Krays ever to quarrel with the Richardsons. There are stories that years earlier there had been a meeting between the Richardsons, Fraser, the Nashes, the twins and the Foreman family over dividing London between them but it had come to nothing. The failure of the meeting was said to have been caused by the refusal of the Richardsons to co-operate, particularly in relation to the money they were receiving from the National Car Parks fiddle.

Whether such a meeting took place, London should have been quite big enough for both the Krays and the Richardsons. As Nipper Read says, 'There was a natural dividing line – the Thames. Soho had for years been

[8] One version of the story has it that Cornell met Fraser in prison and later agreed to join with him in the placing of gaming machines in West End clubs. It is more likely that his allegiance began to change when married Olive, a girl from Bermondsey across the river.

something of an Open City. There was plenty of pickings for everybody. Each firm had the clubs which they protected. There was no need to muscle in on someone else's club.'

Now with the Cornell–Fraser–Richardson alliance the twins began to feel threatened. Whilst Fraser had been in prison following the Spot affair they had assiduously courted him through his sister Eva Brindle, taking her to see him on visiting days, and when he had been released the twins had thrown a big coming home party for him. But Fraser had not been seduced. Instead Fraser, always interested in gaming machines, had taken over a chain of machines once owned by the twins.

George Cornell they saw as a threat because he took a close interest in the pornography market in both the West End and in Essex. The twins also believed they were on the edge of a big deal with the American Mafia and the Richardsons could interfere with it. At one meeting with a Mafioso chief visiting from New York the Richardsons had been present and had made sarcastic remarks. Ronnie also feared that the uneasy truce between themselves and the Richardsons would end. 'I had a gut feeling that something or someone would force us into a full-scale war.'[9]

Worse, there was personal animosity. A meeting was summoned at that gentlemen's club for villains, the Astor, for a discussion between the twins, Ian Barrie and Ron Hart, Charlie and Eddie Richardson, Frankie Fraser and George Cornell. The meeting became heated, with the Richardsons apparently claiming a substantial interest in the Kray–Mafia business arrangements. It was then that George Cornell, never lacking in courage, called Ronnie a big fat poof and told him to bugger off when he asked to be cut into the blue film

[9] R. and R. Kray, *Our Story*, p. 70.

racket. It was not an insult that could be accepted lightly. Ronnie had already slashed little Johnny Cardew from an Islington family for saying, perfectly pleasantly, that he thought Ronnie seemed to be putting on weight. To be called a poof in front of his friends was far too much. There was a discussion about instant retribution but it was put off and instead Ronnie had Cornell's movements monitored.

Shortly after there was another confrontation. This time it was in Al Burnett's Stork Club in Swallow Street, Piccadilly, and this time it was between Ronnie and Frankie Fraser. As a result the Krays called a meeting with some South-East London rivals of the Richardsons and another smaller North London faction. The old talk of an alliance was revived. It was agreed that a defence union should be formed. The Firm was put on war alert. Donaghue recalls:

> We were each given a name. Ronnie Hart and I had to look after Brian Mottram if it came to it. We were all given the names and addresses of clubs, pubs, girlfriends, where our people could be found. Freddie Foreman had a spy in the Richardson scrapyard. If we went south to see Freddie it was like we were going into Indian country. We would go in a hired car with a gun so if we got a pull it wasn't our car and we could say we knew nothing about it. Going south of the river was like going abroad.

Still the Krays did not believe they were strong enough without help. To counter the ferocity of Frankie Fraser someone just as fearless was needed to be their own private man. The person they chose was Frank Mitchell. There was only one problem – he was serving a sentence in Dartmoor Prison.

In the meantime they began wearing bullet-proof vests and a member of the Firm was deputed to be their personal bodyguard, leaving any public house or club first to survey the street. Although they felt themselves in need of protection they did not carry weapons and were becoming increasingly reluctant to allow members of the Firm to do so either. Wednesday nights were when the Krays went visiting around the various local pubs and before these evening visits, members of the Firm would go to the pub or club and hide weapons in lavatory cisterns. They were right to be careful. Shots were fired at the windows of the Widows, the name for the Lion pub in Tapp Street where the Krays used to drink. A few days later a mini-cab owner who resembled Ronnie was knocked down by a car which mounted the pavement.

There had long been a liaison with gangs in Scotland and a Glasgow hardman was recruited to deal with Cornell. He followed him for some weeks but according to legend succeeded only in stabbing him in the bottom when they met in a basement drinking club. The Glasgow hardman returned to Scotland a couple of months before Cornell's murder.

George Cornell survived the Mr Smith's Club affray which had led to the arrest of the Richardsons, only to die on the next evening, 9 March 1966. Ronnie received word that Cornell was deep in the heart of Kray territory, sitting on a stool at the bar of the Blind Beggar public house near Whitechapel tube station in the Mile End Road. Around 8.30 the door opened and in walked Ronnie Kray and Ian Barrie. Had they been a few minutes earlier they would have met a local Detective Inspector having a drink and sandwich. The story is that Cornell looked up and said 'Look who's here'. If he did say that those were the last words he spoke. Ronnie shot him at point-blank range with a Luger pistol.

He justifies the shooting quite simply:

Richard Hart had to be avenged. No one could kill
a member of the Kray gang and expect to get away
with it. . . . Typical of the yobbo mentality of the
man. Less than twenty-four hours after the Catford
killing and here he was, drinking in a pub that was
officially on our patch. It was as though he wanted
to be shot.[10]

Ronnie went into hiding over a barber's shop in the
Lea Bridge Road and the police inquiry got nowhere.
Tommy Butler, the senior detective from the Great
Train Robbery, now on the Murder Squad, was sent
to conduct the investigation. Whilst it was common
knowledge that the Krays were behind the killing –
'Everybody knows Ronnie done it,' one East End villain
told Nipper Read, 'Christ, they did everything but take the
front page of the fucking *Times* to advertise it' – no one
was prepared to admit to seeing anything. The barmaid
had apparently been in the cellar and everyone else had
their heads well down. Butler did, however, organize a
dawn swoop on Vallance Road and put Ronnie up on an
identification parade. He was not picked out by the
barmaid. At that stage she had every reason not to.

Donaghue says he went over to the Three Swedish
Coins in Wapping 'to see a man there to arrange a meet
to see whether the twins could interview the barmaid at
that pub. It never came to anything. I knew that one,
she wouldn't show up and two, if they did she would
never leave.'

Butler was forced to release the twins to their usual
triumphant welcome home. The investigation was put on
ice. But though they might be free of immediate police
attention they were not free of the Cornell family.
George's widow Olive, showing the same courage as her

[10] R. and R. Kray, *Our Story*, p. 72.

husband, mounted a campaign against them, calling at Fort Vallance and smashing the windows. She was brought before the magistrate at Thames Court and fined the derisory sum of £1. At one time the twins seriously considered whether she must join her husband.

Donaghue believes it was then that the twins began to lose touch with reality. Ronnie was on massive doses of tranquillizers and Reggie, besotted with the dead Frances, now believed she had been reborn as a robin he had seen in the cemetery. Ronnie was also putting pressure on his twin to 'do his one'. He would have to wait a year and a half before his brother obliged.

In the meantime, quite apart from managing the day-to-day affairs of the organization, the twins had a long-term and in some ways daring plan. They would arrange the release of the 'Mad Axe-man' Frank Mitchell from Dartmoor where he was serving a substantial sentence of imprisonment. Poor Mitchell, strong as an ox and with the brains of one, had had an amazingly unsuccessful career as a criminal. From the age of eight he had been in special schools, in Borstal at seventeen, and in prison three months later. From then it was downhill all the way, with a flogging for an assault on a prison officer. In 1955 he had been sent to Rampton, certified as a mental defective. In January 1957 he escaped and whilst on the run burgled a house, hitting the occupant over the head with an iron bar. This time he received nine years. Back inside he was sent to Broadmoor, escaped and attacked another householder and his wife. On his arrest he said, 'I want to prove I am sane and know what I am doing.' He received ten years' imprisonment. Involved in the 1962 Hull prison riots he was birched and transferred to Dartmoor.

His behaviour improved and by July 1963 he was removed from the escape list. In May 1964 he was allowed to work outside the prison walls in the quarry party, a small and well-supervised group. In September of that year he was transferred to the honour party, a more loosely supervised group, and now, financed by the Krays, he abused his relative freedom no end. He became a regular in a local pub. Once he took a taxi to Tavistock where he bought a budgerigar. Women were provided by the twins to pass away his afternoons. As one warder said, 'I just could not afford to have Mitchell troublesome.'

For the Krays Mitchell became a special 'away'. Their reputation was on the slide in the East End. Some members of the Firm were now referring to them as Gert and Daisy, after Ethel and Doris Walters, the Cockney music hall act. Others thought they were becoming too dangerous for their own good. Their financial adviser Leslie Payne and his friend Freddie Gore were gone. With the Richardsons in general, and Frankie Fraser in particular, in custody, there was no need for any more strongmen in the Firm. Mitchell was needed more as a rehabilitation or at least damage limitation exercise, showing the East End both how their twins cared for people and, if they put their minds to it, what they could do. On one occasion Mitchell had also protected Reggie Kray against a screw in prison and something of a debt was owed.

Mitchell was becoming querulous about getting a date for his release and the plan was evolved that he would escape from a working party on the Moor and then a campaign would begin to bring pressure for his release. To this end friendly MPs such as the noted homosexual Tom Driberg could be relied on for help. On 12 December 1966 Mitchell went to work at Bagga Tor. The weather that day was too bad for work and the party stayed in a hut playing cards. At 3.30 he asked if he could go and feed some ponies. At 4.20 when the prison officers took the remainder of the party to the bus pick-up point there was no sign of Mitchell. Twenty minutes later the local police were notified. By this time Mitchell was on his way to London. When the hue and cry really went up Mitchell was rather grumpily eating bacon and eggs cooked for him at the Whitechapel flat of a small-time porn merchant and gang hanger-on, Lennie 'Books' Dunn, so named because of the bookstalls he ran in the Whitechapel Road. Mitchell had, it seems, been expecting something more in the way of a red carpet.

When, next morning, his clothing was found in a lay-by some thirty miles from Tavistock it was 'assumed he had made good his escape'. The next and really the last thing the outside world heard of Mitchell was from the newspapers. He wrote to *The Times* and the *Daily Mirror*. Each letter, actually written by Dunn, bore a thumbprint impression to confirm its authenticity and each asked for a release date. At first the Home Secretary agreed to meet with Mitchell but amended this by imposing the precondition of his surrender. The letters dried up. Again it was well known in Barking Road who had helped Mitchell in his escape, but once again, no one was talking to the police.

For a few days Mitchell lived in relative comfort, with the twins trying to keep him happy. A hostess, Lisa, was more or less kidnapped from Winston's night club to provide him with sex and there is little doubt that she became fond of this semi-moron who exercised by holding up members of the Firm two at a time in displays of strength. But Mitchell had in fact exchanged one prison cell for another. Without his surrender he was no nearer obtaining a release date and surrender meant loss of privileges and very probably loss of remission and further time to be served. He began to say he would never be captured alive. And the more he said such things the more of a liability he became to the twins. He wanted to go and see his mother and sister at the family house in Bow and was told a meeting would be arranged, but nothing came of it. He began to rave about going to look for the twins both at Vallance Road and 'all around the clubs'.

On 24 December Mitchell was told by Albert Donaghue that he was being moved to a new address in Kent. He protested at being separated from Lisa but was told she would be following on. He was never seen again, although rather like in the Lord Lucan case, there were reports that he had been sighted in Scotland, Ireland, Germany and, indeed, in most other countries throughout the world. At the trial of the Krays for the murder of Mitchell, Alf Donaghue gave evidence that the axe-man had been shot just as the van left the Barking Road, the gunmen being Freddie Foreman and Alf Gerard, a more or less freelance hitman who died in 1981 in Brighton.

The Firm had a series of codes: 'the dog has won' meant a successful operation had been carried out, 'the dog has lost' meant the reverse. According to the night club hostess Lisa, Donaghue returned to the flat and said, 'The dog is dead.' There was no corroboration of Donaghue's evidence. He himself had been arrested and had turned QE as the trade expression goes. The Krays were acquitted along with Freddie Foreman. Alfie Gerard, who was in Australia at the time of the trial, was never charged.

The third, in chronological order, of the murders for which the Krays eventually stood trial was that of Jack 'the Hat' McVitie, a longtime friend of the family. He disappeared in the autumn of 1967. Apparently he had fallen from favour for a number of reasons.

Tony Lambrianou, one of three brothers and a lesser light of the Kray Firm, who wrote a book on his experiences, described McVitie and his murder:

Reggie didn't do society such a bad turn. Jack the
Hat was a known heavy man. He was six feet two
and hard as nails. He done a lot of imprisonment
in his time. He'd been through the school and he'd
hurt a few people along the way.

His stock in trade was crime and he made money
out of it. He was an active robber and he cared
little for anyone and he was capable of anything. . . . He was on drink and pills and he was
unpredictable. . . . Even having a social drink, he
could suddenly turn vicious for no reason.

He didn't have a care in the world. He didn't
give a monkey for anything, but he should have
done. That was his downfall. . . . The twins only
tried to help him: they put lots of work his way.
But he started making errors, and he brought
trouble on himself.[11]

The work from the Krays had included taking over
part of a drug-vending operation and spying on the Nash
brothers. McVitie was related to Johnny Nash's then
right-hand man. After McVitie's death the story was put
about that he had died when gelignite in his car had
blown up accidentally. It was a story to appease the Nash
brothers.

McVitie at one time had a £25 a week pension. He
worked as a freelance robber and when asked to donate
half the proceeds to the Firm's funds he refused. He was
expelled. Later, after a beating, he was reinstated as a
fringe member if nothing more. He could not be relied
on, however, and he tipped the wink to another
independent robber, Bobby Cannon, when Cannon was
on the line for, at the very least, a bad beating. McVitie
also took to criticizing the twins in public.

[11] T. Lambrianou, *Inside the Firm*, pp. 26–7.

His compounding sin seems to have been his behaviour when given money to kill the Krays' former financial adviser Leslie Payne. He had gone to Payne's house with Billy Exley, an ex-boxer and one-time stalwart friend of the Krays, only to find the potential victim out. McVitie had simply turned away and pocketed the advance fee. Not content with that, he had begun to boast how he had ripped off the twins. It was probably a combination of all these things which led to McVitie's death. They were coupled to one further fact: McVitie was in the wrong place at the wrong time.

He was murdered at a party at Evering Road in the home of 'Blonde' Carol Skinner. She had been sent across the road to a friend of hers for the evening. Tony Barry of the Regency Club had been ordered to tell the Krays when McVitie showed up at the club and to bring to the Evering Road party a gun kept at the Regency. There were advantages in this. The more people who were participants as opposed to mere observers, the more compromised they were and so the less likely to tell the police.

The Lambrianou brothers brought McVitie to the flat and immediately Reggie put the gun to his head. The gun failed to discharge. McVitie began to struggle and to try to escape. Finally Reggie plunged a knife deep into his face and stomach. Reggie commented, 'I did not regret it at the time and I don't regret it now. I have never felt a moment's remorse.'[12]

McVitie's body was wrapped in a candlewick bedspread and taken to South London by Charlie Kray for disposal – something arranged by Freddie Foreman, who, although from South London, was a longtime friend of the twins. Exactly where the body ended is impossible to say. Nipper Read fancied the idea that it

[12] R. and R. Kray, *Our Story*, pp. 85–91.

had returned to East London and had been put in the furnaces of the local swimming baths. Other versions suggest a disposal or burial in farms in Essex or Suffolk. According to Tony Lambrianou, who says the car in which he was taken to South London ended as an Oxo cube in a scrapyard:

> Jack himself is about three miles away from where the car went into scrap, and fifty miles from where we left him. His body will never be found. He and his hat were put in a grave which had been pre-dug, and covered with a layer of soil. A funeral took place the next day, and the grave was filled. So he did get a decent burial.

But by now the gang was splitting. Nipper Read, appointed to the Murder Squad with a special brief to bring down the Krays, had learned from his earlier mistakes. He was not going to move too quickly again. Patiently he began to nip away at the edges of the Firm. Billy Exley, former strong-arm man, was interviewed to no effect. Then Read turned his attention to Leslie Payne, who had after all been the object of the half-hearted attempt on his life made by McVitie and Exley. When would a more adroit one be made? Read obtained an indemnity for Payne against all crimes except those of violence, provided he admitted to them. Over a period of weeks, travelling to town on a daily basis, Payne remained closeted with Read in a police section house away from the eyes of Scotland Yard and other observers as he told the tale of the Firm. Armed with this statement Read was able to obtain evidence from others on the fringes, promising that he would not use the statements unless and until arrests had been made. The inquiries into the murders were shelved as he examined the Krays' involvements with long firm frauds and their dealings in stolen bonds.

Meanwhile at the beginning of 1968 the Krays were moving once more into the international market. They met Angelo Bruno of the Philadelphia family, of whom Albert Dimes was said to be the trusted adviser. Bruno, an associate of American mobsters Raymond Patriaco and Vincent Teresa, and a friend of the financier Judah Binstock, was looking at casino interests in the West End. The Krays promised him a trouble-free life running those interests. They had successfully disposed of a batch of bonds, part of a number stolen in an armed raid on the Royal Bank of Canada in Montreal on 15 April 1965. Now the trade in stolen securities was expanding. They had also met the enterprising American, Alan Bruce Cooper, who effected an entry for them into Europe and the stolen jewellery market in Belgium. It was he who would precipitate the arrest of the Krays.

Read had had Cooper under surveillance for some time when he learned that a man called Paul Elvey was being sent to Glasgow to collect a briefcase. There had long been a two-way trade in villains between Glasgow and London, and there had long been a similar trade of information and assistance between the respective police forces. Elvey was arrested and the briefcase found to contain dynamite, something readily available from the mines around Glasgow. Interviewed by Read, he passed on a story of assassination attempts on Soho strip-club owner George Caruana and others, both in the street and at the Old Bailey. Amazingly, when his premises were searched there was the physical evidence to back it up. Cooper was arrested and to Read's dismay he disclosed that he was being run by John du Rose, a superior officer, as an informer and possibly *agent provocateur*. There was little question of Read being able to charge Cooper; instead he had to use him as a witness.

Read knew that once Cooper disappeared from the streets the Krays would suspect something was up. Luckily the man genuinely suffered from a stomach ulcer and Read placed him in a Harley Street nursing home, from where Cooper telephoned the twins. Read hoped the twins would come and make damaging admissions. Instead they sent one of their henchmen along with Joey Kauffman, a Jewish–Sicilian small-time Mafioso who was dealing in stolen bonds.

In the early hours of the morning of 9 May, after an evening out at the Astor, the Krays went back to their flat and Kauffman to his suite in the Mayfair. At 5 a.m. Read's men swooped, scooping up nearly all the members of the Firm in one hit. Initially they were charged with conspiracy to murder persons unknown. These charges arose from the statements of Elvey and Cooper,[13] and had nothing to do with Mitchell, McVitie and Cornell. It was only after the arrests that Read and his team were able to coax the barmaid to give evidence that she had indeed seen the shooting of Cornell.

The swoop on 9 May had included both the twins' friend Freddie Foreman and their brother Charles. Now, as the police chipped away at the edges of the Firm, several people, including Billy Exley, offered to give evidence. In their book the twins write that they knew their time at liberty was limited; 'the net was closing in. . . . We underestimated the cunning and the cheating of the police.'[14]

With the twins and senior members of the Firm on remand in custody, Read made further progress in obtaining statements from men who might consider turning Queen's Evidence. Although Read thought one of the last who would do so was Albert Donaghue,

[13] Those charges were later dismissed.
[14] R. and R. Kray, *Our Story*, p. 56.

eventually a note was passed to Read at Bow Street asking him to go to see him urgently in prison.

Donaghue, heavily involved in the escape of Mitchell and in the van when he was taken away, had been a well trusted member of the Firm even though he had been shot in the foot by Reggie during an argument in a pub. As far as possible Read had made sure that the members of the Firm were in separate prisons or at least separate wings but, Donaghue says, he went one day for a meeting with Manny Fryde, the Krays' defender:

> We'd been told, don't leave notes about the case in the cell. There were the twins, Charlie and me. I brought out my notes. The girl Lisa had said I had said 'The dog is dead'. I didn't want to dispute it. The dead opposite. We'd had a bull terrier which had to be put down.
>
> Manny Fryde left the room saying he had to go and make a phone call. Reggie just tore my notes up and said 'What we've sorted out is we take all the violence, Scotch Jack takes Cornell, Ronnie Hart takes Jack the Hat and you take Mitchell.' I said 'no'.
>
> Manny Fryde came back and started telling them what he was going to do. 'Just because you're not a Kray don't think I'm not going to look after you,' he said, but I didn't think so. That's when I got my mother to get a note to Nipper. He got me another solicitor, Victor Lissack. I got on all right with him straight away and it went from there.

The trial was split into two sections. The first was that of the Cornell and McVitie murders. The second was for the murder of Frank Mitchell. Trials relating to the charges of fraud and of assault were to be heard at a later date. Before the Cornell and McVitie trial Manny Fryde opened negotiations with the prosecution for deals to be struck over what pleas would be offered by various of the defendants. Nothing came of them.

The Krays received life sentences for the murders of Cornell and McVitie. Charles Kray and Freddie Foreman received ten years each for their part in clearing up after the McVitie killing. Manny Fryde returned to make further offers on pleas before the Mitchell trial. Again they were rejected but this time the twins and Foreman were acquitted of his murder. Donaghue, who pleaded guilty to being an accessory in Mitchell's murder, received two years.

Now that both the Richardsons and the Krays were inside and serving very long sentences, the question was who next fancied themselves as the senior Firm in London.

6

The Dixons
and the Tibbses

Once the Kray trial was over the brass hat brigade at
Scotland Yard had to decide what was to be done with
Nipper Read's squad. In theory, with the Krays and the
Firm put away, there was no need for it to continue, but
once again there were rumours in the press of a takeover
bid for the West End by other interests.

Certainly clubs were paying money to the remnants of
the Nash enterprise but

> it was being done in a very different way from the
> Krays' reign of terror. It was really rather a friendly
> business with this gang – almost a two-way opera-
> tion with benefits to both sides. We thought they
> would jump and occupy the vacuum, but it never
> happened. I think they sensed that if they had done
> that they would have let themselves in for a major
> investigation and consequently all sorts of troubles.
> It was a good example of preventive policing.[1]

Read was sent on the Senior Command Course at
Bramshill, the police training headquarters. He had
been promised the post of Commander when one next

---

[1] L. Read and J. Morton, *Nipper*, p. 266.

became available. Instead he was bypassed twice and sent into exile as the guv'nor of 'Y' division, North London. Unlike almost every other team that had led a major enquiry and operation, his squad, to his continued disappointment, was not awarded a special tie. The cult of the senior police officer, known on radio, television and in the newspapers, was to come to an end. 'Yard takes Star men out of Limelight' headed a newspaper report, which went on to say that the Commissioner, Sir John Waldron, and Assistant Chief Constable Peter Brodie – no lover of Read – were worried about two recent cases which had resulted in publicity for the officers leading them. The cases were the Great Train Robbery and the Kray case. McArthur had not been a Met officer when he investigated the Richardsons and so, for the purposes, did not count.

It was a curious decision. For years Scotland Yard had traded on its stars, from Chief Inspector Dew who chased across the Atlantic after Crippen, to such great names of the decades as Fred Wensley, who arrested Steinie Morrison in 1911 for the murder of Leon Beron on Clapham Common, and Robert Fabian, whose cases had been made into a series of television films after his retirement. In the 1950s Fabian had a considerable rapport with journalists. He would hold court in the local pub at the time he wanted to release the news, leaving the journalists scrambling to meet the newspaper deadlines, but he always had something for them. Now the Yard was to adopt a more faceless policy, with favoured journalists invited on to the fifth floor on a Friday night for whisky and sandwiches with the top brass.

With the snuffing out of the stars came the disbandment of the Serious Crime Squad. Detective Chief Inspector Harry Mooney, Read's junior officer, had kept a lock on the West End in the immediate aftermath of the Krays. No one had jumped into the vacant seat and so the squad was allowed to run down.

But suddenly the regime changed. Waldron died; Robert Mark took his place. Certain elements in the East End were thought once more to be getting out of hand and there was one Scotland Yard 'star' still left to be pulled out of the locker. His name was Bert Wickstead, variously referred to as the Gangbuster and the Grey Fox. As a young officer he had been involved in the Pen Club killing of Selwyn Cooney in 1960 and had worked his way up with stints in the East End and more lately had been involved in the investigation of the collapse of the Ronan Point building in May 1968.

Just as Read took over the Kray enquiry with a couple of officers and no office space, so Wickstead began with no squad and no telephone. It was then that a decision was made to target the Dixon family. But to the outside world who were they? A friend of the Dixons says:

George is a reasonably tough man, a family man, not a man I would call a gangster. He's got a couple of medals for bravery. A kid had broken out of the nuthouse and was shooting at everybody. George was driving past and saw what was happening and disarmed him. The second was when a geezer had a gun in the City Arms in Millwall. George knocked it up in the air.

He had also been a friend of the Krays, although that did not stop Ronnie shooting at him one night in a mock trial held at the Green Dragon Club in Aldgate over some alleged misdemeanour. The gun misfired and Kray gave him the cartridge, telling him to wear it as a souvenir on his watch-chain – and he did. 'His brother Alan Dixon is a big clown, always laughing, joking, extrovert, loves a sing and hasn't got an ounce of violence in him,' says the same friend.

The so called leader of the Dixons was a publican, the 5 foot 2 inches Phil Jacobs, known locally as Little Caesar, whose pubs were the Bridge House in Canning Town, the Royal Oak in Tooley Street, and the Plough and Harrow in Leytonstone, which George Dixon minded. The Dixons had stood up for him when, shortly before their arrest, the Krays had tried to muscle in on his pubs. Now Wickstead believed the Dixons were expanding their own empire under Jacobs' guidance, specializing in protection and long firm fraud.

Jacobs had left school at the age of fourteen and had worked in various restaurants before he went to do his National Service. Unlike the Krays and the Richardsons he must have rather enjoyed it. He became a Leading Aircraftsman. He married in November 1965 with only ten shillings to his name. His wife's parents bought them the Ship in Aylward Street and from then on, with hard work, he prospered. By the time of his arrest he had a Rolls Royce with a personalized number plate.

George Dixon, with former member of the Kray firm Connie Whitehead, had already been acquitted at the Old Bailey of causing grievous bodily harm to a club owner. The allegation was that injuries had been caused after he had refused the offer to have his club looked after. Wickstead's breakthrough in his enquiries came when a complaint was made to West Ham police station by one of the Dixons' brothers-in-law, Micky Flynn. He was immediately taken round to see Wickstead, who wrote admiringly: 'To say he was big was a little like saying that Rockefeller was rich or that Capone was bad. He was huge, one of the most formidable men I'd ever seen.'

According to Flynn, he was one of the enforcers for the Dixons but now he had left his wife, Lynne, he had consequently fallen out with the brothers. They, he said, had retaliated with a bit of nastiness directed towards his

1920: the 'racing fraternity' of Saffron Hill. Darby Sabini and Paesani. From the left standing: Joe Sabini; Micky Papa; Paul Cortesi; Angelo Giannicoli. Sitting: Harry Cortesi; Darby Sabini; Gus Cortesi; Harry Boy Sabini; George Cortesi; Saca Alzapiedi.

1952: warming up for their career. Ronnie (right) and Reggie work out for the camera.

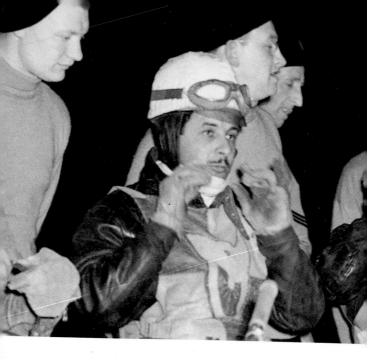

above: Francis 'Split' Waterman in his days as the idol of the speedway fans.

1955: A happy Albert Dimes and his wife leave the Old Bailey after his acquittal in the Battle of Frith Street with Jack Spot.

Bert 'Battles' Rossi.

Fay Sadler; the woman who
captivated Tommy Smithson.

1954: Jack and Rita Spot leave the Old Bailey after her conviction for perverting the course of justice in the Spot-Dimes trial.

1964: solicitor's clerk Manny Fryde (in hat), and colleague Ralph Haeem: (in glasses) with former Kray adviser Leslie Payne, leave the Old Bailey during the Hideaway Club trial.

July 1956: Victor 'Scarface' Russo leaves the Old Bailey after giving evidence which led to Jack Spot's acquittal.

below: A happy day when Reggie Kray marries Frances Shea. Ronnie smiles on the left.

Seventeen years on, Reggie Kray (left) is escorted to his mother's funeral.

Ronnie Kray peeps out at the camera at the memorial service for Red Hot Mama Sophie Tucker.

Connie Whitehead and George Dixon (left and third from the left) with friends.

1967: the interior of the Blind Beggar, Mile End Road, the home of the turn-of-the-century Blind Beggar gang and the scene of the end of Georgie Cornell.

above: Esmeralda's Barn, Knightsbridge; despite appearances for a short time perhaps the smartest of the Kray nightclubs.

George Cornell (aka Myers).

own sisters. One had had her arm broken, another had been threatened.

A friend of the Dixons, and a participant observer in these matters, has it the other way around. 'He'd given his wife a beating and Brian Dixon went round to sort things out.' Translated, this must mean 'sort *him* out'. Despite his size Flynn, the Dixons maintained, ran for cover.

Wickstead sees him in a more heroic light, maintaining that Flynn would have visited each Dixon brother in turn and dealt with him. 'But you see I didn't know how far I'd go,' he told the Commander. 'So I changed my mind. I wasn't going inside for the likes of them.'

It would not have suited Wickstead to have the Dixons as victims: 'If the Dixons had then made a complaint, we would have had to charge him; and with his almost inhuman strength, it might not have stopped at grievous bodily harm. It could so easily have been manslaughter or even murder.' When it came to it no charge was brought over the alleged breaking of Flynn's sister's arm.

It was the familiar pattern of an enquiry. Once one witness came forward it was easier for others. Following a raid on the Greyhound in Bethnal Green, run by a man called Osborne, in March 1971, Wickstead had another witness. Osborne was willing to give evidence about a fight between Michael Young and his cousin Mickey Bailey, which he said had been the usual prelude to a demand for money for protection. The fight was witnessed by two off-duty police officers who were told not to interfere. Instead they withdrew and compiled notes of the incident. Next to come forward was a long-time criminal, Bernard Stringer, who recalled Bailey attacking him in the Court Club in Inverness Terrace.

The arrests came at 5.30 a.m. on 25 August 1971. Wickstead borrowed twenty-nine officers from the Flying Squad and, as a result, nearly came to disaster.

His team was briefed at 4 p.m. and dispersed. Someone leaked the story to the *Evening Standard* which, by the time of the raid, had its early headline prepared: 'Yard swoops on London Gangsters.'

Wickstead learned his lesson. In the future he used only his own squad and the special patrol group. 'We used to get locked in a gymnasium from the time of the briefing until we left for the raid,' one officer recalls.

The Dixon trial began on 12 April 1972 and continued until 4 July. Much of the time was spent challenging the evidence of the police. There had been no written statements of admission and much of the police evidence consisted of verbal admissions. There was also the now fashionable cross-over from the dock to the witness box as some defendants gave evidence against their former friends in return for no evidence being offered against them. Of the defendants who were left, Lambert Jacobs and Brian Dixon were acquitted; Phillip Jacobs, Leon Carelton and George Dixon received twelve years. Alan Dixon went down for nine and Michael Young and Michael Bailey, who had had the fight in the Greyhound, received five each.

Monty Sherbourne defending in the case had called it a 'storm in a teacup' but the judge, Mr Justice O'Connor, had this to say:

> You have mounted a campaign of vilification during the trial against police officers in the hope of saving your skins. Such activity on your part cannot operate on my mind to increase the sentences I have to pass on you. On the other hand, it does show the nature of your guilt. And it removes entirely such compassion as I would have been willing to show.

Moral – plead guilty.

O'Connor called Wickstead forward for a public commendation. 'You and your men deserve the full commendation of the public for bringing this gang to justice. It was a difficult task, thoroughly, honestly, efficiently and fairly discharged.' The encomium did not appeal to the public gallery or the dock, from which someone shouted, 'The end of your reign in the East End is just beginning. We will get you, Wickstead. We will get you.' It was not. They did not. Wickstead and his team were a force to be reckoned with for some years to come.

When George Dixon was released he took a pub in partnership with his father-in-law, then bought a run-down hotel in Hastings, did it up and sold it well. With the proceeds he purchased a caravan park at Frinton and then went into the motor trade. On his release, Alan Dixon first had a wine bar and then expanded into the entertainment business.

The next of the Wickstead successes was the arrest of the Tibbs family. It arose from a longstanding quarrel they had had with a family described derisively amongst some East Enders as 'half gypsies', who were 'not very nice', 'liberty takers' and the ultimate put-down, 'not well liked' – the Nichollses from Stepney.

The feud seems to have begun in 1968 when Georgie 'Bogie' Tibbs, then in his sixties and described by Tibbs' supporters as 'a quiet man', was having a drink in the Steamship public house, managed by a friend of the Nichollses, Frederick Fawcett.[2] He became involved in a row with Albert Nicholls, then in his twenties, who, legend has it, 'smashed into him'. Bogie's eyes were blacked and he lost two teeth. Reprisals were swift and suitable. Albert had a cab office in Poplar near the Blackwall Tunnel where he was visited by Jimmy Tibbs, his brother Johnny and Georgie's son, young George. Nicholls produced a shotgun. It was taken from him, he was knocked down and hit on the head with the stock.

What happened next is variously described. By Wickstead as: 'A shotgun blast inflicted terrible injuries to his legs and to the lower part of his abdomen. There were three large lacerations in the scalp and cuts to the face. The tip of his nose was partially severed and he lost the tip of a finger.' And by an, admittedly partisan, East End historian as: 'Unfortunately the gun went off catching him in the leg.'

That seems to be just how the judge saw it because on his direction at the close of the prosecution case the Tibbs were acquitted of attempted murder and pleaded guilty to minor charges. 'You have been guilty apart from anything else of the most appalling folly. I sympathize with your feelings but at the same time, living in the part of London where you live, there is a great deal too much violence,' said Mr Justice Lyell, handing out suspended sentences of two years' imprisonment coupled with fines of £100 each at the Old Bailey.[3] The Nicholls did not see this as justice being done.

Things simmered for the next two years and then boiled over in November 1970. Robert Tibbs survived having his throat cut outside the Rose of Denmark. Certainly Frederick Fawcett's brother, Micky, was there but just who wielded the knife and who started what, Wickstead was never able to discover.

On Christmas Day one of Fawcett's friends was attacked and severely beaten near his home. Later

---

[3] Albert Nicholls seems to have been out of luck on another occasion. During one of the periods when the Kray twins were seriously feuding with the Richardsons he was knocked down on the pavement outside the Lion public house in Tapp Street. His leg was broken. He had been mistaken for Ronnie Kray.

Michael Machin, brother of Teddy, walked into the Steamship and shot up Freddie's ceiling.

Teddy himself was shot at whilst at home in bed. Two men crept up to his ground floor flat window and blasted him in the backside with a shotgun.[4] Two weeks later Michael Machin was fired on by two men armed with shotguns.

And so it went on. Ronnie Curtis, a friend of the Fawcetts, was badly beaten, as was Lenny Kersey who, it was said, had called the Tibbs pikeys.[5] He was attacked with knives and an axe as he left his flat in Mile End, receiving wounds which required 180 stitches. His wife described the scene: 'I saw the men hacking at somebody on the ground and tried to stop the horrible thing. Then I saw it was my husband. His face was falling apart. I screamed the place down. My friend also screamed and dropped her baby.'

Further attacks took place on the Nichollses and their friends and the Tibbses. Albert and Terence Nicholls were called out of the Rose of Denmark by Stanley Naylor and told to get into their car. As they did so the windscreen was smashed and they were attacked. Albert was stabbed in the leg and a gun was produced. The police arrived and the attackers fled.

---

[4] Teddy Machin, who had been a member of the Upton Park Mob, a friend of Jack Spot and 'a very lucky man', charged in the 1950s London Airport robbery of which he was acquitted, was later shot dead on the doorstep of his home. At the time enquiries were being made into his possible involvement in the death of prostitutes in Soho in the late 1940s. Their deaths were thought to be professional rather than personal. His death was almost certainly a personal matter rather than gang-orientated.

[5] A term of abuse meaning gypsies. The origin is harmless and comes from a user of turnpikes but since the middle of the twentieth century piker has come to mean a thief or cheat.

Terence was taken to hospital but whilst the police were questioning Albert, Jimmy Tibbs returned and drove his car at them. They all jumped for their lives. Albert then drove to the hospital to see his brother. On the way he was hijacked by Jimmy Tibbs and Naylor and hit with a golf club. He managed to push them out of the car as it approached the Blackwall Tunnel. For this attack Jimmy Tibbs was charged with attempted murder.

George Brett, another friend of the Fawcetts and the Nichollses, was shot in the leg.[6] He had tried to separate two men who were fighting in the Huntingdon Arms public house. Eight months later came what he said was the revenge, the incident which determined Wickstead to intervene. Until then, according to his memoirs, he seems to have been observing the situation with something of an Olympian detachment. Quite apart from that, he still had his hands full with the Dixon case.

On 22 April 1971 a bomb was placed under the engine of Jimmy Tibbs' car, near the radiator, and exploded outside a school when his four-year-old son was with him. They would both have been killed had the bomb been positioned properly. The attack came a week after his cafe, the Star in Star Road, had also exploded, although in this case possibly from a gas leak.

'Enough was enough,' wrote Wickstead.[7] Now he augmented his squad and started to liaise with Treasury Counsel Michael Corkery and the late Dai Tudor Price. To the outsider it might have seemed that there was a problem as to which of the rival factions should be prosecuted. Wickstead had no doubts about which faction posed the greatest threat to law and order.

---

[6] For what happened to George Brett, see Chapter 11.

[7] B. Wickstead, *Gangbuster*, p. 91.

The answer to that had to be the Tibbs. They were a highly organized gang. They were becoming steadily more powerful, more ruthless, more ambitious. They were also more wicked and crueller than their opponents. The Nicholls weren't a gang in the accepted sense of the word – more of a loose collection of criminal friends. The same thing could be said about Michael Fawcett and his associates. My decision, incidentally, was agreed and fully endorsed by the DPP.

Nor had he any qualms about taking sides and using one team against another. 'I wouldn't deny it for a moment. In the twilight world of the gangster, archbishops are thin on the ground.'[8] Wickstead settled on Fawcett as the key figure and an arrangement was made with him outside Westminster tube station that he would give evidence.

After the arrests and whilst the Tibbses were in custody awaiting trial, a curious incident took place at Rook's Farm, Stocking Pelham, in Hertfordshire.[9] After the Hosein case the farm had been bought for £17,500 by an East End publican, Tony Wyatt, who also used the name Lewis. On 19 September 1972 a wedding reception for his sister-in-law, Avril Hurst, was held there, at which a number of prosecution witnesses in the Tibbses' case were guests. During the festivities a young man called John Scott was killed with a sickle. The holes in

[8] Ibid, p. 95.

[9] Mrs Muriel McKay, the wife of the chief executive of the *News of the World*, had been kidnapped and held captive there by the Hosein brothers, Arthur and Nizamodeen, in December 1969. They had demanded a ransom of one million pounds. She was almost certainly shot at the farm and her body fed to the pigs. The brothers were sentenced to life imprisonment at the Old Bailey in 1970.

his body were plugged and the corpse was dressed in fresh clothes. It was then placed in Scott's van and driven to the East End, where his body was found the following Monday in Ranelagh Road, Leytonstone, by some schoolboys. A number of people were arrested and taken to Leytonstone police station before being released.

Wyatt was charged with his murder. Scott, he said, had been an uninvited guest who had ridden one of the horses on the farm and had been a general nuisance. He told the police:

> I asked Scott to leave. There was an argument. He pushed me and I fell on the hearth. I got up with something in my hand and I hit him twice with it and he fell down. I realized I had hit him with a sickle. The only reason that this happened was that Scott was making a nuisance of himself to the women of my family and he attacked me when I asked him to leave.

On 9 March 1973 he was convicted of manslaughter and sentenced to three years' imprisonment, most of which was served at Leyhill open prison. He was paroled after twelve months. The farm was sold again, this time for £46,500. Although it is inconceivable that Wyatt managed everything in the way of re-dressing the body and transporting it to Leytonstone by himself, no charges seem to have been brought against any other people.

The month after Scott's death, in October 1972, seven members of the Tibbs family and their friends were gaoled. James Tibbs senior received fifteen years, Stanley Naylor twelve, Michael Machin eleven[10] and Jimmy Tibbs ten. Immediately after the verdict Mrs

---

[10] For footnote, see opposite.

Kate Tibbs, the wife of James Tibbs senior, was taken to hospital suffering from a drug overdose.

This was not generally a popular prosecution amongst the cognoscenti, and the sentences meted out received less than universal approval in the East End. 'They stuck up for themselves, that's all,' was the general reaction Oliver Pritchett of the *Evening Standard* encountered when he canvassed the locals after the case. 'I bet you can go into any pub in Canning Town today and you won't hear a word against them,' said one. 'They've never been liberty takers and that's gospel,' said another.

After the trial a complaint was made that it was Mickey Fawcett who had cut Robert Tibbs. A report was submitted to the Director of Public Prosecutions. Unsurprisingly, he declined to take the matter further.

After his release from prison Jimmy Tibbs worked with the boxing manager Terry Lawless and was eventually given a licence, first as a trainer–second and then as a manager by the British Boxing Board of Control. He is highly respected amongst the boxing fraternity.

Amazingly, the Tibbs' case was the last of the so-called protection racket cases for fifteen years. It was 1990 before Frank Salmon, a market trader from Dagenham,

[10] In October 1973 Machin died in prison after a kidney transplant, donated by his brother Victor, had failed. Robert Tibbs received a short sentence. In June 1991 he received twelve years' imprisonment at Guildford Crown Court. He had left the family's scrap-metal business in 1984 and had run a wine bar. Now he had been convicted following his part in an attempt to smuggle 1.5 tons of cannabis valued at £3.5 million into Britain. Customs officers had foiled the attempt when a yacht, the *Katimavik*, was impounded as she berthed at Oban in Scotland. One-time sculptor and friend of Princess Margaret, Francis Morland, was sentenced to nine years for his part in the importation.

was gaoled at the Old Bailey for seven and a half years. He had been convicted of blackmail, affray and an attack during which ammonia was squirted in a victim's face. Robert Michell, said to be Salmon's right-hand man, was sentenced to three years for blackmail, affray and possession of a firearm, whilst Gary Pollard received four and a half years and Donald Meason twenty-one months.

Salmon had reigned over a part of the East End and Essex for a little over a year, trying to obtain protection money from twenty-three wine bars, clubs and saunas. He had shot up one bar and pressed a gun under the nose of a barman. In 1989 disc jockey Russell Holt, who played the East End pubs, had forty-two stitches in his head and hand following an assault by four masked men. His ankle was broken by a pool cue and he went to the police. He told detectives he had been asked to pay Salmon £1500 as a share in his earnings.

The police used a WPC, Elaine Manson,[11] as the person to trap Salmon. Acting as the friend and business associate of Holt's wife, Denise Seaga, who ran a dress shop, she met Salmon on five occasions, paying out a total of £800. It was thought that Salmon, known as a womanizer, would be less suspicious than if a male officer acted as a decoy. At one meeting she was patted down by him when he came to suspect she was a police officer.

She told the court that one time she was with him he 'shook his arm and a knife slid down inside his left palm'. On another occasion she noticed a bulge in the leg of his trousers and remarked it looked like the outline of a knife. 'Brains of Britain . . .' he replied. 'In this business you get wankers who don't play ball.' On 22 May 1989 she handed over some money and asked Salmon why he

[11] A pseudonym.

referred to the cash as a present. 'I am not going to shout out it is protection money, am I?' he replied.

Afterwards a detective commented, 'He tried to model himself on people like the Krays, though he was never going to be as criminally successful as them. He was a plastic gangster, but he was also a dangerous and violent one.'

7

Prostitution and Pornography

Prostitution, never illegal under British law – the offence is soliciting in a public place for an immoral purpose – has always been a major source of revenue to gangs. It has, however, never really been an 'English crime' and the running of women has been mainly in the hands of Europeans and, in the 1950s and 1960s, particularly the Maltese.

To what extent the operations of the white slave traders have been a fiction of the press is difficult to determine; the pinprick in the cinema, the drugged cigarette undoubtedly made for good copy. There is, however, no doubt that the white slave trade existed in Whitechapel as far back as the turn of the century, when the going price for the vendor of the girl being sent or taken to Argentina was the then very substantial sum of between £200 and £300 per girl.[1]

In June 1912 an effort was made to pass the Criminal Law Amendment (White Slave Traffic) Bill. Supporting it, Ettie Sayer wrote in *The Times*: 'No day passes without several of our girls being duped and trapped and sold into American or continental brothels where life lasts at the most five or seven years, terminating in

[1] B. Leeson, *Lost London*, p. 154.

lingering deaths of the most harrowing nature.'[2] A New York police chief, General Bingham, said in an official government report that at a low estimate 15,000 fresh girls, many from England, were imported in 1909. One syndicate alone was making an annual profit of £40,000.

But whilst prostitution down the East End at the time was certainly rife, it could not necessarily be called a lucrative trade. There were two kinds of girl. Those who went up West and mixed with the toffs would get as much as ten shillings a time or even £1, and they would ride home in hansom cabs. 'The girls who stayed at Spitalfields were very poor. That was what you called a "fourpenny touch" or a "knee trembler" – they wouldn't stay with you all night.'[3]

In the 1920s the white slave trade continued. Advertisements such as: 'Wanted. A few young ladies between the ages of twenty and twenty-five to make up a famous dance act, to travel the Continent and other countries. Apply . . .' The girls who answered were often from the country, with little to recommend them other than a pleasant face. Within a week of their arrival their contract would be torn up by the manager of the club to which they had been sent and, since they had never heard of the British Consul and had no one to whom to turn, they ended up in one of the local brothels.

There has long been a Chinese influence in Soho. Shortly after the First World War a five-foot Chinese, Brilliant Chang, trafficked in women and drugs, and he was almost certainly the supplier of the drugs which led to two well-publicized deaths. After the Victory Ball held at the Albert Hall, Billie Carleton, a pretty young actress, collapsed and died. The inquest showed she had died of cocaine poisoning and was addicted to opium

[2] *The Times*, 11 June 1912.

[3] R. Samuel, *East End Underworld*.

smoking. It was common knowledge Chang had been a close friend but although her companion of the night before, Reggie de Veuille, was charged with manslaughter, nothing was ever proved against Chang.[4] Then in March 1922 Freda Kempton, a dancing instructress, was also found dead from an overdose of cocaine. This time Brilliant Chang did feature. He had been with Freda the night before and faced a hostile series of questions at her inquest. 'She was a friend of mine, but I know nothing about the cocaine,' he told the coroner. 'It is all a mystery to me.'

Chang, gap-toothed with dark hair swept back, was apparently the son of a well-to-do Chinese businessman, and was sent to England to pursue a commercial career. Instead he opened a restaurant in Regent Street and started drug trafficking on the side from his private suite. If he saw a woman he fancied – and he was seemingly irresistible to many – he would send a note with a waiter:

Dear Unknown
Please don't regard this as a liberty that I write to you. I am really unable to resist the temptation after having seen you so many times. I should extremely like to know you better and should be glad if you would do me the honour of meeting me one evening when we could have a little dinner or supper together. I do hope you will consent to this as it will give me great pleasure indeed, and in any case do not be cross with me for having written to you. Yours hopefully, Chang.[5]

[4] In one account the death of Billie Carleton is laid at the door of Eddie Manning (see below); V. Davis, *Phenomena of Crime*.
[5] Quoted in A. Tietjen, *Soho*, p. 25.

From there it was, in many cases, a short step to drugs and degradation.

He operated more or less unchallenged until 1924 when two carriers were arrested. Letters in their possession linked them to Chang. Despite police surveillance nothing was established against him, although, in the flurry of unwelcome publicity after Freda Kempton's death, he withdrew his operations to Limehouse. In 1924 the police raided his premises. They found not only a mandarin's palace in the grimy building but, more importantly, they found, in a secret cupboard, a large quantity of cocaine. He was deported after serving a fourteen-month sentence. During his six-year-reign it is estimated he made over a million pounds from drug trafficking.

When he was driven out of Soho his empire there was taken over by another dope pedlar and white slaver, the balding and hollow-eyed Jamaican-born Eddie Manning. Originally a jazz drummer, Manning ran prostitutes and sold drugs from his flat in Lisle Street and the Berwick Street cellar cafe, known as the Black Man's Cafe, which he owned with his Greek woman friend. Cocaine injections were 10 shillings each and he ran illegal and crooked roulette parties. In 1920 he had served a sentence of sixteen months for shooting a man in a fracas at Cambridge Circus. He received three years' penal servitude for possession of opium in 1922 but continued to flourish until he received his final sentence in 1929. By then he too had been chased out of the drug dealing world and was into receiving.

He was also known to be a police informer and, in turn, the underworld tipped off the police. Manning was found with stolen goods worth some £2000 in his flat. He received another three years' penal servitude and died in Parkhurst, apparently from the ravages of syphilis.[6]

[6] For footnote, see opposite.

A third large operator in the drug market was Sess Miyakawa, a Japanese who ran an international ring in 1923–4. He was sentenced to penal servitude of four years after the capture by the Marseilles police of a shipment of drugs worth £250,000.

Apart from Chang, Manning and Miyakawa, who were to a certain extent independent operators, the leader of the Soho prostitution market in the 1920s was Juan Antonio Castanar. Lithe, dark and handsome, he was an accomplished tango dancer who had at one time had a fifty-pound-a-week contract with the great Pavlova. He opened a school for dance in Archer Street, using it as a front for 'white-birding' – selling women to dance troupes abroad at £50 a time. The reverse side of his talent was to arrange marriages of convenience for foreign women wishing to acquire an English passport.

His great rival was Casimir Micheletti, an Algerian, known as the Assassin because of his ability with a stiletto. Micheletti, who gave his occupation as a furrier, is described as an extremely good-looking young man with dark hair, mild of manner and soft-voiced, who could fight with the savagery of a tiger.[7] Both he and Castanar ran strings of prostitutes; each loathed the other and when Castanar was slashed across the face at the 43 Club in Old Compton Street it was common knowledge that Micheletti was the attacker, although no charges were ever brought. He was also strongly suspected of the murder of another French gangster,

---

[6] According to Val Davis, Manning had a terrible superstition about owls. When he was dying in E2 ward in Parkhurst Prison on the Isle of Wight, he heard an owl hooting and his 'body shook and his eyes rolled in abject terror'.

[7] *Detective-Inspector Henry's Famous Cases* (1942), London, Hutchinson, pp. 91–2.

Martial le Chevalier, who was found stabbed in Air Street.

Micheletti was the more or less innocent witness at another murder trial. On 5 April 1926 yet another Frenchman, Emile Berthier, shot and killed an Italian motor car dealer, Charles Ballada, in the Union Club in Frith Street, Soho. The club had a wooden bar along one side, tables and chairs, a couple of fruit machines and some crude murals on the walls. When the police arrived they found Ballada sprawled in the red chimney corner, shot in the stomach.

According to the evidence of a Juan Gabaron, known as L'Espagnol, Berthier believed Ballada owed him money. He went up to him and said: 'My friends, I respect them, but those who owe me money including my partners will have to pay me otherwise I am going to settle with them. I shall do them an injury.'

Ballada replied, 'You must not talk like that. You must do things not talk about them.'

Berthier then shot him dead with an automatic pistol. A member of the club hit Berthier over the head with a billiard cue but Berthier escaped, stopping only to have his wounds cleaned before catching the train to Newhaven, from where the Dieppe packet sailed. It was there he was arrested.

Berthier had earlier written a letter which was produced at the trial:

> I know the [sic] Micheletti wants to kill me because I do not give him any more money. You must admit I have given him enough. See, actually that makes £1500 all the money I owe and he is asking for more. Whilst he is away for a month I warn you that if he continues to ask me for money I shall do my best to kill him. He has killed two or three others and this man is an assassin.

That was the story according to the evidence but another version is that Micheletti had swindled Berthier of £2000 and Ballada, who closely resembled the 'assassin', was shot by mistake. On the other hand, Robert Fabian, destined to become the great Fabian of the Yard and who, despite the account in his memoirs,[8] played a junior role in the case, believed a feud between Ballada and Berthier had originated in Paris. At the Old Bailey Micheletti gave evidence to the effect that he was terrified of Berthier. Ballada was, he said, his friend.

The pre-trial medical report on Berthier from a Dr W. R. K. Watson at Brixton Prison included a statement: 'He professes to have no memory of the actual case. This, if true, may be the result of the blows to the head which he is said to have sustained after the event.' Berthier, whose father had committed suicide by throwing himself off a building at the Lyons exhibition in 1904, was found guilty but insane. Later he was repatriated to France.

In April 1929 both Micheletti and Castanar were deported from England but within a few weeks Castanar managed to smuggle himself back for a short period before he was once more thrown out, this time permanently. He made his way to Paris and earned a modest living as a tango dancer and by running a small stable of girls. In February 1930 he and Micheletti met in a cafe in Paris and later that night Castanar shot his rival dead. At his trial he blamed the killing on a mysterious man known to both of them as Le Marseillais. It was he who had shot Micheletti, put the gun in Castanar's hand and run away. Castanar was not believed and was sent to Devil's Island.

Six years later, on 24 January 1936, the bullet-riddled body of Emil Allard, known as Max Kessel or Red Max, was found under a hedge near St Albans in Hertford-

8 R. Fabian, *Fabian of the Yard*.

shire. A friend of Micheletti, this scar-faced – due to a fight in Montparnasse in 1922 – well-built man had been shot five times. All means of identification had been removed.

A Latvian by birth, Allard had lived in James Street off Oxford Street and had the occupation of 'diamond merchant', a cover beloved of the procurer. In and out of London since 1913, he was a prime mover in the pre-First World War white slave traffic, selling girls to Latin American brothels. They may have travelled to Buenos Aires in style but that was the last luxury the girls would have seen in their lives. As the police investigated deeper into Allard's background they traced back his connection to the murders of a number of Soho prostitutes, including Josephine Martin, known as French Fifi, strangled with her own silk stockings in her Archer Street flat. She had been a police informer as well as one of Allard's aides looking after the foreign prostitutes smuggled into this country.

Allard's murder was investigated by Chief Inspector 'Nutty' Sharpe, who found the flat at 36 Little Newport Street where he had been killed. The occupier had been George Edward Lacroix, alias Marcel Vernon. He had lived with Suzanne Bertrand, who had gone through a form of marriage to an Englishman called Naylor. Now she was working the Soho streets. By the time Sharpe caught up with them they had fled to France from where the authorities refused to extradite them, although they agreed to put them on trial there for Allard's murder.

The murder was thought to have been because Suzanne Bertrand was working for both Vernon and Allard, and they had quarrelled over her earnings. Marcelle Aubin, Suzanne's maid, gave evidence at an inquest held in London that Allard had called on her mistress and she had shown him in to Vernon. Later she heard the sound of an argument followed by several

shots. Called by Vernon, she and Suzanne rushed in and
found Allard shot in the stomach and back. As he was
dying he broke two panes of glass in the window with his
forearm in an effort to attract attention. It was one of
the matching pieces of glass on the pavement that had
led Sharpe to No 36. Marcelle Aubin had been told to
order a car from a garage in Soho Square owned by
another Frenchman, Pierre Alexandre, and the body of
Allard had been bundled in the back to be dumped near
St Albans.

At the trial at the Seine Assizes in April 1937 the
garage proprietor gave evidence against Vernon, who
was sentenced to ten years' penal servitude and twenty
years' banishment. Suzanne Bertrand was acquitted
after she had laid bare the details of Vernon's partnership with Allard as well as Alexandre's agency for
marrying off foreign women to threadbare Englishmen.
Allard and Vernon, who had first met in Montreal, had
worked the white slave trade together for years and the
breakdown of their relationship does seem to have been
over Suzanne Bertrand, for whom Vernon had left his
wife in Paris in 1933.

Bertrand was also able to throw some light on the
mysterious Le Marseillais who had featured in Castanar's trial six years earlier. At Vernon's trial, another
French gangster, George Hainnaux, known as 'Jo le
Terroir', went into the witness box to say that Red Max
Allard had confessed to him that he had killed Le
Marseillais, really a Belgian called Bouchier, in Canada
in 1930, shortly after the Paris cafe shooting. Kessel,
Micheletti, Bouchier and Martial le Chevalier, he said,
had all been killed in a long-drawn-out battle for control
of prostitution and the white slave trade.

This was the end of the French domination of Soho
prostitution and there is no evidence that the Sabinis
were interested in vice to any great extent. 'I can think

of only two girls who went bad in the whole time I lived in Saffron Hill,' says a resident. 'Darby Sabini protected women, he didn't use them.'

However, from the mid-1930s the Sabinis certainly allowed the Messina brothers – Carmelo, Alfredo, Salvatore, Attilio and Eugenio, into the scene. The Messinas' father, Giuseppe, came from Linguaglossa in Sicily and in the late 1890s went to Malta, where he became an assistant in a brothel in Valetta. There he married a Maltese girl, Virginia de Bono. Their first two sons, Salvatore and Alfredo, were born in Valetta. The family then moved in 1905 to Alexandria and Giuseppe built a chain of brothels in Suez, Cairo and Port Said. The remaining sons were all born in Alexandria and their father ensured they were all well educated. In 1932 Giuseppe Messina was expelled from Egypt and two years later Eugenio, the third son, born in 1908, came to England. He was able to claim British nationality because his father had sensibly claimed Maltese citizenship.

With Eugenio was his wife Colette, a French prostitute, and it was on her back that Eugenio founded his London empire. More girls were recruited from the continent and as the empire grew he was joined on the management side by his brothers. Property was bought throughout the West End and the brothers turned their attention to English girls. The technique used was age-old – good looking girls were given a good time; seduction, possibly with the promise of marriage, followed and then it became time to pay. If the good life was to continue the price for it was prostitution. By 1945 the family's business earnings were estimated at £1000 a week.

The girls were under the day-to-day charge of the French-born Marthe Watts, who had conveniently married Arthur Watts, an alcoholic Englishman, to obtain British citizenship. Born in 1913, according to her story she had been placed in a brothel in Le Havre at the age of fifteen after lying about her age.[9] She had been there only a few days before her age was discovered and had been returned to Paris, where she found her mother had remarried. Within hours she had re-met the *placeur*, the tattooed Francois, who had been responsible for sending her to the house in Le Havre, meeting him in a cafe in the Marais, a then louche *quartier* of Paris. Because of her age it was too risky to send her back to Le Havre, he thought. This time she was put on the night train to Barcelona. There followed a career in the brothels of Europe ending with her marriage to Watts.

In April 1941 she met Eugenio Messina in the Palm Beach Club, Wardour Street, and a month later became his mistress. Within weeks she was out working the streets for him. Her loyalty seems to have been remarkable. Despite regular and savage beatings – the favourite method seems to have been with an electric light flex – she stayed with the family, taking charge of the new girls. As a mark of her devotion she had herself tattooed over the left breast: '*L'homme de ma vie. Gino le maltais*'.

Life with Eugenio Messina was no fun for any of his girls. They were not allowed out on their own, they could not accept American servicemen as clients, they were not allowed to smoke, nor, curiously, were they allowed to wear low-cut dresses or even look at film magazines where the male stars were in any sort of undress. They did not take off their clothes with the customers. Worst of all was the ten-minute rule. Clients were only allowed to stay that time before the maid knocked on the door. It seems to have resembled the

[9] M. Watts, *The Men in My Life*.

Paris and Miami slaughterhouses where girls never leave the bed and a bell rings after fifteen minutes. The other Messina brothers seem to have been more relaxed in their attitudes, particularly over the ten-minute rule.

During the war the Messina brothers had evaded military service simply by failing to report. Warrants had been issued but they were never served and the Messinas maintained a low profile as far as the authorities were concerned. Gino Messina, who had worked with his father as a carpenter, built himself a hiding place in the form of a bookcase with a removable bottom shelf in his Lowndes Square flat. Unknown visitors had to be cleared through a series of front men and women before they were allowed in to see him.

By 1946, with the family's weekly earnings at £1000, the girls were earning £100 a night and were being paid £50 a week. Even if takings dropped after the war the business was still a worthwhile target for other ponces. In March 1947 Carmela Vassallo and four other Maltese endeavoured to muscle in on the enterprise, demanding protection money of £1 a girl a day. Retribution in all forms was swift. At a meeting in Winchester Court, South Kensington, Eugenio Messina took off two of Vassallo's fingertips. But it was not sufficient for the girls. Marthe Watts and two others, now thoroughly frightened by the Maltese and what would happen if they gave in to their demands, went to the police.

Carmela Vassallo and the four others stood in the Old Bailey in April 1947 charged with demanding money with menaces. All the witnesses staunchly denied they were 'Messina girls'. For example, Janine Gilson of Cork Street, Mayfair, admitted knowing the Messinas for three years but denied she had ever spoken to them.

'I know them as diamond merchants and I know them as very wealthy people.'

'Do you know the source of their wealth is the money they take from girls on the streets?'

'No.'

'Do any of these Messina men look after you in your profession?'

'No. I don't have anybody to look after me. If I want protection I go to the police.'

This sort of evidence could not possibly be swallowed by any jury. But there was a back-up. The police had been on watch in Burlington Gardens, off Piccadilly, when the five Maltese drew up and one shouted out to the girls, 'It's better for you to give us the money, otherwise I will cut your face!' In the car the police found a hammer wrapped in newspaper, a knife and a life-preserver. At the men's flat there was a knuckleduster and an automatic pistol with six rounds of ammunition.

Convicted of demanding money with menaces, Vassallo and two others received four years' penal servitude.

The thwarted takeover did however spell the very beginning of the end of the Messinas' reign. Eugenio Messina, who had had no takers for his offer of the enormous sum of £25,000 to anyone who could smuggle him out of the country, received three years for wounding Vassallo. The Messina brothers were now known figures and questions were asked in Parliament: in view of what had emerged at the trials where Marthe and the other girls had loyally lied, denying their involvement with the brothers, would the Home Secretary appoint a commission to enquire into organized vice in London? No, replied Mr Chuter Ede:

It is a criminal offence knowingly to live on the earnings of a prostitute and the police exercise all possible vigilance with a view to the suppression of activities of this kind.

Any enquiry would not help the police because their difficulties arise from the fact that, although they may have good reason to suspect such activities, they are sometimes unable to obtain evidence upon which criminal proceedings could be based.

Then as now.

John Foster, MP for Norwich, who was putting the questions, was not satisfied. What about an examination of the Messinas' bank accounts? Was Mr Ede aware they were popularly supposed to be making half a million a year, that they had no fewer than twenty girls working for them and that they owned a West End estate agency? But Mr Ede was having none of it and the remaining brothers continued to flourish.

All, that is, except Carmelo – Marthe's favourite. Conscious of the privations his brother was suffering he tried to bribe a prison officer at Wandsworth Prison, for which he received two months plus a £50 fine and, on his and Eugenio's release, £700 from the takings. The girls had conscientiously been putting their money in the safe for him – watched, it has to be said, by two of the brothers. On Eugenio's release he bought himself a Rolls-Royce. But, for the purposes of the courts, the Messinas went underground. There was no question now of having knife fights with the Maltese opposition. According to Marthe Watts, complainants were simply framed.

I am sure, from some of the remarks passed by some magistrates, that they did not believe there was such a thing as the Messina Gang. They certainly did not when Sally Wright was charged with assaulting Rabina Dickson Torrance with a knife. Sally Wright pleaded that Torrance was a

Messina woman, that the whole charge had been framed by the Messina Gang, and that she was innocent.

She was by no means the first person who had not been believed after pleading that she had been victimized by the Messina Gang. It seems that when anyone upset the Messinas all they had to do was enlist the aid of the Courts, apparently with police assistance, and that someone was conveniently imprisoned, and incidentally discredited for life.[10]

It took three more years before the Messinas were exposed for what they were, and it was the work of Duncan Webb, who had caused so much trouble for Spot.[11] On 3 September 1950 the *People* published the exposure, backing it with photographs of the Messina girls and the flats from where they operated. Eugenio and Carmelo loaded up the yellow Rolls Royce and left for France via Dover. Though they returned using false passports they were never again seen openly in this country.

The next to go was Salvatore. Attilio and Alfredo remained. Attilio lived in Surrey with one of the girls, the same Rabina Torrance who had brought false charges of assault against Sally Wright when the girl had tried to leave the family. His work in clearing things up completed, he too headed for France, leaving behind only Alfredo, living with Hermione Hindin who worked

---

[10] M. Watts, *The Men in My Life*, p. 207.

[11] Webb was a curious man. A devout Roman Catholic, he believed his mission was to clean the streets of London. After one triumph over the Messinas he put an advertisement in *The Times* offering thanks to St Jude. After the murderer Donald Hume, killer of Stanley Setty, had been convicted Webb married his wife Cynthia.

in Pollen Street, W1, as Barbara.

On 19 March 1951 Alfredo was arrested at his Wembley home, charged with living on immoral earnings and trying to bribe a police officer. He had offered Superintendent Mahon, one of the arresting officers, £200. At his trial at the Old Bailey he naturally gave his employment as that of diamond merchant. No, he did not know Hermione was in fact Barbara. No, he did not know she had over a hundred convictions for soliciting. When she went out in the evening he thought it was to see a relative. It was a great shock to him to learn she was a common prostitute. He had brought his personal fortune, some £30,000, to Britain at the beginning of the war and had dealt in diamonds. He had both diabetes and high blood pressure, which was why he did not really work. What on earth was this vice ring organized by his brothers?

Scott Henderson, who appeared for him and who later conducted the Rillington Place enquiry,[12] did his best for him but Alfredo received two years' imprisonment concurrent on each of the charges and a £500 fine. In fact Barbara worked in the next-door flat to Alfredo's real wife, a Spanish woman, who passed under the name Marcelle.

For the moment it seemed the hold of the Messina brothers – one in prison and four abroad – had been broken. It was not the case. The ever faithful Marthe Watts took over control of the ever younger girls whom Eugenio was sending over from the continent, often after picking them up at tea-dances. Each girl kept her own accounts and it seems that, such was the mixture of loyalty and fear, they never tried to skim for themselves.

---

[12] This was the enquiry into whether Reginald Halliday Christie had in fact killed Beryl Evans, for which her mentally retarded husband Timothy had been hanged.

Every thousand pounds earned meant a trip to see Eugenio in Paris. The money, however, went over by courier.

But now Attilio was making trips to England. Alfredo's solicitors at his trial had been Webb, Justice & Co, and Superintendent Mahon began to follow the firm's clerk, Watson, as he made trips to Europe. In October 1951 Watson went to his home in Chalfont St Giles for a short time, then left and got into another car which drove off towards Amersham. The car was stopped by Mahon and inside, with Watson, was Attilio. He was charged with living off the immoral earnings of Rabina Torrance. At Bow Street court the next morning he was represented by a young solicitor who would become lengendary in the annals of white-collar crime, a man who spun an evil web throughout commercial London in the 1960s and 1970s. His name was Judah Binstock. Attilio received six months' imprisonment, the maximum sentence.

Certainly this should now have been the end for the brothers but it was not to be so. Eugenio, Carmelo and Alfredo controlled matters from Paris until November 1953, when Eugenio was kidnapped and released only on payment of £2000. In some disarray the brothers moved their headquarters to Lausanne. In the meantime Attilio had completed his short stretch and had set up light housekeeping again with Rabina Torrance under the name Raymond Maynard, in Bourne End. Rabina Torrance leased two flats in London in her own name, with payments for rent and rates being made through the Messinas' agents. Attilio, as Maynard, had another flat in Shepherd's Market and the family had interests in a second flat there. Deportation papers were served on him in 1953 but the Italian authorities declined to have him and, once the *People* had traced him to the Hideaway, his appropriately named cottage in Bourne

End, he moved to South London, reporting daily to the police as an Italian national.

But Eugenio had surfaced again, buying 39 Curzon Street in Mayfair from a Mrs Augustine Johans, who continued to manage it as a brothel. In September she was fined £25 but in the raid the police found £14,000 in a safe there. As a result the premises were taken over by Hermione Hindin and Mrs Johans moved elsewhere. Home, however, is where the heart is and Eugenio yearned for England. He obtained another British passport as Alexander Miller, a merchant, and another as Eugene de Bono. For the purposes of travelling here Carmelo became a Cuban citizen, Carlos Marino.

By now, however, girls from respectable Belgian homes were disappearing to England and the Belgian police were actively pursuing their enquiries. Marthe Watts, who had suffered a collapsed lung, was tiring of seeing an ever increasing harem amassed by Eugenio. She travelled to see him in the Residence Albert in Knokke, where he was staying under an assumed name, and severed her connection as quartermaster sergeant of the operation. She was allowed to work independently from a Messina-owned flat in Chesterfield Street.

On 31 August 1955 Carmelo and Eugenio were arrested in the Horse's Neck at Knokke-le-Zoute and charged with being in possession of firearms, false passports and procuring women for prostitution. It was only then that the extent of their current British empire became apparent. Title deeds to four central London properties were found in a safe-box along with long reports from Marthe Watts and Mrs Johans. One of the reports by Marthe Watts showed that one girl, a former nurse working as Therese, had earned £2400 in six weeks. Eugenio had gone through his prospective fiance routine before marrying her off to a stray Englishman recruited for the purpose. Eugenio received seven years' imprisonment. Carmelo was deemed to have served his sentence; he had been in custody on remand for ten months and was released. He disappeared, but not for long.

At the end of 1956 the appeals were heard in the Belgium case. Carmelo had his sentence doubled *in absentia* whilst Eugenio had seven months knocked off. But where was Carmelo?

In October 1958 he was found sitting in a car in Knightsbridge and was arrested as an illegal immigrant. He received a six month sentence and was deported at the end. He died in the autumn in Sicily. But now where was Attilio?

He was working hard, or rather Edna Kallman, initially seduced by promises of marriage and the good life, was. She had been under his control for ten years, put out to work under the tutelage of Rabina. Attilio knocked her about continually until in sheer terror of a further beating she managed to bring herself to return to her parents' home in Derby. They called the police. He was convicted on 9 April 1959 and sentenced to four years' imprisonment. Edna Kallman had earned between £50 and £150 a week over those ten years and had been allowed to keep £7 a week for herself.

'You made a sumptuous but revolting living from the suffering bodies of the women you trapped, seduced and reduced to a form of slavery,' said the Recorder of London, Sir Gerald Dodson. 'You caused great suffering and it is only right and just that you should also suffer.'

Attilio and Eugenio were eventually accepted by the Italian government. Salvatore lived in Switzerland whilst Alfredo, who could claim British citizenship, died in Brentford in 1963.

The year 1959 should have marked the end of the Messinas as an active force but by the late 1960s Eugenio and Carmelo were still paying the rent and rates of premises in Mayfair.

By the middle of the 1960s Soho had an even uglier face than it has today. Dirty bookshops were everywhere and near-beer joints, clip joints and cinemas showing pornographic films attracted the oddest types, plus tourists wanting to see the naughty bits of London. In turn they became the victims of the unscrupulous operators of these establishments, who picked them clean.

Prostitution, clubs and near-beer joints were controlled by the Maltese, who had taken over the territory after the breaking up of the Messina operation and the retirement of Billy Hill and Jack Spot, and had run it with the initial tolerance of Albert Dimes and Bert Marsh. Over the years there had been a constant struggle to determine power and control, and as a result there were spontaneous bursts of violence as one or other faction tried to establish and redefine territories.

At the time the smoothest operator of them all was not Maltese at all but Jewish. Bernie Silver had seen the disasters which happened when rival operators fell out and had the sense to realize that a rapprochement was necessary between at least some of the operators. He therefore formed a liaison with a Maltese, 'Big Frank' Mifsud, a former traffic policeman and a giant of a man who was considered ruthless by lesser lights. A call to visit 'Big Frank' could strike terror into the heart of the recipient of the invitation, who, like as not, could expect a beating handed out not by the man himself but by an underling.

Together Silver and Mifsud effectively ruled vice in the West End for nearly two decades. Initially they ran prostitutes, brothels and gaming clubs in Brick Lane, in the East End, once the preserve of people such as Tony Smithson and Tony Mella, but Silver and Mifsud had a toe-hold in Soho through a strip club in Brewer Street. From there they began to buy up properties using a string of nominees.

The arrangement had been worked out so there would be no rivalry and inter-club warfare between them. Say A and B owned the Star Club, B and C owned the Spangled Club, C and D the Banner Club and D and A the America Club. If, therefore, premises owned by Silver or Mifsud were attacked the other operators would suffer by it, which removed the incentive for causing trouble in another club. The operation was policed by Silver and Mifsud's henchmen, including Anthony Mangion, Emmanuel Coleiro, Emmanuel Bartolo and Tony and Victor Micallef. They ran what came to be known as the Syndicate, owning nineteen out of the twenty-four Soho strip clubs then operating. It worked after its fashion but there was always an undercurrent of feeling and a belief that violence was never far away.

Near-beer joints, again run by the Maltese under the overall supervision of Mifsud and Silver, and of which there was one or more in every street, yard and alley in Soho, worked very simply. Young, attractive and scantily dressed girls stood outside the premises, which were often on the first floor or in the basement of buildings. Subtly, and sometimes not so subtly, they would lure customers inside with the veiled promise of sexual intercourse. Once inside the men were like moths round a flame, unable to resist the flattery and spiel of these 'come-on' girls. They would pay exorbitant prices for non-alcoholic drinks such as lemonade shandy and blackcurrant juice. Each drink came with a cocktail stick and the girl was paid by the number of these sticks she collected during her stint. Their function was only to rip-off the customer for as much as he would pay without complaining. There was certainly no requirement by the management that the girls had to have sex with the clients, although many did as a side operation. If so, they took the man to a local address or hotel.

Two years earlier the Refreshment Houses Act 1964, which required clubs serving any form of refreshment, including soft drinks and sandwiches, to have a licence, had given the police the right of entry into premises. And enter they did, causing a certain amount of trouble to the 'clubs'. Clubs were closed down on a regular basis by magistrates sitting at Marlborough Street and Bow Street, with the result that many proprietors did not bother to renew their licences. The premises reverted to being clip joints where a version of the 'corner game' was played out.

In this there was no pretence that drinks would be supplied or that the girl was a hostess. Money was obtained on the implicit understanding that sexual intercourse would follow. Most of the girls had no intention of having sex and to avoid the predatory punters a delaying tactic had to be introduced. Mostly the girl would persuade the punter that the address was some form of club and that her employer forbade her to leave before a certain time. She would then ask the man to wait around the corner to meet her as soon as she was free. Often the man would wait two or three hours 'around the corner' before he realized he had been done up like a kipper. Under the clock at Victoria Station was a well-worn favourite; Marble Arch, by Big Ben, Charing Cross, outside the Ritz or the Regent Palace Hotel and Leicester Square were frequently named by the punters who had spent many wasted hours waiting there. The one that Nipper Read, then an Inspector at West End Central, liked best, even though he found it hardest to believe, was Morden, a station at the very end of the Northern Line. He asked the Dutch seaman why he had gone that far to wait for a girl and received the reply, in attractive broken English, that he had paid her £100, adding, 'Well, this is where she tells me she is living.'

These men had of course not been unwilling contributors of their money and even when they reported the matter to the police they were often reluctant to go through with the charges because of fear of exposure to their wives, family, friends or employers. Often they were men from the provinces or sailors who would go home or sail before any proceedings could be processed through the courts. It was better to write off their loss and put it down to experience.

As a result of what they considered amounted to immunity from prosecution the girls became more and more brazen, and so occasionally the clients took reprisals of their own. The most tragic example of this was when, on 25 April 1966, three young men out to celebrate a birthday were tricked at a club in Lisle Street and thrown out by bouncers. They found some rubbish in the street, doused it with petrol and threw it into the passageway of the clip joint at No 23. Far from its being the minor annoyance the boys anticipated, the rubbish set fire to other material and soon the whole premises were ablaze. A perfectly innocent man had decided to try to find a lavatory on the premises and, unable to get out in time, burned to death.

All the police had to go on was the first name of one of the boys who had been celebrating his twenty-first birthday. It was announced that there would be a check on the whereabouts of everyone born that day twenty-one years earlier. It would not have been as impossible as it seemed but it certainly would have been boring police work. But, when it came to it, there was no need. A photograph was published of officers starting to make the list at Somerset House and the boys, thoroughly shocked by what had happened, went into Tottenham police station with a solicitor to confess to what they had done. They were later convicted of manslaughter and received sentences of three and four years' imprisonment.

There were of course many other incidents when punters, frustrated by waiting at one or other of the rendezvous, returned to the club and demanded their money back. The normal course of events was that they would then meet one of the club's bouncers and would sustain a black eye or broken jaw for their pains. Once again the fear of disclosure of the illicit sex behind the assault hampered many a prosecution.

Another common scam at the time was the 'blue film' racket. This was another popular version of the 'corner game'. The scenario was usually that of a smooth-talking spiv standing outside an open doorway and inviting tourists to see a blue film. As a come-on he might have postcards showing explicit sex scenes 'from the film'. After taking the punters' money he would direct them up to the second floor and then simply move on to another suitable doorway. There were variations. Sometimes the spiv would actually go to the second floor with the punters and ask them to wait whilst he went into the projection room to check the film. Off he would go down the back stairs. If their luck was in they saw a film made in Scandinavia showing a woman undressing or nudists playing volleyball in long shot.

With the World Cup coming up in July 1966, Read was afraid that both thefts from visitors and more examples of violence would occur over the summer months. Tens of thousands were coming to London and many who would drift into Soho during the evenings would become the victims of the villains who were waiting to fleece them.

There was not only the problem of the clubs and our own thieves but also the con men who would come from Australia, the fraudsmen and tricksters from Mexico and Venezuela, the pickpockets from Italy, second-storey hotel thieves from the States, drug pushers from Holland

and the heavies, the GBH merchants, from Germany. All these and others travel the world and congregate for any international sporting occasion or world or trade fair of sufficient size which runs for long enough. The World Cup was certainly both of those and the thought of the havoc these kinds of villain could create coupled with Soho's local talent was depressing.

So Read formed a twelve-strong squad of officers from 'C' division (West End Central) with the very positive mission first to harass and shut down the clubs, and then maintain a blanket policing operation on the West End. This, he believed, would keep down the foreign villains to a minimum.

The first job was to visit the clubs and take down the names of the girls present. They were also given the 'warning formula'. In other words, they were told in no uncertain terms that their freedom to fleece the suckers was over. It was also explained to the proprietors, or their front men, that they were committing offences of theft or of obtaining money by false pretences and they had better change their lifestyle. It was all to no avail. The pickings were far too easy and the clubs continued to flourish – for a time.

Soon the girls found that the 'punters' were in fact plain clothes officers. In June seven girls were arrested for obtaining money by false pretences or straightforward theft. In the week leading up to the World Cup a further twenty-one arrests were made by the squad, mainly for theft. From time to time Read would lead part of the squad to raid the premises and all present were logged and cautioned. By the start of the Cup only four of the clip joints remained open.

The West End was now divided into nine crime patrols with three sergeants and two detectives, borrowed from other divisions, posted to each. All had personal radios and Read patrolled the division in a radio-equipped car.

It was later acknowledged to be a good example of how effective saturation policing could be. By the end of the operation on 31 July only one clip joint was still in business and that only on a haphazard basis. During the period reported crimes dropped by nearly a half whilst clip joint complaints had gone down from 205 in the first week to 12 in the last.

The bosses, of the police, if not the clubs, were well pleased. Read's report went to the Home Office and commendations were given. It was announced that the squad should be kept on, although, as with everything, gradually it was allowed to run down because of lack of resources. Even so, the crime rate in the West End was stable for some months to come – until nearly the end of the year.

If Silver and Mifsud thought they had a tight hold on Soho and were immune from outside attack, except by the police, they had a shock when Tony Cauci, a one-time friend of Mifsud, fell out with him over the ownership of the Carnival strip club. At the end of 1966 and in the early part of 1967 there was a series of petrol bomb explosions at the Gigi in Frith Street, the Keyhole Club in Old Compton Street and a gaming club in Greek Street, all of which belonged to the Silver–Mifsud connection in which neither Tony Cauci nor his employee, another Maltese, Derek Galea, had a share.

Cauci and Galea's subsequent trial on a charge of conspiracy to cause explosions took place at a time when links between criminals in Soho and the police in the West End were rife and there was considerable concern amongst some officers that the explosives had been planted. Certainly a witness, Harold Stocker, who said that he had seen Galea running from the gaming club shortly after the fire, had given perjured evidence and, on the advice of Mifsud, Galea had turned against his employer. After a retrial at the Old Bailey and an ugly scene when the police had to be called to deal with two dozen Maltese who had suddenly arrived in the lobby to hear the jury's verdict, they were convicted and sentenced to lengthy terms of imprisonment. Once more a fragile peace was restored.

If living off immoral earnings has never been a wholly British sport there is no doubt that some have joined with enthusiasm into its kin folk, strip-tease and pornography. And none more so than James William Humphreys. Born in Southwark in January 1930, he was one of the porn kings of England throughout the 1960s and early 1970s. He was also a major figure in the downfall of many members of the Vice Squad of the time.

There was nothing particularly remarkable about his early career – a burglary here, an approved school there – until, in March 1958, he received six years' imprisonment at Glamorgan Assizes for stealing £8000-worth of postal orders. Freed in the autumn of 1962 he took the lease of a property in Old Compton Street and started a club, a home from home for the criminal and the quasi-criminal, including one of the boxers from the days of the Pen Club murder. He also met up once more with an old girlfriend, June Gaynor, known as 'Rusty', once a barmaid and now a stripper. In the meantime she had had an affair with a Soho frequenter, Peter 'Pookey' Garfath; now she came to work for Humphreys in Old Compton Street. Six months later they married.

On the advice of Detective Sergeant Harold Challenor, then said to be operating his one-man independent protection racket in Soho, Humphreys moved his club to Macclesfield Street. Humphreys had been paying protection money to Challenor as well as providing him with tidbits of information of Soho life. Once in Macclesfield Street Challenor asked for more money and Humphreys paid over two lots of £25. He also made an official complaint, which came to nothing more than a polite rejection from the Commissioner. Challenor was cleared after a brief investigation. It was, after all, the sort of thing an officer would have to put up with.

In fact Challenor had done him a good turn. The Macclesfield Street club prospered and Rusty Humphreys was a good businesswoman. She heard of premises in Walker Court off Brewer Street and suggested Humphreys open another club. It was an immediate and enormous success. For a start it was in the heart of Soho. Secondly, it had the great advantage of being opposite the biggest and smartest strip club in London, Raymond's Revue Bar. Within a year, with his wife at first performing in the three shows the club ran daily, he had become relatively rich. A neighbour in the same small courtway was Bernie Silver, who, with a front man, Joey Janes, as manager, ran a bookshop.

Silver's operations can be traced back to the early 1950s when he ran clubs and brothels in the Brick Lane area of the East End. In 1956 he was arrested and charged with living off immoral earnings. Along with a man called Cooper and acting as an estate agent, he had been carrying on an extension of the Messina trade by letting out rooms and flats to prostitutes at exorbitant rents. Silver appeared at the Old Bailey in 1956 along with a prostitute called Albertine Falzon[13] and seven others in front of the eccentric Judge Maud, who found there was no case for the defendants to answer.

For three months the police had kept observation, in special vans with peepholes and periscopes, on premises in Romilly Street, watching the girls returning with men to their flats and money changing hands. The rent books provided to the girls showed weekly payments of between £3 and £5 but in fact they were paying £25 or

[13] For footnote, see opposite.

£30 in cash. A surveyor was employed by the police to assess the true rentable value of the flats. Many were what he described as 'orange-box' flats, with no heat, light or water, a truckle bed and two orange boxes for chairs. These, he assessed, were really worth three shillings a week. Much classier were the £2 to £3 flats which were properly furnished with an old-fashioned brass bed, a card table, some linoleum but no chair.

Judge Maud ruled that a landlord or estate agent was in the same position as a shopkeeper, doctor or barrister who received money from a prostitute as a customer or client, and that they were living on these monies as their own earnings, not those of a prostitute. 'It may be that the problem is so grave that Parliament must do something about it – but this is not for me.'

Silver may have had a lucky escape but the lesson was learned both by him and by others. Flat farmers, as they were known, took steps to distance themselves from their prostitute tenants by setting up a network of cut-offs and intermediaries. But rent books still recorded only a fraction of the actual rent and key-money of

---

[13] Albertine Falzon later married Silver. In the 1970s she committed suicide by leaping out of the flat in Peter Street, Soho, from which she worked. Other similar deaths in Soho included Frank Holpert, who in November 1973 fell to his death from his balcony (he had been a go-between for Silver and Humphreys), and prostitute Odette Weston, who in May 1975 fell to her death when her flat was fire-bombed. Perhaps the most interesting is that of vice queen Irene Micallef, who ran a call girl racket for her estranged husband Victor. She allegedly jumped to her death from a roof on 25 July 1979 when she was about to leave Soho for a new life with a new boyfriend. When her body was flown home to Sweden and taken to a local chapel, the coffin was found to contain the body of a sixty-three-year-old man named Medcalfe. Her boyfriend went into hiding, believing there was a contract out on him.

around £100 changed hands when a girl took over a flat.

In 1969, shortly before Christmas, Humphreys and Rusty were guests with senior CID officers, including Commander Wally Virgo, at the Criterion restaurant in Piccadilly. Humphreys took the opportunity to complain that Detective Chief Superintendent Moody, then in charge of the Obscene Publications Squad, would not give him a 'licence' to use his properties in Soho as dirty bookshops. Silver, also present, arranged a meeting with Moody in a Mayfair restaurant at which negotiations were opened. Could a bookshop be opened in Rupert Street? Nothing was finalized. Silver and Moody would meet the next day when the porn king would make a formal offer.

When terms were agreed they were staggering: £14,000 was to be paid for the licence; Silver would become a partner, so satisfying Moody, who did not want to see outsiders creeping in; and a further £2000 a month would be paid to prevent raids and closure. It was never a particularly happy association, in part because Humphreys took the opportunity of Silver's absence abroad to begin an affair with his mistress, Dominique Ferguson, a move which soon became Soho gossip and went straight back to Silver. Reprisals were threatened, including a suggestion that Humphreys be fitted up for a crime. In turn, he contacted Commander Drury, whom Humphreys had met at a party given to celebrate the promotion of a Flying Squad colleague, and the threats came to nothing. The fee for this service, said Humphreys later, was £1050. From the moment Humphreys met Drury he seems to have had the Commander in his pocket, wining and dining him and taking him to boxing tournaments at the World Sporting Club.

The first cracks in the empire began to appear in 1971 when the *Sunday People* named a variety of operators as the pornographers of Soho, including Silver, Mifsud and Humphreys along with two others, Jeff Mason and John

Mason. The *Sunday People* also made allegations that there were corrupt dealings with detectives. A Detective Chief Superintendent was appointed to investigate the allegations but, with one exception, all the operators denied they had paid over any money to the police. The exception was Humphreys, who refused to be interviewed, ostensibly on the advice of his solicitor but in fact on the advice of a police friend.

The first exposé by the *Sunday People* had come to nothing. Now in 1972 the paper produced a second round. On 27 February it announced that Commander Drury and his wife had recently returned from Cyprus where they had been guests of Humphreys. The gaff was blown in a curious way. When something went wrong in London one person at whom the police looked was one of the boxers charged in the Pen case, the old-time friend of the Nashes and drinking companion of Humphreys. When the police were looking for Freddie Sewell, killer of Blackpool Superintendent Gerald Richardson, they turned over the boxer's home. Nothing was found to link him with Sewell but he was charged with possessing a firearm and ammunition, a charge he strenuously denied and of which he was acquitted at the Old Bailey. He then had the hump with the Met in general and told a reporter of Humphreys' holidays in Cyprus with police officers.[14]

For a time Drury tried to bluff his way out. Yes, he

---

[14] In the summing up of his trial for possessing the gun and ammunition, the judge told the jury that to acquit would mean that the police officers had committed perjury. At Lewes Crown Court on 31 June 1975 one of the officers on the search, Harold Hannigan, who had been on the same regional crime squad as George Fenwick, was found guilty of trying to bribe a Sussex detective. He was given a conditional discharge by Mr Justice Melford Stevenson who called him 'a very, very conceited fool', and advised him to see a psychiatrist. (B. Cox *et al.*, *The Fall of Scotland Yard*, p. 191.)

had been to Cyprus. No, he had not been a guest, he had paid his share. No, it had not been a holiday, in reality he was looking for the escaped train robber Ronnie Biggs. At the time and for what it was worth, Humphreys supported him. It wasn't worth much. On 6 March Drury was suspended from duty and served with disciplinary papers. He resigned on 1 May. Then, foolishly, he turned on his former friend. He sold his story to the *News of the World* for £10,000 and as part of his confessions he named Humphreys as a grass, something guaranteed to destroy his reputation amongst the criminal fraternity, if not to get him a good beating to go with it. It is not surprising Humphreys took umbrage and gave his alternative version, saying that far from being a grass or getting money from Drury it had been all the other way around. The money, the wine, the good life had all flowed from the Humphreys cornucopia.

But now the foundations of the porn empire were cracking and Humphreys was investigated over the slashing of 'Pookey' Garfath in the lavatory of the Dauphine Club in Marylebone as punishment for daring to have an affair with Rusty. Three days before the attack she had been released from Holloway, where she had served a four-month sentence for possessing a firearm. Garfath named Humphreys as one of six assailants and a warrant was issued for his arrest. Humphreys, who was in Holland at the time, launched a counter-attack. He was not involved in the assault on Garfath, rather it was a frame-up organized by a Detective Inspector in concert with some criminals from Streatham as a reprisal over the resignation of Drury. Meanwhile Rusty Humphreys were arrested and charged with conspiracy to pervert the course of justice and conspiracy to cause grievous bodily harm to Garfath.[15]

[15] She was later acquitted of both these charges.

Now she went to the Complaints Department of Scotland Yard to complain about senior detectives, backing up her claims with details from her diaries which had been taken from her on her arrest three months earlier.

Gilbert Kelland, later to become an Assistant Commissioner, was appointed to lead the investigation. At first he found Rusty Humphreys' statement difficult to accept. If the diaries were all that revealing why had nothing been done for the past three months? Why had they never been sent to the Deputy Commissioner during that time? 'The explanation I was given for this oversight was the pressure of work on the senior officers of the squad dealing with her case, but I have always found this difficult to accept.'[16]

Kelland and his team began their enquiries in earnest and in mid-October they visited Humphreys in prison in Amsterdam where he was awaiting extradition. At first he was prepared to talk but the next day he refused to see them and he maintained this stance until after his conviction on 25 April 1974, when he was sentenced to eight years for the assault on Garfath. Even when, in May, he did consent to make statements and later give evidence, he proved to be a temperamental witness. Looking for a witness who in police terms would remain staunch, Kelland turned to John Mason.

On 27 February 1976 Drury, Virgo and Moody were arrested along with nine other officers. The pool included two ex-Commanders, an ex-Detective Chief Superintendent, an ex-Detective Chief Inspector and a host of smaller fry. It was in any language a major scandal.

In April 1976 at Knightsbridge Crown Court Mason was fined a total of £25,000 for possessing obscene publications and he now began to make detailed statements

---

[16] G. Kelland, *Crime in London*, p. 127.

to Kelland. His revelations were remarkable. One ex-Detective Superintendent had attended Mason's offices once a week to advise on articles for the magazine and generally sub-edit the contributions. He had been paid £10 a week until, on his death in 1972, the job had been taken over by DCI George Fenwick. At the other end of the scale Mason recalled how his routine monthly contribution to the Porn Squad, which had been £60 in 1953, had risen to £1000 by 1971. His relationship with the squad had been such that he was lent a squad tie to go to the basement at Holborn police station, from where, at a price of between £500 and £1000, he could buy material confiscated from other shops and dealers.

At the first of the three Porn Squad trials Humphreys, like Achilles, was sulking in his tent and refused to take part. Even so Fenwick received ten years' imprisonment and four other former officers received between four and eight years. In the second trial, which began the next March, Virgo and Moody, together with four junior officers, faced an indictment with twenty-seven counts alleging bribery and corruption totalling £87,485. This time, faced with the story that his 'bottle' had gone and that Mason was by far the more important witness, Humphreys emerged. All six defendants were convicted, receiving between four and twelve years' imprisonment. Later the conviction of ex-Commander Virgo was quashed by the Court of Appeal.

The third trial involved Drury and two others, and again Humphreys had to be coaxed into the witness box. Now he was an essential witness. Arrangements were made for him to see a journalist from the *Sunday People* who had assured him that a full enquiry was taking place into his own conviction for the assault on Garfath.

Humphreys' evidence at the third trial led to the acquittal of one officer, DI Legge, who had admitted he had gone to stay in Humphreys' apartment in Ibiza.

Humphreys gave evidence that he was one of the very few officers he knew who had never wanted or accepted a penny from him. The case was stopped against Legge, who later resigned from the force. On 7 July 1977 Drury received eight years' imprisonment; the other officer half that sentence.

Humphreys was released at the end of August of that year by exercise of the royal prerogative of mercy. In 1982 he was circulated as being wanted over the manufacture of amphetamine drugs in Eire.

Meanwhile Silver had been pursuing something of a parallel, if more violent, course. As far as he and Mifsud were concerned it blew apart in 1973 when Silver was arrested for living off the immoral earnings of prostitutes; Mifsud went on the run. The girls, run by the Syndicate, had been organized on a factory-line basis. One girl would run the flat from 1 until 7 p.m., when the next shift took over until the early hours of the morning. Each girl would contribute £180 a week to the Syndicate. Silver had been responsible for the recruitment and placing of the girls and their clocking on and off their shifts on time. Strip clubs provided up to six shows a day, with the girls travelling from one to the next on a circuit and making six performances a day. The flats above the strip clubs were owned by Silver, Mifsud and their nominees.

Bert Wickstead had now moved his operations from the East End and had been called in to investigate the Soho vice syndicates. His operation ran side by side with one against dirty bookshops and the investigation into the Porn Squad. One of the first men he wished to interview was George Caruana, who over the years had had three separate attempts made on his life, by any standards a risky one. In 1968 he had been the intended target of a Kray-led attack. Although they had interests in Soho this was to be done as a favour to Bernie Silver, with the possible fringe benefit that they would have a substantial hold over him.[17] The plan had been for Caruana's car to be blown up and, perhaps sensibly, he left the country to work a double act with his wife in a strip club in Hamburg. It was in Caruana's house that Smithson had been murdered in 1956. Now in 1973 Caruana was located and made a statement but when it came to it he declined to give evidence. His retraction was to be only one of a series of early disappointments for Wickstead.

In fact Wickstead had considerable misfortune with his witnesses throughout the case. Apart from Caruana's defection, another potential witness, Maltese Frank Dyer, was kidnapped in London and given a beating, with a gun held to his head, to try to make him disclose what he had told the police. In October 1973 the top men of the Syndicate took off on an extended holiday. An offer of £35,000 had been made for the Serious Crime Squad to drop the charge against Silver. It seemed as though Wickstead's work might have been wasted. One of the officers in his squad had given the tip-off that raids were due. Wickstead went through the motions of having warrants he had obtained withdrawn and then leaked a carefully prepared story that his work had been wasted and his investigation abandoned. For the moment he turned his attention to pornographic books.

Three months later the directors of the Syndicate started to filter back and on 30 December Bernie Silver was spotted at the Park Tower Hotel in London. He was arrested, along with his then girlfriend, Dominique

---

[17] The plan was foiled when as a result of a phone tap the intended assassin, Paul Elvey, was arrested in Scotland with three dozen sticks of dynamite. There had been a considerable trade between the London gangs and Scottish mineworkers, who supplemented their wages by supplying explosives.

Ferguson, as they finished dinner and was taken to Limehouse police station, where Wickstead felt more at home: at West End Central he might run into corrupt officers who could impede his progress.

In the early hours a raid was organized on the Scheherazade Club in Soho. Wickstead had stepped up on stage to announce the wholesale arrest. 'What do you think of the cabaret?' called one reveller. 'Not much,' shouted another. The assembled company, including the band, was arrested and taken down to an East End police station, far from the eyes and ears of the police at West End Central.

But the sweep did not net Frank Mifsud. He had been living in Dublin and was tipped off with a phone call on the night of the Scheherazade raid. By the time the Garda went to arrest him he had gone.

One of the charges against Silver was conspiracy to murder Tommy Smithson. By now Wickstead had most of the story concerning the small-time hoodlum's death. His attempts to blackmail Silver to put up money for Fay Sadler's defence had come at a most unfortunate time. Silver was preparing his moves from Brick Lane into Soho and could not afford any hindrance. Nor could he allow himself to be seen as a weak man. Two contract killers, Philip Ellul and Victor Spampinato, were given the contract and executed their one-time friend Smithson, although they were never paid.

After the murder they had gone into hiding in Manchester, where they received a message from the Syndicate telling them to give themselves up. A deal had been arranged that they would only be charged with manslaughter and once their sentences had been served need never work again. They were betrayed, and both had been put on trial for murder. Spampinato had been acquitted and Ellul sentenced to death before being reprieved on the eve of his execution. He served eleven years and on his release came to London to collect his money. Sixpence was thrown on the floor and he was told to pick it up. Later he was taken to obtain a passport and then to Heathrow.

Spampinato was found by Wickstead's officers working as a wine bar tout in Malta. Ellul was traced by the American police and telephoned Wickstead. Yes, he would come and give evidence. Spampinato gave evidence at the committal proceedings at Old Street Magistrates' Court but did not reappear at the trial. When next traced in Malta he owned a villa on the sea front at Sliema, had a new car and was said to be in possession of £30,000. His contract had been honoured at last.

Ellul was given police protection in a flat in Limehouse. He was kept under close observation but complained, saying that his time in the death cell had left its mark on him and he did not like company. The watch was relaxed and later Ellul said he wanted to return to the States, promising to return for the trial. There is no such thing as protective custody of witnesses in England and so no reason to detain him. He never returned. It is said he was paid £60,000, which would roughly equal the payment made to Spampinato.

Silver was found not guilty on the charge of conspiring to murder Tommy Smithson but guilty to living on immoral earnings. He received six years' imprisonment. Others in the case received up to five years. All that remained was the arrest of 'Big Frank' Mifsud.

He was found in Switzerland, where he had been living in hiding in a small tent on the Austrian border, and was returned to London after fighting a losing extradition battle on the grounds of his ill health. He faced the charge of conspiracy to murder Smithson and also suborning Stocker to give false evidence in the Cauci and Galea case.

Wickstead had already seen both Stocker and Gauci. Stocker admitted he had been promised £100 for his evidence but in the tradition of bilking their employees, Mifsud had paid him only £15. Cauci, a round little man with a cast in one eye, had been set up in a coffee bar in Wardour Mews on his release. He gave his evidence well at Mifsud's trial and a conviction followed. Mifsud was sentenced to five years' imprisonment, only for the Court of Appeal to quash the conviction. He did not remain in England long. He left and returned to Malta to live on the proceeds of his Swiss bank accounts, along with the other members of the Syndicate. Silver returned to the West End but was never again a force with whom to be reckoned.

But, never one door shuts but another opens, and by the 1970s, with the introduction of the escort agency, Soho vice had become an even bigger and more sophisticated business. One of the new kings was not a Maltese but Joseph Wilkins, originally from Stoke Newington but now living the life of a country squire in Surrey. Physically a large man, with thinning and greasy black hair, he had started life as a used car salesman. Following a move to the West End, with interests in fruit machines and night clubs, in 1969 he took over Winston's, then a very fashionable club for tired businessmen and free spending visitors who could be relied on to waste money on indifferent food and expensive drink in return for the opportunity to sit with a hostess, which is what they had come there for in the first place. At one time or another Wilkins had interests in the 800 Club in Leicester Square (formerly the once fashionable 400 Club, home from home for Guards officers out on the town and, in its glory days, frequented by Princess Margaret),[18] the Islet Town Club in Curzon Street and

[18] The premises of the 400/800 now houses a large Chinese restaurant.

the Crazy Horse Saloon in Marylebone run by John Bloom, the former Rolls Razor washing-machine tycoon. But Wilkins also had a string of failed clubs to his name, including the Australian Visitors Club and the Minstrel Restaurant, part-owned by one of the Black and White Minstrels.

The circumstances of his inheritance of Winston's were shrouded in mist. At a licensing application before the then Chief Metropolitan magistrate, Sir Robert Blundell, at Bow Street Magistrates' Court, the former owner, Bruce Brace, maintained that Wilkins had terrorized him into handing over the club. Wilkins agreed that he had paid no money for the 27,000-member club but said that instead of payment he had settled debts of £6000. The licence was granted but the club soon closed.

Wilkins' reign in Soho was a relatively short and certainly a troubled one. An aggressive man, on one occasion in Winston's club he is said to have pointed a gun at the former world middleweight champion Terry Downes for making too much noise. Downes simply turned and took it from him. In November 1970 Wilkins was arrested at his farm and charged with conspiracy to pervert the course of justice over obtaining justices' licences. Charged with him was his helpmate Wally Birch.

This was by no means the end of his troubles. With Birch he was then running the Eve International, Playboy Escort, Glamour International and La Femme escort agencies. Eve had a catalogue of 200 girls who were available as escorts at a fee of £14 a night upwards and the business had a turnover of £100,000 a year. For some time there had been rumours that the more drunken punters from the Crazy Horse had found their way to the 800 Club and, following more drink, had been rolled in the alleyways off Leicester Square. Two of the staff of the 800 were arrested and later acquitted. Wilkins was charged with another conspiracy to pervert, this time along with a solicitor and a Detective Sergeant, to give false evidence in the case of one of the club staff. All were acquitted, as were the staff in their separate case.

On 21 March 1972, whilst awaiting trial for the conspiracy, Wilkins and Birch were shot and wounded in the Beak Street offices of Eve International. Later his then wife Pearl was to blame the Krays for encouraging her husband's enemies but, as the twins were in prison at the time, either their influence must have been marginal or they were wielding considerably more power from their cells than the prison authorities would have wished. Certainly in their youth they had quarrelled with Wally Birch and had been charged with grievous bodily harm following a fight with chains outside a dance hall. On that occasion the Krays had been acquitted.

Wilkins was sentenced to two years' imprisonment for his part in the conspiracy over the club licences, whilst Birch received nine months. Released from prison, Wilkins returned to the escort agency business. In November 1975 he was involved in accusations of the theft of a suitcase from currency swindler Ernest Brauch, a friend and acquaintance of the multi-million-pound fraudsman and property tycoon Judah Binstock. There had been a clever plot, said Brauch, involving the switching of a suitcase at Heathrow Airport, so that he was left with an identical but empty case revolving on the baggage carousel. Wilkins and all the other defendants were acquitted. Nevertheless his empire was crumbling and he was said to owe £90,000 in tax. He complained that his former partner John Bloom had put the skids on him over their dealings in clubs.

By now, however, he had been charged with living off immoral earnings, as had his faithful friend Birch, his long-suffering wife Pearl and some of the girls. The evidence showed that the girls were making £400 a week for themselves, let alone for the agency, which had advertised in the *Diplomatic Year Book*; it was what the trial judge called 'a new and sophisticated form of poncing'. A girl charged £40 for 'a quickie' and £100 for 'longer'. In March 1976 Judge Charles Lawton QC sentenced Wilkins to three and a half years. Birch received thirty months whilst Pearl was given a conditional discharge.

Wilkins had his sentence cut to two years by the Court of Appeal. The trial judge had, it said, been prejudiced by information given at the end of the trial which linked Wilkins to both a notorious Soho gangster and 'Mad' Frankie Fraser.

After his imprisonment he turned to a sophisticated long firm fraud and, following his release from a sentence for that misdemeanour, on 17 August 1987 he was caught sunbathing on a boat, *The Danny Boy*, which was carrying £1.5 million in cannabis. The arrest angered Scotland Yard, which had been hoping to follow the consignment to the South London gang who had ordered the drugs. Now Wilkins claimed he was an undercover agent for the Spanish police and in court named Frankie Fraser as one of the bosses behind the Costa del Sol drugs racket. Wilkins, whose only drink was said to be Dom Perignon champagne, had remarried shortly before he received a ten-year sentence. In September 1990 he slipped his guards when on an outside visit to a dentist from Ford Open Prison. It had been said he was worried about a split with his new wife. He was last reported as being back on the Costa del Sol. In March 1991 it was learned that Coral Edgar, Wilkins' sister, had been paid £2000 by Andrew Neil, editor of the *Sunday Times*, for a statement over Wilkins' links with Carmen Proetta, the witness to the shootings of IRA members in Gibraltar.

Nowadays the Soho industry has taken something of a knocking. But whilst the entrance fee to strip clubs advertising double acts and men and women in bed is low, and the lure that of long-legged girls in fishnet tights on the door, the punters get little for their money. 'The price to get in may be only £2,' says Detective Chief Superintendent Roy Ram, 'but at the foot of the stairs another £8 is removed for "membership". No sooner has the punter's bottom touched the seat than he is presented with the menu – £5.50 for a glass of Coke, £8 for an alcohol-free lager.'

In charge of these operations is another Maltese, Jean Agius – 'short and thin with sparse hair, pale and very unhealthy looking. Over a track suit he wore a showy but moth-eaten fur coat. It was all slightly sad.'[19] According to *The Independent* report, however, he is reputed to be wealthy, with a Rolls-Royce Corniche in London and a Bentley in Malta.

[19] 'The Maltese Legacy' by Peter Popham, *The Independent* magazine, 2 February 1991.

8

Robbers and Robberies

There seem to be two ways of setting up a robbery. The detailed perfectionist method of the highly skilled, or the more rough and ready take your, and everybody else's, chance.

Talking of his time, one villain of the 1960s and 1970s says:

> How did we look out the banks? On a Monday Georgie and I would drive round looking for a bank with a side turning. This was in the days before bandit glass – it was us made them put it in. One of us would go and change a note to see what drawers there were and then we'd go in mob-handed with pick-axe handles. One of us would stay by the door. Sometimes Bertie Smalls used to do that because he was fat and unfit and I'd jump on the counter and cause mayhem.
>
> Security vans were often picked by chance. You'd see them collecting and see them again the next week. You'd watch them doing pick-ups and use your judgement about how much each pick-up was worth and just what the van was carrying.

Teams were often picked up on the *ad hoc* basis you

might expect for a Sunday morning kick around in the park.

One of the labour exchanges for robbery work was the Log Cabin Club in Wardour Street, owned at one time by friends of Billy Hill. It was full of robbers, cut-throats and buyers. I was working with a couple then, called Robin and Mickey, and we used to go direct to the club and say to people, 'You fancy going to work tomorrow?' It could have been a porn shop, it could have been a post office.

Sometimes you got set up. One time I was minding the door of a club down the East End getting £100 a night, basically I was keeping the drugs mob out, and the guvnor says, 'Can you get someone for the back door?' I got hold of Tony and after a bit he said he and a mate had a bit of work, a security van. I was to be the driver. What Tony failed to tell me was that the person who stuck the job up to him was someone he'd given a spanking to a few weeks previous and the man had just set him up with the job and gone to the police.

Wasn't that risky?

Not really. In them days the police never had the informants, and they aren't – well they certainly weren't – as clever as they're made out.

Guns we kept in a slaughter – a lock-up garage in Camden Town. Other people had armourers, like the Krays with Colin 'Dukie' Osborne, but we didn't.

We'd never do less than one a week. Sometimes we'd do two in a day. The first robbery I ever did was in about 1961/2 and I was shitting all the night before – literally. I got £500 and to me it was a million. I bought myself a dark blue crombie coat which all the faces wore at the time and a white Fiat 600, and I had money to spare.

In the sixties a small house could be got for £1000 and I could have bought one – week in, week out. But I didn't – it all went on clubs, cars and women.

Robbery is not of course a twentieth-century phenomenon. There have always been robberies. What were those gallant highwaymen but armed robbers? Even then there wasn't much honour amongst them. Dick Turpin, who never actually made the celebrated ride to York, shot his long-time partner Tom King, accidentally perhaps, but he left him to die and escaped just as surely as John Hilton did two hundred years later.[1]

At the turn of the century a favourite form of robbery was with the garrotte. It was not the Spanish form of execution, a mask with a metal pin slowly tightened, but a neck-hold which, properly applied, brought about unconsciousness. Properly applied was the key phrase. Too much force and the victim died. 'You would come up to a man from behind, put your arms around his throat, with your fists on his throttle. If it went on for more than a few seconds he would choke, so you had to be skilled.'[2] A convicted garrotter could expect a heavy sentence: five years and, worse, a 'bashing' or eighteen strokes with the cat o' nine tails.

The Reubens brothers were not sufficiently experienced. On 15 March 1909 two prostitutes under their control took a couple of drunken sailors, McEachern and Sproull, to 3 Rupert Street, off Leman Street, where the brothers, Morris and Marks, attacked them.

---

[1] See Chapter 11.
[2] R. Samuel, quoting Harding, *East End Underworld*, p. 112.

McEachern was found semi-conscious in the street early the next morning. Nearby, Sproull was dead in the gutter. The case was investigated by Frederick Wensley, who later was the senior officer in the Steinie Morrison case. It appeared that after having sex with the girls, McEachern had decided to return to the ship rather than stay the night, taking Sproull with him. The Reubens brothers had been listening outside the room, expecting to roll the sailors while they were asleep, as would have been the normal practice; if they wanted the remainder of the sailors' money – about £5 each – well, they would be forced to attack them as they left. Apart from his other injuries Sproull had been stabbed.

At the trial at the Old Bailey Morris claimed he did not know his brother had a knife. It was not a defence which appealed to the jury, who convicted them both after a retirement of twelve minutes. They were executed on 20 May 1909.

'From that date, robbery with violence grew unfashionable in East London and few unaccountable dead bodies were found in the streets,' wrote Wensley.[3] It may be that a small industry was born with the hanging of the Reubens. A little later Wensley was sent a whisky glass with a hanging man engraved on the base. The inscription was 'The Brothers Reubens – the last drop'.

But the arrival of the motor car revived the flagging armed robbery business. Now thieves could travel at some speed and with comparative anonymity. In his memoirs George Cornish describes the arrest of what he called the first motor bandits in November 1924. He was certainly wrong in describing Reginald Dickenson and his mates as the first because the Recorder of London, sentencing them to terms of up to seven years, commented, 'I had almost decided to have you whipped . . .

[3] F. Wensley, *Detective Days*, p. 92.

I cannot lose sight of the fact that this class of offence is on the increase.'[4]

In fact it had originated in France long before the Second World War. In 1924 the cashier of one of the biggest French banks was shot dead by a gang which robbed him of 300,000 francs before escaping in a waiting motor car. Later the gang was trapped in a Paris suburb and, on conviction, guillotined. One of them, Saudy, said to the executioner as his head was placed on the guillotine, 'It is very cold. Goodbye all.' In French of course.

Indeed in the first year after the Great War there were sufficient smash and grab robberies with teams using motor cars from which a brick or iron bar was hurled through the window of a jewellers to cause Scotland Yard's Flying Squad to get wheels for themselves. Clearly a new version of the sport was here to stay.

The other form of armed robbery was the highly sophisticated, highly organized version executed with military precision – even though often the nearest the executants had been to the army was the glasshouse.

The first major post-war robbery took place at Heathrow Airport – then called Heath Row – on 28 July 1948. The target was the bonded warehouse which contained £388,000-worth of diamonds and was due to receive a further £250,000-worth. The job had been meticulously laid out, with inside help, and the gang maintained a twenty-four-hour watch on Heath Row over a two-month period. Then a warehouseman approached Donald Fish, chief security officer of BOAC, to report he had been offered £500 to dope the coffee of the warehouse staff. The Flying Squad was called in.

Each morning the organizer, who ultimately did not

[4] G. Cornish, *Cornish of the 'Yard'*, p. 143.

take part in the raid, was watched as he left his home in Ealing, with bowler hat, briefcase, umbrella and *The Times* under his arm, to head for a cafe near Waterloo Station. The plan had been to drug the guards at the warehouse and at first the raid seemed to go according to plan. The messenger with the tea was intercepted, and barbitone was dropped in the jug. But at the last minute the guards had been switched and replaced by members of the Flying Squad. The tea was put on one side and the three 'guards' lay on the floor seemingly unconscious. The members of the gang entered, hit one of the detectives with an iron bar to ensure he was unconscious and then took the keys from his pocket. At the same time other members of the squad attacked the robbers. Of the detectives, John MacMillan had his nose broken and a robber broke Detective Inspector Peter Sinclair's arm. Some of the robbers, including Teddy Machin, escaped. One of them hid under a lorry and, scorched by the exhaust, carried the burn on his shoulder for the rest of his life. The remainder were captured and sentenced to a total of seventy-one years' imprisonment at the Old Bailey.

> King Solly came up trumps. He must have caught a fearful cold as the overheads for this job were certainly very heavy. I believe that he had got a large advance payment from the prospective buyer, but even so, he was faced with the prospect of looking after the families of up to nineteen men for several years, if we all went down.[5]

Who was King Solly? The rumour was that it was a Soho gang leader, perhaps on the basis that four of his men were among those on the robbery, but no charges

[5] Shifty Burke, *Peterman*, p. 129.

were ever brought against him.

The first successful major post-war robbery was the Great Mail-bag Robbery of 21 May 1952, when £287,000 in hard cash was stolen from a post office mail-bag van. According to Billy Hill, the night before the robbery nine men, all of whom had been selected and warned of the raid the week before, and who certainly included Slip Sullivan, had been collected and taken to a flat in the West End, where they were locked in before being fully briefed on the operation. Hill had clearly set Wickstead and Read a precedent on the necessity for keeping a tight hold on their men.

The robbery had been carried out with immaculate precision. The mail-van had been followed every night for months as it left on its journey to Oxford Street. Cars had been stolen specifically for the raid. In the early hours of Wednesday morning one of the team had disconnected the alarm system on the van whilst the staff were on their tea-break. The van was kept under observation when it went to Paddington Station and once it left Paddington a call was made to the West End flat. Four men climbed into one of the stolen cars, a green Vanguard, and the other four into the stolen 2½-litre Riley.

As the van turned into Eastcastle Street off Oxford Street the two cars blocked the driver's path. Six men attacked the three post office workers and then drove off in the van, leaving them on the pavement. It was driven to Augustus Street where the cash was transferred into boxes on a fruiterer's lorry parked there earlier. Thirteen out of the thirty-one bags had been taken. 'The thieves were surprised,' claimed the police.

According to Hill the remaining bags were left because there wasn't any more room in the lorry, which was driven to Spitalfields market and parked there under observation for a further twenty-four hours before it was unloaded. The stolen cars were left in Covent Garden.

At the time Hill was seriously suspected of the robbery and it is now generally accepted that he organized it. Rewards totalling £25,000 were put up by the insurance companies but despite intense police activity for over a year, headed by Superintendent Bob Lee, then second in command of the Flying Squad, there were no charges. Hill recalled:

> All my friends were turned over. My spielers were raided and closed down. Friends of mine going abroad on holidays were turned over by the Customs people. One of my lads even had his car taken to pieces, yet he did not have a criminal conviction. All my telephones were tapped for years afterwards. My mail going through the post was steamed open and read.[6]

In the 1940s there had emerged an apparently highly unlikely gang leader but one who, according to journalist Peta Fordham, was to have a seminal influence over the next thirty years. His name was Ernest Watts and he created the South-Western Gang, so called because most of its members came from that area. He served only one short sentence of imprisonment. He must have been a disciple of the American Von Lamm, whose methods he adopted and improved upon.[7] A job would be cased,

[6] B. Hill, *Boss of Britain's Underworld*, p. 167.
[7] Lamm (?1890–1930), a German officer cashiered for cheating at cards, has been described as America's most brilliant bank robber, on whose technique Dillinger relied. From the end of World War One until the 1930s Herman K. 'Baron' Lamm's men were the most efficient in the business. Lamm's career came to an end when a tyre blew on the getaway car. They seized another which by mischance had a device fitted by a well-meaning son to prevent his elderly father driving too fast. They were overtaken and Lamm died in the ensuing shoot-out.

procedure worked out, the approach, the commission and the getaway timed to a split second, and the rule kept firmly that nothing was to throw out this schedule. If a safe door stuck or the expected haul was not there the timing was still to be strictly adhered to. Around him young Watts gathered Bruce Reynolds and a small band of trusted criminals who were shortly to lead this south-western part of the underworld.

Apparently Watts was an intellectual *manqué*, the clever boy from a working-class family with a chip on his shoulder. His father was almost literally a quack doctor, selling patent medicines around local markets. Watts, a diabetic, had won a scholarship to Christ's Hospital but his family did not allow him to take it up. He served in the RAF and then, seemingly determined to get his own back on society, he turned to a life of organized crime.

According to Peta Fordham, who made something of a career out of the Great Train Robbery,[8] Watts read everything he could about famous criminals and decided the most paying line was in jewel robberies from private houses and shops. In the main he worked alone and received his only prison sentence, one of two years, early in his career. It was shortly afterwards that he met Bruce Reynolds, one of the masterminds of the Great Train Robbery. Fordham attributes to Watts the use of the 'front man', the one who knew only what he had to do and therefore could not embroil others if he 'squealed'. Watts also introduced into England the system of the buying-in of information as well as the scale of compensation for those sent to prison when caught on a job.

---

[8] Peta Fordham was the wife of Wilfrid Fordham QC, who defended a number of those accused of involvement in the Great Train Robbery who were subsequently acquitted. A journalist with the *Sunday Times* and author of two books, she had a continuing interest in the fate of those convicted in the Train Robbery.

Watts killed himself, possibly accidentally, at the age of thirty-two. He had made abortive attempts at suicide in previous years; now he gave himself an overdose of insulin after returning from a job in the Home Counties when he had been without his medicine and had been taken ill. He had, however, committed one of gangland's cardinal sins. He had become involved with a close friend's girl whilst the man was in prison. Fordham tells how at the London Hospital where Watts had been taken one man came to see him only to find he had died. 'A good thing,' he said, 'otherwise we might have had to do a mercy killing.'[9]

The name of Watts does not appear in any account of organized crime at the time but he certainly existed, although perhaps not as the great leader painted by Peta Fordham. 'He was a short stocky fellow with short hair, a good dresser, good thief,' remembers one friend. 'But as the organizer – no. Connie Wilkin was the Daddy-O. He was the business.'

But it was Bruce Reynolds, tall, bespectacled, with the intelligent face of a handsome schoolteacher, to whom the leadership of the South-Western Gang devolved. His father was an active Trades Unionist. Reynolds had served his first sentence for robbery at the age of seventeen and another for an attack on a Jewish bookmaker in Park Lane. He drove an Aston Martin and was happy to let it be known that he had been the youngest major in the British Army. It was Reynolds who led the gang's first, and this time partially successful, major operation – the 1952 London Airport bullion robbery. The team consisted of names which float in and out of the London underworld and society for the next twenty-five-plus years. It included his long-time friend Charlie Wilson, described as a humorous, warm-hearted

[9] P. Fordham, *Inside the Underworld*, p. 77.

man who lived with his wife and three daughters in Clapham, had originally come from Battersea and had been involved in the West End protection rackets.[10] It was Wilson who was introduced to a man working in Comet House who could tell him of the movement of wages for the staff of BOAC.

Another member was Gordon Goody, later the particular favourite of Peta Fordham amongst the train robbers. An enormous thin-faced man, he had tattooed on one huge bicep the words 'Hello Ireland' and on the other 'Dear Mother'. He had already served a sentence that included twelve strokes of the birch for the rolling of a homosexual, and another for robbing a jeweller in Ireland. He liked West End clubs, women and Jermyn Street shirtmakers. Yet another member was the good-looking Buster Edwards, small-time thief, failed street bookmaker and – the straight job he began and ended with – flower-seller.

The drivers were to be Roy James and Mickey Ball, both small in stature and exceptionally talented. Perhaps, like the drummer in a dance band, being small is a prerequisite for success as a wheelman; Danny Allpress, who drove the getaway cars for the Bertie Smalls Gang at the end of the 1960s, and who was said to be able to make a car do almost anything, was not a big man either. Shortly before the London Airport robbery James and Ball had earned over £90,000 from two burglaries in the south of France. They had also blown £30,000 on the tables there.[11] A reserve driver was John Daly, a member of a powerful South London family, later acquitted of his alleged part in the Great Train Robbery. A safe house was arranged in Norbury. It belonged to Jimmy White, an ex-paratrooper.

[10] Piers Paul Read, *The Train Robbers*, p. 20.
[11] Ibid, p. 22.

Most of the team had already worked together in another highly planned wages snatch which had netted around £26,000. Now the prize was much, much higher; the team estimated they would pick up over £250,000. The plan was that the actual robbers would go to Comet House wearing false moustaches and disguised in bowler hats as businessmen and hide in the lavatories until the wage carriers left the building. Then after the snatch they would escape in the cars in which James and Ball, dressed as chauffeurs, would be waiting.

On 27 November 1962 the raid took place. It had been aborted the previous week when police were seen to be escorting the wage carriers. Now things went almost according to plan. The guards and some clerks with them were duly coshed, the wages snatched and away they went.

When they surfaced they found two things were not in their favour. There was only £62,000 in wages and, worse, the public was appalled by the brutal coshing of the guards. Even worse, it was more or less immediately apparent who had carried out the robbery. For a start Ball and James were the only drivers of sufficient class to have driven the getaway cars. Earlier Gordon Goody's flat had been raided over a receiving matter and theatrical make-up had been noticed. Mickey Ball's Mercedes had been seen with a bowler hat and umbrella on the back seat. It was only a matter of hours before the round-up began. Wilson, Goody, James, Ball and another man were put on identification parades but were not picked out. Reynolds had fled to France. Goody now left for Tangier.

In the middle of November a second identification parade was held, this time with the suspects, including Wilson, James, Ball and the newly returned Goody, dressed up in bowlers and false moustaches. Mickey Ball was identified as one of the coshers and broke down, begging the officers to believe he was only the driver. James was not picked out but Goody and Wilson were charged after further parades. Outside help was clearly needed.

And outside help came in the shape of Brian Field, a managing clerk employed by a confused and disorganized solicitor, John Wheater, who had offices in New Quebec Street near Marble Arch. Field had already helped Edwards out over a small matter of a stolen car. Now he began to work on the concoction of an alibi and the bribing of jurors, one of whom was offered and declined £400. It was helped by the fact that, thanks to a singular lack of proper police objections, Uxbridge magistrates had given bail to all the defendants other than Mickey Ball.

During the trial Wilson was acquitted on the direction of the judge but the case continued against Goody. The jury were unable to agree about his guilt or innocence. Meanwhile Mickey Ball received a five-year sentence.

The only way out for the re-trial was to get hold of a witness and this Goody did, with the help of Buster Edwards. Again it appears the witness declined the £200 on offer. Goody, however, was acquitted.

Within three months the money was spent and Reynolds, Wilson and company were back at work doing, or at least trying to do, what they knew best, robbing trains. Sometimes with some success and on other occasions without. And then for them came the big one.

What view you have of the Great Train Robbery depends on whom you believe for the information supplied. Of one thing there is little doubt – the job had been on offer around the underworld for a number of years. Eight, says Peta Fordham. 'The Great Train Robbery was a job which had been hawked like a film script around the underworld for some time. The blueprint had been carefully worked out and had been offered to a number of suitable clients,' says Nipper Read.[12]

It was the biggest theft the world had then known. At 3 a.m. on 8 August 1963 the night train from Glasgow to London was stopped at the remote Brigedo Bridge, Cheddington, in Buckinghamshire. A gang of armed thieves coshed the driver, Jack Mills, smashed their way into the high-valued package coach and stole 120 mailbags whose contents were estimated to be worth over £2.5 million. Even now the Great Train Robbery has a certain romanticism about it which has not attached to later and bigger raids, such as the Security Express and Brinks Mat robberies. There had been thefts from trains not long before that in 1963, particularly on the London to Brighton line, but these had been relatively small affairs.

The first reports of the Cheddington theft were vague but, as the day wore on, it became clear that this was a major robbery. Buckinghamshire was one of the smallest of the county forces and the Chief Constable, Brigadier Cheney, quickly realized he did not have the manpower at his disposal to deal with such a major incident. He used the facility that was available to all provincial constabularies. He called in Scotland Yard.

Officers from Scotland Yard had been made available from 1907 when the then Home Secretary, Herbert Gladstone, wrote to the Commissioner saying he felt that it was desirable that the services of a small number of detectives should be available for enquiries in difficult and important criminal cases committed outside the Metropolitan Police District.[13] It then fell to the officers of Central Office, New Scotland Yard, to take on this

[12] L. Read and J. Morton, *Nipper*, p. 72.
[13] For footnote, see opposite.

responsibility. As the majority of cases they investigated were murders they soon became known as the Murder Squad but they were not used exclusively in this capacity.

The team consisted of ten Chief Superintendents in charge of squads of men who were committed to investigating a variety of criminal cases. These included extradition and fugitive offender cases, banknote forgery and coinage offences, bribery and corruption, international lotteries and crimes relating to government departments. There was no question that these experienced investigators were simply sitting around waiting for a telephone call from a provincial or overseas force. They were well occupied with their daily responsibilities. But there was a rota system with three men on stand-by awaiting call-out. Being one of the three was known as 'being in the frame' and as a call was taken the next moved up a place. Number one had a suitcase ready packed with a current passport in case of an overseas job and had the famous 'murder box'. It meant that an officer had to be available twenty-four hours a day and ready at very short notice to go anywhere in the world.

The number one in August 1963 was Gerald McArthur, who had only recently been appointed to the squad and who, although he had considerable experience in all manner of investigations, including murder, from serving in various divisions of the Met, had never been appointed to assist a provincial force whilst on the

---

13 One of the first, if unsuccessful, investigations was undertaken by Inspector Dew who later arrested Crippen. He was sent to Salisbury to find the killer of a crippled boy, Teddy Haskell. Unfortunately by the time he had arrived all the blood had been cleaned away under the supervision of the local police. Flora Haskell, the boy's mother, was arrested and defended by the young Rayner Goddard who later became the Lord Chief Justice. She was acquitted after a re-trial.

Murder Squad. He chose as his assistant Jack Pritchard. Their role was an advisory and directory one, as was that of any member of the Murder Squad when he was called out. Literally he could advise but if that advice was disregarded then too bad. Although this was standard procedure it did not satisfy the press or the public. Why, it was asked, were only two men detached from the Met to solve the world's greatest robbery? It was decided to supplement McArthur and Pritchard with a larger team.

Meanwhile Aylesbury, where the enquiry was based, throbbed with activity, speculation, rumour and excitement. The world's press swarmed everywhere like mayflies on a Hampshire trout river. Nipper Read recounts the political in-fighting which went on amongst senior officers anxious for their five minutes'-worth of glory and exposure to television and the newspapers.

Each officer wanted some of the glory from this, the world's greatest robbery. Each wanted to be seen as the instigator of this or that line of enquiry, preferably when it had turned out to be a successful one. More senior detectives visited Aylesbury than any scene of crime before and probably since. They all gave notice of their arrival to the reporters and made sure their best side was showing when the cameras clicked. Every senior officer was out to make a name with *his* arrests and have *his* photograph in the papers. All gave short crisp quotes suggesting that they were really overlording the operations and then shortly afterwards they were driven back to London.

Through all this Gerald McArthur maintained an air of unruffled equanimity. He knew who was really in charge. Unfortunately the record never gave him any of the credit for the magnificent job he did. Few members of the general public realized that he was the man at the helm.

The robbery job had been on offer so long that when it happened a number of people were not surprised. It was well known at the Yard that an Irishman was responsible for planning robberies and then selling them on to the perpetrators. The first of these was at Ericson's Telephones in Beeston in Nottingham, and was the first big hijack after the war. He went on to plan many others and detectives would say, 'That's got Mickey's stamp on it,' because the planning was meticulous.

Whilst Nipper Read was at Paddington there was one job Mickey told him about. They never met but he either knew or had heard of Read and there was a series of telephone conversations between them.

I was never quite sure why he blew the whistle but I suspect he had not been paid for the plan for this particular job.

It was a nice job really. Each week money was collected from an office block in Eastbourne Terrace by a GPO van. Mickey told me there would be a Ford Zephyr motor car and four people in it and another bloke on the bus stop and so on . . . when the people came out with the loot etc the men in the Zephyr would attack them and the man at the bus stop would be a back-up helper.

It was a perfectly simple operation to mount and when the raid was scheduled to go off there I was standing in my shirt sleeves on the steps of the office block having an argument with my 'girl-friend', a woman detective, Betty Reid. Two of my men were the office workers there to hand the money over to the GPO men.

Sure enough as the exchange was made the Ford

car appeared with four men in it, drove up and then slowed down. After the exchange was made it roared away up the road.

We arrested the only one left, the man at the bus stop, who had a long steel bar up his sleeve and got five years for conspiracy to rob. When I got back to the nick Mickey was on the phone in a rage. 'You've fucked it up completely.' I said, 'What are you talking about? We had everything laid on. They just didn't stop.'

'No,' he said. 'Of course they didn't fucking stop. These two blokes of yours – the ones in the waistcoats who handed over the cash.' 'Yes,' I said, wondering how he knew they were my chaps.

'They came out of the office . . . the real ones never, never do that.' It was an example of how meticulous his planning was. He had obviously detailed in his plan that the office workers handed over the cash and went straight back to their duties. The fact they did not alerted the robbers and the job was off.[14]

Read was sure from all the information he had that it was the same man who drew up the plan for the Great Train Robbery but that it was Bruce Reynolds who honed, polished and fine-tuned it. There is some confirmation of Read's theory. In Piers Paul Read's book, Gordon Goody and Buster Edwards meet a slightly balding, middle-aged man with a Northern Irish accent who tells them of the high-value package coach on the Glasgow to London mail train.

After the robbery Read recalls standing on the embankment at Brigedo Bridge and realizing what a perfect place it was for the unloading operation. Looking

[14] L. Read and J. Morton, *Nipper*, p. 72.

around, there was only one building in sight, a farm-house, to which the telephone wires had been cut. A short walk down the track was a white flag resting on an overturned barrow. This was the signal for the driver to stop the train so that the high-value package carriage was precisely above the embankment on the bridge. The carriage had been separated from the rest of the train, leaving the sorters, who may otherwise have been a problem wondering what the delay might be, a mile down the track. The exercise had not only involved the uncoupling of the train but the disconnecting and reconnecting of the vacuum pipe controlling the braking system. Read has always believed it to have been a perfectly planned and well-executed operation. The only flaw was the gratuitous violence meted out to Jack Mills, the train driver.

There have been a number of theories about a sinister and mysterious Mr Big, rather like Steve McQueen in the film *The Thomas Crown Affair*, who masterminded everything but who was never caught. Many police discount this and Read believes that the mastermind as such was Reynolds, with the brilliant Gordon Goody as the quartermaster sergeant, the number two. An operation of this size needed financing and the money for it had been provided by the 'City Gent' job at London Airport. Now the planning for the big one could go ahead.

It was another example of fine planning that Leath-erslade Farm had been selected as a temporary hideaway and that discipline over the job had been very strictly observed. Gordon Goody was thought to be the man who kept the troops under control. Before the job he could do this not only because of his forceful personality but by constantly referring to the rewards on offer when the caper was finally pulled.

Things went wrong, according to one theory, after the

team tore open the mail-bags back at the farm, found they had netted over £2 million and realized they had hit a jackpot beyond their hopes. Discipline then went to the wall and from being a well-drilled and regimented body, the robbers reverted to type and once more became individuals blinded by wealth, each eager to go off and spend it for himself.

They were not helped by McArthur putting out an announcement that he believed the robbers were still within a thirty-mile radius. (Leatherslade Farm was about twenty-seven miles away.) When the friend of a neighbouring farmer circled the area in a plane they really thought the game was up and the exodus from the farm was rapid and frenzied. All this led to a break-up of the tight control which had been exercised by the leaders. Believing that it was only a matter of time before the farm was raided, the team began to split up, taking with them suitcases filled with money.

There has also been a theory that there was a Judas, someone who was meant to go to Leatherslade Farm and set fire to it, destroying all trace of its previous inhabitants, but who failed to carry out his task.[15] One story was that a client of Brian Field, the solicitor's clerk involved, had been paid to burn it. But there were about fifteen men holed up there, eating, sleeping, playing games, going to the lavatory, and yet they left virtually no fingerprints. Had it been their intention to have the place burned down, there would have been no need to worry about prints. One would have expected to find them on door panels, light switches, bathroom fittings, the walls, everywhere. But they were simply not there.

[15] The theory was advanced first by Peta Fordham in *The Robbers' Tale*. It was also advanced by Ernie Millen in *Specialist in Crime*. Some underworld sources suggested the Judas was Ginger Marks and that had been the reason for his disappearance (see Chapter 13).

It was only by dusting the most unlikely places that evidence did in fact surface: a sauce bottle, a faint palm print on the tail-board of a lorry, a saucer put out by Reynolds for the cat, and a Monopoly set probably left behind in the mad scramble to get away. In Goody's case there was only the faintest trace of yellow paint on a shoe to connect him to the farmhouse.

Early on at Aylesbury it became quite clear that a London team had executed the job. It had been on offer for some time and informants had done part of their work. Despite the precautions taken by Reynolds and Goody, the Yard knew some major villains were about to pull something big. But it was only after the robbery they knew what.

The police quickly put together a list of those thought to have been involved. After all, there was only a handful of people in the country who were capable of such a job. It was then the real work of finding the evidence began.

Maurice Ray and Ian Holden, the forensic scientists, could provide the foundation on which the detectives could build, but tracing the suspects, their questioning and the breaking of their alibis was left to the Flying Squad under the direction of their newly appointed chief Tommy Butler. It was on this job that he really came into his own. This was what he really loved – chasing top-class villains. It became a personal vendetta. He undertook a totally ruthless and dedicated operation which would finally result in the whole team being netted.

A second base, 'the London End', was established for the enquiry in Old Scotland Yard in the Flying Squad office. Butler, first in in the morning and last out at night, played his cards very close to his chest. His team was given the minimum of information needed for a surveillance operation or to make a quick arrest.

A good example was the way he sent his 'twin', Peter Vibart, the man with whom he was meant to have the greatest rapport, and Read to Leicester after Gordon Goody had been arrested. Goody's had been one of the earliest names suggested as an organizer and prime mover. Police in London had visited his mother's address and some of his known hideouts but with no positive result. On 23 August they had the news that he had been detained in Leicester. Butler sent Vibart and Read to Leicester with no instructions about what they were to do.

> Now usually a superior officer would say either question him in detail there and then, or perhaps ask about an alibi, or just bring the suspect back to the office and talk about nothing but horse-racing on the way down. Not so with Tommy. We had no instructions whatsoever. I suppose we were so in awe of him that we didn't ask before we left Aylesbury. Along the M1 Vibart said to me, 'Nipper, stop at the next service station and give him a ring to see what we are to do.'[16]

At first many of the suspects were brought in, questioned and then released. These included Hussey, Wisbey, Goody, Brian Field and Lennie Field. This gave the impression Butler was only on a fishing expedition and that he had no real evidence to back him up; otherwise he would have charged them. This was a most unusual practice for Butler. Normally, and it was well known amongst the villains, once he had his hooks into someone it was seldom they left the police station except to go to court. As a result some of his junior officers

[16] L. Read and J. Morton, *Nipper*, p. 77.

began to be worried that he was going soft. Nothing of the kind; he was merely playing a game of patience. By seeing them and having a quiet, apparently friendly chat he had persuaded them that, so far as they were concerned, it was a routine enquiry. He had opposed the publication of photographs of some of the leading suspects and had been overruled by Ernie Millen. Butler had rightly feared that men of this calibre would simply go underground or flee the country. The others were lulled into a false sense of security.

When it came to some arrests it was only a question of asking them to report to the Yard, which they did quite happily. This time they did not leave. Within a matter of weeks nine of the fifteen finally charged had been arrested and another five had been posted as wanted.

On 11 August Roger Cordery, a man brought in as the electrician to work the signals on the track, and his friend, William Boal, were arrested in Bournemouth where they had had the misfortune to attempt to rent lodgings from the wife of a police officer. They had bought a vehicle and a substantial sum was found in it. The money was lodged in the Chief Constable's safe and the gloom which had descended over the investigating team lifted a bit. Perhaps the use of Boal, who died in prison during his sentence, is an example of the dangers of using unreliable help. No team of robbers in its right mind should have gone anyway near this amiable but unsuitable little man.

There had been a breakthrough the previous day. A Dorking man, John Ahearn, was giving a lift on the pillion of his motorcycle to Mrs Nina Hargreaves when the small-engined machine began to overheat. They pulled off the road into a sheltered area of woodland where only a few yards from the road, sitting on a tree stump rather like an altar, was a beautiful embossed suitcase. They opened the bag and were astonished to find it crammed with used bank notes. Anyone less honest than Mr Ahearn and Mrs Hargreaves might have been tempted to keep the swag but they knew at once they had stumbled on part of the Train Robbery haul and contacted the police. A dog unit arrived with other officers and began to search the ground. A little further into the wood they discovered another bag. The total count was £100,900.

The police were amazed to see how obvious the case must have been. It would have been visible even from the road. It was almost as if it had been put there to be found. Yet right opposite there was a field of fern in which it was almost impossible to see anything. With a bit more planning the case could have remained undetected for years.

At that time anyone seen with a suitcase was fair game for a stop by an officer. Someone stopped with more than an ordinary roll of banknotes would certainly be invited to 'assist the police with their enquiries'. Hundreds of calls were received from up and down the country giving information about this or that person 'acting suspiciously' by spending money freely. The public was in the grip of GTR mania.

At the bottom of the Dorking suitcase a German hotel receipt was found in the name of Herr and Frau Field. This was Brian Field, the solicitor's clerk, and the £100,900 was obviously his share of the proceeds. Field had been fairly easy to link to the job because Wheater's firm had been instructed in the purchase of Leatherslade Farm. For his part in the Train Robbery he was eventually charged with conspiracy to rob and convicted. He was sentenced to twenty-five years' imprisonment but, on appeal, his conviction for conspiracy was quashed and he received five years as a receiver. Later he changed his name and remarried, putting his past behind him. When he was killed in a road accident his new family was shattered to learn his real identity.

It was after the finding of the suitcase that things started to happen. A caravan owned by James White, one of the robbers, was discovered at Box Hill, Surrey, and on 20 August it was found to contain £30,000. From then on arrest followed arrest. Goody, Hussey, Wisbey, one after another Butler had them. He never let up even after the main body of the team had been charged and convicted. His campaign to trace Charlie Wilson after his escape from Winson Green Prison in Birmingham, his persistent dogging of Buster Edwards until the man lost his nerve and surrendered, and his patient tracking of the leader Bruce Reynolds have all been well documented. The accounts bear testimony to Butler's determination. This obsession persisted until the day of his retirement which, at one time, he postponed.

These men were professional criminals of the highest quality who set out on an enterprise they were convinced would be successful. But even had they known before they started out they would be nicked, Read still thinks they would have done it – just to say they pulled the biggest caper of all.

Ronnie Biggs, Charlie Wilson, Tommy Wisbey, Bob Welch, Jim Hussey, Roy James and Gordon Goody each received thirty-year sentences. Lennie and Brian Field received twenty-five years. Cordery received twenty years and Boal, who in reality was probably little more than a receiver, twenty-four years. Wheater, the solicitor who employed Brian Field and who had partly provided an alibi, was given three years. Some sentences were subsequently reduced on appeal. Arrested later, Reynolds received 25 years.

The police investigation of the train robbery was an outstanding success so far as arrests and convictions were concerned. The failure was to recover no more than a fraction of the money stolen. Of the total of around £2.6 million taken from the train only some £400,000 was recovered. There have been a number of suggestions, apart from the mastermind theory, as to where the money went. First there are always other expenses. If someone puts up some money for finance they are in for a share; if someone provides a lorry or a car or welding equipment, then so are they. Escapes from prison are expensive and so is living in the underworld when your face is on a wanted poster. The members of the gang were blackmailed and ripped off for hundreds of thousands of pounds by their friends in the criminal fraternity.[17] Buster Edwards, Roy James, Jim Hussey, Jimmy White, Ronnie Biggs and Gordon Goody all suffered in this way. Piers Paul Read has analysed the lost money. Hussey lost £110,000 in bad investments; Goody – stolen by a minder – £40,000; Welch – appropriated by a minder – £100,000; James – appropriated by minder – £74,500; White – stolen by minder – £10,000; Edwards – expenses in escape, living and lost money – £140,000.

It was another couple of years before the robbery circuit really spread, and when it did it was for two reasons. The first was the growth of the motorway network and the second was the implementation of the Mountbatten report on prison escapes which had recommended that criminals be dispersed around the prisons in the country rather than being kept with their friends in the same prison near their homes. Now villains from, say, Manchester were put in a Liverpool prison and villains from Liverpool moved down south. As a result there was a wide pool of information to be shared and shared it was. Says one criminal:

[17] See Piers Paul Read's *The Train Robbers*, appendix.

We went to Glasgow to do a job. There was a lad from Wakefield, a guy from Birmingham, me from London and a lad from Devon. When we arrived on the plot there was the happy bag. We went to the scene and fuck all happens. We were all doing speed. We drop the guns in an artificial lake. If they ever drain it they'll find enough to start a small war, and it took us three days to come south. Every town which had a Marks and Spencers we turned over.

'Of course it was a London-based job,' says a Stoke-on-Trent police officer, referring to a major robbery of the time. 'We went round to see the only man remotely capable of putting it together almost as a matter of courtesy and he was flattered we'd been to see him.'

A man eventually put on an identification parade for that Stoke-on-Trent job and not picked out was Derek Creighton Smalls, known to both his friends and the police as Bertie. It was he who led the major London criminal robbery team of the late sixties; certainly it became the most celebrated one. He was also the first person in modern times to become what was to be called a 'supergrass'.

There were of course many, many other robbery teams, including that of John McVicar, who in February 1967 received a sentence of fifteen years for a South London armed robbery which went wrong and in which shots were fired at the police. Eventually the team was trapped and one of the members, Billy Gentry, from a North London family, tried to fire at a police officer at point-blank range. The gun was empty. Gentry received a sentence of seventeen years. McVicar later escaped from Durham Prison and hid out for several years before his recapture. Back in prison, he read for an arts degree and on his release became a successful writer and broadcaster.

Not everyone was pleased with McVicar's reformation, nor had he been universally popular. Such unpopularity may well be mixed with a tinge of envy. 'He's a preacher now, a reformed character and goes on the telly.'[18]

In May 1967 a robbery went off at Bowling Green Lane, Clerkenwell, when £700,000-worth of gold was stolen. Four months later the famous ex-speedway rider, Francis Squire 'Split' Waterman, England's Test captain and twice runner-up for the world title, and his fiancee, Avril Priston, were arrested and remanded in custody at Lewes on 15 August 1967, accused of gold smuggling. Their arrest began a tale of gold, arms and illegal immigrant smuggling. On 14 August a Triumph Herald car driven by Miss Priston accompanied by Waterman had arrived at Newhaven docks for the 7.30 a.m. ferry to Dieppe. When it was searched, three woollen stockings containing twenty-six gold ingots were found concealed in the chassis. The plate over the entry was cut from a sheet of metal. This had been positioned and covered in such a way that it was very nearly invisible.

Waterman, who had taken up arms dealing in Belgium and Biafra after his retirement from the track, said in a statement he was taking the bars to the George V hotel in Paris where the car would be taken from him. 'I was approached by some men I didn't know at the Mayfair Hotel in London. They offered me £100 to borrow a car before I went abroad and I was to let them have it back again after I got to Paris.'

But it turned out that Waterman was making his fifth trip abroad and Detective Sergeant Algy Hemingway asked: 'Have you been selling arms abroad?'

'No,' was the reply. 'But I know that a lot of money

---

[18] Royston James Smith in G. Tremlett, *Little Legs*, p. 39.

can be made if guns can be smuggled from the Continent to Biafra.' According to Hemingway, Waterman also hinted he had been involved with illegal immigrants.

The same day two men, Michael Kenrick[19] and Ivor Bloom, were stopped at Victoria Station on their way to Dover. Kenrick and Bloom were charged with attempted illegal export of forty-five gold bars worth £10,000 and with receiving the bars knowing they were stolen. Bloom had been found wearing a corset containing the bars and at Waterman's address at 149 Elm Road, New Malden, Surrey, fabric scraps had been found in a sewing machine. One of seven children, the attractive, fair-haired Avril was a dressmaker and had been chosen to make the corsets used to smuggle the gold.

Now attention switched to a 150-acre Bedfordshire farm at Manor House, Bourne End, Cranfield, owned by Avril's father, where the police believed a fortune in gold might be hidden. They were unlucky in that respect but what they did find was a box of arms, four rifles, a sub-machine gun and a gas pistol, as well as a large amount of ammunition. Parked on the estate was a van containing a Gallenkamp electric furnace with traces of gold in it. It had been bought by Waterman fourteen days after the robbery. Waterman's 'non-trade' personal enquiry soon after the robbery to a firm that made high-temperature furnaces had alerted customs officers, who had kept observation on the pair.

Another arsenal including two machine guns, two rifles and pistols had been found under Avril's bed.

---

[19] Kenrick received a term of imprisonment and whilst serving it was charged with obtaining money by false pretences in the Kray case. He could not face a further term of imprisonment and hanged himself in his cell. Ironically, because of the heavy sentences handed out to the principals in the Kray trials, it was decided not to proceed against the lesser fry.

Waterman admitted receiving the gold but denied it came from the robbery. He had at the time been hard up and, it was accepted, he had been used by the gang rather than being a member of it. It was estimated he had made less than £1000 from his part in the enterprise.

'I cannot express how I feel about this, of what I have done to Miss Priston, to my family and her. I can only plead most earnestly for leniency for Avril and I am sorry for the trouble I have caused,' he told the Court.

'You were a man who was, by character, prepared to face danger and take risks – a gun-runner in Africa and a man with the quick decisive mind of a speedway rider,' said Carl Aarvold, the Recorder of London, sentencing Waterman to four years' imprisonment. Avril Priston received a six-month sentence which meant her almost immediate release.

After his release Waterman married Avril Priston on 15 September 1970. He was later reported to have business interests in tin and copper mines in Guyana. But it was the activities of the 'gang', none of whom was caught, which attracted the attention of the press and public. There were tales of dealing in diamonds, trafficking in arms to rebel organizations in African countries and smuggling immigrants into the country through the Romney marshes.

Scores of Indians and Pakistanis had been picked up at obscure French ports and landed on beaches in Kent and Sussex. Their relatives had paid £100 in gold for the journey. The bullion was then shipped back to France and on to Switzerland. The trade did so well that an approach had been made to a south coast company to rent an additional boat, the *Sea Rod*, for £20 a week on the basis of a sea-bed survey. It was estimated that a successful trip could net the smugglers between £6000 and £10,000 depending on how loaded the boat had been.

The next the owners knew was a letter from the British consulate office in Boulogne saying the *Sea Rod* had sunk in the harbour there after a fishing smack had salvaged it during a storm off the west coast of France. Four Pakistanis had been on board and had been landed in France but it was not known what had happened to them. Doubtless for many of their compatriots it was a miserable journey which may not have ended so fortunately.

These people, mostly illiterate and ignorant of conditions in the West, are often left shivering with cold and terrified of what awaits them. But, almost without exception, their 'fare' for the trip cost them more than a first-class air ticket. In a sense, those who finish up on the deserted beaches are the lucky ones. Many of their fellow countrymen who attempt the cross-Channel journey, police feel, are deliberately drowned by boat owners who 'pull the plug' in panic when they suspect they are being tailed by Customs or immigration men at sea.[20]

The immigrant smuggling racket has continued intermittently into the 1990s. Early in 1992 immigrants were found on the Kent and Sussex beaches apparently having been abandoned by their importers. When on 13 December 1991 Detective Constable Jim Morrison was stabbed to death whilst chasing a thief in Covent Garden, police enquiries included the interviewing of some three hundred suspects, half of whom were illegal immigrants and many of them Algerian. The first stage of their journey is to travel to Barcelona where false identity papers can be obtained for as little as £30. They are then able to fly to Heathrow where document

[20] C. Borrell and B. Cashinella, *Crime in Britain Today*, p. 120.

inspection of their papers may only be cursory.

On 9 February 1970 the biggest daylight raid on a bank took place when a team of eight or nine men attacked a Security Express van while it was making a stop at Barclays Bank, Ilford, Essex. Their gain had been £237,000.[21] A year later in March 1971 the biggest cash haul since the Great Train Robbery had been grabbed when another Security Express vehicle was ambushed and attacked at Purley, South London. The four guards had stopped to relieve themselves in a lay-by. Twenty-eight bags of banknotes with a value of £456,000 were taken in what was known as the Spend a Penny Robbery.

Then on 2 May 1972 a robbery took place which had reverberations throughout the underworld and which harked back to the Krays. A security van containing twenty tons of silver bullion worth £400,000 was hijacked at Mountnessing, Essex. Although it was a high-class attack it was not so much the robbery itself – though that was still a decent amount of loot for a day's work – as

---

[21] One of the men convicted for his part was Arthur John Saunders. The evidence against him consisted wholly of verbal admissions made to Commander Wickstead. Asked if he was on the robbery he had replied, 'There's no point in saying no, is there?' He put up an alibi defence but his witness let him down. His appeal was dismissed in December 1971 but later Bertie Smalls, the supergrass, said in one of his statements that Saunders had not been on the raid. This presented the authorities with a dilemma. How could Smalls be put forward as truthful in one instance and not in another? The Court of Appeal quashed the conviction, pointing out that Saunders had been drinking when he made the admissions. It ordered £1500 taken from him to be refunded. Saunders was later awarded a substantial amount of compensation for his wrongful imprisonment.

In 1985 Saunders was again arrested for armed robbery. He had led a middle-aged team lying in wait for a security van in Baker Street. This time he received fifteen years' imprisonment.

one of the participants that created the interest because, six months later, George Ince was to be charged with the murder of Muriel Patience, the wife of Bob, owner of the Barn restaurant in Braintree, Essex. And as a second prize for criminologists, George Brett, the brother of John, one of the others charged in the robbery case, was to disappear in very worrying circumstances.[22]

The robbery was a straightforward heist of an MAT lorry which always took the same route and was therefore a perfectly good target. The robbers, armed with a gun and iron bars, attacked the van when they blocked it on a round-about on the A12. Two of the security men were bound, put in a van and taken some two and a half miles to a farm. The police had been targetting one of the men involved and on his arrest he made a statement naming names.

So far as the murder was concerned, both Ince and John Brett were picked out by the Patience family on an identification parade as two gunmen who went to the Barn restaurant in the early hours of 5 November 1972, forced their way in and, when Bob Patience refused to hand over the keys to the safe, shot him, his wife and daughter Beverley in quick succession. Muriel died later in hospital. Brett was never charged. Ince was.

The trial for the murder took place at Chelmsford Crown Court in May 1973. It was presided over by Mr Justice Melford Stevenson, the judge who had tried the Kray twins in their first trial for the murder of Cornell and McVitie, and who was not noted for his sympathy towards defendants.[23] Ince was defended by Victor Durand, who frequently clashed with the judge. Ince continually protested his innocence and was sent down to the cells whilst Beverley Patience gave her evidence that she identified him as one of the attackers. It was

22 See Chapter 13.

23 For footnote, see over.

Gangland

after this that Ince, who had already made an abortive
application to change the judge and who, during the
trial, had had a telegram sent to the Lord Chancellor
asking for Stevenson to be removed, sacked Durand
and his junior, Robert Flach. Now he was on his own.
Both his barristers remained in court, taking no
further part, while Ince stayed in the dock with his
back to the court, interrupting the occasional prosecution witness. He offered no defence until he asked
whether he could be allowed to take the truth drug.
Stevenson said no, 'but would he like his defence
counsel reinstated? Ince replied that he would not and
said once more that the judge was both biased and
rude. After a retirement of six hours, at 9.30 p.m.,
before a tense court, the jury returned to say they had
failed to agree on a verdict.

Within the week Ince was on trial again. This time
before a much more sympathetic judge, Mr Justice
Eveleigh. Durand and Flach were reinstated and this
time Durand called a crucial witness, a Dolly Gray. Ince
had apparently been unwilling for her to appear. He had
thought that when her real name was given, it would act
against him and also that she would suffer reprisals.
Mrs 'Gray' had bravely gone to see her husband,
Charlie Kray, in Maidstone Prison before she testified.
It seems that he did not know she had been seeing Ince
before she told him and this 'Dear John' was a shattering
blow to a man serving a ten-year sentence. To his great
credit, however, he did not attempt to prevent her giving
evidence to the effect that on the night of the murder
she had been in bed with Ince. Reggie Kray, however,

[23] He once sentenced a nineteen-year-old youth to Borstal on his first
offence, saying he hoped 'no soft-hearted official will recommend your
early release'. He had also earlier appeared for Ruth Ellis when he
indicated to the court he could really offer no defence to the charge of
murder.

says he had known of the affair for some time. Unsurprisingly he was not supportive of Ince.

> George Ince . . . was always a slag to me, even though he used to frequent our billiard hall in the late fifties. It was I who first tumbled that he was going with Charlie's wife, so I got hold of him outside the Double R Club and butted him in the face. Ron and I then warned him off the manor of the East End and he made sure he stayed away.[24]

On 23 May the jury retired for over three hours before they acquitted Ince, to wild cheers from the public gallery. Three weeks later a northerner, John Brook, was found in possession of the murder weapon and was later convicted of the murder of Muriel Patience.[25]

Ince, together with John Brett, was convicted of the Mountnessing silver bullion robbery and each received fifteen years' imprisonment. Ince had a hard time in prison. He was made a Category A prisoner and while watching a football match at the maximum security gaol, Long Lartin, he was attacked with a knife by another inmate, Harry Johnson, who was serving eighteen years. True to the Samurai code, when Ince appeared as a witness at the Evesham Magistrates' Court and was asked to identify his assailant, he replied, 'I wouldn't like to take a chance on identifying anyone. You know what I think of identification parades.' Nevertheless Johnson received a further three years for the attack.

A year after the George Ince case came the trial of George Davis, the repercussions of which would set the

[24] R. Kray, *Born Fighter*, p. 58.
[25] The Barn murder case was one of a number of similar cases of mistaken identity which led the Court of Appeal to formulate guidelines on the dangers of identification evidence.

tone of protests for the next twenty years. A robbery was
carried out on the London Electricity Board in Ley
Street, Ilford. A PC Groves who was in the vicinity quite
by chance ran to tackle the robbers and was shot in the
leg for his pains. While he was on the ground another of
the team stood over him threatening to shoot him again.
Groves' colleague was in the police car alerting patrol
vehicles in the area and a series of chases took place. At
one time the robbers were cornered by the unarmed
police, who were forced to back off as they were
threatened with guns. One of the officers involved was
Dave Brady, the driver of a Q car from North London
who, with his colleagues, had ventured into East London
territory to execute a search warrant for some stolen
whisky.

As we were coming to a T junction a battered Ford
crossed us and I could see there were four men in
the car, three of them in crash helmets. This
aroused a modicum of suspicion and then a marked
police car cut in so we were third in line. Then we
heard on the radio that there had been an armed
robbery at the Electricity Board.

We all became blocked in traffic and the driver
of the Ford swung right across two lanes and
then the men bailed out. I ran across towards them
and a fellow in a crash helmet poked a revolver up
my nostril. Then another came round and they
made us kneel down. I had no chance to identify
the men in the crash helmets but I looked at the
fat fellow who was the fourth man and I said to
myself, 'I'll know that sod if I see him again.' I'd
done twelve years in the commandos and a few
months earlier I'd been shot in the aftermath of a
bank raid so though I was frightened I'd had ample
experience.

Another car was hijacked and eventually the robbers escaped.

A name in the frame was George Davis, an East End soldier, no great leader but thought of in the hierarchy as reliable. He had recently been acquitted along with Tommy Hole on a charge of robbery of three lorry-loads of whisky. The evidence had been based on that of one of the newest supergrasses, Charlie Lowe, who admitted attacks on the public with hammers, coshes, ammonia sprays, pistols and sawn-off shotguns, and to having made about £100,000 from crime in the previous four years. When questioned in the case about a conspiracy to cash stolen cheques, Lowe piteously replied, 'Coshing people and robbing them is more my game, sir, not cheques.'

Davis was first seen by the police twenty days after the robbery, when he was arrested and gave an alibi that he had been driving a mini-cab. The books of the firm were gone through and one of his passengers was interviewed. Eight days later the same thing happened but this time the log books were taken away by the police.

He was identified by three officers, including Brady, who had seen some of the gang leap out on to the central reservation at Woodford Avenue. Three months after the robbery a second set of identification parades was held at Brixton Prison. Davis was picked out by two police officers, Appleton and Grove, but another thirty-four people failed to pick him out and three made wrong identifications, two after he had changed his purple shirt with another man on the parade.

However, the jury did not accept his alibi and Davis was convicted in March 1975. He was sentenced to a total of twenty years' imprisonment, reduced on appeal to seventeen. Two others, including Tommy Hole, were acquitted and the jury failed to agree in the case of

Michael Ishmael.[26] An enormous campaign began on Davis' behalf. There were allegations that he had been fitted up and on his conviction his supporters mounted protest marches, demonstrations, and the chalking and papering of most of East London with the slogan 'George Davis is innocent – OK'. In one incident the cricket pitch at Headingley was dug up during a test match. Brady says:

> It was funny the DI in the case had been replaced with a DS and then one day I got a phone call from a copper friend saying, 'I wouldn't fucking go near the East End. Your name's absolute shit because the hierarchy is convinced you've stitched him up.' What hurt me after that was that the coppers came up to me and said they believed it as well. No one believed me. They all believed I'd fucked him up.
>
> The next thing I knew I was out on patrol and I was told someone was here to see me. It was a DCI from Hertfordshire saying he was investigating an allegation of perjury and stitch-up. Now this was

[26] Ishmael was not having a great deal of luck at the time. Shortly before the Bank of Cyprus raid his former lover had run him down in Commercial Road, Stepney, following a row. Unfortunately she also hit a bystander. As Judge Edward Sutcliffe QC pointed out when sentencing Brenda Orsler to two years' imprisonment, 'This was a really dreadful case of using a car as a weapon and injuring not only your man friend but also a nun.' Sister Joan West of the Convent of Mercy, Stepney, had a fractured leg and a cut on her head which required twenty stitches. Ishmael, who sustained injuries to his left knee and arm, but who recovered sufficiently to take his part in the Bank of Cyprus raid, was another to observe the Samurai code. He had been about to leave the pregnant Mrs Orsler at the time and wrote to the judge trying to exculpate his former girlfriend. He had, he said, taken terrible liberties with her and for that reason she would have been so upset she would not have known what she was doing.

the first time I'd been involved in an allegation like
this and what surprised me was there was no old
boy network. I was with them for three hours and
I was giving a right tousing. I was accused of being
as bent as arseholes and this made me even more
angry than when it started.

Then after a bit I started getting iffy calls at
home. 'You stitching bastard, watch your back,'
and things like that.

Then I thought I was being followed but I didn't
know if it was by villains or by the investigation
branch so I got in touch with the DCI in Hertfordshire and told him I was getting iffy calls. Two days
later he came back to me and said, 'It's nothing to
do with them but it won't happen anymore.' I still
don't know who the calls had come from.

Just as Rosie Davis was fantastically loyal to
George so my missus stuck by me, but most people
were sure he'd been stitched up. All I'd done is
made what I thought was a correct ID. After all I
was just a uniform copper from another division.
I'd got nothing to do with it really.

The 'George Davis is Innocent – OK' campaign was
successful. On Tuesday, 11 May 1976, he was released
by the Home Secretary in a blaze of publicity after the
publication of the Devlin report on the dangers of
convicting on identification evidence alone. It appears
an additional alibi witness had also come forward. Davis
travelled back from the Isle of Wight with Charlie Kray,
whom he had met on the ferry; Charlie had been visiting
one of the twins. 'That is my last brush with the law,
never again – never,' Davis told the *Daily Mirror*.

Unfortunately the rejoicing was short-lived. He
seriously blotted his copybook as folk hero when, on 23
September 1977 along with Micky Ishmael, he was

captured *in flagrante* during a raid on the Bank of Cyprus in the Seven Sisters Road, Holloway. This time the police were armed. One of the robbers grabbed an eighty-two-year-old man as a shield as the officers approached. Another passer-by, Mr Albert Carney, grabbed the robber from behind, forcing him to release his hostage.[27] The gang received sentences of up to sixteen years and a number of policemen wrote in their memoirs of the naivety of Davis' former supporters.[28]

Dave Brady's colleagues made sure he wasn't involved this time:

> I got a phone call from a bloke at Holloway saying it was a good idea if I didn't go out on the Q car that day. He said he couldn't tell me why but not to go out. A bit later he rang back and said 'cancel that' and that he would let me know what it was all about. Then I got another call and so I stayed in the nick. Sure enough I got a call to say there'd been a blagging [armed robbery] and Davis had been nicked. They just didn't want there to be any chance I was in the vicinity when it went off.
>
> I don't know if it's true but the story goes that he got away and into a van and a copper poked a pistol through the window. 'I'm only doing a bit of shopping,' George said. 'Well take your balaclava off then,' said the copper.

From the police point of view this was a major success, but the cream turned slightly sour. The next day when the *Daily Express* published a picture of a robber standing outside the bank with a shotgun, it was apparent from the angle that it had been taken from the police control room

[27] He later received the Queen's Commendation for gallantry.
[28] Including G. Kelland, *Crime in London*, p. 205.

from which the bank was being staked out. A Detective Sergeant was suspended. He said he had taken the photograph and passed it to the *Express* because he thought it would be good for the image of the force. He resigned before disciplinary proceedings could be brought.

Davis' sentence in the Bank of Cyprus case was reduced to one of eleven years on appeal. But that was not his last brush with the law. On 21 January 1987 he received another sentence, this time of eighteen months with nine of them suspended, following a raid on the London to Brighton mail train in March 1986. Police guarding postbags on the train tried to enter the mail-van and found Davis blocking the door. He pleaded guilty to attempted theft, while his partner, John Gravell, was sentenced to ten years on his conviction on five charges of theft, attempted wounding and assault.

So far as Brady was concerned the Electricity Board robbery never went away. Years later he was seconded to a police driving school in Norfolk when he heard a young CID officer recounting his time on a course in London and reminiscing about Davis. 'He was bang to rights on the Bank of Cyprus but he was stitched up on the first fucker,' he said. 'I think I became a better officer because of the case,' says Brady.

The decade ended well for the police with the capture and conviction of one of the most successful robbers, Billy Tobin. He was taken in November 1980 when about to rob a security van carrying £1 million in Alleyn Park, Dulwich. The van was to be rammed with the jib of a mobile crane, the driver of which had been kidnapped and tied up in a van. Tobin, on bail at the time for two other armed robberies, was watched by the police following a tip-off. He and another man were shot at by a Detective Sergeant as they approached him moving their hands towards their pockets.

After a re-trial Tobin received a total of sixteen years'

imprisonment. Convicted with him was a member of the team who would himself be executed a decade later, Ronnie Cook. But the police cannot have been wholly satisfied with the outcome of the Tobin case. They had known in advance that he would be on the raid but they had not known the identities of the others. They were not pleased to find that two of the gang came from East London. Now, instead of the polarization which had existed over the years between North and South London firms, it appeared the Thames was being forded.

9

Supergrasses

The early 1970s introduced a new word – supergrass – into the English language.[1] It also gave a new phrase to criminal slang – to do a Bertie, or inform to the police.

Grassing is perhaps the principal method by which the police obtain information which will lead either to the prevention of a crime, or to the arrest of the villains and recovery of stolen property. Any good detective keeps a small, or sometimes large, string of informers who may be active thieves themselves or who may simply hang about on the fringes of the underworld. In the past they were paid out of a police information fund or sometimes out of the pocket of the officer who ran them. It was regarded as a good investment towards promotion. Sometimes in the case of a drug bust the informer was given a part of the bust itself as his reward. Sometimes an informer had a licence to commit crimes, short of violence, in a particular area. Sometimes all three.

One singularly corrupt Flying Squad officer of the 1960s, Alec Eist, is described in admiring terms by a former colleague: 'He was the best informed police officer in London. What he took off one criminal he gave

---

[1] The origin of the term is in doubt. It might come from rhyming slang, grasshopper–copper.

back to another. If he got £200 from a villain for giving him bail, Eist would give £195 to cultivate an informant.'[2]

And another says of the practice: 'You find three pounds of heroin and put only one on the charge sheet. The villains are pleased; less they're found with means less bird, and you give the other two to the informant. The job won't pay the informant so the only way is you give it back.'

The grass could also expect help from his runner if he was arrested. This might well take the form of an intercession to prevent a charge being preferred.

But grassing changed gear on to a wholly different level with the arrest in 1970 of Derek Creighton Smalls. It became the era of the supergrass, the criminal who, to dig himself out of trouble, would inform not just on his colleagues on a particular job but on his associates and their efforts going back years and years. In turn he could expect to receive a minimal sentence compared with that handed out to his former friends. He could also expect, through a nominee, a share of the insurance rewards.[3]

In the late 1960s and early 1970s Bertie Smalls led a highly successful team of armed robbers in a series of attacks on banks, mainly in North and North-West London but on occasions as far afield as Lloyds Bank in

[2] Eist, a florid, handsome, black-haired man, was acquitted in one of the trials of police officers and solicitors in the 1970s. Later he had a dress shop. 'It did no good. He was always having fires and burglaries – it was an embarrassment.' Later he owned a public house near Newmarket. He died of a heart attack.

[3] Although Bertie Smalls was undoubtedly the first of the modern supergrasses, in 1706 John Smith, a convicted housebreaker known as Half Hanged Smith because he had survived an attempt to hang him, was pardoned after he had accused about 350 pickpockets and housebreakers. He may well have been the original supergrass.

Bournemouth. Each time the operational method was almost identical. The robbers wore balaclavas, possibly with a nylon stocking underneath, and masks. The raids were in banking hours. A ladder was used to get over the security grilles put up in the 1960s but not yet made ceiling to counter, and a sledge-hammer was used to smash them. A shotgun would be fired into the ceiling to concentrate the minds of staff and any customers there might be in the bank. There would be one or two getaway cars waiting. The haul was usually substantial.

Smalls' name was in the frame. He had been wanted for the Bournemouth Lloyds Bank job in September 1970 and his wife, Diane, had been arrested along with others, including a Donald Barrett who had made a confession naming names. At the trial at Winchester Crown Court, Barrett pleaded guilty. His reward was a sentence of twelve years and a card posted from Spain from the others, who had all been acquitted, reading 'Wish you were here'.

Smalls had also been identified from a photograph in the Rogues Gallery at Scotland Yard as being involved in the National Westminster raid at Palmers Green in May 1972. The number plate of a Jaguar car which had been used in a trial run had been noted by an off-duty police officer. It was traced back to a garage at Tower Bridge in which Smalls was known to have an interest. That was certainly not sufficient to bring a charge. After a robbery at Barclays Bank on Wembley High Road in August 1972, which had netted over £138,000 in old notes, a special unit was formed by the police under the direction of Jim Marshall. It would eventually become the nucleus of the Robbery Squad.

The team began to accumulate snippets of evidence against Smalls. A woman clerk picked out his photograph as being involved at a robbery amassing £296,000 at Ralli Brothers in Hatton Garden in March 1969. Now the Bournemouth robbery was cross-checked even though he had never been arrested for it. Indeed at one time the Hampshire police had thought he had done away with the principal witness, Stella Robinson, the Smalls' au pair. Only the production of her to the police in London after the acquittal of Diane Smalls and the others had prevented a murder enquiry.

Three days before Christmas 1972 Inspector Victor Wilding went to see Smalls at his home in Selsdon. They now had sufficient evidence to justify an arrest. The only person there was Stella Robinson, who allowed them to look around and who, when pressed, told them Smalls was spending Christmas near Northampton. She did not know the address but she could show them. At 5.30 a.m. the police grouped outside the house and DCI Brewster of the Regional Crime Squad knocked on the door. Smalls in his underpants opened it and the police rushed forward, knocking Brewster over in the rush. Smalls said he had opened the door to let the cat in. It had a trick of scratching to gain admission. Diane Smalls commented, 'You let the rats in, not the cat.'

The arrest was totally unexpected. Members of the gang had paid £5000 each to a 'bent copper' to get an early warning of any arrest. Bertie had not paid his whack. Whether there was such a police officer able to obtain information is doubtful. It may have been a double scam to lure the robbers into a false sense of security.

Smalls was arrested for the Wembley bank robbery and was taken from Northampton to Wembley where he was questioned. On the journey he had made a tentative suggestion about doing a deal but when formally questioned he had said nothing. He was remanded in custody by Harrow Magistrates' Court for committal papers to be prepared. It was when the papers were served on the defence that Peter Donnelly, the solicitor's managing clerk who had acted for Smalls over the years, noticed a reference in them to 'outers'. Smalls would, so the statement of a police officer read, give names if he had 'outers'.

I went to see him in Brixton and asked, 'Did you say it?' He's hedgy. 'I've got to have guarantees,' he said. I went to see either Marshall or Wilding and asked if it was a serious proposition. 'Yes,' was the reply, 'but we don't believe he'll do it.' 'If he does what will you give us?' I asked, and it's then they start thinking it's possible. I went back to Smalls and said, 'Go and sit tight, keep your trap shut.' Then I got word they were interested.

I went and saw him again and told him he's got to put his cards on the table. They wanted robberies, names and so on, but not unnaturally he was reluctant to go into details at this stage. Finally we got a skeleton of the jobs from him in areas.

Then I arranged a meeting with Marshall and Wilding at Wembley. I went up there with Peter Steggles, the senior partner. They've got a clipboard with a list of names and robberies I could see upside down.

I said that everything on the board they could have plus XYZ additional robberies. That seemed to take them off guard. From then we had the advantage. They were reluctant and thought it would be difficult to have anything in writing. Nothing in writing – no deal. They said they'd take instructions. It was then going to have to go to Deputy Commissioner or Commissioner level.

We then tell them that we will draft heads of agreement as to our conditions and the main concerns were, one, the immunity from prosecution and, two, the security. There was no question of a reduced sentence. Another term was that it had to be agreed on by the DPP. We had two more meetings before they agreed to write a letter which was the final document and was basically word for word our heads of agreement.

It was then lined up that on receipt of that letter Smalls was to be produced at Harrow Court. The Bench had been squared to grant him bail – that had been dealt with before we arrived – and he was bailed into police custody and we're taken down to Wembley. We sat down twelve to fourteen hours a day while he reminisced.

By this time I had spread the word I was going on holiday, but the day he appeared people were asking what was happening. Where was he? Where was I? The word was out. That's why I think the rest of the team had paid their money.

Diane Smalls was never happy with the whole business. Donnelly met her on Brixton Hill one afternoon when he had been to see Bertie in prison and explained things. She stood by Smalls but their relationship was effectively over at this time anyway.

By now Smalls had given so much detail – the statement ran to sixty-five pages and covered eleven other suspects and twenty crimes – the police were starting to look for corroboration.

They heaved in Stella Robinson, got a statement from her as to how various robbers, including Bertie, had descended on a flop and when they were playing around with one of the sawn-offs had mistakenly fired it into the floorboards. They managed to identify the address, took the carpet up and the damage was still there with the pellets. But they still needed Diane and I went to her and said, if you don't do it the deal won't be accepted, because we didn't know whether they'd say the evidence was sufficient. Very reluctantly she made the statement, but she then refused to take the oath at court.

One of the final conditions was that if Smalls' statement wasn't used and he was not to be a witness and immunity given, then what amounted to a total confession would remain on police files and not be used against him at a trial.

But there was such a level of corruption at that time that sooner or later it would have got out and he'd have been dead.

During those three days Smalls stayed at Wembley with an armed guard. On the third day the police had to say yes or no. They said yes and Smalls was then produced at Harrow, granted formal bail and taken to a hotel by Wembley Stadium where he and his family were put in the suite in which David Cassidy had stayed the week before. It seemed to please him. Later he was moved out to a couple of addresses, being guarded by shifts of police officers. The only time Donnelly could see him was at an arranged point which he would be given half an hour beforehand. 'I'm sure there was a contract out. Publicity had it that it was £100,000 but I heard from Smalls' friend Jacky O'Connell that it was only £50,000.'

The sweep took place in the early hours of 6 April 1973 when over a hundred police officers rounded up twenty-seven of Smalls' former colleagues. Then the problem was whether Smalls, who was drinking heavily, would actually go through with things when it came to it.

The committal proceedings took place in a heavily guarded gymnasium in Wembley and Smalls appeared to give evidence minutes after his formal acquittal at the

Old Bailey. Jack Slipper, who had chased Train Robber Ronnie Biggs to Brazil and was now one of the senior officers in the case, recounts:

> He stood in the witness box, looking towards the magistrate, resting on his elbow. His eyes seemed dead and he almost mumbled his answers, so that a couple of times the magistrate had to ask him to speak up. I was really worried at that point that Bertie might be about to crack but, just in time, there was an incident which completely changed the picture.
>
> One of the prisoners was a Danny Allpress, a real comedian and a live wire, who had always run around with Smalls and had virtually been his assistant. Danny kept quiet at first then suddenly he leaned across the dock and said in a loud whisper, 'Well, Bertie, who's been having Slack Alice while you're away?' The remark got a lot of laughs from the prisoners, but Danny couldn't have made a more serious mistake. The remark brought Bertie to life. You could see the determination come into his eyes.[4]

Diane Smalls was not popular with the rest of the wives. Once because of friction she had left a holiday in Torremolinos early and had later chosen to spend her time in Tangier. But was the Slack Alice joke as crucial as Slipper believes? Says Donnelly:

> I don't think the Slack Alice joke enamoured them to him, but I don't think it was the end of the world. His attitude was that most of them when pulled in had tried to do exactly the same but he

[4] J. Slipper, *Slipper of the Yard*.

got in first. From that point of view he felt justified. There had also been some trouble earlier when he was on remand for possession of a firearm. He got out but he was skint and one of them was meant to have given Diane money to look after her. He hadn't and I think that annoyed him as well.

In July 1974 at the Central Criminal Court, Danny Allpress received a sentence of twenty-one years' imprisonment, reduced on appeal to eighteen years. Donald Barrett, who had already received twelve years for the Bournemouth job, received another seventeen years, reduced to twelve on appeal. Others had sentences of up to twenty-one years, reduced by the odd couple of years on their appeals.

One of them, Philip Morris, had been involved in a raid in February 1973 on the Unigate Dairies Depot in Ewell, Surrey. Morris had the job of standing guard over a young man, Frank Kidwell, who had just been named Milkman of the Year. The shotgun went off and Kidwell died. The raid netted £148,000. Morris pleaded guilty to Kidwell's manslaughter and received a seventeen-year sentence. For his part in the Wembley raid he received a concurrent sentence of twenty years, reduced by the Court of Appeal to twelve. His appeal against the seventeen-year sentence for manslaughter was dismissed.

The Court of Appeal was none too pleased with the Director of Public Prosecutions, Sir Norman Skelhorne, and his deal with Smalls. 'Above all else the spectacle of the Director recording in writing at the behest of a criminal like Smalls his undertaking to give immunity from further prosecution is one which we find distasteful. Nothing of a similar kind must happen again,' said Lord Justice Lawton.

After the trial Smalls had an armed guard for some

months, but eventually this was phased out and from then on the family lived more or less normally under another name. 'No one ever made threats to me,' says Smalls. 'Of course I didn't put myself about and if I went into a pub and saw someone who was a friend of the others I just left, but no, overall I had no trouble.'

Trouble or not he had set the tone for the 1970s. The opprobrium attached to most supergrasses never seems to have stuck to him. In a curious way he seems to have been regarded as an innovator.

John McVicar, talking about supergrasses in general and Smalls in particular, comments: 'Some of them are very strong people. Look at Bert. He was a good worker, although there was always something odd about him.'

What he did have was a sense of humour. After one bank raid in the Wood Green area a woman witness who was shopping in the High Road ran more or less slap-bang into the men escaping after the robbery. She had heard what she thought was a car backfiring but when three men wearing stocking masks rushed past her she knew exactly what had happened. She backed up against a wall and then started to walk to the end of the alleyway when a fourth man also wearing a mask loped towards her. Again she backed up but as he went past he stopped. 'What a way to earn a fucking living, eh girl?' said a sweating Smalls as he disappeared down the alleyway.

Smalls never did as well as he could have from his story. There was a short serialization in the newspapers, but a book he was planning never came to fruition due in part, perhaps, to both his and his ghost writer's current predilection for vodka.

The next in line to repeat, recant and recount all was a man who did publish his memoirs, designating himself King Squealer. Maurice O'Mahoney had been suspected

for the attack on a Securicor van at Heston in West London. The van had been rammed with a tipper truck but the take had been a disappointing £20,000. He had been the victim of a tip-off that the raid would take place. After his arrest and that of other members of the gang the whisper went around that O'Mahoney was going to squeal. Two members of the team threatened to gouge out his eyes if he talked. O'Mahoney says that this is in part true but he was also worried by the contract of £2000 put out on his girlfriend Sue and his children. He also says he discovered a cyanide capsule had been smuggled into Brixton and the plan was to put it in his tea.[5] According to Jack Slipper, in whose charge O'Mahoney was, this was the turning point. He asked to see a senior officer. In his turn O'Mahoney's evidence led to some two hundred convictions and from then on the floodgates were opened.

After the Court of Appeal's comments on the Smalls deal, supergrasses could not expect to walk free. What they could expect was a sentence of around five years – the supergrass tariff – instead of one of twenty, during which time they would be kept in police custody while they gave their evidence and, allowing for remission and parole, released immediately or very soon after they had completed it. They could expect reasonable accommodation visits from their wives and sometimes the opportunity to go out to the local pubs with the detectives guarding them. There would be reward money and a new identity at the end of their sentence. It is hardly surprising that there has been a steady queue of men – Charlie Lowe, Leroy Williams, Donald Barrett (twice), John McCabe (who claimed to have made £8 million in four years) and many, many more – willing to testify against their former colleagues.

[5] M. O'Mahoney, *King Squealer*, pp. 129–30.

But whatever successes Marshall and Slipper had had with Smalls and O'Mahoney it was nothing to the success which would come to a rising star in the Met, Tony Lundy. In May 1977 Detective Chief Inspector Tony Lundy rejoined the Flying Squad, soon to be reorganized in part as the Robbery Squad with its headquarters at Finchley. It was Lundy who developed the supergrass into a whole business of its own.

Within six months he had his first major success with David Smith, arrested for an attack in September 1977 on two elderly men who collected their company's wages near the Thatched Barn, a restaurant at Borehamwood in Hertfordshire. The money was snatched but then one of the team, Alf Berkley, tore off the glasses of one of the men and squirted ammonia in his eyes. The man was almost completely blinded.

Smith turned supergrass, confessing to over sixty armed robberies. He was kept at Finchley police station for over fifteen months, at the end of which, as a result of his efforts, sixty-nine people were charged, of whom ninety per cent pleaded guilty. Two of the other robbers in the Thatched Barn team were also allowed to become supergrasses. One of them, George Williams, who had been offered the supergrass deal before Smith had rolled over but had initially held out, also received five years for a total of eighty robberies.

His evidence was necessary because there was a small problem with Smith. He had actually killed a man and the DPP's policy was to require a plea of guilty to a murder – which carried a mandatory life sentence – and so he could not be considered a credible witness. Smith had coshed Kurt Hess, an elderly factory owner, during a robbery in Shoreditch. Hess had died three weeks later. However, Smith's luck was in. A statement was obtained from a pathologist which showed that Hess' poor health had contributed to his death. A charge of manslaughter was sufficient and so Smith could be reinstated as a prosecution witness.[6] Later the rules were relaxed and supergrasses who had pleaded guilty to murder were allowed to give evidence for the Crown, in one case with fairly disastrous results.

In fact George Williams' hands were none too clean either. In 1967 he and Smith had kidnapped the manager of a North London supermarket, Walter Price, to get the keys from his safe. The 16-stone Williams, known as 'Fat George', coshed Price, who died eight weeks later from heart failure. Price had staggered home with a lump on his head described by his widow as 'as big as an egg'. When she heard Williams had received the tariff five years she commented, 'That seems a very light sentence for murder.'[7] Judge Michael Argyle, his hands tied by public policy, commented that he considered Smith and Williams as 'two of the most dangerous criminals in British history', adding that whilst he accepted they were telling the truth 'it was nauseating to hear these hypocrites and that as a matter of policy they have only been sentenced to five years each'.

But Smith did not last long on the outside. Throughout his adult life he had been an unsuccessful career criminal and he only spent short periods out of prison. On 29 September 1986 he was caught in a raid on a Securicor vehicle in Golders Green along with another

[6] Smith was also reputed to have killed a bookmaker, Harry Barham, found shot in the back of the head in his car in Hackney; £40,000 had been stolen from him. There was no hard evidence against Smith and he was never charged. In fairness many a name was put up for the Barham killing including that of the ubiquitous Teddy Machin.
[7] For a detailed account of the successes and more importantly the failures of the supergrass system, see Andrew Jennings, Paul Lashmar and Vyv Simson, *Scotland Yard's Cocaine Connection*.

former supergrass, Ron Simpson. Smith again turned supergrass but this time he did not live long enough to testify. In a cell which had been hung with balloons for his birthday five days earlier, Smith cut his throat with a razor blade on Monday, 13 October. Simpson was gaoled for twenty-one years. Perhaps, when it came to it, Smith was the better off.

Recruit followed recruit through the Lundy supergrass factory, some thirty of them defended by Roland Pelly, a Bishop's Stortford solicitor who had been outside the mainstream of criminal defence practice. In fact he had been the DPP's agent in Hertfordshire in the early 1970s when the DPP used to send cases to local firms of solicitors.

One of Lundy's less successful supergrasses was Billy Amies who, dressed as a policeman, had threatened his victim in a robbery with castration and had the man's daughter stripped to her underwear, asking, 'How would you like to see your daughter raped?' Amies served only twenty-four months in prison, but although he had named fifty-eight criminals it seems he was responsible for the conviction of only five.

But in many ways, the seemingly prize catch was nothing to do with Lundy. This was Maxwell Thomas Piggott, who was to turn what the police thought would be the major supergrass and would give evidence against Ronnie Knight, considered by the police to be one of the top figures in London's underworld. Bradshaw, as Piggott became known, had a long and interesting criminal career. In September 1965 he was charged with housebreaking and in November of the same year with throwing acid at the police, for which he was sentenced to seven years' imprisonment. He escaped from Wormwood Scrubs in 1968. In 1969 he popped up in Brighton running a long firm fraud for which he received six years at Lewes Assizes. When on 17 January 1980 he pleaded guilty before Mr Justice Comyn to his part in the Zomparelli murder and numerous armed robberies, he was praised for his courage in naming 105 criminals in a long confession. He was gaoled for life. This was to be the start of a major breakthrough in the war against professional crime. However, when Knight and his co-defendant Nicky Gerard were acquitted of the Zomparelli murder, plans to use Bradshaw in other trials were quickly shelved and he was returned to prison. He served ten years for the murder before his release.[8]

On 24 March 1980 a robbery went off which surpassed the Great Train Robbers' caper. It was also one which would have the greatest repercussions on the credibility of Scotland Yard and, in particular, Tony Lundy. Three hundred and twenty-one silver ingots of bullion, worth £3.4 million, were stolen from a lorry on its way from London to Tilbury Docks, when a gang of bogus traffic officials together with a man wearing a police uniform flagged down the lorry and held up the crew at gunpoint.

The instigator of the enterprise was Michael Gervaise, six foot, a fluent linguist and a skilled burglar alarm engineer, described as a 'balding figure with the mild air of a retail tobacconist'; he was another who would become a supergrass. He had received eighteen months for his part in the 1975 Bank of America robbery but otherwise had no record worth speaking of. Together with an old friend, Micky Sewell, who had been given bail on a charge of armed robbery so that he too could act as an informant, Gervaise put together a team which included Lennie Gibson, Rudolpho Aguda and Aguda's nephew, Renalto 'Ron' Aguda. Ron's specialities included the ability to uncouple trailers from their tractor units at speed.

Gervaise had on his team a number of bent police

[8] See Chapter 12.

officers who were paid to overlook his activities. One, Terence Donovan, who later served a prison sentence, was employed as a 'security adviser' after his retirement from the force. His job was to advise Gervaise of suitable places to burgle. Another bribed by Gervaise was the notorious Alec Eist.

The lorry was stopped by Gervaise, flagging it down wearing his policeman's uniform – supplied by a sergeant in the Met to Billy Young, who had passed it and some other uniforms to Lennie Gibson – and directing it into a lay-by for a bogus traffic census. The guards were threatened that their kneecaps would be blown off if they did not co-operate and away went Gervaise and co with the silver to store it in a slaughter, a rented lock-up garage, near Oakwood tube station at the northern end of the Piccadilly line. Gibson and Aguda senior were the only ones to hold keys to it and they had them on them when arrested.

Sewell was on bail at the time for a £200,000 wages snatch and was being used as a snout by the then DCI Bill Peters, a large and flamboyant officer on the Flying Squad. His mission for Peters was to infiltrate another robbery team headed by Ronnie Johnson and his information led to the arrest of that team hours after they had shot a guard in a robbery at a bank in East Finchley.[9] One of the men soon accepted Lundy's offer to turn supergrass and he named Tony Fiori, an Islington thief, who graduated from grass to supergrass with some facility. In turn he named Gervaise.

It was only a matter of time before Gervaise joined the supergrass circuit. And it was only a matter of time before someone claimed the £300,000 reward being put

[9] Peters was one of the few police officers to sue for libel. On 24 July 1985 he was awarded £10,000 for false allegations of corruption by the *Observer* over the silver bullion robbery.

up by the insurers. The claimant would be Roy Garner, part-owner of a thoroughly disreputable night club, Eltons, which more or less backed on to Tottenham police station, and a man closely associated with Lundy as well as Gibson. He had turned down an approach to do the silver bullion job.

The important thing was the recovery of the silver. Gibson when arrested held out for some time as to its whereabouts until he had spoken with Aguda senior. Quite clearly there was much to be discussed because Gibson then had a two-hour private meeting with Lundy.

On the night of 4 June 1980 the police went to the lock-up at Oakwood, kicked in the door and recovered the silver – all but twelve bars worth £120,000. No one has ever been able to establish where they went to, but there again no one has ever seemed to worry too much about it. Nor has anyone ever satisfactorily explained why it was necessary to kick the door down. After all Aguda and Gibson had been arrested with their keys to the slaughter on them. Gibson and the Agudas received ten years each on pleas of guilty, rather more than the seven they had been half-promised. Micky Sewell had long disappeared – tipped off by a police officer – and Gervaise had his five years. 'Dave Granger', a pseudonym for Roy Garner, the close drinking companion of Lundy, received the £300,000 reward. Garner also submitted claims through Lundy for payment for information relating to a Brinks-Mat security van hold-up in Hampstead in December 1979 and a fraudulent insurance claim based on a faked armed robbery, the reward for which was £75,000. After much haggling Garner received £178,000. Over the years he is believed to have accumulated over £500,000 through rewards recommended by Lundy.

By then the supergrass system was becoming more and

more complicated. There seemed to be competing teams of supergrasses: those who gave evidence under Lundy's aegis and those, such as John Moriarty, who gave evidence against Lundy's friend Garner. Moriarty had twice been shot by rivals and had served periods of imprisonment. Now he decided to give evidence and to implicate Roy Garner.

'I never knew why he did it,' says Dave Brady. 'I was the officer called to the Favourite, the pub in Hornsey Rise where he'd been kneecapped. I asked what had happened and all he said was, "I fell down the fucking stairs, didn't I?"'

In the early 1970s Garner, together with a friend, Kenny Ross, had purchased premises in Upper Street, Islington, and then tried to evict the tenants. When this failed the premises were fired. Now Moriarty was prepared to name them in his statement as the organizers of the arson attacks.

Yet another series of supergrasses was being run from Reading by Number 5 Regional Crime Squad, under the name Operation Carter. In 1977 a security van at Hemel Hempstead in Hertfordshire had been taken for £34,000 and three years later a North London robber, Freddie Sinfield, was arrested. The name he put in the frame was Billy Young, Gervaise's police uniform supplier. And this time a supergrass was prepared to talk about corrupt police officers.[10]

Perhaps 1979 was the Year of the Supergrass. At least twenty leading villains had queued up to give evidence for the prosecution. According to Scotland Yard, serious crime had tumbled from an all-time high in 1977, when it had netted £166 million. James George Gallant had joined the list of supergrasses following the discovery of £1900, his share of a £4600 robbery, in a cornflakes

---

[10] See Chapter 10 for the continuation of this enthralling saga.

packet. He informed on twenty-one major criminals. Assistant Commissioner David 'Crazy Horse' Powis observed, 'London's criminal fraternity is experiencing its lowest ebb ever.'[11]

Another attraction for the supergrass was the attitude of the Home Secretary. In that year, using his 'prerogative of mercy', he cut the prison sentences of seventy-two informers for their 'assistance to the authorities'. Leroy Davies was a particular beneficiary. For his role as informant the Court of Appeal had cut his ten-year sentence to one of seven. The Home Secretary cut it further to four years, seven months and seven days, and released him on parole, after which he gave his life story to the *Daily Express* describing how he had 'repaid his debt to society'.

He disappeared in the 1980s after he had been acquitted of a robbery at the French Revolution public house in Putney. His brother Glanford, who pleaded guilty and implicated Leroy, received five years' imprisonment. It was alleged that Davies had escaped after firing one barrel of a sawn-off shotgun at the police. He had told the jury, which took only ninety minutes to acquit him, that he would never have participated in such an inefficient robbery. Judge Lawson was not so impressed. 'I have no doubt as to the true identity of that gunman,' he told the jury as he invited them to stay behind and listen to the confession of Glanford which had not been in evidence at the trial.

But were the supergrasses all that major? One criminal lawyer commented, perhaps a trifle sourly, 'We seem to be catching the big fish as informers but they in turn are only netting the minnows.'

In recent times supergrasses have not had it all their own way.

---

[11] *Daily Telegraph*, 29 November 1979.

Supergrass trials have fallen into disrepute and supergrasses aren't used quite as much. But what they did was present to your stock gangland criminal a real threat. Gangs haven't stayed together because of that risk. The risk of being supergrassed got very high about seven or eight years ago. Then jurors started to acquit because supergrasses were being offered immunity or extremely low sentences, money was being offered or facilities in custody, so they died off.[12]

More recently life has become more dangerous for supergrasses than in the days of Bertie Smalls. In April 1991 Dave Norris was shot dead in the driveway of his home at Belvedere, Kent. He was reputed to be a grass and, worse than that:

He used to set people up on jobs that he had done himself. He would carry out a warehouse job, tell somebody there was still stuff to be taken and then tip the police off.

The police won't say he's a grass because being bumped off is not a terrific advert for a career in grassing. He was on Rule 43 inside which tells its own story.[13]

---

[12] Michael Mansfield QC in D. Campbell, *That was Business, This is Personal*.

[13] Duncan Campbell, 'Gangland Britain', *Weekend Guardian*, 14–15 December 1991. Rule 43 is protected accommodation away from the mainstream of the prison and is used to house sex offenders and informers along with convicted police officers.

10

Helpers and Hinderers

The underworld cannot flourish without the active co-operation of those in the half-world which straddles crime and respectability. They are the people who, whilst they might not dream of committing a robbery themselves, will assist in covering up, helping obtain bail, standing surety, providing an alibi, giving succour to the relatives of the 'aways'. They are publicans, garage proprietors, scrap-metal dealers, owners of small businesses, betting shop owners, barristers, solicitors and their clerks and, above all, policemen. Sometimes the help is provided for friendship, sometimes for fear, sometimes for money, sometimes innocently, and often for a combination of reasons. Sometimes the helper is a criminal groupie who just does it for kicks.

Jimmy was a bloke who had shops all over London and one of them was a really good one. He used to drink with me and Lennie and then one day just says, 'Can I come with you on a job?' just like that. He was in his early thirties at the time, never done anything wrong at all. He got hooked. From that day he never went back to the shops. Now he's in his fifties doing fifteen years.

Bail has always been an essential requirement of the arrested person. Just as the prudent traveller will settle domestic affairs before going away on a holiday, so will the professional criminal. In essence there is no difference between a trip to the Isle of Wight by a holidaymaker or business person and one by the professional criminal, except that the latter's visit is likely to be of longer duration. It is only sensible that he should provide for his wife and children by doing another couple of jobs while on bail, arranging for their comfort and, if necessary, providing a beard[1] so that the wife will not be tempted to take up with another man during his absence.

On a Friday night we used to collect for the 'aways' in five or six pubs. We each had a book coded to show what people gave and when it was nice and busy we'd start collecting. People would put their hands in their pockets and give what they had. It might be a quid or two or, if they'd done well, a fiver or even a tenner. If they didn't they'd get a hard look and if that didn't do any good then, when they went to the toilet, we'd follow and give them a spanking. Then we'd go with a girl to see the wives and give them the wages. You never visit a woman on her own whilst the old man's away. It looks bad for her and a neighbour might get the wrong impression and say something out of turn.

Sureties would be publicans, garage owners, wives and mothers, anyone without recent convictions to whom the police could not reasonably object.

Sometimes the easy part was getting bail for the client. The most difficult part was to find a surety

[1] A paid escort, usually homosexual.

who was acceptable to the police. In the days before the advent of the Crown Prosecution Service in 1985, when the officer opposed bail himself, if bail was granted he would regard the provision of a surety as a sort of re-match and oppose those proffered on the slightest grounds. The only way round this was to put the surety before the magistrates and see if they were brave enough to overrule the officer's objections.

Although illegal, a sensible surety would require indemnification.

I stood for Harry in £10,000 and the day of the trial he goes back to Ireland. I'm there at the Bailey telling the judge that I'm now out of work and I'd seen him up to the night before so the judge only takes £3000 which I have to pay in a year. Harry's given me the £10,000 and has told me to keep what I'm not fined. He was a real gentleman.

Of course, outsiders as opposed to 'family' would not stand bail without a fee, particularly if they had been required to negotiate with the police in the first place. They were also required to try to eliminate or have watered down certain damaging pieces of evidence.

The first time I ever knew about the police being bent was in 1963 in Borehamwood. A mate and I were nicked in a stolen car with pickaxe handles. The copper comes into the cell and asks if I'm from Kentish Town and I say yes. Then he asks me if I know GB. I think he's on the pump [seeking information] but I still say yeah. That evening I get a visit from a friend who says, 'I've done the business'. And he had. It cost £300 to get six

months and it was good value. We pleaded to the
car and offensive weapons. It could have been a
conspiracy. In them days the police stood by their
word. They dropped evidence or you wound up
with a very small sentence.

Sometimes half the money would be paid in advance
but often it was unnecessary. 'If a publican or bookmaker could get the business done for £500 then I would
expect to pay £1000. In those days the police were
honest. If they agreed something they honoured it.'
There were professional straighteners including one
who owned greetings card shops and was said to have a
lock on a Commander at the Yard. But some could do
better than others.

Old Bill knows you've got a few quid and it's not
your time to go – they can save you for a better
day. They've got two or three of you so they can
afford to leave you out. A friend'll go to a known
man and he'll straighten it up. You get bail to show
good faith. How much? Depending on what you're
on and how much they know you've got in your
pocket. Can be anything. Likely you never see
them. They've got the SP[2] and they won't take
money unless they know you're not iffy.

Sometimes it went wrong. 'I only recall one case when
the cozzer went bent and that was when a West End
copper agreed to get my mate out of a drink driving for
£1000. It all went wrong but I think that was because my
friend was a spade and the copper didn't like spades.'
Sometimes it appeared to have gone all wrong but
hadn't. A solicitor relates:

[2] Literally starting price, but in this context knowledge.

I attended an identification parade at Brixton Prison in the late 1960s for two of my clients charged with bank robberies. The parade took hours with probably about twenty witnesses. Just at the end they were picked out by one person. I telephoned one of the wives to tell them what had happened and she just wailed down the telephone. 'They can't have been; we paid £6000 for that parade'.

Of course, for a variety of reasons criminals like to pretend they have the police in their pockets but I think she was telling the truth for two reasons. The first is that the person turned out to be a police constable who later made a statement saying that whilst he believed the two he had identified were the people he had seen, he could not be sure. The second was that I met one of the wives twenty years later and the first thing she said was, 'I haven't seen you since we paid all that money for the ID.'

On other occasions it was never quite clear whether the money had been well spent.

Just before a bail application in a very substantial jewellery robbery the defendant's wife came up to me and said, 'He's sweet as a nut. You can ask him anything you want.' But any question I asked got a wrong answer. Like: 'He's married with two children? and the reply came: 'I don't think he's married to the woman he's living with. I know the children are by a different father.' It took me half an hour to convince the bench to give the man bail. The client's wife ran up to the police officer afterwards and said, 'Thank you, you were wonderful.' Personally I thought I was the wonderful one. I thought she'd have been better giving her money to me. But then at the trial the officer got up and said the principal witness had gone to Switzerland. There was no point in having an adjournment because he had told him he wouldn't come back.

Negotiations took place in clubs like the Premier off Wardour Street where detectives, barristers, solicitors' clerks and the underworld mixed, or in public houses such as the Prince of Wales in Lant Street in the Borough once run by a member of the Foreman family. Peta Fordham wrote:

> At one end sit the bloods – a lot of failed boxers etc. who are gang strong-arm men. At the other sit the wives, chastely excluded from the conversation of their lords, and drinking port and lemon. This is where the dishonest police get their wages.
>
> The Prince of Wales is a well-known place to fix surrender bargains, as well as to pay over, so that the Flies[3] have legitimate grounds in being there. X and Y [senior police officers] are said to get their wages there through an informer called Z.

But the underworld accepts that in a relationship with the police they are the underdogs. They must expect a certain amount of harassment as part of the toleration of their activities. As one officer says:

> Now this family is a great example. The old man was a great rogue, in fact some of the most spectacular robberies in Kent were his doing, but he lived in abject squalor. There was a huge family.

---

[3] Police officers. Fly was a Victorian term for a police officer and also for a cadger or beggar. Peta Fordham had something of a sense of humour.

The wife was a prolific breeder and it seemed like there were kids from two to forty. Anyway one of the youngsters gets nicked for some shoplifting and we want to give him a caution. You've got to have a parent there and so I was sent to get the old man.

I go round in the car and at his gate is a fucking mongrel Alsatian standing like the Hound of the Baskervilles. I thought 'Fuck, he's going to bite me,' but I got to go in so I ease past him and he follows me up the path.

I go in, dog behind me, and the place stinks. My feet stick to the carpet, and they're burning bits of furniture in the grate and drinking tea out of jamjars.

So I say to Freddy, 'Look we've got the kid, come down the nick and get him.' And he's humming and hawing because he doesn't like nicks and he's pissed off the kid's got caught, when the Alsatian wanders over to the grate and drops three great turds on the fire. Freddy doesn't say a word. Doesn't give the dog a kick or nothing. Doesn't bat an eyelid.

Now, I'm choking and gagging with this dog shit cooking in the fire and eventually I get Freddy to agree that I go on back and he'll follow down in the van in five minutes.

So off I go, get in the motor and there's a rapping at the window and it's Freddy. I wind it down and say, 'What's up now?' and he says, 'Mr Smith, Mr Smith, you've forgotten your dog.'

And if the police could not or would not help, then there was always the possibility of a spot of jury-nobbling to ease passages; and the longer the trial went on the easier it was. Charlie Richardson describes his reaction to the jury in the Mr Smith's Club case:

We was in court and we heard all the names read out and we looked as they come in and you look at the people as the kind of people you can get into. If a man comes in from the East End you find a man who lives in the next road and you ask him what he is like. If they are nice people they go round and fucking see them for you, you understand what I mean. It's all right that way . . .[4]

The jury had been got at in many major trials, including the Heath Row robbery, before the police discovered that, despite the apparent cost in manpower, it was sensible to protect jurors. The jury was protected in the Kray case and has been in most of the major cases thereafter. Nevertheless it was left unprotected in the Dulwich robbery case of 1981, which went to a re-trial. In the first round it was discovered that no less than ten of the jurors lived on Tobin territory in the Greenwich–Bermondsey area and on the third day a juror told the judge her son knew one of the defendants. In the re-trial two members of the jury complained they had received threatening telephone calls but Tobin was still convicted. Now in major trials jurors are kept out of sight of the public gallery.

Even so, with a little ingenuity juries can be got at. For example, a solicitor can obtain names and addresses of jurors quite legitimately. After a re-trial John Reed and Peter Mitchell were jailed for twenty-two years each for a raid on a Brinks-Mat van near Brentwood in Essex – they had sealed off the road, smashed the van open with a hijacked crane and fired at the guards inside, escaping with £500,000.

At the first hearing, after a list of the jurors had quite properly been obtained, a second list came into the

[4] R. Parker, *Rough Justice*, p. 310.

hands of nobblers and they assigned a team to each member of the jury. The trial was halted when four jurors were seen in the same pub as relatives of the two defendants. The solicitor refuted suggestions made by the officer in the case that he had handed over the list for nobbling purposes. 'There had been widespread publicity about the robbery in Essex and we wanted to make sure that no one on the jury came from that area,' he said. He invited the officer to repeat the allegations made in court outside, where legal privilege against defamation does not run.[5] There appears to be no record he did so.

In the pre-PACE days, when access to legal representation was denied to suspects until the questioning had finished, solicitors instructed by major families were expected to have sufficient rapport with a senior officer to be able to get into a police station to provide succour and encouragement. A senior managing clerk says:

This was a murder and a very bad one – a security guard – and my junior clerk is sent down. He rings me at 4 p.m. and says, 'I'm at Leman Street; it's hot in the kitchen and they won't let me near the front door. Can you pop over and see what you can do?'

As I went in, there was a most disagreeable atmosphere and then the DCI walks in with his hat on the side of his head.

'Hello, Sam boy,' he says, 'what you doing here?' And when I explained he told the officers in the case to let my boy in. So then the DCI takes me up to his office and asks for two brandies. When an aide brings them he tells him to take them away and get a proper bottle. 'That's for visitors – bring my stuff,' he says and he pours and pours

[5] *Today*, 11 April 1987.

them out. I was emptying half mine into the rubber plant; it was shameful really. He was legless by the time we finished chatting.

But whilst the underworld is convinced that if things seem to be going badly in a trial the police are not above alleging jury interference even if none has occurred, then help can sometimes come from unexpected sources. According to the *News of the World*, an Acton Crown Court usher boasted he could help if a defendant needed to 'sort out a trial' and would provide jurors' names and addresses.[6] He certainly had the right connections. A relation was the man paid by Jack Spot to mind him when he fell out with Hill and who was out with his girlfriend the fateful night his employer was slashed.

Apart from the police, the occasional too-close involvement of solicitors or barristers in the crime has always been a source of concern. It is still used by some judges as an argument against allowing solicitors rights of audience in the Crown Court.

The first and certainly the most infamous case in modern, or at least Victorian times was that of a fashionable barrister, James Townsend Saward, known in the underworld as Jem the Penman, who employed a gang of safebreakers and con artists to obtain blank cheques. He would then obtain the genuine signature of his proposed victim. He worked on a world-wide basis and on one occasion was able to cash forged cheques in London drawn on a Hobart bank in Tasmania before they had even been missed. Saward was deeply involved in the first Great Train Robbery and when the thieves on that operation fell out he went down with them. He was sentenced to transportation for life.[7]

[6] 25 March 1990.

[7] For footnote, see opposite.

In the early 1900s one of the most adroit and dishonest lawyers was the ex-public school, handsome, charming Arthur Newton, a man with great gifts of advocacy, who duped Crippen into retaining him and who sold both a forged 'confession' to the *Evening Times* and a forged letter said to be by Crippen to the Horatio Bottomley-owned *John Bull*. Newton was suspended by the Law Society and in 1913 was sent to prison for three years over a forged stock deal involving the title deeds to timberland in Canada, a case he defended himself. On his release he became a marriage broker, matching the impoverished holders of titles to those without the titles but with the cash to buy them.

But Newton was eclipsed in the 1920s by the activities of a Charles Sharman, a well-known police court advocate working in the East End. The judge, Sir Travers Humphreys, father of Christmas, recalled that Sharman earned his sincerest respect. 'He struck me as one of the few natural lawyers whom I had come across. He never talked nonsense and seldom repeated himself, with the result that the magistrates, whether lawyers or laymen, always listened with respect to his arguments.'[8]

It came therefore as something of a shock to Sir Travers to find that Sharman, in the best tradition of Saward, had been the head of a gang of international thieves which specialized in stealing mail-bags. In 1922 there had been an incident when a mail-bag containing a consignment of £50 bonds had been stolen from a train somewhere between London and Liverpool. These had been cashed in Belgium by an old gentleman giving the

---

[7] There is a full and most entertaining account of Saward and his associate Edward Agar, who actually carried out the robbery on the London–Folkestone train, relieving it of gold being sent to France, in Donald Thomas' *Honour amongst Thieves* (London, Weidenfeld and Nicolson, 1991).

[8] Sir T. Humphreys, *A Book of Trials*, p. 134.

name of Johnson. Sharman, who was then in his early seventies, was identified by a bank clerk but nothing came of it. Nor did a second incident come to trial. Within a month another mail-bag went missing, this time between Birmingham and London. Sharman was again implicated but said a poor man had picked up the bond certificate and brought it into his office. Next year he was identified as cashing a stolen Mexican bond in Manchester but he provided an alibi. Finally his luck ran out when he was identified by nine people who placed him in Canada selling a stolen war bond from the same bag which had contained the Mexican bond. Because of his age – he was then seventy-five – he received a sentence of three years' penal servitude and was ordered to pay the costs of the prosecution.

Lord Goddard believed there were eleven dishonest solicitors in London and five barristers, and he knew the names of them all. For years Scotland Yard kept a black list of solicitors believed to be too actively involved in helping their clients. Says a solicitor:

The old question asked at parties, 'How do you defend people you believe are guilty?' is easy to answer. Whatever you may think of a client or his case, if he says he didn't do it then you defend him. If you start trying to be judge and jury and only defending the ones you believe to be innocent then you shouldn't be in the game anyway.

I think over all the years I've only defended about a couple of dozen whom I've really thought were innocent and they're the really worrying ones to defend. I remember one who was said to be on a bank robbery begging and praying us to believe he was innocent, and I did. After he was acquitted he was unsporting enough to tell me he was the driver. He was killed in a car accident about three months later. Sometimes I do wonder if there is such a thing as divine retribution.

It's very difficult to walk a line. You are meant to advise the client that he has no defence, so you point out that this and that are fatal flaws in his case so why doesn't he plead guilty? The next thing you know is he comes back and says now this version is the truth, or even worse goes off to a solicitor down the road and says his brief doesn't believe him and you're sacked. Frankly if I couldn't invent better defences than they come up with I'd be ashamed.

Solicitors are at risk from their clients. In 1955 one of the first post-war solicitors found to have been 'middled' was Ben Cantor. He had been one of the solicitors who acted for the Messina brothers and was then acting for Joseph Grech, another Maltese who was sent to prison for three years for a housebreaking offence. Grech had seemingly had an unshakeable defence. Part of the evidence against him had been that the key to the burgled premises had been found on him. Grech maintained that it fitted his own front door and therefore was of no significance. The jury found it was and, from his cell, Grech unloaded a series of legal bombs.

He had, he said, given a Morris Page around £150 to hand to Detective Sergeant Robertson, who had been in charge of the initial case and who made the key to the burgled premises available so that a locksmith could make a lock to be fitted to Grech's front door. There was to have been a further £150 given to Robertson on an acquittal. He also alleged that Robertson had coached Ben Cantor about the questions to be put at the trial.

When Robertson, Page and Cantor appeared at the Old Bailey charged with conspiracy to pervert the course of justice, Grech unloaded some more bombs. His conviction, he said, had been brought about by perjured evidence of other officers acting on the instructions of an Inspector Charles Jacobs, attached to West End Central.[9] Jacobs, he said, had asked him for £2000 so that none of his flats or brothels would be raided. After negotiations the terms were set at £500 down and £30 a week. Cantor, said Grech, had been the bagman taking the £100 to give to Jacobs. According to Grech, Cantor came back saying, 'He wants £500.'

When he came to give evidence Cantor was in difficulties over his relationship with Tony Micallef, a brother-in-law of the Messinas, who had been accepted as a surety by Robertson.

'Can you imagine any honest policeman agreeing to take Micallef as a surety for this man Grech?'
'That is a difficult question to answer.'
'I think it is a simple question. Try to answer it . . .'
'It depends on the circumstances.'

Cantor received two years' imprisonment, as did Robertson; the intermediary, Morris Page, fifteen months.

In November 1955 the *Daily Mail* revealed that Detective Superintendent Bert Hannam had lodged a report with the Commissioner, Sir John Nott-Bower, revealing 'a vast amount of bribery and corruption

[9] In February 1956 Jacobs was dismissed from the force, having been found guilty by a disciplinary board of assisting a prostitute to obtain premises, of failing to disclose in court a man's previous convictions, and of failing to account for property taken from an arrested man. His application to the High Court for an order quashing the verdict, on the grounds that by reason of his mental health at the time he was unfit to prepare his defence, was rejected.

among certain uniformed officers attached to West End Station'. According to Hannam's report the corruption involved 'club proprietors, prostitutes, gaming-house owners, brothel-keepers and men living on immoral earnings'. It appeared that Hannam had interviewed no fewer than forty men serving prison sentences arising out of West End vice.

The extent of corruption can be gauged by the fact that it was found that some uniformed patrolmen in the vice-ridden streets of Soho were receiving up to £60 a week in bribes. Hannam found, so the article said, that 'evidence was "cooked" by police officers to benefit accused people. Details of previous convictions were suppressed in many cases so that men standing on charges were fined nominal sums instead of going to prison.'

Under a heading 'Tipped Off?' readers were treated to the following:

Gaming houses, where faro and chemin de fer were being played quite openly, were tipped off at a fee when a raid was to take place. Proprietors were warned to get 'mugs' in on a certain day, so that the regular customers could escape arrest. Brothel-keepers were told that certain evidence could be adjusted for a price. Huge sums of money changed hands. The 'adjustment' was for an officer to say in evidence that upon the raid taking place he found a number of fully clothed women on the premises, whereas, in fact, they were nude. That gave the premises an air of respectability – and halved the fine.

The hundreds of prostitutes who infest the West End streets are included in the bribery racket. One officer is pointed out by them to be the richest policeman in the Force. Most of these unfortunate girls appear on a special 'roster' due for appearance at a magistrates' court on a certain day for the usual £2 fine for soliciting. If the day does not happen to suit the woman, a 'fee' is paid for postponement.

Nott-Bower acted swiftly. Summoning effectively the whole of 'C' Division, he climbed on to two tables and gave his men a pep-talk.

I wish to tell you how much I deplore the imputations which have recently been made in the press which reflect on the reputation of the whole force and, in particular, all of 'C' Division.

In one of today's papers reference has been made to certain statements regarding the officers of 'C' Division in a report submitted to me by Detective Superintendent Herbert Hannam.

I want it to be known that there is no truth whatever in this, and that none of the subjects referred to in that report have been so much as mentioned in any report submitted to me by the Superintendent.

There was something of what would now be called a damage limitation exercise approach from the authorities. In a statement to the press, Nott-Bower went on to deny that 450 men might be transferred from Central London. 'Nor is there any truth in suggestions that "many officers" have come under suspicion.' Certain confidential papers had gone missing but 'neither is there truth in reports that "top secret" or even "secret" papers have been missed from Scotland Yard. Those that were found in a house have no security importance whatever.'

The next day the then Chief Magistrate appeared at Bow Street to scotch the rumours. The aim could not, he said, 'be other than to sap the confidence of the public in law enforcement, both outside and, perhaps of even greater significance, inside this court.' He went on to exculpate 'C' Division, adding that the article so far as it purported to reproduce the report was 'utterly misleading and most mischievous'. He had not, he said, read the report.

And in the House of Commons Sir Hugh Lucas-Tooth commented that the 'general accusations made in certain' quarters against the police are unwarranted and unsubstantiated'.

The newspapers were not satisfied. Cassandra in the *Daily Mirror* and the then *Manchester Guardian* both rose in defence of the *Mail*. Cassandra wrote: 'The Police Commissioner, the magistrates and the Home Office should reserve some of their congratulations for the day when Central London is cleansed of blackguards, thieves, and pimps who publicly flaunt their power and their riches.'

In December 1955 it was revealed that the wardrobe locker of a Detective Sergeant who had been assisting Detective Superintendent Stephen Glander, who was either helping Hannam or working independently on an enquiry investigating 'allegations of professional misconduct among policemen', had been forced. Papers had been disturbed but nothing had been taken. An enquiry which involved a number of officers submitting their fingerprints for comparison seems to have come to nothing.

Sometimes, of course, the information came out unwittingly. 'We had our own inside tap,' says a surviving member of the Billy Hill organization. 'One of the Assistant Commissioners was having it off with a bird on the strength and she used to tell us everything he told her in bed.'

The next famous name to go was the barrister Patrick Marrinan who had defended so ably in the series of Spot trials. He was disbarred on 28 June 1957 for his association with Billy Hill. His telephone had been tapped and conversations between him and Hill had been recorded. This was in clear breach of the code of conduct of members of the Bar that they should not have direct contact with the client. It is also fair to say that he did not enjoy the respect of the Establishment, with whom he regularly quarrelled. It cannot have helped him that on one occasion he fought Edward Clarke, later an Old Bailey judge and scion of the great legal family, in the robing room at Chelmsford Assizes. He returned to his native Ireland where, with his brother, he enjoyed great success in a criminal practice there.

Throughout the sixties and seventies efforts were made to prosecute dishonest solicitors but, as with police officers similarly accused, juries were unwilling to convict. Solicitors can also, of course, be used innocently.

In the 1960s, the heyday of the Friday bank robbery, you would find your waiting room full of clients who'd brought their friends in to see you. 'Mind if Tommy comes in with me?' they'd ask. Then one of them would ask the time and say 'I didn't think it was so late.' When you went out at lunchtime you'd read a bank had been robbed. There you were providing an alibi if needed. The reason was that all the known faces would be pulled in rather like the round-up of suspects after the German officer has been shot in *Casablanca*. At least the alibi was a genuine one and you did get to take some instructions from the real client.

But it didn't make for a good reputation.

Some solicitors would actively assist:

I had a client accused of an LF in the early 1970s and the principal Crown witness was his former girlfriend. Her statement was to the effect that she had gone with her boyfriend (my client) to see a solicitor in Wembley and the conversation had gone something like this.

'The gentleman asked my boyfriend his name and he said, "John Smith". "Like that is it?" asked the solicitor. "What is it – an LF?" My boyfriend nodded. "Is it too late for a fire then?" asked the solicitor.

Over the years, Norman Beach of the firm Beach and Beach fell foul both of the courts and the Law Society. Unimpressed with the identification evidence against his client, he sought to test the ability of the principal witness to recognize the defendant when he was wearing a ginger wig in the dock. The client was acquitted but Beach was convicted of conspiracy to pervert the course of justice. The jury's finding was overturned in the Court of Appeal in September 1957.

His solicitor son Martin Beach believes his father's action, in the days when identification of a defendant in the dock at court was common, was important in proving that in many cases it was the simple fact of being in the dock which caused the identification. 'The wig case was to prove that by changing the person's appearance the witness may have been briefed that this was the guilty person,' he says. Rules regarding the identification of defendants have been toughened over the years and a dock identification is now almost worthless.

Norman Beach acted in any number of the big criminal trials of the time. Unfortunately for him in 1977 the Disciplinary Tribunal of the Law Society struck him off the Rolls of Solicitors. This time it was alleged that, in a major trial, he had brought a defendant's Uncle Bertie out of the public gallery to sit in the well of the court with solicitors the better to intimidate witnesses. In January 1959 the Divisional Court upheld the decision. Martin

Beach again believes his father was the victim rather than the transgressor.

Perhaps the only real success the police had during this period in prosecuting a solicitor for conspiracy to pervert or related offences – as opposed to those who disappeared with the client account – was with De Mesa, who was involved in the case of Soraya Khashoggi, former wife of Adnan, arms dealer and friend to the mighty. De Mesa received a four-year sentence.

But the most spectacular of convictions of a solicitor has been that of Michael Relton, educated at Westminster, and principal of a very successful practice in Horseferry Road near the magistrates' court. He had made something of a speciality of defending police officers accused of corruption. It is said that of the twenty-eight he defended only one was convicted.[10]

In 1984 Relton was approached to launder the Brinks-Mat money and effectively retired from his practice – leaving it in the hands of a clerk who had served four years for fraud – to run a property company, Selective Estates. In two years using the Brinks-Mat money, say the police, Relton turned £7.5 million into a property portfolio worth £18 million, admittedly with the help of the property boom.

When the balloon went up Relton was interviewed and decided to co-operate with the police to become the first solicitor supergrass. In October 1986 he was charged and remanded on bail with the usual condition he reside at a police station in a suite, where he was visited by his second wife, a barrister's clerk. But, unfortunately for the police, he had a touch of seconds. He declined to assist further and when he appeared at the Old Bailey in July 1988 he pleaded not guilty.

His problems were that he had become too close to

[10] M. Short, *Lundy*, p. 231.

his clients. He had defended a man in 1973 on a drugs trial at Middlesex Crown Court. When the client received three years, Relton had continued to act for him whilst he was in Ford Open Prison, including the purchase of a recording studio in New Cross and a hotel on the Isle of Wight. Relton became his partner.

During the trial Relton said he thought the money had come from the man's father who owned twenty-six betting shops. But even so he should have been alarmed when his client was questioned about the robbery in June 1985, when his clerk, Emmanuel Wein, had acted for him. Instead of demanding a full explanation from his client and declining to act further, Relton had disposed of the money by an even more circuitous route, bringing the money back from abroad to purchase even more property. On his conviction in July 1988 Relton received twelve years' imprisonment. He was released shortly before Christmas 1991.

However astute Relton may have been when dealing in the Brinks-Mat investments, he pales into insignificance beside a man now reportedly living in Switzerland and the subject of a variety of warrants should he care to return to the United Kingdom. 'Judah Binstock is probably the most bent person the world has ever known,' says one City solicitor, not wholly unadmiringly, of the former Messina defender.

Prior to the Gaming Act he sold his businesses for £19 million. He is one of the few people I know who boosted his company by putting his own money into the company and paying tax on it. He owned the Victoria Sporting and the New Brighton Towers in Blackpool.

I went to see him once with a client in Paris. He spoke execrable French – and he gave a small party for about twelve of us. Towards the end he said,

'You're in luck. Madame – I can't remember her name – has got these three girls including this fantastic Eurasian. She's been with Kennedy. We'll have them £150 each the night' – this was late 1969–1970. My client and I looked at each other and Binstock said, 'No, my treat.' And then the client said, 'No, my brief has to go back to London this afternoon for a very important meeting.'

The criminal link was Judah Binstock – George Dawson – Albert Dimes – others. Binstock was not close to clubs; he was a brilliant man with a brilliant mind. He could use criminals in the same way as he used straight people.

Dawson would know all the heavy mob; if something happened Binstock could always talk to him.

Binstock invested a lot of money with Dawson. The deal was they would buy a company which on paper was full of assets, mainly machinery, and when you bought it it was worthless.

At that time I had a substantial indebtedness to a fashionable London solicitor – a dated IOU over a property deal. I had to find the money or extend the note, which would cost more. This got to the ears of Binstock and he approached me to say he would pay off the loan. In return would I guarantee a company in which he had invested to manufacture orange juice for a similar sum. I had already learned the machinery there was worthless and the company was going into liquidation – I didn't take him up. With friends like that you really don't need enemies.

I've never been approached by someone with such a blatant fraud. I knew him – what a rotten thing to do, but that was Judah. Yet a lot of people made money standing alongside him.

But when it comes to it the best helpmate is the police officer, and historically it has always been so. The Met, founded in 1829, was staffed by recruits from the working classes, and they were literally butchers, bakers, plumbers and sailors as well as old soldiers. The aim was to provide a body of honest, sober and unobjectionable men, wearing an innocuous non-military uniform. The pay had been fixed at a deliberately low level to deter the officer class. Immediately, however, there was a high turnover amongst these recruits. In eighteen months, out of a total strength of 4000, some 1250 had resigned and a further 1986 had been dismissed, mainly for drunkenness.

Then in 1877, at what became known as the Trial of the Detectives, one third of Scotland Yard's detective force (admittedly totalling only fifteen) were arrested and stood trial. The reasons for the downfall of Inspector Meiklejohn and his colleagues – associating with criminals, taking bribes, suppressing evidence and giving advance information of impending raids – were no different from the hundreds of their colleagues who followed them down the following decades.[11] As a result the Criminal Investigation Department of Scotland Yard was formed. Fifty years later it was described as a thoroughly venal army.

The Met survived a Royal Commission set up in 1908 to investigate corruption in street crime, and the next major public scandal came in 1928, when a uniform sergeant, George Goddard, stationed at Vine Street and detailed to clean up vice in the West End, did so with such success that when he was investigated he was found, on pay of £6 15s a week, to have a £2000 house. He also had £500 in a Selfridges deposit box and £12,000 in an account in Pall Mall. He had been a police officer for

---

[11] Each detective received two years' hard labour.

exactly twenty-eight years.

From where had the money come? Sir Percival Clarke, for the Crown, said it had come from the person in the dock with him, Kate Meyrick, the undoubted Queen of the Night Clubs. Known throughout the upper echelons of English society as 'Ma', she ruled principally at the Forty-Three Club in Gerrard Street,[12] although in her time she opened dozens of clubs, including Dalton's (in Leicester Square), Brett's, the Silver Slipper and, after her release from Holloway, the Bunch of Keys.

She was by no means a conventional Irish beauty; sad-eyed, drab and dowdy she would sit behind her desk in the narrow entrance hall collecting the £1 entrance fee. But she was an astute businesswoman even if she had not taken up her career until her forties. From the profits she educated her eight children well; one son went to Harrow, the daughters to Roedean. Time and again her clubs were raided, mainly for selling drinks after hours and running unlicensed premises. Kate Meyrick first went to prison in 1924 and continued to do so sporadically throughout much of the next decade, but her most celebrated appearance in court was in 1929 with Goddard.

Goddard certainly could not have come by his money honestly and it was said he had acquired his considerable fortune by gifts from Mrs Meyrick in return for tip-offs over raids. It was something he denied throughout the trial, maintaining he was no more than a successful gambler – £7000 had come from winnings on the turf – and an investor in a music publishing business, which had netted him another £5000. Ever the astute business-man he had invested money in a scheme to sell rock – edible rather than audible – at the Wembley Exhibition

---

[12] She was immortalized as Ma Maybrick in the novel *Brideshead Revisited* by Evelyn Waugh.

of 1924 and then he had dabbled on the foreign exchange market. These ventures had produced £4000 and £2000 each. He had, he said, reported irregularities in the running of the Meyrick clubs.

He was done for by the evidence that a secret observation had been kept by senior officers without letting him know so that in turn he could not tip off the night club queen. Goddard was sentenced to eighteen months' hard labour and ordered to pay £2000.

On his release he was back in court, this time as plaintiff. After his conviction the Commissioner of Police had, somewhat prematurely, confiscated all his money, claiming it to be the property of the Crown. In fact he had been convicted of taking only some £900 in bribes and an order was made that a substantial part of the money be returned to him. Goddard retired to the country and lived off his investments.

After her sentence Kate Meyrick returned to the West End, opening fresh clubs until in 1932, following yet another spell in Holloway, she promised to stop. She died the next year at the age of fifty-six. Dance bands throughout the West End observed two minutes' silence in her memory.

That may be the attractive part of the story. What was unattractive was the fact that as early as 1922 a young officer, Josling, who had arrested a bookmaker, had been warned by Goddard to 'leave the betting boys alone'. In return Goddard would 'see him all right'. The young officer reported the matter to his seniors who charged him with making false statements about Goddard and dismissed him from the force.

Throughout the pre-war period when Sir Hugh Trenchard was Commissioner corruption flourished undercover.

Trenchard, for example, while deluding himself

that he had stopped the rot, had constantly shirked the issue. Detectives played the game according to their own rules, confident that neither their superiors nor the courts would accept the word of known or convicted criminals.

He was constantly alive to the extent of CID corruption and his correspondence with Gilmour during 1934 is a curious commentary on his intellectual cowardice. The man who could talk to kings seemed frightened of corrupt constables.[13]

In 1933 Leopold Harris, a notorious fire-raiser, was sentenced to fourteen years' imprisonment after pleading guilty to eighteen counts of arson, conspiracy to commit arson, conspiracy to defraud, and obtaining money by false pretences. His brother David had received a term of five years following his conviction on two counts of arson. After his conviction Leopold Harris was interviewed at length in Maidstone Prison over allegations that senior police officers, mainly from the East End, had suppressed evidence in return for bribes, participated in mock burglaries for insurance purposes and dropped charges in exchange for cash. Harris told the investigating officer how money had been handed over at a billiard hall in the East End and at a police sports ground. He named two Chief Constables, six Superintendents and three Chief Inspectors. No prosecutions were ever brought.

During and after the war so far as the public was concerned the police were epitomized by George Dixon, the officer who in the guise of Jack Warner was gunned down by the young tearaway Dirk Bogarde near the Metropolitan Music Hall in the film *The Blue Lamp*. There was no point in criminals suggesting that the

[13] D. Ascoli, *The Queen's Peace*, pp. 306 and 240.

police had fabricated evidence, that their confessions were not what they had seemed; the magistrates or the jury, guided by the trial judge, would not believe them. The police were 'our police' and whatever they said and did was beyond both reproach and question.

It was not until the great *Times* exposure in 1969 that the public raised a serious question mark over the behaviour of the police. On Saturday, 29 November, an article was published which led to the convictions of Detective Sergeant John Symonds and Detective Inspector Bernard Robson. It also gave rise to the phrase 'a firm within a firm'. Symonds, Robson and a third officer had been systematically blackmailing a small-time Peckham thief, whilst offering him help if he should find himself in difficulties.

> Don't forget always to let me know straight away because I know people everywhere.
>   If you are nicked anywhere in London . . . I can get someone on the blower to someone in my firm who will know someone somewhere who can get something done.[14]

Robson received seven years, Harris six. Symonds fled the country before his trial but was sent to prison when he surrendered seven years later.

The Times' enquiry led, inexorably, to a full-scale investigation into the Met. In a blaze of publicity Frank Williamson, then Her Majesty's Inspector of Constabulary for Crime, was appointed as adviser to oversee the enquiry. However, Williamson, who had a reputation as an honest and painstaking detective, was seen by the Met as an intruder who, it was feared, would ensure that a positive rather than an inconsequential report was

[14] Garry Lloyd and Julian Mounter, *The Times*, 29 November 1969.

produced. His views on police corruption were well
known and he had stated at many detective training
schools that until the words 'except police officers' were
written into certain statutes, they must be dealt with in
just the same way as any other offender. Nipper Read
recounted:

> At the time of the enquiry I was a Chief Superin-
> tendent at Scotland Yard and Frank, a good friend
> of mine, would confide in me both the difficulties
> he was experiencing and the attitude of some of the
> top brass of the CID. It can be summed up quite
> neatly. One day he asked to see me and I said, 'I'll
> meet you at the Yard.' 'Good God,' he said, 'we
> can't do that, Nipper.' And when asked why ever
> not, he said, 'I'm *persona non grata* at the Yard.'
> I was dumbfounded. Here was a man who had
> been a provincial Chief Constable and who was
> now an Inspector of Constabulary whose presence
> in the Yard was being questioned.
>
> We had to meet in a pub and there he expressed
> his concern at the quality and ability of officers
> seconded to his inquiry from the Yard, giving as an
> example Detective Chief Superintendent Bill
> Moody.[15]

The Drugs Squad was the next to cop it, so to speak.
In November 1972 Victor Kelaher and four other
members of the squad were charged with conspiracy to
pervert the course of justice and, with the exception of

---

[15] Williamson's fears were fully justified. Even whilst engaged on *The
Times* enquiry, Moody was taking vast sums of money from pornographers in the West End. He later received a sentence of twelve years'
imprisonment for his part in an extensive corruption racket. (See
Chapter 7 and also L. Read and J. Morton, *Nipper*, pp. 44–5.)

Kelaher, with perjury. The prosecution was not helped in its case by the evidence of Wally Virgo, whose testimony favoured the defence, but in the end three of the junior officers were convicted of perjury. One received four years, the others eighteen months each. Kelahar, in one of the smart cover-ups favoured by the Yard, was allowed to resign and given a medical discharge. In the shades of Challenor he had spent a year attending St Thomas' Hospital for treatment for a nervous complaint. It did not work as well as it might have. 'I am allowed by the Commissioner to say that, had he not done so, serious allegations would have been made against him in disciplinary proceedings,' said Alex Lyon, Minister of State for the Home Office.[16]

Meanwhile, things were not going well in the City of London police. Following allegations by a supergrass in August 1978, Operation Countryman was set up originally to look into the City of London police but later extended to cover the Met as well. The officers conducting it were derisively referred to by the Met as the Sweeney. In the end eight Met officers were all acquitted of charges brought against them. Three of them were dismissed following disciplinary proceedings, one resigned and four resumed duty.

Nor was there much success for the three-year-long enquiry under the control of Detective Chief Superintendent Stagg. Although the Director of Public Prosecutions was quite content to allow common criminals to be convicted on the evidence of supergrass Billy Young, he was not happy with the prospect of putting serving police officers at such risk. One officer was suspended and, in May 1983, served with internal discipline charges. Would he possibly become the first police supergrass? No, was the emphatic answer. Only traffic policemen bite their colleagues. He knew nothing. He was allowed to resign and a reference was given to him by the Yard, enabling him to become a member of the Institute of Professional Investigators.[17]

The rise and fall of Roy Garner, together with the eclipse of Superintendent Tony Lundy, came with Garner's increasing involvement in the cocaine trade. Before that, in 1982, he had been involved in a VAT fraud which worked by importing exempt coins, such as Krugerrands under £50,000, and then selling them on with the VAT added. This in itself was perfectly legal. The only problem was the VAT had to be repaid within three months. It was not. Given that flights were being made on an almost daily basis the profits were enormous.

In November 1984 Garner went to prison for the maximum term of two years consecutive on two counts and was fined, as well as being made the subject of a criminal bankruptcy order. The Court of Appeal later reduced the sentence by a year and quashed the fine. The Court expressed the hope that the criminal bankruptcy would be pursued by the authorities. It was something of a vain hope. Garner's stud farm belonged to his father, the family home was mortgaged to the hilt, his share of Elton's, the night club behind Tottenham police station, went to repay a loan on the club, and as for the reward money – well that had gone too, probably on his string of racehorses.[18]

By now Garner was well into the cocaine trade – of that there is little doubt – and it is here that the pro- and anti-Lundy camps become polarized. Just what did Lundy know about Garner's dealings? A very great deal, say Jennings, Lashmar and Simson. Nothing at all that

[17] A. Jennings et al., *Scotland Yard's Cocaine Connection*, p. 104.
[18] A. Jennings et al., *Scotland Yard's Cocaine Connection*, p. 112.

was improper, says Martin Short.[19] In any event Garner, put forward as the grass over the Brinks-Mat laundering, was arrested along with a Nikolaus Chrastny and Mickey Hennessey (one of the South London family), over the importation of 57 kilos of cocaine found in suitcases in Chrastny's flat in Harley Street. After sixteen days in custody Garner, through his wife June, got a message to Lundy asking for help. Matters moved quickly. One version is that Lundy was suspended for telling June that 'certain information had been passed at a very senior level from Scotland Yard to senior personnel of the agency dealing with his case'. Lundy says it was for making a complaint about the Chief Constable of South Yorkshire.

Chrastny was given conditional bail. He was to become a supergrass on the usual terms of residence in a police station. Off he went to the wilds of Yorkshire where his wife was allowed to give him £500 in cash for his daily needs, and to while away the time he was given modelling plasticine, paint and glue. By the morning of 5 October he had finished sawing through the bars of his cell, making his escape through the doctor's room and out of the window into a waiting car.[20]

Lundy appeared at Garner's trial, giving evidence *in*

---

[19] *Ibid and M. Short, Lundy.*

[20] Mrs Chrastny was given a seven-year sentence for conspiracy to import and distribute cocaine. She was also charged with helping her husband to escape and was acquitted. It was put on her behalf that of all the people who had an interest in the escape of her husband, Scotland Yard came top of the list. Perhaps one should not think too hard of the officers at Dewsbury police station from which Chrastny disappeared. After all, when O'Mahoney had been in the custody of Jack Slipper he had accumulated a pile of empty cans and bottles which he had hidden in his cell. He only told the police after his release. Chrastny was probably much smarter than O'Mahoney.

camera along with another officer, Detective Chief Superintendent Roy Ramm. The trial judge, Keith Machin, had allowed an application by Michael Corkery QC, former Treasury Counsel who had turned his hand to defence work, to hear this part of the case without the scrutiny of either public or press. Later the *Observer* published an account of the *in camera* part of the trial:

> Lawyers representing HM Customs accused a senior Scotland Yard detective of corruption in a secret session during an Old Bailey drugs trial. . . . Lundy was cross-examined *in camera* about two leaks to the cocaine smugglers which occurred after he allegedly gained knowledge of the case. His answers were inconsistent with subsequent statements by Florida police.
>
> Mr Derek Spencer, cross-examining him for Customs, said the nature of the corrupt relationship was that Garner gave Lundy information to further his career and Lundy gave Garner police information. He told Lundy: 'You found out Garner was being inquired into and you told him.' Lundy denied the allegations.[21]

On his conviction Garner received a twenty-two-year sentence. Lundy was investigated up hill and down dale and in the end a disciplinary matter over the receipt of some fencing for his home was brought against him. He decided not to contest the allegation, maintaining it would cost him over £20,000 to do so. He was allowed to retire on the grounds of ill health and sold his two part story, 'Bent or Brilliant?', to the *News of the World*. There are no prizes on offer for correctly guessing his answer. He is now living in Spain.

[21] 23 April 1989.

Was he bent? Along with journalists, serving police officers are divided on this point.

'He couldn't have done what he did if he was,' says one fervently.

'He had very bad breath,' says another enigmatically.

11

The Killers and the Killed

'We were none of us nice, but you wouldn't turn your back on him,' said Albert Donaghue mildly.

'I thought of him as an original member of Murder Incorporated,' said an acquaintance.

Peter Kelly, a face of the eighties, was more forthright. 'He was a very hard man. Most hateful, frightening man because he was so fucking ugly. He had a horrible disposition. In fact he was the most hateful man God ever put breath into.'

They were all talking about Alfie Gerard, murderer, armed robber, one-time owner of a jewellery business and, amongst the fraternity, a noted cook who at one time ran a restaurant in Bermondsey, the Blue Plaice, in partnership with Mickey Hennessey. He was also noted as probably the nearest London had known to a hired killer who operated for any length of time. Rather like the boots in the film *All Quiet on the Western Front*, the restaurant was passed down the criminal hierarchy as first one and then the next proprietor fell foul of the law.

Since Gerard was acquitted on a number of occasions and not tried on several others, it is not possible accurately to pin the number of murders on him, but the likelihood is at least half a dozen. He also claimed to have disposed of the body of Jack 'the Hat' McVitie.

The killing of Ginger Marks on 2 January 1965 was not
one of his better moves since it was clearly a mistake.
Marks just happened to be in the wrong place at the
wrong time and when the name Jimmy was called it
sounded like Ginger, so he answered. Marks, a small-time
thief, disappeared and immediately there sprang up a
whole series of rumours about him and his whereabouts.
First there was a story he had been involved in the 'Jack
the Stripper' nude murders.[1] Almost immediately petrol
bombs were thrown into the office of a suburban
newspaper after it had run a story linking those murders
to Marks.

From a chip found in the wall in Cheshire Street in the
East End, the police believed Marks had been shot in
the stomach. A dig took place on a local bomb site but
there was no trace of the body. Three weeks later no one
was any nearer a solution. Now came a suggestion in the
Sketch that his body had been thrown in the Thames
in concrete. Next the police thought the killing had a link
with the Great Train Robbery.[2] The *News of the World*
offered a reward of £5000 for information leading to the

[1] The Jack the Stripper murders occurred in the Shepherd's Bush and
Hammersmith areas over a period of a year in 1964. A series of
prostitutes were found naked and strangled. Almost all had had oral
sex. No arrests were made but a man whom the police linked to the
murders committed suicide and the case was closed. A rumour was put
about that the man was the former world light-heavyweight champion
Freddie Mills but neither John du Rose, who investigated the murders,
nor Nipper Read, who investigated the death of Mills on another
occasion, could find any grounds to support this rumour (see J. du
Rose, *Murder was my Business* and L. Read and J. Morton, *Nipper*).
[2] In one version of the Great Train Robbery story Marks was the man
engaged to burn down Leatherslade farm and who failed to do so. His
is one of several bodies said to have disappeared into the parlour of a
South London undertaker.

recovery of Marks or his body. A couple of days later the paper was on the right track. 'It is accepted that he was the unintended victim of a "crime of passion" feud between two South London gangs,' wrote their major crime reporter Peter Earle.

It was ten years before George Evans, known as Jimmy, a hard and quick-tempered Welshman, was arrested for the attempted murder of George Foreman, who at one time ran a club with Buster Edwards and whose brother Freddie was a close friend of the twins. The prosecution's case was that on 17 December 1964 George Foreman was allegedly shot by Evans because he had suspected his wife was carrying on with another man. The prosecution's case was that by hiding out in the boot of her car he had discovered George Foreman. He borrowed a single-barrelled 12-bore shotgun but returned it because it was not powerful enough. He then borrowed a double-barrelled shotgun from a man named Sands and shortened it.

On 11 April, Evans was acquitted both of shooting Foreman and having a shotgun and triumphantly gave an interview to the *News of the World*. He claimed he was continually being framed by police because he would not talk about the disappearance of Marks. 'Think what happens when a car breaker compresses a car into a cube box of metal no bigger than a cornflake box,' said Evans in the witness box, going on to deny that he and Ginger had been up to no good that night.

On 10 January 1975 the police arrested Jeremiah Callaghan, Alf Gerard and Ronald James Everett. By now Evans, serving a seven-year sentence for manslaughter, was prepared to give evidence. He said that he, Marks and three others had been involved in a night raid on a jewellers. When they failed to get in they noticed a red car of the 1100 type following them near the Carpenters Arms in Cheshire Street, Bethnal Green.

The car drew up beside them and a voice called out, 'Jimmy, come here.' Three shots rang out and Ginger fell. Marks thought the call was 'Ginge' and was shot as he stepped forward. Evans ran round the corner and climbed under a lorry, clinging to the transmission link. Marks' body was bundled into a car and driven away. The other two had gone. He named the attackers as Alf Gerard, Ronald James Everett, Jeremiah Callaghan and Frederick Foreman.

On 30 October 1975 Gerard, Callaghan and Frederick Foreman were acquitted by Mr Justice Donaldson. Ronald Everett had been acquitted earlier in the trial. Donaldson said, 'The problems with identification are very real. This crime is ten years old. The first time Mr Evans condescended to say it was these three men who were in the car was last year.' Outside the Old Bailey Alfred Gerard commented, 'This is the end of a nightmare for us. Justice has been done at last.'[3]

In December of the same year as the killing of Marks came the disappearance of Frank Mitchell, the man whom the Krays had at first anticipated would help them if the Richardsons and their allies became too troublesome. Mitchell was killed, so Albert Donaghue said at the trial, after he left the house in the East End where he had been sheltered after his escape from Dartmoor. Reluctantly he had got in the back of a van waiting for him. Alf Gerard was in the van and almost immediately shots were heard.

[3] Marks' wife Anne remarried and never told her son Philip of his father's career. He obtained seven 'O' levels and won a medal for encouraging children to help the police. On 10 February 1987 Philip, then aged twenty, was sentenced to twelve years' imprisonment for masterminding a security van ambush in Limehouse, East London. His stepbrother Robert Judd (twenty-two) received ten years for the same offence. John Samson of Plaistow received eight years.

At the subsequent trial Ronnie and Reggie Kray, Freddie Foreman and others were acquitted of Mitchell's murder, but at the time of the arrest of the Krays and their associates in May 1968 Gerard had fled the country. He only returned after they were acquitted. As a result he was never charged with the murder.

In some camps Gerard is credited with the killing of bookmaker Harry Barham, shot and relieved of over £30,000 in Hackney one evening. But without doubt the most complicated if not the most famous incident in which he was involved, if only parentally, was that of Tony Zomparelli.

In August 1981 Alf Gerard was found dead in a flat belonging to the Callaghans in Brighton, that town of Max Miller and the fading gangster; it was the year his son was put on trial for the killing of Zomparelli. An inquest showed he had died of cirrhosis of the liver. The preferred version, more in keeping with his lifestyle and culinary artistry, is that he choked over a lobster.

The Zomparelli killing came after the death of David Knight, whose brother Ronnie, at one time married to Barbara Windsor, owned the Artists and Recreation Club off the Charing Cross Road. David Knight was badly beaten in a fight with a Johnny Isaacs in a pub at the Angel, Islington. On 7 May 1970 when he was out of hospital, Ronnie took him round to the Latin Quarter night club off Leicester Square to see Isaacs to whom he, Ronnie, had already given a retaliatory beating. He also took with him his brother Johnny and David's friend Billy Hickson, who had, it seems, been the cause of the original fight. As Ronnie Knight put it, 'I wanted they should say sorry to my David, promise him that it was all a big mistake. Then everything would be squared. Then I could forget it. It would be forgotten.'[4]

---

[4] R. Knight, *Black Knight*, p. 100.

According to Knight, Isaacs was not there and whilst he was making his peace with Billy Stayton, Hickson attacked Stayton. In the ensuing fight Alfredo Zomparelli, run-around man for Albert Dimes and bouncer for the Latin Quarter, stabbed David Knight twice in the chest.

Three weeks later Zomparelli, who had fled to Italy, returned and gave himself up. He claimed that the Knight contingent had walked into the club and violence had erupted. He had grabbed a knife to defend himself when two men attacked him. Looking back to the case of Tony 'Baby Face' Mancini, he seems fortunate that he was only convicted of manslaughter, for which he received a sentence of four years. To rub salt into Ronnie Knight's emotional wounds he, his brother Johnny and Hickson were charged with making an affray. Hickson was given a suspended sentence. The jury disagreed in the case of the brothers and the next day the prosecution offered no evidence. The witnesses had either gone abroad or declined to give evidence a second time.

The police version of why the fight took place does not quite match that of Ronnie Knight. According to them the Latin Quarter had been paying protection to David Knight.

After serving his sentence Zomparelli ran a bucket shop travel agency in Frith Street. Much of his leisure time was spent playing the pinball machines in the Golden Goose around the corner in Old Compton Street (and not far from the A & R Club). It was in the pinball arcade he was shot in the head and back by two men wearing dark glasses and moustaches on 4 September, a few months after his release. Appropriately he was playing a game called 'Wild Life'.

'He was a most likeable man,' said Augustus Tedeschi who had known him for fourteen years. 'I cannot understand why anybody should want to do this.'

It is not surprising that the police fancied Ronnie Knight for the killing. He does not seem to have hidden either his loathing of Zomparelli or his intention of seeking revenge. His alibi was that he was in the A & R Club and he named a substantial number of witnesses.

As in all these cases there were a number of theories offered for what was clearly a professional hit. One was that Zomparelli was trying to muscle in to the highly profitable amusement arcade business; another that he was involved in a stolen car racket involving the theft of Lancias and Ferraris in Italy and their resale in London, with claims on Italian insurance companies completing the scam; and a third that he was a drug courier. A Mafia expert, Captain Francisco Rosato of the Rome police, was sent to London to collaborate on the investigation. The police interviewed over a thousand people including Knight but the enquiry came to nothing.

There the file remained shut, if not fully closed, until in 1980 Maxie Piggot *aka* George Bradshaw became the supergrass with most to confess in his generation. On 17 January 1980 he received a life sentence for the murder of Zomparelli with a ten-year concurrent sentence for all the rest. Then he became one of the last of the all-star supergrasses. In his long confession, in which he admitted to over a hundred armed robberies, he named Nicky Gerard, son of Alfie, as his co-hitman, the one who pulled the trigger of a .38 revolver. The shock of hearing gunfire made him involuntarily pull the trigger of his own .22.

He and Gerard had left a flat in Clerkenwell and bought their disguises at a theatrical costumiers on the way to Soho. He also named Ronnie Knight as the financier of the reasonably priced £1000 contract and the supplier of the .38. He said that night he and Gerard received £250 of the promised £1000. He went to his parents' home near Winchester and buried the guns.

Later he would claim that it was not the money which had tempted him but the added prestige in the underworld which such an execution would bring him.

Of course the police were bound to check the story and at least they found the guns buried, as Bradshaw had said, in Hampshire. Forensic examination would match the guns with the spent cartridges found at the Golden Goose.

There is no doubt that Knight had met Bradshaw at the A & R Club. He had been there as a friend of Knight's 'old mate' Alfie Gerard.

'He was a right weirdo, this Maxie character. He had dark, long curly hair, a funny little drooping moustache and a beard.' He reminded Knight of the 'Cisco Kid. 'He must have been blind as a bat because he wore those thick, jam-jar glasses . . . and contact lenses on underneath. Mad as a March hare on the funny powder.'[5]

But by 1980 supergrasses did not always have the ear of the jury. Ten years of practice had taught defence barristers how to overcome the witnesses' all-consuming repentance and a desire to bare their souls so that justice could at last be done. The public was also becoming a little tired of hearing the evidence of men who had committed the most outrageous crimes, and who were serving relatively nominal sentences, which would put away others involved in a single offence and who would then get double or even treble that of the supergrass. They did not like hearing how brave these men had been by telling all, and when they sat on a jury they were rightly sceptical. Knight also had the bonus of his wife Barbara Windsor on his side. The jury acquitted both him and Nicky Gerard.

The Director of Public Prosecutions declined to continue with any further proceedings against the dozens

[5] R. Knight, *Black Knight*, p. 108.

of others Bradshaw had named. Once the police had seen him as a major supergrass he had been placed in police custody at Twickenham outside the prison system under the name of John February. Now he was returned to prison to serve the rest of his sentence.

Gilbert Kelland, the head of the CID at the time, commented:

> Whilst he had been held by us he had been well behaved and co-operative, although he seemed completely cynical about his involvement in murder and other violent crimes. In my view it should be many years – if ever – before such a ruthless criminal is considered suitable for parole.[6]

With hindsight it does seem odd that Knight would have chosen Bradshaw to execute Zomparelli, particularly when his old friend Alfie Gerard was alive and shooting well. For his part Bradshaw complains that the judge was senile and should have listened more closely to his evidence.

The newspapers reported Tony Zomparelli junior, middle name Alberto as a mark of respect to Albert Dimes, as saying, 'The day Ronnie Knight dies, I'll throw the biggest party East London has ever seen.'

Tony Zomparelli believes they exaggerated.

> What I did say was I'll open a bottle of champagne. It wasn't right what was reported. My dad was there [at the Latin Quarter] as a peacemaker. He was hit on the head with a hammer himself. They went round tooled up. I was only eleven when my father died. He was a bit div. There's a story he glassed his best friend but I don't know if it's true.

[6] G. Kelland, *Crime in London*, p. 228.

He was a bad gambler. He and my mother were separated and one day he would have a car full of toys for us and then we'd never see him for three months. When he went to Italy after the killing in the Latin Quarter it was Albert Dimes who told him to come back. He told him he'd only get four years.

Zomparelli went on to say that Knight had loathed his father because Barbara Windsor was always flirting with him.

Bradshaw was released from prison in 1990.

Nicky Gerard did not last that long after his acquittal. In June 1982 he was shot dead in South London. Peter Kelly says that 'Nicky Gerard was a very good friend of Billy Dixon. He was the dead spit of his father but he had a much nicer nature. Personally I liked Nicky. Alfie, when he died in Brighton, was not missed by many. He was a hateful bastard.'

'He [Nicky] would lean on anybody who took liberties,' said another acquaintance. 'But he wasn't only a muscle for hire man. He was known and feared throughout the East End.'

Prior to the Zomparelli trial, in May 1978, Nicky Gerard had been gaoled for seven years for an attack on boxer Michael Gluckstead at the Norseman Club in Canning Town. He had been found not guilty of the attempted murder of Gluckstead, who, widely regarded as a local bully, had his cheek slit from ear to nose and had been shot twice, as well as being hit about the head and being stomped. Gerard would say nothing of his instructions or reasons for the Gluckstead beating. John Knight, brother of Ronnie, was acquitted of all charges relating to the attack.

While he had been in prison Gerard had been sentenced, *in absentia*, by a kangaroo court. Certainly his wife Linda had received threats and a wreath with the message 'Nicky Gerard, Rest in Peace'. Now, on 27 June 1982, when leaving his daughter's eleventh birthday party, he was ambushed by gunmen wearing boiler suits and balaclava helmets at the lock-up garage to which he had driven his Oldsmobile. Shots were fired through the windscreen and Gerard was hit in the stomach. He managed to get out of the car and to stagger a hundred yards but his attackers followed him, smashing him so hard on the head with a gun that the stock shattered. He was beaten unconscious before the gunmen reloaded and shot him.

Gerard had not been sufficiently careful. Over the previous few days he had known he was being followed but he had thought they were undercover police.

'Gerard was one of the most feared men in the London underworld. Although he was acquitted of being a hit man in the Knight case, he was the man who did the heavy business,' said former Commander Bert Wickstead. '. . . His death could easily spark off a gangland war.'[7]

On 22 November his cousin and 'best friend' Thomas Hole was arrested and charged with his murder. Hole's criminal career traced back to his friendship with George Davis and ended on 12 July 1989 at Snaresbrook Crown Court when he acquired a thirteen-year sentence for conspiracy to manufacture drugs, to run concurrently with an eighteen-year sentence for armed robbery.[8] On the way he had acquired a sentence of seven years for the attempted murder of a James Venton. Together with

---

[7] *News of the World*, 27 June 1982.

[8] The prosecution alleged that sufficient chemicals to make 40 kg of amphetamine sulphate had been found at Colney Hall, an isolated mansion near Norwich. The drugs were said to have a street value of millions.

Billy Williams he had been instrumental in holding Venton down whilst a car was driven over him in Daveney Street.

Hole was tried at the Old Bailey in April 1983. He had been picked out on an identification parade by a 'Mr Fisher', the pseudonym given to a protected witness, who said he had seen a man with one rubber washing-up glove acting suspiciously. 'But,' he added, 'I am not sure it was the man I had seen that day in June in the car park.' Despite protests that the Crown had more evidence it had not been allowed to produce, on 27 April 1983 the judge stopped the case at the end of the prosecution evidence.

Thomas Hole was acquitted by the direction of the trial judge, Mr Justice French, who said, 'This, of course, was an appalling gangland murder, and any right-thinking citizen must be dismayed at the thought that no one has been brought to justice for that murder.' Hole, who left court with his friends, said, 'My head is reeling.'

The 'war' had not been long in coming. Within six months of Nicky Gerard's death, Patrick 'Paddy Onions' O'Nione was also executed. On 30 November 1982 he was shot near his son's wine bar, Caley's, in Tower Bridge Road. He had been hit in the back of the head, the right shoulder, the chest and the abdomen. A Detective Sergeant who was passing gave chase to the killer but the man escaped. Paddy Onions had been a major, if shadowy, figure in the South London under-world for some years. As long ago as March 1951 he had been acquitted of being the decoy in a brutal attack in which the Gregory brothers, Ernest and Andrew, received twelve and seven years. In March 1963 he had not been so fortunate. At Lewes Crown Court he received five years in a conspiracy to smuggle watches. The jury failed to agreed in the case of Alfie Gerard, one of three others charged with him.

As always a number of explanations were offered for the execution. O'Nione was thought to be a grass; he was thought to be deeply involved in a drug racket embracing both Europe and the Middle East; perhaps it was a revenge killing for that of Peter Hennessey, one of the South London brothers, who had been stabbed at a Boxing Gala dinner at the Royal Garden Hotel, Kensington.

Two of the Hennessey brothers, Peter and Bernard, after a series of convictions for robbery, had bought a public house, the Dog and Bell, in Deptford. Of course they had a manager in whose name the licence appeared but the pub was theirs. Peter would sit on a stool in the corner of the pub and watch the proceedings. An officer who worked the area says:

> He had a frightening temper. I was scared of him and I was Old Bill. But he did have a better side. At Christmas he and his brother would get a coach and round up all the old-aged pensioners of the area whether they drank in the Dog or not and take them to C & A's in Lewisham and buy them a new hat and coat. It cost them thousands. I think it all went back to Peter being fond of his mother.

Hennessey died at the Royal Garden Hotel at the end of a charity evening designed to raise money for a well-known South London amateur boxing club. 'Every villain in South-East London was there,' says an officer who was involved in the enquiry. 'If the roof had fallen in, South London crime would have been cleared in a moment.'

Towards the end of the boxing, Peter Hennessey, described as 'well drunk', decided to have an informal extra collection in aid of a friend's wife who had multiple sclerosis. He went round the tables and an argument broke out between him and O'Nione. They fell to the floor and during the fight, in which others were involved, Hennessey was stabbed sixty times. James Coleman, a brother-in-law of the Arifs, and O'Nione were charged with his murder. Both were acquitted.

So far as O'Nione's death was concerned, despite the tales of protection of wine bars and pubs in South London and the story that he had been instrumental in financing a web of violence and intrigue spreading as far as Miami and Milan, the likelihood is that he was executed on the instructions of friends of Peter Hennessey.

On 11 March 1983 Jimmy Davey was arrested in Coventry and held in custody to await the arrival of the London police for questioning over O'Nione's death. On their arrival Davey, who had already served a six-year sentence for a brutal attack on a Coventry-based policeman, is said to have lunged at one of the officers, who put him in a choke-hold. Eleven days later, with Davey still in a coma, the life support machine was switched off. The police gave out that they were convinced that Davey had undertaken the hit for £5000.[9]

Seemingly independently of the troubles of O'Nione and Hennessey, John Darke, then aged thirty-two, had fatal difficulties on 21 November 1978. A medium-quality gangster, he had been charged back in 1969 with the BOAC wages snatch and had been acquitted at the Old Bailey in the October. Reputed to be the leader of a South London team known as the Wild Bunch, as well as being a police informer for the last three years, Darke, hacked to death with a machete, had died in a

[9] The going rate for a hit in the 1960s had been £1000, with half that for a shattered arm or leg, but inflation had crept in and in the early 1980s the basic contract was £5000 with a price of up to £50,000 for the death of one of the supergrasses who were proliferating.

pool of blood at the Ranelagh Yacht Club, Fulham – it was also known as Bobby's Club. Tough guy TV actor John Bindon, friend of the model Vicki Hodge, from West London, was arrested and charged with what the prosecution alleged was a contract murder. He was said to have undertaken the contract for a fee of £10,000.

Bindon disappeared immediately after Darke's death and was found a fortnight later in a Dublin hospital. He was said to have staged an amazing escape to foil a gangland execution squad. The *News of the World* thought the amazing escape had been with the full co-operation of the police, who had let him leave hospital after giving vital information about the feud. Bindon, one of whose television programmes had to be postponed whilst he was in custody, walked free from the Old Bailey in November 1979. 'There is a hell of a lot behind this – villains who I'd made enemies with in the past,' he told the *Sun*.

He appeared in various courts throughout the 1980s, mainly on petty matters, and in November 1982 he appeared before the West London magistrate, Eric Crowther, who fined him £100 for possessing an offensive weapon. 'I regret I have not had the pleasure of seeing you act to my knowledge, except here,' said Crowther, with one eye on the evening papers.

Bindon's name came up again in 1984 when the ex-boxer charged in connection with the Pen Club murder of Selwyn Cooney back in 1961, was alleged to have been building an empire of pubs and clubs in South London – and running them through fear. The claim was made by the police at a hearing of an application for a licence in the name of former Bolton Wanderers star, Alvan Williams. The police alleged that the boxer was mixed up with major criminals at home and abroad in organizing serious crime. 'I'm no gangster,' said the boxer angrily, adding that he was taking legal advice. 'Of

course I know villains but I also know very respectable
people.'

In the late 1980s, the boxer, who always maintained
an interest in the sport, was involved in the contract of
a promising South London light-heavyweight boxer. In
1991 he was arrested and charged in connection with a
major drug smuggling operation.

In 1991 both Alfie Hinds and Stephen Jewell died
peacefully. Their lives had been rather less so. Hinds'
criminal career had led to a change in the law, while his
great friend and business partner, Tony 'The Magpie'
Maffia, was killed by Stephen Jewell, who served a life
sentence on his conviction. Throughout his trial Jewell
constantly implicated Hinds in the killing.

Alfie Hinds, who died in January, had a number of
claims to fame. With an IQ of 150 he certainly had the
intelligence to qualify for the dubious epithet Master
Criminal – his old adversary Chief Superintendent
Herbert Sparks thought he was 'the most cunning and
dangerous criminal' he had met. In those pre-Ronnie
Biggs days of the early 1960s he was certainly the best
known prison escaper and he was generally regarded as
the best non-lawyer advocate of his time who appeared
on his own behalf in the criminal courts.

Hinds was born in 1928, the son of parents who had
both seen the inside of prison. Indeed his father had
been sentenced to ten strokes of the cat on being
convicted for a bank robbery in Portsmouth. He had
died soon after and Hinds believed that the flogging had
contributed to his death. As a young man and a skilled
safebreaker, he was in and out of Borstal and army
detention centres but after the war, apart from what he
described as 'a foolish incident in 1946', he had seemingly settled down and worked in the demolition
business for his brother. He had a small bungalow (or
the largest on the island depending upon whether the

commentator is pro-Hinds or not) at Wraysbury on the Thames. On Thursday, 24 September 1953, the furniture and department store, Maples in Tottenham Court Road, London, was burgled. The thieves struck lucky. When the safe was blown there was a considerable amount of jewellery discovered. Four days later Hinds was arrested at his bungalow along with two others. For his part in the burglary he received a sentence of twelve years' preventive detention from Lord Goddard.

Hinds bitterly and continually protested his innocence. The theft had been an inside job and the evidence against him consisted of that of accomplices, some scientific evidence (particularly dust in the trouser turn-ups of a suit Hinds said he had not worn since it had been cleaned) and some verbal admissions. He maintained that he had had poor representation – a last-minute change of counsel with the substitute refusing to call his alibi witnesses – as well as suffering at the voice of an interrupting Lord Chief Justice whose interjections and questions ran into the hundreds in a two-day trial. And, he maintained, perjured police evidence.

There is no doubt, however, that, at best, Hinds had been in the wrong place at the wrong time. On the Monday prior to the theft he had gone to Tottenham Court Road to buy a carpet from one of the co-accused in a pub. He had lent the man his Land Rover and when it had not been returned had telephoned the police and reported it stolen. He maintained that had he been involved he would never have put himself on offer. The counter-argument was that this was a diabolically cunning move to divert suspicion if his vehicle had been seen on a reconnoitre – just the sort of thing a Master Criminal, class of '53, would have thought of doing.

Hinds was nothing if not resourceful. While in prison he wrote a leaflet detailing his innocence, and had it printed and circulated. His first escape came two years later when he left Nottingham Prison in November 1955 using a hacksaw blade and a prison workshop key he copied from memory. He stayed on the run for 245 days, circulating his pamphlet and recording interviews for later use on the television and radio.

The newspapers and the public loved him. Almost all the popular papers recruited 'experts' to comment on his escape. Major Pat Reid from Colditz wrote for the *Sunday Dispatch*, Geoffrey Household, author of *Rogue Male* – the story of a man on the run from the Nazis – had his say in the *Daily Mail* and even the now released 'Mad Parson' John Allen, who had himself escaped from Broadmoor and had stayed out for two years before recapture, gave his comments. Hinds, caught in Dublin on 31 July 1956, successfully defended himself on a charge of prison breaking and continued to use the legal process to try to have his case reopened and provide the opportunity for another escape. In the meantime the *Star* published his version of events, 'This is My Case', in July 1957.

His next escape chance came when he went to the Law Courts in the Strand to argue a case against the Prison Commissioners. With the help of a friend, Tony 'The Fox' or 'The Magpie' Maffia, he locked his escorts in a lavatory and was gone. This time he did not last long on the outside. He was caught in Bristol, recognized by an alert stewardess who later said she felt mean for giving him away, about to board a plane to Ireland. For his part in the affair, Maffia was later sentenced to twelve months' imprisonment. It was back to prison for Hinds and this time he stayed until in 1958 he escaped from Chelmsford with another copied key. His old safebreaking experience was standing him well. Two years later, as William Herbert Bishop, he was arrested, again in Ireland. Back in prison he continued to seek the reopening of his case, at one time arguing in person before the House of Lords.

In June 1961 one of his co-accused gave his story to the *News of the World* saying 'Alfie Hinds wasn't in on the deal but he had been promised a cheap carpet.' Hinds was still trying unsuccessfully to have his case reopened when a short time later Herbert Sparks, on his retirement from the police, published his memoirs in the *People*. In them he said Hinds 'couldn't admit that he had been out-thought by the police', adding, 'I think it is a pity that Alfie did not take his medicine manfully.'

Now on the hostel scheme under which prisoners go to a halfway house before their release, Hinds sued for libel, offering to withdraw the case if his appeal against conviction could be reopened. This time his case was far better prepared and he was represented by James Comyn, later to become a High Court judge, who called experts to throw cold water over the scientific evidence. His alibi witnesses stood up and, in a test of will, Hinds came over much better to the jury than an emotional Sparks. Hinds was also fortunate in that the police were going through one of their bad patches. The Challenor case had not been forgotten and when at one point during cross-examination Sparks buried his face in his hands, a wag in the gallery called 'Watch out! He's doing a Challenor.'

Despite an unfavourable summing-up the jury awarded Hinds the then huge amount of £1300. Disregarding James Comyn's advice not to put his head in the lion's mouth again, the award emboldened him to go one more time to the Court of Appeal. But that court was not as easily persuaded as a jury. For the last time his appeal was rejected. By now, however, he had been released and for some time he lectured on the criminal justice system at polytechnics. The law was later changed so that a criminal conviction was effectively a bar to subsequent civil proceedings to claim it was wrong.

In the Channel Islands Hinds became not only the Secretary of Mensa for the islands but a successful property developer. 'Plumbers are like lawyers,' he said. 'I found I couldn't rely on them so I learnt to do it all myself.'[10]

Throughout the rest of his life he kept in touch with his friend and helpmate, the small but flamboyant Tony Maffia. They acquired a coppermine in Portugal together and worked in various enterprises. They also both knew Stephen Jewell.

For outside purposes Maffia was a car trader with a small firm, Justice Motors. His card carried a drawing of the Old Bailey figure but with the scales of justice weighed down rather than evenly balanced. Described as having bundles of personality and a man who couldn't keep his hands off a quick deal, he was one of the largest receivers of stolen goods to be found.

He disappeared in 1968 soon after he returned from Belgium, where he had shown an interest in forged notes over which he might have been deceived. On 27 May he met a recent acquaintance, Stephen Jewell, a Manchester coal merchant, who hoped to sell him forged £10 notes and to whom Maffia hoped to sell his cruiser, the *Calamara*, then in a marina at Wallasey Island. The price for the notes was £8000 in real money against £32,000 paper value.

According to Jewell, when he saw Maffia's house in Buckhurst Hill he liked it so much he suggested buying it. The price, which now seems nominal – £12,000 – was even then a bargain. Maffia was separated from his wife

---

[10] Sparks outlived Hinds and at the end of 1991 was in retirement in Sussex. On Hinds' death he wrote a rueful letter to the *Police Pensioners* magazine warning ex-officers against publishing their memoirs.

and a sale was needed. They then drove in Maffia's green Jaguar MCC 932 to the marina to see the boat. Jewell carried a gun which, he said, Maffia had instructed him to bring. The gun, with its magazine housing bullets with a hole in every nose, was put on the front seat covered with a cloth. Jewell's car was then left in a pub car-park. They certainly went to the marina, where Maffia reversed a call to London to say he would be back in about an hour. After they left the marina he was never seen alive again. Maffia had been planning to fly to Jersey later that day. Apparently he had important papers to sign.

'Everybody's wondering what happened to Tony,' says a friend. Well, the Krays were no friends of his. When Charlie Kray was in a spot of trouble in Africa and needed money to repatriate him, a whip had been organized. Maffia had told them to bugger off and get the money the hard way as he had done, by grafting.[11] However, the twins were in custody and, for once, blame could not be laid at their door. Tony's older brother, the much shyer Arthur, was missing as well. He was wanted for questioning over a spot of LF.

Negotiations were opened with the police by a retired wrestler, 'Man Mountain' Dean, who arranged the surrender of Arthur Maffia. The long firm enquiries came to nothing but Arthur could not explain where his brother might be.

Four days later on 1 June it became quite apparent where he was. On the Whit Saturday one of the staff at the Midway Restaurant, so called because it was between Southend and London, saw a dog sniffing at a

---

[11] It was over this that Buller Ward was striped. He warned Maffia in the Regency Club that the Krays were about to do him over. Maffia escaped through a back door, but for his treachery Ward received 110 stitches in his face.

green Jaguar which had been in the car-park for the last few days. In the front passenger seat covered by a tarpaulin was Maffia. It had been a hot few days and his body was so bloated it was recognizable only by finger-prints and a gold ring he wore. He had been shot twice, by the right eye and behind the right ear.

Two days later Jewell, of his own volition, arranged to see Detective Chief Inspector Kenneth Drury.[12] His story was that shortly after he and Maffia had left the marina, they were stopped by three men in a Ford Zodiac who told Jewell to go away while they talked to Maffia about a deal. When he returned both Maffia and the Zodiac were gone, as was the pistol and ammunition from the Jaguar. The car itself was still there. Jewell's overcoat which he had left in the car was blood-stained. He described the men, saying that one had a scar on his cheek.

He said he drove off in the Jaguar for London and after a time stopped to throw the overcoat into a field. It was just as well he admitted that, for the coat was found containing a live bullet and sale particulars of Maffia's house. A witness would later say he saw Jewell wipe the passenger door with the coat before it was thrown away. He agreed he left the Jaguar in the car-park of the Midway Restaurant.

It was not a good story. Quite apart from the forensic evidence against him, how did Maffia's body get into the Jaguar if it was not in it when Jewell drove to the Midway? It is impossible to believe that when Jewell dumped the Jaguar at the restaurant, the killers then happened upon it quite by chance and in full view put Maffia's body in the passenger seat. Or had they

[12] Drury was later implicated in the great Porn Squad enquiry, convicted and sentenced to eight years' imprisonment, reduced to five on appeal.

followed him all the time, watching what he was going to do? Jewell was convicted by a ten to two majority. Throughout the trial he had repeatedly sought to implicate Hinds, answering questions by saying that Hinds should be asked about the subject. After the trial Hinds was allowed to have counsel, Mr Roger Frisby, make a statement in court denying any knowledge of the murder.

Why did Jewell go to the police in the first place? There were probably enough local candidates to keep the police happy in their enquiries for months. Presumably he wanted to get his story in first in the hope it would be believed. Unfortunately he changed the details on a number of occasions, although he stuck to the basic details throughout his trial and sentence. Whilst he was in Wandsworth he wrote to Arthur Maffia denying, yet again, that he had been his brother's killer and giving descriptions of the men whom he said had stopped the car. Arthur Maffia and other friends made what are quaintly described as 'their own investigations' and were satisfied the killer was Jewell. But Jewell could still find supporters for his story and in 1991 a television programme was made advancing his version of events.

Once the police began their investigations into Maffia's background they unearthed a series of safe-boxes containing the proceeds from a string of robberies in the Home Counties, including a gold bar from the £750,000 gold bullion robbery in Bowling Green Lane, East London, a year earlier. There were coins, diamonds, Dresden porcelain and jewellery. His name 'The Magpie' was completely justified.

There seems no really good reason why Jewell should have killed Maffia. It certainly wasn't a robbery. When the body was stripped, cash and cheques totalling over £700 were found, together with some rare gold coins. As always a number of theories were advanced. It was a contract hit – in which case it was extremely clumsily executed; Maffia was shot because he would not join in a forgery racket, which seems unlikely as offers such as this are made and declined on a daily basis without such major reprisals; Jewell had swindled Maffia and Hinds, which doesn't account for why he then shot Maffia; that he was swindled by Maffia and Hinds, which would. There is no suggestion that Maffia was a grass. Another theory advanced by friends is that Jewell showed Maffia three £10 notes and said pick the right ones for £4 each. They were all genuine and Maffia put £12 on the table saying he was not being taken for a mug and that was all he was going to buy. The theory is that on the way back to London Maffia ('he had a spiteful tongue') taunted Jewell, who shot him in temper.

Maffia was thirty-eight at the time of his death and, assuming you count other people's property as his, was worth well over £500,000.

Another killing which brought back the past was that of fashion expert Beatrice Gold, who on 8 September 1975 was shot through the head at point-blank range at the dress factory she owned in Islington. The killing was certainly a contract one and thirty-one-year-old Errol Heibner, a self-confessed jewellery store robber, was gaoled for life with a recommendation that he serve a minimum of twenty-five years for the killing. But why was she killed?

The link with the past was the second defendant at Heibner's trial, Robert 'Battles' Rossi, who had previously been sentenced to seven years for the slashing of Jack Spot. Now it was alleged that he was the contact man who had set up the murder, for which Heibner had been paid £8000, and had provided the pistol with which Mrs Gold was shot.

But there were many things to muddy the waters. Her lifestyle had been bizarre. She was the author of two

unpublished novels on sex and was what was impolitely
known as a fag hag, a woman who favoured the company
of homosexuals, whose parties she and her husband
regularly attended. She was also said to be involved with
the Soho porn market and was thought by Bernie Silver
to have documents which could be used for blackmailing
purposes. Indeed, according to the evidence at the trial,
there had been a meeting between Silver, Zomparelli
and a Frankie Albert (who later fell to his death from a
roof during a police raid) to discuss her position. There
had been nearly fifty keys to her factory floating around
to make it easy for the killer to gain entry, but who but
an intimate would know she would be alone and in
position at exactly the right moment?

Rossi was an old friend of a Hatton Garden villain,
George Miesel, himself a friend of Albert Dimes and
one-time bookmaker on the point-to-point courses.
Rossi lived over Miesel's spieler at one time. The case
was that Rossi had handed a package containing the gun
to Heibner in the Strand only a few hours before the
killing. In evidence Rossi told the court he thought the
package had contained jewellery. He was found not
guilty.

For some years after the murder a television producer
worked on the theory that a prominent London solicitor
had been involved in the killing. The proposed documentary programme was never shown.

Other killings were definitely linked to past crimes.
Sid Kiki, the betting shop proprietor, was a regular
police informant, providing them with good information.
One evening in May 1967 he telephoned Nipper Read.
'Listen,' he said, 'you've got another Ginger Marks on
the manor.' Did Read know of a man, Jack Buggy?
When Read said he had never heard of him Kiki asked
if he knew of the Mount Street Bridge Club. At one time
it had been quite a fashionable card club but as the years

had passed it had become little more than an illegal gaming club run by Franny Daniels and his nephew Charles 'Waggy' Whitnall.

'Well,' said Kiki, 'this fella Buggy was knocked off in there a few nights ago and his body has been done away with. Apparently he was making a right nuisance of himself. Albert Dimes was called in at the end.'

American-born John 'Scotch Jack' Buggy had come to England with the American forces and had become a Glasgow hard-man. In 1961 he had been sentenced to nine years' imprisonment following the shooting of Robert Reeder outside the Pigalle night club in Swallow Street. Buggy had endeavoured to go backstage to invite singer Shirley Bassey, who was the cabaret act that night, to attend a private party. He was turned away shouting loudly. Reeder, who was dining in the club, complained and Buggy smashed a plate over his head. Both men were ejected and Buggy shot Reeder at point-blank range. He was acquitted of shooting with intent to kill but convicted of shooting with intent to cause grievous bodily harm. During the time he had been in prison Buggy had served part of his sentence, and become friendly, with one of the Great Train Robbers, Roy James.

Read and his Superintendent, Arthur Butler, walked round to the bridge club from West End Central to see what was going on. Both noted that there was a new carpet on the club's floor. But there were no signs of nerves from either the punters or the staff. The club was hardly a hive of activity. Butler sent Read to make some enquiries and he went to Buggy's address in Kilburn. He discovered that his girlfriend, Ann Phillips, had received a telephone call from him on 12 May telling her to meet him at her mother's stall in Kingston Market. Buggy had not shown up and two days later she had told the police in Sutton he had gone missing.

Now all sorts of rumours started to fly around the West End. The night before Buggy disappeared a gelignite bomb had gone off in the hallway of the club in Mount Street. He was known to have been involved in protection rackets in the past. Could the bomb and his disappearance have been connected to them? Ann Phillips told the *Evening Standard* that he had given up that part of his life, but could she really know that? Then there was a suggestion that he owed £20,000 to a big-time syndicate. Another version was that it was a Mafia-backed killing and yet another that Buggy had been protecting a man who had turned against him.

There was also the story, and it was the one which lasted the longest, that he had gone in search of money belonging to Roy James and said to be held, but unaccounted for, by a man who frequented the club. It was also said that the man had been given the money to mind but when the Train Robbers' appeals were dismissed he had gone on a spending spree and blown it all.[13] Buggy's mission was to try to recover at least part of it. As to Buggy's death, the firm rumour was that he had been shot in the club at around 3 p.m., his body wrapped in a carpet and taken away. There was yet another story that he had eventually been killed in a garage in Kingston upon Thames.

Buggy's red MGB sports car turned up in Maida Avenue by the Grand Union Canal. In it was a key to a safe deposit box which he always carried. It was now clear that he was dead and a murder investigation was started. Police frogmen dived into the muddy waters of the canal while other police, along with forensic

---

[13] In his book, *The Great Train Robbery*, Piers Paul Read endeavours to account for the total monies stolen in the raid, apportioning shares to each man. He lists £76,000 as having been stolen by the man deputed to guard Roy James' share.

scientists, began the search of the club's Regency-striped walls and its spanking new carpet.

There was no help at all from the members who had been in the club. They knew nothing or, if they did, they certainly would say nothing. It had all the hallmarks of a gangland execution. Two men whom the police thought could assist and so wished to interview were out of the country.

The body surfaced, so to speak, in a slightly unusual fashion. Two off-duty police officers out fishing off Seaford in Sussex had seen something floating. They had cast for it, hooked it and reeled in Buggy's body. It was wearing his black polo-neck sweater and the arms had been bound with baling wire. He had also been gagged. In his back pocket was his driving licence and some correspondence. An examination by the pathologist Francis Camps showed he had been shot twice.

The police made little more progress the second time around. One of the men whom they wished to interview, Waggy Whitnall, was in Vienna, where after negotiations he agreed to be interviewed in the presence of a London solicitor, Andrew Keenan. Nothing came of that interview and he remained in Austria. When it came to it no one was arrested and charged that year, nor for the next six.

There was, however, an interesting sequel to the story. On his deathbed in 1973 Albert Dimes is said to have ordered that the police be told the truth about Buggy's death. In any event enquiries were renewed and then Donald Wardle, a member of a team of Australian shoplifters who was serving nine years for blackmail, made a statement. As a result Whitnall's uncle, Francis Daniels, then aged sixty-three, and Abraham Lewis, who was two years older and had been working at the club at the time of Buggy's death, were charged with his murder. Wardle maintained that he had been in the gaming room of the club on the afternoon of Buggy's death when he had heard three shots. Daniels, he said, had come out and told him and other players to go home.

In November 1974 both men were acquitted and so the death of 'Scotch Jack' Buggy still remains a mystery. Like all unsolved crimes it has been taken out and dusted down over the years and even more reasons have been put forward for the slaying.

Read still believes it was something to do with the Train Robbery money. Shortly before he left 'C' division a Mr Field had called at Savile Row asking to see him. Read was surprised to discover it was the former solicitor's managing clerk, Brian Field. He told Read he knew Buggy because he had served part of his sentence in the same prison and that there was no doubt in his mind that Buggy had heard the story of the handing over of the money from the robbery for safekeeping. According to Field it was common gossip in the prison.[14]

A final footnote is provided by Tony Lambrianou, one of the Krays' runners. He had been turned over and questioned in the investigations into Buggy's death. Years later he met Roy James in Gartree.

And the Weasel was asking me why Buggy had to go.

He said, 'The money doesn't matter to me. I just wouldn't like to think Buggy died for it.'

I was happy to tell Roy that we genuinely hadn't had anything to do with the murder.[15]

One murderer managed to evade justice for so long that the warrant against him was eventually withdrawn.

[14] L. Read and J. Morton, *Nipper*, p. 124 et seq.
[15] T. Lambrianou, *Inside the Firm*, pp. 118–19.

John Gaul, procurer to the rich and with a conviction for living off immoral earnings, set up the contract killing of his estranged wife Barbara, a former children's nanny, who was shot outside the Black Lion Hotel, Patcham, near Brighton, where she had been visiting her daughter Samantha on Monday, 12 January 1977. She died eleven weeks later.

On the basis that when a wife is killed the first person to be questioned is the husband, John Gaul was taken in to Cannon Row police station but was later released. Almost immediately he fled to Rio de Janeiro. Later that year he was found with a new nanny, Angela Pilch, in Switzerland before moving on to Malta.

Originally Gaul had been a property dealer, who diversified into motor trading and then returned to his first love when in 1952 he took over Sun Real Estates, a publicly quoted company which had not paid any dividends for some time. In 1958 it had paid an 8.5 per cent dividend and had a trading profit of £37,000. In 1962 the profit was £122,000 with premises worth £3 million.

On 11 October 1962 Gaul had been fined £25,000 for living off prostitution. Through a firm called Rent and Management he had leased out flats in Soho to prostitutes, charging £20 a week for old squalid properties with poor furniture. Of the £20 only £8 8s was entered in the rent book. It was collected by a pair of old Soho characters, Thomas Jenkins and Anthony Deguilio.

Now, in theory, all that was behind him. In practice it was not. His name came up in both the Profumo and Lambton vice scandals.

It was not difficult for the police to trace the actual killers of his wife. On the way from the killing the shotgun used was dropped from a car window and later the car was traced to a breakers yard in East London. The contract had been arranged in Norfolk with two

East End brothers, Roy and Keith Edgeler.

The brothers were gaoled on 24 June 1976. In the witness box Roy said that from his limited knowledge he did not believe it was John Gaul who had arranged the contract for which he was to have been paid £10,000. Roy Edgeler was given a recommendation of a minimum of twenty years to serve.

On 3 April 1978 Gaul was arrested in Malta, where he was living on a boat in the harbour, having defied efforts to have him returned to the United Kingdom. There had been troubles with the United Kingdom's extradition treaty with Malta because the Home Secretary had refused to extradite a Maltese woman on a forgery charge. Gaul had high political connections in Malta.

Why should he be involved in the killing? he asked. Barbara had agreed to an undefended divorce, claiming neither alimony nor costs, and had already relinquished claims to the child, Samantha. There was no reason why he should have had her killed, he argued plausibly.

On 24 April 1978 a blast destroyed a mini-cab office and flats in Hackney Road, owned by Printing House Properties Ltd, a £100 company owned by Gaul. It was thought that a Maltese, John Borg, who had been involved in West End properties over the years and who had been gaoled for ten years for gunning down another Maltese outside a Stepney cafe in 1953, had died in the blaze. This turned out to be correct. Borg's body was found in the wreckage on 3 May. Curiously, no smoke was found to have been in his lungs, a clear indication he had died before the fire. Things were made more complicated when it became known that a Portuguese, Carlos Amazonas, had made a statement to the police that Borg had been approached to kill Mrs Barbara Gaul. This statement had somehow found its way into the Soho underworld.

By 1981 Gaul was assumed to be safe in Malta because

of his political connections. Officially the explanation was that insufficient evidence had been supplied by the British police, but Gaul was now well established – he had built and leased out a 240-room hotel. In March that year he was reported to have had a serious heart attack. On 17 July 1981 a magistrate in Malta said the prosecution case was weak and refused to order extradition.

By April 1984 it was reported the English police had given up. Even if he came back, the passage of time had made witnesses' memories unreliable. Gaul was said to be ill and medical certificates were sent to the Director of Public Prosecutions and the warrant was dropped on his orders. Gaul at once flew to Switzerland and then came back for his son Simon's wedding in September 1984. He died in September 1989 in Italy. He had been reported missing but it was three days before it was realized he had died in a Milan hospital.

According to the *Sun*[16] Keith Edgeler, then in Ford Open Prison, named Gaul as the man who had ordered the contract. It was, he said, because Gaul feared Barbara was about to expose shady deals. He said he never received the payment for the murder. Despite offers by the police for a deal he had refused to talk on the basis that if a man could have his wife murdered, his own family was in danger.

In two connected gangland killings there still seems to be no general consensus of opinion as to why the victims were executed, nor for that matter is there complete certainty amongst the cognoscenti that the right men were put away. The Legal and General Murders was the last major case investigated by Bert Wickstead and it concerned the deaths of two second division robbers –

[16] 31 October 1989.

the gaunt, gangling Billy Moseley and his close friend, Micky Cornwall, the first of whom disappeared in the autumn of 1974 and the second in the spring of the following year.

The Legal and General Gang[17] was headed by Reginald Dudley, a hard-man with convictions for violence, and a most unlikely villain, Bobby 'Fat Bob' Maynard, a roly-poly amiable man who had a terrible speech impediment caused, it was said, by being severely beaten in a fight in a club in Tottenham Court Road. He spoke extremely slowly with long gaps between words and was seemingly unaware of this problem because if interrupted by the recipient of his telephone call with a 'Hello Bobby', he would reply 'How-do-you-know-it's-me?'

By the mid-1970s Dudley had become a professional receiver. 'He didn't mess about with anything except high-quality stuff', dealing alike with the underworld and the police, for whom he was also said to be an informer.

'He was well respected in the fraternity. I always thought he could go as far as the Krays and the Richardsons. He had a team and he had the ability and the sense of purpose to do to North London what the Krays did to East London,' says one police officer who knew him.

On his release from prison in September 1974 Moseley was horrified to find his old schoolfriend Maynard had teamed up with Dudley. On 26 September Moseley set off for a meeting at 6.30 p.m. with Ronnie Fright at the Victoria Sporting Club in Stoke Newington. He had been having an affair with Frankie, Ronnie's wife, whilst

---

[17] The soubriquet Legal and General Gang came about when Dudley and Maynard appeared in a Kentish Town public house wearing identical overcoats which resembled a popular television commercial for the Legal and General insurance group.

Fright was serving a seven-year sentence for armed robbery and the meeting was to clear the air between them. Moseley was never again seen alive. Parts of his body started to surface a week later in the Thames near Rainham. Although the head and hands were missing it was possible to make a positive identification of the body since Moseley had suffered from a rare skin disease. The autopsy also showed he had been tortured. His toe-nails had been pulled out and he had been burned.

Moseley's other great friend, Micky Cornwall, was released from prison a fortnight after the bits started floating along the river. He was tied in to Dudley through a short liaison he had been having with Dudley's daughter Kathy. Kathy had once been married to a John Dann, known as Donuts possibly because he had worked in a bakery but also because it was said he cut holes in people who offended him. That marriage had broken down and she had taken up with a Ray Baron. When, in turn, he went to prison, she took up with Cornwall. In theory this was just as heinous a crime as Moseley's affair with Frankie Fright but neither Baron nor the paterfamilias, Dudley, seems to have objected.

Cornwall, along with any number of criminals before and after him, was looking for a 'big one'. He now had a new girlfriend, Gloria Hogg, and was looking for sufficient money to buy a place in the country. Cornwall, again like many other criminals, lacked discretion. He confided his plans to John Moriarty, hardly the best person because Moriarty later turned supergrass after being shot in the leg for the second time. Cornwall left Gloria for the 'big one' on Sunday, 3 August 1975. He had been renting a room from another police informer, Colin Saggs, and left shortly before two men came looking for him. Sharon Saggs, his daughter, would identify them as Dudley and Maynard at the trial. Moriarty saw him at a bus stop in Highgate on 23 August and that seems to have been the last sighting of him before his body was found in a newly dug grave at Hatfield, Hertfordshire. He had been shot in the head.

The old 'gangbuster' Wickstead's last swoop was on 22 January 1976. Seven people out of eighteen taken were charged. They had been interviewed over a period of four days[18] and included Dudley and his daughter Kathy, Maynard and Ronnie Fright. During the period in custody they were said to have made admissions which amounted to evidence against them. Dudley was alleged to have said of Cornwall, 'I told him if he had sex with her, I would kill him.' Maynard allegedly admitted going to the Saggs' house looking for Cornwall. 'It was business,' he said. As for the question put to him that he had told Fright to be late for the rendezvous at the Victoria Sporting Club, he is said to have replied, 'I'm not answering that, otherwise I'm finished.' Apparently, Wickstead had had a tape-recorder fitted into his desk at the police station but had never switched it on. Why not? asked the defence.

'I am a police officer who believes in police methods and tape-recorders are not used in police interviews,' replied the Commander.

The prosecution's case was that the killings had occurred because (1) Moseley had had an affair with Frankie Fright, (2) he had fallen out with Dudley ten years earlier, (3) Moseley had been suggesting Dudley was a grass, (4) he, Moseley, was sitting on the proceeds of a large jewellery robbery, (5) out of sheer sadism, (6) Cornwall had set out to avenge Moseley's death, (7) he

---

[18] The effective implementation of the Police and Criminal Evidence Act of 1984 was nearly ten years away. At the time suspects in serious cases could be interviewed almost endlessly. Then such protection as was available to suspects was the informal Judges' Rules. These did not include the right to the presence of a solicitor during interview.

had discovered Dudley and Maynard were the killers and so (8) had had more than a brief liaison with Kathy in order to find out the truth. It was said Moseley had been shot with a single bullet. The case against Ronnie Fright was that he was deliberately late for his meet with Moseley outside the Victoria Sporting Club and so had lured him to his death.

Apart from the confessions and the liaisons between the various dead and accused there was not, as the judge, Mr Justice Swanwick, told the jury, 'evidence on which the Crown could ask you to convict'. The police had stated on oath the confessions were accurate and the defence had said they were fabricated. Whom were the jury to believe?

Much of the rest of the evidence was the rag-bag of serving prisoners who, having seen the light, were able to give evidence against their former cell-mates.

In the end Ronnie Fright was acquitted, as was another defendant, while a third had been acquitted at the direction of the judge. Bobby Maynard was found guilty on a majority decision on the third day of the jury's retirement. He and Dudley were sentenced to life imprisonment; Kathy received a suspended sentence along with an old-time villain, Charlie Clarke. Six weeks later Moseley's head, wrapped in a plastic bag, was found in a public lavatory in Barnsbury, North London. Perhaps significantly the copy of the *Evening News* wrapped around it was dated 16 June 1977, when the jury had been in retirement.

Some facts emerged from the inquest. The head was in 'extremely' good condition, Professor James Cameron, who had undertaken the initial autopsy, told the coroner. Traces of car paint indicated it had been in a garage for some of the three years since Moseley had choked on his own blood. That removed one of the pillars on which the Crown had based its case. It had also been in a deep freeze, for it was on the thaw when it was discovered.

After the appeals were rejected the families of both Dudley and Maynard launched a campaign to prove their innocence. It did not take the extreme course adopted by the friends of George Davis. T-shirts were sold and there was a march through Camden Town to Hyde Park Corner. Bobby Maynard junior stood as a candidate in the European Parliament elections in June 1984. Inevitably, however, the campaign suffered with Davis' conviction for the Bank of Cyprus raid. Dudley appeared on television in the 1984 BBC programme *Lifers*. Nor was the North London underworld convinced of their guilt. Whilst it was accepted that Dudley was capable of great violence, few could believe that Maynard had the same capacity. Over the years various names have been put up as the potential killers but no real enquiry has been undertaken by the authorities.

In 1991 'Liberty' adopted the Maynard–Dudley case as one for special consideration in a campaign against wrongful convictions. With the passing of the Police and Criminal Evidence Act of 1984 it is doubtful if there would have been convictions in the Legal and General case.[19]

Several years later, in November 1985, two more heads turned up. They seem to have been thrown one night at the door of Harold Hill police station, Essex. They belonged to hard-man David Elmore and James 'Jimmy the Wad' Waddington (so named because he always carried a wad of money) who had vanished on St Valentine's Day 1984, thereby giving the press a good deal of licence to use the word 'massacre'. Elmore, a night club bouncer, and Waddington, who happened to

---

[19] For a more detailed account of the case, see B. Woffinden, *Miscarriages of Justice*.

be in the wrong place at the wrong time, were bound hand and foot, then attacked with a ceremonial sword stolen from a sports club and throttled with a tablecloth in the Kaleli restaurant in Station Road, Barking. According to a witness, Brian Wilson, Elmore began reciting the Lord's Prayer and when he reached 'Thy will be done', he was interrupted by one of his attackers who said, 'You're dead right, son'. The killing was said by the prosecutor, William Denny QC, to be the culmination of a longstanding feud between the Elmores and another East End family, the Maxwells, which had included an axe attack on a relative, Mickey Maxwell, ten years earlier. An alternative theory was that Elmore had been running a protection racket and that he and Waddington had been attacked as they had finished their meal at the Turkish restaurant.

Bar steward David Maxwell was acquitted of the murder in January 1985 after just an hour's retirement by the jury. 'I am off to celebrate with my family,' he told reporters.

> I have been held in prison since March for crimes I had nothing to do with. The jury accepted what I told them about prosecution witnesses lying through their teeth. We had only got the word of the police that these two men were murdered in the first place.
>
> The only reason that I can put forward as to why the staff at the restaurant implicated us is that they have something to hide and they wanted a fall guy.

David Reader, who was acquitted of assisting in the disposal of the bodies, added, 'It's all been an ordeal. The allegations against us and my brother are totally without foundation.'

His brother Ronnie Reader was in Spain at the time

of David's and Maxwell's arrest, and in November 1984 announced that he would be returning to England. 'I'm giving myself up,' he told the *Sun* in an exclusive article, in which he said he would return home after Maxwell and his brother had faced their trial. 'I'm taking a terrible chance,' said Ronnie, who at the time lived in a small flat in 'picturesque Nerja' on the Costa del Sol. 'If I am found guilty, it means life imprisonment.'[20] He wasn't.

After his acquittal the senior detective in the case said the police 'are not looking for anyone else'.[21]

After the heads were found, Jimmy Waddington's mother Winifred told the *Daily Express*, 'I felt desolation not knowing where his last resting place might be or what exactly happened to him. I wanted to have him found in one piece but it looks like it could be him.'[22]

Others victims, such as Tony Mella, seem to have been killed almost pointlessly. Mella, a small-time thief and one-time proprietor of a spinner,[23] had been a boxer. In his early days he thought he had promise as a heavyweight. He fought at the Mile End Arena where his friends had arranged that his opponent should throw the contest. In the next match he came up against Dennis Powell, a southern area champion, who would not agree to the fix. Powell gave him a bad beating before knocking him out.

Later he became semi-respectable and took to running

[20] *Sun*, 7 November 1984.

[21] *Today*, 21 March 1986.

[22] *Daily Express*, 6 November 1985.

[23] A spinner, now rarely seen, was a cross between the three-card trick and a roulette wheel. Played outside racecourses and dog-tracks, it consisted of the punter betting on which suit of cards came up. It was, of course, fixed by using a stick, known in the trade as a Haley, to stop the wheel.

clubs such as the El Ababi in Soho. He was heavily involved with gambling machines with interests throughout England. There are a number of colourful stories about him. One is that a bayonet was rammed into his backside and left there for several hours. The metal cauterized the wound and it healed. He also fell foul of the dwarf Roy Smith, who wrestled as Fuzzy Kaye:

> . . . I opened this club for dwarves in Gerrard Street. Tony Mulla [sic], who was a big villain in those days, had two clip joints down the street. He thought I was taking away his business. He was angry and was wailing up and down the street, just across from my club, shouting at me: 'You think you're Jack the Lad', 'Midget mafia', and so on, trying to tell me that I was being cheeky and was out of order opening a club on his patch. . . . Anyway I wasn't having that and took him up the stairs above his clip joint, took his trousers down and slashed him across the arse with a razor; gave him noughts and crosses.[24]

Another story is of his death. He had, the story goes, offended a rival organization and a button man had been sent from America to carry out the hit. He went to Mella's office, asked if he was Mella and shot him. The gunman turned and walked calmly down the stairs. Mella, badly injured, managed to take his own gun from his safe, followed the American on to the street, shot him and then died himself.

The truth is more prosaic. One of Mella's minders was Big Alf Melvin, another man with a long criminal history. Over a period of time Melvin was treated appallingly by Mella both in front of the hostesses and

[24] G. Tremlett, *Little Legs*, p. 100.

A family snap of Jack 'The Hat' McVitie.

below: Eugenio Messina arriving handcuffed for the trial, accused of illegal possession of firearms and attempted procuring.

1970: 'To a fine gentleman': the wreath sent by the Twins to Albert Dimes's funeral.

Soho Rangers F.C. Left to right includes: Stanley Baker, George Wisbey, William Stayton, Tommy McCarthy (Bert's brother), Albert Dimes, Frankie Fraser. Front row includes: Bert McCarthy (boxing promoter) Eddie Richardson and others.

'The Sinister Scrapyard' said the newspapers. The Richardsons' yard at New Church Road, Camberwell.

Charles and Eddie Richardson.

left: Frank Fraser, friend to the mighty, doyen of both Soho clubs and the British prison system.

November 1980: a delighted Ronnie Knight leaves court after his acquittal on a charge of killing 'Italian' Tony Zomparelli.

right: George Brett, victim of Henry 'Big H' Mackenny

below: Terence Eve: victim of Big H flexes his muscles.

Friend of the famous, Ronnie Knight (left) with his wife Barbara
Windsor and Frank Norman, author of 'Fings Ain't What They Used
to Be'.

The Great Train Robbery case remembered: Gordon Goody (in dark
glasses back right) Bruce and Frances Reynolds, Micky Ball and, far
left, Roy James.

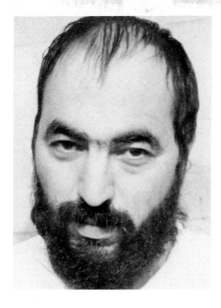

left: 1991: Dennis Arif, acting head of the Arif family jailed for 22 years after the shoot-out with the police in Surrey.

below: The scene of the Arif-police shoot-out.

Off to prison goes the Black Widow Linda Calvey after her conviction at the Central Criminal Court.

Mrs Meyrick's coming out party from Holloway Prison.

friends and the punters. 'Like he was a serf,' said Buller Ward. There was also the possibility that Mella had pulled a fast one and deprived Melvin of his interest in one of the clubs.

One afternoon in the Bus Stop Club in Soho, Melvin said to Tony Mella, 'You've took a right fucking liberty there. We been pals all these years. I been more like a brother to you and now you've gone and took a liberty like that.'

He fired at Mella, who ran out of the club shouting, 'The silly bastard's shot me.' Mella died on the pavement with his head being held by one of the hostesses who had followed him outside. Melvin sat in the club for some time and then put the gunbarrel in his mouth and pulled the trigger.[25]

English criminal law has always been a bit squeamish about convicting defendants of murder if no body has been found. It dates back to the seventeenth century when a man was executed for murder, only for his supposed victim to appear some years later. For a long time it was the case that there could be no conviction for murder without a body. Then in the 1880s came the case of Dudley and Stephens where the cabin boy was eaten at sea. In the case of James Camb, he was convicted although the body of Gay Gibson had been pushed through a porthole.

Then after the war came the case of Onufrejczyk, who was convicted of the murder of his partner in a farm even though the body was not found. From then on there was a series of cases where death was presumed beyond a reasonable doubt from the surrounding circumstances. Mrs McKay (killed by the Hossein brothers), Frank Mitchell, Jack 'the Hat' McVitie and Ginger Marks were

[25] H. Ward, *Buller*, p. 130.

all cases where there was no body. However, perhaps the most amazing series of cases where no bodies were found resulted from the killings by John Child, Henry MacKenny and Terence Pinfold.

Unlike Gerard who seems to have been a one-man hit squad, the three set themselves up as a team of contract killers and, for a time at least, they appear to have been very successful. In 1972 John Childs, more usually the getaway driver on armed robberies, discussed the prospect of providing contract killing with Henry MacKenny, a huge man who had his fingers tattooed with LTFC on his right hand and ESUK on his left, and Terence Pinfold. These two were partners in a firm which made both life-jackets and cuddly toys, working out of a small hall belonging to St Thomas' church in Haydon Road, Dagenham, Essex.

The idea met with mutual approbation but it was not until two years later that it was put into execution, partly because Childs was given a prison sentence for burglary in October 1974. The third partner in the cuddly toy firm, Terence Eve, was thought not to be pulling his weight. According to Childs, who became the chief prosecution witness, he and MacKenny were waiting when Eve returned to the church hall in Dagenham one October evening after making some deliveries of toys, coincidentally to Bob Patience at the Barn Restaurant in Braintree. Eve was beaten senseless with a metal pipe and then strangled with a rope. There were two witnesses, Pinfold and Robert Winston Brown, an odd job man in the workshop but a one-time none too successful professional wrestler who had worked small halls as one of the many masked White Angels about at the time. The police made enquiries but they came to nothing.

The first actual contract, according to Childs, was George Brett, a haulage contractor and receiver. He

disappeared along with his ten-year-old son Terence on
the first Saturday of 1975. The fee was said to be £2000
and was paid by Leonard Thompson, who had been
beaten up by Brett. It was a fee reduced by ten per cent
because, so Childs told the court, Thompson supplied a
sten-gun and two hundred rounds of ammunition.
Brett's wife had been approached earlier in the week by
a man who gave his name as Jennings. He had asked her
to make sure Brett was about on the Saturday. He
turned up again, this time as a 'city gent' wearing a
Homburg hat and carrying an umbrella. Brett said he
would follow him in his own car to look at a load the
man had for disposal. As he was leaving, Brett's son
Terence ran out and climbed into his father's Mercedes.
Neither were seen again but the car was found near
King's Cross station.

There were considerable rumours about his disappearance. Brett was believed to have been a police informer
and it was said he had informed once too often. Another
version was that he had stumbled on a crime syndicate
ready to take over the remainder of the Krays' operations. Or he was the victim of a 'group who organize
revenge beatings and shootings from prison' – a clear
and erroneous reference to the Tibbs family, who were
named in the newspaper article. Nevertheless it was
announced that Bert Wickstead had been called in to the
investigation. Finally it was suggested that he was
enquiring too deeply into a bullion robbery which had
netted £400,000 and for which George Brett's brother
John was serving a fifteen-year sentence.[26] Yet again the
police enquiries came to nothing. It was even thought
possible that Brett would return one day.

Childs' version of events was that he had been the city
gent. He had taken Brett and his son to the workshop,

[26] For footnote, see over.

where only three rounds had been required out of the two hundred. MacKenny had fired the shots at George Brett whilst Childs gave the child a worn teddy bear to hold as he was killed.

In November 1975 the White Angel was the next to go. Brown had earlier escaped from prison, where he was serving a short sentence, and it was feared that when recaptured he might trade off information about the Eve killing. He was lured to Childs' council flat in Poplar, where he was shot and then stabbed and struck with an axe. As befitted a man able to take punishment in the ring he survived these injuries and only died when run through with a sword by Childs.

Nearly three years later the team pulled off another contract. This time it was conducted, so Childs said, on behalf of Paul Morton-Thurtle who had had sour business dealings with a Frederick Sherwood, a constant companion of criminals, who ran a nursing home in Herne Bay. On 31 July 1978 Sherwood took his Rover car to a potential purchaser and was never seen again. The car was found in Earls Court. Childs' story on this occasion was that the price of the contract was £4000, payable by instalments of £1500 down and £500 a fortnight. Sherwood was taken to MacKenny's bungalow, near the workshop, given the £480 he had asked for the motor and shot while he checked the money.

The team's last success was on 12 October 1978 when a roof-repairer, Ronnie Andrews, disappeared. He had been having marital troubles with his wife Gwen. The

---

[26] On 29 November 1973 John Brett, together with three others including George Ince, was convicted of the hijacking of a £400,000 consignment of silver bullion at Mountnessing, Essex. 'You played for very high stakes – something over a third of a million pounds – and the penalty must be severe,' said Mr Justice Milmo sentencing them. (See Chapter 8.)

police made enquiries and also spoke to his best friend, Henry MacKenny, who was able to confirm that Andrews had both personal and business problems and might have moved on. What he did not say was that he was himself infatuated with Gwen. Andrews' Lincoln Continental was found the next day in the River Nene in Lincolnshire. A postcard signed Ann and postmarked nearby Wisbech was produced by Mrs Andrews, who said her husband had received it. The implication was that he had left home to set up a new life. A more convincing theory advanced by the police was that he had accidentally driven into the river while drunk and the body had been swept out to sea. The deep tidal currents were extremely strong and a half-empty bottle of vodka lay on the back seat of the car. Despite the connection of MacKenny with two of the victims, again the enquiry lapsed. Childs' version was that he had been given £500 to lure Andrews to his own flat, where MacKenny shot him whilst Tina, Childs' wife, made a pot of tea.

It was only when Childs was arrested following the hijacking of a Security Express armoured van in Hertford in June 1979 that he began to talk. He was arrested through his own carelessness in what had otherwise been a well-planned and executed robbery. The robbers had cleared £500,000 by impersonating Security Express employees. After the robbery they changed out of their uniforms in a public lavatory, leaving the clothing behind. In the pocket of one of the overalls were the keys to a BMW. It was not difficult for the police to trace the vehicle to its owner, an East End greengrocer. In a deal for a light sentence he returned the money which had been left in his care and then implicated both John Childs and MacKenny as part of the robbery team.

The case was initially investigated by Tony Lundy, then a Detective Inspector. He rightly supposed that this was not the first raid the team had carried out and interviewed each member with a view to getting confessions of other jobs. One of the team was even more forthcoming and named Childs and MacKenny as being involved in the killings of Andrews, Eve and the Bretts.

Lundy's initial inclination was to laugh at him but the man went on:

'There's going to be another murder shortly – and you know the victim.'

'What are you talking about?'

'Do you know a police officer called Treen?'

I said 'yeh' because John Treen had been one of my inspectors on the Flying Squad in 1977, so I knew him well. Treen had arrested MacKenny and Terry Pinfold in December 1976 but then the Director of Public Prosecutions dropped the case against MacKenny.

He said, 'MacKenny is going to murder Treen and Butcher,' who was the sergeant on the same case.[27]

Lundy recalled that MacKenny had been arrested in December 1976 over two bank robberies at Romford and Woodford. He was then placed on a total of eight identification parades but was not picked out. Nevertheless he was detained on the basis of witnesses' remarks of a big man – he stood 6 feet 6 inches. He was an associate of Terence Pinfold and, so the detectives investigating the case said, he had made verbal admissions. MacKenny denied these verbals and wrote out a statement giving a detailed notice of alibi.

The case against him had been dropped in July of the next year, whilst Pinfold was gaoled for ten years. When

---

[27] M. Short, *Lundy*, p. 74.

the allegations were dismissed he shouted threats at Treen, the officer in charge of the case. Later MacKenny had endeavoured to interest the media in a number of cases in which he said miscarriages of justice had occurred.

In turn Lundy had difficulties in getting senior officers to accept that the stories told by his informant were credible and it took him some time to persuade Commander Arthur Howard that the matter should be investigated further.

In December 1979 Childs became the first serial murderer in modern times to confess and give evidence against his accomplices. He had a hard time in the witness box, saying that he was drinking a bottle of whisky a day to try to obliterate the memory of killing Terence Brett. He did admit he had thought about writing a book on the killing but denied the potential title 'East End butcher'.

The juries' verdicts were curious. As to the murder of their partner Eve, Pinfold was convicted and MacKenny acquitted. Both were acquitted of the murder of the White Angel, Brown. MacKenny was convicted of the murder of Brett and his son, while Leonard Thompson, charged along with him, was acquitted and left court without a stain on his character, as did Paul Morton-Thurtle, acquitted in the case of Sherwood, the nursing home owner. MacKenny was convicted in that case as he was over the killing of Ronnie Andrews. He and Pinfold received life sentences, with, in MacKenny's case, a recommendation that he serve not less than twenty-five years.

He was not happy, shouting that he had never killed anybody but that through his life-saving jacket he had saved plenty. 'Straight people need protection from you,' he told Mr Justice May, 'and from mongols and mugs like you,' he added to the jury before the court was cleared.

But where did all the bodies go? Although there had been considerable forensic evidence of bloodstains and traces of hair which went to corroborate Childs' story, there was no trace of any of the six bodies. According to Childs, initially the idea had been to cut up the bodies using a butcher's mincing machine. This had proved too blunt to deal with Eve and the idea was abandoned.

The next suggested method was simplicity itself and extremely efficient. The bodies were cut up and then burned in a standard-size fireplace with an anthracite fire augmented by a gas burner. Bones which did not dissolve could be pounded on the hearth. The ashes were then emptied on waste ground. The disposal of a complete body took about twenty-four hours.

Professor James Cameron, the pathologist, was asked whether it would be possible to cremate a body in this way and tests were carried out. An 11-stone male pig, calculated as being the equivalent of a fully developed average-sized man, was taken to Childs' home. Cameron, using brute force, sawed up the carcass, taking just over five minutes. He described it as 'perfectly simple, requiring no anatomical knowledge'. The police and the pathologist then sat down to burn the body. Later Cameron told Philip Paul:

The temperature in the fire reached over 1000 degrees but the room never went above 75. It was all properly measured, logged and photographed. But when we put the intestines on the fire it almost went out. Because, as soon as it burnt through, the fluid ran. Later on we were told that MacKenny had washed out and dried the intestines before they were burnt.

The total burning of the pig took thirteen hours. We ended up with remains of ash, bone and whatnot which filled two large plastic bags. We then went over it twice with a hammer, as we were told MacKenny had done, and eventually finished up with a small plastic bag of ash with not a remnant of teeth or bone visible to the naked eye.

Repeated checks had been made outside the building during the burning, but no smell of roasting pork or other odour had been detected.[28]

Death from a striping, traditionally a slashing of the buttocks and anus rather than the face, was uncommon but on 24 August 1986 Michael Collins of Canning Town, said to have been trying to install a protection racket in the area, bled to death on his way to hospital. He and a friend, Mark Natrass, had been over powered in the Moonlight public house in Stratford Broadway, once owned by former England and West Ham football star Bobby Moore, when they were first sprayed with ammonia and then slashed by four men. One of the cuts to Collins severed an artery in his left leg.

A week later wealthy night club owner Peter Morris died after being stabbed with a flick knife, hit with an axe and finally shot three times as gangs battled outside the Telegraph pub, also in Stratford Broadway. The incident was said to be a revenge attack following the death of Collins.

[28] P. Paul, *Murder Under the Microscope*, p. 156.

12

The Last Decade

Over Easter bank holiday 1983 a particularly unpleasant robbery took place. A gang led by a 'toff' with a 'posh' accent carried out what came to be called the Great Banknote Raid in Curtain Road, Shoreditch, East London. Seven million pounds was removed from the Security Express headquarters when six masked bandits burst in at about 10.30 a.m. One guard had petrol poured over him and was threatened that if he did not hand over the combination for the safe, he would become a human torch. The guards were then tied and blindfolded for the duration of the raid, which would last a further five hours.

As with the Great Train Robbery it was a job which had been on offer for some years and one which had taken a considerable time in the planning. The Security Express building had been known as Fort Knox and had been thought to be a virtually impregnable fortress. The underwriters put up the then staggering sum of £500,000 as a reward. But it was police work which paid off. One of the men involved had been under observation for some time and when he was being questioned about another major robbery he told the police he had stored Security Express money at his home. This led to the arrest of an Allen Opiola, who was later given three years and three months with a recommendation he serve this in police custody. Opiola was to turn Queen's Evidence against the rest of the gang.

He had allowed his home – the money would fit into most people's living rooms – to be used for counting and laundering the money. For this service, and for providing suitcases, making coffee, fetching a Chinese take-away whilst the money was being counted and later doing a certain amount of laundering, he received £30,000.

On 10 June 1985 John and James Knight – brothers of Ronnie who was aquitted of the murder of Tony Zomparelli and was once married to actress Barbara Windsor, herself a former girlfriend of Charles Kray – were arrested along with Billy Hickson.[1] Hickson, who had been shot accidentally by 'Colonel' George Copley, and the brothers were three of five men convicted. John Knight received twenty-two years, James eight for handling stolen monies and Hickson six. With his new wife, Ronnie Knight now lives in Spain, one of the so-called Famous Five from the Kray days, unwilling to return to England. The Five were reduced to four with the conviction of Frederick Foreman, who in 1990 received a nine-year sentence for his part in the handling of the Security Express monies. The remaining three are Ronald Everett, once a close friend of the twins, John James Mason, who was acquitted of conspiracy in the £8 million robbery of the Bank of America in 1976, and Clifford Saxe, one-time landlord of the Fox in Kingsland Road, Hackney, where the robbery is said to have been planned. Saxe is reputed to have bought two villas for just under £170,000 with part of his share.

Within six months the Security Express robbery had

[1] For further details of some members of the Knight family and friends' alleged involvement in organized crime, see Chapter 11.

paled into insignificance. On 26 November 1983 at 6.40 a.m. the biggest of the biggest of robberies took place when £26 million in gold was lifted from the Brinks-Mat warehouse on the Heathrow trading estate. Its ramifications would run for nearly a decade. Again the guards were threatened: one with castration; others had petrol poured over them; another was coshed for not producing keys sufficiently speedily and was then punched in the stomach as he lay on the ground. The gang drove off with 6400 bars of gold. It was clearly a job executed with help from the inside. The premises had been opened with a key and the gang knew the guards' names as well as the workings of the vaults and locks.

It was only a matter of days before the police latched on to the last guard to arrive that morning – Tony Black – who had missed the robbery because he was ten minutes late for work. Black confessed. His sister was living with Brian Robinson, who had been on the Williams & Glyn's robbery in 1978 and in 1981 had benefited through the mistakes of the No 5 Regional Crime Squad.[2] Black identified two more of the team, Tony White and Michael McAvoy.

---

[2] Robinson was one of a number of criminals who were known as 'The Colonel'. The most famous example is Ronnie Kray and another is George Copley. It was Copley who was instrumental in sabotaging the efforts of the No 5 Regional Crime Squad when in June 1981 he and Frankie Fraser junior were on trial at Oxford on charges of robbery. Three months previously a Sergeant Pook visited him in Reading gaol and was secretly taped by Copley in a conversation in which Pook confirmed an offer that if Copley was to admit his part in the Williams & Glyn's robbery and also give evidence of corruption against certain London detectives, he would receive only a five-year sentence. The tape was produced at the trial and the case was stopped. It was 'hopelessly compromised' said Stephen Wooler for the Director of Public Prosecutions.

In December 1984 Robinson and McAvoy received twenty-five years each; White was acquitted. Later there was said to be £50,000 on offer to free McAvoy and Robinson. Black, who had given evidence for the Crown, was handed a six-year sentence. That still left a number of villains at large and a very large amount of property missing. The gold, in the form of marked ingots of extremely high quality, could not be offered to legitimate dealers; instead it was being smelted by a small bullion firm, Scadlynn, on the outskirts of Bristol.

A surveillance operation on a Kenneth Noye ended in disaster. An undercover police officer, John Fordham, clad in a balaclava helmet, was stabbed to death in the grounds of Noye's home at West Kingsdowne in Kent. Noye, charged with the murder of Fordham, gave evidence that 'I just froze with horror. All I saw when I flashed my torch on this masked man was the two eye-holes and the mask. I thought that was my lot. I thought I was going to be a dead man.' He stabbed Fordham eleven times.

In November 1985 he and Brian Reader, who was with Noye at the time, were acquitted of murder. In July 1986 both were convicted of handling the Brinks-Mat gold, along with Garth Chappell, a Scadlynn director. Reader received nine years and Noye, whose defence was that he was a gold smuggler and VAT fraudster as opposed to a thief and receiver, ended up with fourteen years. However, there are still plenty of figures in the underworld who believe that his defence was correct. No Brinks Mat gold was ever found on his premises and, although £100,000 of gold was discovered, tests showed this could not have been from the Brinks-Mat robbery.

Garth Chappell received ten years, whilst Matteo Constantino, sixty-eight, a longstanding Hatton Garden villain who had allowed his company to be used in a false VAT claim, received a suspended sentence of twelve months for conspiracy to evade VAT on the gold. After being melted down it had then been delivered in small parcels to London. The gold was sold on the legitimate market to dealers who were charged VAT at fifteen per cent. Constantino had been acquitted of dishonest handling and was suffering from cancer at the time.

The convictions of Noye and Reader were the greatest successes the police had on the Scadlynn side of things. The next year John Palmer, a former director of Scadlynn who had been invited to leave Spain by the authorities and who chose to be deported to Britain from Rio de Janeiro, was put on trial at the Old Bailey. He was charged with conspiring with Noye and Reader dishonestly to handle the gold. He was acquitted and went to live off the proceeds of his time share business in Tenerife.

Nor was there any greater success in the case of John Fleming, who was deported from Florida in 1986. In March of the next year, with evidence given against him by a new supergrass, Patrick Diamond, Fleming was charged with dishonestly handling nearly £500,000 of the Brinks-Mat proceeds. At the committal proceedings at Horseferry Road Magistrates' Court he was found to have no case to answer. Fleming told reporters, 'I feel a great relief. It has been a bad year,' before he returned to Spain where he was involved in a car accident and again deported.

The year 1991 proved fatal for Noye's former friend, forty-three-year-old Nick Whiting, who ran a garage at Wrotham in Kent. Whiting had been questioned back in 1983 over a Range Rover sold to Noye and bought back. Now on 6 June Whiting vanished from the garage along with five cars. At first it seemed to be a straightforward kidnapping but when all the cars stolen in the raid on his garage were recovered within a few days, unkind suggestions came on offer, including one that Whiting had staged his own disappearance over the Brinks-Mat spoils and that he had gone on the run with a friend of his, Lennie 'Little Lew', who was also wanted in connection with Brinks-Mat.

Ex-racing driver Whiting had secured a plot of land during the period of falling property prices and had borrowed bent money to finance a building deal. One suggestion was that the mortgagor wanted his money back. A variation on the theme is that Whiting owed money on the cars. At the beginning of June his body was found in marshland in Essex, nearly a month after his abduction. It appeared he had been beaten up, bound hand and foot, and stuffed in a car boot. He had then been shot in the back of the head, seemingly after being frog-marched across at least three miles of boggy ground.

Throughout the late 1970s and 1980s the police had adopted a more aggressive policy towards armed robbers. Stake-outs were followed by shoot-outs. One of the first to go was Micky Calvey, shot in a robbery in 1978. The old-timers didn't have it so good any more. On 9 July 1987 Nicholas Payne and Michael Flynn were shot dead in Plumstead as they tried to attack a Securicor van. Four months later, in November, Derek Whitlock died in a hail of bullets in Woolwich as he mounted a similar operation.

On 13 April 1989 Terry Dewsnap and James Farrell failed to batter their way into the post office strongroom at North Harrow and died. They had been staked out by the police for over a month. Dewsnap, once related by marriage to night club owner Joe Wilkins, had served six years for receiving monies stolen from the Dunstable branch of Barclays Bank following the kidnapping of the manager in 1976. Farrell had served twelve years for holding up the National Westminster Bank at Isleworth after his conviction in June 1977. 'They needn't have shot him quite so many times,' said one of the relatives.

One of the oldest surviving armed robbers of recent times has been John Hilton who, in September 1991, was jailed for life. He was then sixty-two, frail and grey-haired, but he had killed three people during his thirty-year career which had ended in Burlington Gardens, Piccadilly. In 1963 he had been given a life sentence for the murder of a man in the celebrated raid on the Co-op dairy in Mitcham, South London. He was freed on licence in February 1978 and a month later he and Alan Roberts robbed a Hatton Garden jeweller, Leo Grunhut, outside his home in Golders Green. He accidentally shot his partner in the thigh and as the jeweller tried to escape shot him in the back. The proceeds of the raid were £3000 in cash and £277,000 in diamonds. Hilton managed to get his partner into their getaway car and drove him to a garage in South London where he bled to death. Roberts was buried on a railway embankment at Dartford, Kent. Grunhut died a month later.

Hilton told the police, 'The course of history of armed robbers is littered with bodies. If it had been me then Roberts would have done exactly the same thing. Roberts got in the way and I shot him in the thigh. The jeweller was running to his front door so I shot him in the back from three feet.'

In June 1981 Hilton had received fourteen years for seven robberies, an attempted robbery and two charges of conspiracy. On 6 October 1990 he escaped from Kingston Prison in Portsmouth and raided a jewellers shop in Brighton. The haul this time was jewellery worth £90,000. His career has seemingly closed with a raid by him and his partner on a jewellers in Burlington Gardens when, on 4 December 1990, they terrorized two brothers into handing over £420,000 in jewellery. The brothers gave chase and Hilton fired three shots before he was tackled and overpowered by police, the brothers and other jewellers. At his trial he refused to allow his counsel to put forward any mitigation.

With the police on the alert for armed robbers, the pattern changed. The year 1987 was that of the international inside job, which surpassed, on paper at least, even the Brinks-Mat robbery. In July of that year the Knightsbridge Safe Deposit Box Centre, opposite Harrods, was robbed of £40 million by American antiques dealer Eric Rubin working with Italian Valerio Viccei and the manager of the deposit company, Parvez Latif, the black sheep of a wealthy Pakistani family who had been promised a third share of the proceeds and had taken out £1 million insurance on the company.

Latif, then in serious financial difficulties, agreed to let Rubin and Viccei into the building. The guards were tied up and threatened and the 120 safety deposit boxes were stripped. Once again it was a grass who brought about the team's downfall. Rubin, a shadowy man who held neither bank account nor credit cards, had commuted from New York for the robbery. Valerio Viccei, who had links with neo-Fascist terror groups in Italy going back to his teens, had lived the life of a playboy with tastes in women, Gucci shoes, fast cars and cocaine, not necessarily in that order. He was wanted in Italy for a series of bank robberies. In January 1987 Rubin had teamed up with Viccei to rob Coutts Bank in Cavendish Square, the first time in its three-hundred-year history that Coutts had been robbed. To make things even cosier amongst the conspirators Viccei was also sleeping with Latif's girlfriend, Pamela Seamarks. Viccei, whose fingerprint was left at the scene when he cut himself – some police think deliberately – had intended to return to Colombia, taking with him his black Ferrari Testarossa. He had difficulties in obtaining an export licence, delayed his departure and was arrested. He received twenty-two years while Latif received sixteen. The member of the gang who turned Queen's Evidence to put them all away had the now almost statutory five. Later Rubin, said to be a dying man, was extradited back to Britain and received a twelve-year sentence.[3]

On 24 April 1990 the Great Train Robber Charlie Wilson was shot dead beside his swimming pool at his home in Marbella. He had been hosing down the pool area when his wife, Patricia, answered a knock on the door. There was a man with a South London accent asking for her husband. She fetched Charlie and he and the young man went off together.

At the inquest held in London in November 1991 Patricia Wilson said:

I heard the man say 'I am a friend of Eamonn.' I had a feeling there were two people there, although I couldn't say why.

I heard two very loud bangs and at first I thought it was from the building site next door, but then I heard the dog screaming.

Charlie was lying at the side of the pool face down. The man had gone and the gate was open.

I saw blood coming from his mouth and Charlie did a sort of a press-up and gestured in the direction the man had gone.

Initially it was reported he had been killed with a single karate blow but the autopsy showed he had been shot in the side of the neck and the bullet had lodged there. As the shot passed through the larynx it would have caused heavy bleeding and as he inhaled blood he would have been unable to cry out. The dog had a

---

[3] Viccei wrote his own acount of the affair whilst in Parkhurst in *Knightsbridge* (pub. Blake hardbacks).

broken leg and had to be destroyed.

The inquest was told by Detective Superintendent Alec Edwards that although there was no direct evidence to link Wilson with drug dealing, there was much circumstantial evidence, such as his lifestyle and his visits to Morocco.

> As far as the Spanish police and the British police are concerned, there is circumstantial evidence that this is a drug-related incident.
>
> We know of his meeting British criminals who are known drug dealers and who have since been convicted of drug dealing and with one who has also been executed in a gangland killing.

A verdict that he had been shot by persons unknown was recorded. Paul Spencer, a solicitor for the Wilson family, said after the inquest that the drug allegations were strongly denied.

After his release from prison in 1978 – he was the last of the Great Train Robbers to be freed – Wilson had led something of a charmed life so far as the courts were concerned. In 1982 he had been one of seven men charged in a £2 million VAT fraud involving the melting down of £16 million-worth of gold Krugerrands. Charges against him were dropped when the jury had disagreed twice and he paid £400,000 to Customs and Excise. In 1984 he spent four months in custody awaiting trial for the alleged armed robbery of a security van. He was freed amid allegations of police corruption.

The executed man referred to by Edwards was Roy Francis Adkins, whose inquest was heard the next day. In the convoluted way of life in the underbelly of society, James Rose had pleaded guilty to drug offences at Chelmsford Crown Court in January 1990, naming Adkins as the leader of the gang. Apparently Rose had been authorized to say this by Wilson and it was something which, not surprisingly, upset Adkins, who then had ordered the execution of Wilson. There was, however, no suggestion that any of Wilson's friends had killed Adkins by way of reprisal. It was an entirely separate matter.

On 28 September 1990, the night of his death, Adkins had met two Colombians in the Nightwatch bar of the American Hotel in Amsterdam. He had been the middleman in selling parcels of stolen emeralds in Amsterdam; he had been approached by a Sean O'Neil and several successful runs had been carried out. Then one of the parcels had been stolen from O'Neil and the Colombians wanted their money as a matter of urgency. Adkins persuaded O'Neil to attend a meeting to explain in person what had happened.

According to O'Neil he had gone to the Nightwatch bar and had seen Adkins with the Colombians. Adkins gestured to O'Neil to continue walking. O'Neil had then heard eight gunshots and had run out of the hotel. He had not known Adkins was dead until he read the papers the next day.[4]

In the 1970s some members of various families had great influence in South London: the Tobins, the Hennesseys, the Smiths in Deptford, the Frenches in Lewisham and the Porritts and their quasi-cousins, the Reddens. 'Flash' Harry Hayward had the Harp of Erin, the Frenches had the Deptford Arms, and Peter and Bernie Hennessey, with a manager firmly in place to

[4] This evidence was given by a Customs and Excise officer. Earlier in 1991 O'Neil had been acquitted at Isleworth Crown Court of charges relating to £10 million-worth of cocaine. Three Colombians co-accused were sentenced to terms of up to eighteen years' imprisonment. Now, although he had previously made a statement, O'Neil could not be found to give evidence in person at Adkins' inquest.

hold the licence, ran the Dog and Bell. In 1966 Peter Hennessey had served a sentence of ten years for warehouse breaking and his brother Bernard had a conviction for conspiracy to rob. The third brother, Micky, friend of Alfie Gerard, would later be a party in the big drug-smuggling case involving Nikolaus Chrastny.

During the decade a new name appeared on the South London scene, that of the Arif family from Stockwell, originally from Turkish Cyprus and now the kings of the Old Kent Road. 'It doesn't matter whose name it is over the door of the pub in some areas,' says one police officer, 'it's the Arifs who own it.' Pubs, restaurants and clubs, including the Connoisseur in the Old Kent Road, are said to have been bought with the proceeds of a series of major armed robberies.

The head of the family is forty-two-year-old Dogan Arif, currently serving fourteen years' imprisonment for his part in an £8.5 million drug-smuggling plot. At the time of his sentence he had followed the tradition of porn king James Humphreys (Hastings United) and master fraudsman Robert Maxwell (Oxford United) in owning a football club, non-league Fisher Athletic, in South-East London. During his time as chairman, the club, which at one time rose to the so called Fifth Division, the Gola League, was involved in paying substantial transfer fees for well-known players and had as its manager Malcolm Allison. In 1983 Dogan was acquitted of taking part in a bogus arms deal plot to swindle the Ayatollah Khomeini out of £34 million.

The family first came to some sort of national prominence when in May 1977 Osar Arif was acquitted of the murder of security guard David Cross in a robbery when £103,000 was stolen from a security van on the A2. The windscreen was smashed with a sledgehammer and the crew blasted with a shotgun. Photographs of the

fleeing robbers were taken by a passer-by while other
onlookers chased them up a bank at the side of the road
before they too were fired upon. Bekir Arif was
convicted of disposing of guns which had been found in
the Surrey Docks; he received five years.

In 1981 Dennis and Bekir Arif were seen in the market
square in Bromley near a Securicor van by an off-duty
police officer. He was suspicious of their behaviour and
went to intercept them in his car. A chase ensued, with
the raiders throwing away crash helmets as they drove.
They were convicted of conspiracy to rob.

On 27 November 1990 the police shot dead Kenny
Baker, one of a four-man gang armed with enough
weapons for a small war, including a Brazilian-made
revolver, a 12-bore Browning self-loading shotgun, a US
Army self-loading Colt, an Enfield Mark II revolver and
a Browning 1922 pistol. He and three of the Arif family
had ambushed a Securicor van parked on a garage
forecourt in Reigate whilst the woman guard and a
colleague went to buy drinks from a cafe. It was due to
deliver some £750,000 to various branches of Barclays
Bank. They were forced back into the van at gunpoint
by Dennis Arif wearing a 'grandfather' mask. The plan
was for the van to be driven away followed by a pick-up
truck driven by Mehmet Arif, Dennis' brother, with
Kenny Baker in the passenger seat.

The police, however, working in Operation Yamato –
named after the Japanese sneak attack on Pearl Harbor
– had been targeting the Arifs. Squad members rammed
the van and Dennis Arif and his brother-in-law,
Anthony Downer, threw down their weapons. Mehmet
Arif and Kenny Baker did not do so.

'I felt a muzzle blast across the left side of my face and
realized he [Baker] was shooting at me and I could tell
my life was in danger,' PC William Hughes said in a
statement at Dennis Arif's trial. 'I fired two shots at

Baker and then I heard two shots on my left and saw the passenger window disintegrate.'

Mehmet, who was wounded, and Downer both pleaded guilty to conspiracy to rob and possession of a firearm with intent. Dennis Arif ran the defence of duress, saying that he owed Baker £60,000 because of gambling debts – he had lost over £100,000 gambling in the previous twenty years – and that Baker had threatened to shoot him if he did not pay it back.[5] He had taken it seriously when he heard that Baker had previously shot a man. He was not believed. Earlier in the year both men had attended an Arif family wedding at the Savoy along with the other powerful South London families, the Colemans, Frasers, Whites, Adams and Hiscocks.

The jury took only an hour to convict him and afterwards friends of Baker pooh-poohed the idea that he would force anyone into committing a robbery. 'But Kenny wouldn't have minded being an excuse,' one of them told reporter Duncan Campbell. 'It is accepted that if someone is on their toes or dead you can drop them in it.' Perfectly sporting behaviour. Dennis Arif received a sentence of twenty-two years; Mehmet and Anthony Downer eighteen years each.

At the trial Dennis had asked to be tried under another name because of the prejudice the name Arif might have on a jury. After all, in the 1981 case involving Dennis Arif for conspiracy to rob and firearms offences, the police were convinced that there would be an attempt to nobble the jury. The first sign seems to have been as early as the first week of that trial when Michael

---

[5] In English law the defence of duress is extremely difficult to establish. In essence the accused must show that he, or his family, was in a life-threatening situation and had no opportunity to report the matter to the police. It was a defence run with success by Tony Barry in the Kray trial.

Arif, another brother, was seen with a man who could be described as a minder outside the court waiting for the jury to come in. On the road outside, a BMW was seen moving slowly. Michael Arif may have seen the police observation and he jumped into the car, later traced to the ownership of a defence witness. The next day a woman approached a woman juror on the underground offering money for a favourable verdict. The juror had the courage to report the incident.

In hindsight it seems incredible that the trial judge did not order blanket protection of the jury, or that the prosecution did not think to ask for it, but when the judge asked who wanted protection only five said they did. They included the woman who had been approached. In the end the jury failed to agree and when the police took the woman home she broke down, saying she had done a terrible thing in pressing for an acquittal because she was in fear of her safety. She claimed she had been terrified by a large man sitting in the public gallery. At the re-trial the following year Dennis was convicted.

Despite his sentence for drug-smuggling it was believed that Dogan Arif had masterminded his empire from prison and according to some sources the aim of the 1990 robbery had been to accumulate sufficient funds to organize an escape attempt.

'The Arifs are undoubtedly feared,' a detective told the *Independent*. 'People are not daft enough to cross them. There will be a void in the Old Kent Road area now which will be filled. It will be the survival of the fittest.'[6]

'We reckoned they made millions,' said another detective. 'We believe they have been active armed robbers for about twenty years. Every job was always

[6] *Independent*, 10 December 1991.

meticulously planned and ruthlessly executed.'[7]

But by now the sensible families had moved into drugs. So even if the aim was to put together enough money to free Dogan, what were the Arifs doing with an attack on a security van?

The explanation of one police officer is, 'They're dinosaurs, that's why. Look how old that Kenny Baker was.' He was fifty-three.

Others do not agree. 'For every drug man who succeeds he has to have the stake money from somewhere and drug deals are financed by money from armed robberies. Robbing security vans is the best way. You can pick up £1,000,000 without too many problems,' says a senior South London officer.

The theory is that the exodus from armed robberies by the sensible gangster came about with the rise of the supergrass, the lengthy sentences which were being imposed by the courts and the fact that the police were now very often armed and were adopting a tougher line with gangsters they encountered.

These days are very different from those of the early 1970s. Between 1971 and 1973 shots had been fired on only three occasions by the police. On the other hand the number of occasions when firearms were issued in connection with a particular incident had more than doubled, from 1072 to 2237 in 1973.

In that year PC Peter Simon, armed with a Webley revolver and on his way to guard the Israeli Embassy, was told that the National Westminster Bank in Kensington High Street was being robbed by three armed men. He walked into the bank to be confronted by a robber with a sawn-off shotgun. Simon stood in the middle of the bank and shouted, 'I am a police officer. I am armed.' He was shot in the arms and chest before he shot

---

[7] *Sun*, 10 December 1991.

and killed one of the raiders and injured another. Public reaction was all praise for this young officer.

It was not the same for two other members of the Special Patrol Group three months later when they encountered three young Pakistani men holding hostage the staff of the Indian High Commission in the Aldwych. They shot and killed two of the men. The third gave himself up unharmed. It was then discovered the weapons had only been imitations. Now the public was less pleased and there were suggestions that the police should have used tear gas or rubber bullets.

Public support had been fickle, but in 1966 Harry Roberts had shot dead three policemen in Braybrooks Street, Shepherd's Bush. He, together with his two friends, John Duddy and John Witney, had been on their way to rob a rent collector when the police approached Witney about the out-of-date tax disc on his car. Roberts shot DC David Wombwell through the head and DS Christopher Head through the back before going over to the police car where he shot PC Geoffrey Fox. Roberts and the others were sentenced to life imprisonment with a recommendation they serve at least thirty years. Previously Roberts had been fortunate. In November 1958 he had attacked and robbed a seventy-nine- year-old man, who died a year and three days after the attack. Had he died two days earlier a murder charge could have been preferred. Roberts was saved by the time limit. He received a seven-year sentence. It was after his release from that sentence that he teamed up with Witney and Duddy, ensuring they were always armed for their work. It was this predilection for guns that caused the death of three police officers during a routine stop and questioning.

On 23 August 1971 Frederick Sewell shot and killed Superintendent Gerald Richardson, head of the Black-pool Borough Police, in an armed robbery in The Strand in Blackpool. Sewell and four other South London gangsters undertook what they considered to be a simple job which would net them £100,000 of jewellery. Things did not go simply. One of the staff managed to set off the alarm, the first police officer on the scene saw the men escaping and followed them, and others joined the chase. Finally Richardson caught up with Sewell, who shot him twice at point-blank range as the officer wrestled him to the ground.

Sewell escaped and hid out in London for the next six weeks until a succession of offers of reward, including £10,000 from the *Daily Mirror*, brought about his betrayal. He was sentenced to life imprisonment, again with a recommendation that he serve a minimum of thirty years. Sewell's comment on the man he killed – 'He was too brave.'[8]

On 20 October 1979 Peter Bennett became the first customs officer to be killed on duty for nearly two hundred years when he was shot by Lennie 'Teddy Bear' Watkins, proprietor of Edward Bear Motors, Fareham. Bennett, married with a one-year-old son, had been part of a stake-out team on a surveillance known as Operation Wrecker.[9] Some well-known faces were fringe members of the enterprise. In 1976 Watkins was serving a sentence in Maidstone Prison for a supermarket snatch when, together with his minder Graeme Green, he planned to switch from armed robbery to drug smuggling. Deals were set up in Pakistan and secret compartments fitted to the containers shipped abroad. With high-quality cannabis being imported – blocks were embossed with the Rolls-Royce symbol – the trade was

[8] There are few accounts of these cases but one does appear in C. Borrell and B. Cashinella, *Crime in Britain Today*.
[9] There is a memorial to him in the form of a pair of doors at All Hallowes Church in Mark Lane, London EC3.

highly lucrative. Four runs brought in £10 million-worth
at street prices. Watkins bought his garage. High living
was his downfall. Reports began to filter through to the
police that £20 notes were being used to light cigars. A
joint police and customs observation was mounted.

The customs officers watched as a container was fitted
with a false bottom and despatched by lorry with sanitary
ware to Karachi. They waited until its return when,
driven by Watkins, it was filled with shoes and with £2.5
million-worth of cannabis in the false floor. It meandered
for a period of days around the Suffolk countryside after
unloading at Harwich. The shoes had been dropped off
in Saffron Walden and one morning a bag containing
guns was seen to be handed to Watkins as the lorry was
parked.

The surveillance ended in the Commercial Road when
it became apparent to the officers that there had been a
'show-out' and their cover was blown. Watkins, who
knew he was being watched, had doubled back and forth
in an effort to shake the observers. Now he parked the
lorry, leaving two sawn-off shotguns inside, and called
his team for further instructions. He was told to stay near
the telephone box and wait for an orange van which
would guide him to a slaughter in Limehouse. Watkins
was by a bus stop when he was approached by Bennett
and Detective Sergeant John Harvey. Watkins had a
Lady Beretta inside his parka and he fired at both
officers, hitting Bennett in the stomach. A seventy-six-
year-old pedestrian came to the men's aid and began
beating Watkins with his stick as other officers surrounded him.

At his trial for murder at Winchester Crown Court in
October 1980 Watkins endeavoured to leave the witness
box. 'I am not going to answer any more questions from
made-up note books and rubbish from your firm, from
the trickery department who pull more strokes than an

Oxford blue,' he told prosecuting counsel. His defence was that he thought a rival gang was about to hijack the lorry and he had shot in self-defence. It was not a story the jury accepted and Watkins left the dock hoping the judge would die of cancer, after he had been given a life sentence with a recommendation that he serve a minimum of twenty-five years.

If there was not too much in the newspapers about the case it is not surprising. It was a vintage month for trials. On the day Watkins was convicted, Ronnie Knight was acquitted of the murder of Zomparelli whilst the jury in the MacKenny case was hearing about the time it took to reduce the carcass of a pig to ashes.

But there were a number of differing verdicts at the trial of the others said to have been involved in the conspiracy to import the drugs in the container. Brian Bird and James Johnson, who both pleaded guilty, were sentenced to six and five years' imprisonment respectively. Green received six years. Frederick Foreman, recently released from his sentence in the Kray trial, received two years on a plea of guilty at a later trial, whilst George Francis was acquitted after a re-trial.

Within a month an effort to free Watkins had failed. A ladder had been left propped against the wall of Winchester Prison and a yellow lorry had been parked nearby.

One man who did not stand trial was Colin 'Duke' Osbourne, one-time armourer and gofer of the Krays. Immediately after the arrest of Watkins it was made known that the Duke was wanted for questioning as a potential organizer of the enterprise. He was sought by both the police and other firms who believed he held a list of pushers. Osbourne was never arrested. On 3 December 1980 he was found dead on a playing field at Hackney Marshes. He was aged fifty. It was said in some quarters he died from natural causes, that he had had a heart attack. A less charitable view is that he died of a drugs overdose. An open verdict was returned at the inquest.

In February 1987 Dennis Bergin had died in a raid on the Sir John Soane's Museum in Lincoln's Inn Fields. In July of that year Nicholas Payne and Michael Flynn were killed by police officers as they threatened the crew of a Securicor van in Plumstead, and four months later Anthony Ashe was shot dead and Ronald Easterbrook was wounded after a robbery of a Bejam store in Woolwich, South London.

If this was not sufficient to spread alarm through the underworld, the generation who had executed the great armed robberies of the 1970s and early 1980s, even if they weren't in prison, were getting a bit arthritic for this kind of pavement work.

If you're organizing an armed robbery too many people know about it – there's often the man inside, then there's the people you approach who may decline because they're on holiday or have another bit of business, but now they know what you're doing on a particular day and there's always the chance they'll grass you up for the reward money. Then there's the fact the police would fucking shoot you if you were caught in a stake-out. And even if they don't end up dead, you end up with a twenty.

So what did these old South London villains do?

First there was the refinement of the bank robbery by kidnapping the bank manager and his family, holding them hostage overnight and then taking the manager down to open the safe in the morning. The team could be a relatively small one. Three to guard the hostages and two to go to the bank. In a kidnapping for ransom the team would be of the same number, again with three members guarding the victims, the fourth negotiating with the police and the fifth administering the technical details such as supplying cars etc.

Until the mid-1970s kidnapping had never been a part of British crime. As Mark Bles and Robert Low point out, 'Almost all the major kidnaps for ransom in Britain since the first in 1969 were carried out either by foreigners or by loners who were outside the criminal mainstream.'[10] However, in 1985 the British underworld kidnapped Shirley Goodwin who was taken from her home in Hackney. At the time her husband, John, was in prison.

In the early 1980s John Goodwin had been a regular visitor to the Old Bailey, first as defendant and then as prosecution witness. He was charged with the burglary of a bank in Whitechapel in 1982 and on his first trial the jury could not agree. The second was abandoned when he feigned a heart attack and on the third, when he produced a tape-recording of a detective taking money from him, the case was stopped. But in April 1982 he was back again in the dock along with Brian Reader, later convicted of handling some of the Brinks-Mat gold and acquitted of the murder of John Fordham. This time Goodwin's accuser was the redoubtable Micky Gervaise and the charges related to burglaries totalling over £1.25 million. Gervaise by now had become a double agent supergrass and was saying that not only did he not wish to give evidence but also that Robbery Squad officers had told him to implicate Reader and Goodwin and give false evidence against them.

---

[10] M. Bles and R. Low, *The Kidnap Business*. They cite the cases of the Hossein Brothers from Trinidad, Greek Cypriots in abductions in 1975 and 1983, and Donald Nielson as the loner in the kidnapping of Lesley Whittle in 1975.

Despite Gervaise's turnaround the trial judge abandoned the trial amidst claims of jury nobbling and on a retrial in October 1982 both Reader and Goodwin were acquitted. In March 1983 Goodwin was convicted of nobbling and received a seven-year sentence. This was quashed by the Court of Appeal on 25 May 1984. 'However suspicious we are, we have to look at the quality of the evidence and the quality was lacking,' said Judge Lawton. As for the detectives Goodwin had taped, two were acquitted, one after putting up the ingenious defence that he had taken the money but had told the truth so he could not have committed perjury. The third had his conviction quashed by the Court of Appeal.

In the meantime, however, Goodwin had fallen out with yet another old-established South London family, the Pitts, and Shirley was kidnapped. At 11.30 one evening four men with sawn-off shotguns burst in, grabbed Mrs Goodwin, took £1500 from the wall-safe and handed over a ransom note reading, 'If you call the law then I will teach you mob a lesson you will never forget.'

Mrs Goodwin was kept chained up in a deserted holiday camp from which messages were sent by the gang demanding £50,000, a sum it appears the team thought Goodwin owed them and which, it was believed, he had in an account in a Jersey bank. Goodwin was provided with a telephone in his cell and he, together with the family solicitor, Jeffrey Gordon, co-operated fully with the police. Negotiations continued and the gang was lured into collecting a letter from Goodwin's sister which, it was said, was of vital importance. The mini-cab in which the letter was collected was followed to an address in Rennethorne Gardens. From then on it was relatively easy to trace the gang to the Isle of Sheppey in Kent where Mrs Goodwin had been held.

She had been released in Mitcham, South London, in the meantime.

Charles Pitts and his son-in-law, Sean McDonald, were charged and appeared in May 1984. On 22 June 1984 Pitts was gaoled for eighteen years and McDonald for eight.

Whilst hostage-taking of bank employees had become relatively common during the 1970s, it was not until the £1 million Millwall Security Express robbery in 1983 that a security guard and his family had been taken hostage. But there are real problems with this line of work. A Robbery Squad officer says:

> You need at least six people for a successful hostage situation and you have the logistical problem of keeping them overnight. Straight attacks on security vans are so much easier. If cash is being transferred there is little the carrier can do to protect himself. He has to rely on the honesty of the people who work for him and who are often paid peanuts. He has also to rely on their self-discipline. And even then, no matter how impregnable you think you make the van the people have to get out of it some time. Hostage taking will only take off in a big way if other robberies become too difficult to do.

Where one door opens another shuts. The great days of the commercial burglary are probably gone for ever. A former participating expert says:

> All the major commercial burglaries throughout the country in the sixties and seventies were carried out by a loosely associated team of eight. If you look back you'll find they end in 1982. I'm not talking about the Knightsbridge job because that

had shooters and was an inside job anyway. I'm talking about the proper burglaries. The last one was Lloyds Bank at Holborn. There hasn't been one since. They're things of the past. Security is tightened and to be frank the professional expertise isn't there. Nor is the money.

But what of those off the field of play down there in Spain? A Drugs Squad officer says:

They were sitting down in Marbella, which anyway was the cannabis route, and they've got to do something with their money. In the old days no self-respecting villain would have had anything to do with drugs but now it's different. We've had flower power and we've had the permissive sixties and so cannabis is not that bad. And even if it is, they're not actually doing the villainy, all they're doing is putting up a bit of scratch to finance it. It's not hands on so to speak.

But, of course, once the apple had been bitten it was realized the money behind the taste of cocaine was considerably greater than that of cannabis. The old-timers were sitting on top of an even more lucrative trade. Moreover, possession of cocaine for one's personal use was not an offence in Spain, which provided the bridgehead for the Colombians into Europe. A kilo of cocaine may have weighed the same as a kilo of heroin but the profit was many times greater, and so shipping in bulk was not the problem it was with the Class B drug.

One drugs deal is worth £3 to £4 million. Drugs is a victimless crime; there's no one embellishing the figures. With drugs there's no one screaming.

It's greed, pure greed, why people go on in

drugs. You'd think after one go they'd have enough. Put it in the bank at ten per cent and it's £100,000 a year – but no. A pal of mine and me received information that our car number had been taken. Now it was a straight car and so we put ourselves about and found it was tracked when we went to see a man we knew. They'd been on him for three months for drugs. So we say to him, 'Look, why don't you give the game up?' And what does he say? 'How do you turn up winning the pools every week?' He got caught on his sixth 10-ton run. His whack must have been £5 to £6 million. He got a ten and he's been done again since. They think it's for ever.

There wasn't even all that much risk.

You had a man pick it up in Spain, drive through Customs into France, which are a joke anyway, with the van or truckload. Sometimes it's concealed in the skin walls of the caravan and sometimes in the roof of a Range Rover. It's a three-day job and £5000 top whack for the driver for a big load.

Anyone except a totally amateur drug smuggler will employ a cut-out system so that the courier knows only his or her superior, and perhaps not even them. Nor will they know what is in the package. The drugs can be compartmentalized. Once the main cargo has been imported then the drugs can be left to sleep until the time personally chosen for the pick-up. With a robbery there is no knowing just how secure the operation is.

And the police see the sentencing in drug cases as rather a joke. 'It's all cock-eyed. You give a bimbo courier twelve years and in reality the same for the organizer. It may look great on paper but with parole and remission it's about one and the same.'

They are also unhappy about the press handouts which magnify out of all proportion the value of the quantity of drugs seized.

> You buy a kilo of cocaine in Colombia for $2500. Now to buy that in the UK will cost £28–30,000 from the importer. That will have cost him £5–10,000 in Spain. Once it's on the streets in the East End then it can realize between £80,000 and £100,000 in gram deals, but it's still really only $2500 of drugs.

And what happens to the money from a successful drugs run? It is laundered back to Spain where a bigger villa, a better bar may be purchased or, more likely, it is changed into dollars or Swiss francs. And what is the discount – bearing in mind the Train Robbery money was laundered at ten shillings in the pound? Probably a fee of between ten and twenty per cent depending on the amount, together with an up-front fee of between £20,000 and £30,000 for a one-million-pound launder.

But as the traditional English gangs shifted their position from robbery to drugs there grew up two other major operations: the Triads and the Yardies. The first would work independently and the second, sometimes at least, in a reluctant partnership with their traditional counterparts. Although some police officers decline to accept the existence of the Triad operation in London and the United Kingdom, the late 1970s and the 1980s have produced a rise in this and other ethnic minority gangs.

> I was reluctant at first to accept that any Triad groups existed in London. I was anxious that any

criminal elements that existed did not have their street credibility, and in consequence their ability to intimidate, enhanced by being labelled Triads, with all the fear that such a term generates.[11]

But Detective Superintendent James Boocock soon changed his mind.

Quite distinct from these street gangs, however, there exists a number of very close-knit groups whose criminal empires are networked throughout the United Kingdom and beyond. They are shrewd, ruthless individuals who have no compunction in resorting to extreme violence in order to punish, intimidate or impose their will on vulnerable Chinese businessmen.

In February 1976 Mr Kay Wong, a restaurant owner from Basildon, was kicked to death in an illegal gambling club in a basement in Gerrard Street as he sat playing Mah Jong. He suffered fourteen broken ribs as well as a ruptured spleen. The kicks were so savage that the toe of one of the attackers' shoes had split, and later the police were able to trace a shop in Leeds where a new pair of shoes had been bought and to retrieve the old ones.

Just what was it all about? The attackers had wanted to know the address of Wong's son, Wong Pun Hai, whom they believed to be a member of the 14K (a Triad gang formed in the 1950s, named after 14 Poh Wah Road, Kowloon) and partly responsible for the murder in December 1975 of one of their relations, drug dealer Li Kwok Bun (sometimes Pun), in Holland. Li Kwok

[11] Detective Superintendent James Boocock, *Police Review*, 21 June 1991.

Bun had failed to make a heroin delivery and the 14K had displayed its displeasure by putting eight bullets into the man's chest.

There had been no problems with the Amsterdam police. The body, decomposing quietly in the dunes at Schevingen, was not found until a fortnight after Kay Wong's killing. In Bun's pocket 1500 guilders (then £300) had been left, indicating to all who could read the message that it was not a robbery gone wrong. Bun may also have died because of his involvement in the murder of the so called Godfather of Amsterdam, Fookie Lang, who was believed to be an informer who had co-operated with the Royal Hong Kong Police in one of their periodic and often unsuccessful blitzes on Triad crime. Lang had been shot dead outside his own restaurant on 3 March 1975. After exacting their revenge on him, 14K had fled to London where in turn they became the hunted.

Kay Wong was unfortunately in the wrong place at the wrong time. His attackers headed north to Leeds where they split up. Two returned to Amsterdam whilst one went to Wales. They were charged with murder and appeared at the Old Bailey in November 1976. Convicted of manslaughter they received terms ranging from five to fourteen years.

Some days after his father's death Wong Pun Hai went to Vine Street police station with the dual purpose of claiming his father's body and clearing his own name of the death of Li Kwok Bun. In turn he was arrested and put on trial for murder in Amsterdam with two others. All were acquitted.[12]

The following year, on 11 January 1977, Shing May Wong, educated at Roedean, was sentenced at the Old Bailey for conspiracy to deal in drugs. With one of those

[12] For footnote, see over.

splendid passages of hyperbole which judges love to use when they can see the morning papers in their crystal balls, Judge Michael Argyle had this to say:

> When your tiny shadow fell on Gerrard Street, metaphorically the whole street was darkened and you and your confederate walked through the valley of the shadow of death. When you drove to the West End of London it was to become spreaders of crime, disease, corruption and even death.

He was rewarded. The *Daily Mail* faithfully recounted, 'At that her serenity was gone, she sobbed.'

Hers was a curious story. The reason she gave for becoming involved in the drug world was to avenge her father. He was a bullion dealer who had been kicked to death in Singapore by a gang of nine youths who lured him to a deserted spot when he was carrying a hundred gold bars. Six of the youths were hanged but for May Wong that was not sufficient. She told the court she believed he had been murdered on Triad orders, so she decided to infiltrate the group.

She abandoned her business, a beauty salon and boutique, and became a hostess in Singapore. Here she met Li Mah, the man who was to become her lover and who also received fourteen years' imprisonment. He, it was said, had fallen foul of the Triads when he owed them money and had agreed to work for them when his family was threatened. He was sent to Britain to peddle

---

[12] According to Fenton Bresler in *The Trail of the Triads*, Wong Pun Hai returned to England where in the late 1970s he was running a fish and chip shop in the Midlands. In September 1984 he was later alleged to have been involved in an attempt to extort £2000 from a Soho waiter but was acquitted.

drugs coming in from the Golden Triangle of Laos, Cambodia and Thailand. May Wong left her husband and came with him.

Their first consignment was to sell low-grade heroin and when they proved themselves they were issued with two pounds weight of good-quality 'smack', then worth £92,000 on the London streets at £15 a fix. Over the next six months she and Li Mah brought in £500,000. In two years her gang brought in £20 million. They were promoted, replacing a restaurateur, Chin Keong Yong, known as Mervyn, who had become an addict himself and had started stealing from the Triads.

May Wong's third partner was Molly Yeow, a beauty consultant whom Judge Argyle described as 'chief of staff'. She received ten years. It was during a search of Molly's home in Montpelier Grove, Kentish Town, that the police discovered May's address to be in St Mary's Avenue, Finchley. May was away in Singapore but she had left behind two little red books setting out in neat columns the names of retailers, stocks of heroin and the price paid for supplies. To lure her back the police gave out that Li Mah and Molly Yeow had been seriously injured in a car crash. She returned and was promptly arrested.

Argyle was not convinced by her tale. 'I cannot judge the truth of this,' he said.

By June 1990 four Triad gangs, Wo Sing Wo, Wo On Lok, 14K and San Yee On, each said to have a hard core of ten members, were systematically working the six streets of Chinatown – Wardour, Gerrard, Macclesfield, Lisle, Newport and the southern side of Shaftesbury Avenue – demanding protection money from restaurant owners and the gambling interests. As an indication of the amount of money involved, 14K are said to control a multi-million-pound racket of gaming and protection. A swoop was made in Glasgow in July 1990 and a number of restaurateurs there were charged in a multi-million-pound credit fraud said to be masterminded by 14K. However, they may be under siege. A Singapore-based group is said to be taking over from them.

Wo Sing Wo are undoubtedly seen as the most powerful of the London Triad operations, a position they established in August 1977 with a ruthless attack on their then principal opponents, Sui Fong. It came in the Kam Tong restaurant in Queensway, the second most important London base of the Triads after Chinatown. Three customers were slashed with traditional swords and another who ran into the street was chased by a man carrying a meat cleaver. In those few seconds Wo Sing Wo established a control they have not relinquished. Sui Fong have been effectively banished to operations in West London.

By June 1991 the situation in London had deteriorated substantially, with the intimidation of Chinese restaurant owners rising to such an extent that the chairman of London's Chinatown Association called for the government to proscribe the different Triad gangs.

Triad organizations require the euphemistically named 'tea-money' as a tribute, and the traditional chopping using a 14-inch beef knife is regarded as the ultimate sanction. If, for example, the restaurant owner does not pay on the first approach a negotiator is sent in. This meeting will be formal with tea and perhaps a meal in the private room of a hotel. Before a chopping takes place a knife wrapped in a Chinese newspaper may be presented as a final warning. If the man remains intractable then he will be killed.

Apart from protection and straightforward blackmail the Triads offer such services as loan-sharking. In certain areas of Glasgow, permission from a high-ranking Triad member is required before a Chinese businessman may approach a bank for a commercial loan – and such permission is only granted in return for tea-money. Also on offer are credit-card fraud, gambling, video-pirating and prostitution. The Chinese-operated brothels throughout the country are staffed by Malay or Thai girls usually brought into the country as secretaries or tourists who work a three-month stint before returning home.

As with most communities the problem the police have is in persuading victims to come to court. After a number of arrests in a very serious case in 1990 the victim left Britain and simply disappeared. No evidence was offered.

It is feared that the Triad problem will get worse as 1997 approaches and Hong Kong reverts to China. The Chinese Intelligence Unit based in the West End has no doubt that Triads resident in Great Britain are arranging for other gang members to join them here.

The second major operation, the Yardies, basically Jamaican-run gangs, merged at some point with their more powerful American equivalents, Posses, a name taken from the Western film, with their leaders known as Top Guns. The influence of the Yardies in Britain can be traced back to around 1980. They were blamed for up to 500 murders during that year's Jamaican election campaign in which they supported Michael Manley's People's National Party. When that regime was toppled by the more moderate Labour Party they fled first to New York and Miami and then further afield, including England.

Suggestions of the meaning of their name are diffuse. The Yard can mean home in general, a patch of territory or manor, Jamaica more specifically and a dock area in Kingston quite specifically.[13] Membership of the senior ranks is restricted to between thirty and forty men from Jamaica who are said to rule their members with iron

---

[13] In American prison slang it is also the exercise area.

discipline. 'Quite a few gained admission [to England] saying they were reggae musicians but their main aim was to take over drug supply lines,' said an observer.[14]

They were reported as having established a base within the year in Railton Road, the scene of the Brixton riots in 1981, running protection in the drinking she-beens and prostitution as well as illegal gambling and drugs. Two years later they were reported as having moved the scene of their operations to the All Saints Road area of Notting Hill Gate.

Three years on there were reports that they were back in South London attempting to hijack the booming cocaine market. In May, June and July there were six shootings which included two murders, the second of which, on 23 May, bore the hallmarks of a cold-blooded drugs execution. The victim, a thirty-one-year-old man, was standing in the doorway of the Old Queen's Head public house in Stockwell Road, London, when a blue Mercedes pulled up. A man got out, walked up to the victim and shot him at point-blank range with a sawn-off shotgun. The other victim was a doorman at Cynthia's night club in Acre Lane. He was shot through the head when trying to stop a gang entering the club and shooting their real target. At that time street robberies were running at around twenty-five a day in the Brixton area alone.

The same West Indian observer commented: 'Even among the violent elements, the Yardies are known as the worst. They first moved in on All Saints Road in Notting Hill, then into Hackney and now they are trying to take over Brixton. They are well armed and highly dangerous.' A detective said, 'They won by being totally ruthless and the situation in Brixton is looking like a carbon copy.'

[14] *Evening Standard*, 8 July, 1991.

On 25 May 1987 what the press described as the first Yardie killing took place. The deaths in Brixton three years earlier seem to have conveniently been forgotten, but perhaps they were just killings by the prior incumbents. Michael St George Williams, thirty-one, from Stoke Newington, was found slumped over the steering wheel of his car in Stamford Hill with gunshot wounds in his back after leaving a night club. Williams, who had left Jamaica at the age of three, had convictions for minor drug dealing but there was no hard evidence to link him with any criminal group. Described perhaps accurately as a street trader – in fact he ran a small baby-clothes stall – he was known for his lavish spending. He drove a Porsche.

The Yardies were closely watched by the police throughout the late 1980s but to no great effect. One problem was the adoption by members of street names such as 'The Scorcher', or 'The Executioner', which would be changed at will. A second problem was, and still is, that many of their assaults would go unreported both from a fear of further reprisals and a general mistrust by the black community of the police. In the summer of 1991 two events came to light. In one an armed gang had raided and robbed three hundred people at a disco. In the other an armed gang had fired shots at a fund-raising event attended by over four hundred people in a South London community centre. Neither had been reported to the police at the time.

At present the home of the Yardies is in South London, where a gang can consist of as little as four and as many as forty loosely associated people. Each will have one or two leaders, known as the Big Man, who will return to Jamaica for a month or two to buy and supervise the despatch of drugs. Then he will exchange positions with his opposite number.

Back in London, where police believe up to a hundred

people a day are dealing crack on the streets, there are the generals, who supervise the gangs' particular activities such as the dealing and prostitution, and the enforcers, lower in the hierarchy, who will collect money owed by drug dealers.

'In gang fights over territory, they don't take out the top man. They'll hit the second in charge to show how close they are. Otherwise they would lose all power and information.'[15] Kidnappings are relatively common. The Yardies 'are always ripping each other off. Someone might owe money for some drugs, but won't pay. So he's kidnapped until relatives, or other gang members, pay the ransom.'[16]

In October 1987 a swoop was made in Dallas, Texas, and thirteen other American states, rounding up the major Shower Posse, based in New York, and other Posses throughout the country. From documents seized it was apparent that the Posse operations stretched into Great Britain. The documents showed clear links with Yardies, not only in London but also in Birmingham and Bristol as well as in Sheffield. It appeared they had moved on from cannabis and cocaine to heroin dealing.

Three months later Scotland Yard began its first organized major offensive against the Yardies when a lengthy surveillance was undertaken on the New Four Aces, a club in Dalston. On 25 February 1988 it was announced that Commander Roy Penrose, formerly of the Drug Squad, was to head the new team. Two weeks later it was learned that one of America's top Yardies, Lester Coke, aged forty, known as 'The Executioner' and leader of the Shower Posse, had flown into Heath-

[15] Detective Superintendent Bob Chapman, quoted in 'Living on the Front Line' by Ken Hyder, *Police Review*, 22 November 1991.

[16] Detective Superintendent John Jones in 'Living on the Front Line', op. cit.

row on false papers. Happily throughout his visit he was tailed by the Jamaican Defence Force.

Six months after Penrose took over, the strength of his squad was doubled and a week later the so-called Godfather of British Yardies, Errol 'Rankin Dread' Codling, was deported to Jamaica where he was taken into custody. But the killings continued. On 1 September 1988 Rohan 'Yardie Ron' Barrington Barnet of Vaughan Road, Harrow, died from two shots in his chest after an exchange of gunfire in Harley Road, Harlesden. On Christmas Day Steven Mendez, twenty-two, was shot dead as he sat in the rear of his car during a street battle between rival gangs in Camden.

Penrose and his men had rather more success throughout 1989. On 21 July Philip Baker, described as a 'top Yardie drug trafficker', was sentenced to fifteen years' imprisonment for conspiracy to import cocaine and possession with intent to supply. On 4 August 'The Scorcher', Neville Edmond August Grant, also known as Graham Johnson and Noel Folkes, was arrested. A week later four men, Hubbert Millwood, Courtney Murray, Paul Lemmie and Stephen Fray, were convicted and sentenced for running Britain's first 'crack' factory. On 13 August 'The Scorcher' was deported. Altogether he would be deported four times in four different names.

In 1992 it has become clear that the problem of the Yardies–Posses is no longer an isolated one but is at the very least on the fringes of big-time crime. In November 1991 Leroy, from Rankers, the New York Posse, and Victor Francis were arrested while selling crack on the third floor of a council block in White City, London. Leroy, who claimed to be Norman Smith, and Victor, who gave his name as Ivan Thomas, were both wanted for questioning involving a murder in the United States.

Romeo Hugh Dennis used his real passport to come to England in late 1987 and when here acquired the passport and identity of Andrew Clarke, a serving soldier. Dennis set up home with his girlfriend and claimed social security. It was only when he was arrested for a failed bank raid that his identity became known. He had served two sentences totalling thirty years in Jamaica before being released on parole in 1981.

Genuine passports are now being obtained for the price of a single £30 hit of cocaine, Detective Superintendent John Jones announced. Drug pushers are offering addicts a deal they can't refuse – free drugs or a substantial discount in exchange for their birth certificates, which contain the necessary details to obtain a passport. One Yardie is known to have entered Britain eight times in a year, on each occasion using a different passport.[17]

At the same time, with shootings in South London averaging two a week, there has been a substantial increase in the use of firearms. Prices are incredibly low. An average semi-automatic pistol with ammunition costs about £250, with a sawn-off shotgun a bargain at between £50 and £100. On the other hand a sophisticated handgun such as a 9mm automatic costs £600.[18] For

[17] *Daily Mail*, 3 December 1991.

[18] The price of an automatic in 1954, according to Robert Fabian in *London After Dark*, was £10, with a big revolver costing £5. Most were war souvenirs or were smuggled in from France, Belgium and Eire. In the *Sunday Times*, 8 March 1992, Simon Bell wrote that he obtained a Smith and Wesson handgun for £300 on three days' notice. Ten years ago, he wrote, the price of a Browning was £60, reflecting its age and its probable involvement in several crimes. The following week it was said in an East End spieler, 'Shotguns are easy to buy and if you want a handgun then you can get one for £150, but you can guarantee it's been used. If you want to do a bit of work then you've got to buy it off someone sensible. There's a drought at the moment and you might have to go as high as £800.'

those who cannot afford the purchase price, guns can be rented from armourers for the night or week. Certain named guns, as opposed merely to makes, are highly favoured. 'I want Brown Annie tonight.'

In the three months to November 1991 the specialist squad aimed at tackling the problems of the Yardies made fifty-eight arrests. There were six charges of armed robbery, a kidnapping, two threats to kill, five of attempted murder and twenty-six drugs offences. Ten firearms were recovered along with ammunition and £40,000-worth each of heroin and cocaine.

The killings have continued throughout 1992. It is believed there have been some forty to fifty shooting incidents in Brixton alone, most of them unreported. Seizures of crack have risen from around two hundred rocks in 1990 to two thousand in 1991.[19]

But not everything has been centred on London. In 1991 in Manchester the Yardies, with the Gooch Close Gang and the Pepperhill Mob, were fighting for control of the lucrative Moss Side estate, dubbed Britain's Bronx by some newspapers. On 29 October, in the fourth gang-related murder there that year, Darren Samuel tried to escape the Mountain Bike gang, who chased him into a baker's shop and fired six shots at him as he tried to leap over the counter.

Yet just as there has been no general acceptance amongst police officers of the Triads as a force in the underworld, nor is there of the Yardies. A senior officer told journalist Duncan Campbell:

It is the Jamaicans who come over here and are not worried about using guns to sort things out who are the most dangerous. They use their baby-mothers to bring drugs over. But what happened was that

---

[19] *The Times*, Saturday review, 14 March 1992.

every time a West Indian guy was done for drugs or firearms, it was described as a Yardie thing, so their reputation grew. Some of the blokes themselves took advantage of it because their name had a certain menace to it which worked for them.[20]

'In a way the Yardies are the only real gang operating,' says Bill Waddell, curator of Scotland Yard's notorious Black Museum, perhaps a trifle optimistically.

Certainly Asian gangs have never been a threat to London's established hierarchy although they have been around nearby Southall for the last 20 years. There two classic styled gangs, the Tooti Nung and the Holy Smokes, operated more or less unchallenged except by each other from the early 1970s until the beginning of the 1980s. The Tooti Nung, possibly a rough translation of the Punjabi words for worthless or no good, were regarded by the community as downmarket Sikhs. Primarily groups of youths with membership handed down from brother to brother they and their arch rivals the Holy Smokes lived in comparative anonymity, with their sport consisting mainly of gang fights, stealing cars, 'and the rather less palatable abduction and rape of unaccompanied women, usually Sikh girls, whose families never reported the attacks to the police', according to one local solicitor.

Another area of activity was the financing of trips to India.

The way to do this was to report a lost Cortina (there wasn't a youth in Southall who didn't have a complete set of Ford keys), take it to a garage where it would be stripped, the parts stored and the shell dumped in a side street. The police would

[20] 'Gangland Britain' in *Weekend Guardian*, 14–15 December 1991.

then find it and the insurance money would be paid
out. The car would be reassembled by the garage
and returned to the owner less a fee. The de luxe
version of this is for the garage to dump the car
with one sports wheel so the loser could claim for
the other four.

The gangs, whose origins dated back to 17th century
Indian groups, surfaced so far as the police and public
were concerned in 1982 when outsiders became involved
in the fights and were injured. In 1989 there was
something of a police crackdown on Tooti Nung–Holy
Smoke crime which had expanded to stolen credit cards
and traveller's cheques as well as drug dealing and
immigrant smuggling. Shopkeepers in the district,
mainly Indian or Pakistani, were also the victim of minor
protection rackets run by the gangs. In the view of the
solicitor:

> They dominate communities like Southall . . . it's
> a place where as soon as you have some money you
> go and live in Hounslow or Wembley. What there
> is is drug dealing. It's a way of escape. A high
> percentage of businesses in Southall have been
> financed by drugs. Restaurants are a particularly
> easy way of distributing drugs. There is a high
> turnover of staff, storage space and no one needs
> an excuse to go into a restaurant.

In August 1989 the police announced that more than
165 suspects had been held in the crackdown which had
begun in January.

This is organised crime on a grand scale with many
of the participants having amassed large sums of
money. Several are now multi-millionaires leading

apparently respectable lives,

said Detective Superintendent Roy Herridge.

Until recently the London gangs seemed to honour the supposed Mafia tradition that women were left unharmed. Well, maybe they were threatened and worked over but at least they were left alive. This now appears to have gone by the board and the so-called Colombian mob method of wiping out everyone in sight is beginning to prevail.

In October 1991 Mick Smithyman was gaoled for life for the killing of his former girlfriend, April Sheridan. On 6 January 1990 he had shot April, mother of three young children, in a Kentish wood, because she knew too much about his underworld activities. Following a conviction he had burgled a neighbour's house and provided the shotgun used in the contract killing of another woman, Kate Williamson. Smithyman was afraid April would inform on him. Two others, Paul Smith and Ygar Salih, were in the car which took her to the fields where Smithyman marched her into nearby woods and shot her.

She pleaded with Smithyman, telling him she was pregnant. 'Just shut up. You know you are going to get it anyway. You know where grasses go and you don't deserve to live,' was Smithyman's reply according to Michelle Miles, Salih's girlfriend, who gave evidence at the trial. In turn she was told she'd get what April had got. 'Say goodbye to my kids and give them a kiss and tell them their Mummy loves them,' were April's last words to Miles.

Women gangsters are rare. At best, or worst, they are normally minders of property, cheque fraudsters, alibi givers and general supporters, trailing to prison taking food, changes of clothes and until a couple of years ago a half bottle of wine or a pint of beer a day to the men on remand. Now they pass drugs as they kiss their husbands and lovers goodbye. Fay Smithson, the Black Widow of the 1950s and 1960s, seems to have been in that mould. Much tougher was Linda Calvey, another 'Black Widow', who boasted she was the original of one of the characters in the popular ITV series, *Widows*.

In 1978 her husband Micky was shot dead during an armed raid and she earned her nickname by shouting 'murderer' at the police officer who stood trial for the shooting. He was acquitted and given a bravery award. Shortly after that she became involved with robber Ronnie Cook, going with him on trips abroad, including one to Las Vegas in which it was said they spent £30,000 in just over a week. He lavished gifts on her – clothes from Harrods, jewellery, money, a car, even £4000 for cosmetic surgery. There was, however, a down side. Cook's wife Rene was almost in penury and he was obsessively jealous, forbidding Calvey to speak to other men, beating her savagely and, according to reports, subjecting her to sadistic sexual practices.

Three years later he was jailed for sixteen years for his part in what was described as one of the 'most spectacular and well-planned robberies in the history of crime'. Whilst this is quite often a phrase used by prosecuting counsel opening the case to a jury, this robbery did have the hallmarks of brilliance. It was in fact Billy Tobin's Dulwich raid, when a hijacked mobile crane was rammed into the back of a security vehicle containing almost £1 million near a school in Dulwich.

Calvey promised to wait for him and as a mark of her fidelity had 'True Love Ron Cook' tattooed on her leg. But, it seems, she could not give up the lifestyle to which she had grown accustomed. Almost certainly Cook had had money salted away and she began to spend it, taking up with one of his friends, Brian Thorogood, whom

Cook had arranged to act as a 'minder' for him whilst he was inside. Thorogood left his wife, bought a house in Harold Wood, Essex, and moved in with her. Later he too was sentenced and served three years of a five-year term for conspiracy to rob. Linda also seems to have supplemented her income by being the armourer for various robbery teams.

Fearful that on his release Cook would find out about both her infidelity and her dissipation of his money, she planned to kill him, offering a £10,000 contract. Finding no takers, she turned to Daniel Reece, a convicted rapist whose evidence had assisted the police in convicting David Lashley, the killer of Australian heiress Janie Shepherd. Quite apart from the money Reece too was enamoured with Calvey and agreed to do the job.

In theory Ron Cook had a cleaning job outside the prison but, as with so many before him, he took to more palatable days out. Linda Calvey collected him on 19 January 1990 from Maidstone Prison and drove him to London, whilst Reece, whom she had already collected from another prison, waited outside her flat. Cook brought in the milk and as he stood holding it Reece followed him in and shot him in the elbow. He could not, he later told police, bring himself to kill the man. 'I shot to his side and he fell backwards into the kitchen. I moved forward and stood over him. I could not kill him. I have never killed anyone.' Linda Calvey had no such qualms. She grabbed the gun from him, ordered Cook to kneel and then shot him in the head.

Reece took a train back to the West Country to continue his thirteen-year sentence for rape, buggery and false imprisonment.

At first it seemed as though Calvey had been success-ful. The police appeared to accept her story that an unknown gunman had burst in and shot Cook whilst she cowered in a corner. Then it was discovered Reece had been with her over the weekend and had been her lover. It was curious he had not been mentioned in the statement. Under questioning Reece cracked first, telling all.

Reece, who was not notedly popular in prison following the evidence he gave against Lashley, thought twice about squealing again and withdrew his confession in court. Linda Calvey told the jury his confession was a fabrication. 'Ron meant everything to me,' she said. This gesture of solidarity did Reece no good. They both received life sentences for murder. Just as the men in Fay Sadler's life had ended up dead or in prison so did those in the life of Linda Calvey, a classic gangster's moll turned gangster.

1991 might be described as a vintage year for violence in what *Today* called the Bermondsey Triangle,[21] and much of it related to the Arif family and their rivals. Possibly some of the violence dated back to the shooting of Stephen Dalligan, a nephew of Tony White, at the Connoisseur Club. He had gone there by invitation to try to calm things down between his brother Mark and Ahmet Abdullah, known as Turkish Abbi, a suspected drug dealer and adopted son of the Arifs, who had quarrelled earlier. Stephen was shot in the mouth and back. He was unable to give a full description of his attacker and no charges were ever brought. Although there had been a number of witnesses none of them was able to make any identification. Dalligan would not even authorize the release of the bullets which had lodged in him.

On 11 March Ahmet Abdullah himself was killed in the William Hill betting shop in Bagshot Street, Walworth. Hit in the back after pleading with his attackers not to kill him, he had tried to use another customer as

[21] 4 December 1991.

a shield and had managed to escape from the shop before he was shot. He reached a nearby flat and then died within a few minutes. Tony and Patrick Brindle were acquitted of Abdullah's murder at the Old Bailey on 16 May 1992. Witnesses had given evidence from behind screens and were themselves only identified by number. Tony Brindle gave evidence that he had been playing cards and drinking in The Bell. Patrick did not give evidence. After the hearing Grace Brindle, their mother, told how the boys helped old ladies across the road and cried when their pet budgie died. In turn, the police said the enquiry was closed.

The next month, on 28 April, David Norris, a South Londoner suspected of grassing on gangsters, was shot at his home in Belvedere, Kent. Two men wearing crash helmets approached him and one opened fire with a handgun. Things cooled down for much of the summer until, on 3 August, David Brindle, another of Tony's brothers, was shot dead in the Bell public house in East Street, Walworth. Two masked gunmen burst into the crowded pub shortly before closing time and screamed 'This is for Abbi' before they fired on Brindle as he tried to scramble over the counter. No one is quite sure if the cry was something of a blind.

It was a shooting to be followed a few days later by that of the now legendary Frankie Fraser, apparently well out of his ground outside Turnmills night club in Farringdon. When questioned by the police about the shooting, which had removed part of his mouth, the sixty-seven-year-old fiancé of Train Robber Tommy Wisbey's daughter gave his name as Tutankhamen and said 'What incident?'

Over the years his relations had shaped up nicely. In July 1984 David, then thirty-seven, received a sentence of fourteen years' imprisonment for his part in the hold-up of a director of an airline and his family in Hyde Park

Gardens. In November 1986 James, who had an interest in the Tin Pan Alley club, a wine bar off Charing Cross Road, was sentenced to a term of imprisonment in Bruges, Belgium, for his part in a drugs conspiracy.

Ten days after the shooting of Fraser, William Walker was shot in the leg and arm as he was out walking with his wife in Rotherhithe. It was reputedly another gangland incident.

A man who typified the term footsoldier, John Masterson, one-time Scots hard-man and a friend of the Krays – he has a watch inscribed 'To John from the Kray brothers' – was more fortunate. On 17 October 1991 Masterson, a miner from Hamilton near Glasgow, smartly turned out in suit, shirt and tie and thick spectacles, had been drinking in the Heaton Arms and other pubs in South London with his and the Krays' friend Bernard O'Mahoney. On the way home they were attacked with ammonia sprays and there was a report a shot had been fired. Masterson was bundled into a car and disappeared. He reappeared at the Royal Infirmary, Edinburgh, three days later, doused in petrol. 'He was a walking petrol bomb,' said a member of the staff. It was a case of mistaken identity, said Masterson.[22]

In November Perry Donegan, a friend of David Brindle, was shot in the leg in the Green Man in the Old Kent Road. On 3 December Kenneth Neal was shot dead with a bullet in his chest and two in his head by a man described as young and blond who jogged away laughing. At first it was thought Mr Neal had been killed by mistake. Later it transpired that he had been involved with a married woman and had recently resumed the relationship.

---

[22] For an account of his career, remarkable for his prison experiences rather than work on the ground, see 'The Footsoldier' in D. Campbell, *That was Business, This is Personal*.

By the end of 1991 there had been forty murders in
the South London area, a hundred per cent rise on the
figure for 1990. But not all the violence has been
confined to South London. There has been just as much
violence across the river and in Essex, but with no press
magnet such as Frankie Fraser, the North London gangs
have been able to go about their business almost
unreported, as two longstanding families, one with
substantial South London connections, have waged war
for control of a drug and protection market.

> If I knew they knew the Xs I wouldn't deal with
> them. They are today's equivalent of the Krays and
> the Richardsons. Say a man owes you £15,000 for
> a legit piece of business, then he goes to the Xs and
> says he doesn't want to pay. They say they'll get
> you off his back for £5000 and they do. I'm not
> frightened but I'm not going up against them. Why
> don't the police do something about them? I don't
> know. There's three of them on bail at the
> moment. One for a big drugs thing and the others
> for possessing shooters. Maybe the police have a
> grander plan. I don't know.

Mad 'Scouse' Alan Smith, a moneylender and enforcer, was shot in a pub in Islington, as was former
armed robber Brendan Carey in September 1990. He
went down in the bar of the Prince of Wales in the
Caledonian Road, shot at point-blank range. At first the
police had difficulty in making an identification and a
neighbour said of him, 'I believe the victim was Irish and
named Jimmy. I think maybe the shooting was a
punishment or something to do with drug dealing.'[23]

[23] *Evening Standard*, 28 September 1990.

On 2 January 1990 a shooting took place in Huntingdon Street, N1, which led to the arrest of a former footballer, now a garage owner in the area. He was later released and brought a number of libel actions against the newspapers which alleged he had been part of this gangland shoot-out.

Later that month, William Fisher was shot dead on the doorstep of his home in Islington when a man in a motorcycle outfit opened fire. Fisher had long been a name in the frame and the police had interviewed him over a bogus Hatton Garden robbery, although drugs and not the spurious insurance claim were thought to be the reason for his death.

Masseuse Debbie Lee Parsons (forty-three) disappeared on 23 June 1990 and was found shot with a cross-bow in Epping Forest. She had been due at her boyfriend's restaurant to help out at a special party that evening. She never arrived. Despite wide-ranging police enquiries and the attention of the *Crimewatch* programme, no one was arrested and charged. The officer in charge of the case, Detective Superintendent Harvey, said it was an execution by any other name.

That month the former supergrass John Moriarty was dragged out of a bar in Benalmadina on the Costa del Crime and thrown under the wheels of a 32-ton lorry. Moriarty, who had survived two shooting attempts, did not on this occasion.

In December 1990 at Southwark Crown Court, high-living Peruvian Rene Black – he had wanted to be both a top-class racing driver and show jumper – who had planned to flood the market with cocaine, earned a fifteen-year sentence and the stripping of his £1.5 million fortune. His slightly reduced sentence was an acknowledgement that he had turned Queen's Evidence. His distribution partner, James Laming, was gaoled for eleven years and stripped of £23,950 of his profits. The

defence of former car dealer Laming had been an
ingenious one. He had not been dealing with Black at all
over cocaine, about which he knew nothing, but rather
over an attempt to organize horse-racing coups. He had,
he said, invented an ultrasonic stun gun which could
bring down a horse at three furlongs distance. All you
had to do was point and shoot. Laming tested this at
Royal Ascot in 1988 when jockey Greville Starkey was
brought down on Ile de Chypre when leading the field
in the Kings Stand Stakes. Very sportingly Starkey
allowed the defence to test out the machine again, this
time in the peace of his paddock. But the jury would
have none of it. Laming was found guilty on two charges
to supply cocaine and one of conspiracy to supply.

In December 1990 Laming's partner, John Lane, alias
John Gobba, was found shot in the back. Lane had been
arrested along with Laming at his Holborn flat but had
been released when no drugs were found on him. He had
been a close associate of Lionel Webb. In January 1991
Webb, supposedly an estate agent, was shot at his
premises in North London, which he used as a front. His
safe was found to be stuffed with narcotics.

On Sunday, 24 March 1991, antiques dealer and
cocaine user Peter Rasini was shot dead at his home in
River Avenue, Palmers Green, a North London suburb.
A sole gunman came up behind Rasini as he walked
down the path and shot him four times in the back.
Loyally, his family said they knew he had no enemies in
the world. A re-run of the events on *Crimewatch* has
failed to produce a charge and Detective Chief Superintendent Bill Peters told *Time Out* that 'the cold-blooded
way the murder was executed, the lack of clues, the
absence of any motive at all, point towards a hired
killer'.[24] One theory is that Rasini may have stumbled

[24] *Time Out*, 22 January 1992.

across a major criminal activity, whilst another is that he angered a member of the criminal fraternity and had to be killed.

On 17 July 1991 publican Alan Brooks was dragged from his bar at the Clydesdale pub in Loughton and hacked to death by a six-man gang with machetes. He had only taken over the pub two weeks earlier.

Whether innocent by-standers who have suffered include Maxine Arnold and her boyfriend Terry Gooderham, found shot dead in their black Mercedes in Epping Forest on 22 December 1989, is open to speculation. Certainly she was a bystander; he may have been more of a player, which resulted in what was certainly a gangland execution. As always a variety of suggestions were offered. Terry had an active life, for he shared it with Maxine part of the week and another blonde, Carol Wheatley, for the remainder. One suggestion was that there was a third Ms Gooderham in the background and she had organized the hit, but enquiries came to nothing. Nor did they in relation to the theory that he was involved with Brinks-Mat monies.

Gooderham had been a stocktaker for a number of clubs and pubs in London and Hertfordshire, and one anonymous friend put it: 'It is nothing to do with his love life or his own business but a lot of money is involved.' There were claims that he had been the victim of part of a drugs war and indeed a small amount of drugs were found in the car, but the police became convinced these had been planted and were a red herring. Then there was a claim in the *Daily Mirror* on 4 January 1990 that he had tried to muscle in on the lucrative Spanish ice-cream market and had so upset suppliers that a £50,000 contract was put out on him. Finally there was yet another solution offered. This time it was that the killing was over £150,000 which was euphemistically described as having been redirected.

Possibly the killing related to the North London gang war which had been simmering throughout the 1980s. 'Sometimes we take out one of them, and then they take out one of ours. Or the other way around,' said a fringe participant.

Commentators have seen the gaoling of Freddie Foreman, Eddie Richardson and Dogan Arif, along with the death of Charlie Wilson, as the basic causes of the present instability in the underworld. 'Two or three new gangs started to take over, with drugs as the base of their power. One of them has been ruthless in its bid to get to top dog position,' reported Jeff Edwards in the *People*.[25]

Life is cheap in North London at present. According to the *Sunday Mirror*,[26] contract killers will carry out the murder of a top criminal for £25,000, down to as little as £1500 for a surplus wife or boyfriend. According to the article the gang, so far unpenetrated by the police because of a wall of fear, operates on a kill now pay later basis. If this is correct they are the legitimate descendants of Henry MacKenny.

With spoils on offer of which Darby Sabini, the Cortesis, even Billy Hill, the Krays and all the other long dead or imprisoned heroes can never have dreamed, there are likely to be more killings and near-misses. It promises to be a long struggle for power.

[25] 7 October 1990.
[26] 5 January 1992.

And then . . . ?

It would not be right to finish this saga without at least a comment on the relationship the gangs have had with their national and international counterparts, in particular the so-called Mafia. There must also be some effort to lift the curtain of the future and to see if, and how, things will change over the next decade. Although there has been organized crime on a large scale in some provincial cities, the police usually seem to have stepped on the participants sufficiently hard and sufficiently quickly to stamp out gangs similar to the Krays and the Richardsons. One case in point was Sheffield, where gang wars raged in the 1920s and where Sir Percy Sillitoe, later head of MI5, suppressed them in a way that is quite alien to today's liberal attitudes.

The gangs there, led by George Mooney and Sam Garvin, controlled organized betting in the area. The game was called tossing and odds were laid against which of five half-crowns landed heads or tails. According to Sillitoe, each gang had hundreds of members who, quite apart from running the pitching rings, controlled the poor quarters such as the Crofts, Norfolk Bridge and the Park, collecting protection from the publicans.

I called my senior officers together and asked them

to select very carefully for me some of the strongest, hardest-hitting men under their commands. . . . It was not difficult to pick a dozen of the best of these to form a 'flying squad' specially to deal with the gangster problem. These men were taught ju-jitsu and various other methods of attack and defence, and it was surprising how little teaching they needed. They had just been waiting for the chance to learn![1]

Motorways and airports have certainly contributed to the improved mobility of the London-based criminal. France, Spain and in particular the Mediterranean have long been happy haunts of teams, initially of burglars and shoplifters, now of drug smugglers. On the other side of the coin there have always been visiting teams. Describing the build-up to the World Cup in 1966 Nipper Read wrote:

There was not only the problem of the clubs and our own thieves but also the con men who would come from Australia, the fraudsmen and tricksters from Mexico and Venezuela, the dipsters from Italy, drug-pushers from Holland and the heavies, GBH merchants from Germany.[2]

If there is any doubt that travel broadens both the mind and the opportunity, the case of Jamaican gunman Leon Virgo should assuage it. Virgo lived more or less quietly in a council flat on the North Peckham estate in South London whilst commuting to New York on false passports using the names of Kenneth Smith and Kenneth Barnard to carry out contracts for the Jamaican

[1] P. Sillitoe, *Cloak without Dagger*.

[2] L. Read and J. Morton, *Nipper*, p. 122 and see Supra p. 161.

Spangler Posse. In July 1987 in Manhattan he killed James Fernandez, shooting him nine times, and a week later he shot drug courier Tanya Lang, who was believed to be an informer. A further fifteen cases were left on the file at his trial at the Manhattan Supreme Court.[3]

And on the subject of travel there has been a resurgence of immigrant smuggling. Throughout the winter of 1991–2 there were reports of immigrants being found on the beaches of the Kent and Sussex coasts and in March 1991 fifteen Indians were found in a lorry at the Heston service station on the M4 west of London, the latest in the lucrative immigrant racket. In 1991 over four hundred people were found to have been smuggled into England – well over twice the number for 1990.

According to a report in *The Times* most of those smuggled are from Bangladesh, India, Turkey and Pakistan, with suggestions that between £1000 and £3000 is paid per person for the trip made by air to Germany or Denmark before being loaded into lorries for the crossing of the Channel.[4]

How far does basic street-level crime reach up into the world of the City and finance? One London solicitor traces the hierarchical structure of the 1960s from solicitor Judah Binstock, one-time owner of the Victoria Sporting Club, then protected by Corsican connections, to George Dawson, the orange juice king who later went to prison for fraud, through to Albert Dimes. John Bloom, the washing-machine tycoon, was deeply involved with Joe Wilkins, relative of Bert Wilkins who stood trial with Bert Marsh for the Wandsworth dog-track killing of 1934, who in turn was the man behind Dimes, and so on. Even the seemingly small-time Tony Mella of the one-armed bandits mixed socially with his

[3] *Daily Mail*, 5 March 1992.
[4] *The Times*, 24 March 1992.

solicitors and the directors of publicly quoted companies. The links are both endless and indissoluble.

And as for the Mafia? There can be little doubt that from the days of the Sabinis there have been close links with Italy and later with American-organized crime both at blue- and white-collar level. Dimes was closely linked with Angelo Bruno, whilst Bert Marsh assisted the Giotti family from New York when they were trying to establish a foothold in English gaming. Although Bruno seems to have declined close involvement, saying the English ways were 'quaint', his friend Meyer Lansky, the Mafia financier, was a friend of the malevolent Binstock and together they went to Brazil with Sir Eric Miller, chairman of the Peachy Corporation, not long before Miller shot himself on the Jewish Day of Atonement. The Krays had close links with New York crime. When they were endeavouring to shut down Nipper Read's enquiry, a hitman was brought over from New York. He was arrested at Shannon and put on the next plane home. The Richardsons had interesting deals in South Africa. The Soho connections have always been with France, Malta and Cyprus. When Gaul, the property magnate, wanted a hitman to remove his wife, Barbara, he knew where to find one – in the East End underworld.

It was only the vigilance of the immigration authorities which kept the Mafia out of London when the Gaming Act of 1960 was passed. The big junkets of American gamblers which followed provided an opportunity to launder money through the casinos. According to Peter Gladstone Smith it was then that Angelo Bruno endeavoured to forge links through Albert Dimes – and Judah Binstock. Apparently he wished to establish the American numbers racket in the United Kingdom. Basically the numbers game is a variation of the Italian National Lottery or the Pools. For a very small stake the punter has the opportunity to bet on a single three-digit number with the winner determined by the results at a major race meeting that day. The odds against winning are 1000 to 1 whilst the pay-out is a maximum of 599 to 1 less ten per cent commission on winning bets. Punters will choose their lucky numbers, birthdays, houses in which they live, etc, and it is possible to buy part of a ticket, when the odds paid out are considerably reduced. Bruno, along with film actor George Raft and other prominent American-organized crime figures, was subsequently refused entry to the United Kingdom.[5]

More and more the really intelligent criminals are turning to computer fraud. It is less dangerous to subvert a bank employee into passing over the numbers of an account than it is to attack a security van and risk being shot at by the police. Moreover conviction, which may be rare, carries less in the way of a sentence.

Of course such computer crime is not new, and one of the first exponents was Roderic Knowles, who in 1968 came within an ace of removing $600,000 from the Bank of America. Knowles, an Old Etonian, led a team – of all people, public schoolboys could never be called a gang – of gold smugglers. To finance the enterprise, one Sunday he obtained entrance to the Bank of America in Seoul and photographed the documents needed for the fraud. He and his colleagues obtained the Bank's secret code which authorized the branch's immediate payment from an account to a person named in the message. Knowles decided to try the scam on two branches, one in Zurich, the other in Amsterdam. The money was obtained from the Zurich branch but the innate cautiousness of the Dutch in paying out a large sum of cash close to a weekend led to Knowles' arrest.[6]

[5] P. Gladstone Smith, *The Crime Explosion*.
[6] P. Deeley, *The Manhunters*, p. 119

Perhaps even easier is the money to be made out of cloned credit cards. *The Times* reported a worldwide card fraud involving the embossing of personal account details on to a 'cloned' card and using a non-existent bank. The profits are said to be channelled into drugs and pornography.[7]

On a smaller scale it is possible to rent a stolen credit card at certain London clubs and public houses for an hour or for a day. The days when forgery, for this is what the scam amounts to, brought about a three-year sentence are long gone. The girls who are involved at the mule end of the trade can, at the worst, expect a fine or probation for a first, second or third offence unless they are extremely unlucky with their choice of magistrate. It is rare that they know the person from whom they obtained the card in the pub or wine bar for £25.

Now, with the booming cocaine and heroin trade, international co-operation between criminals is essential. Already there are tenuous links between Yardie gangs and the traditional London underworld. The immigrant smuggling racket requires cross- border co-operation. There is evidence that the Peruvians and Colombians have moved into the London drugs market. Once these presently tenuous links are properly forged we could see a whole new game. The only major criminal organization which does not seem to have established any real hold in London – possibly because of the relatively small community here – is the Japanese Yakuza, but no doubt, despite the country's new laws to kill off organized crime, it is only a matter of time before that happens.

[7] *The Times*, 23 March 1992.

Bibliography

Ascoli, D., *The Queen's Peace* (1979), London, Hamish Hamilton

Ball, J., Chester, L. and Perrott, R., *Cops and Robbers* (1979), London, Penguin Books

Beveridge, P., *Inside the CID* (1957), London, Evans Brothers

Biron, Sir Charles, *Without Prejudice* (1936), London, Faber and Faber

Black, D., *Triad Takeover* (1991), London, Sidgwick & Jackson

Bles, M. and Low, R., *The Kidnap Business* (1977), London, Pelham Books

Borrell, C. and Cashinella, B., *Crime in Britain Today* (1975), London, Routledge & Kegan Paul

Bresler, F., *The Trail of the Triads* (1980), London, Weidenfeld & Nicolson

Burke, S., *Peterman* (1966), London, Arthur Barker

Campbell, D., *That was Business, This is Personal* (1990), London, Secker & Warburg

Cannon, J., *Tough Guys Don't Cry* (1983), London, Magnus Books

Cater, F. and Tullett, T., *The Sharp End* (1988), London, Bodley Head

Challenor, H. with Draper, A., *Tanky Challenor* (1990),

London, Leo Cooper

Cherrill, F., *Cherrill of the Yard* (1953), London, Harrap

Cheyney, P., *Making Crime Pay* (1944), London, Faber & Faber

Chinn, C., *Better betting with a decent feller* (1991), Hemel Hempstead, Harvester Wheatsheaf

Cole P. and Pringle, P., *Can you positively identify this man?* (1974), London, Andre Deutsch

Cornish, G., *Cornish of the 'Yard'* (1935), London, Bodley Head

Cox, B., Shirley, J. and Short, M., *The Fall of Scotland Yard* (1977), Harmondsworth, Penguin

Davis, V., *Phenomena of Crime*, London, John Long

Deeley, P., *The Manhunters* (1970), London, Hodder and Stoughton

Dew, W., *I caught Crippen* (1938), London, Blackie

Dickson, J., *Murder without Conviction* (1986), London, Sphere

Divall, T., *Scallywags & Scoundrels* (1929), London, Ernest Benn

Du Rose, J., *Murder was my Business* (1971), London, W. H. Allen

Fabian, R., *London After Dark* (1954), London, Naldrett Press

— *Fabian of the Yard* (1955), London, Heirloom Modern World Library

— *The Anatomy of Crime* (1970), London, Pelham Books

Felstead, S., *The Underworld of London* (1923), New York, E. P. Dutton

— *Shades of Scotland Yard* (1950), London, John Long

Finmore, R., *Immoral Earnings* (1951), London, M. H. Publications

Fordham, P., *The Robbers' Tale* (1965), London, Hodder & Stoughton

— *Inside the Underworld* (1972), London, George Allen

& Unwin

— Gladstone Smith, P., *The Crime Explosion* (1970), London, Macdonald

Goodman, J. and Will, I., *Underworld* (1985), London, Harrap

Greeno, E., *War on the Underworld* (1960), London, John Long

Grigg, M., *The Challenor Case* (1965), London, Penguin

Henry, J., *Detective-Inspector Henry's Famous Cases* (1942), London, Hutchinson

Higgins, R., *In the Name of the Law* (1958), London, John Long

Hill, B., *Boss of Britain's Underworld* (1955), London, Naldrett Press

Hinds, A., *Contempt of Court* (1966), London, Bodley Head

Hoskins, P., *No Hiding Place*, Daily Express Publications

Humphreys, Sir Travers, *A Book of Trials* (1953), London, Pan Books

Janson, H., *Jack Spot, Man of a Thousand Cuts* (1959), Alexander Moring

Jennings, A., Lashmar, P. and Simson, V., *Scotland Yard's Cocaine Connection* (1990), London, Jonathan Cape

Kelland, G., *Crime in London* (1986), London, Bodley Head

Knight, R., *Black Knight* (1990), London, Century

Kray, C., *Me and my brothers* (1988), London, Grafton

Kray, R., *Born Fighter* (1991), London, Arrow

Kray, R. and Kray, R., *Our Story* (1988), London, Pan

Lambrianou, T., *Inside the Firm* (1991), London, Smith Gryphon

Laurie, P., *Scotland Yard* (1970), London, Bodley Head

Leeson, B., *Lost London* (1934), London, Stanley Paul & Co

Lewis, D. and Hughman, P., *Most Unnatural* (1971), London, Penguin Books

Lucas, N., *Britain's Gangland* (1969), London, Pan Books

McConnell, B., *The Evil Firm* (1969), London, Mayflower

Millen, E., *Specialist in Crime* (1972), London, George G. Harrap

Narborough, F., *Murder on My Mind* (1959), London, Allan Wingate

O'Mahoney, M., *King Squealer* (1978), London

Parker, R., *Rough Justice* (1981), London, Sphere

Paul, P., *Murder under the Microscope* (1990), London, Macdonald

Payne, L., *The Brotherhood* (1973), London, Michael Joseph

Pearson, J., *The Profession of Violence* (1977), London Granada, (1985), London, Grafton

Read, L. and Morton, J., *Nipper* (1991), London, Macdonald

Read, P., *The Train Robbers* (1978), London, W. H. Allen

Richardson, C., *My Manor* (1991), London, Sidgwick & Jackson

Samuel, R., *East End Underworld* (1981), London, Routledge & Kegan Paul

Short, M., *Lundy* (1991), London, Grafton

Sillitoe, P., *Cloak without Dagger* (1956), London, Pan

Slipper, J., *Slipper of the Yard* (1981), London, Sidgwick & Jackson

Taylor, L., *In the Underworld* (1985), London, Unwin Paperbacks

Thurlow, D., *The Essex Triangle* (1990), London, Robert Hale

Tremlett, G., *Little Legs, Muscleman of Soho* (1989), London, Unwin Hyman

Tietjen, A., *Soho* (1956), London, Allan Wingate

Tullett, T., *Murder Squad* (1981), London, Triad Grafton

Viccei, V., *Knightsbridge* (1992), London, Blake Hardbacks

Ward, H., *Buller* (1974), London, Hodder & Stoughton

Watts, M., *The Men in My Life* (1960), London, Christopher Johnson

Webb, D., *Deadline for Crime* (1955), London, Muller
— *Line up for Crime* (1956), London, Muller

Wensley, F., *Detective Days* (1931), London, Cassell & Co

Wickstead, B., *Gangbuster* (1985), London, Futura

Wilkinson, L., *Behind the Face of Crime* (1967), London, Muller

Woffinden, B., *Miscarriages of Justice* (1987), London, Hodder & Stoughton

Index

Gibson, Lennie 285–7
Giotti family 430
Gladstone Smith, Peter 430
Glander, Det. Supt.
  Stephen 307
Glinski, Christopher 59, 61,
  119
Gluckstead, Michael 335
Glyn-Jones, Mr Justice 58
Goddard, Lord Chief
  Justice 243n, 302, 341
Goddard, Sgt. George
  313–15
Gold, Beatrice 348–9
Goldstein, Morris ('Moisha
  Blue Boy') 61
Gooch Close Gang 413
Gooderham, Terry 425
Goodman, Arnold 144
Goodman, Jean 106, 109,
  125
Goodwin, John 396–7
Goodwin, Shirley 396,
  397–8
Goody, Gordon 239,
  240–41, 253–4
Gordon, Jeffrey 397
Gorman, Mr Justice 82–3
Grant, Neville Edmond
  August ('The
  Scorcher') 411
Gravell, John 269
Gray, Dolly 262–3
Great Bank Note Raid
  375–6
Great Mailbag
  Robbery 235–6

Great Train Robbery xvii,
  73, 90, 117, 118n, 156, 170,
  237–54, 260, 285, 326, 350–
  53, 375, 383, 384, 401, 420
Grech, Joseph 303–4
Green Gate Gang x
Green, Graeme 392
Greeno, Det. Chief Supt.
  Edward 15
Greenwood, Anthony 71
Gregory, Andrew 336
Gregory, Ernest 336
Groves, PC 264
Grunhut, Leo 381

Hackney Gang 28, 31
Hainnaux, George ('Jo le
  Terroir') 193
Hall, Roy 102, 103, 110,
  111, 114, 125, 127–8
Hannam, Det. Supt.
  Herbert 304–5, 306, 307
Hannigan, Harold 215n
Hanratty, James 89
Harding, Arthur xi, 6–10,
  12–13
Hargreaves, Mrs Nina
  251–2
Harris, David 316
Harris, Leopold 316, 317
Harris, Lucien 109–10,
  114–15, 118
Hart, Richard 120–23, 124,
  156
Hart, Ronnie 139, 140–41,
  153–4, 166
Harvey, Det. Sgt. John 393

Gangland Volume 2

Contents

For Dock Bateson, with love

Introduction

In the years after the trial of the Kray twins in 1969 the reporter Brian McConnell was sent around the countryside, on behalf of the *News of the World* for whom he was then writing, offering up to £100,000 reward for information which would lead to a conviction in an unsolved murder in the area. Wherever he went he saw senior local police officers and was confronted both with the statement that there were no gangs operating in the area of the force he was visiting and the belief that there had to be something seriously amiss with the Metropolitan Police to have allowed the Krays to have flourished at their peak for as long as they did – something in the region of five years with one abortive prosecution in the middle.

It is an attitude which still persists in many forces. That there have been gangs in the area in the past but certainly there are none today. Nothing like London. They couldn't possibly flourish with the control we have of criminals in our town. We're a small community. We know them all and who's doing what and what they're capable of.

To a certain extent the comment about the knowledge of the local hook's capabilities are, or at any rate were, justified. Some years ago a bank robbery went off in a city in the Midlands and a client of mine who went on to national notoriety was hauled up from London as a probable suspect. Chatting with the officers before the identification parade, I asked why they suspected it was an out-of-town job. It was easy, they replied. There was only one man in the town capable of such a robbery, 'and he was flattered when we went to see him'.

From my client's point of view the identification parade went off smoothly. He was a stoutish man and, on hearing of his arrest, friends travelled to the Midlands to give help and support. One of them, Peter Hubbard, now deceased, a celebrated horse doper, closely resembled my client particularly in relation to the number of pounds overweight he was carrying. For once the police officer in charge of the parade was prepared to let my client have a friend stand on the parade as a foil or dummy. Naturally he selected the position next to Hubbard and at the last minute changed ties with him. Hubbard was identified and, since he had a deal of trouble even climbing stairs in those days, was quickly eliminated from the inquiry.

The parade had been held in an upstairs room in the police station and on the way down I followed behind the witness and one of the police officers. There were some recriminations going on and the witness said, with some reproach, 'But you told me he was the one with the red tie.'

That night I broke one of my golden rules about not travelling with my clients and their friends. The last train to

London had gone and the choice was staying in the town overnight or getting a lift back with my client. Hubbard had an interest in a boy boxing on the undercard at the Albert Hall and was keen to see his protégé in action. It was a foggy night and he drove at breakneck speed passing, for some reason or other, through Newmarket. My client was urging him to slow down but Hubbard was in ebullient form. 'No worse than when I doped that horse before the Guineas,' he said, naming a racing *cause célèbre* and the bookmaker who he maintained had paid him. And as we swished through the fog he pointed out the stables where he had worked his art over the years.

I asked to be let out at the first underground station to which we came. I have no idea whether they reached the Albert Hall in time although I noticed their boy won. I idly followed his career from then on, but he never amounted to much.

The attitude that the police are on top of crime in their area still persists. Last year whilst trying to research professional crime in Dublin, I met a Gardai officer who was keen to impress on me that there was no such thing in Ireland. 'You're wasting your time,' he said. 'Stay and have a good holiday, but you're wasting your time.' The following morning the papers were full of a professional hit which it seems had been directed at the wrong man. The next few days revealed a chapter of crime which the Krays and Richardsons at their peak had never approached.

As with *Gangland*, I have tried to distinguish between crime committed for profit and for political or social motives. I have therefore omitted the details of the dozens of miners who were accused of rioting and other civil disorder offences in Wales during mining disputes with the mine-owners. Nor is there any account of the extortion by some members of Dev Sol and the Kurdish Workers' Party who are said to have been targeting Turkish businesses in London, Hull, York, Harrogate and Liverpool for funds – £100 per worker is reported to be the going rate. Shortly before Christmas 1993, demands ranging from £5,000 to £100,000 were made on Turkish North London shopkeepers. One restaurant owner from Stoke Newington who refused to pay was savagely beaten. A special unit was set up at Stoke Newington police station and the Metropolitan Police had plans to extend this throughout the whole of London.[1] There had been a similar protection racket run on the Cypriot community in the 1960s. Similarly disturbances and quarrels in the cause of religion, even though the participants have often been gangs in all but name, cannot feature and so there will be nothing in the chapter on Liverpool about the death of John Kensit, the founder of the Protestant Truth Society, on 25 September 1902. He was attacked by a large Catholic crowd as he left a meeting, and died after being struck by a file thrown from the crowd. John McKeever was charged with the murder and acquitted.

Domestic crimes have therefore had to be excluded, even though this means the loss of such fascinating cases as that of Ernest Clarke whose conviction at Newcastle Assizes in 1980 of the killing of 16-year-old Eileen McDougall ten years earlier ended in the Court of Appeal in 1986, when Mr Justice Lawton said that it was inconceivable that the murder could have been committed by anyone else.[2] It was a blow for JUSTICE, the organization which had

---

[1] *Observer*, 5 December 1993; *Sunday Telegraph*, 2 January 1994.
[2] See F. Bresler, *An Almanac of Murder*, p.37.

investigated his case and campaigned for his release[3]. Nor can there be any detailed look at Joseph Clarke (no relation) who on 3 February 1929 had one of the shortest murder trials on record. At Liverpool Assizes he was sentenced to death in a case which lasted four and a half minutes. He had strangled his landlady.[4]

Politically motivated crime on the mainland has once again been excluded, hence the Workers' Party of Scotland will not receive the coverage which the activities of its members – Ian Doran, a second-hand-car dealer; William McPherson, professional gambler; Colin Lawson, former monk in a closed order at Nunraw Abbey, West Lothian (later a 'soldier of the proletariat') and their leader, bookseller Matthew Lygate – perhaps deserve. Their aim was to turn the country into a Communist republic. To finance the revolution they committed a series of robberies in 1972, armed with shotguns and ammonia sprays. Lygate, a man of previous good character who defended himself at the trial, received twenty-four years, Doran twenty-five and McPherson twenty-six respectively. Lawson did best of all: he received a mere six years.

Crime in Belfast has been omitted on the basis that it is too intricately connected with political matters. Given the situation in Ireland, this exclusion has not always been possible. The interconnections between organized criminals and major

[3] JUSTICE was founded in 1957 following the joint effort of leading lawyers of the three political parties to secure fair trials for those accused of treason in Hungary and South Africa. It is now an all-party association of lawyers (with membership open to non-lawyers) to strengthen and uphold the rule of law in the territories for which the British parliament is directly or ultimately responsible: in particular, to assist in the administration of justice and in the preservation of the fundamental liberties of the individual.
[4] See J. Bland, *True Crime Diary*, p.40.

and fringe political groups there have been, at times, almost indissoluble. I have tried, however, to avoid the murders, robberies and kidnappings which can be clearly shown to be the work of political extremists. Even that is not always possible, but sadly I have had to exclude both the Sallins Train Robbery, which was a miscarriage of justice to rank with some of the better British efforts, and the Kerry baby case, a wholly domestic matter but important because it led to a change of attitude by senior officers to the workings of the Gardai.

I had intended that once more the starting point should be the turn of the twentieth century. However, I cannot bring myself to consign to oblivion without at least a mention the engagingly named Paisley Mohawks, who sound like an ice-hockey team, but were in fact a collection of racecourse bullies in the mid-nineteenth century.

The time scale should also eliminate the so-called High Rip Gang which may or may not have flourished in Liverpool in the mid-1880s. There is no doubt that there was a considerable amount of violence in the Scotland Road area where the police patrolled in couples. It was there the legend of the High Rip Gang grew up, much to the annoyance of the Chief Constable William Nott-Bower:

> It was suggested that the large number of crimes of violence in the Scotland Division was due to the work of an organized gang, banded together for purposes of plunder and violence, and executing vengeance on all who ventured to give evidence against them or their nefarious work. And, not content with inventing the Organization, a most euphonious name for it was also invented, and it was stated that this organization was known as the 'High Rip Gang'. Of course all this created considerable, and entirely unjustifiable,

alarm, though there was never the very faintest shadow of foundation for the suggestions made. But letters from all sorts of irresponsible persons, Press comment, and a certain sort of public opinion assumed the impossible, and accepted the fact of a 'High Rip Gang'. It was impossible, for such a gang could not have existed without the police ever hearing of it, and the circumstances of the various crimes were such as to render it impossible to assign them to such a cause.[5]

Whether there was such a gang may be open to question, but there were certainly a great number of robberies with violence and woundings in the list for the November Assizes of 1886 presided over by Mr Justice Day. He dealt with them sternly. After each verdict of guilty, and there seem to have been about twenty of them, the defendant was put back to await sentence at the end of the Assize. On the last day he was brought up and sentenced to a term of imprisonment coupled with twenty or thirty lashes of the cat. As a reminder, this was to be administered in two instalments, the second just before the man's release from prison. Crimes of violence in Liverpool, High Rip Gang or not, decreased sharply for a time after that.[6]

However, the overall picture of Manchester and its policing

[5] W. Nott-Bower, *Fifty-two Years a Policeman*, p.148.
[6] Certainly the *Daily Telegraph* thought there were High Rips. As part of Mr Justice Day's swingeing sentencing, two lads of 19 said to be High Rips received fifteen years penal servitude for stabbing a member of the Logwood gang. One man, said the newspaper, had had to have police protection because he would not allow the High Rips to use a goods shed of the Lancashire and Yorkshire Railway Company, the keys to which he had been entrusted.

cont'd overleaf

would be poorer without an account of the good Inspector Bannister who ran the brothels and probably a good deal more in the 1890s. Nor, even though it occurred in 1895, would it really be possible to omit mention of the theft, and subsequent fate, of the first FA Cup from a Birmingham shop window.

In 1895 Aston Villa won the FA Cup, beating West Bromwich Albion 1–0 at the Crystal Palace ground. On the night of 11 September it was stolen from the window of William Shillcock, football and boot manufacturer, in Newton Row, Birmingham. The shop was a lock-up one and the zinc covering was removed from the roof, allowing a man to be lowered in.

A £10 reward was offered by Shillcock, who also said that if the Cup was returned there would be no questions asked. It was well insured and it was proposed that a new gold Cup should be purchased at a cost not exceeding £200, the insurance money. This suggestion was turned down and it was agreed that another Cup – as closely resembling the old one as possible – should be purchased. Aston Villa was fined £25, the exact cost of the replica.

Nothing was heard of the Cup for over half a century until in February 1958 the *Sunday Pictorial* carried a scoop that Harry Burge, an 83-year-old Birmingham man, had stolen the trophy. Burge said that he and his two companions had jemmied the

cont'd
(*Daily Telegraph*, 15 November 1886.) There is some oral evidence that there was such a gang. In an interview in the *Liverpool Echo and Express* on 19 October 1960, Elizabeth O'Brien, then aged 86, recalled that, 'There were women in the High Rippers who identified themselves with a flower or plume in their hair. They were more vicious than the men'. She also said that the only control of the High Rippers came from a policeman known as Pins. When he approached the gang scattered, calling, 'Pins is coming.' She would have been nine at the time Mr Justice Day dealt with the gang.

back door, stolen the Cup, money from the till and some boots, and had then melted it down and used it to fake half-crowns, some of which were passed in a public house belonging to Dennis Hodgetts, the Villa forward. There were a number of discrepancies in his account, but that may be attributed to a recollection of events which had taken place over sixty years earlier. Burge had been in and out of prison for forty-six years, and two years after the Cup was stolen he was convicted of theft himself, so he had the right pedigree for the job.

Shillcock later wrote in *The Book of Football*, 1906:

> It was an incident which seemed to me at the time a great and unprecedented calamity. I pictured myself a ruined man. I seemed to see myself a hated individual – to see my business boycotted. Why, I was the man who lost the English Cup . . . I am not joking when I say that I believed that incident was destined to ruin my connection with football, but happily such has not been the case. But you see that I shall ever be a man with a record unique in the annals of football.[7]

[7] Not quite unique because on Mothering Sunday, 26 March 1966, the World Cup was stolen from the Stampex exhibition at Westminster Hall. The thieves removed the screws from the plates of padlocked double doors and the lock from the back of the glass-fronted cabinet. Several days later a demand was received, along with the detachable top of the trophy, and following a telephone call a 47-year-old docker was arrested.

Shortly afterwards a Dave Corbett was out with his dog Pickles on Beulah Hill, Streatham, when the animal sniffed out the trophy hidden in the bushes. Pickles was given a year's supply of goodies by a dog food manufacturer and a medal by the National Canine Defence League. Mr Corbett undoubtedly also did well from the recovery of the trophy. Unfortunately, so the story goes, Pickles did not live long to savour the benefits from his triumph; whilst chasing a cat, he strangled himself with his lead.

So far as the end of the time scale is concerned, it has become increasingly difficult to separate the history of crime in any major town or city from that of international drug trafficking. However, for the purposes of chronology I have included in chapters on the towns themselves some individual crimes, such as the apparently random killing of Benji Stanley in January 1993 in Moss Side in Manchester, rather than looking on his death as part of the national and international scene.

One of the problems with writing a sequel is that there is bound to be a certain amount of repetition. I hope I have kept this to a minimum. Although in the chapter on London I have referred to the Krays, the Richardsons and the Sabinis, the last at some length, I hope that I have provided new stories about the various gangs and, although presenting a chronology, I have not repeated in too much detail their exploits which have already appeared in *Gangland*. The behaviour of London criminals is crucial to an understanding of the rest of the country. There have been links and exchanges in a series of cases. In the 1960s Glasgow hardmen wanted for crime in their city were sent for rest and recuperation, and possibly to do a job at the same time, in London. For example, when the Krays wanted to deal with Georgie Cornell, before he was shot, a Scot was recruited to shadow and pay (in the sense of punish) him. Criminals from the provinces would set up the jobs to be carried out by London teams, thereby providing a measure of protection for both, and conversely when a safe needed blowing, London criminals would hire a man from Glasgow or the North East where there were mining communities from which men experienced with explosives could be recruited.

In the case of supergrasses and particularly the Brinks-Mat robbery, I have had to restate the facts of the cases which have appeared in *Gangland* before bringing the stories up to date. In general I have omitted the lives and careers of the great individual jewel thieves such as Peter Scott, Raymond Jones and George 'Taters' Chatham. In a curious way although a part of, they were also apart from, the Underworld and often moved in a completely different society. I had intended to look more closely at some of the great art robberies, but with the exception of the loss of the Beit collection (twice) that subject will have to await another day or another book.

As for this book itself, I would like to claim it is a complete history of what has recently become known as designer crime, but it would be idle of me to do so. As I wrote in the Introduction to *Gangland*:

> Of course much of this book is oral history and the narrators of the tales may not be wholly reliable. Quite genuinely their memories will have faded but also there are axes to grind, scores to be settled, no longer with knives but in print, proving yet again that the pen is mightier than the sword. It also has to be said that some of the reporting in the old days, as since, was not aimed at a sociological study but at the number of copies of the newspapers or magazines to be sold . . . One of the major causes of the break-up of the Spot-Hill partnership was their rivalry over the publication of their respective memoirs. Wearing one of his less attractive hats, the newspaper reporter Duncan Webb was used by Hill, whose autobiography he ghosted, to discredit and embarrass Spot.

One example of the difficulties faced in writing a social history of crime such as this is that the protagonists played under a variety of different names, often their mothers' maiden ones. Ruby Sparkes, for example, appeared in court as Watson. When I was trying to trace his former girlfriend Lilian Goldstein, I was confidently informed that she was, 'Nona Hayes, you know, the daughter of Timmy, Guv'nor of West Ham'. This was firmly denied by others who knew her and who placed her as coming from North-West London. When eventually I found details of her career in the Public Record Office which seemed to confirm that she was no relation of the Hayes family, I mentioned this to my informant. He was sceptical and suggested she might have been some sort of illegitimate daughter; it was almost as if he wished her to have a legitimate criminal pedigree. Generally speaking Goldstein was thought at the very least to be attractive, and she must have had a good deal of skill and bravery as can be seen from the grudging tributes by officers who followed her in 1940 in the hope she would lead them to Sparkes who had just escaped from Dartmoor.

Contrast this then with the recollection of Val Davies, who wrote a number of books on the pre-war London Underworld:

If we rule out Peter the Painter and the Bonnet gang, a woman has the distinction of being the suspect pioneer of smash-and-grab crime in this country. But I must hasten to add she was by no means a glamorous bobbed-haired bandit. On the contrary, she was an unwashed, foul-mouthed, illiterate, drink-sodden Amazon with a reputation of being able to use her fists as ably as a man, however tough he may be.[8]

[8] V. Davis, *Phenomena in Crime*, p.136–7.

You might not think the descriptions could be of the same woman, but it is accepted that there was only one girl smash-and-grab raider at the time so he must have been referring to Goldstein.

Other examples of multiple names include the old villain Arthur Harding who was also known as Tresidern, whilst Harryboy Sabini was also called Harry Handley and Henry Handley. Jack Spot was variously named Camacho and Comer.

Another problem is the absence of documentation about these heroes. In the early days many could not read and write, and those who could were not too often willing to commit themselves to paper. By the time records are released by the Public Record Office, those to whom they refer will have long passed out of memory. When they did commit themselves to paper the events had happened long before and, even allowing for scores to be settled, recollections could be genuinely faulty and inconsistent. Take Arthur Harding remembering his companion Jack 'Dodger' Mullins. In *East End Underworld* on p.132, Harding refers to Mullins as 'ignorant as bloody hell and brutal with it'. By p.149 Mullins has become 'a thief but not a violent type', but by p.185 he has reverted to being 'one of the biggest terrors in London at the time'.

The final problem is, perhaps, a technical one. We are long past the days when cases were disposed of with anything approaching celerity; now, a simple shoplifting case can take two days and a murder case with two or three defendants will last a month. In 1959 Ronald Marwood was suspected of killing a police officer in a fight outside a dance hall in the Holloway Road. He was not arrested immediately but thirteen of his companions were. In those days there was no such thing as a paper committal; every word of evidence against a defendant had to be taken down, usually in long-hand. This included witnesses such as a plan drawer or photographer, let alone anyone whose evidence might be challenged. The remaining defendants were committed for trial by the end of the year. Marwood gave himself up in early January. His trial at the Old Bailey was in March (after a full committal hearing) and he was executed in April. Now cases which once would have been heard within weeks will take a year or more to come to trial. Juries, where in 1911 they had taken twenty-eight minutes to convict Steinie Morrison[9] against whom the case was never strong,

---

[9] Steinie Morrison aka Alexander Petropavloff was charged with the murder of Leon Beron, found dead on New Year's Eve 1909 in some bushes on Clapham Common, London. He received a few shillings a week rent from properties he owned, but lived in a sevenpenny-a-night lodging house. However, Beron did carry on him both jewellery and fairly large sums of money – up to £70, which could then buy a house. The victim's skull had been fractured and he had been stabbed. His money, watch-chain, and a £5 gold piece he carried were gone, and his forehead was incised with several cuts that looked like the letter 'S'. This was the initial letter of the Russian word for *spic* or double agent. A reward of £500 was offered for information leading to the conviction of his killer.

His death came only a fortnight after the Houndsditch murders by the Russian anarchists who, whilst carrying out a burglary, had been surprised by unarmed police and had shot them dead. Three days into the New Year there had been the famous siege of Sydney Street in which the murderers died in a blazing house after a long gun battle with the Scots Guards. Was there any evidence that Beron knew the Houndsditch murderers? No, said Inspector Frederick Wensley in charge of the investigation. It was, he believed, purely a matter of robbery.

The evidence against Morrison was that he knew Beron and was seen with him in the East End shortly before midnight on the night of his death. He also knew the area; just before his arrest he had

will, following the American example, retire for hours, if not days. As a result it is not possible to give the outcome of cases which have happened in the last year or sometimes even two. There are inevitable lacunae.

All I can really hope is that this book is the most comprehensive so far. When I completed *Gangland* a number of those mentioned telephoned me to say they had acquired – even if they had not actually purchased – copies and pointed out some errors. I hope that there will be even fewer in this book, but of course there will be omissions. Once more, if those who feel unfairly left out,

cont'd

obtained work in a bakery at Lavender Hill a few minutes from Clapham Common. He had given a parcel to a waiter in an East End restaurant, saying it contained a flute, but at Morrison's trial the waiter said it was far too heavy to be a flute and seemed more like an iron bar. Again, there was evidence that Morrison had been thoroughly unpleasant to him and the man had every reason to hold a grudge against him. There were spots of blood on Morrison's collar when he was arrested; he seemed to have come into money just after Beron's death; and in those days, when identification evidence was accepted quite readily, he was identified by two cab-drivers who firmly put him on Clapham Common at the time of the murder.

The trial started at the Old Bailey on 6 March, almost two months from the day of his arrest, before Mr Justice Darling. His defence was an alibi. After midnight he had been in his lodgings. Some of the witnesses called to place him with Beron before midnight were prostitutes, and the waiter who said he had been given an iron bar rather than a flute to mind had tried to commit suicide (then a felony). Morrison's counsel, Edward Abinger, tore into them, ignoring the judge's warning of the consequent damage to Morrison's character in evidence. The identification evidence was not strong; Abinger called a John Greaves, of the Royal Institution of British Architects, to deal with the inadequate lighting at the Clapham Cross cab rank, and he threw considerable

and that they have done better than some of the named participants, care to write to me stating their credits, I will endeavour to ensure they find themselves in any subsequent edition.

As always I am grateful to a considerable number of people for their help and advice and who have allowed me to quote from their books. This time they include, in strictly alphabetical order, Joe Beltrami, Julian Broadhead, Lisa Brownlie, Doug Cluett, Dani Garavalia, Frank Fraser, Frances Hegarty, Brian Hilliard, Dick Hobbs, Cal McCrystal, Brian McConnell, John Morris, James Nicholson,

cont'd

doubt on the identification. Also, it was shown that Morrison had at least ten collars and that he was a fastidious dresser. Nor was he a fool. Surely he would not have worn an unwashed collar for a week – particularly one stained with Beron's blood?

The difficulty came when his alibi about seeing two sisters at a music hall was effectively broken. The girls were muddled over their evidence; they could not say who paid for their tickets and, worse, could not remember who was on the bill. Morrison did not help himself when he went in the witness-box. He could not prove that the upturn in his finances had not come from Beron's pockets. Then Abinger's tactics in cross-examining the prostitutes rebounded against his client. Morrison's character was put in evidence – prison record, false names and all.

Darling was not sure of Morrison's guilt and he certainly did not sum up for a conviction. He told the jury that Morrison had no convictions for violence and, more importantly, that a foreigner on trial for his life might do things an English person would not do. Merely because he had concocted a false alibi did not mean he had committed the crime. This did Morrison no good; the jury took only a short time to convict. Morrison now told the court that the money he had came from a bank forgery. It was normal for judges to add that they agreed with a jury's verdict, but instead Darling told Morrison to be advised by his solicitor and learned counsel.

Even though they upheld the verdict it is clear the recently

Douglas Skelton, Edda Tasiemka, Stuart Tendler, Leon Williams, Frank Williamson, and Richard Whittington-Egan, to whom I owe a special debt for the references he obtained from his library, as well as the staff at the Public Record Offices both in Chancery Lane and at Kew. There are also a great number of journalists and others who have assisted me but have asked not to be named. Faults and frailties are mine alone. The book could not have been written without the endless support and encouragement of Dock Bateson.

cont'd

formed Court of Appeal did not like the conviction, but under the terms of the Criminal Appeal Act 1906 there was nothing they could do:

> Even if every member of the Court had been of the opinion that he personally would have acquitted the prisoner the Court must yet have upheld the conviction, unless they were of the opinion that the verdict was so perverse that no reasonable jury would have given it.

Nevertheless it, plus Darling's summing-up, was enough to save Morrison's life. Churchill commuted the death sentence to one of penal servitude on 12 April 1910. Morrison could not accept the verdict, and time and again petitioned the Home Secretary to have his case re-opened. He is also said to have petitioned for the death sentence to be carried out. After starving himself for three months he died in prison on 24 January 1921.

1

London – The Families

The battles for control of London, in particular the East End and Soho, have been charted before, albeit from different perspectives.[1] Briefly the history traces through such early gangs in the East End as the Russian immigrant Bessarabians and Odessians at the turn of the century, Arthur Harding and his Vendetta boys in the first few years of this one, running through the Titanics, a team of pickpockets and burglars destroyed in around 1915, to the Sabinis, initially a racecourse gang after the First World War, and their long-lived rule of Little Italy in Clerkenwell and Soho.

The Sabinis, five brothers born of an Italian father and an English mother named Handley, led by the redoubtable Darby, had first seen off Billy Kimber and the Brummagen Boys, a Birmingham-based racecourse gang (but with many members from around the Elephant

---

[1] See J. Morton, *Gangland, London's Underworld*, and R. Murphy, *Smash and Grab*.

and Castle) and later the Camden Town Mob, led by Fred Gilbert but in which their old rival Kimber had a considerable interest. The leader was not present in July 1922 nor was Kimber – he had been shot the previous year and survived – when the Sabinis visited their regular haunt the Red Bull on the edge of Clerkenwell to find members of the Camden Town gang in what they could justifiably call their bar. There had been a rumble a few weeks earlier, as a result of which Joseph Sabini would be sentenced to three years' imprisonment. Now the knives (Sabinis) and guns (Camden Town) were out. Fortunately, as on other occasions, either the weaponry was faulty or they were extremely bad shots because Detective Constable John Rutherford, who had been in the bar and had followed the Camden Town boys as they chased the Sabinis, was shot at at close range. The bullet missed. In November a number of men were sentenced for this little fracas. Joseph Jackson received seven years and George Baker five years' penal servitude. Birmingham men George Martin and George Hillier were acquitted and presumably went back home.

Then when there should have been peace and prosperity they faced internal difficulties from their senior lieutenants such as the Cortesis, and also from other smaller organizations over the division of the spoils and the allocation of pitches on the racecourses.

The Cortesi brothers were already serving four-year sentences for their assaults on Darby and Harryboy Sabini in the Fratellanza club in Clerkenwell when another ally of the family, Edward Emmanuel, was attacked in September 1924 by which time the Yiddishers, who foolishly and temporarily had aligned themselves with the Cortesis, were back in the Sabini fold.[2]

The prosecution of Alfie Solomon for murder in the Eden Social Club, Hampstead Road, London came about over an incident earlier in the evening when former prize-fighter Barnett 'Barney' Blitz, also known as Buck Emden, set on Emmanuel with a broken glass. He believed Emmanuel had been responsible for grassing him up the year before over an affray at Epsom races. He suggested that Emmanuel, who organized the bookmakers' concessions, had paid the police £20 to have him arrested. Given Emmanuel's 'in' with the police, it seems a perfectly reasonable belief. Solomon came to Emmanuel's aid and stabbed Blitz with a carving knife. The boxer died in hospital some days later and the Sabinis rallied to the assistance of their supporters.

It was the strict custom in the 1920s for members of the Bar to see their clients only in their chambers. Not many years previously it had been the custom not to see the clients on capital charges at all, leaving their solicitors to transmit messages of succour and support to the prisoners. Now Darby Sabini and his friends descended on Sir Edward

---

[2] Emmanuel had a long-lived history in the East End. At one time, before seeking an alliance with the Sabinis, he had run with Arthur Harding. In his later life he was regarded as being a great 'fixer' with the police. His son, Phillip, was among the first eight stewards appointed in 1921 at a wage of £6 per week each to assist the Racecourse Bookmakers and Backers Protection Association. The other stewards included the Sabini brothers. In 1926 Netley Lucas wrote of the Sabinis in *London and Its Criminals*, '. . . the gang is backed and upheld by one of the best known and most powerful bookmakers on the Turf. A member of all the racing clubs, a man who pays out thousands after each big race, and retains twice as much, he has a smart flat in the West End, several expensive cars and a still more expensive wife.'

Marshall-Hall KC in his flat in Welbeck Street and, with the help of a bundle of the old white £5 notes, known as Bradburys, and said to total £1,000, persuaded him that he was the only man at the Bar able to save Solomon from the gallows.

They were right to select Marshall-Hall. In one of his most impressive displays of forensic theatricality, he smashed a glass on counsel's bench in front of him and held it so that the jury could see the jagged and dangerous edge. Surely, confronted with this and an enraged boxer, there was every reason for poor Solomon to panic. The jury thought so and returned a verdict of manslaughter. Solomon was sentenced to a term of three years' imprisonment.[3] On his release he asked the police for protection against other race gangs.

The Sabinis' control of matters declined in the 1930s. They were under siege from the up-and-coming White family who had initially been amongst their supporters,

[3] Marshall-Hall was probably the greatest of the old-style advocates of the twentieth century. His behaviour in court was often spectacular and the glass-smashing demonstration at Solomon's trial echoed that of his earlier defence of Marguerite Fahmy, a lady who had married a rich Egyptian, Ali Kamel. Apparently he both treated her with violence and subjected her to sexual brutality. When finally he demanded anal intercourse she shot him. In his speech to the jury, Marshall-Hall, demonstrating to the jury how she snatched the gun to protect herself from this anti-social behaviour, dropped the weapon just as she had described dropping it after shooting her husband. He said later it was by accident, but the effect was described as 'an attack on the nerves as violent as a physical blow'. Mme Fahmy was acquitted to an outburst of cheers and clapping. Hall is the model for the performance by Charles Laughton in the film *Witness for the Prosecution*. In later years the character of Mme Fahmy has undergone something of a downgrading. She was, it now appears, a Parisian prostitute rather than a high-born lady.

and also now from Alfie Solomon to whose defence they had rallied a decade earlier. Darby Sabini could no longer control the disparate Jewish and anti-Semitic factions in his organization. A slashing of a member of the Hoxton mob at Liverpool Street Station led to the fight on 8 June 1936 at Lewes racecourse when Sabini bookmaker Mark Solomons (once acquitted of the attempted murder of Billy Kimber) and his clerk, Mark Frater, were badly beaten. An accommodation was reached. Now the Whites took King's Cross whilst the Sabinis retained Clerkenwell and Soho.[4]

During the War the Sabinis were dealt some rough treatment, not only by rival gangs but also by the British government. Some of the brothers were interned as enemy aliens. Darby Sabini was detained in June 1940, and by the November had still not appeared before a tribunal to determine whether the reasons for his detention were justifiable. Harryboy (alias Harry Handley, Henry Handley and a few other names) was detained at the same time. In the War Darby Sabini served a short prison sentence for receiving. Curiously, although he maintained he had been framed possibly either by Alf White or Alfie Solomon, he

---

[4] The celebrated battle at Lewes racecourse was the last of the big gang racing battles. There are grounds for thinking that the Sabinis tipped off the police who were then able to prevent considerable punishment being dealt to Frater, the clerk. Certainly, according to DCS Greeno, an anonymous telephone call had been received telling the Squad, 'It's going to be off at Lewes on Monday.' (*War on the Underworld*, p.64.) Sixteen men were arrested and the ringleaders drew five years' apiece at the next Lewes Assizes. One of them was Jimmy Spinks, leader of the Upton Park mob. It spelled the end of him as a real contender for the control of the Underworld. It is said that the men's families were supported during the sentences by the founder of one of Britain's largest bookmaking firms.

pleaded guilty. His son was killed in the Battle of Britain and this effectively destroyed him and what power his family had retained.

Like all good gang leaders, Harry's convictions were modest and the evidence of his bad character was minimal. George Cortesi had taken out a summons for assault against Harry, Darby and a number of others. At Clerkenwell Police Court on 22 October 1922 Harry had been fined £3 and £2 costs. The conviction brought into play a bind-over earlier in the year at Marylebone where he had been charged with assaulting a Fred Gilbert at Paddington Railway Station with an automatic pistol. Harry had not been convicted but had been bound over to be of good behaviour, with a surety, each in the sum of £5. Now both he and Edward Emmanuel, his surety, forfeited the money. This was the incident which led to the shooting of Harryboy and Darby by the Cortesis in the Fratellanza Club. There was also evidence that sixteen years later, in 1938, Darby had been seen in Tattersall's enclosure at the Ascot races kicking a Richard Hutton. Harry had gone to give a bit of extra help to Darby who was said to be drunk. Darby was expelled from the meeting and a black mark was registered by DI Ted Greeno against Harry, later to be used in evidence against him. Conviction wise, the worst that could be said about the family was that Joseph, another of the brothers, had been sentenced to three years' penal servitude in 1922. There had also been a small matter of the attempted bribery of prison officers whilst he was in Maidstone.

The police report leading to Harryboy's arrest described him as

. . . one of the leading lights of a gang of bullies known as the Sabini gang who under the cover of various rackets have by their blackmailing methods levied toll on bookmakers . . . He is a dangerous man of the most violent temperament and has a heavy following and strong command of a gang of bullies of Italian origin in London.

The report concluded:

We have no knowledge that he has previously engaged in any political activities but . . . he can at best be described as a dangerous gangster and racketeer of the worst type and appears to be a most likely person who would be chosen by enemy agents to create and be a leader of violent internal action.

Harryboy appealed against his detention under regulation 18B. The reasons for his detention were given as 'hostile associations' but more likely he, together with boxer Bert Marsh, also known as Pasquale Papa – who had been acquitted of murder following a fight at Wandsworth Greyhound Stadium in 1934 – had been detained because they were suspected of a successful bullion raid at Croydon Airport. This dated back to the 1920s and was believed to have netted the then very substantial sum of £80,000.

There is no doubt that security at the recently opened Croydon Airport was lax, as was the discipline with the pilots. In theory the buffet-cum-restaurant was open only to passengers and customers, but the pilots kept overcoats in their lockers to wear over their uniforms so as to gain access. Nancy Johnstone, who worked in the buffet, recalls that one pilot, Paddy Flynn, used a code 'a little more sugar this morning' to mean a measure of whisky in his coffee before he flew. He lost a leg in an air crash whilst flying for Imperial Airways in the early 1930s.

Opposite the restaurant was the bullion room in which gold bars, the universal currency, were stored. If a transfer of currency was made between countries then the gold bars were literally moved. The security was in the hands of guards of the Civil Aviation Transport Organization, but from time to time the door to the bullion room was left open with the key in the lock.

The staff noticed that a man was hanging around the airfield, and it is thought that he took a wax impression of the key when one day it was left in the lock. Nancy Johnstone remembers locking up the canteen one afternoon after the last flight – there were no such things as night flights – and when she returned to the premises the next morning she found it in an upheaval. Gold due to be flown to France was gone.

Shortly afterwards a Sabini bookmaker, in tribute to or financed by the robbery, began betting using the name Nick Gold.

The appeal was delayed and so Harryboy, ill-advisedly as it transpired, applied for a writ of *habeus corpus*. He had already offered his house, worth some £15,000, as surety if he could be granted bail. In his affidavit in support of the application for leave to be granted the writ, he said he had never been known as Harry Handley. The evidence of his arrest was that the police had gone to his house at 44 Highbury Park, Highbury New Barn in North London on 20 June 1940 and asked Sabini's wife where Harry Handley was. The reply had been 'upstairs'. It was also successfully argued that he could be described as being of 'hostile origin' even though he had an English mother, Eliza Handley, and his father had died when he was a child. His brother George Sabini had a daughter in the ATS and a son in the RASC who had joined up after war had been declared with Italy. The authorities were none too pleased when Harry was released from detention on 18 March 1941. He was promptly re-arrested for perjury, and on 8 July that year he received a sentence of nine months' imprisonment.[5]

Arthur Swan, himself detained under the wartime 18B measures at what he described as the Ascot Concentration Camp – the authorities later preferred to regard it as an internment camp – remembers them:

Amongst this diverse community were two men, the Sabinie [sic] brothers, the Soho gangsters who had achieved great notoriety as the result of their raid on Croydon's airport strongroom and the theft of £80,000 of gold bullion. Always with them, but slightly to the rear was a 'Papa' Marsh, a short, stocky individual who, I was informed, carried out the Sabinie orders. I might add that they were held in great awe by the Anglo-Italian section. I recall at one time we were having a spot of bother with the Anglo-Italians and when I was walking around the compound they came up beside me and said, 'If you can get us a bottle of Chianti from the other side of the wire you will have no further trouble from the Italian section.' Shades of Chicago!![6]

---

[5] There is a full and critical account of the regulation 18B process under which the Sabinis and many others were detained in A. W. Brian Simpson's *In the Highest Degree Odious*, Chapters 13 and 14. Home Office papers TS27/496A.

[6] Unpublished memoir of Arthur Swan. Swan, who was Mosley's British Union District Treasurer of the Lowestoft Branch, was Camp Leader at Ascot Concentration Camp. There he represented all detainees, not simply Mosley's Blackshirts. He died in 1993.

One Sabini man who survived the purge was 'Italian Albert' Dimes, who became Billy Hill's right-hand man when he and Jack Spot controlled Soho. Once the anti-Italian orders had been signed, reprisals were taken against the Italian-owned clubs in Soho. Italian-Jewish fights broke out and continued for some time. The main aim was to inflict the maximum damage on the rival club owner's premises. One of the fights was in the Palm Beach Bottle Parties club in Wardour Street. It was there that Antonio 'Babe' Mancini stabbed Harry 'Little Hubby' or 'Scarface' Distleman to death. Rather against the run of evidence and certainly the judge's summing-up, he was convicted of murder. 'Italian' Albert Dimes, an increasingly powerful figure as the years went by, was present and charged with affray. In the second trial for the affray witnesses were becoming increasingly reluctant to identify Dimes or his co-defendants and he was bound over to come up for sentence. On his release he was returned to his unit in the RAF from which he had deserted.

The Whites had an uneasy tenure in office. They were not really hard (or hard enough) men. As early as 1939 their leader, old Alf White, had taken a bad beating at Harringay dog track by some young tearaways from Stoke Newington, and there seems not to have been the expected swift reprisal. Their serious and rapid decline began at the end of the War, first with their ousting from control of Yarmouth racecourse in October 1946 when their hardman Eddie Raimo, who had earlier slashed Billy Hill, backed down in the face of Jack Comer, known sometimes as Jack Comacho and most often as Jack Spot, who wished to install a Jewish bookmaker on one of the prime pitches. Later Spot, with the help of Arthur Skurry of West Ham, took over the pitches at Ascot from the family.[7] In January the next year they were comprehensively evicted by Spot in an alliance with Billy Hill.

Frank Fraser, longtime friend and assistant to Billy Hill, recalls the family:

Then [pre-war] they had a good team with men like
Jock Wyatt and Billy Goller on the strength but now
Alf White was old and Harry, his son, was a lovely man
but with no stomach for a fight. Harry was in Wandsworth in 1944. He'd hit a geezer with a walking stick
and got a few months. That was all the time he'd done
and he didn't like it. He was very big, impressive, full of
bonhomie, hail-fellow-well-met. And Alf was as well. If
you had a crooked copper they were the ideal men to
handle it. If anyone was in trouble and could get a bit
of help they were the ones to go to, but as for leaders
they didn't really have the style. All in all they were a
weak mob and they were ripe for taking.

Billy Hill didn't really have time for racing people.
He thought they were phonies, frauds who'd never
really done any proper bird. He booked them as sort of

---

[7] R. Murphy, *Smash and Grab*. Murphy's always interesting
account of the Underworld is in parts, as he freely admits, the
Gospel according to Spot. Neither Murphy nor Spot's other
detractors would claim that the man with a thousand cuts was
always completely accurate in his recall of events. One story on
which Spot traded for his working career was how he had felled the
wrestler Roughneck, the bodyguard of the fascist leader Mosley, in
his march down the East End in 1936. In its edition of 23 January
1955 the *Sunday Chronicle*, which was running Spot's memoirs at
the time, published a retraction of the Roughneck story: 'No
attack occurred on Sir Oswald Mosley, or the procession. The
story of Sir Oswald Mosley being attacked is therefore complete
fabrication.'

bullies. So I don't think he thought of turning them out but there again he didn't have any time for them either. Jack Spot was the one who wanted control. Now Spot wasn't a thief. He would run a million miles from nicking something himself but what he'd do was he'd then nick it off the thief. He was what they call a thieves' ponce. What he was was an enforcer. His real name was either Comacho or Comer. He reckoned he'd got the name Spot because he was always in the right spot when there was trouble. He'd got great ideas about protection at the races and Bill was friendly with him. Spot could see Bill would be a great asset and when Spot had the row with the Whites he pulled Bill in. Bill had a tremendous amount of respect and clout and that was the overwhelming factor.

Spot had good hard people like Teddy Machin and Franny Daniels, who were on the airport job, solidly behind him then.[8] They were all getting plenty of money where the Whites never had that muscle. They had some good people but not enough. Harry White never fancied a mill and when Spot did White's team at the end of 1946 in Al Burnett's The Nut-House off Regent Street, he hid under a table.[9] That's when Billy

---

[8] The 'airport job' was a raid in 1948 on London Airport said to have been organized by Jack Spot. It ended in disaster when the police discovered the plot in advance of the raid. Detectives were substituted for the baggage handlers who were to be robbed and a battle took place. Several men were convicted and received up to twelve years' imprisonment. Teddy Machin escaped, as did Franny Daniels who held on to the chassis of a lorry and received severe burns whilst doing so.

[9] Al Burnett owned a number of clubs and night-spots over the years, all of them frequented by the Fancy. When Nipper Read investigated the Krays' hold on the West End, Burnett vehemently

Goller got his throat cut. The one who would have been terrific and who would have defended the territory was Alf White's son, also called Alf, but he had died in 1943. The other brothers, Johnny and Billy White, were really racing people and not involved in clubs. The Whites were literally eliminated. I wasn't surprised at all, but they still kept the race meetings. Old Alf and Harry were clever there.[10]

Nothing was too small for Hill.

Jimmy Farrell's father used to sell pigeon food in Trafalgar Square and paid Hill to let him do so. Hill took money off the smudge, off the clip joints. He was like Tony Mella, he took everything off everyone. He says he wasn't involved in vice but he took money off the Messinas to allow them to operate.[11]

Of course, whilst Spot and Hill controlled Soho, the epicentre of crime, there were still other teams who had non-competing interests in inner London. For example

cont'd
denied paying them protection money although it is apparent that he was doing just that. Burnett was a follower of greyhounds, in which he had some success. His dog Pigalle Wonder won the Greyhound Derby, and on retirement was a prepotent force in breeding. Burnett also wrote his memoirs *Ace of Clubs*.

[10] F. Fraser, *Mad Frank*, p.46.

[11] The smudge was a photography racket operated in London and at the seaside. Punters had their photographs 'taken' with a camera with no film. They then paid a ten-shilling deposit for the non-existent photographs. Tony Mella ran clubs in Soho. He was shot in a quarrel by his long-time friend Alf Melvin, who promptly killed himself. See J. Morton, *Gangland*, pp.364–5.

Frank Fraser, twenty years later associated with the Richardson brothers in South London, was then operating a small gang of jewel thieves and robbers. Aldgate was another Soho. It was riddled with clubs, including Jack Spot's Green Dragon, catering for East Enders in general and seamen off the ships which had just docked in particular. Prostitutes lined the pavements. In Sanders Street, just off Henriques Street and Berners Street, was a row of brothels run by the emerging force of Maltese.

Running a drinking club was a traditional small- (and sometimes quite large-) time way of making money through illegal sales of drink, illegal gambling, possibly coupled with a certain amount of prostitution and receiving. Clubs and 'parties' had proliferated during and after the War, with the police waging a battle against them. In London, prosecutions had been at the rate of two a week, from the club on the marshes which catered for Pitch-and-Toss punters, through the Pavilion Bridge Club in Shepherd's Bush run by a family from its home – the police had moved against it when they received ten complaints, including one from a woman who wrote that her husband gambled away his money and kept her short of food – to a similar Temperance Club in Brighton, up to the Gateways in the King's Road which had 700 members and was 'very tastefully decorated' but which 'unfortunately' had gaming machines, back down again to the Ninety Club in Clapham which was

. . . frequented by men and women of the lowest order, and troops of the Allied Nations . . . A young woman made spasmodic noises on an accordion . . . anyone could get admittance by giving three rings on the bell, and they could then drink to their hearts' content. The people . . . were mainly of the worst possible type: thieves and women of the lowest order. The conversation was foul, and some dancing went on with women high-kicking in scanty clothing . . . the place was in effect an unlicensed public house. In two previous incarnations as a club it had been struck off the register twice and on the last raid was making a substantial profit.[12]

Another more identifiable gang, however, was the Elephant and Castle mob who had flourished as an amorphous group since the 1920s when they had aligned themselves with Billy Kimber against the Sabinis and had suffered for it.[13] They were credited with being a gang not only with its own slang – a bit of an exaggeration because it was only Cockney back

---

[12] *South London Press*, 16 October 1942.
[13] 'In a series of lightning raids, the Sabinis proceeded to hit rival gangs where it hurt most. The Irish Mob in Camden Town had seen their most lucrative night club, the Blue Angel, torched to the ground. The Townsend Brothers, the vice lords of Paddington, had two of their brothels visited by the Sabinis, the girls and their clients driven into the street, too terrified to return. And tonight the Sabinis had smashed up six spielers belonging to the Elephant Gang and had helped themselves to the loot;' Edward T. Hart, *Britain's Godfather*, p.103. In July 1922 the police nipped another major fight in the bud with the arrest of Fred Gilbert, said to be the leader of the Camden Town Gang or Brummy Sage's Mob. He had been heard to talk about a raid to be undertaken that evening saying, 'Alf White and the Sabinis will be done for certain.' He was acquitted at the Old Bailey of slashing George Droy and shooting at him and his brother Trixie as well as blackmailing a bookmaker Harry Margules. Efforts, including an offer of £150 to leave the country, were made to get Margules to change his story. On this charge Fred's brother, John, and two others were also acquitted. MEPO3/366.

and rhyming slang – but also in allowing women to be members, but again this intelligence seems to have been a bit of reporters' licence.

Now some of the younger male members of the Elephant and Castle team were in extreme difficulty. They were involved in the murder of Alex de Antiquis. On 29 April 1947 a robbery took place at Jay's, a jeweller's near what used to be the Scala Theatre in Charlotte Street where the magicians Maskelyne and Devant played an annual Christmas season. The raid was a failure from the start. The staff was held at gunpoint but one member managed to press the burglar alarm. When a director of the firm, Ernest Stock, leaped over the counter and shut the safe door, he was rewarded with a blow from a revolver. Seventy-year-old Bertram Keates threw a stool at one of the gang and a shot was fired in return. By now the raid was clearly in difficulties and the men ran into the street to their car. Because a lorry was blocking the way the three men involved could not reach their getaway car and instead ran off down the street waving their guns.

The men were almost caught at the scene when a surveyor Charles Grimshaw, who was passing, tackled them. Those were the days when members of the public would 'have a go'. He was fortunate to escape with his life.

At that moment a motor-cyclist drew up in front of me. He more or less stood up from his machine on one leg, as though to dismount, and I heard a shot and saw him fall. I saw two men come round the front of the machine, which had fallen over, still running towards me across Charlotte Street. They were side by side and the taller of the two was removing a white scarf from his face. There seemed to be a third person on the other side of the fallen motor-cyclist.

I stepped off the kerb behind a stationary car and as they drew near me, trip-kicked the shorter man. He fell full length on the pavement and dropped the gun he was carrying. I jumped on top of him, but his companions, who had run on a few paces, turned back and kicked me on the head. That made me release the man as I was dazed, and he pushed me over and stood up . . . He picked up the gun, pointed it at me and said 'Keep off.' I stayed where I was.[14]

The shot motor-cyclist was 34-year-old father of six, Alex de Antiquis. He had tried to block their path by stalling his motor-cycle. As he lay dying in the gutter he said, 'I tried to stop them . . . I did my best.'

The robbers turned out to be Harry Jenkins, his friend Christopher James Geraghty, and 17-year-old Terence Peter Rolt. They were traced through a massive police hunt led by Robert Fabian, the legendary 'Fabian of the Yard'. A raincoat was found in a room in a building in nearby Tottenham Court Road, and in turn that was traced to a shop in Deptford where it was identified as having been sold to Jenkins' brother-in-law.

Jenkins, with a record of assaults on the police and known by his associates as 'The King of Borstal', who had only been released six days earlier, was brought in for questioning. Now he told the police it looked like his coat but that he would say nothing more. His friend, Christopher Geraghty, who had twice escaped from a Borstal with Jenkins, was also picked up. His story was that he had been in bed with an attack of boils; he was released. Rolt was also known as a friend of Jenkins; he too had apparently been ill

---

[14] R. Higgins, *In the Name of the Law*, p.126.

in bed at time of the raid, and he too was released. Jenkins was also allowed to go after twenty-seven witnesses on an identification parade had failed to pick him out.

The next day, however, Fabian had Jenkins in again. This time he told Fabian that he had lent his raincoat to a man in Southend. This man was eventually found and admitted to a robbery in Queensway, West London, with Jenkins and Geraghty. After that they had all gone to Southend where he, Walsh, had tricked the others out of their money. He admitted casing the premises in Charlotte Street but denied being on the raid. That, he said, was down to Jenkins and Co. He later received five years for the Queensway robbery.

A loaded .45 revolver was then found in the mud at Wapping and ballistic tests showed it was the one which had been fired in Jay's. Jenkins' parents-in-law lived only a quarter of a mile from where the gun was found. Geraghty was the first to be arrested. He made a confession naming Rolt but refused to put Jenkins in the frame. Rolt was next to be pulled in and he too confessed, but this time he named Jenkins. The so-called 'King of Borstal' was arrested within hours.

The whole story came out in dribs and drabs. The bungling of the raid appears to have been largely that of Rolt. He had been told to wait for his colleagues outside the jeweller's but instead blundered in, leaving the others to follow. It was Geraghty who shot de Antiquis as they fled from the scene. Neither Geraghty nor Rolt gave evidence, but Jenkins produced an alibi calling a number of witnesses. His story was not accepted; he and Geraghty were hanged on 19 September 1947. Rolt was ordered to be detained during His Majesty's Pleasure.

The executions of Jenkins and Geraghty had a salutary

effect on London's gangland, says ex-Detective Superintendent Robert Higgins:

> [The Antiquis case] had the effect of breaking up much
> of the gang warfare which was brewing in London's
> Underworld at that time. Many criminals went as far
> as throwing away their guns when they heard that two
> young men were destined for the gallows.[15]

When it came to it, the Jenkins family were fortunate that on an earlier occasion both Harry and an older brother, Thomas, had escaped the hangman. On 8 December 1944 they had taken part in a raid on a jeweller's in Birchin Lane in the City. Ronald Hedley, known as 'Silver' because of his blond hair, was the driver who had knocked down Captain Ralph Binney, who ran into the road with arms outstretched to signal the getaway car to halt.

Hedley did not stop and passed right over the gallant retired naval captain. Hedley put the vehicle in reverse and then, with Binney trapped under the car, drove off at high speed. Binney[16] was dragged for over a mile before being dislodged. At the trial Hedley was found guilty of murder and Jenkins of manslaughter. Hedley was sentenced to death, reprieved and released after serving nine years. Thomas Jenkins received eight years.

Harry Boy wasn't charged. When they took Harry Boy into the police he had this brilliant idea and he chinned the police sergeant, knowing full well he'd be merci-

[15] Ibid p. 135.
[16] A medal for civilian gallantry was struck in honour of Captain Binney.

lessly beaten up. As a result everyone on the ID parade had to be plastered up with tape and so he wasn't picked out. He eventually got Borstal for the assault on the copper.[17]

For the next seven years peace more or less reigned in the London Underworld as Spot and Billy Hill, with the tacit approval of the police, kept the capital under control. Who was the dominant figure of the ill-assorted pair really depends upon whose version of events is believed. It would seem that at the start Spot was the senior partner. Hill at the time was having some small localized trouble. He was arrested for a warehouse-breaking which, for once, he did not commit. On bail he removed some stolen parachutes from the original thieves and with the proceeds headed for South Africa. There in Johannesburg and in association with Bobby Ramsey, later to run with the Krays, Hill opened a gaming club, Club Millionaire. This was directly in opposition to the wishes of the South African ex-wrestler Arnold Neville, known as the 'Guv'nor of Guv'nors'. Permission would normally have to be sought from him and, in turn, he would expect a percentage.

Reprisals were swift. Neville and his henchman launched an attack on the club and were badly beaten by Hill, who had been given a gun, and Ramsey. Neville was nearly scalped, needing a hundred stitches, and given a striping by Ramsey for his pains.[18] Hill vanished to Durban where he was arrested; given bail, he again absconded. Ramsey stood

[17] F. Fraser, *Mad Frank*, p. 30.
[18] A striping was done not, as might be expected, across the face but across the buttocks. It was also called noughts and crosses. The victim would remember the damage, as for some time he would not be able to sit down.

his ground and received a sentence of five months for assault. A week later Hill was back in England, hiding under the protection of Arthur Skurry in Upton Park in the East End.

After a job in Manchester in which he, another man, and Teddy Machin netted £9,000 – they had been told the proceeds would be not less than £35,000 – Hill gave himself up on the original warehouse-breaking charge. He received three years and according to Spot was penniless when he was released in 1949. Spot then maintains he allowed him to manage some of his spielers.

Hill and his friends tell it rather differently. The money to finance clubs came not from Spot but from a former brothel-keeper Freddy Field. Hill, who was a fine gambler, had a share in a club with Sammy Samuels who describes his play:

> With Billy Hill the game was the thing, quick and fierce, win or lose that's how he liked it. Where another man would turn nasty over a losing run, Bill simply shrugged. Money was not all that important to him.
>
> I have seen twenty players round a dice table calling bets and when Bill arrived watched those same people play to double the stakes. Players who had hesitated to call on a pound now called to fifty-pound bets. Whatever the amount they knew they would be accommodated. B. H. not only livened up a game, he brought the money with him to make the play interesting.[19]

By 1952 there was no question whose star was in the ascendancy. Jack Spot had organized the failed bullion

---

[19] S. Samuels with L. Davis, *Among the Soho Sinners*, p.84.

raid on London Airport, whilst on 21 May of that year Billy Hill pulled off the stunning Eastcastle Street mailbag robbery which netted him and his associates some £287,000, closely followed in 1954 by a bullion raid in Holborn. Hill, now a celebrity both in and outside the Underworld, never needed to work again. Spot did. Worse, he saw his old henchmen changing allegiance. Each was courted by newspapers but Hill, with the shady reporter Duncan Webb[20] behind him, had the better press and Spot, enraged with Webb's championing his rival, broke the reporter's arm one night. It cost him dear: a conviction, damages and later bankruptcy.

In August 1954 came the celebrated fight in Frith Street between Spot and Albert Dimes, friend to the Sabinis and now Hill's right-hand man. It was one more battle for control of social and political supremacy of the West End. Now, it appears that Spot sought out the relatively amiable Dimes in an effort to get at Hill. Both Spot and Dimes were acquitted after considerable shenanigans involving perjured witnesses at the Old Bailey. It was, however, effectively the end for Spot. A year later he was badly slashed by Frankie Fraser and others at Hill's instigation. Later clubs he owned were torched. He dropped out of the scene whilst Hill assumed the role of 'Godfather', buying himself a villa in Spain to which he went with a new friend Gypsy Riley. His wife Aggie stayed behind running a couple of Soho clubs. Dimes went into betting shops, gaming machines and another half-dozen dubious enterprises. He was believed to be the trusted representative in England of the Bruno family from Philadelphia.

[20] For further details of the late Mr Webb's escapades, see fn. p.282; J. Morton, *Gangland* and F. Fraser, *Mad Frank*.

Soho was, it seems, up for grabs and for a time the Nash family from Islington – six brothers once lovingly described by a newspaper as the wickedest brothers in England – reigned supreme. They had started life protecting Cypriot cafés at £2 a week, and had moved up in the world and into Mayfair where they had interests in fashionable clubs including the celebrated Astor nightclub, the beloved haunt of the Underworld on a Friday night. By today's standards their exploits have paled into insignificance and, over the years, several of them have gone on to build respectable businesses.

Seemingly the beginning of the end of the Nashes came over a stupid fight following a minor car accident. Others, such as Bert Wickstead, who rose to become a Commander in the Flying Squad, read it as chance providing an opportunity for a significant move in the power-play for control of the West End.

Selwyn Keith Cooney, manager of the Billy-Aggie Hill-owned New Cabinet Club in Gerrard Street, and no friend of the Nashes, was in a relatively minor car accident with one driven by hostess Vicky James, known as 'Blonde Vicky' and a friend of Ronnie Nash. Cooney, instead of doing the more sensible thing and forgetting about the matter, sent the bill for 54/9d for the damage to the girl. She was not insured and the bill remained unpaid. Quite by chance Cooney met Ronnie Nash in a Notting Hill drinking club. Words were exchanged and each suffered a black eye in the subsequent fight. Two days later Cooney went to the Pen Club, said to have been bought with the proceeds from a robbery at the Parker Pen Company and named as an Underworld joke, in Duvall Street near Spitalfields Market. It was a club which was frequently raided by the police and, almost as regularly, it changed hands.

Reports of the background to the incident on 7 February 1960 vary. Apart from Wickstead's theory one version is that

Jimmy 'Trunky' Nash, who worked as a minder at the Astor Club in the West End in which the family had an interest, set out to avenge his brother's beating. Another is that Jimmy, the mildest of the brothers, was sucked into the incident.

Jimmy, together with his red-headed girlfriend, a hostess named Doreen Masters, Joey Pyle and another former boxer, John Read, arrived at the Pen Club a little while after Cooney. According to witnesses Cooney was pointed out to Nash by Doreen Masters and, together with Pyle and Read, he went straight over, broke Cooney's nose with one blow and proceeded to give him a severe beating. 'That will teach you to give little girls a spanking,' he said. Cooney, protesting he had done nothing of the kind, fought back and there was a cry 'He's got a gun.' Two witnesses were adamant that Nash then shot Cooney in the head at point-blank range.

Others in the club then attacked Nash and Read, who was hit over the head with a bottle. They ran out of the club and Nash was driven away by Pyle whilst Doreen Masters drove off with Read. Two witnesses in the club were brought in for questioning. The first was Cooney's girlfriend, a 19-year-old barmaid from the New Cabinet, Joan Bending. The second was Johnny Simons, who had hit Read over the head with a bottle. Both were to point the finger at Jimmy Nash, Pyle and Read. Joan Bending had picked out both Pyle and Read at an identification parade.

Two days later James Nash surrendered himself at City Road police station. He, Pyle, Read and Doreen Masters were charged with the capital murder of Selwyn Cooney. What followed was one of the worst examples of post-war witness interference and jury intimidation.

It began on 16 March with a razor attack on Johnny Simons in a Paddington café. His face needed twenty-seven stitches to repair it. The assault was followed by two on his girlfriend, a 23-year-old model, Barbara Ibbotson. On the first occasion she was snatched in broad daylight in Soho, and thrown into a car where her face was slashed four times. Three weeks later she was the victim of another attack when three men broke into her flat whilst she was taking a bath, held her under water and slashed her again. This time she received wounds also requiring twenty-seven stitches. Now Bending and Simons accepted the police protection offered them.

The trial began on 21 April with the public gallery filled with 'faces' including members of the Billy Hill organization, and the Kray twins as well as the Nash family in force. Only Nash, Pyle and Read stood trial; the charges against Doreen Masters had been dismissed.

Of the ten male jurors one, who was later found to have a conviction for dishonesty as a juvenile, had appeared to nod towards Billy Nash in the public gallery. The police overheard a remark that one of the jury was to be nobbled, and a watch was kept on this particular juror. One day after court he was followed by officers who had seen a young man run away from his car. 'You won't catch me putting a foot wrong now,' he said with the emphasis on *now*. Meanwhile it seems that one of the two women on the jury, a Mrs Doris Reed, had a husband on remand in Brixton. He is alleged to have told Nash, Pyle and Read that his wife had made up her mind that Nash was guilty of capital murder.

The facts were reported to the judge by both the prosecution and defence, and on 25 April Mr Justice Gorman discharged the first jury.

In the second trial the defence case was reached and a surprise witness, David Sammons, was called to say that at the time Cooney had been shot Johnny Simons had been drinking in another bar, and that Joan Bending was so drunk she had had to be helped out of the bar before the fight. Pyle and Read were acquitted on 2 May and then next day James Nash gave evidence that he had never had a gun but that he had hit Cooney 'twice on the nose with my fist because of the things he was saying'.

The all-male jury took ninety-eight minutes to acquit Nash of Cooney's murder, but at a second trial which began an hour later he was found guilty of causing grievous bodily harm and was sentenced to five years' imprisonment. For his part in the affair Pyle received a sentence of eighteen months, and that was the last substantial sentence he received for thirty years.

Now with the Nashes seemingly vulnerable, the police mounted a campaign against them which ended when several of the family and friends were found in a club in Queen's Gardens, Bayswater with, so it was said, guns, something they vehemently denied. Prison sentences followed.

On his release from the assault charge Pyle kept well in the background but it was he who advised small-time villain, Michael Perry, to go to *The Times* over his black-mailing by three policemen, which led to the great inquiry of 1969 and the subsequent gaoling of the officers.

In 1971 Pyle's home was searched when the police were looking for Sewell, the killer of Superintendent Richardson in Blackpool, and, it was alleged, a firearm and ammunition had been found there. In the summing-up at his trial, the judge told the jury that to acquit Pyle would mean that the police officers had committed perjury. They did. Some months later one of the officers on the search, Harold Hannigan, was found guilty of trying to bribe a Sussex detective. He was given a conditional discharge by Mr Justice Melford Stevenson, who called him 'a very, very, conceited fool', and advised him to see a psychiatrist.

In 1978 Pyle was suspected of having helped actor John Bindon flee to Dublin after an incident in which John

Darke, a small-time thief and police informer, was hacked
to death at the Ranelagh Yacht Club, Fulham. Bindon,
charged with murder, later returned and was found not
guilty. The charge of perverting the course of justice against
Pyle was dropped. He now became interested in unlicensed
boxing and at one time was said to have had a share in the
contract of a prominent South London light-heavyweight.

In 1984 his name surfaced once more when police
opposing the granting of a pub licence to a former football
star alleged that he was being backed by Pyle who, they
said, had been involved with international crime figures.
They also alleged he had been building a South London
empire of clubs and pubs based on protection. Pyle challenged this, saying, 'I'm no gangster. Of course I know
villains but I also know very respectable people.' Later
another allegation against him was that he had close links
with the Mafia.

On January 4 1995 time ran out for club owner Ronnie
Knight, once married to the actress Barbara Windsor. In
the past he had been acquitted of the killing of Tony
Zomparelli in the Golden Goose pinball arcade in Soho,
following the death of his brother David in a fight in the
Latin Quarter in Wardour Street[21]; since Easter 1983 he had
been on the run following the £6 million Security Express
raid at a depot in Shoreditch, during which petrol had been
poured over the guards. His younger brother Johnny
received a sentence of 22 years over the matter and another
brother, Jimmy, eight years for handling some of the stolen
money which was thought to have been divided into parcels
of between £400,000 and £500,000 immediately after the
raid. Ronnie Knight fled to the Costa del Sol.

---

[21] see James Morton *Gangland* p254 *et seq.*

Now two weeks shy of his 61st birthday, Knight's plea to dishonestly handling £314,813, a part of the proceeds, was accepted and he was sentenced to seven years' imprisonment. There was considerable speculation about the reason for his return to face his trial. The official handout was that in true East End tradition he wished to see his elderly and ailing mother but there was also speculation that he had run into serious trouble with an up and coming league of new criminals in Spain. The high profile given to him by the press cannot have helped in an area where a 'heads under the parapet' attitude is regarded as best for the community.

There was a story that shortly before he returned to England, courtesy of *The Sun* newspaper, he had pulled a double-cross on one of the bright young things on the Costa Del Crime. This may have stiffened his resolve to return home. It is said that he had persuaded a firm to invest £10,000 to buy a consignment of Moroccan cannabis which would sell at three times the price. Unfortunately after receiving the money he never came up with the drugs and, the story goes, a gun was put to his head.

Back in England he was said to have only the clothes in which he stood and six pairs of Italian shoes. It was thought likely that Security Express would try to seize his villa near Fuengirola.

According to the police Knight's conviction left just three old friends from the Security Express days on the beach – John Mason, Clifford Saxe and Ronnie Everett. Mason and Everett, both in their sixties, had adopted a very low-key but substantial lifestyle since their arrival some twelve years ago. Saxe was said to be almost penniless.

John Bindon also left the scene. He died in October 1993, it was said of cancer, but, more probably, of an AIDS-related illness – the death certificate said broncho-pneumonia –

from which he had been suffering for some time. A small-time criminal with convictions for petty violence and living off immoral earnings, he had starred with Carol White in *Poor Cow*, one of the kitchen-sink dramas beloved in the 1960s. His greatest claim to fame had been the number of beautiful women with whom he had associated, maintaining that Princess Margaret had been one of them. There is little supporting evidence for this claim, save that they were on the West Indian island of Mustique at the same time and that Her Royal Highness came across Bindon whilst he was posing naked on the beach. There is a photograph of them together, with Bindon wearing a tee-shirt emblazoned 'Enjoy Cocaine'. Certainly model Vicki Hodge, the baronet's daughter with whom Bindon lived on and off for a stormy ten years, was in the number and proud of it.

It was during their relationship that he came to the aid – with a machete, so he told the court – of his friend, Roy Dennis, who was being attacked by Johnny Darke, one of the well-known family, at the Ranelagh Yacht Club on 21 November 1978. This was not the version of the prosecution, who maintained Darke's death was a contract killing by Bindon for a fee of £10,000 said to have been put up by a John Twomey. It was difficult for the police to establish the pattern of things because by the time they reached the yacht club most of the debris had been stowed away. Darke, acquitted of a wages snatch at BOAC in 1969 and the leader of the South London Wild Bunch, had been a police informer for some years. He had been paid £850 for information about men arrested for armed robbery in October 1977. The previous year he had been acquitted of murder. In 1978 there had been a contract of £5,000 on his life after he had spirited away a consignment of marijuana. It was thought he was about to rip off another drugs dealer when he died. An associate said of him, 'He was the type of man who would carry a knife into church.'

Aided, so said the police, by Joey Pyle and Lennie Osborne, the severely wounded Bindon fled to Dublin, wrapped in a red blanket to hide the blood, accompanied by a girlfriend, a former Bunny girl and friend of football manager Malcolm Allison. Others suggested the flight was with the connivance of the police in return for help given. Some witnesses suggested it was the girl who had given Bindon the 10-inch knife with which he killed Darke. He had it, so he said, for protection from a mysterious Mr X, 'an 18-stone lunatic', who knew about his previous existence and threatened him in some unspecified way. For fear of prejudicing the outcome, an episode of the popular TV series *Hazell*, in which Bindon played a heavy, was postponed until after his trial. He returned of his own accord to face the charges and was charged with murder and affray along with Raymond Bohm and George Galbraith, friends of Darke. Lennie Osborne and Ernest Begbe, who were also charged, failed to appear at the Central Criminal Court. Meanwhile rival factions staged benefits; Flash Harry Hayward, landlord of the Harp of Erin and brother of Billy who had been involved in the Richardson fight at Mr Smith and the Witchdoctor's Club, supported Darke's widow, whilst Dave Barry, a long-time friend of Spot and Billy Hill, organized one for Bindon.

The evidence that it was a contract killing came from the familiar source of a cell-mate to whom Bindon was said to have confessed. The £10,000 contract was the story of prisoner William Murphy, also on trial for murder. Asked why he grassed Bindon, he piously replied, 'I don't think it's right people should go around killing other people and getting paid for it.'

In giving evidence in his defence Bindon described the incident as 'almost like a ballet', presumably from *Gayaneh*. Bindon was stabbed in the chest and eye and, so he said, Darke was threatening him saying, 'I'll cut your head off.' 'I held my arm out with my knife in it. I was trying to keep him off me . . .' said Bindon.

For a time after his acquittal in December 1979 Bindon – for whom actor Bob Hoskins had given evidence, calling him 'Biffo the Bear' and so obtaining a rebuke from the trial judge – was temporarily lionized by London's café society. One of his party tricks was to get down on all fours and thump the floor asking, 'What's it like down there, Darkey?' His particular trick, however, was to balance a number of half-pint beer glasses on his erect penis; this was done by inserting the member through the handles rather than balancing them budgerigar style.

Bohm and Galbraith were not so fortunate. They received three and four years respectively for their part in the affray.

As the years passed Bindon faded from the scene. In the long run the case had done his television career no good and he appeared in magistrates' courts throughout London on minor charges on an irregular basis. He had always been a 'Jack the Lad' and there is a story that a journalist found him near his home in Chelsea at the wrong end of the attentions of a George Wright. Mr Wright, who died in 1976, had apparently pointed a gun at Bindon's head and said, 'Go on, John, now lick the sole of my other shoe.' He was, he said, trying to teach Bindon some discipline.

By the end of his life Bindon[22] was in a sorry state, racked

---

[22] John McVicar paid a tribute to John Bindon in *Lucky For Some* in the *Evening Standard* reprinted in *Prison Writing*, No.4 1994.

with pain and drawing social security. 'I couldn't go and see him,' says one London face, 'he'd see it in my eyes, no matter how I tried to hide it.'

If Bindon ended his life alone, Lennie Osborne ended his in disgrace. After such a good start, he went bent on his former friends and colleagues and became a supergrass.

Meanwhile, back in the 1960s, with the Nashes out of the way the path was clear for two brothers who were to some extent their protégés. Ronnie and Reggie Kray built an empire in the East and West End.[23]

The East End had always had a series of 'Guv'nors,' most of whom had flourished over a period of years with little or nothing to show for it at the end. They had, however, never thought to extend their territories, or if they had they were not capable of it. John Pearson describes some of them:

Jimmy Spinks, Timmy Hayes, old Dodger Mullins: none of them admirable men, but they were recognized for what they were and did what many better men would like to have done. They never worked. They'd scare money out of bookmakers, publicans and successful shopkeepers. Dodger would work his own protection racket round all the small-time bookmakers calling each Monday for his 'pension'. Shopkeepers paid him something too; sort of insurance to keep the lesser tappers away.[24]

Even their brutality was memorable: 'Jimmy Spinks ordered some fish and chips, and when they cut up rough

[23] John Pearson, *The Profession of Violence*, p.31. Reg Kray pays tribute to a number of these men in *Villains We Have Known*.
[24] John Pearson, *The Profession of Violence*, pp.28–9.

because he wouldn't pay, he threw the fish-shop cat in the frier.'

There were also the families who ran the London docks, such as the Butlers, and who did not need to extend their territory. An East End Londoner says:

> The London Docks were No.6 and No.7 at Wapping and Bermondsey. If as a new boy I went onto a ship and there was thieving of say Ronson lighters, then I might be allowed to steal six. Everyone clubbed together to give the ship worker his cut. If you stole you had to chip in to Jimmy Butler who ran Scruttons, a big docking firm, or you paid the Collins or the Maddens. I reckon on the docks out of 3,000 then 2,000 was thieving.

Meanwhile in South-East London Charlie Richardson with his brother Eddie, said by some to be even smarter than his sibling, were also erecting a series of companies and an organization which set them apart from the other powerful South-East families of the time such as the Haywards, the Hennesseys and the Frenches. In Canning Town in the early 1960s there was what was derisorily known as the Brown Boot Gang. Members and affiliates dressed snappily, so they thought, in 50-guinea suits, but spoiled the image by wearing brown boots and the white stock favoured by East Enders. They did however prosper, and moved out to Noak Hill near Romford and points further East.

Even less known are some of the families who have controlled sections of West London, a more or less un-chronicled hive of activity, including the Mills brothers one of whom, Alan, gave evidence for the prosecution over the death of McVitie, and the Cannons, of whom Joey was the best known but not the most favoured amongst the fraternity.[25] Other well-known faces from South and North London, such as Ray Rosa and Bert Rossi, had clubs there.

Some of the families were involved in running prostitutes as well as club protection, but, 'The brasses weren't the sort of scrubber you saw in Park Lane, they were more film-star-like looking. I couldn't believe they were on the game,' recalls one habitué.

The Krays have had far more publicity than the head-below-the-parapet Richardsons which, if anything, may point to how much more intelligent the latter family was. Certainly their interests were better organized and their public profile less clear. They were perhaps unlucky to meet their downfall as they did – another fight in a club.

The lucky venue was Mr Smith and the Witchdoctor's, a barn of a place with cabaret and gambling in Catford. Again versions as to the reasons for the fight vary. The official version is that the Fraser–Eddie Richardson axis had been asked to take over what could be euphemistically described as security for the premises. Unfortunately no one had told the present incumbents, the Haywards and Hennesseys, that this was to happen. Another version is a splendid conspiracy theory that this was an attempt by the Krays – with whom the Richardsons were, at the time, in serious disagreement over the rights to provide security for a blue-film racket in the West End – to dispose of their rivals once and for all.

Frank Fraser in his memoirs suggests that, as is often

---

[25] Cannon gives a graphic account of running prostitutes in his book *Tough Guys Don't Cry*. He fell foul of a number of people in West London and was the subject of attacks in prison by men who suspected him of being too close to the authorities.

the case, it may have been nothing more than domestic feuding:

> What I heard years later, and I think it's right, is what they were afraid of was really a domestic matter. Roy Porritt had worked for us, me and Eddie, on the machines. He was a great mechanic. He'd left us to go on his own but we were still friendly. Billy Hayward had been having it off with Roy's wife. Roy had found out and told her to drop it out otherwise he'd tell us and there's no doubt we'd have been cross with Billy.[26]

Whatever the cause or causes may have been, fighting broke out about 3.30 a.m. A small-time villain and friend of the twins, Dickie Hart, produced a gun and shot Henry Rawlings. In turn Hart was shot dead. Fraser, who himself was badly injured with a bullet in his thigh, was acquitted of his murder. Eddie Richardson, Fraser, Billy Hayward and a number of others were convicted of affray and each received five years' imprisonment. Now the police, led by Gerald McArthur who earlier had been a leading investigator into

[26] F. Fraser, *Mad Frank*, p. xi. There have been many accounts of the rise of the Kray twins and the Richardson family. Perhaps the best are John Pearson's *The Profession of Violence* and Robert Parker's *Rough Justice* describing the Krays and the Richardsons respectively. Another example of a domestic dispute is that of Ray Moore, brother of Charlie Kray's ex-wife Dolly. In October 1984 he was shot at close range by Thomas Murphy shortly after leaving the home of a relative in Eltham. For a time it was believed to be in connection with the Brinks–Mat robbery, and the police were also investigating Moore in relation to a lump fraud during the building of the £500 million Thames flood barrier. It turned out to be more prosaic: Murphy believed Moore had been involved with his wife.

the Great Train Robbery, made inroads into an empire of long-firm frauds, protection and violence. Charlie Richardson received ten years, as did Eddie and Fraser. Charlie Richardson also received five years for conspiracy to pervert the course of justice; he had tried to bribe a juror during the trial of his brother on the affray charge.

Was the meeting with the Haywards and Hennesseys for a show-down over control of the club planned? Probably not. If it was, where was the fearless East End hardman George Cornell, now a close friend of Fraser? It was he who had called Ronnie Kray 'a big fat poof' in what was meant to be a meeting of reconciliation at the Astor Club. Three days after the affray at Mr Smith's, Cornell was shot in the Blind Beggar in Whitechapel. He had been visiting another friend, Jimmy Andrews, who was in hospital having had his leg blown off in another shooting incident. It is unlikely that the Fraser–Richardson axis would have been without Cornell if they had planned trouble that night.

Ronnie Kray has it that he and his brother owned a small share of Mr Smith's.

. . . nothing heavy, nothing serious. Some said that the Richardsons had been tipped off that Reggie and I and half our firm would be in the club that night, and that was why they hit it. But only one member of our firm was there at the time – a young guy called Richard Hart, who was having a quiet drink. He was an extremely nice fellow, with a wife and little kids, but they shot him dead.

Richard Hart had to be avenged. No one could kill a member of the Kray gang and expect to get away with it. The problem was both of the Richardsons and Mad Frankie Fraser were in custody and likely to remain so.

That left Cornell. He would have to pay the price. And let's face it, who better?[27]

One member of the Richardsons who survived the fight in Mr Smith's and the subsequent trial, and who later went on to far greater things, was James Alfred Moody. He helped carry the wounded Fraser out of the club and Eddie Richardson to hospital, and was acquitted of affray after a retrial.

Moody had always been a shadowy figure in the London Underworld. He was known as a hard man – his first conviction in 1967 was for manslaughter of a young Merchant Navy steward William Day, at a South London party, for which, along with Moody's brother, Richard, he received a six-years' sentence. It was his last conviction but by no means his last involvement in crime.

At school in Hackney he was said to be a mother's boy but later, a committed body-builder, he was enormously fit and strong. He became an invaluable member of the so-called Chainsaw Gang – and also of Billy Tobin's Thursday Gang – of the late 1970s, which specialized in hi-jacking, often with considerable violence, security vans in the South-East London area. On one occasion Moody, dressed as a policeman, jumped out of a car in the Blackwall Tunnel and

---

[27] R. and R. Kray, *Our Story*, pp. 71–2. Ronnie Kray is wrong; Charlie Richardson was not at that time in custody. He was in South Africa from where he returned to try to assist in his brother's defence. There have been numerous other suggestions over the reason for the fight. One is that it was set up by another South-East London family with feet in both camps who saw the chance to divide and rule. Given the volatility of members of the Underworld, particularly when in drink, there may be a bit of truth in each of them.

forced a security van to stop. To prevent the alarm being given he took the keys from a number of nearby motorists. The end for Tobin, and in a way Moody, came when he was arrested at Dulwich in the act of hi-jacking a security van with a mobile crane.[28] The ever-resourceful Moody escaped and hid out in a lock-up garage which he furnished with books, food, body-building equipment and a chemical toilet. Caught when he visited his son's flat in Brixton, he was charged with a series of robberies totalling £930,000 and sent to Brixton prison to await trial. In the 1980s it was still possible for remand prisoners to have food, wine and beer brought in by friends and relatives. Moody's brother Richard brought, with the Sunday lunches, hacksaw blades, drill bits and other tools.[29]

Moody had noticed that outside his cell was a flat roof and it was to this that he and cell-mates Gerard Tuite, a Provisional IRA bomb-maker, and Stanley Thompson, veteran of the Parkhurst prison riot of 1969 and now charged with armed robbery, cut through the brickwork.

[28] Billy Tobin had led a charmed life. He had been acquitted of a gin robbery in 1974, and a year later, despite the identification evidence of eight police officers, had been acquitted of a warehouse robbery. In March 1977 he was acquitted of a £115,000 robbery at the Express Dairy, Wembley and in 1978 was acquitted on ten counts of conspiracy to rob and possession of firearms with intent in relation to the £197,000 raid at the *Daily Mirror* offices during which a security guard was shot. It was in this case that Tobin alleged he had paid Hugh Moore, later Assistant Chief Constable for the City of London, for help. The allegation led to *Operation Countryman*. Finally Tobin received sixteen years for the Dulwich hi-jack.

[29] There is a full account of Moody's life and death in Cal McCrystal's 'The Hit at the Royal Hotel', *Independent on Sunday*, 8 August 1993.

Every morning the rubble was removed in their chamber-pots at slopping-out time. On 16 December 1980 they pushed out the loosened brickwork of their cell, stepped on to the roof where a ladder had been left by roofers and were away.

Thompson need not have bothered. The escape took place whilst the jury was out in his trial at St Albans and, in his absence, they found him not guilty. Tuite was later arrested in Dublin, becoming the first person to be charged in Ireland with criminal offences committed in England. He received ten years. Richard received two years for the help he had given his brother.

And James Moody? He simply vanished. Some Underworld faces say they received irregular Christmas cards from him but, apart from that and an unsuccessful raid on a flat in West London where his fingerprints – and nothing else – were found, there was no sign at all for the next thirteen years.

Then on the night of 1 June 1993 while drinking at the bar of the Royal Hotel, Hackney, where he was known as Mick, he was shot dead by a man described as in his early forties and wearing a leather jacket. The man had ordered a pint of Foster's lager and put two coins down on the bar to pay for it. Then he had moved towards Moody and fired three shots. As Moody slumped to the floor, a fourth was fired into his back before the man was driven away in a stolen white Ford Fiesta XR2.

Where had he been and why was he shot? As to the first, there were suggestions that he had been hidden out by the Provisionals, but clearly he returned to England some years ago, if indeed he ever left. At the time of his death he had been living in Wadeson Street, a back alley off Mare Street in Hackney. As to why, one theory was that it was a killing done on behalf of a cuckolded husband, for Moody was very much a ladies' man – he is said to have required the services of a different woman each evening. A second version is that it was a part of the long-drawn-out struggle for power between the Arif family and other South London interests, and that it was in revenge for the killing of David Brindle in the Bell public house in Walworth in August 1991.

According to the prosecution evidence, on 11 March 1991 Patrick and Tony Brindle allegedly shot Ahmet Abdullah, known as Turkish Abbi, in a Walworth betting shop. They were both charged with the murder. This, it was said, followed the shooting of a Stephen Dalligan, a nephew of a senior London figure, Tony White.[30]

The killing of the Brindles' brother, David, was said to be in revenge for the death of Ahmet. The brothers were wrongly said to be the nephews of the old villain Frankie Fraser, and this led credence to the story that it was all part and parcel of a gang war. In fact Grace Brindle, their mother, is at pains to deny any family connection with the famous Frasers or Brindles. Now that he is dead the most convenient name in the frame for the killing of David is that of Jimmy Moody. Moody is also fancied for the killings of Terry Gooderham and his girlfriend Maxine Arnold in Epping Forest in December 1989, and antique and cocaine dealer Peter Rasini in Palmers Green in March 1991.[31] There is also speculation that he carried out the

[30] One theory is that Dalligan had gone to the Connoisseur Club to act as a peacemaker following a quarrel between his brother Mark and Ahmet Abdullah.
[31] On 24 March 1991, 47-year-old antiques dealer and cocaine user Peter Rasini was shot in the garden of his home in River Avenue, Palmers Green. A solo gunman had come behind him as

killing of Peter and Gwenda Dixon, whose bodies were found near an arms cache in 1989. It is thought that they stumbled upon him accidentally. Attributing all these deaths to Moody may, however, be another way of clearing up crimes.

As for Tony and Patrick Brindle, neither of whom had any convictions, they were both acquitted of Abdullah's murder after an extraordinary trial at the Central Criminal Court in which screens were fitted so that witnesses, who were identified by numbers and not by name, could not be

cont'd

he walked down his garden path and had shot him four times in the back. Loyally his family said they knew he had no enemies in the world. Maxine Arnold and her boyfriend Terry Gooderham were found shot dead in their black Mercedes in Epping Forest on 22 December 1989. Most likely she was a bystander; he may have been more of a player which resulted in what was certainly a gangland execution. As always a variety of suggestions were offered. Terry had an active life for he shared it with Maxine part of the week and another blonde woman, for the remainder. One suggestion was that there was a third Ms Gooderham in the background and she had organized the hit, but enquiries came to nothing. Nor did they in relation to the theory that he was involved with Brinks-Mat monies. Gooderham had been a stocktaker for a number of clubs and pubs in London and Hertfordshire and one anonymous friend put it, 'It is nothing to do with his love life or his own business but a lot of money is involved.'

There were claims that he had been the victim of part of a drugs war and indeed a small amount of drugs were found in the car, but the police became convinced these had been planted and were a red herring. Then there was a claim in the *Daily Mirror* on 4 January 1990 that he had tried to muscle-in on the lucrative Spanish ice-cream market and had so upset suppliers that a £50,000 contract was put out on him. Finally there was yet another solution offered. This time it was that the killing was over £150,000, euphemistically described as having been 'redirected'.

seen by the defendants. Tony gave evidence that he had
been playing cards in the Bell. Patrick did not give evidence.
Their mother told the newspapers how they cried when their
budgie had died, and of their partiality for helping old ladies
cross busy roads. In their enigmatic way the police said that
the inquiry into Turkish Abbi's death was now closed.

There is, however, another theory over David Brindle's
death which fits the facts but has nothing to do with the
overall game plan of the South London warlords. It was
simply a personal matter:

It now turns out that Jimmy Moody was working in a
pub at the back of Walworth under the name Tom.
He'd been in the area for ten years. He wasn't an out-
and-out nightclubber so he could have been there and
very, very few people would know who he was. He'd
done quite a bit of bird and now he took it as a
personal thing to keep out. It was a personal challenge
for him. There's a lot of other guys been in that
position and they've been out nightclubbing it and
soon got caught. Jim did have that determination
and single-mindedness to keep that low profile and
trust no one. He could be stubborn and obstinate, a
good man but a loner. He'd be content to do his work
and watch the telly knowing that every day was a
winner. That's how he would look at it. I think David
had had a row with the publican and Jimmy had crept
behind him and done him with a baseball bat. David
was badly knocked about and told Jimmy it wouldn't
be forgotten. Next night or a couple of nights later
Moody and another man went into the Bell in East
Street and shot David and a bystander. Immediately
afterwards he went over to the East End.

Much as I knew Jim well, I can understand the feelings about David's death and that it was one that had to be done. I suppose if someone who knew it was going off had really pleaded for him it might have made some difference but I doubt it.[32]

Once Moody had been traced to Hackney it became common knowledge in South-East London that reprisals were to be taken, and Fraser absented himself from London on the night of the killing. No doubt a number of others did so as well.

As might be expected reaction to Moody's death was mixed. His son, Jason, an actor, told the *Sun*: 'I'm not ashamed of my dad, because he did what he did for his own reasons. All I know is he'd be proud I didn't turn out like him.'

David Brindle's mother appears to have been convinced her son was killed by Moody.

I'm glad Moody's dead. My family is overjoyed. The police rang to tell us this morning. He got it the way he gave it out. I'm glad he didn't die straight away – nor did David. That man was evil and I hope he rots in hell.[33]

The Richardson empire toppled in 1965 and the Kray one some four years later. Theirs had been an endlessly recounted story of protection, long-firm frauds and a murder each. Ronnie had carried out his promise and shot down George Cornell in the Blind Beggar. Reggie had removed

[32] F. Fraser, *Mad Frank*, p. 221.
[33] *Sun*, 3 June 1993.

Jack 'The Hat' McVitie, a long term hardman now drinking heavily who, given money and orders to kill Leslie Payne, one-time financial adviser to the Firm, had not only conspicuously failed to do so but also had boasted about ripping off the twins.[34]

Another suggestion for the quarrel with the Richardsons is the refusal of that family to give up a lucrative car-park racket at Heathrow Airport. In fact Heathrow, or Thiefrow as it came to be known, was a long-time haven of criminal activities. In the 1960s and 1970s property was stolen almost at will. Part of the reason for the thefts was that at the time the Universal Postal Union required that registered mail-bags had a distinguishing label so that special care could be taken for their protection – at the same time, giving special notice to a thief. Some thought the thieves were unfortunately amateurs with no real network for disposing of the millions which passed through their hands. An old-time villain laments:

> One time I dived in the river for a load of industrial diamonds which had just been chucked. £38,000 it came to. The people who'd nicked them didn't know what to do with them.

This was not the view of the authorities. In an investigation carried out by Captain John Gorman, then head of BOAC security, he found that the dead letter-box beloved of the spy story was being used. Thieves would put the stolen industrial diamonds in prearranged hiding places one of which was, rather chancily, under a stone beside the Great

---

[34] There are a number of stories of McVitie in his heyday in F. Fraser, *Mad Frank*.

West Road. These would be collected later and the thief would receive £1,000 a few days later.[35]

Once the Krays were out of the way the police were keen to ensure no upstarts took over their patch. Certainly they had their eyes on a potential return by the Nash family but none materialized. Nipper Read recalls:

The work done by Harry Mooney [an officer on Read's squad] to put the lid on the East End had been so effective that no one was daring to occupy the vacuum left by the dismemberment of the Kray Firm. However, I was now to look at target criminals, and one North London gang fell neatly into my catchment area. They were the obvious first choice and we looked at them intently for a period of time, but they certainly weren't doing the things you would expect them to be doing if they had taken over from the Krays. They had one or two clubs in the West End who were paying them money but it was being done in a very different way from the Krays' regime of terror. It was really rather a friendly business with this gang – almost a two-way operation with benefits to both sides. We thought they would jump in and occupy the vacuum, but it never happened. I think they sensed that if they had done that they would have let themselves in for a major investigation and consequently all sorts of troubles. It was a good example of preventive policing.[36]

[35] P. Gladstone Smith, *The Crime Explosion*, p. 86. In 1970 Smith wrote that the annual loss in diamonds, jewellery etc. at Heathrow was £500,000, 30 per cent of which came from passengers' luggage, with only 20 per cent recovered.
[36] L. Read and J. Morton, *Nipper*, p.266.

It was not until April 1972 that the Dixon brothers – also from the East End, and who had been fringe members of the Kray coterie – met their match in Commander Bert Wickstead, and it was he who brought down James Tibbs and members of his family six months later. In the latter trial particularly it appears that the complainants could just as easily have stood in the dock, and there are still many in the East End who believe that the Tibbs family was merely defending itself rather than making any pro-active moves towards domination of the East End.

Curiously that seems to have been the last prosecution of any protection racket in either the East or the West End by families or even individuals until 1990. That year Frank Salmon, a market trader from Dagenham who ran a small-time racket covering wine-bars, saunas and clubs, received seven and a half years at the Old Bailey.

South-East London was, however, a different proposition. It was here that the powerful families controlled the Underworld community more or less untroubled by authority in their day-to-day life. It was over this world that the Arif family, Turkish Cypriots who settled in Rotherhithe, wielded substantial influence. They were the 'most heavily investigated criminal "firm" since the Krays.'[37] The Arif empire extended to clubs, pubs and restaurants – 'it doesn't matter whose name it is over the door of the pub in some areas, it's the Arifs who own it' – and for a time the head of the family (though the third brother), Dogan (born February 1949), owned the Gola League club, Fisher United. Principally their art-form was the armed robbery. The list of their convictions and unsuccessful prosecutions is a history of the 1970s and 1980s, as is the genealogy of the

[37] N. Darbyshire with B. Hilliard, *The Flying Squad*, p.5.

Arif family in which few of the brothers have not swum into the notice of the police.

Ozer's (b. September 1947) principal claim to fame was his acquittal in 1977 on a charge of the murder of security guard, David Cross, on the A2 near Dartford during an attack on a Securicor van in which £103,000 was stolen. Bekir (b. September 1953) was convicted of disposing of the guns used in the robbery and received five years. Ozer had already been convicted of a minor part in a West London bank robbery in 1975.

In 1981 under surveillance during the so-called police Operation Kate, Michael McAvoy, sentenced to twenty-five years' imprisonment in the Brinks-Mat robbery which netted £26 million of gold bullion in London on 26 November 1983, was photographed with a member of the family. At the end of Operation Kate, Dennis (b. April 1956) and Bekir were convicted of conspiracy to rob when they were seen too near another Securicor van, this time in Bromley.

On 27 November 1990 the police ambushed the Arifs in another raid on yet another Securicor vehicle as it toured the Reigate area delivering £750,000 to branches of Barclay's Bank. Kenny Baker, Dennis Arif, Mehmet (b. December 1950) and Anthony Downer (a close friend of sister Susan) were cornered when the police vehicle rammed their van. Dennis and Downer threw down their weapons; Mehmet and Kenny Baker did not. Baker was shot dead and Mehmet wounded.

At the trial, at which Mehmet and Downer pleaded guilty and received eighteen years apiece, Dennis Arif ran the ingenious – if difficult to establish – defence of duress. He owed Baker £60,000 in gaming debts and Baker had threatened to shoot him if he did not pay it back. As a result he had taken part in the raid. This defence was not a great success; the police had been able to show that both he and the late Mr Baker had been at a family wedding at the Savoy earlier in the year. Dennis Arif received a sentence of twenty-two years.

Dogan was already in gaol serving fourteen years for his involvement in an £8.5 million drug-smuggling plot for which Eddie Richardson received twenty-five years. In 1983 Dogan had been acquitted of taking part in a bogus arms deal designed to separate the Ayatollah Khomeni from £34 million. Bekir followed shortly after Mehmet and Dennis when he was caught in another police trap, this time in Norwood.

The Arifs had integrated well with the South-East London community. Apart from their sister Susan's relationship with Anthony Downer, Dogan's brothers-in-law include Peter and Terry Cunningham, serving eight and sixteen years respectively for conspiracy to steal and rob and firearms offences. James Coleman, another brother-in-law, had been acquitted of the murder of Peter Hennessey, one of the brothers who owned the Dog and Bell in Peckham.

Meanwhile the North London teams seem to have been keeping their heads out of the range of police fire. Reports are that nothing much has changed in the territory, with the two most powerful families seeming to have reached at least a temporary accommodation. The East End, thought perhaps to be unified under Kray control in the 1960s, is now split into areas with one family and friends in control of Canning Town and another masterminding operations in Barking. Others operate in Bow and Stepney. In part they are based on school acquaintanceships, as well as allegiance to football clubs and in particular Millwall.

2

London – the Robbers and the Others

Crime in London is not, and never has been, purely family-controlled. There have always been a number of individuals and joint enterprises which have worked either independently of, or in conjunction with, the fraternal businesses. Nevertheless family ties do bind more than friendship. A traditional way of solving crime has been through the use of the informer, or by persuading a minor member of the operation that he, or sometimes she, is better off in the witness box than in the dock. The annals of criminal trials are littered with witnesses who have shared cells with prisoners and who have heard from them a valuable and timely confession denied to the police. One instance of the former is the Kray case, where Read was successful in persuading a number of fringe players to 'go QE'. Indeed, a good part of the art of detective work is turning or bending the small fry as it is known. Curiously, if the defence attempts to bend back that same small fry it is known as conspiracy to pervert. The Bindon trial is an example of the use of the cell-mate who has heard the hitherto silent defendant cough his lot.

In the 1970s, however, a new breed of witness was born. It was the era of the supergrass; usually an armed robber who had seen daylight fading through the prospect of prison bars and had decided to tell all he knew about his former colleagues in return for a nominal sentence, served very often in a police station and accompanied by booze, television, evenings out with his minding officers and sometimes conjugal visits. The first of these reformed villains was Bertie Smalls, who gave his name to the phrase 'to do a Bertie' or to inform.[1] He secured the best deal of them all. Much to the fury of Mr Justice Lawton he was never prosecuted. He was followed in quick succession by Maurice O'Mahoney, who wrote a book about his life and time, Charlie Lowe, Billy Amies, Leroy Davies and dozens of others. All were keen to repent at the expense of their friends and, for a time, with lawyers not knowing how to cross-examine them effectively and with help from the trial judges, very successful they were too. Instead of the fifteen and twenty years' imprisonment terms they merited, and which were handed to their former friends, they received fives. Then as the years went by, and the convictions mounted, juries became more sceptical. It was apparent that some of the behaviour of the Crown's witnesses was infinitely worse than that of the driver on a minor bank

---

[1] At the time when Smalls dictated his epoch-making statement, a 'very senior detective who knows the form book backwards' estimated that there was a pool of some 3,000 criminals in London readily available for bank robberies. J.A. Mack, *The Crime Industry*, p.60. Recruiting for jobs was often done on an *ad hoc* basis in such clubs as the A&R and the Log Cabin in Wardour Street, see J. Morton, *Gangland*, p. 230.

robbery. Billy Amies who, dressed as a policeman, had threatened his victim with castration and had the man's daughter stripped to her underwear, asking, 'How would you like to see your daughter raped?', could not have appealed very much to jurors. He named fifty-eight criminals but was responsible for the conviction of less than half a dozen.

It also became clear that these men were not completely born again. A number of them returned to their old trade. Donald Barrett was allowed to become a supergrass on two occasions and survived to tell the tale, but David Smith, who had actually killed a man and received five years for his part in over sixty robberies, soon took up where he had left off. On 29 September 1986 he was caught in a raid on a Securicor vehicle in Golders Green and five days after his birthday on 8 October, in a cell still festooned with balloons to mark the occasion, he cut his throat with a razor-blade.

Some, however, were much tougher. One figure from the 1970s who re-surfaced and survived, in a little reported case, was Bertie Smalls' immediate successor in the supergrass stakes, the self-styled 'King of the Squealers' Maurice O'Mahoney, now known as Peter Davies. In the summer of 1993 he was to be found in the dock at the Old Bailey flaunting a Flying Squad tie and charged with robbery.

Following his successful career as a bank robber, and a subsequent equally gratifying one as a supergrass, O'Mahoney kept out of public vision until he was arrested in Reading in 1990 on a charge of shoplifting. He had been found, along with his young son, pushing a shopping trolley out of a store. His defence was that he was on his way to the electrical department to obtain some guarantees before paying. The case was stopped by magistrates at the committal proceedings.

Three years later his defence to a charge of robbery was that it was a snatch carried out on the instructions of the police to incriminate another man. In the witness-box he told a strange story. After his acquittal at Reading, when curiously his custody record had disappeared, his cover was blown. He now tried to see a senior officer whose job it had been to protect supergrasses, and received no substantial help. In the November he went to see a DI whom he knew at Brixton police station, and asked what help he could have. Again there was a negative response, but this time O'Mahoney asked when and where the station's Christmas party would be held. He entered the raffle, which carried the first prize of a ticket to Paris.

According to O'Mahoney he was later contacted by a DI, the man whom he had seen at Brixton police station, and asked to carry out a small commission for him. What the police wanted, said O'Mahoney, was for him to carry out a smash-and-grab at a sub-post office, leave behind the main money and instead take a money-bag containing £250 worth of 20p pieces from outside a post office in Shepherd's Bush. The robbery was to take place on 30 June. The idea was that when O'Mahoney handed the bag over to the police they would then plant the money on another man.

O'Mahoney went on to say that, since he had packed in the job of supergrass, or more probably it had packed him in, and he had served his five-year sentence in Chiswick police station, he was a frequent visitor to Briefs wine bar, a popular haunt of villains, barristers, solicitors and the police, not necessarily in that order, which was opposite Inner London Crown Court in Newington Causeway. Briefs had been opened by three police officers who had subsequently left the Metropolitan Police, along with solicitor Michael Relton who later had received twelve years' imprisonment for his part in laundering the money from the Brinks-Mat robbery. O'Mahoney told the court he spent much of his time in Briefs, and his function in life was collecting and laundering money and generally helping Relton. The wine bar was one which, from time to time, had been placed off-limits by Commissioners.

According to O'Mahoney's evidence he was introduced at the Brixton party to an officer known as Basher, whom he said had acquired the nickname because, every time he was drunk, he started to fight. It was then the proposition was put to him and it was suggested he should recruit someone who was clean to carry out the raid with him.

O'Mahoney found a man in Bristol and duly appeared in Shepherd's Bush. A white Ford Escort car was, he said, to be near the shop and a red one for the getaway outside a local public house, the Fox and Hounds. As he looked round the area before the robbery he saw a Rover motor vehicle with three officers in it, as well as two mounted police officers near by. Something, he told the court, was wrong. He had intended to do the snatch himself but now he sent the other man in. It was completed but the alarm went off. The man got back into O'Mahoney's car, and as he did so the police started shooting.

In the car provided by the police, according to O'Mahoney, was a bag of guns – one a starting pistol, a second which had been tampered with – and cartridges which had been sprayed with oil. The effect of this would make them extremely unreliable. He maintained, and there was no evidence to contradict him, that neither he nor his friend ever shot back.

According to the Home Office expert eight shots were fired, all by the police. O'Mahoney never attempted to reach the exchange getaway car; instead he took to his feet, was caught and taken to Shepherd's Bush police station where DS Fuller, who had looked after O'Mahoney when he was in custody in Chiswick in his supergrass days, arrived. The custody record showed that no one knew who O'Mahoney was, and that Fuller took his prints to identify him. According to O'Mahoney, Fuller told him that everything would be sorted out.

In the witness-box O'Mahoney listed the officers with whom, he said, he had had corrupt dealings going back as far as the early 1970s. Efforts to suggest that he had turned up uninvited to the Christmas party and had been summarily booted out foundered when he produced his winning raffle ticket which, sensibly, he had not cashed.

It was, wrote Duncan Campbell of his behaviour in the witness-box, '. . . a virtuoso performance. The prosecution dismissed his case as rubbish but the jury acquitted him.'[2]

As Campbell went on to write, this has left Mahoney in something of a dilemma and his lawyer, Adrian Neale, wrote to the Home Office and indeed went to see the Home Secretary, Kenneth Baker, asking for a guarantee of his client's safety. He has been given no promises. An inquiry by the Police Complaints Authority carried out before the trial exonerated the officers involved in the Shepherd's Bush case.

Certainly the greatest British robbery in terms of money obtained rather than in public interest had been the 26 November 1983 Brinks-Mat case. With £26 million, even allowing for inflation, it dwarfed the Great Train Robbery as the most successful operation of its

[2] *Guardian*, 16 July 1993.

kind, but neither it nor its perpetrators ever captured the imagination of the public in the same way. A good deal of this has to do with the reporting restrictions imposed by the Criminal Justice Act 1967. Before then, every week when defendants in custody were brought before the court the prosecution would outline the facts of the case to the magistrates, particularly the most unattractive ones from the defence point of view. They would be duly reported in the early editions of the evening papers. The 1967 Act imposed substantial restrictions on what could be reported in the papers without the consent of the defendants. In a flash all the fun went out of local court reporting, and people who week by week had been front-page national figures were relegated to a small paragraph on page seven.

The Brinks-Mat robbery was another example of the escalation in violence offered to victims. At 6.40 a.m. the robbers, wearing balaclavas and armed with machine guns, burst into the vaults of the Brinks-Mat security company near Heathrow and terrorized the guards. Two had the crotches of their trousers cut open and petrol poured on them; the team leader then threatened to set fire to them or to cut off their penises. £26 million, in the form of 6,800 gold bars waiting to be sent to the Middle and Far East, was loaded and transferred into waiting vans.

It was really only a matter of days before the police latched on to the last guard to arrive that morning – Tony Black – who had missed the robbery because he was ten minutes late for work. Black confessed. His sister was living with Brian Robinson, one of a number of villains over the years known as 'The Colonel'. Robinson had been on the Williams & Glyn's robbery in 1978 and in 1981 had benefited through the mistakes of the No.5 Regional Crime

Squad.[3] Black identified two more of the team, Tony White and Michael McAvoy.

In December 1984 Robinson and McAvoy received twenty-five years each; White was acquitted. Later there was said to be £50,000 on offer to free McAvoy and Robinson. Black, who had given evidence for the Crown, was handed a six-year sentence. 'Never again will your life be safe. You will be segregated at all times and you and your family will forever be fugitives from those you so stupidly and wickedly helped,' said the judge, the late Mr Justice David Tudor-Price, in another of the homilies senior judges like to hand down, for the benefit more of the press than the defendants who no doubt know it already.

That still left a number of villains at large and a very large amount of property missing. The gold had been in marked ingots of extremely high quality. It could not be offered to legitimate dealers; instead it was being smelted by a small bullion firm, Scadlynn, on the outskirts of Bristol.

A surveillance operation on another suspect, Kenneth

---

[3] Robinson was one of a number of criminals who were known as 'The Colonel'. The most famous example is Ronnie Kray and another is George Copley. It was Copley who was instrumental in sabotaging the efforts of the No.5 Regional Crime Squad when in June 1981 he and Frankie Fraser junior, a nephew of 'the great man', were on trial at Oxford on charges of robbery. Three months previously a Sergeant Pook visited him in Reading gaol and was secretly taped by Copley in a conversation in which Pook confirmed an offer that if Copley was to admit his part in the Williams & Glyn's robbery (another problem for the City of London Police) and also give evidence of corruption against certain London detectives, he would receive only a five-year sentence. The tape was produced at the trial and the case was stopped. It was 'hopelessly compromised' said Stephen Wooler for the Director of Public Prosecutions.

Noye, ended in disaster. An undercover police officer, John Fordham, clad in a balaclava helmet, was stabbed to death in the grounds of Noye's home at West Kingsdowne in Kent. Noye, charged with the murder of Fordham, gave evidence that, 'I just froze with horror. All I saw when I flashed my torch on this masked man was just the two eye-holes and the mask. I thought that was my lot. I thought I was going to be a dead man.'

And, as the jury found, in self-defence he stabbed Ford-ham eleven times. In November 1985, Noye and Brian Reader, who was with him at the time, were acquitted of murder. In July of 1986 both were convicted of handling the Brinks-Mat gold, along with Garth Chappell, a Scadlynn director. Reader received nine years and Noye, whose defence was that he was a gold smuggler and VAT fraud-ster as opposed to being a thief and receiver, ended up with fourteen years. However, there are still plenty of figures in the Underworld who believe that his defence was correct. No Brinks-Mat gold was ever found on his premises and, although £100,000 of gold was discovered, tests showed this could not have been from the Brinks-Mat robbery. Garth Chappell received ten years, whilst Matteo Constantino, 68, a long-standing Hatton Garden villain who had allowed his company to be used in a false VAT claim, received a suspended sentence of twelve months for conspiracy to evade VAT on the gold. After being melted down it had then been delivered in small parcels to London. The gold was sold on the legitimate market, mainly to dishonest dealers who were charged VAT at 15 per cent. Constantino had been acquitted of dishonest handling and was suffering from cancer at the time.

The convictions of Noye and Reader were the greatest successes the police had on the Scadlynn side of things. The next year John Palmer, a former director of Scadlynn who had been invited to leave Spain by the authorities and who chose to be deported to Britain from Rio de Janeiro, was put on trial at the Old Bailey. Charged that he conspired with Noye and Reader to dishonestly handle the gold, he was acquitted and went to live off the proceeds of his time-share business in Tenerife.

Nor was there any greater success in the case of John Fleming who was deported from Florida in 1986. In March of the next year, with evidence given against him by a new supergrass, Patrick Diamond, Fleming was charged with dishonestly handling nearly £500,000 of the Brinks-Mat proceeds. At the committal proceedings at Horseferry Road Magistrates' Court, he was found to have no case to answer. Fleming told reporters, 'I feel a great relief. It has been a bad year,' before he returned to Spain where he was involved in a car accident and again deported. He was back in London in December 1993 when he was attacked in the Horseferry Road near Victoria Station, receiving wounds which required some forty stitches.

1991 had been a fatal year for Noye's former friend, 43-year-old Nick Whiting, who ran a garage at Wrotham in Kent. Whiting had been questioned back in 1983 over a Range Rover sold to Noye and bought back. Now on 6 June Whiting vanished from the garage along with five cars. At first it seemed to be a straightforward kidnapping, but when all the cars stolen in the raid on his garage were recovered within a few days unkind suggestions came on offer, including one that Whiting had staged his own disappearance over the Brinks-Mat spoils and that he had gone on the run with a friend of his, Lennie 'Little Lew', who was also wanted in connection with Brinks-Mat.

Ex-racing driver Whiting had secured a plot of land

during the period of falling property prices and had borrowed bent money to finance a building deal. One suggestion was that the mortgagor wanted his money back. A variation on the theme is that Whiting owed money on the cars. At the beginning of June his body was found in marshland in Essex, nearly a month after his abduction; it appeared he had been beaten up, bound hand and foot, and stuffed in a car boot. He had then been shot in the back of the head, seemingly after being frogmarched across at least three miles of boggy ground.

As for McAvoy and Robinson, they were awaiting the hearing of their appeals when Fordham was stabbed and realized that, without a substantial sweetener, any slim chance they had of getting a few years off their twenty-five years had evaporated with his death. They put up a deal to DAC Brian Worth. If they gave back half their share of the bullion, then a good word could be put in to the Court of Appeal. The proposition foundered when they found their friends on the outside and in possession would ante up perhaps a million or two, but nothing like the required amount required for any possible reduction. McAvoy, in particular, was annoyed. He wrote from Leicester prison in November 1986 that he was considering informing, he was not going to be 'fucked for my money and still do the sentence'. But when it came to it he was not prepared to turn informer.[4]

The Brinks-Mat laundering trials continued into the 1990s, by which time several of those convicted early on in the proceedings, such as solicitor Michael Relton, had been released. In November 1991, after five months of evidence, the trial of McAvoy's ex-wife Jacqueline,

[4] N. Darbyshire with B. Hilliard, *The Flying Squad*, p.232.

Gordon Parry, Brian Perry, Jean Savage, Patrick Clark and his son, Stephen, was halted by Judge Henry Pownall who would not reveal the reason but told the jury, 'Believe me, it is a proper reason.'

By 1993 Noye was in Latchmere House in Richmond, Surrey, once a boys' remand centre but now a resettlement centre for villains coming to the end of their sentences. The regime is fairly relaxed, with the men allowed out to work during the day and being given extensive weekend leave. It was believed that Noye had been involved in a plan to import cocaine from America as well as laundering dirty money. Unfortunately it appears that a detective may have tipped off one of Noye's partners in the operation, as a result of which a shipment of drugs was cancelled. It is said that Noye paid £500 to the police officer for the information.

It is not the first time that Noye has been involved in bribery since his imprisonment. In 1988 he is said to have offered £1 million to a senior officer who, in turn, was cleared of any misconduct.[5]

In real terms little of the Brinks-Mat money has been recovered, and civil actions have been started to try to retrieve some of the outstanding losses. Several actions have already been settled by those convicted.

McAvoy was probably right when he decided to observe the code of silence. In recent years, and in contrast to the days when Smalls and the others walked about seemingly impervious to the large prices said to be on their heads, informers have had a hard time. In turn the police have gone to lengths to try to convict those they suspect of killing them. After all, if they do not, then potential informers may get discouraged.

[5] *Sunday Times*, 5 December 1993.

In February 1989 informer Alan 'Chalky' White was killed. He was last seen walking to the off-licence in Minchington, Gloucestershire to get some lager. Three months later his body, wrapped in a blue tarpaulin, was spotted by a family at the Cotswold Water Park near Cirencester. He had been stabbed in the heart.

White, who had several minor convictions, was due to give evidence against a Danny Gardiner with whom, so White said, he had robbed a petrol station in Stroud netting £4,800 in 1986. White, who had a drug problem, had declined the police offer of a new identity. He was given a 'panic button' to use if he felt threatened, but most nights he could be found in the local Crown public house. With the death of White, the case against Danny Gardiner collapsed and he went abroad.

With the help of Interpol the police conducted inquiries in Egypt – where Mr Gardiner was wrongly reported to have died in Cairo – France, Spain, Morocco and Israel. On 4 January 1991 Mr Gardiner flew back voluntarily from Tel Aviv. He had been found there working in a tourist hotel, having apparently entered the country under a false name. Gardiner was later convicted of White's murder.

In 1990 another informer was killed. He had previously told the police of a planned contract killing resulting in the arrest of the hit-man. Before the trial the judge accepted the argument of the defence that it needed access to police information; this would have meant a disclosure of the identity of the informant, and the trial was abandoned by the prosecution. At the time of his death, the man had been resettled in Germany – the cost of relocating an informer, names, passports and driving licences for him and his family, is around £100,000 – and he was murdered shortly afterwards.

A second killing occurred in Amsterdam and involved a man who had given police information about a gang of drug traffickers; and the third, early in 1993, was in Ireland. It seems the link to the identification of the informant had come about through the withdrawal of the case by the prosecution.

In May 1993 the trial of four men, whom the prosecution alleged brought over hired killers from Northern Ireland to dispose of supergrass David Norris, collapsed with little publicity at the Old Bailey. Indeed, for such an important case the press had been remarkably silent. After nearly six weeks the trial, which had cost almost £1 million, was halted when the Recorder of London, Judge Lawrence Verney, ruled that the evidence of the two main prosecution witnesses, Renwick Dennison and Stuart Warne, was unsafe for the jury to rely on. Patrick Doherty, George McMahon (both from South London), Terence McCrory from Belfast and John Green from Falkirk, were all acquitted.

The prosecution had outlined a curious but ultimately not compelling story of hitmen hired through Northern Ireland drug dealers who were promised cheap cannabis in return for the completion of the contracts. Two men who were never arrested, Thomas McCreery and Stephen Pollock from Kent, were said by the prosecution to have helped organize the murder squad. McCreery, so the prosecution said, had come to London from Belfast after he had been shot for supplying Catholics with drugs.[6]

[6] McCreery seems to have had a chequered and eventful life. According to evidence given in the case he had been active in the Belfast Loyalist Underworld since the middle 1970s as both a drug dealer and the recruiter of Protestant hitmen. At one time he was on the run and thought to be in Spain after he had been shot in a

At an earlier trial Warne, the link between the English drug dealers and the Irish, and Dennison, one of the hitmen, had been sentenced to life imprisonment after admitting conspiracy to murder. Warne had told the jury how one of the defendants, Patrick Doherty, had met him in a South London public house and had whistled up £20,000 in half an hour by using his mobile phone. This was, he said, the price for the unsuccessful killing of a second man, John Dale, 'the object of dislike and hatred apparently because he was in the habit of ripping people off in drug deals', said Timothy Langdale QC for the prosecution. Dennison took over the contract and shot him in the back outside his London home in April 1991, and then missed at point-blank range when he shot at his head. So far as Norris was concerned, the 45-year-old informer was shot as he begged for mercy with his wife watching helplessly.

Norris' death was just another in the series where the prosecution had inadvertently blown their man's cover by dropping the case. He was shot in July 1992 at his home in Belvedere by a motorcycle-riding killer.

In 1987 the *Sun* newspaper, in one of its more public-spirited displays, had a photograph taken of five super-grasses in Bedford Gaol. The men, David Medin, Clifford Barnes, Fred Scott, Steven Henry and John Davies, were photographed at exercise. The *Sun* pointed out that if their photographer could take a camera shot of them, with a reported £1.8 million on offer for their collective

cont'd
car outside a social club in the Shankhill Road area. The IRA had indicated that he was under sentence of death. He had been lucky to survive for so long for he was thought to have had contacts with the IRA and INLA. A close relative of his, Ned McCreery, was killed by the UDA in 1992.

deaths, then a hitman could just as easily take a real shot at them.

Nevertheless, some still thought it was worthwhile to exchange twenty-two years inside for a lifetime of looking over their shoulders. Lawrence Cain, known as 'The Snake' and said – a trifle optimistically, given the going rate – to have a £250,000 contract on him, was one of them when, in 1991, he received just seven years for armed robbery. He had given 'valuable help' to the police after admitting taking part in twenty-seven raids in South-East London over an eight-year period. The money had gone on foreign travel and a £300-a-day heroin habit. Amongst those who went down as a result of his evidence were his former partner Alan Condon, who drew twenty-one years, Cain's best man when he married a Thai girl who collected sixteen, and William Harding who netted a year less. Cain's counsel told the court that he had turned informer for the highly praiseworthy reason of divorcing himself from the criminal community. 'No one will come near me unless it is to kill me', said Cain whilst giving evidence.

Two spectacular snatches, if not quite of the magnitude of the Brinks-Mat raid, seem to have been carried out by the same man. The first in December 1990 happened when Eddie Maher was apparently a victim. Maher was a Securicor guard when thugs burst into his driving partner's home, held him and his wife hostage for fourteen hours and told him she would be killed unless the money was handed over. The guard together with Maher drove to the Securicor depot, collected £2 million and handed it over in Rotherhithe. They were then put in the back of the van and later released. The other man's wife was subsequently released in Epping Forest. Securicor offered £100,000 as a reward leading to information and conviction of the robbers but it was never claimed.

Then on 22 January 1993 Eddie Maher disappeared with £1,327,500 packed in fifty white Securicor bags. The 'robbery' had taken place outside a bank in Felixstowe. Maher and his regular colleague delivered cash to a branch of Lloyds bank; whilst the other man was inside the police allege Maher drove off in the two-ton van, which was found an hour later a mile away, with the secured cash compartment empty. Maher's lover, Debbie Brett, and her son had left their rented home in Woodham Ferrers near Chelmsford a week before the Felixstowe robbery. It is possible that this second 'hi-jacking' was the work of one man working alone.

Another more or less solo effort was by the man the newspapers named 'Florida Phil' Wells. He was thought to have decamped to the warmer climes of that State with something approaching £1 million taken from his security van at Heathrow in July 1989. The van, from which he should have delivered the money to a branch of Thomas Cook, was found forty-eight hours later at the Colnebrook estate near Heathrow. Also gone was his wage packet; those of his colleagues were still in the van. It was a crime which captured the imagination of the public.

In 1991 Wells telephoned from France that he was on the run both from the law and gangsters. In March 1993 he – or at least someone closely resembling him – surfaced in the pages of the *Sunday Mirror*.[7] The robbery, he (or his doppelganger) said, had been forced on him when he was threatened by West Indians who had poured petrol on his son Christopher. No, he had not gone to Florida. He had been hidden in a caravan park at Clacton, been on the Norfolk Broads, lived on a canal barge near Shrewsbury.

[7] *Sunday Mirror*, 14 March 1993.

He had also had a heart attack, and he believed there was an £80,000 contract out on his life. Indeed at one time it had been thought he was dead. The police were reported to be furious that they had not been tipped off.[8]

Wells did not last long on the outside after that. In May another daily newspaper, this time the *Sun*, was approached by an intermediary and invited to buy an interview for £25,000. The police were alerted and Wells was caught in a trap; he had only £4 on him. On 9 December 1993, after a two-week trial at Isleworth Crown Court, he was found guilty of stealing £928,000 in foreign currency. The story now came out. The £2.50-an-hour security guard had collected the money in nine shoe-box-shaped bags from an aeroplane and loaded them into his Ford Fiesta van which he had dumped only a few miles away; to cloud the trail he had telephoned a relative to say he was off to Florida. His story to the *Sunday Mirror* was not wholly accurate; the Norfolk Broads and the caravan park at Clacton had not featured all that prominently. He had certainly stayed in Clacton – indeed the police had raided the park and missed him by a few hours – but his real base had been in Malta where he landed first in October 1989. He was on and off the island constantly, visiting Hungary, Tunisia, Bulgaria, Sicily and finally Russia where he married his third wife, Olga (described variously as a gymnast/ night-club stripper) in Uzbekistan. He had told her he was a wealthy greengrocer. He seems to have forgotten about another wife in America. After the trial she announced she wished to have nothing more to do with him.

On 14 January 1994 he received a sentence of six years. Neither the police nor the trial judge were by any means

[8] *News of the World*, 24 January 1993.

convinced he had acted alone. Prior to the theft he had, it seems, been bragging about his employment in East End public houses.

If blue, or black, plaques were to be awarded to houses and flats for their significance in crime, then a candidate would be Welbeck Mansions in Marylebone. It was here that Bert Wilkins, convicted of the manslaughter of the Montecolumbo brother at Wandsworth dogs in 1934 and later a shadowy but influential figure in Soho, lived until his retirement to the South Coast. It was also here that businessman Donald Urquhart lived with his Thai girl-friend, Pat Lamspithone, until he was gunned down in Marylebone High Street on 2 Jan 1993. The millionaire property tycoon and owner of Elstree Golf Club was on his way home from a meal in a local restaurant when a man in a white crash helmet walked up, pulled out a .32 pistol and shot him twice in the head. The man then jumped on a black Yamaha 250 motorcycle and disappeared. Urquhart's kill-ing was said to have been worth £20,000 and, according to persistent newspaper reports, the assassin was said to be an ex-boxer who worked for a South London gang.

The police were able to trace the bike. It had been advertised in the 23 November 1992 issue of *Loot* magazine for £275, and sold for £200. A similar ten-year-old bike had been used by the killer of ex-boxer Roger 'The Growler' Wilson, then manager of an off-licence and a jewellery fence. He had been shot in the head as he got out of his Mercedes in Kensington on 5 March 1992. Again the motorbike which the killer used had been advertised in *Loot*.

Another motorcycle killing came on 21 June 1993 when Tommy Roche (42) was shot three times as he worked in a lay-by near Heathrow Airport, said to be over a drug deal which went wrong. Roche had been the minder to Donald Urquhart and was also said to have been a grass. As a teenager he had tried to work with the Krays.

The technique of murder by motorbike comes from Columbia where teenage hitmen were first hired in the 1980s, but the London version seems to have been cut-price in the extreme. 'What's amazing is that they're using ten-year-old clapped-out bikes to flee the scene. Obviously they are really cutting costs,' said Detective Superintendent Bill Scholes.[9]

At the other end of the scale, by the early 1990s patterns of crime had also changed. Gone were the days when a handbag was merely snatched. Now, too often, the victim is stabbed as well, often for the fun of it. Nineteen-year-old crack addict Duane Daniels led a team of muggers through the streets of South London in general and, in particular, on the notorious William Bonney Estate in Clapham. By the time his criminal career was suspended at the Old Bailey in December 1993 he had committed 959 identifiable offences to finance his habit, which was said at his trial to be a daily intake of half an ounce of cannabis, twenty rocks of crack, ten pints of extra-strength lager, two doses of LSD, a quarter of a bottle of spirits and handfuls of tranquillisers.[10] At his arrest Daniels, whose rocks of crack cost £25 a

---

[9] *News of the World*, 14 February 1993.

[10] This was not the largest number of offences taken into consideration at the Central Criminal Court. Brian Reece wrote to *The Times* saying that in the 1970s he recalled a case of a man who had had 1,187 offences taken into consideration. They had all arisen from a nationwide operation to defraud banks by cashing stolen cheques each to the value of £30. The man had received a sentence of two years' imprisonment suspended for two years. *The Times*, 5 January 1993.

rock, had nothing to show for his crimes except the clothes in which he stood. His team, the 28 Posse, recognized by a special mark in their closely cropped hair, was a motley assortment of both willing and frightened recruits. One boy who declined to join had his coat set on fire.

In one month alone Daniels stole £100,000 worth of television and video sets in burglaries, but before the end of this part of his career he and his gang had turned to a much more sinister form of crime. His victims were kidnapped and tortured to reveal their personal identification numbers which would allow Daniels to obtain money from the cashholders at banks.

One victim was working alone in the evening in the offices of a building contractor's when Daniels tricked him into opening the door, claiming he was a cleaner. The man was hit on the head with a bottle and tied with telephone wire before being stabbed in the legs to make him reveal the PIN number. Daniels and other members of his gang fled and the victim then threw himself through a window in an effort to get help. Another, a woman who was attacked in a veterinary surgery, was threatened with the decapitation of her guinea-pig. In 1991 he had been jailed for three and a half years for a series of similar violent crimes.[11] Now he received nine years.

Another victim of an indiscriminate shooting was barrister's clerk Amaranath Bandaratilleka who was gunned down by Avie Andrews, aged 16, the middle-class son of an actor. His victim was in a newsagent's shop in Hammersmith when Andrews, together with Sam Perman aged 18, son of an antiques dealer and director of the Poetry Society,

[11] *Sunday Times*, 5 December 1993; *The Times*, 24 December 1993.

robbed it. Mr Bandaratilleka was shot in the stomach after being ordered to turn out his pockets and revealed he had only 26 pence, a pocket calculator and an office organizer on him. Andrews, the father of a five-month-old baby by a 20-year-old girl – and who was being supported by another middle-class girl – also admitted robbing drug dealers of £650 of cannabis with a sawn-off shotgun bought from Underworld contacts for £200 as a defence weapon for his bogus drug racket – a thriving trade in cold cure pills crushed to resemble Ecstasy tablets, to pay for his heroin addiction. He later confessed to his sister and then to his father. He had, said Edward Quist-Arcton for the defence, started taking cannabis at 11, and was addicted to heroin by the age of 15. Now the Court was told that during his time on remand he had tried to commit suicide but had, after an escape from a secure unit, kicked the heroin habit. 'The Avie Andrews before the court now is a far, far different person from the drugged, befuddled teenager of earlier this year. He has manfully accepted full responsibility for the death and nobody regrets the senseless waste of life more than he does.' Apart from Mr Bandaratilleka's family and friends presumably.

The 1990s saw the continued rise of the contract killer. The targets, apart from Moody, included those involved in drugs deals which had gone sour, and supergrasses. There was also the suggestion that one killing had been a community action with the death of a drug dealer who had been warned off a territory. Of course, contract killing is not a new phenomenon. Earlier examples included the killing of Paddy O'Nione and Tony Zomparelli.

In April 1993 Judge Michael Coombe sentenced James Brooker and his brother Mark to terms of nine and eight years following an attack on a mechanic, Thomas Kennedy, in the Simla public house in Thornton Heath. They had been acquitted of charges of attempted murder. Kennedy required more than a hundred stitches after being attacked with a knife, a cosh, a beer glass and a bar stool. The subsequent trial was littered with missing witnesses. The judge said:

> I haven't the slightest doubt that there has been interference with witnesses in this case. It is proved to my satisfaction that certain witnesses had been put in fear, a grave fear. It is an indication of the violence surrounding this case that the terror which began on June 20 [1992] could extend all these months later.[12]

By the end of the trial two witnesses were still missing, another had changed her statement and a fourth had been declared 'hostile' by the judge. At first he had been seen as an important witness, but later claimed he could not remember the incident.

The intimidation of witnesses and, in particular, the victim, is nothing new but with the time between arrest and trial in serious cases now up to a year, it is much easier for offers and threats to be made. Nationwide, over twenty major trials involving serious violence have collapsed and some three hundred investigations, including murder hunts, have been abandoned during 1992–3. In June 1993 a pregnant woman received a month's imprisonment at Newcastle Crown Court for failing to give evidence at the murder trial of her former boyfriend; she said threats had been made against both her and other witnesses. It was slightly different in Merthyr Tydfil when Ali Khan, a

[12] *Sunday Times*, 11 April 1993.

shopkeeper whose shop had been under siege in a racist attack, declined to give evidence. The men were convicted when local residents told the court they had heard the men threatening to burn Mr Khan's shop. In 1992 a trial in Manchester collapsed when a woman who had named several people she said were involved in a machete attack on Carl Stapleton, disappeared. She had insisted on anonymity in court, but the judge had refused. As a result the prosecution offered no evidence. There have been other instances in both Manchester and Liverpool.

It is not always private witnesses who seek protection. In December 1993 the much vaunted Operation Mensa trial collapsed at the committal stage when the officer who had allegedly infiltrated the gang told the court he wished to be shielded from the view of the public gallery and to give a false name. When this was refused the prosecution had the charges dismissed by the stipendiary magistrate, Mr David Fingleton, saying they were intending to apply for a voluntary bill of indictment.

The great individual jewel thieves are men of the past. George 'Taters' Chatham is in his eighties; Peter Scott is a tennis coach; Raymond Jones, once said to be the greatest climber in the country, is retired. Jewel thefts have never had great attraction for the run-of-the-mill criminal.

Whoever you go to to sell, it will always be, 'Oh how difficult this particular jewellery is. It will require resetting and cutting and this will devalue it because there's been such a hue and cry about it.' And there's no challenge to this type of market. The thief has to put up with whatever price comes up unless he finds someone who personally fancies a piece or pieces of the jewellery for his own personal use, and that man would have to go to the expense of having it altered. If you're not lucky enough to find that person you're lumbered. But jewel raids will always go on. It's easy to carry away and you might be lucky to get that particular diamond or two which could come to a lot of money. That's the chance you're looking for. It is a very precarious commodity to sell. Sometimes you can get a commission, that's the better thing because you know exactly what you're going for and what you're going to get for it.

A few years ago a pal of mine did a jeweller's, a tie-up, and I believe officially it was said that nearly £2 million pounds worth of jewellery was stolen. I think about five of them were engaged on this endeavour and my friend who took a leading part, which meant that he would have at least an equal share, he received £7,500 altogether. That was getting it in dribs and drabs as well. They just couldn't sell the tom.[13]

As Fraser says, there will always be thieves who are prepared to try their luck at a snatch and resale. For example, 13 July 1993 saw the end of one the world's best professional safe-breakers, Roy Saunders, who had opened locks on behalf of Scotland Yard, and another locksmith, Robert French. They had led a five-man team including Robert Reed on a raid on the New English Artworks workshop, which manufactures watches for Cartiers in New Bond Street. It had been a highly professional job with one of the gang, posing as a window-cleaner, checking the fire alarm the day before. Bugging devices had been planted to deal with video cameras. Unfortunately they ran

[13] F. Fraser, *Mad Frank*, p.30.

into a police surveillance unit which was watching the area, not for them but as a result of a series of lesser burglaries. Two men escaped by abseiling down the back of a five-storey building in New Bond Street, but the others were caught in the basement of a nearby shoe shop. Saunders was unable to tell the police what either he or his equipment were doing on the premises. He and French told the police that by chance Reed had wandered into the shop to urinate after finding the door open. Equipment worth several thousands of pounds was found in his car. At the trial Saunders said he had been too drunk to remember anything of the evening. It was not a defence which appealed to the jury. Sentencing them to four years each in prison, Judge Fabyan Evans said on 6 August 1993, 'This must have been one of the most sophisticated burglaries of commercial property that has taken place in recent years. It is rare nowadays that an offence of this kind that involves such considerable profit involved no violence. Quite why men of your age became involved in an offence like this is a mystery to me.' The target had been £1 million, but it would have been likely to fetch only one-fifth in the market. The answer is both money and excitement. Anyway, older men than they had been at it for years.

On 28 November 1924 some wild colonial boys Dennis Harris and John James, along with John Russell and Edward Flood, were charged with breaking into Ewarts in Euston Road. They were seen coming out of the premises and promptly arrested. Scotland Yard's records describe them as 'a gang of dangerous warehouse breakers, safe-breakers'. Harris, known as 'Dare Devil Dennis', was 64 at the time and received three years' penal servitude, as did the 60-year-old James. Both had convictions in Australia and South Africa where they had ridden as steeplechase jockeys.

Only three years earlier Harris had received four years for receiving stolen property from big London robberies.

But when one door shuts another opens, and a recent example of a well-researched target was in July 1993 when, in a snatch lasting ten minutes, three thieves raided Graff jeweller's in Hatton Garden, said, 'Don't move or we'll shoot' to the staff whom they forced to lie on the floor, and escaped with diamonds, rubies and sapphires totalling some £7 million.

It took place in the middle of the morning rush hour when the thieves, who had the codes to the security room doors, took one £2-million diamond intended to be the centrepiece for a brooch and a £1-million ruby and diamond necklace. They were interrupted by another member of the staff who had been out for a cup of coffee, and left behind another diamond valued at £2.5 million before escaping into Farringdon station. This was the second attack on a store owned by victim Laurence Graff. In March 1993 the West End branch of his firm was robbed of jewellery worth £2 million.

Nevertheless by now drugs were the mainspring of the whole of the Underworld, both London and nationwide.

3

Glasgow

Perceived wisdom has it that there were no gangs in
Glasgow until after the First World War. Sir Percy
Sillitoe, the Chief Constable of the 1920s, chronicles the
Redskins and the Black Hand gangs with their 'childish
names' as being the first of many[1], whilst the old *Daily
Mirror* crime writer, Norman Lucas, with a fine disregard
for such worthies as Arthur Harding, Darby Sabini, Billy
Kimber and a whole host of Londoners, suggested that
Peter Williamson was the 'first true gangleader in Britain'.[2]

Quite apart from the racecourse gangs which flourished
in the nineteenth century and which operated out of the
city[3], both seem to have overlooked the existence of the

[1] Sir Percy Sillitoe, *Cloak Without Dagger*, p.140.
[2] Norman Lucas, *Britain's Gangland*, p.5. Others, including John
Mack in *Crime in Glasgow*, agree with him.
[3] In 1848 the *Renfrewshire Advertiser* noted that the Glasgow
Fancy had attended Paisley Races and had used brute force to
obtain a levy from the owners of stalls at the meetings. In the early
part of this century the Redskins, so known because of the razor

Penny Mob which operated in the 1880s in Townhead and the East End of Glasgow.

> This gang had a common fund to which all contributed, and when members were fined at the police courts, the money was always forthcoming – hence the name 'Penny Mob'. Their picturesque name should not disguise the fact that they were 'a gang of hooligans, who for long were a source of serious annoyance to the community'.[4]

But the Penny Mob whose leaders, as was common at the time, were known as Chairmen, was not alone. There were at least three other fighting gangs, the boys of the Wee Do'e Hill and the Big Do'e Hill along with the Drygate Youths. Twenty years later there were two rivals in central Glasgow, the San Toy Boys and the Tim Malloys. The former had the helpful chant:

> We are the young San Toys,
> and we can fight the Tim Malloys.

After them came the Mealy Boys, the McGlynn Push, the Village Boys and a few years later the Gold Dust Gang. They all seem to have operated in much the same way, fighting being the principal ambition coupled with a certain amount of leaning on local shopkeepers for protection money to pay off the inevitable fines.

The Redskins came a little later, flourishing during the First World War, but this gang, reckoned at one time to be

cont'd
slashes on their faces, roamed the Scottish racecourses in much the same way. See Carl Chinn, *Better Betting with a Decent Fellow*.
[4] *The Times*, 19 January, 1920.

over 1,000 strong, was far better organized than its rivals such as the Kelly Boys from Govan, the Baltic Fleet from Baltic Street, the Beehive Corner Boys, the Waverley Boys, the Cowboys and the Bell On Boys. Again the members' speciality was inter-gang fighting, but they also demanded protection money from shopkeepers whose premises were otherwise ransacked. The unfortunate owners would find all their goods mixed in a heap on the floor with, if they were extremely unfortunate, themselves deposited in the middle of the debris. On the way out the gang would break the shop windows.

Robert Colquhoun, who later became a detective chief superintendent and who was then a young beat constable, thought 1923 was a vintage year for Glasgow gangs, citing the Cheeky Forty and the Black Diamonds in the St Rolox area as his immediate concern:

> They were street corner thugs, who fought one another in head-on clashes a hundred strong or more – though they usually preferred it if some unsuspecting rival gangster strayed alone into their territory and could be 'done up' in the appropriate tradition. Sometimes girls attached to a gang would provide the necessary lure to achieve the catch.[5]

From time to time fights were more straightforward, one-on-one, affairs and there seems to have been no disgrace in recruiting a champion to promote your cause. Colquhoun recounts the story of two hardmen who fought each other with razors, then stopped and went to hospital together to be patched up.

[5] R. Colquhoun, *Life Begins at Midnight*, p.18.

That night had been enough for Jacko. He still kept up his quarrel with Chopper, but he hired a strong-arm man from the Gorbals to fight the next round of the battle. In gangland code, Jacko's standing didn't suffer by his decision to employ a deputy. After all, it was argued, he was still willing to continue the quarrel – and that was the important thing.[6]

It was, however, the Beehive Corner Boys, later abbreviated to the Beehive Boys or Gang, who moved up a gear. Under the leadership of Peter Williamson, described by Sillitoe as powerfully built and coming from a respectable family, who was aided by his lieutenant Harry M'Menemy and a man called Howie, they were into straightforward theft, burglary, armed robbery and, with the help of a London criminal recruited for the purpose, safebreaking.

Williamson, who apparently preferred one-to-one fights rather than gang battles and who had the ability to spot a policeman a mile away, could often be seen at the end of a gang fight appealing to the brawlers to behave. For some time it stood him in good stead but eventually the convictions began to pile up and M'Menemy, true lieutenant that he was, served a nine-month sentence for Williamson. He allowed himself to be put forward as the attacker of a man whom Williamson and a Dan Cronin had assaulted. His captain would undoubtedly have earned a term of years rather than months on conviction. Later the gang moved away from being a traditional fighting gang and into theft, safeblowing, house-breaking and armed robbery.

In 1924, at a time when there was open warfare between the South Side Stickers and the long-lasting San Toy Gang,

[6] Ibid p.77.

one of the major gangland fights of the era took place in the Bedford Parlour Dance Hall in Celtic Street not far from the football ground. It was, however, between two of the smaller affiliated teams, and James Dalziel, the leader of the Parlour Boys, died in it.

Dalziel, aged 26 and described as snub-nosed and sturdy, was known to his friends as Razzle-Dazzle. Although traditionally Glasgow gangs had many 'queens' or girl hangers-on who could be used to secrete weapons if the police arrived, Dalziel, whose favourite weapon was a pickshaft which weighed nearly three pounds and was three and a half foot in length, considered it effeminate to dance with them; he would only take the floor with the other male members of the gang. The Parlour Boys, as befitted its name, had proprietorial rights over the dance hall and did not have to pay admission. Instead members observed a two-part ritual. They would troop past the cashier saying they 'knew the boss'; the second and equally important part of this quasi-masonic ritual was to wipe their boots.

On 2 March 1924 the Bedford Boys went into the hall, to be followed in the early hours of the morning by the Bridgegate Boys, a group affiliated to the San Toys. Possibly they had merely come in to avoid the heavy rain, but it is more likely that to pass their rivals' headquarters without a murmur would have been a major loss of face. They cleared the first hurdle of the ritual muttering that they 'knew the boss', but when they failed to wipe their boots the cashier, Mrs Stevenson, sounded the alarm.

In the traditional phrase of the police, 'Fighting broke out', and during it Dalziel was stabbed in the throat by a youth, Collins. Later at the Assizes the jury acquitted him of Dalziel's murder and he received a twelve-months' sentence for affray. Fines imposed on those convicted of affray were paid for by a levy on local shopkeepers. Immediately the convicted men were elevated to the status of hero.

Many of the fighting gangs had junior sections, just as today the Crips and the Bloods of Los Angeles and other gangs have wannabees and graduating ranks for pre-teen children. In 1928, four years after the Dalziel murder, another gang killing ended with heavy sentences. This time the participants were from the junior division, and the fight broke out over a minor injury to one of the queens belonging to the South Side Stickers, sustained in a cinema fight. Now three girls went to see Frank Kerney, the 16-year-old leader of the Calton Entry gang, to say that Abraham Zemmil of the Stickers challenged him to a fight on the Albert Bridge. For once, instead of all-out warfare the terms were that the battle should be five-a-side. Lining up with Zemmil were Alexander McCaughey and James McCluskey. McCaughey had a sword, as did Kerney. McCluskey, who had a dagger, hit James Tait of the Calton gang supporting Kerney. Kerney and his team then attacked McCluskey, who stabbed Tait in the back.

McCluskey, Zemmil and McCaughey, along with Archibald Gaughan, James Walker and George Stokes, appeared at the Assizes charged with causing the death of Tait. They were between 15 and 17 years old. Unsurprisingly and unfortunately, none of them could explain how Tait had come to be stabbed in the back. The charges against Walker and Gaughan were withdrawn. Zemmil and Stokes each received a year inside. McCaughey, who pleaded guilty to rioting, received eighteen months' imprisonment and McCluskey, who pleaded guilty to mobbing, rioting and culpable homicide (an equivalent to manslaughter), was sentenced to a term of five years.

That was the year when the very powerful Billy Boys were born. There has long been a sectarian element in Glasgow life, let alone street life. For example, the major football clubs in the city were, until the 1980s, conducted on strictly religious lines. Only Catholics played for Celtic; only Protestants for Rangers. The Billy Boys, taking their name from William of Orange, the persecutor of the Irish Catholics and victor at the Battle of the Boyne, faced up to the Norman Conquerors, known as the Norman Conks, who came from Norman Street and were Catholics.

The leader of the Billy Boys was William Fullerton, a fighting man who worked in Gilmours Club in Olympia Street and who tended to leave the thefts undertaken by the gang to other members. The Conks were led by Bill Bowman, who saw the march of the Communist-led National Unemployed Workers' Movement on 19 January 1932 as a splendid way of invading the Boys' territory. Fullerton and his gang diverted the march into Abercrombie Street where rioting took place. In accordance with local tradition, the fines levied were paid for by the local shopkeepers who had already had their plate-glass windows broken.

At one time the eight hundred members of the Billy Boys had membership cards on which a weekly payment of 2d a week was marked. The money, which once totalled £1,200, went into a Bridgeton bank. Even in church the members were armed; in the 1920s Fullerton attended the wedding of one of his gang:

> The bridegroom stood before the minister with a sword concealed in his morning dress. The best man had a gun in his pocket . . . I'll never forget the scene as they left the Church. The gang waiting outside threw bottles instead of confetti.[7]

[7] *Evening Citizen*, 17 January 1955.

Sunday was church parade day, when the Billy Boys would march through their enemies' territory to the Church of Scotland in French Street. Participation in the service was not obligatory for the members who, satisfied with their efforts, returned home. Later, in 1934, Fullerton organized a fife-and-drum band to accompany them on all Catholic Holy Days. The band would march playing Loyalist tunes such as 'The Sash My Father Wore' until they encountered the Conks. The end of these parades came when the Chief Constable, Sir Percy Sillitoe, decided enough was enough. Sillitoe, who had already been responsible for treading with some brutality on the Gavin-Mooney gangs in Sheffield before his move to Scotland, now organized what came to be called Sillitoe's Cossacks.

When one day the band marched towards Celtic Park along Norman Street, two officers ordered them to turn around. As they were brushed aside two police vans emptied officers, armed with long riot batons, on to the streets. The whole band was arrested and charged with assaults and disturbances. Only one of the players escaped injury. According to legend, Elijah Copper dived into his own bass drum and hid there until the fighting had ended.

That was the beginning of the end for the Billy Boys and their eclipse came shortly afterwards when a drunken Fullerton, carrying a three-year-old child, was leading his men towards the Toll Gate. Two police officers tried to remove the child and were pushed aside. They followed the gang at a distance until they saw a Sergeant Tommy Morrison, known as 'Big Tom' from Toll Gate. By now the march was a little over a quarter of a mile away from the Toll Gate police station. The gang was allowed to turn a corner and then Morrison and the two officers intervened. Fullerton, told he was being arrested for being drunk in charge of a child, struck the sergeant who 'drew his baton to defend himself'. Billy Fullerton received twelve months' imprisonment, and when he was released his leadership was over. The Conks, with no Billy Boys to fight, also seem to have gone into decline and pined away.[8]

What Sillitoe optimistically saw as the end of Glasgow gangsterdom as such came in April 1935. John M'Namee, his brother Andrew and a third man, Kennedy, set on a John M'Allister. Andrew M'Namee had an iron bar, the other two had knives. According to Sillitoe, M'Allister said, 'If that is your way, then we will fight it out man to man, one at a time. There are three of you.' M'Namee is said to have answered, 'There are no fair fights here.' A passer-by, Angus Doherty, tried to help M'Allister and was set about by Andrew and his iron bar. Then Charles Smith, outside whose house the fight was taking place, came home from work. He stopped to help Doherty, and as he did so John M'Namee ran back and stabbed him through the shoulder-blade. Smith died instantly.

In the witness-box Doherty was unable to identify his attacker, but not so Mary Smith, the 15-year-old daughter of Charles, waiting and watching for her father's return. John M'Namee received fifteen years' imprisonment for culpable homicide, Andrew M'Namee four and Kennedy three.

Just as he is credited, partly through self-proclamation,

---

[8] In 1939 Billy Fullerton joined the Army and, it seems, served with distinction. Later he worked in a Clydebank shipyard. After his death in 1962 some 600 people followed his coffin, laden with floral tributes including a cushion of marigolds, to Riddrie Cemetery. Massed flute bands played 'Onward, Christian Soldiers' with which his 1930s band had always ended their tour of Catholic territory.

for cleaning up Sheffield, Sillitoe did the same for Glasgow. His technique was simple. John MacLean, a constable for thirty years in the City of Glasgow Police, recalls:

> He got together the biggest and hardest men in the force, and ordered them to go out and batter the living shite out of every Ned who scratched his balls without permission. I'm telling you we didn't have to be asked twice.[9]

When they heard of a gang fight, the technique was now for the police to trundle along in nondescript vans – the aim was certainly not to break it up in advance – watch the participants battle each other and then beat and kick the survivors. As in Sheffield, Sillitoe's conduct in Glasgow has been severely criticized:

> Before long, the batter squads acquired a reputation for violence that was quite as high as that of any of the gangs. But just how effective they were in reducing the number of street battles is open to question: they certainly had *some* effect, but nothing like as much as Sillitoe claimed. It is possible that, in the long term, they gave a sort of seal of approval to acts of violence, for the only apparent difference between them and the gangs was that they were paid to cause physical harm. If the guardians of the law used strong-arm tactics, didn't it show that might was right? Whenever Sillitoe boasted of his success against the people he described as 'unemployable louts', he stated that his purpose was

[9] John MacLean, quoted by Jonathan Goodman and Ian Will in *Underworld*, p.76.

to make them *heed* the law; he never said anything about getting them to *respect* it.[10]

But the gallant Sir Percy was deceiving himself and others if he thought that the M'Namee case was the end of the Glasgow fighting gangs. In reality the continuity of the gangs has survived two World Wars and flourishes today. Rather, it is the chronicling of them that has faded.

Over the years Glasgow juries have proved resistant to convicting men charged with capital murder, and from 1928 to 1946 there was no single person executed. The fights, however, went on.

However, on 20 October 1945 John Patrick Smyth was walking along Argyle Street around 10 p.m., when eight men approached him, asking, 'Where are the Dougie Boys?' Smyth, seeing a bayonet under one of the men's coats, tried to leap on to a passing tram, decided that it was going too slowly, leaped off and ran for it, leaving behind the girls with whom he had been walking. He also left behind 19-year-old John Brady, who had simply been out walking and who had no connection with the Dougie Boys. Brady, who had been discharged from the Navy only four days previously, was stabbed to death. Four men appeared in the North Court in Glasgow charged with his murder; one of them was only seventeen years old at the time, and under the prevailing rule he could not be sentenced to death if the trial ended before his eighteenth birthday. It did not; the jury retired that day. He and two others were convicted, but in the end he and one man were reprieved. Twenty-one-year-old John Lyon was hanged on 9 February 1946 at Barlinnie prison, the first man to go to the scaffold for eighteen years.

[10] Ibid., p.76.

He was, however, soon followed by another fighting man, Patrick 'Carry' Carraher. He had been the fortunate recipient of the benefit of a Glasgow jury's dislike of the death penalty when, in October 1938, he had been acquitted of the murder of a regular soldier, James Shaw. By then Carraher, who would fight without fear using boots, fists or weapons alike, had already racked up eleven convictions including assault, housebreaking and carrying explosives. On 13 August 1938 he had sent a message via a young girl to a prostitute that he wanted her company. She refused to go with him and ran to her protector, James Drurie, on whom Carraher, unused to disobedience, pulled a knife. The men faced each other and then suddenly Carraher turned away.

By chance, they met later that night and again matters might have quietened down until Shaw bravely, if foolishly, butted in and tried to act as a peacemaker. He was unsuccessful. Peter Howard, one of the men who had been with Drurie, told the court: 'Suddenly I heard a scuffle. When I turned around, Carraher had disappeared and Shaw was holding his neck.'

His jugular vein had been slashed and he died on the way to the Royal Infirmary. Howard was taken to the police station and Carraher, when he heard of his arrest, said to a girl: 'I stabbed Shaw – he was very cheeky. But I won't let Howard swing for it. I'll give myself up.'

In fact he didn't. A Detective Sergeant, John Johnson, found him sitting by the fireside in a house in Florence Street in the Gorbals. Carraher had already thrown away the knife.

In what was described at the time as a brilliant defence, Carraher's counsel made much of the fact that in the few seconds before the blow was struck none of the witnesses could actually say what had happened. Carraher received three years for culpable homicide.

Now he rejoiced in the soubriquet 'Killer' and was back in prison in 1943, this time for slashing a man with a razor, for which he received another three years. Two years later he went to the assistance of his brother-in-law, whom he had been told was in a fight at a public house in Rottenrow. There he saw John Gordon, an ex-Seaforth Highlander, who had been captured at Dunkirk and who had recently been released from a prisoner-of-war camp in Germany. Gordon, a bystander, was thought wrongly by Carraher to have been one of his brother's attackers. He cut Gordon behind the left ear, a wound measuring four inches deep. The soldier died almost immediately after he was admitted to the Royal Infirmary. Curiously, it was John Johnson who again found Carraher; this time the man was fast asleep in bed. The blade of Carraher's knife was only two and a half inches long and therefore, said the defence, it could not have caused a four-inch-deep cut. Medical evidence for the prosecution convinced the jury that it could. Carraher's appeal was dismissed and his petition for a reprieve refused. He was hanged at Barlinnie on 6 April 1946 and according to Patrick Meehan, safebreaker and Glasgow hardman who would himself be convicted of murder, fought all the way to the gallows.

After the Second World War the city planners began moving Gorbals' dwellers from that slum to high-rise estates on the edge of the city. One, unintended, effect was for gangs to name themselves after areas rather than mere streets.

In the 1950s there was a youth gang called the Bingo Boys in Govan, but again fighting rather than theft seems to have been their main activity, just as it was in the late 1960s when

James Patrick – the pseudonym of a teacher who, for social research purposes, joined a juvenile fighting gang, the Young Team from Castlemilk – was able to list twenty youth gangs in the city. Several called themselves Tongs as a mark of respect for the old-time Calton Entry or Calton Tongs. But by the end of the 1950s there had already been the Torran Toi, the Bal Toi and the Bar-L (a diminutive of Barlinnie) on the new Easterhouse estate.

According to the writers Goodman and Will, the old-fashioned weapon the cut-throat razor, faced with obsolescence because of an increase in the use of its safety counterpart, was now at a premium. Flick-knives and steel knitting needles were the choice weapons of the time, replacing ice-picks, meat-cleavers and the spud-grenades (potatoes studded with razor-blades) of earlier times.

If there were any lingering hopes that the fighting gangs had disbanded by the 1960s, James Patrick's book should swiftly dispel them. There is also evidence that by now the older members of the gangs had moved into illegal money-lending or loan-sharking, as opposed to say the London and Dublin sport of club and pub protection. Ronald Maxwell wrote:

> Big money for protection of clubs, casinos and book-makers, does not exist in Glasgow. Most gangsters live from illegal money-lending. The interest rate is 4–5/s in the £ per week. So someone who borrows £5 must repay £6 the next week.[11]

Maxwell recounted the story of one man who borrowed £10 and could not keep up the interest payments. He eventually

[11] *Sunday Mirror*, 18 February 1968.

owed £100 after paying back £30. The debt was cancelled on the understanding that he paid £2 per week for life.

Sometimes it was hard to tell whether the accounts by players were genuine and, if they were, should they actually be included in a list of gangs since they clearly saw themselves as 'White Angels'. In 1965, *News of the World* reporter Ron Mount interviewed what could be described as such a band who operated from a fifth-floor office next door to Wendy's Restaurant in West George Street, Glasgow. The decor was bizarre, with a stuffed stag's head in a corner on the floor and a shrunken head on the mantelpiece. Ranged around were a number of ancient guns, spears and daggers. More usefully there was a large tape-recorder. There John Muir Lindsay, Lieutenant in the Royal Marines Reserve, sometime estate agent, sometime insurance claims investigator, ran a commando outfit which promised to do anything required. They had placed an advertisement in the *Sunday Times*;

Have Gun, still travelling. We are a rather unusual firm. Our service is world wide and strictly confidential. In our ranks we have commandos, parachutists, snipers, lawyers and insurance claims investigators. We will go anywhere anytime.

We will try anything. James Bond has nothing on us. If you are a corporation and want a difficult job well done, contact us. If you are an individual with a problem or are in trouble or just plain desperate, drop us a line. It will probably surprise you how we can help. Our fees are – well, let's say it again, depends on how we like the job.

Lindsay told Mount that he had about fifty former officers on call in the UK and 250 agents worldwide. Letters had poured in and the firm had now been going for a year. The requests had included demands to murder the Prime Minister, which they had not taken seriously, and one from three men in Africa who had written about a comrade's dying wishes to find and kill a man who had raped his wife. The woman was still in a mental hospital because of the experience. They had taken this seriously and made inquiries, tracing the man to Israel where it was thought he had already died.

Most of their work, as reported to Mount, seems to have been along the lines of assisting women of whom advantage had been taken following a laced drink to obtain retribution from their violators. One poignant tale concerned a vicar's wife who many years earlier had had an illegitimate child. Now quite by chance the father turned up in the town and recognized her. He required her to submit to him every Friday afternoon and, Lindsay told Mount:

> . . . after a few weeks of hell she wrote to us. We sent two lads who told the man that unless he left her alone we would deal with him and his own mother would not recognise him afterwards. That stopped him and his nasty little game.

In Lindsay's pile of mail the morning Mount interviewed him was a letter from a 'distraught father who alleged his daughter was being kept in a Home Counties' convent against her will'. The man had enclosed a map of the place, asking Lindsay and his men to raid it and kidnap her.[12]

And if that seems just too fantastic to believe, think now

[12] *News of the World*, 16 June 1965.

of the retrieval and the subsequent de-programming of children who have joined the Moonies and other out-of-the way sects.

The year 1967 saw the break-up of the definitely serious Tallymen. The violence which led to the demise of that gang began on 14 July, Glasgow Fair week. A pimp, 'Babs' Rooney – who had fallen behind with his repayments – and Sadie Cairney were celebrating the Fair in Kinning Park when Rooney was knifed to death over the £7 debt. James 'Babyface' Boyle and William Wilson, brother of the gang boss Frank 'Tarzan' Wilson, were charged. Jimmy Boyle received life imprisonment, with a recommendation that he serve fifteen years' minimum for the murder. Wilson was found not guilty of Rooney's murder but received twenty-one months for theft and assault.

Later that year Frank 'Tarzan' Wilson, along with his chauffeur John 'Bandit' Rooney and the crooked Glasgow lawyer, James Latta, were jailed for a total of twenty-four years for plotting to have the two men freed. All three were found guilty of inducing people to give false evidence at the trial of Boyle and William Wilson. Frank Wilson, who had wanted to do better than be a simple loan-shark – to further his education he had borrowed books from the public library on Sicily and the Mafia – was jailed for twelve years and Rooney for four. The third man in the dock, James Latta, had been on a retainer from the gang; he was a frequenter of the Hi-Hi bar in the Gorbals where he discussed the fabrication of alibis, bribery and the suborning of witnesses and the jury. The gang had not been wholly successful in their efforts in the Boyle-Wilson case, although Sadie Cairney left the witness-box at the High Court saying she was in fear of her life, and a bomb exploded in the front room of another witness, 15-year-old Eddie McGill, in Hutcheson Town

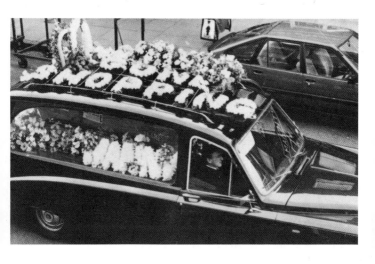

Goodbye to:

Shirley Pitts
(above)

Arthur Thompson
(below)
(*Glasgow Herald and Evening Times*)

Goodbye to:

David Brindle
(above)
(*Martin Goodwin*)

Lee Duffy
(below)
(*North News and Pictures*)

The end of:

Jimmy Moody
(above)
(*S&G Press*)

Thomas Roche
(below)
(*Topham*)

**The six faces of
Howard Marks**
(above)
(*Enterprise News*)

**Billy Hill attends
the funeral of
Billy Blythe**
(right)
(*Hulton Deutsch*)

**Martin Cahill,
the man they called
the General
(and who denied it)**
(Russell Banks)

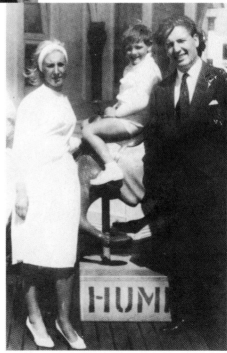

**Family man:
'Mad' Frank Fraser and
family**
(S&G Press)

**Another family: Jack Spot
and Rita**
(*Syndication International*)

**A flashback to the days
of the Sabinis:
Joseph Jackson**

Court. Before sentencing Latta the trial judge, Lord Grant, commented that he believed because of the lawyer's activities the administration of justice in Glasgow had been seriously compromised over a long period.

The demise of the gang soon followed. With the leaders gone, the police were able to make swift and considerable inroads into the affairs of the Tallymen who apart from their six-for-five loan-sharking had been into safe-breaking and extortion. Owners of businesses in the financial district of the city had been pleased to pay protection money rather than go to the expense of having the aerosol paint removed from their office façades. Said one Scottish judge:

> Crime in Glasgow is dominated by money-lending. It is an unspoken theme. These so-called motiveless crimes – slashings and beatings – are not motiveless at all. The victim is very often in debt and he is trying to dodge the column. The last thing he'll do is go to the police and tell the real story.

James Boyle's earlier career was in the best tradition of the Glasgow hardmen. His father had been one of Peter Williamson's lieutenants in the pre-war Beehive Gang, and before the Rooney stabbing James Boyle had accumulated a formidable record of assault both on the police and civilians. He attended St Bonaventure's school, from which eight former pupils were serving life sentences in the 1970s, and almost all of the old boys at that time had, at the very least, been on probation. Between 1965 and the 1970s he was acquitted of one murder and the charge in another case was dropped. The police had had considerable difficulty in obtaining witnesses. In two cases, parcels of gelignite had been dropped through their letterboxes.

It was never expected that Boyle would be a model prisoner, and at first he kept up his reputation. Within a year he had eighteen months added to his sentence for assault on a prison officer, and in October 1967 he received a further four years for attacking two more officers. In 1973 he was acquitted of the murder of a fellow inmate in Porterfield. The same year he was one of several prisoners convicted of attacking prison officers, for which he received another six years consecutive to his existing sentence. Amongst the cognoscenti he was not thought to be likely to live out the initial sentence anyway; he had received a beating from the Porterfield batter-squad of prison officers and it was believed that another bad beating would do for him. Even if it did not, he was always at risk from another inmate from a rival gang.

Then came the transformation scene. Boyle was selected to be sent to an experimental unit in Barlinnie where he was encouraged to indulge in 'self-examination, self-awareness and self-expression'. Given a knife for wood-carving, he never abused his privilege. A prison visitor Sarah Trevelyan, daughter of Sir John, the former film censor, married him during the latter part of his imprisonment. He was released in the early 1980s and has subsequently spent much of his time in social work with young people. On Friday 13 May 1994, Boyle's son, twenty-seven-year-old James Boyle junior, was found dead from stab wounds near a tenement block in the Oatlands district of Glasgow. Police refused to comment on suggestions that local people had complained of drug dealing in the area.

It turned out, as so often is the case, to be a domestic matter. In October 1994 Gary Moore, described as one of Scotland's most violent criminals, was sentenced to eight years' imprisonment for the culpable homicide of Boyle.

Both had had a relationship with Janice McEnery. At first she had been Moore's girlfriend but when they separated she took up with James Boyle. On the night of Boyle's death Moore was staying with Janice whilst on home leave from a sentence of armed robbery. Boyle had been warned to stay away but came to the house. Moore ran downstairs and stabbed him through the heart. In court Moore said he thought Boyle was pulling a gun on him. He claimed that Boyle ran forward and accidentally impaled himself on the knife.

Moore had been charged with murder in connection with the Ice-Cream War, and in 1991 with the murder of Diane McInally, whose body was found in Pollok Park, Glasgow but on both occasions the charges had been dropped

The decline and fall of one gang is exemplified by the Y Y Shamrock (Young Young Shamrock) which could boast about 150 members in 1968. One boy said he joined because he couldn't walk in town without being attacked. Now the YYS were on top of the pile with Real Mental Shamrock, the parent group (note the same structure of the Crips and Bloods in Los Angeles, with its ranking organization). The Shamrock gang, or 'team' as it was called by its members, began as the Emeralds Football club which failed through apathy.[13]

By 1968, of the original founders of the Shamrocks eight years earlier, two were serving life, one six years for attempted murder, another member three years for attempted murder; three were in prison for a serious assault, and three were detained at Her Majesty's pleasure. Their arch-enemies were the Fleet from Maryhill. A Fleet member was killed and the Fleet grassed the Shamrock,

[13] Ken Martin, *Observer*, 1 December 1968.

hence the sentences and a perfectly good reason for the continuance of warfare but, as Voltaire might have said, if reasons did not exist they would have been invented.[14]

A total of eighty-three years' imprisonment was handed out by Lord Cameron following the attempted murder of 17-year-old John Muir who strayed into a fight between the Spur and the Nunny gangs. There was a shout of 'get that one' and a blade was put through Muir's arm. William Donnelly received twelve years' detention and another youth the same. He had convictions for theft, attempted housebreaking and attempting to pervert the course of justice. After this incident, whilst on bail, he had been in trouble again. By the early 1970s the once powerful Shamrock Gang had gone, according to Glasgow's Assistant Chief Constable, William Ratcliffe.

By now it was thought that there were probably about twenty-five gangs in the city, each with a hard core of six or seven boys. Glasgow was rated the most violent city in the United Kingdom, and ranked among the six most violent in the world in company with Mexico City, New York, Chicago, Palermo and Bogota.

A short-lived gang flourished briefly in the autumn of 1969, and they were certainly not boys. Two of the four were ex-Glasgow police officers. On 16 July 1969, dressed as businessmen, they were each carrying a briefcase before they reached the doors of the British Linen Bank in Williamswood, Renfrewshire. There they put on nylon masks and held up the staff, blindfolding and tying them all up except the manager who was forced to open the safe and hand over £21,000.

Three of them tried again on 30 December 1969, and this

---

[14] *News of the World*, 24 June 1968.

time successfully robbed the Clydesdale Bank in Bridge Street, Linwood of £14,212 which they put into two suitcases. They also took a quantity of silver and this they put in a metal box. It was as they reached safety, the flat in Allison Street where Howard Wilson (who had served ten years in the force) lived, that they were approached by Police Inspector Andrew Hyslop. He had recognized Wilson, seen the box and along with Constable John Sellars went over to investigate. By the time they went into the back court of the flats Wilson had disappeared. Hyslop called for reinforcements and met Wilson again in Allison Street. The man denied having a box or suitcase and Hyslop asked if he could search the flat. There in the living-room were the two suitcases full of money. He went to look for the box, could not find it and returned to the front room where Wilson shot him at point-blank range, taking away most of the left-hand side of his face. He also shot through the head Constable Edward Barnett, who had joined the search, and Acting Detective Constable McKenzie who was shot a second time whilst he was on the ground. One officer locked himself in the lavatory to use his mobile radio to call for assistance and another, Detective Constable John Campbell, with enormous courage, tackled Wilson, knocking him to the ground and capturing the gun. A second robber in the flat took no part in the shooting and a third escaped only to be retrieved later.

Wilson accepted full responsibility for the shooting. There was no question of joint enterprise, so although at first charges of the murder of DC Barnett were preferred against the other two men, it was accepted they should only stand trial on the charges of robbery. Each received twelve years' imprisonment. Wilson received life, with a twenty-five-year minimum recommendation. The fourth man at the

July raid was never found; the police had reason to believe he was dead.[15]

Nor were Walter Norval and his team, known as Norval's Criminal Syndicate, by any means a boy's gang. For a time he was at least one of the Kings of the Glasgow Underworld. In November 1977 he and eleven others stood trial for a series of armed robberies. The trial was delayed when the Glasgow High Court building was damaged by petrol bombs; it was thought the attack had been carried out by supporters of the team with the aim of destroying the documentary evidence against them. Norval's daughter was charged with conspiracy to destroy the building, but was acquitted.

Again the case was surrounded with accusations of witness intimidation. Norval's son-in-law was sentenced to five years' imprisonment for threatening to kill a man who was due to give evidence against Walter. A leading prosecution witness, although kept under guard and in solitary confinement, had scalding water thrown over him. Round-the-clock surveillance was provided for the jurors and an armed bodyguard for the judge and prosecuting counsel.

Norval received the modest sentence of fourteen years. At least it was modest in comparison with those meted out to the Workers' Party of Scotland some five years earlier (see p.73). The Norval trial did not break the gang; the remaining members recruited suitable candidates to fill the temporary vacancies.

Shortly after the Workers' Party of Scotland had been broken up with heavy prison sentences, there was a

[15] Joe Beltrami gives a full account of the legal aspects of the case in his *The Defender*, pp.125 et seq.

straightforward criminal enterprise, an armed robbery, which went tragically wrong. On 21 December 1973 a team of robbers stole £20,000 from the British Engineering works in Charles Street, Townhead, Glasgow and when tackled by Jim Kennedy, a security guard, a member of the gang shot him in the stomach. The Glasgow police learned the men were travelling back to London.

In theory it had been a well-planned job organized by Robert Marley at the Railway Tavern in Cowlairs. He had anticipated that the take, swollen by Christmas bonus pay packets, would be over £50,000. He approached James Aitken and in turn they recruited heavies including Steve Doran and Jim Murphy. Murphy then contacted two more young men, Sid Draper and Alan Brown. Members of the squad travelled to Glasgow from London and met on Friday 21 December.

Equipped with high-powered binoculars and a two-way radio, Aitken stayed in a multi-storey car park which commanded a view of the works' yard. Brown, Murphy, Marley and Draper, together with another man, armed with two sawn-off shotguns, an automatic pistol and two pistols, hid themselves by the entrance. As other security guards began transferring money boxes from the strongroom to a fork-lift truck Aitken gave the signal. The fork-lift driver was squirted with ammonia and both guards were shot in the arm and back. Jim Kennedy ran to challenge the robbery, was clubbed to the ground and tried once more to prevent the theft. This time he was shot.

The gang was traced because one of its members had mentioned the name 'Big Jim' on the raid. An anonymous caller provided another name. Glasgow police travelled to London to mount a joint operation with London officers led by Detective Chief Superintendent Jack Slipper (who later chased Ronnie Biggs, the Train Robber, to Brazil). They staked out the flat of Robert Marley's girlfriend and he was arrested within hours. He soon made an eleven-page statement giving details of the preparation for the crime; the gang had held what amounted to board meetings to determine in what way the robbery should be carried out, and whether they should have guns.

Within twenty-four hours all but one of the robbers had been arrested; the last was arrested some weeks later in Brighton. The team received a total of 119 years. Brown received a life sentence with a twenty-five-year minimum recommendation. Steve Doran's brother Ian had already been jailed the previous year for twenty-five years for the more politically motivated bank robberies of the Workers' Party. The police believed that they had been part of a 'travel anywhere' Robbery Inc. whose other members had carried out robberies including one in Dundee (£11,000 from the Royal Bank of Scotland) and another in Erskine, Renfrewshire, where bank raiders had taken £2,000, as well as at least one other robbery in Glasgow.[16]

One of the great Glasgow gang wars took place in the 1980s, culminating in the murder of six members of the Doyle family including an 18-month-old baby in April 1984 when the door of their flat at 29 Bankend Street was soaked

---

[16] There is a full account of the police work leading to the arrest of the men in J. Slipper, *Slipper of the Yard*, Chapter 10. Draper escaped from Gartree prison by helicopter on 10 December 1987. Andrew Russell had hi-jacked the helicopter and forced the pilot to land in the prison's exercise yard. Draper and 38-year-old John Kendall climbed aboard and escaped. The helicopter was obliged to put down in poor weather on a nearby industrial estate and the men held up car drivers to get clear of the area. Draper was later caught in Enfield, North London.

in petrol and then fired.[17] The war was over territorial rights to ice-cream concessions. Much of the post-war troubles in Glasgow originated in the housing schemes. There had been a policy to shift the Inner City slums to the outskirts and building had commenced by the beginning of the Second World War but had then been suspended. One of these was Carntyre in the East End. Unfortunately the building work was not always of the highest quality. The houses and flats were invaded by rot; on the other hand the allotments bloomed. It was here and on estates like it throughout Scotland and the rest of the country that the mobile ice-cream van flourished.

The ice-cream – like the hot-dog – trade has always attracted competition, and not infrequently violent competition. Traditionally, the tricks employed to temporarily disable the opposition have been at a fairly low level such as squirting raspberry flavouring on to a rival's windscreen or stopping either directly in front of or behind a rival and so creating instant competition. Extreme examples could, however, include putting nails under a van's tyres. Fights between rival drivers were not all that infrequent. Other ploys adopted to deter or maim the competition were for drivers to damage their own vans and then report the incident as criminal damage by their rivals.

Youths could be hired for a few pounds or even a drink to carry out an attack on the opposition, and it was not unknown for a driver to pay someone to threaten him in the presence of a witness so that the matter could be reported to the police. This could then be stored up as a

---

[17] There is a very full account of the case, and comprehensive analysis is put forward as to why the convictions were unsafe, in Douglas Skelton and Lisa Brownlie's *Frightener*.

kind of goodwill with the police against the day when allegations would be made against that driver.

In Dundee there was considerable trouble between rival van owners and drivers, whilst Edinburgh had introduced a licensing system based on zones. A driver found in the wrong zone could lose his licence. The Glasgow Council knew of the ice-cream troubles and in the 1970s did have some control over them, but this lapsed with the Civil Government (Scotland) Act 1982. Glasgow estates became an open city, with escalating violence being used to increase the market share. The violence which followed has been ascribed to a war over the drug trade, but in their book Douglas Skelton and Lisa Brownlie maintain that this particular quarrel in 1983–4 had nothing to do with drugs but was purely and simply over the profit which could be made – £200 a week more or less tax-free, or up to £800 if the driver sold stolen cigarettes and soft drink – on a lucrative van round.

Drivers could either be owners of their vans and pay the ice-cream distributors such as Fifti Ices for garaging space, or lease the van on a weekly basis. The big companies which offered this facility included the Marchetti brothers, who were connected by marriage to Fifti Ices.

Instead of a squirt of strawberry on the windscreen, or deflated tyres, the early 1980s saw the use of the baseball bat, then firearms and finally the petrol bomb. The troubles were not between the owners of Marchetti (although it was their vans which suffered) and Fifti, but between the drivers. By the end of 1983 vans operating in the Garthamlock area would return to their depot with the windows and headlights smashed, as did the vans which lodged at Fifti. By then it was on a twice-weekly basis. Helpers were recruited and Andrew 'Fat Boy' Doyle was given a

**Eugenio Messina arrives
handcuffed to a police escort at the start
of his trial in Belgium**
(*Associated Press*)

Albert Dimes celebrates his acquittal in the Jack Spot case (above) (*Topham*)

Arthur Thompson, **the 'king of Glasgow'** (right) (*Glasgow Herald and Evening Times*)

Marchetti van rent-free to try to run the opposition off the road.

The first use of firearms in what came to be known as the ice-cream wars seems to have occurred around 8 p.m. on 29 February 1984, when shots were fired at driver Doyle and his 15-year-old assistant Anne Wilson as they made the rounds in Garthamlock. A shotgun was fired by a man who had climbed out of a Volvo car and the pellets broke the windscreen of Doyle's van. Earlier that month there had been an attempt to set fire to the Marchetti building in Glentanar Road.

The attacks continued throughout the month and in the middle of March a police sergeant who knew the warring drivers spoke to James Mitchell, a Marchetti man, and Agnes Lafferty and Tony Capuano (Fifti Ices). Marchetti would agree to nothing except an unconditional surrender in the shape of the withdrawal of Fifti Ices from Garthamlock. Lafferty and Capuano said that although they would not be frightened away, if Mitchell would agree to a compromise they would. Unfortunately, as it turned out, the name of a major Glasgow hardman was mentioned by Agnes' brother Thomas who was with her. The name was Thomas Campbell known as 'TC' – partly because those were his initials, partly because he wore steel-capped Big T boots, but also after the cartoon character 'Top Cat.' The last thing wanted, said Lafferty, was for 'TC' to be involved.

Campbell was the brother of one of the Marchetti drivers, Sadie, who was paying protection money. If she gave credit it was never repaid; if she refused credit her van was attacked. Campbell was a genuine Glasgow hardman who ran the Goucho gang with a razor of iron. He was sentenced to ten years for mobbing and rioting after a fight in a car park at a Glasgow dog-track. After his release he associated with the Barlanark Team, which then numbered about forty and worked in groups 'tanning' or robbing post offices and cash-and-carries throughout Scotland. He was acquitted of complicity in a prison-break from Barlinnie in 1980. Escapers included John and James Steele, the brother of Joseph who would stand trial with Campbell for the Doyle murders. Later Campbell bought a van with his wife Liz and worked the route. Attacks continued both ways and spread to an attack on a Viking Ices van in Castlemilk, an area also used by Fifti Ices drivers. In one incident a van operated by two girls was attacked and a minder, John Shepherd, travelling in it was stabbed.

The fire occurred at 2 a.m. on 16 April, the night – as many of the witnesses recalled over the years – Tommy Cooper died on television. During it or shortly afterwards Christine Halleron, Anthony Doyle (aged 14), Mark Halleron (aged 18 months), James Doyle junior, Andrew Doyle and James Doyle died. Stephen Doyle jumped with his dog from a window, Lilian Doyle was rescued from a window-ledge. Daniel Doyle survived when he managed to get his head out of a broken window and so avoided inhaling the fumes.

There were two possible eyewitnesses to the fire-raisers. One, John Whitefield, described four young fellows aged 15–16 running past him, and another said he thought he might recognize the men involved. Neither was asked to attend an identification parade.

At first the police considered whether the fire might have been started because of the Doyle brothers' work in the nightclubs, where they were thought to have upset punters. However, slowly but surely they hardened on the theory that it was to do with the ice-cream wars. They came to this conclusion in part because as Andrew Doyle lay in the ambulance in Bankend Street he said to a police officer, 'I told you the bastards would torch me. If this is because of the ice-cream hassle I'll get the bastards.' Apparently on an earlier occasion he had said to the same policeman, 'Look, they've battered me, shot me, all I'm waiting on now is the petrol bomb.' The officer duly reported the second conversation to a superior.

The first man arrested to confess was Joe Grainger, who admitted that he, Thomas Campbell and others had been keeping clock, or look-out, whilst Joseph Steele and others actually started the fire. He retracted his evidence at the trial and as a result served five years for his pains and perjury. He appealed successfully to the European Court of Human Rights, which ruled that he had not had a fair trial, but the Scottish Office took no action. The second plank of evidence on which the prosecution would base its case was that of Billy Love, who said he had been in the Netherfield bar when Thomas Campbell had asked for volunteers to firebomb the Doyle household. Steele had been with them.

The other evidence against Steele and Campbell amounted to little more than one sentence of verbal admissions. Campbell was alleged to have said that he intended the fire only to be a frightener, whilst Steele had said it wasn't he who had lit the match. A further piece of supporting evidence was the finding of a map in a briefcase belonging to Campbell which circled Bankfield Street and marked the Doyle flat with a cross. Steele and Campbell supporters point out that there was no need for their clients to have such a map: they both lived in the area and knew it like the backs of their hands. Steele's alibi was that he was home in bed with the flu; his mother was his witness. Campbell said he had been watching a video with his wife, Liz. Both men were convicted. Campbell received a life sentence with a recommendation that he serve at least twenty years. Steele's sentence carried no recommendation.

After the trial the press had a field day. After all, here were two men both of whose families had been involved in heavy gang crime in Glasgow for years. There were suggestions that instead of raspberry ripple in the cones there had been heroin at £10 a bag, something which had not been mentioned at the trial. It is a claim which Campbell fervently denies. The fighting between Fifti Ices and March-etti did not end with the convictions. There were even allegations, again denied, that Campbell was controlling things from his cell.

Since the trial there have been persistent attempts to re-open the case. Billy Love has from time to time changed his story back and forth. In the latest version given to a BBC journalist in 1993 on his release from Dartmoor, he said, 'I couldn't even ask Thomas Campbell or Joe Steele to forgive me for what they've been through. I know I've shortened their lives.' Campbell has said he will neither shave nor cut his hair until his release. Filmed in Barlinnie prison, he spoke bitterly of the Serious Crime Squad which he called the Serious Fit-Up Squad. 'They're called in to assess of all villains in the area who has the least defence. Then if they've no alibi or only one witness they'll do.' Steele has escaped three times, once glueing himself to the railings at Buck-ingham Palace. On his last escape on 25 May 1993 he spoke to the BBC reporter, saying that although he was now nearly eligible for parole he would not apply. 'Only guilty men take parole.' He surrendered by climbing a scaffolding tower in front of the prison, staying there for an hour to be filmed by the press.

The chances of either Campbell or Steele winning their hoped-for re-trial are slim. Two of the senior officers in the case are dead; one committed suicide shortly after the case. All they can hope for is a pardon, or that the case will be referred back to the Court of Appeal. One of the defence counsel in the case who referred to the evidence brought against the men as 'rotten to the core' is now an Appeal Court judge, and the men and their supporters hope he will somehow intervene on their behalf. One difficulty regarding Love's retraction is, as a Scots lawyer put it, 'Technically it is not what the Appeal Court would base any decision on. They have said before they will not entertain an appeal merely because a witness changes his story.'

Steele believes that unless he wins a re-trial he will only leave prison in a box. 'If I don't win my case, I don't think I'll get out.'

In March 1992 a man who had a genuine claim to be the King of Glasgow's Gangland, possibly even that of Britain, died peacefully. Arthur Thompson, who had survived countless attacks and attempts on his life, died of a heart attack. The weekend before his death he had been out dancing with his wife and friends. Perhaps of all Glasgow hardmen he could be said to have been a genuine Gangland Boss in the old traditional style. His lawyer, Joe Beltrami, who said that Thompson had 'gun-metal eyes', wrote:

> [Thompson] was an impressive-looking figure – about five feet ten inches tall and weighing about 12 stones. He was well-built, in a not-so-obvious way – his suits were well-cut and sober, his ties and shirts conservative. Distinguished-looking and slightly older than I, his face displayed small marks of by-gone conflicts. He had more acquittals to his name than most.[18]

[18] J. Beltrami, *A Deadly Innocence*, pp.58–9.

Thompson was born in 1931, the year of the introduction of
the Means Test. His parents lived in a tenement in Glasgow's North Side and were eventually rehoused in Blackhill. His brothers became barmen-cum-bouncers in the
Provanmill Inn near the family home, but Thompson
himself had greater ambition; he wished to be a landlord
and not merely a bouncer. His efforts to acquire the
necessary capital foundered when he and Paddy Meehan,
a noted peterman who had learned his trade with the
legendary Johnny Ramensky, blew the safe at the Commercial Bank in Beauly, Inverness-shire.[19] The raid was not
a success. The bank contained five safes, one of which
housed a sixth. There was little in them except for documents and £400. On the way back to Glasgow they stopped
for petrol and the garage owner took the number of the
Humber Snipe because it was 'not the sort of car one usually
associates with such men'. They were further out of luck, for
the key to Thompson's house was found in the road where
he had dropped it on leaving the bank. Meehan, convicted
on a majority verdict, was sentenced to six years and
Thompson to half that.

In the 1950s and 1960s he built up a reputation as a

[19] Ramensky, Glasgow-born of Lithuanian parents, was a bril-
liant cracksman. He was employed behind enemy lines during the
Second World War and awarded a Distinguished Conduct Medal.
Another safebreaker used in the war was the Englishman Eddie
Chapman, later a close friend of Billy Hill. Glasgow has always
had a tradition of providing class safebreakers. In *Life Begins at
Midnight*, p.85, Colquhoun wrote, 'Petermen are commonplace in
Glasgow. In fact, if I was asked to name the type of specialist
criminal most often produced by the city, I'd plump for the
safeblower. There's a strong suggestion that a school for safe-
blowers, where novices can learn their trade from experts, has
more than once been organised in the city.'

hardman dealing with villains such as Gorbals street baron, Teddy Martin – described as having the Italian looks which drove women wild, and a ferocious temper – who was shot on 25 March 1961, and Algie Earns who was beaten up at Glasgow Cross. Both had run protection rackets involving clubs, pubs and street bookies.

Thompson was described by Meehan as:

> . . . at least as tough [as Martin] and one of the most single-minded men I have ever known. He is happily married, dotes on his children, and never drinks anything stronger than a bottle of beer. He is, however, not a man to cross . . . Both Teddy [Miller] and Mac-Tampson were quite capable of cool, extreme violence but, I hasten to add, only within a very strict set of rules. Neither, for instance, would attack an ordinary member of the public, either on a job or in one of the pub brawls which are not an uncommon feature of Glasgow life. Neither would countenance violence towards a woman, or to a man whose womenfolk were present. But they were leading members of a very hard society and would protect their position in that society with any force they considered necessary. Other criminals who 'crossed' them did so at their peril. An insult, delivered to them personally, or to a friend, would be quickly and forcefully avenged.[20]

Thompson had had an uneasy relationship with Martin for some years and the shooting seems to have been over an

[20] P. Meehan, *Innocent Villain*, Chapters 3, 4 and 5. Thompson is described as MacTampson. Teddy Miller appears under his own name. For the prison break Meehan received fifteen months; Thompson was never charged.

initial suggestion that Thompson was tight with his money. This was rather harsh since Thompson had, in part and along with Meehan, engineered Martin's escape from Peterhead prison in 1954, which had been the first successful escape from the jail. Meehan and John Harvey collected Martin when he came over the wall, whilst Thompson put up a diversionary scheme. He arranged for prison clothing to be smuggled out of Barlinnie and had it marked with Martin's Peterhead number. Once Martin was out of prison and in fact drinking in a nearby hotel, he made an anonymous call to the police telling them that the man was hiding in a loft at Blackhill. It was there the police found the clothing and presumed he must already be in Glasgow. Now Martin was safe to take the road from the Highlands to home, secure in the knowledge that there would be no police blocks on the way.

The quarrel was over the financing of a robbery at the Westminster Bank at the junction of the City Road and Old Street in London. The idea had been promoted by a London criminal and was to be a safeblowing. Meehan and Martin had been down in London reconnoitring the situation, and had expended a certain amount of money on the enterprise. Thompson was due to go on the raid with them and, as a full partner, was expected by Martin to put up his share of the capital required for the expenses. When he produced a £100 note in a public house, Martin changed tack and suggested that Thompson was trying to set them up, a far worse insult. The implication was that a £100 note, rare at the time, could have come from a robbery and therefore its serial number could be traced if Martin tried to cash it. A week before the robbery was due to take place, Thompson shot Martin in Meehan's flat.

Meehan's wife Betty, who was nine months' pregnant,

ran into the room. Now, according to the code of the Samurai, Martin, who was bleeding heavily, could not be touched again. The standard practice would have been for him to be given a coaxy (or piggy-back), put in a van and dumped. Instead Meehan called an ambulance and Martin was taken to hospital in a coma.

The next day he was, however, fighting fit and so far as he was concerned the robbery could go ahead. Thompson was clearly out and so another Glasgow safebreaker was recruited. The robbery was a disaster; Martin and the second man were caught *in flagrante* when an office worker heard the safe blown. Meehan escaped only to look around for another job. The London contact Billy suggested that a Co-op store in Edmonton would be suitable. Meehan appears to have been reluctant but the job went ahead and, at the last minute, Meehan was persuaded to actually blow the safes. He was standing over them unpacking dynamite, of which far too liberal a use had been made, when the police walked in. Billy received five years and Meehan eight. Meehan believed he had been grassed by the woman, Sheila, with whom he had been staying.

Thompson had effectively been apprenticed to bookmaker and gambler, Mendel Morris, who also had an interest in nightclubs, betting offices and casinos for which at the time only a drinks licence was necessary. He became a partner and when Morris retired to England Thompson took over. He rarely served a sentence. In 1951 he received three years for assault and robbery, in 1953 eighteen months for extortion, and in 1955 three years for the Beauly bank. From the 1950s he maintained links with English criminals. He was a friend of Billy Hill, and visited Frank Fraser when he was in prison serving seven years for the attack on rival gangleader Jack Spot.

When Robert 'Andy' Anderson escaped (rather by chance with Ronnie Biggs, the Train Robber) and appeared on the doorstep of Atlantic Machines, run in Tottenham Court Road by Eddie Richardson and Francis Fraser, looking for assistance, it was to Thompson that Fraser turned for help. Within forty-eight hours Thompson met Fraser and Anderson in Edinburgh and found the escapee work for a period of months until Fraser arranged for Anderson to move south to Manchester to join Bobby McDermott.

Fraser recalls admiringly:

There was a lot of trade between Glasgow and London; a lot of help and friendship. If a Scottish fellow was in London who needed help we'd put him up. It was a two-way thing but it showed the strength of the friendship. You wouldn't get too many people who could get on the phone and ask if they could put up someone who had escaped doing 12 years. Not only that, he'd escaped with Biggs. They never blinked an eyelid. The answer immediately was 'Yes'. It was not for financial gain. They wouldn't take one penny.

But it was over his twenty-five-year-long war that he and his family had with the powerful Welsh family, also from Blackhill – five times as long as the London feud between the Brindles and the Carters – that Thompson really made his mark. First, Patrick Welsh and his friend James Goldie died when their van hit a wall and then a lamp-post. Thompson was charged with causing their deaths by running them off the road and was acquitted after the jury retired for rather less than an hour. The original charge of murder had been reduced to one of unjustifiable homicide.

Three months later Thompson and his mother-in-law, Maggie Johnstone, climbed into his MG parked outside his house in Provanmill Road. When he started the car there was an explosion; she was killed, he was injured. Three of the Welshes were later acquitted. In July 1967 Rita Thompson went to prison after admitting leading a raid on the Welsh family's home. The police, if not actually frightened, were certainly wary of Thompson. One senior officer evacuated his family from his home during the prosecution for the deaths of Welsh and Goldie, fearing it would be bombed. Another officer emigrated after the case.

Through his son Arthur Jr, known as the Fat Boy, and some of his London contacts, Thompson reluctantly moved into drugs, operating from a base in Blackpool. But by the end of the 1980s attempts to overthrow him were coming thick and fast. In November 1989 he was shot whilst washing his car in front of a lock-up garage. He booked himself into the private Nuffield Alpine Clinic and told police and the doctor who removed the bullet that he had injured himself with a drill bit which had sheared off during use. Three years later he was run down outside his council house home which by now he had converted into something like a luxury fortress – two houses knocked into one, and heavily barricaded with steel doors. Again he survived.

Arthur Jr did not survive, however. Drugs proved to be his downfall. In 1985 he went to prison for eleven years on heroin dealing charges. The case was a curious one and until his death the Fat Boy maintained his innocence, claiming he had been framed by a Jonah McKenzie. For a time Arthur Jr was able to demand a cut from his team, the Barlanark Gang, but he was by no means a popular leader and a rival organization was in place within the year. Although he may have assisted his son, Arthur Snr was no more anxious to join him in the drug trade than the Godfather, Don Corleone, had been keen to join Sollazo. Thompson firmly denied that his daughter Margaret had died from a drugs overdose in June 1989. Instead it was put about that she had choked to death on her own vomit after a drinking bout. Her drug addict boyfriend fled Scotland. Nevertheless, Thompson loyally protected his son against drug-dealing allegations, maintaining that the Fat Boy had been framed by the police. 'The trouble for young Arthur has been that the cops have long memories,' he told the *Sunday Times*. 'When they couldn't get me they took my son.'

By 1991 it was estimated that up to £200,000 a week was being generated in gang money by the manufacture, supply and distribution of cheap drugs. But so far as the Fat Boy was concerned he was isolated when the gang fractured. His percentage had dried up. Meanwhile, a hand-grenade had been thrown into a public house where the Barlanark team once drank. Before he came out on home leave as part of a parole plan in 1991, he vowed to kill the five men he said had ripped off his earnings. The circumstances of his death were curious. Released on weekend home leave after serving some seven years of his sentence, he arranged to have a meal with his sister in an Italian restaurant. Although the house in which he lived was part of Thompson's fortress, the Fat Boy apparently took no great protective measures for his safety. Almost at the last minute the venue was changed and he went to Café India, a smart Indian restaurant in the centre of the city, with his mother and common-law wife, Catherine. Shortly before he arrived at the restaurant a man, later said to be a Paul Ferris, had approached the manager, asked if there was a Thompson there and insisted on searching the dining area with its two hundred plus customers before he was satisfied there was not. After his meal Thompson returned to the fortress, had a word with his father, and then walked to the end house to check whether his brother, Billy, was recording a film on the video set. He rang the bell and a woman in the house, who went to the door, sensed something was wrong. She saw the Fat Boy staggering away, shot. One bullet had grazed his cheek, one fractured two ribs and the third hit his heart. His last words were, 'I've been shot, hen.[21] I'm going to collapse.' The family did not wait for an ambulance but drove him to hospital where he was found to be dead on arrival.

The police and Arthur Thompson had various theories about the killers. From the point of view of the police, the killing must have smelled of an inside job. Who knew at which restaurant Arthur would be? Or when he would return home? Would outsiders really linger outside the well-protected house awaiting his return? Could a message have been sent to them from the time he left the restaurant?

Now, say Underworld acquaintances, it was the moment for Thompson to show who really was the master. As his son's cortège went to the graveyard it passed a car in which the bodies of the two men Joe 'Bananas' Hanlon and Robert Glover, suspected of Arthur junior's killing and shot in the head with a .22 pistol, had been left. Overall, Hanlon had not led a lucky life. A car he owned had been blown up, his ice-cream van from which he also sold heroin had been torched and he had been shot on two occasions, once in the penis.

Stephen Guy, a friend of the Fat Boy, had been charged over the torching of the van but was acquitted. However, Guy's troubles did not end there. Within the week shots had

---

[21] A term of endearment sometimes used ironically.

been fired at his house and a lodger Robert Johnstone, who had nothing at all to do with Guy, was hit in the neck.

The obligatory police swoop on Fortress Thompson, real name Southfork, over the deaths of Hanlon and Glover, came to nothing. The family was arrested, released and returned to what was now a compound kitted out with surveillance cameras and floodlighting.

In 1992, after a trial lasting fifty-four days, a third man, Paul Ferris, suspected of being one of Thompson junior's murderers, was acquitted. The thread of the case – possibly not the best ever handled by the prosecution – was that all three men had been involved in the killing. It may be that the prosecution had followed, too closely, Arthur Thompson's thought processes, reconstructed the case and found the evidence which would fit the theory. Much of that evidence was from a fellow-prisoner and supergrass Dennis Woodman, a Geordie, who told the jury Ferris had confessed to him in prison. Woodman and his then common-law wife and her brother had been involved in a nasty kidnapping of a farmer in Dumfriesshire in an effort to get him to withdraw money from his bank accounts. How had Ferris made the confession? Shouting through the bars of his cell to Woodman, conveniently in the next cell, whom he had never seen? How had Woodman been placed in the next cell? Well, apparently when he had been in another prison he had been found with escaping tools in his cell, something he, Woodman, said had been planted by the authorities, and as a result he had been transferred. Cross-examined by Donald Findlay, a flamboyant lawyer and Vice-Chairman of Glasgow Rangers, Woodman told of the tragic death of his children in a road accident, something for which everyone had sympathy for several days until it was revealed that the children were alive and well and living in England and, indeed, Woodman had sent them a Christmas card from prison after their 'death'. Most of his evidence about the case could be traced, almost word for word, to pages from the Scottish editions of the *Sun* newspaper. As the trial went on the normally pro-active Findlay quietly demolished Woodman, who became more and more wild in his allegations, including a suggestion that Ferris's solicitor had endeavoured to bribe him. It was evidence which badly backfired on the prosecution for Woodman was not believed, something which by the end of his two weeks in the witness-box surprised few. Indeed, the surprise was that the prosecution still clung to his evidence instead of chucking their supergrass overboard and relying on the other evidence. And what was that?

Partly, another odd piece from a former girlfriend of Robert Glover who said that he, Glover, had called her in the middle of the night saying he had to see her. At the time she was living with another man, but Glover came round and they sat in a parked car for some hours during which time he told her of his and Ferris's involvement.

This presented something of a problem. Glover was dead and could not be cross-examined on the veracity of his statement. It was admitted into evidence but with considerable warnings from the trial judge, Lord McCluskey, as was the identification evidence that it had been Ferris in the restaurant combing the tables to find the Fat Boy.

There is little doubt that at the very least Ferris had been in the wrong city at the wrong time. Coming from a spectacularly criminal family he had moved to London where, as one Scots lawyer put it, there was evidence he had been 'repotting' himself. Nevertheless he had admittedly flown to Glasgow on the day of the killing to buy clothes for his child by a woman in the city, heard of the shooting and had absented himself smartly, hiring a car and driving south throughout the night.

Ferris – 'clever, articulate and passionate', says one trial observer who adds, 'the most convincing accused are either those who are innocent or those who are guilty but who know the police have manufactured the case against them' – was also cleared of charges of supplying drugs, knee-capping a former member of the Barlanark team, Willie Gillen, and attempting to murder Arthur Thompson himself.

Ferris's defence was, in part, that the killer of young Arthur was in fact 'Blind' Jonah McKenzie, a man who at the age of 37 had acquired thirty-six stab wounds and who had been blinded by 'Bananas' Hanlon in an attack in May 1991. This it was said was as a reprisal for the attack on the ice-cream/heroin van. McKenzie, a staunch Thompson man, who had received seven years when young Arthur picked up his eleven, vehemently denied the allegation. The jury accepted Ferris's alibi for the murder and the shooting of Willie Gillen; he had sensibly written on sixty-three pages of a notebook before his arrest. The reason for doing this was that he had, so he said, been fitted up by the police on a previous occasion and as a result kept a detailed account of his movements. He had, he said, been assisting another man in Glasgow who had been slashed: 'There was blood spattered all over his face – that's when I noticed his right hand. You could actually see the white muscle tissue and the blood streaming from it.'

Curiously, part of the defence was also to prove that the dead men, Glover and Hanlon, were also innocent and a substantial number of witnesses were found who, if they could not completely alibi the men, could go a long way towards doing so.

So far as the attempt on Arthur senior's life was concerned, this could not possibly have been done by Ferris for Arthur himself, a great performer, went into the witness-box to say he regarded Ferris almost as a son.

After Ferris's acquittal the *Daily Record* reported there was a £30,000 contract on his life. Indeed, in the ensuing troubles Ferris's family had not escaped unscathed. Willie Ferris, his father, required over a hundred stitches following an attack. He was beaten with a hammer and baseball bat and his car, bought with a disability pension, had its tyres slashed and was later set on fire. Ferris's brother Billy, himself convicted of murder, asked to be moved to a prison nearer to his father.

The Fat Boy's funeral itself was graced by the attendance of lawyers, MPs and entertainers. 'What a stroke,' said a South-East London friend of the Thompsons with approbation of the killing of Glover and Hanlon. 'And what a send-off for the boy.'

By now Arthur Thompson senior, who owned a holiday home in Rothesay as well as one in Spain, was moving into the role of businessman, making donations to charity and mixing with prominent political figures. As was befitting, his own funeral in March 1993, an all-day and night affair, was a splendid one with another full turnout by sportsmen and politicians as well as more than one criminal. First, there had been a scare that there was a suspicious device at the cemetery and an Army bomb disposal unit carried out a controlled explosion of what turned out to be a hoax device. After a quiet service at the home for family and friends, it was off to the cemetery, and then to the Provomills Public House where those who had not been able to attend the religious formalities were able to pay tribute to the family.

In August 1994 Ferris was fined £250 for possession of

crack cocaine. 'I'm no gangster,' he told the court in Manchester, adding that he smoked the drug to alleviate the soreness of his sensitive skin.

Billy Thompson, the remaining son of the Thompson family, was due to be released from Barlinnie in February 1995. Only time will tell whether he will be able to assume the position his father held in Glasgow. In the meantime Ferris does, however, seem to be regarded as the new King of Glasgow.

Meanwhile what had been happening to Thompson's old mate Patrick Meehan? He had certainly been in the wars and had barely survived. Many of his problems stemmed back to Thompson waving the £100 note about in the Glasgow public house.

Meehan had not settled down to do his eight years' preventive detention, imposed by Judge John Maud at the Old Bailey, the easy way. His wife, the long-suffering Betty, had decided enough was enough and began divorce proceedings. In prison Meehan had refused to work and had quarrelled with officers. In December 1962 he tried unsuccessfully to escape from Nottingham prison and his efforts had been rewarded with 180 days' loss of remission, along with cellular confinement and nine days' bread and water. Even before his sentence he had had an unnerving experience. According to his memoirs, whilst changing down the £100 note to more manageable proportions he had been approached by a man who had suggested that, in view of his success with Martin's escape he, Meehan, might be able to assist with the springing of the spy George Blake from prison. It was suggested that Meehan would probably have to go to East Berlin for further instructions.

Meehan succeeded in his escape, again from Nottingham, on 20 August 1963 when, during a diversion in a cricket match, he and three other prisoners escaped through a fence to a waiting car. He and a prisoner named Hogan went to Glasgow, from where Meehan caught a flight to Dublin and then another to Germany, where he recounts that he was questioned about his ability to help to free certain Russian spies including George Blake.

What is absolutely clear is that in early 1967 the recaptured Meehan was transferred from Blundeston prison in Suffolk to Parkhurst on the Isle of Wight. It was there he met a man who was nearly his nemesis, 32-year-old Lancastrian James Griffiths, whose early claim to fame was that he was the first man to escape from a prison on the Isle of Wight and actually get off the island.[22] He and Meehan became friends, along with another Glasgow villain, Roy Fontaine.

Out of prison in August 1968 Meehan, who had served seven of his eight years, returned to Glasgow. He went through a variety of jobs until in the spring of 1969 he started a little business installing spy-holes in front doors at £1 a time. That summer Griffiths turned up in Glasgow selling stolen antiques; he stayed with Meehan on and off

---

[22] Griffiths was taken before the Rochdale Juvenile Court by his mother as being out of control at the age of nine. Following a career of relatively minor crime, he took part in a nasty armed robbery in Blackpool in 1963 for which he received four years. His escape from Parkhurst in December 1965 was simple. He walked away from an outside working party, caught a bus to Ryde and boarded the ferry to Portsmouth from where he caught a train to Scunthorpe where he lived in a caravan. His time on the outside did not last long. He took part in other armed robberies and eventually, in March 1966, he received a further four years' imprisonment at Lindsey Quarter Sessions for housebreaking and theft. This was consecutive to the sentence which he had left unfinished.

during the next weeks, and on Saturday 5 July went to Stranraer to look over a possible burglary at the motor taxation office there.

On 8 July 72-year-old Rachel Ross died at the County Hospital, Ayrshire. She had been the victim of a tie-up robbery off Racecourse Road, Ayr, and one of the robbers had knelt on her chest. Her 67-year-old husband, Abraham, had been hit with an iron bar and stabbed in the neck. Very much in the frame for the robbery and killing were Meehan and Griffiths. One reason was that Abraham Ross said that the two men involved had called themselves Pat and Jim. It was also accepted by Meehan that he and Griffiths had been in the area. At a voice identification parade in which Meehan was the only one who spoke, Mr Ross identified him. He had been asked to say, 'Shut up, shut up, we'll send for an ambulance.'

Two girls to whom Griffiths and Meehan had given a lift also identified Meehan in another identification parade. Griffiths could not be identified; he was already dead. Whilst in prison he had been one of the subjects of a BBC documentary in which he had said he would never do another sentence. He was proved right.

Shortly after Meehan's arrest at 10.30 a.m., the police went to 14 Holyrood Crescent, Griffiths' home. The reason was simple: Meehan had given them Griffiths' name and address as an alibi witness. When there was no reply to their knockings, they kicked the door down and were faced with Griffiths wearing bandoliers of ammunition about his body and firing at them. A Detective Constable William Walker was hit. The other officers retreated, taking Walker with them and pursued by Griffiths firing at them from the window. By the time Griffiths left Holyrood Crescent four more officers had been injured. He then shot a man, Jim

Kerr, who was getting into his car, and when Kerr collapsed out of the vehicle Griffiths took it and drove off to the Round Toll Bar in Possil Road, where he fired two shots into the ceiling and with the third killed William Hughes who had moved only to put down his drink.

Griffiths was chased out of the bar by the extremely brave chargehand, John Connelly. He then shot two more men during his escape until he holed up in 26 Kay Street off the Springburn Road. It was there that Chief Superintendent Malcolm Finlayson, peering through the letter-box, saw Griffiths aiming at the door: 'It was either Griffiths or myself. I took my .38 and aimed it through the letter-box and fired at his shoulder.'

Griffiths, hit in the chest, died after firing further shots at the officers as they burst through the door. That day one civilian was killed and eleven were injured, along with five police officers.

Meanwhile there were rumours in the Underworld that despite Griffiths' suicidal behaviour and his record for unpleasant robberies, he and Meehan had not been responsible for those robberies. The name to come up regularly was that of Ian Waddell. Joe Beltrami, the veteran and probably best-known Scottish solicitor, who acted for Meehan, recalled:

> As one detective told me, 'Waddell's name is mentioned a lot.' A client said, 'The dogs in the street are barking the names of Waddell and Dick. Even they know Meehan's innocent. The police must know too.'[23]

[23] J. Beltrami, A *Deadly Innocence*, p.62.

Under Scottish procedure, if a defendant alleges that another has committed the crime then he must impeach or name him in pre-trial procedures and Waddell and another man were duly impeached by Beltrami. At the trial Waddell was invited to repeat the words, 'Shut up, shut up . . .' and Ross, hearing him, said that although he was not sure it was like the voice.

In his book Beltrami complains of the trial judge Lord Grant whom he believed rescued the Crown whenever necessary. The prosecution was 'rescued' now when he asked Ross, 'Is your recollection as clear now, three months later, as it was when you went to the parade?'

Waddell had been on the Crown's list of witnesses but was not called and so had to be called for the defence. He admitted that he was one of the first people questioned after the murder, but denied that he had paid the substantial sum of £200 to a solicitor to attend the police station with him. Later he denied that he had given the money to the solicitor, William Carlin. The reply would later earn him a sentence of three years' imprisonment for perjury.

Meehan's legal team – Beltrami had briefed Nicholas Fairbairn and the late John Smith, former leader of the Labour Party, for him – were hopeful, if not confident, that a verdict of not proven, that intermediate verdict available to a Scottish court, would be the worst that could happen. They were wrong. A majority (and in Scotland a bare 8–7 majority of the 15-member jury will suffice) found him guilty.

Beltrami never gave up. A solicitor with the greatest experience of the Underworld, he used his contacts, notably the influential Arthur Thompson, to discover the real killers in an endeavour to have the conviction set aside.

Beltrami had been half correct in having Waddell and the

other man impeached. The correct half was Waddell. His actual partner turned out to be an unlikely one, the noted hardman William 'Tank' McGuinness. He had been a client of Beltrami's for some fifteen years (as had almost every other self-respecting Glaswegian villain at one time or another) and was known for his partiality for tie-ups along with his penchant for violence. In 1968, along with John Farrell, he had been accused and acquitted of the murder of a man named Richards. At first sight Waddell, thought to be something of a blabbermouth in drink, would not seem a likely partner for the very canny and experienced McGuinness, the latter's name not being one to be bandied about lightly. Although not at present on a charge McGuinness began to pay visits to Beltrami's office on an informal basis, leaking more and more clues about the robbery. By the time of his last visit he had admitted that it had been Waddell's responsibility to telephone the police to get the Rosses released. He had also taken the lawyer and Ludovic Kennedy, of the Free Meehan Campaign, around the drainage system of Ayr trying to find rings and keys from the robbery. Beltrami's problem was that these were confidential statements by a client. Without his express permission to use them, he was bound by the lawyer's equivalent of the seal of the confessional. To do so could easily have meant his being struck off the roll of solicitors.

In early 1975 McGuinness' home was broken into late one night by two masked men armed with a sawn-off shotgun. He was not there but his wife and daughter were; they were terrified as the shotgun was fired into a cupboard. On 12 March 1976 he was found in a coma in Janefield Street close to the Celtic football ground. He had been beaten unconscious and died thirteen days later in the Royal Infirmary. He had never recovered consciousness.

Although it was never proved, it was put about that McGuinness had been killed over his involvement in the Ross murder.[24]

The death of McGuinness did at least release Beltrami from the confidentiality of the statements made to him by the man. It was established that Waddell's alibi was false and that although he was unemployed at the time, shortly after the Ayr robbery he had been in possession of substantial funds. Meehan was pardoned in May 1976. Now Ian Waddell was charged with the murder of Mrs Ross and put forward the defence of impeachment against Meehan and Griffiths. He was acquitted by a majority verdict of the jury who retired for just over an hour.

His acquittal brought him little fortune, however. In 1982 he was murdered in Blackthorn Street, Glasgow by his friend, Andy Gentle, who received a sentence of life imprisonment. The men had been involved in the death of Mrs Josephine Chipperfield, and the prosecution's case was that Gentle felt that Waddell might turn him over to the police.

---

[24] In June 1976, shortly after Meehan's pardon, John 'Gypsy' Winning, another of Beltrami's clients, was charged with the murder of McGuinness, his close friend. In 1962 he and McGuinness had escaped from Barlinnie together and later stood trial in Glasgow for safeblowing at a Dalry bank. McGuinness was acquitted and Winning received a sentence for reset (dishonest handling of stolen goods). Each received nine months for the prison break. Some of the evidence against Winning was that he had blood of McGuinness' rare type on his coat. Evidence was given that it could have come from a previous instance when Winning broke up a fight between McGuinness and James Bruce in the Braemar Bar in London Road. There were also evidential difficulties about the taking of the blood sample from McGuinness. The jury was directed to return a verdict of not guilty.

'Gipsy' Winning had already gone. In 1980 he had picked a fight with James McLellan, yet another of Beltrami's clients, when drunk at a house in Rosebank Cottage, Dunfermline. McLellan was more than a match. His father had been a well-known Glasgow cobbles fighter and had passed on his talents. McLellan's plea to culpable homicide on the grounds of provocation was accepted and he received a sentence of thirty months.

In due course there was an inquiry into the Meehan case undertaken by Lord Hunter. Published in 1982, it offered a new and curious theory that all four men, Griffiths, Meehan, Waddell and McGuinness, had been involved. Meehan finally received the sum of £50,500 in compensation. Beltrami had been hoping for £100,000 and had to work quite hard to persuade Meehan that this was a reasonable sum.

It would be pleasant, but inaccurate, to record that Meehan was grateful for Beltrami's efforts over the years on his behalf. Perhaps understandably given the pressures of prison life, Meehan's letters to Beltrami during his sentence were filled with recriminations. After his release and compensation he appears to have been only marginally more grateful. There is a photograph of him being shown the dotted line by Beltrami as he signs for his compensation, in which he looks reasonably happy. His gratitude did not last. In 1990 he produced a book which was highly critical of Beltrami and partly blamed him for his conviction. After some thought Beltrami decided not to apply for an interdict (injunction). The book was not on general sale.

Meehan died in a Swansea hospital on 14 August 1994. He had left Glasgow ten years earlier to live with relations in Wales. Sir Nicholas Fairbairn commented: 'He was a vagabond and I am glad he is dead. To hell with him. He was a psychopath, just a horrible, nasty, evil, loathsome crook'. Beltrami was genuinely surprised and saddened that Meehan had turned on him. He described him as being an egotistical megalomaniac adding, 'And being so, while he would take advantage of as much support as he could, in my opinion he grew to resent those who helped him because he felt he should not have required their assistance in the first place.' Another solicitor described him as not having a single redeeming feature. [*The Scotsman* 16 August 1994]

At the lower end of the scale, in 1992 David McDermott argued with Alan Auld over the loan of £5. McDermott hit Auld twice with a machete, for which he received a sentence of nine years and three months for attempted murder. It was unremarkable. Knives had been the weapons used in 382 attempted murders in 1992 in Strathclyde, and in slightly over half the 92 murders. Once, said David Bryce, a former member of the Calton Tongs, it was about areas. 'You couldn't go from Barrowfield into Calton – you might get killed. Now people go from Barrowfield into Calton to score.'[25] Drugs have taken over once more.

[25] Stewart Hennessey, *Slice of Life*, in *The Times*, 15 May 1993.

4

Liverpool and the North West

The century started badly for the Birkenhead police. On 9 September 1900 the third robbery of the year took place at the Birkenhead Post Office. George Fell, shoemaker, auxiliary postman and caretaker, failed to answer the gate when other postmen arrived for the evening shift at about 4.50 p.m. They forced the door and discovered a pool of blood inside the doorway. Fell was found in the postmaster's room, his face covered with a postbag. A broken poker lay on the floor and a coal shovel had several dents in it. It seemed as though Fell had used it as a shield against the blows from the poker. £19.15s.2d had been taken from the safe, along with £50 in £10 notes and three postal orders. Although details of the notes were circulated and their numbers printed in the national newspapers, no single one was ever tendered.

Nor was the killer ever found. One theory is that he may have had the gate opened to him by Fell sometime during the day and immediately attacked him, which would account for the blood in the doorway. Another is that he may even have hidden himself in the cellar amongst postal baskets whilst the office was open, and was later surprised by Fell. Fell had a great send-off, with the Post Office band playing the 'Dead March' from *Saul* and a crowd of 10,000 mourners at Flaybrick Cemetery. A trust fund was set up for his widow. The robber was never caught despite inquiries nationwide and indeed in Australia. At one time the Birkenhead police fastened on a man in the Grimsby area, but that line of inquiry came to nothing.

On the two previous occasions when the Post Office had been robbed, the employees were made to make good the loss. Each had a small amount stopped from his weekly pay until the money had been repaid. This does not seem to have been done the third time.

Probably the robbery was committed by an individual rather than a gang. If so it would conform to the consensus of police, lawyers' and sociologists' opinion that on balance there has been no organized crime in Liverpool; certainly not on the scale seen in London.

It is a secondary economy, the economy of the streets with relatively low class crime. Most Liverpool crime relates to casual employment. There are gangs of kids who do a bit of thieving one day, a bit of violence the next and a bit of shoplifting the third. It relates to the economy of the City. Apart from the docks there's nothing worth stealing.

Mike Brogden,
Professor of Law, John Moore's University

The criminal classes in Liverpool are mainly deprived children who've grown up in overcrowded Catholic homes – mainly of Irish extraction.

E. Rex Makin, Liverpool solicitor

> It is essentially small time, haphazard, lacking in central organization and carried out by individual villains each working more or less alone and for his own nefarious purposes.[1]

It is a view which may partly be true if one ignores that at one time in the early part of the century half the Chinese community was estimated to be actively concerned in the manufacture of opium, that there was dock related crime – including the rolling of drunken seamen – in the days when 18,000 men were employed there, that there have been such active gangs as the Kellys, the Brodies and the Throstles, and that at present there is a thriving drug connection and there appears to be a drug-linked protection war centred on the provision of bouncers for the discos and nightclubs. It may be played down as minor league compared with the great days of the Richardsons and the Krays in London, but it isn't particularly small-time when we are speaking of drug deals in the sum of £67 million.

There is also little doubt that the Liverpool City Police were regarded as the toughest of the tough, and that they controlled the street bookmaking, the shebeens and the drinking clubs. But again a view is that their protection rackets were strictly second rate.

> It only amounted to a bottle here, 200 cigarettes there. Not proper money. There wasn't any about.
>
> *Mike Brogden*

They were also protecting their snouts, warning them of raids by the uniformed police. The amount of actual

[1] R. Whittington-Egan, *Liverpool Roundabout*, p.175.

detection was very low. I should think 95% depended upon the snouts.

E. Rex Makin

When on 11 February 1901 the Chief Constable of the Liverpool City Police reported to the Watch Committee he was quietly self-congratulatory. True there had been a slight increase in the number of indictable offences, 3,742 compared with 3,504 the previous year, but twenty years earlier it had been, with a much smaller population, 6,236. Crimes of violence at thirty-five in number were three less than the previous year, burglary and house-breaking four less and forty-four fewer than five years earlier.

The increase in larcenies was due, he wrote, to minor thefts of loose cotton, rope, sugar on the Dock estate. A new class of offence was emerging, however: the theft of bicycles from office doors, passages and shops. In fact so great had been the decrease in crime that the previous year the strength of the force had been reduced by 100 and had worked 'without loss of efficiency'. There was 'no better tribute to the improved conditions in Liverpool'. Thirteen constables received medals, clasps or votes of thanks for stopping runaway horses.

The next year the Chief Constable was even happier. 'Serious crimes of robbery with violence and assaults with intent to rob, seem to be practically stamped out, there being only eight of these crimes during the year compared with 28 the previous year. Some years ago from 80 to 120 cases per annum was a common number.'

By 1911 Liverpool was 'the most criminal, the most drunken, the most lawless city in the United Kingdom. Why is this?' demanded an anonymous writer in a long-forgotten publication of the time. There was a tendency to blame 'those Irish' but this was not borne out statistically. The Chief Constable lamented, 'There is a general decline of personal honesty in many relations of life. Every year I am more convinced of the fact and every year the remedy seems harder to find.'

The writer went on to show that per 100,000 of the population in 1909 Leeds had 182 tried for indictable offences, London 212, Birmingham 250, Cardiff 264 and Liverpool nearly double London's score with 456. There was an enormous rise in crimes against the person.

In 1929 over 900 bicycles were reported as stolen and the Chief Constable now had this to say about a newer form of transport:

> Owing possibly to the mistaken notion that a motor car may be taken from the street, used and afterwards abandoned without the risk of prosecution, we have had a continuance of so-called joy-riding. In all 75 motor cars were reported as stolen. All these cars were recovered, several within minutes of their being reported missing, and the police obtained sufficient evidence to prosecute in 22 cases for larceny of the car, and in 11 cases for larceny of petrol.[2]

Shortly before the War there was an outbreak of protection in 1937 at the Grand National meeting, always a Mecca for outside criminals. A gang led by another of the so-called Colonels and unusually for the time including two Australians were in operation. Herbert Balmer, then a relatively young officer who later became Deputy Chief

[2] Report on the Police Establishment and the State of Crime, for the year ending 31 December 1929.

Constable, was on duty at the racecourse when he noticed the Colonel and his squad. He reasoned that any trouble would occur after the National was run, at a time when the crowds would begin to leave the course without waiting to see the remaining races. He was right. He and his men found two bookmakers who had been slashed. One had eighteen stitches and the other fifteen. Initially they refused to talk, saying that the fault was theirs and they should have paid. According to his memoirs, which appeared over a lengthy period in the *Liverpool Echo* on his retirement in 1967, Balmer arrested the Colonel after a struggle in which Balmer's coat was slashed to pieces. The Colonel received four years' imprisonment after asking Balmer merely to charge him with an offence triable only in the magistrates' court which would have meant a maximum of six months.

Where there are docks there is crime should be one of the easiest of maxims for a sociologist to memorize. Or is it a stereo-typical generalization? Whichever it is

. . . the war brought an increase in Sailor Town in Liverpool [which] had gangs of youths indulging in inter-gang warfare – coshes, tapes, with the radius of operations around Park Lane, Paradise Street and Back George Street. Sailors were being lured out of the safe haven of milk bars and the YMCA with the offers of visits to illegal drinking clubs and being rolled on the way to a girl's flat. There were allegations by the Recorder of Liverpool of Police Brutality. H. B. Balmer, a sergeant who acted as police court advocate, told magistrates that the US forces had found it necessary to organize a special corps of soldiers to stop pilfering mainly of cigarettes which were being stolen from American stores and ending up on the Black Market.[3]

Balmer had done rather better than that. He had infiltrated a ring of men stealing from the American PX stores. In fact there was a huge trade in watches and jewellery and Balmer and a colleague made arrangements for sale to him of two jeeps and five cases of watches and jewellery for £10,000. When he arrived at the rendezvous with the money he was told they had been outbid. Balmer and his friend appeared to leave but, in fact, climbed through a window at the back of the premises and when the other buyers arrived they were arrested.

At the end of 1945 the Report on the Police Establishment and the State of Crime for the seven years from 1938 commented:

Crime had increased 68.9 per cent since 1938. The raids on the City left many premises very easy to break into, and premises made unfit for occupation provided cover from which to attack adjoining premises and also for hiding stolen goods. The shortages of all kinds of food and clothing made it easy for thieves to dispose of stolen property and also made it worthwhile to steal what before the war would not have repaid the trouble and risk. Crimes on a large scale were often instigated by operators in the black market and on many occasions a whole lorry load of goods was stolen. Many such large scale operations were detected by the police and successful prosecutions resulted but it was seldom possible to obtain the evidence necessary to establish

[3] *News Review*, 11 March 1943.

the guilt of the principal offender. Deserters from the Forces and Mercantile Marine were responsible for many offences and were not easy to catch as their visits were often of short duration. The darkened streets provided opportunities for 'hold ups' and snatch thieves but the number of such offences was surprisingly small considering the unusual opportunities.

Two years later, dock thefts were up by 10 per cent and seventeen of the people prosecuted – who came, said the Chief Constable's Report, from all walks of life – were watchmen.

And after the War there was a further great influx of prostitutes to assist the spending of money earned by sailors. Liverpool became a big post-war city of murder and violence. Twenty men and four women received substantial sentences for rolling. The *Daily Herald* returned to the theme of violence and crime on 27 July 1950. 'What makes it our wickedest city?' asked Alan Clarke. (Runners-up were Manchester and Blackpool.) Outside the station Clarke had a cup of tea; it cost 8d including a 5d deposit on the cup (no saucer). The stallholder told him that even with the deposit he lost five dozen cups a week. Goods were scarce on the home market. There were pretty girls who could be used in come-on operations. He heard of one eight-year-old leading a gang of housebreakers armed with a blowlamp. Lime Street was thronged with pimps and prostitutes. However, the Kelly conviction had split up the great organized criminal gangs such as the Swallows who had the eponymous bird tattooed on their wrists. In 1948 it was reckoned there had been over 200 juvenile gangs. There were still dozens in 1950 including the Peanut Gang, so-called because they began their career by splitting open bags of peanuts on the docks, before they graduated to splitting open the heads of seamen decoyed into alleys off Lime Street for their wage packets. There was, said Clarke, a well-established cover system by which a wanted criminal was smuggled from family to family. There was still ingrained mistrust of the law – old-timers could remember the police baton charges in motor-cycle chariots. However, the article ended on an encouraging note. By fairness and intelligent public relations, the police were breaking down the old hostility. There were fewer tensions between Catholics and Protestants, for example.

One crime which had been running since the 1920s was grid-lifting to get into cellars and so burgle houses. In 1947, 115 such entries were reported. It seems the householders either did not have them mended when the grids rusted, or that coalmen failed to put them properly back in place after delivering.

But the implication of one paragraph of the Report was that the black population was to blame for much of the disarray:

> I visited a coloured men's 'social' club within a stone's throw of the cathedral. In a room about 15 feet square, I counted 60 black men and white women – packed together and jiving strenuously on the steel-reinforced floor which pulsated with their weight. A Negro drummer beat time on the mantelpiece.

This was clearly particularly wicked.[4]

In 1951, 72 people were proceeded against for brothel-

---

[4] It was however a view which prevailed at the time. The part of Liverpool by the Cathedral where the black community lived was known as The Jungle.

keeping and/or living off immoral earnings. More sinister was the fact that one-third of all dangerous drugs prosecutions throughout the country came from Liverpool.

Things hadn't improved by the year 1952. Liverpool was 'Crime City – and nobody really seems to care,' said Douglas Howell in the *Daily Mirror*. Edward Devlin and Alfred Burns had just been hanged for the murder of Beatrice Rimmer, a middle-aged widow.

Four months may be a long time in journalism, but nothing had changed when 'Our Crime Reporter' from *Reynolds News* went to investigate 'The Quiet City – where terror stalks as night falls'. The town was quiet by 11 p.m., probably because the police went down the streets stick-swinging and in pairs. It was a delusion that the gangs who were the successors to the Devlins, the Burns, and the Kellys had been wiped out by the now Chief Superintendent Balmer. Gangs paraded the streets marking out territories to be invaded only in disputes over women. The crime schools were now in the inappropriately named Hope Street and Upper Parliament Street.

After the War there was an outbreak of rolling in the Lime Street area, near the station and known for prostitution.[5] Rolling, or mugging as we now call it, had always been a known Liverpudlian sport.

Rolling has had a long tradition in Liverpool and been traditionally associated with sailors and prostitution and the taking of the pay packet which was flashed around too openly.[6]

[5] The Liverpool ballad *Maggie May* includes the line, 'She'll never walk down Lime Street any more.'
[6] *Crime in the City*: Report of the Steering Group, November 1974.

This time, however, it was businessmen who were being rolled and subsequently blackmailed. The Throstle Gang operated with a girl who it was said had once been a model in London. She would pick up men in hotel bars and then on the way back to her flat they would be attacked and robbed. Again Balmer was involved, allowing himself to be picked up by the girl who asked him to walk home with her. On the way, in Benson Street, she asked for a light for her cigarette. This was the signal for the robbery, but Balmer had men following him and after a fight in which he engagingly recounts, 'X had to strike him with his truncheon', the Throstles were arrested. The girl, who first denied all knowledge of the men and then later alleged that they had forced her into the scam, received twelve months and the men up to seven years. It was thought they had committed up to eighteen similar offences during their career. Two of the victims were still being blackmailed by the gang at the time of the arrests, but despite the arrests they refused to give evidence against them.

Balmer rose steadily through the police and his three finest cases came in the period between 1949 and 1951. The first of them was the Cameo Cinema murder which broke the so-called Kelly gang.

George Kelly had had a life of petty crime. His first conviction had been at the age of 10 when he was discharged under the Probation Act for breaking and entering. It was the first of a long list he acquired before he joined the Royal Navy, from which he deserted five times. In 1943 he was sentenced to nine months' imprisonment for assault. In 1945 he received a sentence for what is now dishonest handling, and the same year three years' penal servitude for desertion along with a year's hard labour.

On his release he worked in a café, as a street trader and

as the barker for an escapologist. Then he took up pimping and ran a small string of prostitutes. His gang was a pretty pathetic affair by today's standards. His henchman was Charles Connolly, also a Royal Naval deserter and, after the War, a one-time railway porter. He was a capable amateur boxer who was always looking for a street fight. There were also two girls involved.

According to Norman Lucas, gang leaders such as Kelly were using their cars as mobile brothels with the girls under their control obliged to hand over up to 75 per cent of the night's takings. The girls were also expected to steer punters into clip joints where the men would be overcharged for their drinks but, in contradistinction to the London clip-joint, there would be at least a chance that sex would be available. Usually a couple of rooms were set aside for the girls to take their clients.[7]

One of the girls in the Kelly milieu was Jackie Dickson, who may well have had tuberculosis and who after the War was befriended by Jimmy Northam, known as 'Stuttie' from a speech impediment suffered as a result of an accident in the War, during a part of which he had been involved in a gang which rolled servicemen. Dickson had married a sailor who had deserted her immediately after the wedding. She was summoned by Kelly, and the party was joined in the public house by Marjorie Dawson, known as 'Norwegian Marjorie'.

Kelly, it seems, put up a number of propositions including the waylaying of a taxi driver known to be a police informer, a shopbreaking expedition and the robbing of the fun-fair in New Brighton.

It seems to have been Connolly who originally suggested

[7] N. Lucas, *Britain's Gangland*, pp.30–31.

the theft of the takings from the Cameo Cinema in Wavertree. It was agreed that a gun would be needed to frighten the manager and one was produced without difficulty by Kelly. 'Norwegian Marjorie' told him to put it away in case it was seen by other people in the pub, but Kelly calmly loaded it. There was some discussion about a disguise, and Dawson was made to hand over a small green apron for Kelly to use as a mask, whilst Northam surrendered his overcoat.

The next evening Kelly and Connolly went to the cinema. Connolly remained outside, whilst a little after 9 p.m. Kelly climbed the stairs to the office and demanded the takings from the manager, Leonard Thomas. He refused to hand over the takings and Kelly shot him, as he did Leonard Catterall, the assistant manager. Now he panicked and dropped the bag of money he had snatched. On his way out he was seen by Patrick Griffin, the cinema fireman.

Connolly was long gone by the time Kelly reappeared; he had left at the sound of the first shot. Kelly then started to compile an alibi, going into the Leigh Arms and buying a drink for a James Currie, a man whom he hardly knew. Currie would later give evidence that Kelly seemed nervous and out of breath; he asked him what was the matter and whether he had been in a fight. Kelly agreed he had. Connolly had gone off separately to join his wife and sisters in a local dance hall.

The next day the papers were full of the news and Connolly, a very frightened man, said he was going to leave the country, something for which Kelly roundly denounced him. He also threatened 'Stuttie' Northam and Jackie Dickson with a seeing-to from his brothers if they should open their mouths. Shortly after this, Norwegian Marjorie committed suicide.

A month after the murders Northam and Dickson decided to write to the police. Northam, helped by the girl, printed the anonymous letter which read:

THIS LETTER IS NOT A CRANK'S LETTER OR SUCHLIKE. NOR AM I TURNING INFORMER FOR GAIN. I KNOW THREE MEN AND A GIRL, NOT INCLUDING MYSELF, WHO HEARD ABOUT THIS PLAN FOR ROBBERY. I WOULD HAVE NOTHING TO DO WITH IT AND I DON'T THINK THE GIRL DID. WHEN I MET HER ON SUNDAY, SHE HAD NOT BEEN OUT WITH THEM. ANOTHER MAN DROPPED OUT ON ACCOUNT HE WANTED TO UNLOAD THE REVOLVER BEFORE THEY WENT. THERE WERE ONLY TWO MEN WENT. THE MAN HE TOOK WITH HIM LOST HIS NERVE AND WOULD NOT GO IN WITH HIM, BUT SAID HE WOULD WAIT OUTSIDE BUT DID NOT.

It was not wholly accurate but it was something for the police to go on.

The reference to 'another man who dropped out' was to a window-cleaner, whom Kelly had tried to recruit but who had refused the offer to participate when he heard of the loaded gun.

The letter continued to the effect that the writer could give more details of the murder if the police put an advertisement in the local newspaper offering immunity from prosecution. By the time they did place a notice in the personal column of the *Liverpool Echo*, 'Letter received. Promise definitely given', Northam and Dickson had disappeared in the direction of Manchester.

The one outstanding recollection Griffin had of the gunman was of his dark eyebrows, a feature of Kelly's face, and even before the letter Herbert Balmer had pulled Kelly in for questioning but his alibi stuck. His girlfriend Doris O'Malley swore that before he went to the Leigh Arms he had been with her in another pub, the Coach and Horses.

Balmer eventually heard the story that Jackie Dickson had been involved, and after a huge search over the North of England she was retrieved from Manchester. So was Northam, but it was not until six months after the robbery that he gave up the names of Kelly and Connolly. When they, in turn, were arrested, they denied knowing each other and Kelly said, 'I never had a gun in my life. I don't know how to handle or fire one . . .'

Kelly was by no means pleased to find he was being defended by Rose Heilbron (who later became a High Court Judge), the first time a woman had led in a murder case. 'I want no Judy defending me,' was said to be Kelly's opening gambit. It wasn't as if Miss Heilbron was making a fortune; she was receiving 15 guineas under the Poor Persons Defence Act, with her junior 10 guineas and her solicitor 2 guineas a day and expenses.

There really wasn't much evidence against Kelly and certainly less against Connolly: an identification witness against the former and the tainted evidence of Dickson and Northam against both. Help was at hand, however, in the shape of a serving prisoner, Robert Graham, doing six months for receiving stolen property. He bolstered the prosecution's case with the evidence that Kelly had told him of the sixty witnesses he had in the Leigh Arms to give him an alibi. Connolly was even less discreet; he apparently told Graham he had had nothing to do with the murders, but admitted he had been to the cinema with the man who did them. He said he had run away when hearing the shots.

All three witnesses, Northam, Dickson and Graham, told the court how frightened they were of reprisals from Kelly's family and friends. 'Stuttie' and his girlfriend, who were now rehoused and living under assumed names, even refused to write them on a piece of paper for the judge.

Worse was to come for Connolly when his alibi was broken. He said he had been at a dance hall from about 8.20 in the evening, and that his wife had joined him twenty minutes later. He also said he had entered a rhumba competition and his wife, two of his sisters and their friends all put him in the dance hall before the murder was committed. Unfortunately it all went wrong. The Master of Ceremonies was sure that Connolly had not arrived until after the pubs closed. He remembered the man specifically because he had been wearing his hat on the dance floor and had been asked to remove it.

Even so the jury was unconvinced. After the thirteen-day trial, the then longest in an English court, they disagreed, were sent out again and failed to reach a verdict after another four hours. This time the prosecution had the idea of trying the men separately and, much to Miss Heilbron's unease, the re-trial was fixed for a week later. She made a series of applications to both Mr Justice Oliver and Mr Justice Cassels, who was to take the second trial, and merely had her ears boxed for her pains because she had made the application without her client being present. One of the reasons for the urgency was that Jackie Dickson was said to be suffering from a fatal and progressive disease.

This time Kelly was found guilty of murder – a decision in which the judge heartily concurred – with the jury retiring for only fifty-five minutes. As Kelly left the dock he said, 'Get Balmer and I'll . . .' No one heard how he intended to complete the sentence. Northam and Dickson each received £20 reward from the court, with the thoughtful Mr Justice Cassels saying, 'There might be a Liverpool lady or ladies who could show a real act of kindness' – whatever that meant. Miss Heilbron took the case to the Court of Criminal Appeal with a novel if ultimately unsuccessful point. She argued that because there was a juryman who had a felony conviction the trial was a nullity and the conviction should be quashed. It was not an argument which Lord Goddard, the Lord Chief Justice, found attractive. Kelly's appeal was dismissed and he was hanged on 28 March 1950 at Walton Prison. No evidence on the murder charge was offered against Connolly in his separate re-trial, and he pleaded guilty to the robbery of the £50 takings and was sentenced to ten years' imprisonment.

Balmer received a series of threatening letters, but these died away. He was sent to police college, and on his return it was decided he should have a bodyguard. In his memoirs published in the *Liverpool Echo* over a three-month period, he wrote that he did not think much of this idea and did a round of the pubs such as the Beehive where Kelly and his gang had hung out. He had no trouble except that on one evening in Park Street two men alighted from a taxi and ran towards him. Three others de-taxied and hauled them back to the cab.

One of the members of another team at the time of Kelly's trial, the Brodie Gang, boasted a wife who was known as the 'Strong Arm Man', as opposed to woman. She took umbrage at the evidence given in a case and as the witness left court, attacked her with a razor. She received four years' imprisonment and the gang lost its heart.

Balmer's second famous case involved the murder of Beatrice Rimmer, a middle-aged widow who was reputed to have a cache of money in her house. Edward Devlin and Alfred Burns had known each other for some years before August 1951 when Burns was on the run and being harboured by his friend. In one of the all-night cafés in

Liverpool frequented by young criminals, Devlin and Burns explained to Marie Milne the opportunity there was for robbing Mrs Rimmer without too much difficulty. Milne, a 16-year-old who had been recruited by June Bury, Devlin's girlfriend, was not completely enthusiastic; she said she would think about it. The next day the men explained the plan to the girls. June Bury said she wanted nothing to do with it but Milne, thoroughly frightened, hedged her bets. Burns and Devlin then recruited George MacLoughlin, a youth who had spent eleven of his 20 years inside, and who at 14 was the youngest person admitted to Walton jail. The plan was simple enough in theory. It is one which has been operated over the years with great success by con-men, gypsies and even young children. Marie Milne was to keep watch until she was sure Mrs Rimmer was in, knock and then engage her in conversation whilst Burns, Devlin and MacLoughlin broke in at the rear.

Things went wrong almost from the start. MacLoughlin was fortunate enough to be arrested for burglary two days before the planned robbery of the 19th. Milne was still not happy with her role. Thoroughly frightened of her part in the robbery, and more so when Devlin pulled a knife from his pocket and threatened her, she was still more frightened about what might happen if she went to the police.

Burns and Devlin decided to go ahead without waiting for MacLoughlin's release – which might have been quite some time in the future – and on the 19th went by taxi with Milne to Cranbourne Street where Mrs Rimmer lived. When they arrived she appeared to be out and Milne was sent to a local cinema and told to wait outside. The men broke the kitchen window and were searching the premises when Mrs Rimmer returned. They attacked her, beating her with a piece of wood, and left her to die on the floor; she had fifteen wounds in her head. When they met up with Milne, she refused to go back to Manchester with them but she still did not inform on them. That was done by MacLoughlin who, whilst serving his sentence in Walton, discussed the crime with other prisoners. Word was passed to the Governor and then to Balmer. In court he justified his informing on the basis that he was a professional burglar and did not approve of violence.

The girls were traced – June Bury was now pregnant – and then the taxi-driver. Milne told them that when she had met the men after the burglary Devlin had asked, 'Will the woman live?' and Burns had replied, 'To hell with the woman. We will be out of Liverpool before long.' Devlin was arrested inside twenty-four hours and Burns three days later.

Richard Whittington-Egan, then one of the leading crime reporters in Liverpool, told barrister Fenton Bresler:

> I was present at the magistrates' court during the committal proceedings. Devlin was insolent – whispering and sniggering to his companion in the dock. I never saw two people on a serious charge so unaffected by the circumstances in which they found themselves. I was later to see them at the trial. I expected to see a change in their demeanour after their long weeks in prison. But they were still as cocky as ever. They saw themselves as gangster heroes.[8]

They ran an interesting if not unique defence at the Assizes, claiming that they had been engaged in a robbery at a clothing warehouse in Manchester from which they had stolen raincoats, suits and trousers, and had spent the night at the home of a Joan Downey. Another man gave evidence

[8] F. Bresler, *Scales of Justice*, p.43.

that he was on the warehouse breaking with them but Mrs Downey flatly denied their story. The factory had been broken into some time between midday Saturday and early Monday morning when the crime was discovered. The trial judge pointed out that there was no reason why the men could not have committed the burglary to which they admitted and the murder to which they did not.

It was after the jury had found them guilty and the Court of Criminal Appeal had rejected their appeals that Rose Heilbron, who had defended Devlin, produced a statement from a 15-year-old Elizabeth Rooke that she had heard June Bury say the men were innocent and that the real killer was the father-to-be of Bury's baby. This caused considerable upset. Lord Goddard refused to admit new evidence.

What was urged upon us was that we should hear fresh evidence of a most important character . . . and it went to show that June Bury, the importance of whose evidence I have already emphasized, had committed perjury and had admitted that she had committed perjury, and, secondly, that another man had admitted that he had committed the murder.

We declined to consider that evidence, and we declined for very good reasons. Matters of this sort have often previously been before the Court of Criminal Appeal, who have always in these circumstances refused to hear such evidence mainly on the ground that they have no power to order a new trial.[9]

[9] Lord Goddard speaking on a House of Lords' motion that the Court of Appeal should have the power to order a retrial. (*Hansard*, Lords, 8 May 1952, cols 745 *et seq.*) The power was not granted to them until the Criminal Justice Act 1967, since when it has been sparingly used.

So the matter went to the Home Secretary. He appointed Albert Garrard QC and Commander Harold Hawkyard of Scotland Yard to inquire whether a possible miscarriage of justice had taken place. They found that the man named had been away from Liverpool at the time of the Rimmer killing, and that the story of Elizabeth Rooke could not stand up. Both men were hanged on 25 April 1952; both affirming their innocence.

There were reprisals in the Liverpool Underworld. It was decided that Marie Milne should have her throat cut, but in the end she was merely beaten unconscious in a back alley and needed thirty stitches. June Bury was beaten up in an all-night café and later was the subject of a further six beatings. She went to London, underwent plastic surgery and returned to Liverpool secure in the knowledge that she could not be recognized. She could; and was beaten yet again. MacLoughlin, correctly regarded in Underworld terms as a grass, was continually beaten both in and out of prison. Joan Downey, who had refused to corroborate the Burns-Devlin alibi, had her home set on fire.

Even the minor witnesses suffered. The taxi-driver who had taken the trio to Cranbourne Street was beaten up; another prosecution witness was shot and dumped in Blackpool. It was, wrote Norman Lucas, five years before the witnesses felt safe from the wrath of the remaining members of the Burns-Devlin gang.[10]

The third of the famous murder cases in which Balmer was involved at the time was the killing of the semi-crippled junk dealer-cum-recluse, 82-year-old George Hugh 'Daddy' Walker, on 14 January 1953. This time it was not a gang matter but the maniac work of unemployed labourer John

[10] N. Lucas, *Britain's Gangland*, p.45.

Lawrence Todd who hit Walker thirty-two times with an axe. After the death in 1944 of his wife Madam Pepper, a dancing teacher, Walker, who had been a master tailor, lived in a twelve-roomed house at Warbreck Road near Aintree, increasingly surrounded by junk. When his dog would not stop howling, neighbours went to investigate and found his battered body. The axe had been clumsily hidden in a chimney. Todd went to the police to explain why he might have been seen in the area, but he was identified through a watch stolen in the robbery which he had sold. He was hanged at Walton jail on 19 May 1953.

Even so Balmer was not without his critics. There were allegations both in and outside the police that he had stitched up Kelly as well as Devlin-Burns. Doyen of the Liverpool criminal solicitors, E. Rex Makin, recalls:

After those cases I used to give a lift to a Detective Sergeant who was involved in them. He wasn't an ordinary sort of copper, a supercilious type of man, and when I told him I wasn't happy with the Devlin-Burns case, he replied, 'Does it matter? They're scum.' That was his attitude and it's stuck with me all my life.

Balmer had been a ship's carpenter. He was a publicity seeker and a bully. His methods were purely verballing. He was the archetypal detective who believed the best evidence was a cough whether genuine, forced, induced or voluntary.

By 1957 there was a general clean-up of the city in anticipation of its 750th birthday. The drinking clubs could be raided on one warrant three times a night. But three years later *Today*, in the form of John Godwin, reported: 'This is Liverpool . . . City of Violence', and included such gems as the tailor who 'includes automatically a special cosh pocket in all suits he makes for teenagers; . . . the Liverpool kiss gripping lapels and ramming the forehead into the nose'.[11]

Violent crime was up: murders from nil to four; cases of robbery with violence from 47 to 69; there were attacks on policeman every two days. According to Godwin, a police inspector told him:

> Our chief problem here? Same as it's always been – violence. We've just about licked the drug traffic, we've chased the prostitutes off the streets, we've closed down most of the shebeens and we've never had much trouble with gambling. But we can't stop people from bashing each other over the head.

Nightlife shifted sharply to the east of the city around Parliament Street, Park Road and Grove Street.

The only Underworld boss in Liverpool in recent years, thought Godwin, was Rudolph 'Bull' Gardner who arrived as a stowaway with £11 from Jamaica. He began operating, buying marijuana from American seamen and selling it in the black community (known, in the days when such a phrase could be used without even the slightest lift of an eyebrow, as Jungle Town) near the cathedral. He opened a shebeen and then the Fortune Club in Princes Road on which he spent over £8,000. It was estimated he was earning £50 a night. But he forgot to have front men, and when in 1955 the Fortune was raided he took the fall of two years personally. He returned to Liverpool after his sentence, but was no longer any sort of power and was effectively run out

[11] 20 August 1960.

by the police. He then went to London where at the Inner London Quarter Sessions on 12 October 1959, then aged 36, he received another two years for possessing 4lb 3oz of marijuana.

Probably the popularity in the 1960s of the Beatles had as much as anything to do with cutting youth crime in Liverpool. The sociological argument runs that crime is most prevalent amongst middle-teenagers, and that as youths get older they will pair off with girls who will lead them out of the gang. Friday night was fight night and there had been splendid fights with such gangs as the Holly Road and Park Gang. Then members of the gangs began to play instruments. A boy who fought was now regarded as just a man without a woman. Status was no longer dependent on winning a rumble but on how the band within the group had performed. This is to a certain extent the same today when drugs gangs adopt a reggae band of their own.

Suddenly Liverpool became OK. The cathedral was built, the docks were gentrified. On the back of the Beatles came a whole Merseyside culture, much of which has endured – Cilla Black, Alan Plater, George Melly, the Barrow poets. But as the Garden of Britain was planted, the flowers of the city withered.

With the new prosperity came a taxi-war which was waged intermittently for ten years, with licensed taxis being sprayed with graffiti and private vehicles having their tyres slashed. Two of the early casualties were two brothers who on 1 July 1966 received three years each for conspiracy and demanding with menaces – they were acquitted of setting fire to the Stretton Club in Wood Street. They had tried to take over taxi-cab services in the city, setting up the so-called Private Hire Association whose aim was 'to bring together all the private firms in Liverpool'.

Again where there is money to spend crime is almost invariably organized to skim off part of it. By 1979 it was believed there were twelve crime families who ran nearly fifty pubs and clubs in the centre of town. The police believed that the clubs, which ran from the back-street shebeen to smart nightclubs, were being used to launder money and also to generate the capital for more ambitious enterprises outside the city. The calendar of crime for a year in the city was impressive.

On 16 May 1978 fifteen men raided five houses in the Fazakerley, Dovecot, Walton and Bootle areas. They were carrying an arsenal of weapons including sawn-off shotguns, baseball bats, swords, axes and hammers. Their three victims included a man whose ankles were repeatedly hit with one of the axes in an endeavour to cut off his feet; he needed 107 stitches. Another was found in his underwear hiding in a cupboard; his underpants were taken from him and he was striped, before he escaped naked through the streets, by the men in two cars and a taxi. The raid was thought to have been over skimmed takings of a club in which one family held an interest.

In September 1978 three brothers, Colin, Robert and Brian Fitzgerald, were involved in a bottle and knife fight with two other men in the Indiana Club, Berry Street. One of the men received wounds requiring 48 stitches, and in February 1979 Colin began two years' imprisonment to go alongside the three years he was already serving following a fight in the Babalou Club in which two men and a woman were slashed. In the same month a shotgun was fired in a fight in the QT Club in Manstys Lane. The manager, Peter Stockley, received shoulder wounds. In May that year three men were acquitted at the Crown Court of possessing the shotgun and ammunition and causing £400 worth of damage.

In the meantime there had been a couple of arson attacks. The Knightsbridge Club in Duke Street had gone up in flames after an explosion on 1 November 1978, and three months later the Palatine Club in Dale Street was gutted by what the police were convinced was an arson attack. No one was charged with either offence.[12]

But, so far as the police were concerned, the most serious incident had involved the Flying Squad's Detective Sergeant Bernard Craven, who suffered brain damage in an attack on him whilst guarding the London supergrass Billy Amies. Versions of what exactly happened and how vary.

Amies, it will be recalled, was one of the more unpleasant of armed robbers. Amongst his other roles, he was the 'policeman' who had threatened one of his victims with castration and the rape of his daughter. He had also been at work on Merseyside. In the first of his three cases there a middle-aged woman had been repeatedly punched in the face; in the second another middle-aged woman, her Down's Syndrome daughter and her son had all been tied up; the latter had also been threatened with castration. In the third incident a garage owner and his family had been tied up, and the owner had had his testicles bitten to persuade him to open his safe.

Tony Lundy, who turned Amies into a supergrass, described him as follows:

> In some ways Billy was a nutter. He was also known as Billy the Queer because he's a raving homosexual. A big hard man, over six foot, a real animal, a compulsive armed robber who was really feared, but clever too.

---

[12] *Guardian*, 2 July 1979.

Amies was in serious difficulties. He was caught out of his territory and had been arrested with one of Liverpool's real hardmen John Tremarco. Lundy was told by another supergrass, David Smith, that Amies wanted help because he feared a corrupt Liverpool police officer, John Keating, was trying to lighten Tremarco's load by placing it on Amies' shoulders. It appears Amies was being pressured into pleading guilty. Lundy went incognito to Walton jail and saw Amies who, once he had read Smith's statements involving him, decided that the path to safety was for him to turn supergrass. Much to the fury of the Merseyside police Amies was transferred to Brixton on Rule 43 and then to Acton police station. There he told his version of his life of crime, implicating Tremarco and also Keating.

In October 1977, he went back to Liverpool to plead guilty. His statement was then shown to the solicitors for the other defendants who, as soon as Amies walked into the witness-box, in turn were forced to put their hands up. The public gallery howled revenge and the case was adjourned until the Monday for the sentencing of everyone including Amies.

The new and reformed supergrass was, unsurprisingly, unhappy about staying in the North West for the weekend. He wanted to do the round trip to the safety of London. It was agreed he should be returned on the Sunday night to be lodged overnight in a Liverpool police station. So far so good, except that on the Sunday night the London sergeants who had custody of Amies could not find him a home; nor could they manage to contact the local Serious Crimes Officers. They turned up with Amies in tow at the hotel in Liverpool where Lundy was staying. Further efforts to find Amies a bed in a cell failed, so he was booked into the hotel along with his guarding officers Craven and

O'Rourke. On a toss of the coin it was decided that Craven should sleep in the room with Amies, and O'Rourke outside.

Unfortunately Amies thought it would be a good idea to go out for a last drink. This was by no means an uncommon situation with supergrasses, and the officer agreed. Off he and Craven went to a pub in the docks called the Crow's Nest. Even more unfortunately it was the haunt of Tremarco's friends. Lundy seems to have been full of admiration for his protégé.

> Typical of the fearless animal he is, off goes Amies with Craven into the lions' den. But as soon as they walk in, they're set upon! Amies, big strong beast, fights his way out and escapes, but Bernie Craven gets an almighty kicking. He's almost kicked to death but he manages to stagger out of the pub, he's found in the front garden of a nearby house and he's rushed to hospital.[13]

Amies was badly cut and had a broken arm by the time he returned to the safety of the hotel. Craven was not so fortunate; he had severe concussion, a broken nose and a fractured cheekbone. He never really recovered, and retired from the force on health grounds. The next morning Lundy managed to have Amies' case remitted to London where he could be sentenced for all his offences. Tremarco received fifteen years. Back in London Amies served only two. Two

---

[13] The quotations are from M. Short's *Lundy*, pp.51–2. There is a full account of Amies' career in Chapter 4 of the book. An alternative view is expressed in A. Jennings and others, *Scotland Yard's Cocaine Connection*. They point out that apart from the two men in Liverpool, Amies' evidence only served to convict three more people.

years later Keating was convicted of attempting to extort half the money an insurance company had paid to a police informer. He received two and a half years.

The story in the Underworld was that Amies had been punished in the pub by a Liverpool hardman, Billy Grimwood, assisted by two London brothers from a well-known and influential family. The mystery remains as to why Amies chose the Crow's Nest, of all Liverpool pubs, in which to drink.

One outcome was a purge on the Liverpool drinking clubs. The Chief Constable, Kenneth Oxford, objected to the renewal of the licences of twenty-five establishments. They were suspended for one month, after which Mr Oxford withdrew his objections.

> We felt the little fish were going to go under. While they had transgressed, they weren't the people we were really looking for. But the effect has been to say to the club-owners and licensees: 'You have been warned.'[14]

Peace was at least temporarily restored, although the Merseyside police were well aware that many clubs were operated by front men, that there were two sets of books being kept and that the proceeds from the bar takings were going to finance heavy crime committed by Liverpool criminals throughout the country. Now with the recession the great days of the clubs are over and the powerful families have moved into international credit-card frauds.

Meanwhile the Triads had finally been successful in establishing something more than a foothold in the community. There had been a large Chinese community in the

[14] *Guardian, 2 July 1979.*

city dating from mid-Victorian times and in 1927 the *Echo and Daily Post* had trumpeted, 'What the police found in a Liverpool Chinaman's premises'.[15] By today's standards it was pretty tame, but the bags of opium and morphine (let alone the gun with two hundred rounds of ammunition) was sufficient to kill 10,000 people, said the city analyst. A year later the community was in the news again. This time there had been raids on the gambling joints, and thirty-nine Chinamen appeared before the city's magistrates. By and large they were a stable and well-respected community; however, there was one celebrated murder case involving a Chinese businessman, which was by no means a gangland killing although it had its origins in a club fight.

Lock Ah Tam had come to England as a ship's steward in the 1890s. He had settled in Liverpool and become a wealthy man through restaurants and clubs. He was thought to be the most respected Chinaman in England and was European representative of a Chinese dockers' union. Unfortunately, in 1918 he was hit on the head with a billiard cue by a drunken Russian sailor and underwent a personality change. He took to drinking heavily, flew into terrifying rages, lost his business and went bankrupt. On 1 December 1925 he gave a party for his son, but when the guests had gone began to abuse his family. His son went for the police, but by the time he returned Lock Ah Tam had shot his wife and daughters before telephoning the police to say, 'Send you folks please, I have killed my wife and children.'

He was defended by Sir Edward Marshall-Hall QC, paid for by the Chinese community, and offered a plea of insanity. It was rejected by the jury in twelve minutes. He was hanged on 23 March 1926.

[15] 10 November 1927.

In 1980 Fenton Bresler reported that a former head of the Drugs Squad in Merseyside had 'no knowledge of any criminal Triads working in the Merseyside area'.[16]

By 1986 however, the picture had changed and, it has emerged, there had been a Wo Sing Wo – a powerful Triad gang – presence on Merseyside for some time. Lau Kam Keung, a relatively minor member of the operation, moved up a grade or two when his immediate boss left for the richer pickings of Soho. Now Lau Kam Keung, or Freddie Lau as he was known, decided it would be a good idea if Wong Mai Cheung, the owner of a restaurant in Nelson Street, paid him £200 a week protection money. To emphasize the seriousness of the suggestion, various of Lau's friends would sit all day in the restaurant over a single bowl of rice. Wong agreed a figure of £100 and paid this for two years until he rebelled. He was beaten with rice flails and went to the police. He was given a tape-recorder, and taped conversations when it was suggested that Lau should buy his restaurant to pay off some wholly imaginary debts to Lau. Lau eventually pleaded guilty and received a sentence of ten years' imprisonment.

It came out later that Lau had been operating a loan-sharking arrangement offering Chinese gamblers credit in the north of England casinos. Minimum repayments were £100 a week to keep the interest at bay. As with all good loan-sharkers, the nut or capital sum owed was never touched. One case showed that over two years a punter had paid £4,000 in respect of a £350 debt. The unfortunate men could, however, join Wo Sing Wo as a way out of clearing the interest; though the capital debt was still never voided.[17]

---

[16] F. Bresler, *The Trail of the Triads*, p. 151.
[17] D. Black, *Triad Takeover*, pp. 86–8.

By the early 1980s Liverpool was racked with political scandals with widespread allegations of corruption against officials, councillors and political leaders. A decade later the story in the city was much the same as in the rest of the country. Although with the recession much of the club scene has faded there was a battle, if not a war, between groups of bouncers over who should mind the clubs and the lucrative drug trade that goes with the control of the door. Indeed, drugs were once again paramount although officers maintain, almost certainly correctly, that the trade is minor compared with that of Manchester from where, in the main, the local dealers get their supplies.

Nevertheless it has proved too much for some. Jean Larkin, who ran a company selling window-blinds, and her boyfriend Gary Pettitt, who ran an enterprise selling drugs, left their flat in Aigburth on 27 April 1993. The television was left on and her dog, Bruff, unfed. Pettitt had had a call to a meeting in a McDonald's in Markey Street, Chorley, some 25 miles away, and Jean Larkin went with him. It seems they kept the rendezvous because a van marked 'Calypso Blinds' had been seen in the neighbourhood. It was later found at Manchester Airport.

On 1 June the police began digging in woods at Coppull, three miles outside Chorley. Some jewellery belonging to the couple was found, as was burned clothing. The police were convinced they had been killed and their bodies burned. Two men had been seen camping in the area the week Pettitt and Jean Larkin had disappeared; it was believed the men had a brown Rover 213 and a silver Accord which had been seen in the Gateshead area. The Rover was later found in Barry, South Glamorgan. There was no suggestion, said the police, that Miss Larkin had been anything other than an innocent bystander in what appears to have been a drugs deal which went wrong.

On 4 October 1994 brothers Francis (31) and James Mullen (25) were convicted of the killing of Pettitt and Larkin. They were sentenced to life imprisonment. The trial judge indicated that he would recommend that each should serve a minimum of twenty years before being eligible for release on licence.

So, in 1994 Liverpool is like almost all of the other cities. Drugs are the main source of criminal behaviour. Says one senior detective:

> At the bottom end 10-year-olds with a habit break into your house or my car to feed their habit; in the middle there is a battle for control of the clubs to see whose drugs go in, and at the top end there is major distribution.

In the meantime at least two players have disappeared. Michael Showers, who established credentials as a 'community worker' in Toxteth, was jailed for twenty-one years in 1991 for his part in the importation of heroin to the value of £2 million. More permanently off the scene is Brian 'Snowy' Jennings who, when he died, was said to be one of the richest men in Liverpool. He kept his wealth concealed, he drove a second hand car and lived in a council house. 'He was dressed like an unmade bed,' said a friend. He died in 1994 in Strangeways prison awaiting trial over his role in the importation of cocaine said to be worth £500 million. His partner, 62 year old Tommy Comerford, was recently released after serving his 14 year sentence for importing heroin. (*Sunday Times*, 15 January 1995).

5

Newcastle and the North East

In his novel *Jack's Return Home*[1], Ted Lewis – who was brought up in the North East – paints a portrait of club life in Newcastle in the 1960s when in the evenings the winnings from one-armed bandits spilled on to the carpets of the plush nightclubs and prosperous working men's clubs, and at dead of night into the pockets – with a rake-off to the barman or club steward – of the collectors who were skimming from the machines they had been sent to empty. His was an accurate picture of local hardmen and violence linked to London gangsters. At one time, said BBC producer David Seymour, '. . . it was a bit like the Wild West in Newcastle . . . the London gangs squabbled and three nightclubs were burned down.'[2]

On 7 January 1967 two company directors were accused of murdering a fellow director in a fruit machine business who had been found shot dead in his car. It became a

---

[1] Filmed as *Get Carter*.
[2] *Daily Express*, 28 March 1980.

complete *cause célèbre* and has featured in many compilations of miscarriages of justice in the British legal system. Dennis Stafford, aged 23, and Michael Luvaglio, 29, who appeared at Peterlee magistrates' court in Co. Durham, were charged with murdering 33-year-old Angus Sibbett who had been found shot the previous Thursday in the back seat of his car parked beneath a bridge at South Hetton.

Sibbett, burly, bearded and handsome, had been a key figure in one of the biggest gambling set-ups in the country. His territory was in the North East, at that time stuffed full of one-armed bandits, which at that stage were a major source of Underworld income.[3] He had served his apprenticeship in London with one of the biggest gangs, and this connection lasted until his death. He was a larger than life character who had served in Korea, been a shoe salesman, run a Chinese restaurant and done twelve months for receiving before gravitating to Newcastle where he worked for Vince Landa, otherwise Vincente Luvaglio,[4] who had set up Social Club Services Ltd, a company with many subsidiaries which installed gaming machines, then mainly the old-fashioned one-armed bandits, in clubs.

Dennis Stafford, one of the two men charged with the murder, had led what can most charitably be described as an interesting life. His father Joe Stafford, whose real name was Siegenberg, had been, and indeed still was, one of the great go-betweens and fixers for criminals who wanted to do business with the police over bail or the dropping of

[3] Frank Fraser gives a long account of the troubles he and Eddie Richardson had in installing their machines in preference to other people's around the country in *Mad Frank*.
[4] *News of the World*, 19 March 1967.

charges. The good-looking, if also brilliantined and spiv-like, Stafford junior made his name in the Underworld as a high class con-man, burglar and prison escaper.

At the Inner London Sessions on 26 July 1956, he was sentenced to a seven-year term for breaking and entering and being in possession of a loaded revolver. He had pleaded guilty. Four months later on a wet and windy 8 November he escaped over the wall from Wormwood Scrubs, along with Anthony Hawkes, another con-man who in previous metamorphoses had been a cavalry officer, an Irish peer, a foreign trade attaché and a Rumanian butler. Hawkes was serving a six-year sentence for false pretences over a textile swindle which curiously he had been operating in his own name. It is idle to think the pair did not have substantial outside help, because exactly twenty days later they both turned up in Newcastle if not loaded with money then at least presentably dressed, and with enough cash to pay for rooms, offices and the necessary props to open a wholesale cloth long-firm fraud, which they operated successfully until the balloon went up in February 1957. By this time Stafford had a fiancée, Sandra, a 19-year-old model in a make-up fashion house.

As with all well-organized operators of long-firm frauds, by the time the creditors moved in Hawkes and Stafford were gone. Just as the police had been tipped off that the morose Mr Whelby and the nice Mr Hutton were Hawkes and Stafford respectively, so someone had tipped off the pair that the police were in close pursuit.

Whelby had once more become Mr Hawkes when he was found in the King's Hotel off the Bayswater Road in London ten days later, but of Mr Hutton there was no sign. He had become Wally Birch[5] and had gone to Port of Spain, Trinidad. Unfortunately, as was always the case with Stafford, he was irresistible to women. In the time he was out and about in London before he fled, he had acquired another fiancée, an actress, Eileen. Before taking the boat from Liverpool he told her where he was going and when she sent a telegram to say she was joining him the police, who had been watching her, made four. DI George Mullen and DS Jack Huntley retrieved him – watched, it was said, by a silent crowd of 500 people including several pretty girls.

Stafford was properly and righteously penitent. In an exclusive story he wrote for the *News of the World* whilst in a Port of Spain prison awaiting his extradition, he had this to say:

I'm most sorry for the friends I let down and grateful to the friends who didn't let me down. Most of all I'm sorry for my parents – they never let me down. I only wish I could do something for them. But of course, I can do something for them – from here on I promise them solemnly that I will go straight and stay out of trouble.[6]

Meanwhile his father, Joe, once a landlord of an East End pub and now described as a Soho commission agent, said of his son:

[5] The choice of the name Birch was interesting and should have been a dead giveaway. Wally Birch and Stafford had been involved in a fight with the Kray twins in their teens outside the Mayfair Ballroom in Tottenham. The Krays had been acquitted but Ronnie Kray never forgave Stafford for grassing on him. The real Wally Birch went into clubs in Soho with Joe Wilkins, nephew of Bert who had been acquitted of the murder of Massimo Montecolumbo at Wandsworth Greyhound Stadium in 1934.
[6] *News of the World*, 20 October 1957.

It all began in the War. He was evacuated to Cornwall and I was in the Army. He missed his father's right hand. His big trouble is his big ideas . . . After school he began as a waiter but before he was 17 he was in the fruit business with his own office and doing well until someone let him down over money.[7]

On his return he was sent to Durham Assizes, where he received an additional eighteen months for the Newcastle long-firm.

He settled down for a while in Dartmoor until Monday 5 January 1959, when he escaped along with William Day, a house-and garage-breaker, also serving seven years. It was his third attempt at escape. By the Wednesday it was thought that Stafford, armed with a new passport, was already abroad. An admirer said that the break had been planned with extreme care:

That's the mark Stafford gives to all his work. He is admired by the real criminal element which makes up about 10 per cent of the prison population. They look up to him as a man with a brain, always waging war on the law, and often winning – and a man who doesn't give up when he loses one contest and lands in prison . . . he can always get someone to tip him off about prison routine and events which he, as a man under closer guard, couldn't obtain.[8]

Unfortunately Day did not make it off the Moor. He was found drowned in a reservoir. It seems he had blundered

[7] *Daily Mail*, 18 October 1957.
[8] *Daily Mail*, 1 January 1959.

into the water and Stafford had thrown him a lifebelt but had not raised the alarm.

Stafford had not made it out of the country however. On 20 February, forty-four days after his escape, he was arrested in Leicester Square and returned to Dartmoor where he was regarded with something less than critical favour by the other prisoners who held him responsible for the death of Day. He was put in solitary confinement and allowed out by the Governor, George Brown-Smith, to reassure his father that he was not being victimized over Day. Stafford said that he had not merely thrown him a lifebelt but had gone in the water after him and grabbed him, but had lost hold in the dark.

But the original case of housebreaking and possessing an offensive weapon was far from over. In August 1960 John 'Happy' Sambridge swore a statement that it was he who had planted the gun in Stafford's car.

Sambridge, who later was shot by Frankie Fraser over an incident at Brighton Races in 1955,[9] said that on the day of Stafford's arrest he had been approached by a detective who told him he had the needle to Stafford and wanted him nicked. Sambridge had been given a gun by the officer and left it on the shelf under the dashboard. For this service he had received £5. The statement was passed to Lord Stoneham at the Home Office. Joe Stafford, who throughout his son's escapades always campaigned totally on his behalf,

[9] Fraser was working a pitch on the free course at Brighton owned by Albert Dimes, then in custody over the Spot fight in Soho, when he was arrested by Chief Superintendent Greeno and questioned over suggestions that he was in Brighton to kill one of Spot's men. Fraser was released without charge but believed that Sambridge had identified him to the police. When Fraser was released from prison in 1962 he sought out Sambridge and shot him in the leg.

said he thought that the finding of the gun might have been an influence on the judge who passed the sentence on the housebreaking charge. As so often happens with statements and confessions and petitions, it was a false dawn. Nothing came of the inquiry.

Stafford was released on 23 March 1961 to join a catering firm as assistant – an ideas man earning the then handsome four-figure sum plus car and expenses – to one of the directors. Again a bright future was prophesied. 'He got into trouble originally because he lived above his income, but now with responsibilities I am sure he will settle down,' said a friend.[10]

Wrong. He lost the job and then worked as a chauffeur to a London car hire firm. After that he was jailed for three months for being in possession of a Browning automatic, and then under the name of Fielding he was back inside for a year after pleading guilty to stealing a car from a car park in Brighton. On his release in 1965 he made his way to Newcastle where he too joined the employment of Vince Landa, working as booking agent for the cabarets playing the clubs. He was now earning a basic £25 per week and could possibly double it with commission.

Landa, whose younger brother was Michael Luvaglio, the other defendant in the Sibbett killing, had at one time been an officer in the RAF police before he had moved to the North East and established a gambling empire. At one stage he was in the multi-millionaire category; he owned a substantial country house with thirty acres near Bishop Auckland, he had a villa in Majorca and he ran a Rolls-Royce, a Jaguar and half a dozen other cars. In a gesture of family solidarity he moved his parents and Michael to the

[10] *Sunday Express*, 22 March 1961.

North East. Michael also became an employee of Social
Club Services Ltd and its myriad of interlocked companies.

Sibbett's body was found at about 5.15 a.m. on 5 January
1967 in a Mark X Jaguar badly parked near Pesspool
Bridge, Front Street at South Hetton. He had been shot
at close range. A pit worker had seen there was someone in
the vehicle, thought he was asleep and opened the door to
wake him and tell him to move.

Stafford was not lucky with informants in the North
East. Someone had tipped off the police about his long-firm
in 1957. Now ten years later someone told the police that a
damaged red E-Type Jaguar was in a Sunderland garage to
which it had been taken for repair.

In what became an increasingly misty case, one thing was
clear. Michael Luvaglio had driven the red E-type on 3
January. He had been to his brother's home in Majorca
with his parents, Stafford and their respective girlfriends.
Everyone had flown back to London, then all except Landa
had flown up to Newcastle. Landa had stayed behind to see
his accountant and then had returned to Majorca. On 4
January Luvaglio had telephoned his brother who told
Stafford to use the E-type as his own car was in for repair.

The evidence against Stafford and Luvaglio ran as
follows. The red E-type Jaguar had been in some sort of
collision with the Mark X. It was common ground that
Stafford and Luvaglio had arranged to meet Sibbett that
night. They said he had not turned up for the meeting and
whilst they waited at the Bird Cage Club, Stafford went
outside to the Jaguar to get some duty-free cigarettes he had
brought back from Majorca. He noticed that the E-type was
damaged and drew it to the attention of a Matthew Dean,
the acting doorman. There were tyre marks in the snow
which suggested a vehicle had collided with the E-type and

had then reversed away. Both men were well alibied by their girlfriends Pat Burgess and Selena Jones, the singer. Much of the prosecution case depended on the time of death and whether the defendants could have driven from the club, killed Sibbett, dumped his body and driven back within three-quarters of an hour.

The trial judge Sir Patrick O'Connor QC, in his summing-up, did not assist the defence and, in one of those pieces of rubric so favoured by judges, offered this little homily.

> Luvaglio has told you that Angus Sibbett was his friend and it is a matter which you will give careful consideration to. As human beings you will, of course, know that friends are of two types. True friends and false. Today [March 15] is the exact anniversary of that famous cry, which has run down the ages, when Julius Caesar lay dying, 'And you, Brutus', whose dagger was in his heart; his friend. Seventy-five years later one greater than Caesar was betrayed by Judas with a kiss.

The jury was out three hours before returning a guilty verdict. The Court of Appeal was unsympathetic and although in March 1972 Reginald Maudling, the then Home Secretary, referred the matter back to that court for a re-hearing of the appeal, there was no joy there. Luvaglio's parents stuck loyally by him, instructing Sir David Napley (soon to be president of the Law Society) on their son's behalf. In his book Napley firmly maintains his belief in Luvaglio's innocence.

> I had then been practising for over thirty years, and was not unfamiliar with the questioning in and out of

court, but not one of us – or, for that matter, any of the other experienced lawyers and non-lawyers who afterwards questioned Luvaglio – was ever able to catch him out or fault him. Jimmy Comyn (later Mr Justice Comyn) shared the belief that Luvaglio was innocent of the murder. John Mathew, a Senior Treasury Counsel at the Central Criminal Court, who at the time spent almost his entire time prosecuting, while unwilling to commit himself to the view that he was convinced of his innocence, was far from convinced of his guilt, and was abundantly satisfied that on the evidence a jury ought not to be satisfied beyond reasonable doubt that he was guilty.[11]

In turn Joe Stafford did what he could, approaching such diverse people as the police officer Nipper Read – offering assistance with the Kray case if help could be given to his son – and to the then Prime Minister, Harold Wilson. In January 1973, in an echo of the 'Happy' Sambridge statement, two men swore statements which were handed to the *People* alleging they had been offered £5,000 to kill Sibbett. George Shotton, a Newcastle car dealer with a long criminal record including convictions for violence, said he had been approached in the Bird Cage Club by a man who seemed to be Italian. A second man, whose name was not given, said the man who approached him appeared to be Greek.

But, despite representations by MPs, lawyers, newspapers and by JUSTICE, Stafford and Luvaglio languished

[11] Sir David Napley, *Not Without Prejudice*, p.289. There is a very full account of the Luvaglio case in Sir David's book in Chapter 21. David Lewis and Peter Hughman, then an articled clerk and now a solicitor, wrote what must be the definitive account of the case – *Most Unnatural: An Inquiry into the Stafford Case.*

in prison. In October 1973 their appeal to the House of Lords was rejected. This was the end of the matter so far as legal avenues were concerned. Both men were paroled in 1979 and the next year Stafford did neither of them a favour. In an exclusive interview with David Mertens in the *News of the World* for a reported fee of £10,000, he confessed, 'I did it'.[12] He said he had committed the crime whilst Luvaglio was in bed. Once more he was out of favour with the Underworld, and to compound his problems he was on the run for a drink-driving offence, and was also wanted in connection with some credit-card frauds. Luvaglio, unavailable for comment, was said to be in Oberammagau with his mother to see the Passion Play. During his stay in prison he had obtained an Open University degree, and since his release he had been working with handicapped children. Later he and Sir David Napley issued a statement pointing out discrepancies in Stafford's account.

Stafford back-tracked quickly. He clearly could not retract to the *News of the World* and so he did the next best thing. He made a statement to the *Sunday People* for their edition of 28 September, saying his confession was a lie and he had only made it for financial reasons and '. . . to prove how hypocritical the system is and how people will believe what they want to believe. We did not commit the murder and the evidence and the facts of the case remain as they were.' Earlier he had told the *Guardian* that Luvaglio had nothing to do with the shooting. In 1989 the *Mail on Sunday* reported Stafford as being under arrest, along with South African banker Gotz Gunterhoner, over a multi-million-pound international fraud on the Trust Bank of Johannesburg.[13]

[12] *News of the World*, 7 September 1980.
[13] *Mail on Sunday*, 30 April 1989.

What was the truth behind the killing of Sibbett? Was it over his continuing womanizing? Or was it over the machines? It later emerged that he had been skimming substantial profits from the gaming machines he was minding for Landa.

That was certainly the theory advanced, immediately after the trial, by Patricia Sacre, an old friend of both the Luvaglio brothers and Sibbett: 'The trouble was so many people were on the fiddle. Everybody was setting up their own private companies and milking the kitty in various ways.'[14]

Landa's empire collapsed after the trial. It emerged that Sibbett had been organizing thefts on a wholesale basis from the clubs which had rented machines from Coinamatic, a subsidiary of Social Club Services Ltd, to the tune of £1,600 a week. Landa, it was said, knew of the thefts and had turned a blind eye to them. When the police went to his home in Bishop Auckland they found him gone – to his villa in Majorca.[15] For the next few years he led a peripatetic life, wandering like a second division Flying Dutchman around the Mediterranean. In 1977 he was still abroad living in poor circumstances in Malta. He was held twice by the police; once in Italy after the sinking of his yacht in Sicily. Two years later he surrendered himself on charges of fraud to the police in Chester-le-Street. He now had a fiancée, 19-year-old Julie Hamblin, who was standing by him. On 22 February 1980 Landa pleaded guilty to seven frauds on the working men's clubs. The judge, taking into account the time he had spent in prison abroad awaiting extradition, fined him £2,750 with £1,000 costs. On his release Landa

14 *News of the World*, 19 March 1967.
15 *People*, 20 August 1967.

told the press that, had he known the outcome of the case, he would have surrendered himself much earlier. He still lives in some style near Durham.

The Stafford-Luvaglio affair was on any reckoning by far the most important case in the North East for decades. Life there generally progresses at a level almost divorced from the more vibrant and wealthy areas of the country. Says Professor Dick Hobbs of the University of Durham:

> It's a very run-down area with a very sparse population and a very small market centred on Newcastle City centre where the amount of drinking establishments is quite phenomenal. On a Friday and Saturday people just flock in and get pissed. They queue half an hour in their party clothes to get in a pub in freezing weather.
>
> There is no economic mobility. You go down the pit at 15 and come up at 65. Culturally they are used to that even though it last happened two generations ago. There is no opportunity for people to move around. In some cases by the age of 25 you have gone through economic cycles but it isn't the case in the North East.
>
> The traditional jobs have been the pits, shipbuilding and engineering. People in the workplace were restricted to these masculine stereotypes and the same thing applies to crime in the North East. All you need is cropped hair and big shoulders.
>
> In the rural areas there is still dog-fighting in the villages, and in an evening you can see men in camouflage clothing leading three lurchers out. The gamekeepers shoot the dogs with guns with infra-red sights.

Nevertheless, says one local solicitor:

Although there is a twenty per cent unemployment figure, the remaining 80 per cent do very nicely. They earn their money and they spend it. The cost of housing is low and beer is £1.25 a pint. In Newcastle there is a lot of night life both high and low. There is the Royal Shakespeare Company here for three months, the Scottish National Opera and then there are the wine bars and the clubs. They spend their money and a proportion of it is going to be spent illicitly. Drugs are professionally operated, the amateur approach has been swept aside even in Hartlepool. The drugs come in from everywhere but particularly from the ports such as Newcastle and Middlesbrough.

There have been a number of celebrated murder cases in the North East including the unsolved murder of Evelyn Foster in 1931.[16] This, however, was a domestic matter and murders committed in the course of theft or robbery in the area included that of Police Constable Shiell, in which the evidence was remarkably similar to that of the case of Craig and Bentley. The murder was committed by two young men. Ostler, himself the son of a Leeds police officer, and Appleby were found by Shiell breaking into the Co-op store at Coxhoe, County Durham on 29 February 1940. He chased them into Westley Place where he was shot. He had already blown his whistle to summon help and he was soon found; he was taken to the local hospital

[16] Evelyn Foster was found on 6 January 1931 lying beside the burning wreck of her car. She had suffered appalling burns and died a few hours later. Before she died she accused a bowler-hatted man of setting fire to her. No one was ever arrested for the crime or really even suspected, although Jonathon Goodman puts up a plausible argument naming a possible murderer in *The Burning of Evelyn Foster*.

where he said to his Superintendent, 'They've finished me Super.' The local justices' clerk was called to take a dying declaration from the gravely injured Shiell: 'I cornered them. One pulled a revolver and the other said, "Let him have it, he is all alone," and he shot me, just one shot in the stomach at the side.'

The men ran a cut-throat defence which was inevitably to bring down both of them. Ostler ran the defence of an alibi, whilst Appleby said he was present when Ostler fired the fatal shot and gave evidence to that effect. Appleby denied saying, 'Let him have it. He is all alone.' His version was that he had said, 'Come on, let's give him a clout.' Mr Justice Hilbery in summing up said:

> If you accept the deceased's account, you may have to ask yourselves if it were not for Appleby's remark, 'Let him have it, he is all alone', the foul hand of Ostler might not have pulled the trigger.

Both were convicted at Leeds' Assizes and sentenced to death.

According to Professor Hobbs:

> So far only Ecstasy appears to be a problem on the drug scene in the North East. There is really no cocaine in general use up here. There is a general conservative culture. Legitimate fashions reach the North-East late. Ecstasy took off two and a half to three years after it did in London.
>
> You can get cocaine in Middlesbrough at £50 a gramme, the same price as in London. It's still a yuppie drug here.

Part of the reason is that there is no real ethnic minority community. There is a very small Asian community in Newcastle and an enormous Hassidic community in Gateshead, but 'they're invisible'.

There is little doubt that cocaine will arrive and that crack is the ideal substance for a depressed inner city estate where nothing has happened for 25 years. But as yet there is no demand. Crack is a ghetto drug and there are plenty of white ghettos which have no economic vitality legitimate or illegitimate.

This trailing behind the fashions of the remainder of the country seems to be echoed in the attitude in the North East to crime. The Chief Constable's annual reports mark a depressing but relatively slow upward progression in the use of firearms – in 1987 the use of the shotgun doubled and that of the sawn-off shotgun was up by a third – and of attacks on the elderly. There have been instances of force by career criminals, as when in 26/27 April 1977 a customs officer was tortured to make him reveal the whereabouts of his money. Three men later received sentences of up to five years.

There have been sporadic incidents of gang violence, such as the 1980 Saturday lunch-time fight when the West Denton gang took on the Benton gang in the Eldon Square shopping precinct. The victim had cuts running the length of his spine, and the ringleader of twelve received three years. A year later a fish and chip shop in West End was petrol-bombed on 23 April 1981, earning nine years for the ringleaders. That year, at the more professional end of things, it was discovered that forged American $20 bills were being printed in the Newcastle area. Eight men including three from Newcastle were found guilty and given three years each. Generally speaking, however, the Chief Constable's report on interesting crimes in his annual survey was devoted more to domestic incidents than to the activities of the career criminal.

By the middle of the 1980s there were rumours that the various warring Newcastle factions had joined together into what would be a formidable alliance; but, if a temporary alliance was formed, it soon splintered. There had always been some solidarity amongst North East criminals. It is said that when the Kray twins wished to explore the possibility of taking an interest in the North East, and indeed took Joe Louis, the former world heavyweight champion, on a tour there, locals explained that their continued presence was unnecessary. From time to time North Easterners have been recruited for their ability to handle gelignite on one-off operations in the South, but generally they have remained a league apart.

One of Newcastle's most famous criminal sons is the independent safebreaker, Eddie Chapman, now in his late seventies. He had been apprenticed in the shipbuilding trade and then had joined the Guards before, on his first leave, he deserted and received 112 days in the guardhouse. On his release and back in prison, he joined up with Jimmy Hunt who took him on a break-in at Fyffe's, the banana importers. Now he learned how to open safes, and Odeon cinemas became his principal target; there was always a substantial sum kept overnight. His technique involved the use of a condom which was filled with gelignite and water and then pushed through a lock. This stopped the gelignite dropping into the safe.

Eventually Chapman was captured in Jersey, where he had fled while on bail in Newcastle. He had been arrested there following an escape from Scotland where he and his partners were caught blowing a safe in a local Co-op. He was sentenced in Jersey to two years' imprisonment and while serving them the Germans invaded the Channel Islands. He was recruited as an agent but immediately became a double one, working for British Intelligence and being parachuted into Germany. He was allowed to keep his German earnings, and there would be no prosecution over the forty or more safes he had blown. He wrote his memoirs and his story was made into the film *Triple Cross*. In later life he ran a health club and hotel in Hertfordshire, and spent some time trying to prove that a senior Metropolitan police officer was crooked. He finally retired to Spain, one of the very few criminals of the old school who actually held on to their money.[17]

In August 1993 a bizarre crime was committed. In a scenario reminiscent of the 1870s in Arizona, a gang took over the remote town of Rothbury, Berwick-on-Tweed, to steal £15,000 from the post office there.

Early on Monday 23 August five men, dressed in camouflage clothing and wearing ski-masks, appeared in the village, cut the telephone wires and threatened some of the 2,000 residents with crowbars. They took over the main street with a stolen council van and told the residents who were looking out of their windows to go back to bed and stay there. They then forced their way into the post office and escaped with £15,000 in cash, pension books and stamps.

It was not the first attack on this tiny village. In 1992 the village store had been the subject of a ram-raid, a popular

---

[17] Apart from his own memoirs, there is an account of his exploits and capture in E. Greeno, *War on the Underworld*, Chapter 10, in which Chapman is referred to as Mike.

form of sport which had originated in the North East in the 1970s.

The last months of 1993 were not a happy time for Newcastle hardmen and bystanders alike. From the middle of October six men were shot in nightclubs and discos, and two men, rumoured to be connected to the city's leading families involved in drugs, disappeared. It was part of a continuing story that, however isolated the North East may be and however 'behind' in fashion, it is not always immune from the crime problems which beset the other areas of the country. The shooting of Viv Graham has its roots in the late 1980s; the cause was almost certainly drugs. There was a bouncers' war in 1988. As Hobbs says:

Here the bouncers are weightlifters and ex-boxers, huge men and they are used for their size. Some have been on steroids. In other places it's their hardness. The clubs are involved in Ecstasy. It's easy to make your name here. You don't get the challenges you would in Manchester or Liverpool.

Apart from the truth, one of the first casualties was Robert Bell, builder and bouncer of Gateshead. On 22 August 1988, he was dining in Santino's Restaurant in Newcastle's Cloth Market when two men burst in. One man, who was never identified, cut the telephone lines, and it was alleged by the prosecution that a Peter Donnelly went to the table where Bell was sitting and pointed a shotgun at him. Fighting broke out and the gun was taken from Donnelly by Viv Graham who was at the table; he smashed it against the wall and told Donnelly not to be so stupid. According to the prosecution, Donnelly, of Lemington, Newcastle, and the second man then fought Bell who was stabbed first in the shoulder and then in the chest, penetrating the heart. He was saved by emergency surgery. Graham had again intervened and given Donnelly a good beating before the police arrived.

The motive, said David Wood, prosecuting, was revenge for a fight earlier in the evening between Bell and Donnelly over two girls, which had been broken up by the police who arrested one of Donnelly's friends. The prosecution's case was that Donnelly had then gone home, changed his clothes and come out looking for Bell armed with a gun and carving knife. In a written statement made after the fight, Bell claimed that Donnelly was his attacker. At the trial the following April, when Donnelly was charged with attempted murder and various ancillary offences, Bell changed his story. On reflection he could now not be sure that it was Donnelly who attacked him nor how his injuries occurred. Nor could Bell's brother, Ian, help in the question of identification. He had chased the second man who had tried to take another customer hostage.

There were cheers from the public gallery when Donnelly, who had declined to answer police questions and to give evidence, was acquitted by the jury after a retirement of forty-five minutes.

Graham was not long out of the news. Before the trial of Donnelly, he and his friend Rob Armstrong had been the victims of a drive-by shooting outside Newcastle's Manhattan nightclub in April 1989. At about 1.30 a.m. the rear window of their Bluebird Nissan was shot out, and four other shots put sixty pellets into Armstrong. Graham escaped unhurt. Both men, unable to identify their assailants, denounced them. Rob Armstrong said:

> We are the good guys. We try to keep the peace. I am no angel but I can say outright I haven't done

anything to anybody to warrant being shot at. I know I have more friends than enemies in Newcastle. Licensees ask us to keep an eye on their premises during the weekend in case there is an outbreak of trouble. I would only use a reasonable amount of force to eject troublemakers.

I have heard it suggested we were shot at because of some sort of protection war. That is pie in the sky. Newcastle is too small for anybody to operate protection. Licensees ask us to help them out. I have heard it said that an outside operator from Leeds is moving in to slap a protection racket on Newcastle pubs but to me that is just stupid talk.

Viv Graham added:

We are not doormen. Doormen stand outside and try to prevent potential troublemakers from entering the pub.

If a situation gets out of hand, which can happen in packed city pubs and clubs when people have had too much to drink, we will try and calm it down.

A 'city centre pub landlady' was sure there was no protection:

There are good doormen and bad doormen. Just as there are some good police officers and some who go in heavy-handed.

You pay for security because Newcastle is a rough city, but nobody is demanding money by threats. I know of no protection racket.

But the police were not so convinced. A spokesman said that intelligence units had been moved into premises named by licensees as being under protection: 'We know who these gangsters are. This situation will not be allowed to get out of control . . . We will not tolerate gang warfare or intimidation on the streets of Newcastle.'[18]

Initially they were not notably successful in their efforts. Two months later, doorman Mark Stephenson had his ear bitten off at Idols, a club in the seaside town of Whitley Bay. It was stitched back on and five men were charged. Then in the July of that year former championship contender boxer Howard Mills, who was now working as a doorman at Hanrahan's Bar, was shot in the leg which he had to have amputated. Two months after the attack on Mills, Billy Robinson, the under-manager of the Cotton Club, was shot at a party in Felling; hours earlier he had been threatened at Bentley's nightclub. Another man, Paul Basey, was also shot simply because he got in the way. Amid cheers and handshakes Alan Swindon, also of Felling, was acquitted of wounding with intent. William Robinson had told the jury at the Newcastle Crown Court that he could not identify his attacker.

The next year Viv Graham received three years for wounding Stuart Watson, the doorman of Hobo. Along with him were members of some of the North East's powerful families. Alan Tams received two and a half years, as did Stephen Sayers. David Lancaster and Viv's friend Rob Armstrong also went down for a similar period. This had been a high-profile police exercise, with up to fifty officers cordoning off the magistrates' court when the defendants were brought in. Members of the Sayers and

---

[18] Neil McKay and John Merry in *Sunday Sun*, 7 May 1989.

Tams families had been up in court only a few weeks earlier when John Henry Sayers[19], along with Stephen Sayers, was charged with a variety of offences including conspiracy to handle stolen vending machines. Alan Tams was charged with a variety of assaults. Tams, who admitted biting a policeman on the arm – he threatened to bite his nose off if he came any closer – had a month added to his two-and-a-half-year sentence. The policeman had intervened in a food fight in the Elswick Road where eight men had been throwing eggs, flour and ketchup at each other. Tams was seen walking from a general shop with a tray of eggs whilst the others continued fighting. The defence, at one time, suggested the police officer had over-reacted.

At the end of the Watson trial the doorman said he was sorry for what had happened, and went on to accuse the Regional Crime Squad of using him as bait to get Graham and the others. There had been an undercover officer posing as a customer when the incident took place, who had been under orders not to intervene. Unsurprisingly, he came under heavy fire from the defence lawyers and was asked whether when he realized one of the men had a spiked weapon he should have stepped in. 'No,' replied the officer, 'I had been briefed and instructed not to.' A security video of the incident had been a 'chilling picture', said Judge Mary MacMurray.

[19] In January 1995 the *Sunday Times* reported that John Sayers was still a force to be reckoned with – still operating from his cell in Frankland prison, where he was serving a sentence of fifteen years for armed robbery. His great rival is Paddy Conroy, now in Spain after being freed from a prison escort by an armed gang.

On 22 January 1995, 54-year-old John Brian Sayers, father of John junior, was shot in the jaw. He declined to tell the police about the incident. Later a man was charged with attempted murder.

In November 1991 Alan Swindon left circulation after he took too much Ecstasy once too often, and was given twenty-four years for the murder of Paul Furness with a hunting knife. Swindon and Roy Storey had been stabbed in their stomachs in April 1990 in the Rockshots area, where they had been at an Easter pyjama party.

The troubles had led to a registration scheme for nightclub doormen. Organized in May 1992 by the Northumbria police, and the first of its kind in the country, it required the vetting of all doormen at premises which held a public entertainments licence. 'Incidents involving door supervisors have nose-dived. As well as violence, the registration scheme has addressed the problem of protection rackets and drugs,' said Superintendent Peter Durham towards the end of 1993.[20]

Not everyone had received the message, however. Paul Short suffered a fractured skull, two fractures to his left wrist, two broken ribs and a broken right wrist when he was dropped over a balcony twenty feet on to a concrete floor, allegedly by a bouncer at the Sirocco nightclub in Washington. Magistrates at the court there were told that he did not wish to press charges against his attacker. In fact it was Short who appeared in court. On 22 June 1991 he was fined £50 and ordered to pay £140 for smashing the windows of the nightclub before the bouncers dealt with him.

Now, in the last hours of 1993, Viv Graham was killed by three shots from a .357 Magnum handgun as he walked to his car in the Wallsend district. It seems his attackers had been shadowing him for most of the evening. Graham had been drinking for most of New Year's Eve in the Anchor and Queen's Head public houses. He crawled thirty yards before collapsing outside a newsagent's shop.

[20] Quoted in the Newcastle *Journal*, 3 January 1994.

Graham had also been credited unofficially with the attack in September 1991 in Walkers, yet another New-castle club, on the footballer Paul 'Gazza' Gascoigne which damaged his knee and nearly ended his career. The police were unable to find witnesses to give evidence and the inquiry was ended after Gascoigne told them he wanted the matter dropped. The near killing of a pub customer who failed to drink up sufficiently quickly is also attributed to Graham. Whilst he was serving the sentence for the attack on Stuart Watson, he is said to have calmed a riot in Durham prison.

Just about the only unchallenged facet of the killing is that Graham is indeed dead. The permutations of reasons proffered are seemingly endless and depend upon whether the speaker has a pro- or anti-Graham stance. He is thought to have been negotiating with black dealers in Leeds – he was seen in the Hilton there in the summer of 1993 – and there had been attempts by a Yorkshire team to muscle in on the North-Eastern trade. Alternative suggestions have been that the killers came from suppliers in Liverpool or London, or that the men were Italians brought up from London on contract to do the business.

One neutral observer offers the thought that Graham had been crossing-up North-Eastern criminal families in general and South Shields ones in particular for far too long. He also suggests, more interestingly, that it may have been related to the death of a young girl in a club which Graham was minding at the time. His third offer had been mooted in the papers; that it relates to the death of Graham's arch-rival Andy Winder who died in Tenerife in 1993.

The 34-year-old Andy Winder, who had previously run a modelling agency in Darlington before leaving in 1986 to go into a time-share scheme, was in charge of the touts for a major time-share company in Los Cristianos, Tenerife. Winder, who had taken over touting in Lanzarote and Gran Canaria, now wanted control of South Tenerife, an area which had been the fiefdom of another hardman who was said to have bitten off a rival's nose and had subsequently left for Portugal.[21]

One version of that story is that there had been a savage bare-knuckle fight between Graham and Winder after which Graham, who had needed substantial surgery, had placed a £10,000 contract on the body-builder. Winder is said to have taken out a bizarre form of insurance, or at least revenge, in the form of a £30,000 contract on Graham only to be executed after his death, which came in late September 1993.

There had been a fight involving four other 'very large men' at a time-share in Tenerife. It appears that Winder tried to stab 26-year-old Richard Cashman from Teesside and, when others intervened, he stabbed them as well. A shot was fired and Winder fell dead. David Coates, from Stockton-on-Tees, was stabbed and broke his arm jumping from a balcony.

Another North-East hardman is also suggested to have been offered substantial terms to deal with Graham. Lee Duffy, from Eston near Middlesbrough, who already controlled lucrative protection rackets in Cleveland, had been offered a large stake in organized crime in the North East. Duffy had survived three attempts on his life and had

---

[21] Along with the Costa del Crime, Portugal has been a haunt of English gangsters. According to a report in the *Guardian* a group arrived in the late 1980s and 'until recently' were taking £1,000 a week off the managers of Vale Vavio in Portugal on the promise of not breaking the legs of their timeshare salesmen. Nick Davies, 'Who killed Rachel?', in *Guardian Weekend*, 14 August 1993.

apparently tried to meet Graham on a number of occasions before he himself was killed, stabbed to death in a fight with David Allison in Middlesbrough. After being told that Allison had been fighting for his life, the jury acquitted him.

Then there was the question of whether Graham was indeed in the rackets. His father, Jack, was convinced he was not. Citing the fact that he was being taken to court over the repossession of his son's car, he argued that if Graham had been in the drug and protection scene he would not have allowed this to happen. On the other hand, this was not the view taken by New Year's Eve partygoers who on hearing of Graham's death toasted the event saying, 'Viv no more for '94.' A pub landlady told the Newcastle *Journal and Echo* that his protection racket had made the life of a pub owner a misery.

Pubs were forced to pay £200 a week to him or there would be some sort of trouble. If you refused to hand over the cash someone would be planted and a fight would break out on the premises. There was no way landlords could stop drugs being sold on the premises. He was a hard man, a bully, who threatened both men and women.

But another pub manager said:

I have never heard anything bad about Viv. You didn't see him much, but if any of the pubs had bother they would give him a ring and he would sort it out. He was a gentle giant really.

'People are upset because Viv was much loved round here,' said one lady, referring to the theft of flowers left at the murder scene. One wreath left behind said: 'Uncle Viv: Our hero. You will always be in our hearts.' Journalists were chased away from the scene by heavily-built men.

Within a week of Graham's death £50,000 reward money was on offer and there were reports that it might soon be doubled, as it was by his fiancée and long-time companion Anna Connelly. Two other claimants for Mr Graham's affections surfaced. In addition to a wife and two children, and Ms Connelly, it was discovered he had had a red-headed lady friend by whom he had another two children.

In the meantime something approaching anarchy was said to be rife amongst the clubs, with Graham's competitors demanding £100 a night to protect the bars he used to control.[22] Whether this was newspaper hype remains to be seen. In the first few weeks following Graham's death there was no apparent take-over of his empire, if indeed one existed.

[22] See Howard Foster, 'Gangland war looms after drug killing' in the *Sunday Times*, 9 January 1994.

6

Manchester

The history of crime in Manchester over the last hundred years resembles a clockwork doll whose mechanism has broken and is now running around in all directions, creating mayhem as it does so. The officers who retired perhaps twenty years ago, when professional crime was the old-fashioned theft, robbery, a little prostitution and a little protection, would have trouble recognizing parts of the city today.

Perhaps it is cheating a little to stretch back a decade before the end of the century to begin the account of crime in Manchester, but it is also instructive to see the state of the police at the time. It was in something approaching disarray, at least 'D' division was. The public inquiry into 'allegations bearing upon the efficiency and discipline of the Manchester City Police' ordered by the Home Secretary began on 24 May 1897 at the City Sessions courthouse before J.S. Dugdale, Recorder of Birmingham. It particularly related to the retired and disgraced William Bannister.

The now ex-Superintendent William Bannister had been

a constable in 1871, a sergeant in 1875, an inspector in 1880 and a superintendent in 1882. In the 1890s he was in charge of 'D' district in which there was an abnormally high number of brothels and disorderly houses. In particular in Shepley Street, houses were kept by a woman named Sarah 'Mother' Wilson, and a man named Taylor. These were, said Mr Sutton, appearing at the inquiry for the Solicitor to the Treasury, houses which should have been suppressed. Bannister was a close friend of 'Mother' Taylor; he not only drew up her will but also was a beneficiary. After her death the houses continued to be used for immoral purposes, and there was evidence from constables that Bannister was the one who carried on the management of them. This was a problem which had been raised in the early 1890s. When challenged then, Bannister had explained that his father and Sarah Wilson had been intimate friends, that he was the executor and that he had disposed of his interest in one of the houses for £12.

In 1893 Bannister had been brought before the Watch Committee on two charges of misconduct, and at one time in the debate it seemed as though he might be dismissed. Some members of the committee then protested that this would mean the loss of his pension, and a reprimand was substituted for dismissal.

All the constables involved with the 1897 inquiry gave the seeming protection of Bannister by the Watch Committee as a reason why they were afraid to move against him. They were also afraid of being 'swamped by their colleagues', and in the case of one senior officer he too did not want to be responsible for Bannister losing his pension. Others said that 'D' division was no worse than other divisions.

In the Chief Constable's report for 1896, the number of brothels was listed as twelve and houses of accommodation as three. The Chief Constable of Liverpool had commented that he could find fifty in the Oxford Road area alone. Brothels apparently were only regarded as such when it was 'fully proved to have been so'.

Bannister was also seen in company with a Mrs Julia Davis, separated from her husband, in the Falstaff public house in Hulme, behaving in a way which 'if true would have degraded him'. This was the evidence of a Constable Wilkinson before the Watch Committee. Bannister had told the Committee that he was in the pub for the purposes of making a will – he seems to have had a healthy sideline in this occupation – and anyway that there had been a robbery committed which he was investigating. Wilkinson had resigned.

In 1893 Julia Davis took another public house, the Derby Arms in Vine Street. She must have given this up after she had troubles with her licence, because in 1895 she was living at 34 Greenheys Lane. Bannister was regularly seen coming out of the back passage of the house at 8.30 in the morning, and once constables had seen Davis hitting him with her umbrella in the street.

Bannister, described as a bold bad man, had also brought an action against the Reverend John Kelty for defamation. Kelty had complained to Bannister's superior officers that Bannister had gone in a cab, drunk, with two prostitutes to Braby Street police station. At a slander trial at Carlisle Assizes the words had been held to be privileged, but Mr Justice Kennedy had whitewashed Bannister, telling him he left the court without a stain on his character. Bannister had, in effect, won the action and a celebratory testimonial dinner for him was paid for with £200 donated by local licensees. Constables had been invited to sign a testimonial and had been charged sixpence for 'meat and potatoes and plenty of beer'. One officer had become so drunk that when he tried to sing, cymbals had to be brought to 'knock him off'.

How many constables were present? asked R.B. Batty at the inquiry.

'I could hardly see any one absent,' replied Constable Thomas M'Dermott.

Officers gave evidence that they were afraid to make a report to the Chief Constable, making excuses such as that by Constable P. Lacy who feared 'being shifted'.

Q: Is it looked upon as a disgrace in the force to be shifted?

A: The man is looked upon as a mug for interfering.

'All applications for the Watch Committee or the Chief Constable must be submitted through your superintendent, and you are not allowed to write on official subjects to any personage whatsoever without the permission of the Chief Constable,' Lacy added.

There were complaints about the number of prostitutes who frequented the annual police ball. 'The policeman would not have a very happy time if he had no amusements at all,' replied the Commissioner. There were also allegations that the Chief Constable had received £60 or £70 (sensation) as part of a testimonial from local brewers. One witness complained that he was being charged with being given two guineas, when the Commissioner's subscription list reached a thousand pounds. The Chief Constable tired of the complaints and was content to let Bannister wait until he could draw his pension and then he would go.

Inspector Burroughes had made a complaint about a beerhouse, and in turn the keeper complained about him. When the licensee was convicted Burroughes wished to go and see the Chief Constable to have the complaint expunged, but Bannister merely deleted it from the charge book. Burroughes went on to say that he believed Bannister had warned prostitutes of raids.

On 7 December 1896 Bannister resigned before the Watch Committee. His last act had been to help his old friend William Taylor escape a charge of brothel-keeping.

According to Dugdale's report, issued on 19 July 1897:

[He] must have had friends on the Committee who persuaded the majority, probably out of good nature, to retain him in his position and override the opinion of the sub-committee and the Chief Constable without any risk of any individual responsibility being fastened on themselves.

The report also stated that Bannister had been promoted over four other inspectors and against the recommendation of the Chief Constable:

This false step was the starting point of all subsequent mischief. A superintendent of police commanding a division of more than 200 men must necessarily exercise very great power; his good word or disapprobation would naturally have great effect in regulating the promotion of the men . . .

In sharp contrast to Bannister was Jerome Caminada, regarded as the father of the Manchester police, who joined the force in 1868 at the age of 24 at a time when the worst areas for crime were the Ancoats and Angel meadow districts. By 1874 Caminada had racked up a staggering 20,000 arrests.

Crime figures are notoriously difficult to explain and

justify. A difference may arise because one force cautions all shoplifters on the first occasion they are caught, another may not even document domestic assaults; nevertheless it is difficult to satisfactorily explain the 60 per cent rise in crime in Manchester between 1944 and 1945 (against a London rise of 25 per cent and a Leeds rise of 4.3 per cent) and a tenfold rise in the value of property stolen from £26,375 in 1938, of which half was recovered, to £262,432 in 1946 with £76,985 retrieved – unless someone was, to use a phrase, well at it. And not just someone: several people. The reports of the Chief Constable were silent on an explanation but housebreaking, shopbreaking and warehouse raids showed the greatest increase, conforming to the London pattern. What lay behind both, suggests Edward Smithies, was the insatiable demands of the black market. Manchester's geographical position at the centre of the textile trade made it particularly vulnerable. What was worse was the almost complete collapse of the clear-up rate, down by 32.9 per cent from the 1942 figure of 63.8 per cent.[1]

As with the other major cities the black market flourished during the War in Manchester, with petrol and stolen clothing coupons as favourite commodities. A Manchester syndicate was able to distribute forged clothing coupons to nearly forty firms both there and in London. In fact the forgeries seem to have been pretty amateur ones. The forger had failed to note that most genuine coupons were torn off a sheet; his were cut from it. The ring was broken up by a tip-off and the police found the owner of a London factory with the coupons. Others were traced when a Manchester man was found giving others into a post office in exchange for vouchers. It seems that the word was that if you wanted

[1] E. Smithies, *Crime in Wartime*, p.189.

coupons in Manchester they were freely (well, for payment) available in Great Ducie Street. Twenty-two people found themselves in the dock, mostly charged with handling, and most maintaining they did not know the coupons were forged. The rich defendants had counsel who were able to argue the technicalities, and only ten were eventually convicted. The forger received four years' imprisonment.[2]

It was also a time when, because of the perilous state of the economy, forgery was treated very seriously. Towards the end of the War well-made forged notes had been circulating in the north of England, and it must have seemed to the police that a major counterfeiting gang had been broken when in June 1945 Herbert Winstanley was discovered passing a forged £1 note at the Albion Greyhound Stadium in Salford. When they raided his home there were 2,498 forged £5 notes and 6,651 £1 notes stacked up awaiting distribution. It turned out, however, not to be the work of a major crime syndicate, rather a cottage industry. The work was entirely that of Mr Winstanley, who told the police that he had been passing notes for about seven years.

> I was practising on the £1 notes for 11 years before I issued a single one. I started it as a hobby [said the 60-year-old signwriter]. I have done everything myself. With regard to the £5 and £10 notes I have never tried to pass a single one as they are not good enough yet.

He was sentenced to 10 years' imprisonment.

Policing was tough in the 1940s. Sir Robert Mark recalls:

---

[2] *Manchester Guardian*, 13 May 1942.

I can remember a very successful, fairly senior detective in Manchester, who, when dealing with hardened criminals had his own version of the Judges' Rules. It consisted of greeting the prisoner with the blunt enquiry, 'Will you talk or be tanned?' If the reply was in the negative, sometimes colourfully so, the prisoner was removed smartly to the lavatory where he was upended and his head jammed down the bowl. It usually took two to hold him, whilst a third repeatedly pulled the chain until a waggling of the feet indicated a more compliant attitude. He then signed a form headed by the usual caution against self-incrimination. My point in relating this is to make it clear that practices such as this were perfectly well known to solicitors, to counsel, to judges and to the Press, but that no one did anything about them because there seemed no obvious way to achieve a fair balance between the public interest and the rights of wrongdoers. To pretend that knowledge of such malpractices was confined to the police alone, as people occasionally do, is sheer hypocrisy.[3]

After the war there grew up a now legendary collection of characters including the Black Prince, Chuck Taylor, who wore a wig and had a dance trio in which he played the bongo drums, and in the summer used to steal ladies' handbags from the park; and Bobby Critchley who had a bullet-proof car. According to Manchester legend it was Critchley who saw off Jack Spot when he came to the city in search of a nightclub to mind. Critchley had himself been involved in racecourse protection, and the club Spot fancied was his Jacaranda in the Stretford Road.

[3] Sir Robert Mark, *In the Office of Constable*, pp. 52–3.

'When God made heaven he made Manchester,' recalls an old-time face. 'Do you know where you could drink all afternoon? In the Crown Court. They had a bar open there the whole time.'

Old-time police officers are keen to impress that there was little, if any, organized crime in Manchester. 'It was still villagey enough for people to notice. We never had anything which hadn't had someone as a witness,' says one former Detective Chief Inspector.

There was prostitution, of course, run by the Camilleris, a Maltese family. Street bookmaking before the Betting Act was unofficially tolerated. Everyone came before the courts in their turn, and there were no complaints from the bookmakers as long as no one was left out.

Clubs abounded, but it seems to have been fairly harmless entertainment. Clients were sold sponges for 2/6d and encouraged to throw them at the stripper, who collected them at the end of her act for re-sale. The ex-wrestler 'Big' Bill Benny[4] owned clubs including the Cabaret Club – 'The South of France comes to Manchester' – and Chez Joey with roulette and blackjack tables at the back. 'When the police came the doorman would delay them a while to give breathing space for the punters.' According to folklore Benny, who had a hairlip and was by all accounts a genial giant, died in bed and had to be lifted off the girl. The cabarets themselves were fairly homely at the beginning of the sixties, perhaps a wrestling bout, a bit of striptease, and sometimes a freak act such as Tom Jacobsen the armless wonder who shaved punters with a cutthroat razor and his

---

[4] One of his regular opponents was the Geordie, Charlie Scott, and the billing would read: 'Big' Bill Benny [Afraid of no one not even 'Big Boy' Charlie Scott] *v* 'Big Boy' Charlie Scott [Afraid of no one not even 'Big' Bill Benny].

feet, opened beer bottles and played the piano. Later came the top-line acts, the expense of which would close many of the clubs.

The view of some police officers is that the small spielers catered for the Jewish immigrant community in particular:

> They were real workers. They raincoated the world.
> You'd see them from 6 a.m. until midnight. Then when
> their children were 18 or 19 and off to University, the
> last thing they wanted was to be seen over a hot sewing
> machine. That first generation went to clubs, private
> illegal gambling clubs, to play chemmy and baccarat.

The legalization of gambling ruined clubs such as Chez Joey. Once Mecca opened in the city, no one wanted to go to the smaller clubs. The middle sixties saw the end of the teenage coffee bars where soft drugs had been freely available.

That period also saw the last executions 'in the manner prescribed by the law'. Two relatively minor criminals, Peter Anthony Allen and Gwynne Owen Evans, young Preston dairymen, were hanged on 13 August 1964 for the murder of John Alan West.

The murder had been committed in the drab mining town of Workington. West, who worked for the local laundry, lived in a semi-detached house in Seaton, one of the suburbs. He was killed, hit by a poker and stabbed, in a robbery which went wrong and in which Evans left behind his macintosh together with a Royal Life Saving Society medallion bearing his name and initials. Apparently Evans had known West for some five years. At the time of the murder Evans had been living with Allen and his family and they had been behind with the rent and rates. They had also been on a small crime spree together, committing a series of shopbreakings and other thefts for which they were fined by Preston Borough Magistrates. It seems they committed their murder, in part, to pay their £10 fines. Evans told Allen that West had money lying around, and they drove to Workington. Evans went in to see West in the early hours of the morning and in turn he let Allen in about 3 a.m. Each blamed the other for hitting West with an iron bar, and the jury convicted both after a retirement of three and a quarter hours. It cannot have helped that it came out that Mrs Allen had been 'more than a landlady' to Evans. Their appeals and applications for a reprieve were refused. The letters signing their death warrants were sent on Tuesday 11 August. The Permanent Under-Secretary of State at the Home Office said, 'It seems kinder to let the prisoner go on hoping until the last possible moment.' Allen was hanged at Walton, Liverpool and Evans at Strangeways, Manchester. At the last meeting Allen had with his wife he 'went berserk, really berserk. He was strong, you know, and the glass in there, they say it's supposed to be bullet-proof, but he smashed it. He went berserk.'[5]

It depends on one's outlook whether by the 1960s Manchester crime was free of protection or was firmly controlled by the so-called Quality Street Gang which included the redoubtable ex-boxer Jimmy Swords. The

[5] Mary Allen quoted in E. Jones, *The Last Two to Hang*, p.100. 13 August seems to have been a popular day for hanging celebrated criminals. In 1868 the first so-called private hanging took place when Thomas Wells, aged 18, was hanged after being convicted of the murder of Edward Walshe. He had been sacked for poor work and within minutes returned with a gun to shoot the Dover Priory stationmaster. In 1915 George Joseph Smith, the 'Brides in the Bath' murderer, was hanged by John Ellis at Maidstone.

police view is that they were a group of minders and enforcers who, as the years passed and they grew older, had moved into the more respectable lines of club and restaurant owning. Even their critics do not rate them highly. 'They are given credit they didn't deserve.' On the other hand, as property developer and local Conservative Party chairman, Kevin Taylor, recalls:

There was never any such gang, but several Manchester characters had styled themselves that way as a joke, in commemoration of a Quality Street TV advertisement of the 1960s depicting rather suave debonair crooks. In fact, they worked hard almost every day on their car sales pitches, in all weathers, which is hardly to be expected if they were indeed criminals.[6]

The local faces had a good relationship with the police, to whom they could turn if they were threatened by outsiders. There are various versions of the story of what happened when the Kray twins came to Manchester in one of their forays to find a club outside London, and it was on the Cromford Club that they set their sights.

One variation is that they were met on the platform at Piccadilly station and put on the first train back. Frank Williamson, who was in charge, recalls it slightly differently:

Owen Ratcliffe was a charming man. He was a great gambler. He owned the Cromford Club at which Jack London [the ex-heavyweight champion], who by this time was nearly punch-drunk, was the doorman.
I went to the Midland with Douglas Nimmo, my

[6] K. Taylor, *The Poisoned Tree*, p.21.

sergeant. It was no later than 1961. A house detective, Tabby Booth, who'd been a sergeant in the railway police, alerted me. He rang me at home saying he'd got boxers called Gray from the East End of London who were being difficult and throwing their weight about. He also told me that Owen Ratcliffe had been in the Midland earlier in the evening with a large meat cleaver under his Crombie coat. They'd knocked poor old Jack London down the stairs of the Cromford and there was no need. He was no menace by then. I rang the police in London and asked about the Grays. They told me they had nothing on them. This was patently false because Grays from the East End who were boxers was an easy link. It was only the next letter in the alphabet.

Douglas Nimmo, my sergeant, and I waltzed into the Midland, told them to get on the next train and we never saw them again in Manchester. Len 'The Barber' Carter who had a strong link with London teams was with them. Nimmo just dismissed him. Told him to go away.

The Cromford Club was certainly an object of police attention.

It was the only one which caused us any trouble; not that it wasn't well appointed and well run. It was who went in there and the amount of money gambled there we were interested in. The gaming was run by a man called The Aga because he looked like the Aga Khan.

One person on whom everyone is agreed, however, is that Bobby McDermott was the King of the Barrow Boys and, the police believe, was the King of the Fences. Possibly if

Manchester had anyone in the 1950s, '60s and '70s who could be regarded as approaching major criminal status, it was he. According to Frank Williamson, 'We looked at him long and often but we could never pin anything on him.' From McDermott's Cellar in New Barn Street near the Cromford Club, he rented out a series of barrows to the stallholders across the city and would provide work for any man who approached him on his release from prison. He was also regarded as being a high-class receiver, was certainly well connected with major crime figures in both London and Glasgow and could be relied upon to provide safe lodgings for prison escapees. When Robert Anderson escaped by chance with Ronnie Biggs from Wandsworth, it was to McDermott that his London connections later turned for help.

McDermott was also loyal to Manchester officers. At the height of the investigation into the Flying Squad in 1969, in an effort to discredit Frank Williamson who was overseeing the inquiry, officers from London were sent to sniff out any dirt that might be clinging to his uniform: 'These two officers went to see McDermott and tried to get him to say something about me being dishonest but he wouldn't.'[7]

Kevin Taylor, himself once a successful businessman, fell foul of the police. Amidst political manoeuvrings, allegations, counter-allegations and certainly a multitude of recriminations, John Stalker, the Deputy Chief Constable of Greater Manchester, had been suspended and then reinstated before he finally resigned. His acquaintance Taylor, himself a friend of the so-called Quality Street Gang (if it existed), and who had built his fortunes on his

[7] Frank Williamson, quoted in J. Morton, *Bent Coppers*, p.138.

skill as a professional card player, had been ruined by a prosecution which eventually collapsed.

In May 1984 John Stalker was appointed to lead an inquiry into the shooting of six unarmed men in 1982 by the Royal Ulster Constabulary, an appointment which if it was by no means welcomed enthusiastically by the RUC Constable, Sir John Hermon, was certainly not welcomed at all by others.

Within the year Stalker had made substantial progress in his inquiry. By February 1985 he was chasing what was known as 'the Hayshed' tape, which, if genuine, he believed would prove that RUC officers had shot an unarmed teenager without warning and in cold blood. Despite requests and assurances, he was never to see the tape, and fifteen months later he was told that a squad had been set up to investigate a Manchester policeman. Simultaneously Greater Manchester police were beginning their investigation into Kevin Taylor.

The inquiry was pursued ruthlessly. Surveillance equipment had been set up to spy on his palatial Bury home. Friends and relations were being quizzed by senior detectives. His phones were being tapped, his mail opened and (on one occasion) his accountant's office burgled. His bankers all over the world were getting requests from Manchester detectives for confidential documents. Taylor asked his lawyers to find out what the police wanted. They would not say. Taylor told the police he was ready and willing to talk to them at any time they wanted. He got a promise from the Chief Constable James Anderton that if the police ever wanted to speak to him, they would get in touch with his lawyers. That was not the way it happened. When Taylor's house was raided in May 1986 there was no advance warning. The police took away a few old papers from the 1970s – and the real loot: three photographs of John Stalker.[8]

Inquiries continued into the working of Taylor's bank accounts. Certainly he had borrowed £1 million, but the properties were valued at £1.6 million and no customer or client ever suggested that Taylor was involved in fraud. Nor did bank officials. The next step was to approach the Crown Court and ask for access orders to seize Taylor's accounts. In a sworn statement to Judge Preest, DI Arthur Stephenson suggested that Taylor was involved with drugs. Preest granted the orders. The statement was kept in a sealed envelope for over two years. In the trial, counsel for the Crown was to admit there was no evidence at all on which the application was based.

Now Taylor was charged, along with his accountant, a Co-op bank official and a surveyor, with conspiracy to defraud the bank by over-valuing the property. The result was a disaster for him. His companies collapsed, as did the prosecution, but not before Taylor was effectively ruined.

Senior police officers told lie after lie, and were exposed as telling countless others in the course of their investigation. The two chief investigating officers committed a blatant contempt of court for which many an ordinary citizen would have been fined or imprisoned. They were fortunate to escape with a reprimand.[9]

As the trial progressed Stephenson, one of the officers to be reprimanded, was under severe cross-examination by Taylor's counsel, David Hood. Driven ever deeper into damaging admissions over the conduct of the case and, in particular, into the evidence given on the application before

8 Paul Foot, *Spectator*, 9 June 1990.
9 ibid.

Judge Preest, Stephenson's credibility in the case was destroyed. At lunchtime on 18 January 1990 Michael Corkery, a London barrister who had unexpectedly been instructed on behalf of the Crown rather than a local member of the Manchester Bar, received instructions from the Director of Public Prosecutions to offer no further evidence.

As for Stalker, by this time he had resigned. He had been removed from the Northern Ireland inquiry on 29 May 1986, and had been given extended leave pending the outcome of disciplinary offences. Inquiries into his relationship with Kevin Taylor continued for the next three months until after a 36–6 vote by the Police Committee he was reinstated on 23 August of that year. At worst the allegations were reduced to the use of a police car for his own purposes. On his reinstatement he maintained an unhappy relationship with the Chief Constable James Anderton who had, by all accounts, been smitten with religion. It was clear to Stalker that he had no future in the force, particularly when Peter Topping was appointed Chief Superintendent in preference to Stalker's choice, John Thorburn. It was Topping who had been the senior officer in the unhappy prosecution of Kevin Taylor. Stalker retired on 13 March 1987.[10]

Police supporters have been keen to point out that Taylor's writ for malicious prosecution has never been actively pursued, adding by way of explanation that Taylor is an incorrigible gambler spending much of his time playing kalooki in Greek-owned gaming clubs. Others know just

[10] There are three basic accounts of the two cases. *Stalker*, and *The Poisoned Tree*, are in one pan of the scales, *Topping* is in the other. All are intensely personal.

how much it would cost to pursue a claim without the benefit of legal aid. Stalker went into journalism which was, perhaps, his first love. There is little doubt he had been treated badly by the force. His legal costs for defending himself before the Police Committee had amounted to something over £21,000. Despite his reinstatement without charges, the Police Authority refused to make any contribution to the costs, which were paid for largely by public subscription and a concert organized by a Frankie 'Frou-Frou' Davies.

But putting the Stalker-Taylor problems to one side, at last there was a triumph. In May 1989 came a great feather in the force's cap. It had rooted out from its ranks the 'bullying and crooked' police officer, Thomas Gerald 'Ged' Corley, a constable with wide-ranging contacts in the Underworld. The list of complaints compiled against Corley, described as a 19-stone thug, and certainly a 6ft-4in. weightlifter, included conspiracy to rob and supplying a firearm. It was alleged that for a decade he had conducted a regime of crime and intimidation whilst serving in Greater Manchester. His superiors had failed to act despite there having been twenty-four complaints from the public. Now in 1987 Chief Inspector Peter Jackson was ordered to investigate Corley after a report that whilst off-duty sick he had been working as a nightclub bouncer. It was then Jackson discovered that Corley had devised cruel initiation routines for new police recruits.

At Manchester Crown Court, on a charge of conspiracy to rob – an attack on a security guard at Walkden near Manchester in 1987 – and transferring a firearm, despite his continued protestations of innocence and that he was being fitted-up, Corley was found guilty and received a sentence of seventeen years' imprisonment.

Within a matter of weeks, the cream on the top of the milk had soured. An inquiry began into the investigation which led to Corley's conviction, and it became clear that two officers had trawled criminals for evidence, offering incentives for assistance. Corley was identified after criminals were shown photographs, and then picked him out on an ID parade. In return for this valuable information charges were reduced to simple robbery, and they received sentences of ten years reduced to six on appeal when the court was told of their great assistance. Another criminal who had implicated Corley in the supply of a gun was given bail and committed more robberies. Jackson made a complaint into the conduct of officers in the inquiry – notably the conduct of the man in overall charge, Chief Superintendent Arthur Roberts. An outside force from West Yorkshire, led by Assistant Chief Constable Colin Bailey, was called in to investigate.

The basis of the complaint was that the original investigation into Corley and his behaviour had shown that other police officers may have had potentially unlawful contact with criminals. Jackson had, it appears, repeatedly requested senior officers in the Greater Manchester police to check out this information as thoroughly as the investigation into Corley was being conducted. He maintained this had not been done. After the Corley trial he sent a memorandum to Roberts, then another which insisted on a decision from an assistant chief constable. He was promised the matter would be taken up with the deputy chief constable. Then he found that not only had there been no progress on his memorandum but that his conduct during the Corley inquiry was being investigated. He went to his solicitor and made a formal complaint against Roberts.

The complaint was, in effect, fourfold. First, after the Corley conviction two criminals had said they knew certain officers, one a senior one, had consorted with criminals and they planned to blackmail the officers. The second strand concerned a conversation between Jackson and another informant who said that officers sympathetic to Corley had colluded in an attempt to discredit evidence given against him at his trial. The third was that a member of the Regional Crime Squad had arranged for the police to see defence documents removed secretly from the defence solicitor's office. The fourth suggested that a criminal who was an important witness at the Corley trial had revealed a plot the basis of which was to frame a police officer by planting evidence on him. Apparently it was decided not to make this evidence available at the trial, where it might have damaged the witness. Jackson was concerned that an attempt might be made to say the evidence had come to light after, and not before, the trial.

At the end of August 1992 Roberts, along with a Sergeant Bob Meek, was suspended, not because of Jackson's complaint but because of an earlier one by Corley against the whole team which investigated him. There were then rumours that Jackson himself would be suspended. If this happened what, asked *Police Review*, would be the effect on Jackson's complaint against Roberts and indeed the Corley conviction?[11]

What did happen was that in March 1990 'Ged' Corley who, when one considers the treatment meted out to convicted police officers, rightly described his last two years as a nightmare, was acquitted by the Court of Appeal

[11] Stephen Cook, *The Inquiry Goes On, and On, and On*, 6 October 1989.

who described his trial as having been a travesty of justice. He had previously been released on bail by the Court of Appeal in the autumn of 1989, not something which that court does regularly or lightly. If the Crown Prosecution Service had known only a quarter of what had emerged since the trial, Corley would never have appeared in court, said Lord Lane, the Lord Chief Justice.

The evidence against Corley had been implication by three men who had admitted their part in the £11,000 wages snatch. Another criminal had claimed the officer had supplied him with the sawn-off shotgun used in the raid. Now the Court of Appeal heard that inducements, including reduced charges, bail and cash, had been offered to the criminals to persuade them to name Corley.

By this time Jackson had resigned from the force and had retired on medical grounds. He claimed that his complaint against Chief Superintendent Arthur Roberts had been followed by a 'vicious campaign' against his sanity and his integrity by a small group of officers. He declared:

> It must be a matter of concern to the public that there are people in the police service who find it unacceptable for an officer to raise doubts about an investigation and consequent conviction. It is the kind of unhealthy atmosphere which makes possible such cases as the Guildford Four.[12]

On 24 January 1992 Salford robber Brian Sands, said to have devised the set-up against Corley, received seven years' consecutive to a sentence of eight years he was already serving.

[12] *Police Review*, 12 January 1990.

In May 1992 summonses of perjury and perverting the course of justice were issued against Roberts, Jackson and a Detective Sergeant Kevin Ryan. A month earlier Corley had received the massive sum of £230,000 compensation for wrongful imprisonment from the insurers of the Greater Manchester police. Part of the money was spent on a green Rolls-Royce, in which he drove to watch the men involved in the investigation against him arrive for the remand hearings of their own case.

At Leeds Crown Court in March 1994 the former Chief Superintendent Roberts was acquitted of two charges of misconduct and received a nine month sentence suspended for two years on a third. Inspector Jackson was in hospital receiving treatment for a mental illness and was unable to stand trial.

Criminals grew younger. In July 1992 a boy was sentenced to fifteen years' youth custody for armed robbery. He and a team had not known that the old-fashioned bank robbery would surely lead to arrest. They had been smashing the security screens. Still, sometimes variations on the old methods were the best. On 6 May 1993, at least four men were involved in a wages snatch at Armaguard at an industrial estate at Carlisle. The first man is believed to have acted as a decoy by feigning problems with his car which stalled, causing a tailback of traffic around 7 p.m. at a roundabout on the outskirts of the city and causing the crew of a Security Express vehicle to stop. It is thought that whilst the van was stationary two others attached themselves to the chassis of the vehicle and were driven on to the estate by the unsuspecting crew. Once inside Armaguard, the gang seized around £1 million. The fourth member then drove the robbers away in a white Transit van. The men apparently had worn a special harness to attach themselves to the van, a none-too-far cry from the days when Teddy Machin escaped in a similar manner, but using only his hands and feet, after the abortive London Airport bullion raid in 1948.

Until the 1970s one of the more rare forms of crime in Britain was kidnapping. Generally when it occurred it was not for money, but of children as pawns in the custody game played by their parents. When it broadened out again it was not always for ransom as such but to enable a relation (often a bank or building society manager) of the kidnapped person to produce the keys to the safe vault or produce not his own money but that of his employers.

August 1992 saw a Mancunian example of an old-style kidnapping when Elizabeth Kerr, whose husband Derek managed a branch of Barclays Bank in Sale, Greater Manchester, found a man wearing a police officer's uniform at her door telling her that her husband had been injured in a road accident. She went with him, as she thought to the hospital, but the man drove off the road and into a field. He got out, hit her in the face and then after taping her mouth bundled her into the boot of the car. Derek Kerr then received a call demanding £40,000 and telling him that his wife would suffer extreme harm if he did not do so. He took the money towards a junction of the M63 motorway where it was collected by the kidnapper. Mrs Kerr was left tied up in a wood at Over Alderley in Cheshire.

The kidnapper turned out to be soldier turned financial adviser, Tony Bosson-Williams. He was identified when fourteen months after the incident a palm print of Bosson-Williams was found on a piece of paper in the Kerrs' home. At first he denied the matter but then admitted having spent the ransom – giving his wife £1,800 a month, taking holidays in America and Lanzarote and buying a speedboat.

A week before the Kerr kidnap, Bosson-Williams had attempted a similar one involving a Solihull bank manager, but he had gone to the wrong house. On 14 January 1994 at Chester Crown Court he was jailed for twelve years for the kidnapping of Mrs Kerr and two years for the attempt to run consecutively.

A year earlier it was not so much a question of kidnapping, more of hostage taking when on 6 March members of the Wilson family were held in their home outside Chorley. The attack took place shortly after 9 p.m. when Mrs Wilson, one of her daughters, Lisa, and Lisa's boyfriend went to visit a friend. Within minutes two men wearing balaclava masks and surgical gloves burst into the house, knocking aside the remaining daughter Michelle. On their return Mrs Wilson and her family who had been joined by her accountant husband, David, were tied up and made to lie on the floor. David Wilson was ordered outside and the family assumed he was being taken hostage. When they heard two bangs they concluded it was a car backfiring. It was not.

When they later freed themselves they found the telephone wires had been cut and they drove to get help from a neighbour. On their return they found David Wilson's body face down. He had been shot at point-blank range.

Initially the police said they knew of nothing to the detriment of Mr Wilson, who had been a partner in a local firm of accountants, was the owner of a former cotton mill and printing firm as well as being the sleeping partner in a number of other businesses. Then newspapers began to speculate about links with such diverse interests as Underworld and drug gangs and the IRA. It was noted that he had been concerned in an investigation into a shipping fraud. Just over eighteen months later the full story came out at the trial of Stephen Schepke, a former art restorer, charged with conspiracy to murder Mr Wilson. The shipping fraud over a non-existent cargo of cigarettes had involved £26.5 million. The original plan had been to pass off cheap Mexican cigarettes as Marlboros but Hector Portillo, alleged by the Crown Prosecution Service to be Michael Austin, with whom Wilson had been dealing, pulled a double cross. There were no cigarettes. Wilson, who had been involved with Portillo in deals relating to the sale of 90 tonnes of gold bars from Mexico to an Isle of Man company engagingly known as Fergie Ltd – the gold, along with the cigarettes, failed to appear – was furious and had spoken to the Crown Prosecution Service about his role in the affair.

Portillo then wanted Wilson silenced. The man was far too dangerous to have as a loose cannon sounding off. Probably he contacted Schepke. Six days before his death Wilson, who had been warned earlier in the year that Portillo wanted him dead, had himself fired off a salvo by fax complaining to Portillo that he had 'set him up', saying he would never forgive him and threatening that one day he would 'have his day'. Schepke had stood to make some £60,000 out of the deal if it had gone through. The contract had been carried out by two professional hit-men and it was not suggested that Schepke had been other than an influential cog in the wheel.

On 20 October Schepke was found guilty of aiding and abetting Wilson's murder. The jury was unable to agree a verdict that he had conspired to have Wilson killed. He received life imprisonment.

Now the major action focuses on the infamous Moss Side district, barely a mile from the city centre, home of the drug gangs with an estimated turnover of £20 million plus a year, which bedevil the community and which, for a number of reasons, the police seem to be unable to control let alone eradicate.

Like so many other inner city areas, Moss Side has come down in the world. In the 1850s, when it was known as Twenty Pits, it was wet with pit-like indentations. In the great expansion of Manchester the land was drained and substantial houses built. Then came the large terraced houses which until the 1930s were owned by teachers, bank clerks, and what ex-officer Tony Fletcher describes as 'comfortable' tradesmen.

During the years of the Depression, more and more of these people found it necessary to take in what were at first termed genteel guests, then lodgers, in order to make ends meet. In some cases rooms were let with the provision of meals, or partly furnished for self-catering.

After the War those who wished to move and could do so made their escape to the more salubrious parts, nearer the Cheshire boundary, and the whole area began to deteriorate. Eventually entire houses, often with twelve or fourteen rooms, including cellars and attics, were let room by room to individual tenants.[13] At first the tenants were immigrants from Europe and then from the West Indies. Finally the Alexandra Park estate was built. It was planned as a neighbourhood community, protected from through traffic with little clusters of brick houses facing on to cul-de-sacs and connected by what the planners fondly believed would be companionable footpaths. But it turned out to be an area extremely difficult to police, a warren of rat-runs into which fleeing hoodlums and drug dealers could easily escape. As mob rule took hold and the estate deteriorated, families began to move out. Vacated houses were quickly

[13] T. Fletcher, *Memories of Murder*, pp. 45–6.

vandalized, adding to the aura of despair that now pervades the area.[14]

The first death was that of Ivan Preston, the doorman of a shebeen, who was shot in 1987. From then on it seemed that much easier for the drug dealers to kill those who stood in their way.

The major dealer in the Ordsall end of Salford, on the other hand – who has the overall control of the supply of designer drugs, amphetamines and Ecstasy – is a man who, whilst dealing in substantial blocks of cocaine, publicly denounces its supply and use. He has a network of both youngsters and older dealers. 'He is practically untouchable,' says one officer. 'He has kids who will shoot you.' Ordsall is an estate built in the 1970s and – with streets truncated into cul-de-sacs so that criminals could not escape through them – is now covered in graffiti. The local park has been ringed with fencing to keep out stolen cars. This was the scene of the troubles and riots in July 1992 and the *Sunday Telegraph* postulated that the Mr Big of Salford who had a posse of fifty youths at his command could be blamed for fanning them. It was then that a woman found an AK-47 gun in her son's bedroom. Guns brought back from the Gulf War as souvenirs are now coming into circulation. In the area a handgun could go for as little as £70.

Much of the trouble in the inner city area stems from the employment of doormen in the nightclubs and discos. The aim of the drug dealers is to have one of their own men on the door, to enable their dealers to get in to the exclusion of other dealers. So there is a form of both protection and extortion in evidence. The nightclub or disco will be

[14] Russell Miller and Peter Warren, 'A Cry From the Streets' in *Sunday Times*, 7 March 1993.

protected from the trouble which would ensue if there was a free drug market, the sponsor gets a clear run at the distribution of his product. When the Cheetham Hill-based Thunderdome Club decided to hire its bouncers from an out-of-town firm in June 1990, revenge was swift. Three of the bouncers were knee-capped in full view of more than 300 people by masked men wearing shotguns. Seven people were later arrested, but the Crown Prosecution Service decided there was insufficient evidence on which to mount a successful prosecution.

Moss Side and Cheetham Hill, Salford are the main drug and gang districts, with Moss Side divided into segments. Pepperhill no longer exists since the pub of that name closed and its members have now regrouped at Doddington. The Gooch Gang suffered a substantial blow to its pride when twenty-one members were caught in Operation China during which undercover police had filmed them selling drugs to members of the public. In a series of raids on forty addresses in the Alexandra Park area, drugs, a loaded semi-automatic weapon and a crossbow were seized.

The police operation came at a time when the Pepperhill-Gooch feud, in which Cheetham Hill aligned themselves with the Gooch, had become more or less totally out of control. Later, sentences ranging from three years' youth custody to eight years for possession of a loaded firearm were handed down at Manchester Crown Court. The Gooch Gang was dead. Children could now play football on the estate without the fear of walking into sniper fire. Peace reigned for about four months. Then – long live the Young Gooch. Seven or eight of the younger members of the Gooch who had not been involved in the swoop reformed. In fact the Gooch Gang itself was not dead at all – it was merely sleeping until it realigned itself in prison, putting pressure on prison officers and governors by demanding, in return for co-operation, such privileges as exclusive use of the gymnasia.[15]

The ascending scale of juvenile and young adult crime in the area ran from theft *from* cars to theft *of* cars, then racing round the streets daring the police to chase them. The next step was into a different league. Across the road from the Moss Side estate is a red light area, and the teenagers then put the arm on prostitutes to take their clients to a certain area where they could be attacked. In one case the client was forced, at knifepoint, to divulge his telephone number, and when he returned home the Gooch Gang member telephoned and threatened to contact the man's wife unless he came to meet him with his cashpoint card. From there, it was on to dealing in heroin and crack.

[15] Prisons have always been controlled by powerful figures and gangs. At the time of the Parkhurst Riot in 1969 the cinema show could not start until the leader of the prison had taken his seat in the audience. In 1993 Judge Stephen Tumim, the Chief Inspector of Prisons, said that drug-taking including heroin had been an epidemic at Long Lartin prison in Gloucestershire, where prisoners drank their home-made hooch in front of staff. There were protection rackets with weaker prisoners paying insurance in drugs, tobacco or cash. A-wing was dominated by white prisoners, mostly London gangsters, who permitted only non-threatening ethnic minority prisoners, usually Asian, to join them. Even these were only tolerated if they were prepared to carry out menial tasks. Lynne Bowles, the No. 3 Governor at Whitemoor Prison at March, Cambridgeshire, spoke of criminals winning control of the prisons. Calling for a tough regime where criminals had to earn privileges such as television in their cells, she said that the 'senior prisoner and his rent-a-mob are selling drugs, booze and the benefits of refusal to cooperate' and organizing mass disobedience over issues such as the price of chicken in the prison shop. *Daily Mail*, 18 August 1993.

The catalogue of violence dealt by one gang to the members of another is astounding for such young people – a gang on mountain bikes circling a 19-year-old in his BMW before opening fire, two men jumping from a bedroom window after being shot by a gunman from the doorway, a young man on a mountain bike firing indiscriminately in the street. As the Gooch estate has steadily been evacuated the violence has spread to nearby Old Trafford where on 26 April 1993, in an incident in which five houses were hit with bullets, an 18-year-old student Andrea Mairs was shot in the stomach by a stray bullet as she pulled back the curtains from her bedroom window. Although severely traumatised she lived. Some were not so lucky. On 29 October 1991 Darren Smith tried to escape a gang on mountain bikes by running into a baker's shop; he was killed when six shots were fired at him as he leaped the counter. The men charged were acquitted. A principal prosecution witness had taken a drug overdose rather than appear at the trial. Between January and November 1992 there were six murders.

There is, of course, a steady trade on the estate in guns with the going price of a clean pistol (one which has not been used) anything from £500 to £800 depending upon how urgently it is needed. As for a used weapon – 'anything you care to offer' says one police officer.

At the adult level a feud developed between senior members from Moss Side and a highly organized team of good professional armed robbers led by yet another military gent, 'The General', from Cheetham Hill. The problem first arose in 1989 when a team from Moss Side came to do an armed robbery and found The General and his men *in situ* bent on the same target.

One of the most appalling pieces of gratuitous violence

which exceeded almost anything the London armed robbers have had to offer in recent times came, when in 1989, an armed robbery in Royton, Oldham at the Coin Controls factory went seriously wrong. Just after 10 a.m. the robbers struck when the Security Express van was making a wages delivery. They were approached by two armed robbers who demanded the money and, when told that the chute which contained the cash was jammed, attacked them. In November 1990, at Manchester Crown Court, Judge Rhys Davies was told that Chinadu Igheawara attacked one guard with a machete. As the man lifted his arms to defend himself he was knocked to the ground and then tried to crawl under the van. Stephen Julian then shot the other guard in the groin shearing off the top of his left thigh. Unfortunately the first guard had not crawled far enough under the van and Julian shot his ankle which was protruding, almost blowing it off. His leg was amputated from below the knee. As the second guard tried to escape he was shot in the back at almost point blank range. Amazingly both survived.

Stephen Julian had fled to Jamaica assisted by a Raymond Odoha. Julian made a fraudulent application for documents in Jamaica and was deported.

In October that year the driver of the getaway car, Mark Mann, decided to give evidence in return for a lighter sentence and this led to the trial of Julian, now back in England, and Igheawara in November 1990. Both men admitted two other robberies from branches of the Royal Bank of Scotland netting over £50,000 and conspiracy to rob the Security Express van. Julian received 22 years and his companion 20. Mann's sentence was a more modest eight years. The court had been told that whilst on remand he had been moved to six different prisons.

Odoha was now wanted for assisting Julian in his escape, so he decamped to London where he was helped by a man who was to become a close friend, Tony Johnstone.

Johnstone, who usually wore body armour, was originally a Moss Side boy who committed a shooting just to prove himself before transferring his allegiance. By a curious coincidence his mother, Winnie, is also the mother of Keith Bennett, still missing from the time of the Moors murders. By now Cheetham gangs were more or less in control of the nightclubs in the city. One favourite trick in a raid was to take cash from the tills on the bar and then use it to pay for champagne.

Johnstone became 'the man', carrying guns and driving Ford Cosworths which, with an easy speed of 120 mph, made surveillance almost impossible. 'He just took off,' say the police who were trying to keep him under strict observation.

The night before he was killed in February 1991, he walked into a nightclub where the Cheetham Hill men had gone for a drink, grabbed the microphone and said words to the effect that whilst he would be happy to sort things out with them they were no match for him. Sensibly they declined the challenge. Although they were no doubt quite happy to see him go, thoughts that the Salford team had been involved in his death were red herrings. In the end Johnstone died over a quarrel which wasn't strictly his. The Salford comment was that if he had not died that Friday, he would not have lived six months.

He and three others did an armed robbery at Monksbridge in Oldham when the security van was literally kidnapped and some £360,000 stolen. A further £1 million was left on the van solely because the robbers were unable to carry it away. Within four hours of the robbery

Johnstone and his friends were locked up, put on identification parades and then released.

All that was recovered were six £20 notes found in a Wendy House belonging to a relation of Craig Bulger. Bulger was charged and convicted of dishonestly handling the money. The police believe that Johnstone's serious troubles began when he then went to ask for £80,000, his share of the takings, and was told by Desmond Noonan, a member of a Cheetham Hill family, that there was only £40,000 left. Bulger was not pleased and told him he was going to complain to Tony Johnstone.

This, in turn, could not have pleased Noonan who that night went to visit Paul Flannery, then in a Southport hospital. Flannery had served eight years for an armed robbery. On his release he had made serious threats to a policeman and when other officers went to arrest him Flannery, possibly because he thought his visitors were from a rival organization rather than policemen, dived through a window seriously injuring his back.

A week later Johnstone was killed. He had gone out with his friend Tony McKie, who became a prosecution witness, in his new fine white Cosworth when he was flagged down by Desmond Noonan, so said McKie, near the Penny Black public house about 10.30 in the evening. According to his evidence, McKie saw a Ford Orion parked nearby with three men sitting in it, including Paul Flannery making his first ambulatory outing from hospital in the front seat. McKie told the court that Flannery nodded to Noonan and then fired shots at him, McKie. Clearly something was wrong and Johnstone tried to climb a wall to escape; he was shot in the back. At the trial in the summer of 1992 Noonan, his brothers Damien and Derek, Paul Flannery and a prison escapee Michael Sharples were all acquitted.

One of the hardmen from Moss Side was Delroy Brown, known by the police as Public Enemy Number One which, said an officer, 'isn't far from the truth'. Brown led a charmed life. In 1986 he was an unknown who appeared from Birmingham, 'dripping in gold and driving a BMW', and teamed up with members of the Pepperhill mob. The belief is that it was Brown who triggered off the war between Cheetham Hill and Pepperhill, not through any drug deal but simply over a domestic matter. Brown was seen out with the girlfriend of a Cheetham Hill man doing five years for robbery. The information relayed back to The General began a feud between the two. Brown's car was taken from him and he was held up at gun-point. He retaliated and then received a visit from four masked men at his home; shots were fired. And so began the Moss Side-Cheetham Hill war with Tony Johnstone a leading soldier.

One attack came in 1990 when Johnstone led a group of men into the International Club in Longside where Brown was drinking. Johnstone, according to accounts, emptied a .38 at the luckless Delroy. It was after this that Jonathan Quartey received a visit from the police at his home on the Alexandra Park estate where a Colt .45 automatic was found. He received thirty months' imprisonment, reduced on appeal.

Meanwhile Brown, together with a friend, had ventured into Cheetham Hill territory, the PSV Club in Hulme. There Stephen Jackson, a friend of the General, was shot in the testicles and Delroy (who did not do the shooting) was dragged into the car park where serious efforts were made to cut his head off. Eventually he escaped with the help of friends and fled to Liverpool where he treated the wounds with Dettol, hiding in Embledon Street off Granby Road in

Toxteth until matters quietened down and his injuries
healed. Jackson later received ten years for the possession
of cocaine. He had objected to being tried in Manchester,
but this did not help him. In 1990 the judge, known as
'Wacko' by the community, gave him the sentence in
Liverpool.

The final Cheetham attack on Brown came when his car
was overturned in Alexander Park. After that things
quietened down, mainly because of Johnstone's problems
with the Noonans. However, that was not the end of Delroy
Brown's localized troubles. Once again it was almost a
domestic matter.

One of the more popular shebeens on the estate where
Red Stripe, curried goat and red snapper is on offer is off
Gooch Close, and was a favourite haunt of Delroy Brown
and his friends. It was from outside there that his car was
taken by two 13-year-olds, driven away, damaged and
dumped. Unfortunately the report to Delroy gave the
perpetrator of the incident as another man entirely; in turn
his car was attacked, with the tyres being slashed and the
vehicle set on fire. This was now the start of the Gooch-
Pepperhill war. Machete attacks became prevalent. A
classic drive-by shooting resulted in a 14-year-old boy
being hit in the eye and partially losing his sight.

After that, say the police, there was real war. There were
mountain bike and motorbike attacks on people and
property and then, in 1991, came the first death – that of
Carl Stapleton. It was perhaps extraordinary that, with so
many violent attacks, there had been no deaths before.
Stapleton, who was related to a major player in the game,
was found alone, out of his ground, and stabbed eighteen
times with a survival knife. It was at this trial that the
principal witness completely changed her evidence; she had

been in what amounted to protective custody from which she had regularly absconded, returning time and again to the estate. At first she had identified a Stephen Morrison, who in a previous incident had himself been macheted, but at the trial she said she had picked him out from a parade because she fancied him rather than because she had seen him get out of a car at the place of the killing.

Delroy Brown was becoming increasingly suspect even amongst his friends. There were rumours that he was an informant, and he was chased by a gang of Gooch into the Big Western public house in Pepperhill where he was attacked by a dozen youths. 'He is incredibly brave,' says one police officer with some admiration. 'If you see his body it is a mass of scars and holes.' He managed to grab the knife from one of his assailants and then barricaded himself behind the cellar shutters. When the police arrived he was the only one remaining. In his pocket they found fifteen rocks of crack which he alleged had been planted. He was charged with possession with intent to supply, and at the Manchester Crown Court in June 1993 he received six years' imprisonment.

In January 1993 one of the seemingly more horrific random killings took place in Moss Side when 14-year-old Benji Stanley was shot in the heart while he was queueing to get pies in the popular Alvino's Tattie and Dumplin' shop. The killer had driven up in a silver Rover and fired through the window at Benji; he then walked into the shop and shot the boy once more through the chest.

It was a crime which for a time provoked if not national outrage, then at least national publicity. All investigations showed, as Detective Superintendent Terry Smith told the inquest held in December, that Benji was not involved with crime or gangs. However, unfortunately for him he was wearing khaki clothing and a coloured bandana, a badge of one of the Moss Side gangs.[16] Detective Superintendent Smith said that Benji's clothing was part of growing up, and the coroner commented: 'He was a young man going about his normal life, getting some food with a friend and he was brutally murdered. The indications are that it was basically an assassination.'

The court was told that 16-year-old Tito Gunning, who had been with Benji when he was shot, had later told the police that a version of the events and description of the gunman he had given immediately after the killing had been made up.

There may have been a truce for a short while, but in the first seven months of 1993 there was a string of shootings which culminated in a sub-machine gun attack on a public house in Whalley Range district which borders Moss Side. Almost a year to the day of Benji's death, another killing dispelled any lingering doubts that it and the ensuing measures taken by the police might have brought a new and improved era to Moss Side. Despite the fact that he was wearing a bullet-proof vest Julian Stewart, aged 21, was found shot to death on 12 January 1994.

Not all the killings were shootings. When Ian Marriot, assistant manager of the Ritz – a club only a few hundred yards from the Hacienda – was attacked, a bottle of acid was thrown in his face one afternoon. He took seven hours to die. No one was arrested.

---

[16] Red for Gooch, blue for Doddington. In this way the gangs match the colours of the Crips and the Bloods from Los Angeles gang wars or, looked at another way, the respective colours of Manchester United and Manchester City.

Cardiff and the South West

Crime in Cardiff in this century is spanned by two murder cases – one in which justice was demonstrably not done, and the earlier one where many people still believe it was not done either.

'I was brought up being told they were innocent,' recalls one old-time villain.

'They' were Edward and John 'Tich' Rowlands, accused of killing a boxer turned bookmaker on 29 September 1927 in St Mary Street, Cardiff. Dai Lewis, a former professional welterweight boxer, ran the 'chalk and water' protection,[1] a small-time protection racket at Monmouth races, and in doing so fell foul of the Rowlands brothers who regarded that unnecessary service as one which they and their followers alone would provide for the bookmakers. It appears that Lewis, despite the protection racket he ran, was popular with the bookmakers. Presumably they were

---

[1] Providing chalk for the bookmakers to write the odds on their boards, and water for their sponges to change them.

happier paying private enterprise than the local big machine.

The day before, he had been warned that the Rowlands were not pleased with him and despite a certain amount of bravado he took the precaution of staying away from home that night and slept in a hotel in St Mary Street.

The next day was business as usual. He went back to the races at Monmouth and in the evening returned to St Mary Street and the Blue Anchor public house where he drank all evening, ignoring the Rowlands brothers and their friends Daniel Driscoll, John Hughes and William Price.

He was set on shortly after closing time outside the Blue Anchor. John Rowlands had previously warned Lewis about muscling in and he was the instigator of the attack, as he had been of many others. Lewis's throat was slashed in a wound seven and a quarter inches long and one and a quarter inches deep. As he lay dying on the pavement, 'prostitutes rushed to his aid, ripping off their petticoats in a desperate effort to staunch the flow of blood'.[2] He was taken to the Royal Infirmary hospital where the police went to his bedside waiting for him to name his attackers. It was while they were there that two calls came inquiring after the state of Lewis. The second was traced to the Colonial Club in Custom House Street, and there the police found the Rowlands, Driscoll, Hughes and Price.

In the early hours of the morning it became clear that Lewis was not going to survive, and a local magistrate and the Clerk to the Justices came to his bedside to take a dying declaration which could be used in evidence at any subsequent trial. A dying declaration was what was called an

[2] D. Thomas with R. Grant, *Seek Out the Guilty*, p.39.

exception to the hearsay rule, which only admits in evidence statements made in the presence of the accused. In this case there would have been no breach of the rule because Edward Rowlands and Daniel Driscoll were brought to Lewis's bedside.

The boxer maintained the code of the Underworld: 'I do not know how I have been injured,' he said. 'I do not remember how it happened. There was no quarrel or fight. Nobody did any harm to me. I did not see anyone use a knife.' Then he added to Eddie Rowlands, 'You had nothing to do with it. We've been the best of friends'; and to Daniel Driscoll, 'You had nothing to do with it either. We were talking and laughing together. My dear old pal.' To his wife he gave £3.5s 0d – what was left from his earnings at the races.

The funeral on 5 October was attended by up to 25,000 people who lined the streets as the cortège passed. It was a week after that John Rowlands made the admission that he had stabbed the boxer. Lewis had, he said, attacked him with a knife, they had wrestled for it and Lewis was accidentally stabbed. Driscoll and Eddie Rowlands both said they had seen the fight but had made off not anxious to be involved. At the magistrates' court John Hughes was discharged and the other men committed for trial at the Glamorgan Assizes.

The queue for seats in the public gallery began thirty-six hours before the trial itself commenced on 29 November, with Lord Halsbury prosecuting for the Crown: 'This was murder as cruel and beastly as you can possibly imagine, premeditated and carried out – I might almost say flaunted – in Cardiff's main street.' In fact, however, the evidence was confused; witnesses were not able to agree on what had happened. Some said that John Rowlands had the knife as he approached Lewis, but a police officer said Driscoll was holding Lewis whilst Edward struck him in the face.

Driscoll did not help himself. He called a patently false alibi, as a result of which he became one of thousands who have been convicted not for what they have actually done but for telling lies. His discredited alibi cannot have helped his colleagues. Although Price was acquitted, the jury found Driscoll and the Rowlands brothers guilty after an hour's retirement.

The jury may have been certain at the time but the public, the police and politicians were not. £600 was collected for an appeal and a petition mustered a quarter of a million signatures demanding that the Court of Appeal look at the verdict. That Court, with Mr Justice Avory amongst its members, was never likely to be over-sympathetic and the appeals were dismissed on 11 January 1928. On the way to the appeal hearing, however, John Rowlands went berserk and, certified insane, was sent to Broadmoor where he died many years later.

A Harley Street doctor returned from a holiday in France to give his opinion that Lewis had died from a heart attack rather than from loss of blood. Three Cardiff doctors who attended the post mortem supported him.

The case had already been raised in the House of Commons and two members of the jury travelled to see T. P. O'Connor, the Father of the House, with a petition from eight members of the jury:

We, the undersigned, hereby state that we are of the opinion that the sentence of death should not be carried out. There has been so much brought into the case at the Court of Criminal Appeal and in other ways, as to cause us great anxiety since we made our decision. Sentence of death should be waived as an act of mercy.

O'Connor managed to obtain an interview with the Home Secretary, but this did not produce any result. 'No regard can be paid to expressions of opinion by individual members of a jury by which a prisoner has been convicted.'

The night before the execution the man Driscoll asked for a bottle of port; Edward Rowlands told his family, 'I have told the truth all through. Don't forget me at eight o'clock tomorrow. They can break my neck but they can't break my heart.' Rowlands was apparently shaking and had to be helped when he went to the scaffold, but Driscoll remarked, 'Which is mine?' when confronted with the two nooses. Both maintained their innocence to the end and Driscoll's last words were said to be, 'Well, I'm going down for something I never done, but you don't have to pay twice.' Outside the prison a crowd of over 5,000 gathered and sang hymns.

The men were certainly unfortunate; their position reflected the Home Secretary's attitude towards racecourse violence. Two years earlier he had refused a reprieve for one of the Fowler brothers from Sheffield. Later a more liberal attitude prevailed, and it became the custom that if one man of two due to be hanged was found to be insane before the execution, then the other was reprieved. This was the situation in the famous Chalkpit murder case in 1947 when Thomas Ley, one-time Minister for Justice in New South Wales, and Lawrence John Smith, a joiner, were found guilty of the murder of John Mudie, a hotel barman. The body was discovered in the chalkpit which gave the case its name on 30 November the previous year. Ley, then aged 67 and clearly in a state of dementia, had fallen in love with a

231

lady in her sixties but wrongly believed she was carrying on with Mudie, a much younger man. Smith was recruited to help obtain a confession from Mudie, who was later killed. After the trial Ley was sent to Broadmoor where he died on 24 July 1947. John Smith's sentence was commuted to one of life imprisonment.

Ex-Detective Superintendent Power took the view that Driscoll had indeed tried to stop the fight, and that if he had not given the false alibi he might well have been acquitted. As for Eddie Rowlands, the belief was that all he had intended was that Lewis should be marked rather than killed. The case became known in Cardiff as the Hoodoo murder. John Hughes died within twelve months, and one of the prostitutes who had given evidence committed suicide by jumping from a second-floor window. One of the detective-sergeants committed suicide, two other officers died – one from tuberculosis and another from cancer – whilst a third died from a stomach complaint. All were relatively young men. In September 1928, Harold Lloyd – the solicitor who represented Price – was sentenced to five years' penal servitude for embezzling clients' monies.

The most famous area of Cardiff crime was Butetown, better known as Tiger Bay, where the Lewis killing had taken place. From the end of Victorian times it had become the home for seamen whose boats docked in Cardiff. By the beginning of the First World War there was a black population of around seven hundred, and it was there in 1919 that the first race riot of the century broke out. The causes given are varied, but those who had returned from the War were angered that their jobs had been taken and worse, they believed, so had their women – even worse still, that they had been taken by the coloured men who were thought to be nearer the animal than their white counter-parts.[3]

The flashpoint, so far as Cardiff is concerned, occurred on 11 June 1919 – although there were almost simultaneous riots in Liverpool and in the North East – and is described by PC Albert Allen writing in the *South Wales Echo*:

> I was the only PC on duty at the Wharf when it started and I was on duty the whole time it lasted in the Docks area. First of all I would like to point out the cause. In Cardiff there were quite a number of prostitutes and quite a number of pimps who lived on their earnings. When conscription came into force these pimps were called up. Then a number of prostitutes went to the Docks district and lived with these coloured people who treated them very well. When the war finished the pimps found their source of income gone as the prostitutes refused to go back to them. The night the trouble started, about 8.30 p.m., a person who I knew told me to expect some trouble. I asked why and he explained that the coloured men had taken the prostitutes on an outing to Newport in two horse wagons and that a number of pimps were waiting for their return.[4]

Fighting and rioting continued for some days, leaving one dead, numerous injured and very few men charged.

Bute Town was where the action was. In Bute Street alone in the 1920s, when the place was 'bad and dangerous',

---

[3] Editorial in the *Liverpool Courier* quoted by J. Williams, *Bloody Valentine*, p.18.
[4] Quoted by J. Williams, *Bloody Valentine*, pp.18–19.

there were said to be 42 cafés, a dozen pubs and sundry brothels. In 1952 there were 106 convictions connected with prostitution; not exactly a high strike rate. In 1954 the whole community was 8,000 strong: white, coloured, Arab, Indian, Somali and Maltese. At the time of the murder of Lynette White in 1988, there were thought to be some 150 prostitutes working in the rebuilt area.

But while Bute Town may have been dangerous the crime was strictly small-time, fencing, prostitution and related offences, a certain amount of rolling and mugging drunken sailors, theft from the docks. It was the sort of crime associated with an economically poor area. There were, however, more talented people at work in the city.

On the afternoon of 4 December 1928, a mailbag bearing a pink label was placed in the luggage van of the train which left Cardiff at 3.15 p.m. for Paddington. The bag was later found, including all the unregistered packages and some of the registered ones, on the banks of the Thames near Cannon Street the next afternoon. £5,500 in currency notes and £600 in Bank of England notes were missing.

From the police investigation it seems that the guard did not leave his van except for five minutes near Reading, when he was spoken to by a man who complained of sickness and who rushed into the lavatory with his head in his hands. However, this seems to have been a red herring, for the package was received by a porter at Paddington. Police inquiries showed that some well-known faces had been travelling that day. A George Rogers was the man who had been sick and Danny Davies, a bookmaker – confusingly associated with a man giving his name as Daniel Davies but really James Foster – had been on the train. Foster had already been acquitted of a similar mail theft the previous year. Danny Davies was suspected of all the big coups in South Wales and of master-minding robberies.

George Rogers was also known as Bastable, as well as having the more engaging soubriquet 'Portsmouth George'. He had been licensed to stand as a bookmaker at Wembley greyhound track, but had been thrown out for bad language and had been arrested with Coleman and Jack Davies in 1925.

The following Sunday in the *Empire News*, and much to the fury of the police, Joseph Foster kindly explained how on a previous occasion he had been duped into being a 'staller' for the gang. A staller was the last man in such a scam, who would set up an argument with customers or officials in order to allow the men carrying the proceeds of a theft time to make their escape.

According to reports, the £5 notes stolen in the robbery were thought to be in Cardiff. It was believed that a wholesale effort would be made to launder them at a professional athletics meeting due to take place in Powderhall in Edinburgh in the first week of January.[5] Instead, the notes in the main turned up at dog tracks.

A letter very neatly written by a Mr George Evans from Lambeth Hospital arrived at Scotland Yard on 19 February 1929, offering to name the perpetrators. When he was seen by the police he named a totally different collection of men – 'Jeweller George', George Spiers, a man named Willis and another by the name of Ryan – from the ones whom the police suspected. Unfortunately for Evans' theory, Spiers was serving a sentence for a mailbag robbery and was in custody at the time of the Cardiff-Paddington snatch.

[5] Amateur athletes such as Rugby Union players would run in masks to protect their non-professional status at these meetings.

'There is no doubt that Evans' mental faculties are some-what impaired and I am given to understand by the Infirmary Authorities that he is given to fits of delusion,' wrote a policeman who investigated the claim.

Davies, Foster and Co lived to fight another day. And, it seems, fight again they did.

A year to the day a mailbag containing £3,500 in bank notes was stolen between Swindon and Paddington. Marked for delivery to London, the bags were made up and placed in the last van on the train as it stood in Swindon station. Shortly before the train left Swindon a lady approached the guard, Maurice Sherrick, and asked him to find her an empty compartment; she said she was feeling ill and asked him to look in on her during the journey. He found her a compartment three coaches away from his van, and during the journey he did indeed go and look her up and spent some minutes talking with her. This was the only time he left the guard's van. Bags were unloaded at Reading, but everyone questioned was adamant that the London bags were left untouched.

It is not difficult to guess whom the police had in mind for this little escapade. Davies, Rogers and three other men, including William Arnold – an ex-Superintendent of the GPO who had been discharged following a conviction in 1921 for stealing mailbags in Birmingham – were highly favoured.

A week later the police received an anonymous letter putting George Bastable firmly in the frame. He was, it was said, the originator of numerous Post Office thefts including a Cardiff job and one in Hull: 'He is hand in glove with every crook in London and in the provinces and was said to visit Cardiff once a week to keep a check on the progress of his war on the Post Office.'

The letter was signed 'One of Bastable's victims', and presumably was from a former member of the team with whom Bastable had fallen out. Watch was kept on the men but nothing came of it. The notes started filtering into circulation, all in the London and Essex areas, and a good number, as might be expected, from various greyhound tracks. Every tenderer was questioned, but each was able to account satisfactorily for his possession of the note. By 3 May 1930, the investigation was effectively closed. Davies, Rogers and Co., if indeed it had been them, appear to have retired.[6]

There were 2,000 people in the auditorium and a queue outside the Odeon Cinema, Bristol, on 29 May 1946 when cinema manager Robert Parrington Jackson was shot in the temple. The cinema was showing *The Well-Groomed Bride* starring Olivia De Havilland and Ray Milland, with a support of *The Light That Failed* starring Ida Lupino and Ronald Colman. Just at the moment when a boy actor in the film shoots a cap pistol, so did Jackson's murderer. Jackson died the next morning. Curiously Jackson had his own gun which was never found, but weeks later a gun was found in a static water tank in Bristol's Park Row. The police ran the usual 'developments expected' announcements, but it was all hot air. There was speculation first of all that this was a robbery, but the theory seems to have been discounted in favour of another that it was a disgruntled member of staff or a relation or perhaps a wronged husband or boyfriend. Jackson had the reputation of being a womanizer and it seemed all of the takings had been left behind. Yet another theory was that it was an American robber who went straight to the Midlands and was then

[6] PRO: MEP03/501/509.

shipped back to the States by the American authorities; and still another that it was the work of a local thief, Blackie Alan. There the case stood for nearly fifty years until, in October 1993, a man walked into Bristol police station to say that the killer had been his father.

Then *Today* revealed the name of the killer, Billy 'The Fish' Fisher, and the motive. 'The Fish' was so-called because he was so slippery.

Short of money, he and a friend, Dukey Leonard, had jumped on to a train from the South Wales coalfields and broken into Parrington Jackson's office. He had reached for the alarm and they had shot him before escaping with loose change. As is usually the case the police had retained a 'secret clue'. This time it had been revealed that Jackson had been shot once, but in reality he had been shot twice and the son who reported the killing knew this. Fisher told his family in the 1980s and died in 1989, by which time Dukey Leonard was also dead. Surviving members of the Odeon staff seemed pleased that it had been a robbery rather than a personal attack on Jackson.[7]

Another killing which is likely to remain unsolved for some time is that of former car dealer Wayne Lomas of Hengrove, Bristol, who disappeared in August 1988. Three years earlier he had been acquitted of attempted murder after it was alleged he had fired a sawn-off shotgun at a man outside a Bristol nightclub. The day before he disappeared he had been arrested twice for fighting.

Six days later the police went to his home and found the dogs roaming loose in the garden, the tumble-dryer still switched on and five days of newspapers on the hall floor. An uneaten meal was on the table. The police suspected it

[7] 3 November 1993.

was a gangland killing; Lomas had been thought to be involved in drug dealing and protection. On 11 October 1993 the police received a tip-off and went to the house of a couple, not involved in the inquiry, who were away in America. There, eighteen inches under the dining-room floorboards, was a concrete block, and inside the remains of Mr Lomas. Four men were arrested and released without charge.

Not everything goes right all the time for armed robbers. David Lewis, who had a conviction in 1987 for robbery at a post office, obtained a job with Securicor as a guard; he had used a man he met in prison as a referee. One of Lewis's longer-term aims for 1993 was to hold up Bookers Cash and Carry in Leckwith, Cardiff, but unfortunately he and and his colleague and referee Paul were thwarted when, having taken £90,000, a rival organization opened fire and relieved him of the takings.

But the police maintain, perhaps with more justification than is often the case, that career criminals in Cardiff did not flourish as they have done in other major cities. They point out its relative isolation by road from the rest of the country until the late 1970s. Certainly London criminals were imported to carry out bank robberies, but because of the relatively low crime figures the CID was, they say, able to devote sufficient attention to big-time crime to make it unprofitable.

There was also the possibility that the local outlying communities might take the law into their own hands. In his book, *How Green Was My Valley*, based on stories he was told as a child about a mining community, Richard Llewellyn recounts the hunt for – led by the local minister – and subsequent killing of a child molester. The events of the first weekend in June 1992 were equally dramatic for the village of Penrhys near Tonypandy. There, in the garden of his home, Ronald Penrose was beaten so badly that he did not recover. His son Jason was kidnapped. After the attack on Penrose, who himself had a conviction for theft, Jason was apparently bundled into a car, taken to a quiet spot by a lake and roughed up. It was believed that the actions had taken place because of a heart attack suffered by an elderly lady who found her house being burgled.

This was not the first time that otherwise completely respectable members of a community have carried out their own brand of justice. There have been several such events in Wales, let alone other parts of the country. Indeed it had happened only the previous month. In the small community of Newborough in Anglesey some two hundred villagers, disheartened by the failure of the authorities to deal with what they saw as the criminal activities of a local youth, met in the village square and decided to run him out of town. The youth was eventually taken into what amounted to protective custody. His family left the village shortly afterwards.

In recent years, perhaps the most extreme example of the vigilante in England, and the community's sympathy towards him, occurred when Stephen Owen was acquitted of attempted murder by a Maidstone Crown Court jury in May 1992. Owen, described as mild-mannered, had shot and wounded a lorry driver who had been responsible for the death of Owen's 12-year-old son in a hit-and-run incident. After serving twelve months of an eighteen-month sentence, the man had seemingly expressed quite the reverse of remorse.

The murder which stands at the opposite end of the century to the killing of Dai Lewis is that of the death of prostitute Lynette White, slashed to death on St Valentine's

Day 1988. It had, however, been preceded by another killing in which arrests were made and, after a campaign by JUSTICE, two young men Wayne and Paul Darvell, local misfits, were freed.

The Darvell case occurred in Swansea. On 19 June 1986 they were convicted of the murder of a sex-shop manageress, Sandra Phillips. In June the previous year she had been sexually assaulted, savagely beaten, and her shop then set on fire in an effort to cover the traces of the murderer. Wayne Darvell, suggestible and with limited intelligence, was a compulsive confessor. He had earlier admitted to the murder of a dentist which he could not possibly have committed. Now he admitted this murder and implicated his brother Paul.

When the case was referred back to the Court of Appeal in July 1992 the defence alleged that there had been a planted earring, false sightings and a doctored confession. The Crown Prosecution Service did not contest the appeal.

One crucial piece of evidence, that of a palm print found on a pay-phone attached to the wall near the dead woman's body, was neither hers nor that of the brothers. This information was not passed to the defence; instead they were told that the tests had been insufficient for positive identification. Certain officers were investigated but there have been no prosecutions.

Lynette White, then aged 21, was killed in a frenzied attack on 14 February 1988. She had been the girlfriend of – and had worked for – a small-time pimp, Stephen Miller. The week or so before her murder she had fallen out with Miller. Most of her earnings, between £10 and £25 a time, were disappearing up his nose and she believed he was having an affair with another girl. She was also due to give evidence in two cases, one involving Francine, a sister of the powerful Cordle brothers, who was alleged to have stabbed a prostitute, Tina Garton, in the lung. Lynette had met Stephen when his older brother Tony was living with Francine. Tony had returned to London at the request of her brothers after he had beaten Francine once too often. Stephen and Lynette had begun to live together.

The English Collective of Prostitutes argues that it is desirable for a working girl to have a man who will protect her, and that such a person should not be prosecuted for living off immoral earnings. It is, they say, safer for the girl to have someone who knows where she is and may be in a position to help her if she gets into difficulties with a client. Certainly at the start of their relationship Miller seems to have been boyfriend rather than pimp. As her death approached, their relationship may have altered.

In *Bloody Valentine* John Williams interviews a lesbian pimp, Debbie Paul, who explains how such a relationship can work:

Most of the girls are working for themselves. And some of the girls are working for themselves and their man as well. Round here the way it works is that if you've got a man dealing with drugs, and you've got a prostitute and they connect, then half of his money's with her and half of her money is with him, it's all mixed up together. If you've got a relationship with a pimp you've got to have some sort of agreement – I give you some of my money and you give me some of your money; you're making off drugs, you've got to compromise. But I don't think Stephen ever compromised, he would just take all the time.[8]

---

[8] J. Williams, *Bloody Valentine*, p.61.

Lynette's body was found in the squalid Bute Town flat where she took her punters. She had been stabbed more than fifty times and, from the defence wounds on her hands, it was clear she had tried to fight off her attacker. Her head and one breast were almost completely severed, but there had been no rape nor mutilation of her genitals.

For ten months the South Wales Regional Crime Squad had no evidence except that it seemed a white man had been seen covered in blood a hundred and fifty yards from her flat shortly before her body was found. Then in December five black men, Stephen Miller, Tony Parris, Yusef Abdullahi and two cousins, Ronald and John Astie, were arrested. The reason for this was that two prostitute women Angela Psaila and Leanne Vilday suddenly told the amazing story that they had been present when Lynette was killed by the men, and they had been forced to participate in the slashing of her body.

What, if any, corroborative evidence was there? So far as Miller was concerned it was his own admission. He was questioned at length and, after denying the offence, he confessed. A supergrass, Ian Massey, said that Parris had confessed to him in prison and Abdullahi's girl-friend, Jacqui Harris, put him in the frame; she said that Yusef had told her he had been in the room when Lynette was killed. There was no corroborative evidence against the Asties and there was no forensic evidence against any of the men – this from a room which must have teemed with forensic material. The motive, the police decided, was revenge by Stephen Miller for Lynette's bad behaviour.

There is no doubt that from the start Psaila and Vilday told lies. Psaila seems to have had some racist feelings; in court she called the defendants 'black monkeys'. The police were so concerned about Vilday's evidence, and the changing of her statement between committal proceedings and the trials, that she was taken to a hypnotist, something which had been effectively discredited if not outlawed in both the English and American courts by the mid-1980s.[9] Vilday had named Martin Tucker as one of the killers and then withdrawn the allegation, and Psaila made and withdrew an allegation against another man.

For trials there were in the plural. The case was transferred to Swansea and the evidence had been heard by Mr Justice McNeil when, at the start of his summing-up in February 1989, he died of a heart attack. The second trial began in front of Mr Justice Leonard – the judge in the so-called Vicarage Rape Case – in the May and ended in

---

[9] Hypnosis has been used for a variety of legal and quasi-legal purposes including the obtaining of quick information by Israeli troops. There are two basic techniques, the crystal ball and the age regression. In the first the hypnotised person is invited to 'look into this ball and tell me what you see'. In the age regression the person is taken back in stages to the moment he is trying to recall. There are considerable difficulties in gauging the accuracy of the evidence obtained. Witnesses can lie deliberately or unknowingly and tend to guess at answers anyway. Once a person has been hypnotised the recollection, right or wrong, becomes that much stronger. Dr Martin Orne, a leading opponent of hypnosis in American courts, said at a Home Office conference in 1981 that 'hypnosis decreases reliability whilst making the witness more compelling'. In a trial at Maidstone Crown Court on 19 June 1987, the police had used a self-taught hypnotist who had learned his craft from reading books in the public library. The evidence he had obtained was ruled inadmissible. Earlier in 1987 the Home Office had issued guidelines to the effect that there be an uninterrupted video of the session, and that a witness who may be called to give evidence on material matters should not normally be considered for hypnosis.

November.[10] At 197 days it was Britain's longest murder trial. He warned the jury of the dangers of convicting on the uncorroborated evidence of the girls alone, and they must have listened to him because they acquitted the Asties. The others received life imprisonment.

Now began the campaign for the release of the Cardiff Three. It became known that the supergrass Ian Massey had given evidence against 'Ged' Corley, the Manchester policeman whose conviction was quashed by the Court of Appeal. Massey, a man with a record for violence, serving a fourteen-year sentence for robbery, was released after his first parole hearing. He had served a third of his sentence. Jacqui Harris retracted her evidence and made a statement saying that Yusef would often say weird things and that she had made her statement to hurt him. That left the confession of Miller, a man with an IQ of 75, a point above subnormal. It transpired that he had denied the offence some three hundred times before confessing. As Lord Justice Taylor said in the Court of Appeal:

> If you go on asking somebody questions, and tell him he is going to sit there until he says what you want, there will come a time when most people will crack. Oppression may be of the obvious, crude variety or it may be just by relentlessness.

[10] Mr Justice Leonard was criticized over his sentencing in the Vicarage Rape Case in February 1987 when he handed down a substantially less severe sentence for the particularly unpleasant rape of a vicar's daughter than for a burglary (see R. Herridge and B. Hilliard, *Believe No One*, p. 1). He retired on the grounds of ill-health at the end of 1993, not long after the Court of Appeal decision in the White Case.

How did the trial judge not exclude a confession obtained in these circumstances? It appears he was never asked to hear the transcript of the tape made of that part of the questioning. The solicitor who was with Miller during the interviews was blamed for not trying to intervene on Miller's behalf.

Twenty-nine days after the conviction of the men, the body of another girl was found in the Fairwater area of Cardiff about two miles away from Lynette's flat. She too had been savagely slashed. No one has been arrested for her killing.

8

Birmingham and the Midlands, Sheffield and Yorkshire

On 1 June 1921 a team of thirty-eight, including some of Birmingham's most notable criminals, went for a day at the races. They were on their way to the Derby, as indeed every English racing gent should. But perhaps they were not exactly going to the Derby. They were going to waylay the Italian boys, the Sabinis, who had usurped the position of every rightful Englishman, that of racecourse bully. Believing that it was time the thieving Italians were taught a lesson, they had gathered, armed with an arsenal of weapons including razors, coshes, axes and knuckle-dusters, outside the Malt Shovel public house in Milk Street.

They had been geed up, if not exactly financed, by Horatio Bottomley, proprietor of the magazine *John Bull*, swindler *extraordinaire* and protector of all things British, and his equally opportunist friend Reuben Bigland, known as 'Telephone Jack'. Bottomley apparently began ranting about the scandal done to the British boys who had served

so valiantly in the trenches, only to find that on their return
the Sabinis had stolen their pitches at the racetracks. On the
eve of Derby Day a Birmingham boy had been attacked in
Covent Garden and had needed seventy stitches in his legs
alone. The combination was irresistible.

It was certainly correct that the Sabinis, together with the
backing of the Jewish team the Solomons, were running the
Southern courses, but it was not correct to say that the
British boys had been edged out by foreigners. Billy
Kimber, the leader of the Brummagem Boys, was certainly
British. But if the Sabinis, with their Italian father and
English mother were not, then how could the Birmingham-
Italian Mancinis, some of Kimber's henchmen, be either?

A meeting was arranged in a hotel off the Bull Ring and
instructions were given to attack the caravan of London
bookmakers taking taxis back home from the races.
The aim was to ambush them in the Ewell Road. Steve
Donoghue won the Derby on the courageous horse Humorist[1];
the Birmingham men left and duly blocked the road with

[1] Humorist was indeed a brave horse. He began to haemorrhage
shortly after the race and died within a few weeks. A post-mortem
showed he had been running on only one sound lung. Bottomley
and Bigland soon fell out. Bottomley was running a crooked
Victory Bond draw and it was arranged that Bigland should
receive a £500 prize. They met at King's Cross Station and
according to the story Bigland asked where was his monkey.
'Up a stick,' replied Bottomley, displaying enormous wit. It was
the end of their relationship. Bigland was so annoyed that he
published a 2d pamphlet which Bottomley saw as defamatory,
sued for libel and lost. He was prosecuted and received a seven-
year sentence. In prison he is said to have retained his sense of
humour. He was seen on the prison machine by a visitor who
commented, 'Sewing?' He replied, 'No sir, reaping.' But the story is
also told of Oscar Wilde. P. Baker, *Time Out of Life*, p. 35.

their charabanc and attacked the first cab in sight. One of the men inside lost three fingers to a meat cleaver. The cabs were overturned and the occupants routed.

Unfortunately, somewhere along the road to Epsom the wheels of the Birmingham coach had become crossed and, instead of attacking the Sabini bookmakers, the Brumma-gem men waylaid some bookmakers and their friends from Leeds who until that day had been wholly sympathetic to the Birmingham cause. There was worse to follow.

At first, when they heard of the affray, the police thought it was a Sinn Fein riot, but when PS Dawson arrived on the scene he found it was far more easily controlled. First he removed the sparking plugs from the charabanc and then he used the expedient of threatening to shoot the first of the men who moved. He was then able to keep twenty-eight Midlands ruffians (ten escaped) under wraps until help arrived.

Ruffians they were. Here is a small selection of some of the finer representatives.

John Allard had a conviction for manslaughter in March 1912 after pushing the point of an umbrella into his victim's eye and served seven years' penal servitude. For his part in the Epsom affray he received eighteen months' hard labour.

Edward Banks had been involved in the shooting (of Darby Sabini) at Alexandra Park the previous year, and there was a suggestion that he had been going to get some Mills bombs from Birmingham.

John Lea(e) had a conviction for manslaughter and three other cases of wounding.

William Graham was described by the police as a ruffian and bully known as Cockney Bill. He was living with Annie Moran, a well-known thief and prostitute, off the proceeds of robberies by her. On 4 March 1912 he had received five years at Birmingham Quarter Sessions for wounding. He was one of those acquitted of the affray. In all, seventeen out of the twenty-eight were found guilty. Two received three years' penal servitude and three eighteen months' hard labour.[2] Shortly after, following a raid on a public house in which shots were fired, the ringleaders at the Assizes received up to five years' imprisonment.[3]

If that was the end for a number of Birmingham trouble-makers, there was plenty going on in Sheffield. There had been for years. In the 1840s there had been an alliance between Sheffield men and others from Manchester, Nottingham and Liverpool to form the Northern Mob who had controlled betting at cock-fights, prize-fights and race meetings, and later there had been indigenous to Sheffield the Gutterpercha Gang and another led by a man called Kingy Broadhead whose speciality was a sort of protection racket involving gentlemen and tall hats. If they did not wish to see their headgear in the mud, they paid a tribute.

In the First World War in Sheffield there were the Red Silk and White Silk gangs, named after their neckerchiefs, who were principally muggers but who could, if roused, be persuaded to deal with local soldiers on leave at the Blonk Street fairground. Most towns and cities had such banditry. At the time Hull, for example, had the Silver Boys.

The early 1920s witnessed the bitter battle for the control of Sheffield by two rival gangs, the Mooneys and the Garvins. One of the principal reasons for their wish for

---

[2] The Brummagem Boys eventually reached an accommodation with the Sabinis and the race tracks of Britain were divided between them on a rough North-South split. Billy Kimber is said to have ended his working life as the manager of a London greyhound track.
[3] PRO: MEPO/3/346.

supremacy and control over a large percentage of the working-class element in the town was simply that, in June 1921, 69,000 from a workforce of 512,052 were jobless. As a result betting was rife with, according to evidence given to the Betting Tax Committee in 1923, some 90 per cent of the adult working-class population of industrial areas either participating themselves or assisting others to do so. The potential takings were enormous, with a successful local bookie taking up to £100 a day and employing forty runners each receiving commission of up to two shillings in the pound.[4] This was nothing really new. It was estimated that in 1913, in a survey of four large works in the city, 486 out of 600 men were habitual gamblers.

Betting was not confined to horses and greyhounds. There was semi-professional athletics and, as in other large cities, bare-knuckle fights. There was also Pitch-and-Toss. This was one of the simplest of all gambling games, a variant of which is the staple Australian gaming diet of Two-Up. Generally three or more coins are spun in the air with betting on whether the majority fall heads or tails.[5]

The major Pitch-and-Toss rings in Sheffield, and there were many others around the countryside, were at Sky Edge, Wadsley, Five Arches and Tinsley. They were run

[4] I am most grateful to Julian Bean for permission to quote from his books, *Crime in Sheffield* and *The Sheffield Gang Wars*. Both provide a detailed and fascinating account of life and crime in Sheffield in the 1920s.

[5] Pitch-and-Toss had as many variations as venues. It was also known as 'Nearest the Mottie' and 'Nudgers', 'Hoying' and 'Burling'. Playing had been banned on Sundays in Victorian England. It was played on any waste ground with rings on pit banks in Lanarkshire and on the beaches near Swansea. It survived in places as a regular sport until the 1950s. See C. Chinn, *Better Betting with a Decent Feller*, pp. 95–103.

by the rival gangs of Sam and Bob Garvin and George Mooney. The clientele came from a wide area, Rotherham, Chesterfield and Barnsley.

The Sky Edge ring was old-established. It had been run before the First World War by 'Snaps' Jackson and, when he went into the army, his brothers. Control then passed to a local bookmaker, William Cowan. After the War Cowan passed control to George Mooney, then in his late twenties and living in West Bar; his gang was much more a racecourse mob than a street gang, palming betting slips, running the protection of local bookmakers and beating up recalcitrant ones and their clerks. Indeed the Sabinis might have been proud to call him a brother.

Mooney drew the members of his gang from two separate areas of Sheffield – West Bar and the Park. Things worked well until the end of 1922 when profits began to slip. The reason for this was first that the 'Sankey' money, a payment of 10 shillings a day added to the wages of 8/6d, was withdrawn, and second a determination by the welfare authorities to cut off allowances from families whose members were found gambling. The gang began to disperse with Mooney – who not unnaturally saw his position as leader requiring the most money – dispensing with lesser lights, particularly the Park mob.

They now teamed up with the slippery Sam Garvin. After all the Sky Edge ring was on their own horizon, if not doorstep. The Park Brigade was formed and within weeks, using superior numbers, ousted Mooney and his men from control. Reprisals were not long in coming and William Furniss, a former Mooney man, was attacked by Frank Kidnew and Albert Foster as he lay in bed. Furniss was dragged out of his home on 29 April 1923 and knocked unconscious with pokers. It is easy to see how matters escalated. This clearly could not go unpunished and three weeks later there was a full-scale riot in Corporation Street. Only one man was arrested, and on his appearance before the city magistrates he was fined £1 for assaulting a bystander who was hit by a brick and £6 for assaulting a police officer. He had, apparently, been at the Licensed Victuallers' Ball in the Cutlers' Hall. On 27 May it was the turn of Frank Kidnew to suffer. He was set on, receiving one hundred cuts which required a stay in hospital. Asked about his attackers he replied, 'Reckon they've spoiled my suit.'

Matters escalated from there onwards and on 16 June the police arrived at West Bar to find the Mooney house there under siege from the Park Brigade. They also found one of its members, George Wheywell, shot in the shoulder. Inside the house Mooney's small arsenal was revealed – two guns and three life-preservers. Mooney and his mates and the Park Brigade members were arrested this time. All were remanded in custody at their own request except for Thomas Rippon who, immediately he left the court, was chased and slashed by George Wheywell and part of the Park Brigade. This time they ended in custody – except for Wheywell.

A week later George Mooney pleaded guilty and the rest of his team not guilty. They ended by being bound over in the sum of £25 each, as were the Park Brigade. Then came the case of the attack by Wheywell on Tommy Rippon. Mr Rippon decided he did not wish to give evidence and the 'extremely dangerous' Wheywell lived to slash another day.

The Mooney team was back in court within the week. They were unable to find sureties until after Carpatheus won the Northumberland Plate, the Pitman's Derby, at 4 to 1.

Now it was suggested by the Watch Committee that stricter controls should be exercised by the police over the gangs. In turn they replied that they were under strength and not getting the support of the courts. On the Underworld front it was said that Mooney had been to Birmingham to reach an alliance with Billy Kimber and those of his boys who were left, whilst Sam Garvin and the Park Brigade were looking for help from Darby Sabini. Mooney also gave an interview to the *Sheffield Mail* explaining that there was no such thing as a Mooney Gang whereas the Park Brigade were a hundred strong. The troubles, he maintained, were because of a threat to his legitimate hold on Sky Edge. Unfortunately Mooney went on to name his five supporters, who were none too pleased to see their names in the newspapers. One of them, John James 'Spud' Murphy, had it out with Mooney in the street, as a result of which little altercation each was bound over in the sum of £5. Nothing was done about the clear breach of the previous week's £25 bind-over. The police had some justification in thinking they needed more help from the courts.

By the end of 1923 Mooney had become something of a pariah. His 'four supporters' had taken real umbrage about being named. In September Murphy had been sent for trial charged with an assault on Mrs Mooney; he had thrown a brick at the pregnant woman, knocking her unconscious. Again the police may have thought he got off lightly. The Assistant Recorder, C. Milton Barber, was long on homily and short on sentence.

People in the city of Sheffield, be their names Mooney or Murphy or Smith or Jones, or anything else, must know that if they come up to these courts and are convicted of crimes of violence they will all be dealt with in a suitable manner. Taking into consideration all the circumstances you will be sentenced to six months' hard labour.

The Mooney family did not have a very happy Christmas. By now Sam Garvin's Park Brigade ruled supreme. On Christmas Eve Frank Kidnew led a razor attack on the house, but failed to find George Mooney hiding in a cupboard. Bail was allowed in the sum of £20 each to Kidnew, Sam Garvin, Sandy Bowler, a one-time boxer, and Robert Crook, but not before they had spent Christmas in the cells. In January Mooney had the humiliation of being protected by the police as he went to court to give evidence. Cross-examined, he admitted to fifty-three convictions. Curiously, although all four had, they said, been distributing tickets for a charity boxing tournament at the time of the attack, only two were believed. Garvin and Crook were acquitted, Kidnew and Bowler received a modest three months each. The damage had been done to Mooney. His close friend Albert Foster had already sought refuge in Birmingham. Now his brother John emigrated and in early January Mooney left the area. Garvin reigned supreme; at least for the moment.

Garvin was a man born in 1880 who had convictions around the countryside for assault, illegal gaming, housebreaking and theft. He was well-built and well-dressed, and popular not only with his followers but also for his assistance when he organized a boxing tournament for the relatives of men killed in a colliery disaster at Nunnery. Whilst on bail for the attack on George Mooney, with Kidnew as the referee at the tournament and Barlow as the secretary, he raised £130. He wrote to the *Yorkshire*

Telegraph and Star thanking people for their support and, at the same time, pointing out just how many 'congratulations have been showered upon me'. It was an action which would be repeated over the year by any sensible gangleader who knew the benefits of some well-advertised charity work. He took an interest in politics, breaking up Labour Party political meetings, and his family was one of the first to move into the Walkley estate which had the unheard-of luxury of an indoor bathroom.

Over the next two years gangs roamed the streets of Sheffield stealing and mugging passers-by and fighting each other. As well as Garvin's Park Brigade who committed themselves – apart from some thefts and robberies – to the destruction of what was left of Mooney's team, there was now a Junior Park Gang and a rival organization, the Smithfields Gang, constantly at war with each other. The local magistrates seemed afraid to hand out heavy sentences and now the prospect of meeting violence with violence occurred to senior police officers.

At the New Year of 1925 an arrangement was made over the running of Sky Edge. Six delegates from the former Mooney organization and six from Park Brigade would supervise the division of proceeds. The public was pleased, the Mooney men were pleased, but what was in it for the Garvin team? On the face of it not much – after all, they were in control. Looked at a little closer, things became clearer. The price for the concession was the withdrawal of yet more summonses against Sam Garvin, Barlow, Kidnew and William Wareham. They had been in a bit of horseplay after which a Mooney man, George Newbould, had needed several stitches. Magistrates and defendants wished each other a happy New Year.

The troubles began again by the end of January. Four

former Mooneys went – together with the assistance of a
Birmingham thug Tom Armstrong – to Sky Edge to sort out
their percentage and were told that any deal they might
have thought they had was off. They were chased by about
fifty Park Brigaders (should that be Brigadiers?) into a
house from which they had to be rescued by the police.
By now things were hotting up once more. George Mooney
had returned from his abdication but his gang was being
run by Foster (who had defected from Garvin), Wheywell
and Tom Armstrong, one of Billy Kimber's Brummagem
boys who was living at George Newbould's home.

Attacks and counter-attacks followed one another with
frequency. Now George Newbould was seen as the leader of
the forces opposed to Garvin. He had two pitching rings
under his control and the police were raiding Sky Edge on a
regular basis. Patrons were looking for other rings where there
were no such tiresome interruptions. Apart from running the
pitching rings, however, the gangs controlled the poor quarters such as the Crofts, Norfolk Bridge and the Park,
collecting protection from the publicans and shopkeepers.

It was the death of a bystander which brought matters
home to the citizenry of Sheffield. There has long been a
tradition that the Underworld should be allowed to play by
itself provided it does not cross the boundary dividing its
representatives from decent folk. The line was crossed on 28
April 1925 when William Plommer, an ex-Sergeant in the
First World War, a labourer and father of two children, one
a three-week-old baby, was stabbed to death. A fight had
taken place near Plommer's home in which a 23-year-old
Garvin gang member, Wilfred Fowler, had been defeated.
Plommer had only been a spectator, but the next night
Fowler and his friends had toured the area threatening to
do for Plommer and two of his friends.

Plommer came out of his house to meet them and was attacked by a gang of eight men. Plommer who, towards the end of the fight, was hit over the head with a child's scooter, had received stomach wounds which seemed to have been caused by a bayonet. A policeman in the vicinity found Wilfred Fowler, his younger brother, Lawrence, and a third man George Wills sitting on the steps of a shop. Plommer lay nearby.

Meanwhile the gang had gone looking for Plommer's friends and had caught up with Harry Rippon who was slashed with a razor. He identified his attackers as Sam and Bob Garvin and William Furniss.

In all eleven men were finally charged with the murder of Plommer. They included the Fowler brothers, Frank Kidnew, Sam Garvin and George Wills. In those days a coroner's jury was entitled to return verdicts of murder against named defendants and they did so in the cases of the Fowler brothers, with allegations of aiding and abetting against seven of the others including Garvin and Kidnew. The defence was that Plommer had run a tossing ring under the railway arches at Norfolk Bridge and had been the attacker of the Fowlers, going for them with a poker and razor. Efforts by the defence to substantiate either allegation in the police court failed. The men were committed for trial at the Leeds Assizes.

Plommer had indeed been unfortunate to be involved. Wilfred 'Spinks' Fowler had argued with a man called Harold Liversidge in the Windsor Hotel. Liversidge had been struck and had then gone to Plommer's house to get help. Quite clearly there were a number of spectators and encouragers at the fight because James 'Spud' Murphy was one of the watchers. Liversidge and Fowler had fought with the latter, ending on the floor. As Plommer helped Fowler up he was told, 'Jock, you have got to have a tanning for this tomorrow.'

The next day Plommer was advised by a friend to leave his home but he refused. Evidence was called that he was approached by seven men, each of them armed. He offered to fight them one by one and knocked down Lawrence Fowler before he was overpowered. It was the case for the prosecution that one of the Fowlers had struck the fatal blow.

Kidnew was acquitted on a submission of no case to answer at half-time. So was Robert Garvin. Sam Garvin was acquitted by the jury. George Wills and two others were found guilty of manslaughter. Both the Fowler brothers were convicted of murder. Before sentence was passed the brothers were asked if they had anything to say and Lawrence replied, 'I spoke the truth. I only struck one blow with the poker. I am innocent. If his wife would only speak up. It is an impossible decision.' Wilfred said nothing. George Wills was sentenced to ten years' penal servitude on the manslaughter charge.

An appeal was lodged and unsuccessfully argued. The Court of Appeal took the view that, rather than the Fowler brother having been unfortunate to be convicted of murder, some of the rest had been fortunate not to be. There was still the hope of a reprieve, particularly when it was rumoured that Wilfred had made a last-minute confession exculpating his brother. Surely the Home Secretary had to act? He did not. There had been trouble during the summer at a series of Northern racecourses and law and order was in the air. The brothers were executed on consecutive days – Wilfred first – at Armley Prison, Leeds. Lawrence had asked to be executed with his brother, but for no clear reason this small act of clemency was denied him. Another man,

Alfred Bostock, who had battered his mistress to death and thrown her in the river at Rotherham, shared the scaffold with Wilfred on 3 September.

What, meanwhile, had happened to Sam Garvin? The answer was that on Saturday 1 August, the day after his acquittal in the Plommer case, Garvin was back in the dock on a charge of wounding Harry Rippon, Plommer's friend. This time he was found guilty but, yet again, the sentence does not seem to have been the swingeing one which this old bully merited. He received twenty-one months' hard labour. His brother, Robert, received a modest nine months.

And what about George Mooney? On the day Garvin was sentenced he came unstuck on the way back from pony races at Worksop. He had the misfortune to find himself in a railway carriage with William Cowan whom he had ousted six years earlier from the Sky Edge ring, an action which could be said to have started off the whole present state of affairs. At the end of the journey Mooney was charged with grievous bodily harm; Cowan had three fractured ribs and a bitten ear. When questioned by the police, Mooney did not mention the ribs but denied the attempted cannibalism. He received nine months' hard labour.

Albert Foster received eighteen months' hard labour for a fight outside a boxing tournament Sam Garvin had promoted in the happier days when he was at liberty; and Peter Winsey, another Garvin man, struck old Patrick Mooney, George's uncle, splitting his head; he received two months' hard labour. Inroads were being made into the teams.

What was also breaking up the gangs was the attitude of the new police Special Duties Squad, formed four days after the Plommer murder. According to former Chief Constable Sir Percy Sillitoe, who is generally credited with the destruction of both the Sheffield and Glasgow gangs:

I called my senior officers together and asked them to select very carefully for me some of the strongest, hardest hitting men under their commands. I had 700 policemen, each with a minimum chest measurement of thirty-six inches, all fit and healthy men, and none of them was disinclined to play the gangsters at their own game and meet violence with the strong arm of the law. It was not difficult to pick a dozen of the best of these to form a 'flying squad' specially to deal with the gangster problem. These men were taught ju-jitsu and various other methods of attack and defence, and it was surprising how little teaching they needed. They had just been waiting for the chance to learn![6]

The squad was led by ex-Coldstream Guardsman PC Walter Loxley, who weighed in at 19 stone 8 lbs and stood 6 feet 2 inches. Its other members probably needed no ju-jitsu lessons. Jerry Lunn was an ex-heavyweight boxer, and Julian Bean describes a third officer as 'another hardman well versed in the techniques of rough-house and back-alley brawling'. According to Sillitoe another member could not only hold seven tennis balls in one hand but could also pick up five loose tennis balls in his fist. They were soon in action against the gangs and dealt out heavy punishment in the bar-room and street brawls which preceded arrests. If cross-summonses were taken out suggesting that the officers had acted outside the scope of their authority, then help was at hand from the courts:

On the other hand, if you are satisfied that at the time when this man Wheywell was assaulted, that he had

[6] P. Sillitoe, *Cloak Without Dagger*, p. 79.

begun by striking the officer, as, I believe, the evidence shows, and that what the officer did was after that, believing he was going to offer further violence, then you must find a true bill against Wheywell.[7]

And the jury did just that: Officer 0. Wheywell 3 months.

Sillitoe is undoubtedly mistaken when he recalls forming the Special Duties Squad. It had been done by the former Chief Constable Lieut. Colonel John Hall-Dalwood, who had fallen out with the Watch Committee in the autumn of 1925. There had been considerable difficulties in the force, with allegations of heavy drinking by senior officers. Hall-Dalwood retired in early 1926 and Percy Sillitoe took up duties on 1 May 1926, the first day of the General Strike. There is little doubt, however, that he honed the Squad. Perhaps like many another officer time had dulled the cutting-edge of his recollections. In this passage we are almost into ex-police officer Tom Divall's fond remembrances of Darby Sabini and Billy Kimber as 'good allies'.

The Mooney and Garvin gangs had a final clash, as a result of which both leaders were sent to prison. After George Mooney came out, when his sentence was completed, I sent for him and saw him alone in my private office. I spoke to him like a father. I said: 'Well, Mooney, you see what my attitude is. If you chaps do this sort of thing I am going to see that you go to prison, and it's not getting anywhere. Now what is the sense of it?'

Mooney did not answer. I went on: 'Why don't you

[7] Mr Recorder W. J. Waugh quoted in J. P. Bean, *Sheffield Gang Wars*, p.111.

stop this damned nonsense of fighting Sam Garvin's men? I shall stamp out his gang just as I shall stamp out yours, but if you have any decency in you, as I believe you have, you won't wait to be stamped out like some sort of dirty pestilence. You will come to your senses while there is time and keep your dignity.'

When he got up to leave I said, 'I really believe you will try to better yourself, Mooney, and I want to shake your hand.'

He stood and looked at my proffered hand for a long moment without saying a word. As I was about to withdraw it, he burst suddenly into tears, grasped it and said: 'You are the first gentleman I have ever had the privilege of shaking hands with, sir.'

All good stuff from *Eric or Little-by-Little* or *Tom Brown's Schooldays*. There is no record, however, of Mooney and Garvin having been in prison over the same incident, but there were suggestions that they might have a man-to-man fight for control for a purse of £100. It was thought it would draw a bigger crowd than a Sheffield United *v.* Sheffield Wednesday Cup-Tie. It never took place; after all Garvin was 47 by now.

By 1927 the police had bent, if not broken, the gangs – there were still sporadic outbreaks by the Junior Park and Smithfields gangs – and indeed Mooney and Garvin went their separate ways. Both became bookmakers on the northern courses. Garvin, wearing a white hat, was Captain Mee, and Mooney metamorphosed into George Barratt, betting at the Owlerton Stadium until well after the Second World War. Perhaps the homily described by Sillitoe did happen and did take effect, for Mooney had no more convictions. Garvin, who had not had the benefit of

Sillitoe's uplifting speech, continued to associate with thieves and pickpockets and added to his list of convictions until his death in the 1960s.

Although it was estimated that at the height of the armed robbery escapades the great bulk of large-scale criminal enterprises in the South of England and the Midlands were organised from London and carried out by groups which included London-based operators, this did not stop there being a very substantial number of local operators. A 1964 study showed that there would be 1 in 10,000 major full-time operators in a town of 80,000. Such an operator would of course be extremely low in the pecking order of London.[8] But it was to the Midlands and North West that London criminals turned when they had to leave 'the smoke' for some reason. For example, when Eric Mason received a bad beating at the hands of Frankie Fraser, could get no sympathy from the Twins and was also none too popular with some other London faces, he went to Blackpool. There he was joined by some brothers who had also fallen out with the Krays. In turn they moved back through the Midlands where they ran some girls and owned a club or two.

On 31 October 1984 Police Sergeant John Speed was murdered in Leeds when he went to assist another colleague who had also been shot whilst investigating two men seen tampering with car-door handles opposite Leeds parish church. The gunman was chased for over a mile before he managed to escape by hi-jacking a car at gun-point. The killing led to suggestions that an 'affable and dangerous' Irishman had devised an ideal way of carrying out robberies in the United Kingdom and had carried them out for about

[8] J. Mack (1964) 'Full-time Miscreants etc', in *British Journal of Sociology*, vol. XV, pp. 38–53.

fifteen years. The procedure was simple – that of hit and run. Within hours of the robbery the perpetrators were back in the Republic.

Inquiries led to the police interviewing 10,000 people and 18,000 leads being checked out. Finally, after an anonymous telephone call the police were pointed in the direction of Eamonn Kelly. Kelly, born in Dublin, had spent the greater part of his life in Leeds. Detectives flew to Dublin and it was found that there were a number of applications pending for Kelly's extradition on bank robberies. He was already serving fourteen years for his part in the kidnapping of Jennifer Guinness in Ireland. However, it became clear that so far as the killing of Police Sergeant Speed was concerned Kelly could not have been the killer.

Kelly was, however, linked to an Irishman who had lived in Yorkshire, Gerald Stone, and through him to Dave Graceworth, known as 'The Mechanic' because of his ability to soup-up all manner of motor vehicles. Graceworth was seen loitering in the car park of a supermarket and was approached. He took off and was killed in a high-speed chase when he lost control of the vehicle he was driving. His guilt was confirmed by an accomplice on the day of the robbery which led to the murder of Sergeant John Speed.

Anything Londoners can do Yorkshiremen can do better, including tampering with witnesses. In 1992 Judge Jonathan Crabtree lifted reporting restrictions at the Newcastle Crown Court and revealed a massive trial-fixing plot described with some justification as the 'worst in history'. After a six-month trial at Leeds Crown Court, Scarborough antiques dealer John Walsh had been convicted in 1989 of handing £1.25 million of antiques and valuables which had been stolen over a ten-year period in a series of often violent raids on country houses in the North of England. Walsh's haul had been discovered by some Scouts who camped on land near the home Walsh shared with his mother. The police dug up five beer barrels and freezer bags containing silver, porcelain and jewellery. He received seven years' imprisonment.

This was only the beginning of the story. The police set up Operation Judge to inquire into what they considered was perjured evidence given on Walsh's behalf. The defence had been that the witnesses had sold the items to Walsh. In fact many had been bribed with cash or gifts of clothing to give perjured evidence. Over a period of eleven months thirty of the witnesses, including a former Yorkshire cricketer, a Hatton Garden diamond merchant and other antique dealers were convicted. Sixteen went to prison for their part in the conspiracy and Walsh received a further three years and was ordered to pay £40,000 costs. His brother Ivor was sentenced to five years, and his sister-in-law Susan received twelve months.

After the last trial Detective Superintendent Ian Peacock, who had headed the twelve-strong team of detectives, commented:

I think most of Scarborough must have known what was going on and it must have seemed for some that justice had just simply ceased to exist and the Walsh family were above the law.

Back in Sheffield, drugs have taken a hold not dissimilar to that in other cities. There was, however, a slightly unusual case in 1992. Another 'Mr Big' Craig Allen ran a drugs ring from a police cell block at Bridge Street. Described as 'short and flabby and not a user, something which gave him the power of ten over lesser mortals', he had already escaped from a prison bus in Grenoside in May 1991. Whilst on remand for a post-office break-in he used the now fairly liberal facilities which allow the use of the telephone to an inmate to keep in touch with his family, to mastermind a drug distribution centre. The cell block was being used at a time when prison cells were not available to remand prisoners because of overcrowding. Allen fed £30 a day into the telephone to organize a distribution network of couriers to deal in heroin, amphetemines and cannabis across South Yorkshire, Nottinghamshire and into Manchester. Eventually staff at the cell block became suspicious of his almost total monopoly of the telephone and it was tapped. The police now heard how Allen's middle-aged parents had kept drugs in a dog kennel and in a specially built floor safe in the burglar-alarmed shed in the family home in Parson Cross.

Allen's mother, Marjorie, collapsed in the dock when she received two years. His father had half that sentence, Allen's girlfriend received five years. In all fifteen people received sentences and Allen himself collected ten years for supplying, eighteen months for the post office and twelve months for escaping from the prison bus. The police described him as having a mind like a computer. 'He rang all his contacts from memory and was able to work out weights and prices straight away,' said an admiring officer.

Any doubts that crime was not alive and well in Leeds were dispelled in December 1993. Apart from a place for local talent to thrive, it has long been one of the safe havens for London gangsters who need some time away from 'the smoke', and it was to this city that Jack Spot had fled in November 1943 after a small spot of trouble in a Paddington spieler. Here, according to his memoirs, he had protected a club owned by a man named Milky against

267

the predations of a Polish mobster. This led to Spot being given a share of a book at a local dog track, and the general enhancement of his reputation.

Leeds was also a city which had difficulties with its police force in the 1950s which led to a series of prosecutions of serving officers and the eventual jailing of a former inspector for the manslaughter of an immigrant.

Now yet again clubs and drugs with linked dealing and protection have become rife in the Chapeltown area, the drug and red-light district of Leeds. In December it was alleged that two men, Robert Samuels and Clifton Bryan, were seriously attacked and wounded as a reprisal for their earlier behaviour. They had, Leeds magistrates were told, kidnapped a teenager, Mark Smith, and then blackmailed his associates into paying £2,900 as a deposit for his release. It was a complicated series of affairs with Smith being kidnapped for allegedly assaulting a Michelle Midgeley, a friend of Samuels and Bryan.

A further instalment of £7,000 was due to be paid for Mr Smith's release and arrangements were made to collect the money from a bank in Chapeltown. When Bryan and Samuels arrived on Monday 13 December they found no Mr Smith and instead, said Stephen Fox for the prosecution: 'Another car was parked further along. It followed them. They stopped, the car pulled alongside and someone fired off a double-barrelled shotgun.' It was the first of nine discharges that night. Samuels was badly injured and Bryan thought him to be dead. He drove towards the local hospital, pursued by gunmen who shot at the pair once more as they reached the hospital's Chancellor Wing.

Smith, however, was the one who ended in court when he appeared accused of conspiracy to murder. Reporting restrictions were lifted at the request of his solicitor.

This violent incident is not an isolated one. According to a report all the small Asian businesses live on their nerves. A fish-and-chip shop has lost its till twice during frying hours; robbers have simply walked in and taken it. The local community fears that, if things are not controlled and the disaffected young black community does not have its energies channelled in the right way, then Chapeltown could become another Moss Side.

The penchant for motor-cycle killing spread to Northamptonshire in October 1993 when John Reynolds, a local property dealer, was shot to death whilst walking his golden retrievers with his daughter. The motor-cyclist shot him five times.

Over the years Leicester has also had its share of troubles. In the 1960s the Lambrianou brothers, two of whom were convicted in the Kray trial, had what seemed to be an unhealthy interest in the mini-cabs in the city until they were spoken to on the subject by Charles Kray. That was the decade of the first hot-dog wars of which Bob Black, who used to work for burger baron 'Mr Big' Gary Thompson, said: 'In the Sixties there was a lot of rivalry. In those days a burger stand would get turned over, or if somebody stole someone else's pitch they would get a good hiding. Today, they are using shooters.'[9]

In the early 1990s things were much more serious. 'Mr Big' Gary Thompson, known by the soubriquet not merely because he weighed 25 stones but because of his control of the business, and his assistant, John Weston, died on 27 August 1990 outside Thompson's Victorian home in Oadby. They had been followed from the Thompson catering business in Aylestone Road, Leicester.

[9] *Independent on Sunday*, 2 September 1990.

Thompson had been shot three times with .22 bullets; one bullet had passed through his right leg and into his left. A second had gone through his arm before entering his spleen, and the third had been fired at close range into his head. His companion was found curled up, shot in the legs and head. The opinion of the pathologist was that both had been shot whilst on the ground. It was thought that a large sum of cash, certainly £30,000 and possibly as much as £80,000, had been taken from Thompson's Bentley.

Thompson, who had worked up his father's hot-dog barrow trade from the time he was 12, was undoubtedly the King of the Midlands burger business. In 1978 he had been fined £400 for assaulting a rival hot-dog salesman. He had seen off his main rival Geno Loizo by purchasing his business after a long-running battle in which Thompson had sent two men to steal all Loizo's hot-dog equipment, including not only his freezer but also 1,000 bread rolls and his tomato sauce. Now between 1981 and 1987 Thompson's business turned over £3 million. That year he went to prison for a VAT fraud involving over £400,000.

On the August Bank Holiday weekend that he died, Thompson had his vans at three local shows as well as at York races and in Devon and Essex. A little after midnight on the Monday, he and Weston transferred the substantial takings to the boot of his Bentley at the depot and drove home. They were followed by Terence Burke and Warren Slaney in a gold Ford Sierra. Weston was shot first and, according to Mavis Thompson who saw the fight, her husband was standing his ground against Slaney before he was shot. The men then drove off with the money.

The prosecution put the case as a simple robbery which went badly wrong. Slaney ran an alibi defence, whilst Burke said that he had been recruited with Thompson's knowledge to 'do an insurance job'. The gun had been taken to kill the Rottweiler guard dog; he, Burke, did not know there would be any shooting of humans. He said that while on remand Slaney had threatened to kill him and he had been warned to wear a bullet-proof vest while on trial at Northampton Crown Court in February 1992. Slaney did not give evidence but called witnesses to the effect that he was at the engagement party of his cousin at the time of the shooting.

Given what amounted to a cut-throat defence – Burke's counsel described Slaney as 'the cool executioner' – it was not surprising that the jury convicted both men. Slaney, a former professional boxer, cried out, 'They've convicted an innocent man – I've been framed.'

Were either of the versions of the case the correct ones or, as Mr James Hunt QC, counsel for Burke, suggested, were 'some very big men behind the scenes'? Certainly troubles continued in the hot-dog business for some time after the killings with Joe Persico – who ran vans and who had, at one time, worked for Thompson – finding them vandalized and daubed with graffiti. An unlit petrol bomb was found on the steps of his parents' home in Equity Road. Shots were fired through the front windows, and the windows of the car showroom belonging to Persico's brother, Tony, were smashed.

Then a dead pig with 'THE GRASS' and 'JOE' written on it was dumped outside Tony's garage. The pig had been artistically made-up with a receding hair-line and heavy facial scarring. Its eyelids had been cut off.

Joe Persico, who in the past had received a sentence of five years for kidnapping and grievous bodily harm, went into hiding after being warned there was a £25,000 contract on his head. Fly posters began appearing around Leicester suggesting 'Joe Persico sold Lee Oswald the gun'. Another more colourful one was a 'wanted' poster for 'Joe Per-Sicko' and suggesting he was impersonating Postman Pat, a hardman, a plank, a chicken carcass and that, amongst other things, he had 'tiny genitals'; 'a Max Wall lookalike trophy, no business (soon) and no chance'. The posters were signed by local body-builder Ramzy Khachik, who owned a gymnasium and provides doormen for clubs in the Midlands.

Persico was, quite understandably, extremely alarmed. He spent a considerable time at the offices of the *Leicester Mercury* putting his side of the case. One former reporter remembers him as being 'almost paranoid with worry'.

But paranoid or not, fight back he did. He sent videos of Thompson's funeral to his rivals and rang them to play dirges down the phone. Eventually he and Khachik met. There had been a problem with Persico's sister in the ice-cream van depot. Marie Persico believes a gun was pointed at her. Khachik says she held a knife and he leg-swept her to the floor to disarm her. The knife ended in the possession of the police and no charges were brought.

The Persico-Khachik confrontation came in the Holiday Inn, Leicester in April 1991. Names were called and Khachik invited Persico to sort matters out in a man-to-man fight. Apparently Persico did not move; instead he began to dial on his mobile phone, as did Khachik. The manager of the hotel called the police who 'arrived to witness the stand-off'.[10]

That had not been the end of the Persico troubles. In 1991 he was charged with reckless driving and threats to shoot his former business partner, Clifford Taylor. It was all part

[10] *Independent*, 6 April 1991.

of a long-running feud in which a year earlier Taylor had obtained an injunction against Persico. Taylor had bought the vans of the murdered Gary Thompson and according to his counsel, Persico had raided his lock-up garage and made off with the mobile food stalls. Persico's counsel denied any involvement by his client in the incident. His explanation did not appeal to the judge, who said at a later hearing that he had 'an abundant opportunity' to reveal where the fleet had been hidden and had not done so. He received a four-month sentence for contempt of court and ignoring an injunction.

Earlier in the year Persico had been acquitted at Leicester Magistrates' Court when on 8 April 1991 the prosecution abandoned a case of common assault, criminal damage and threatening behaviour. Mr Walter Berry, prosecuting, said that two out of four prosecution witnesses had failed to appear and the other two were refusing to give evidence. Three were said by Mr Berry to be 'terrified'. Earlier Persico's counsel had asked for the matter to be adjourned because of a film the previous night on television. In the Cook Report on the mobile burger business Cook's hot-dog operation – established by Roger Cook for the purposes of the programme – was closed down and towed away by rival traders. The film appeared to show Mr Persico in a bad light. The magistrate declined to grant the adjournment, saying he had not seen the film.

Things were even better when at Leicester Crown Court on 27 November 1992, to cheers from the public gallery, he was acquitted of the threats to kill Clifford Taylor but convicted of reckless driving.

The Persico family had earlier had difficulties when in June 1985 Joe, then known as John, was sentenced to five years' imprisonment. He was described by Mr Justice

Hayden Tudor as the ringleader of a gang who had kidnapped and then tortured 18-year-old Mark Coulson following an incident in Tops nightclub in Leicester in which Coulson, said Persico's counsel, had challenged him to a fight. When Persico had declined he had been attacked by other people and a broken glass had been pushed in his face. The judge pointed out that according to Coulson he had never seen Persico before.

As Coulson and another friend left the Range Inn on the Melton Road, Coulson was kidnapped and his friend chased away. Coulson was taken to Persico's home where he was punched and kicked and a wire put round his neck. He had a finger broken and his feet were stamped on. Finally he was thrown in a canal, fortunately in a shallow part.

Yorkshire has not escaped the growing trend of the kidnapping of relations of workers who have access to substantial funds rather than being rich in their own right. Sometimes, however, the victims have been able to strike back. In February 1994 two masked men broke into the Huddersfield house of a security van driver, bound and gagged his wife and then took Polaroid photographs of her with a shotgun pointed at her temple. She was forced to write a message to him. They then approached him after he and a co-driver had picked up cash to deliver to a local sub-post office. As he left the van to make the delivery, one man passed the co-driver a note to be given to the husband. He recognized the writing and drove after the men who were in a BMW. Along the road he rammed the vehicle but, after a chase, it got away. Some hours later his wife was found shaken but otherwise unharmed in the boot of the BMW where she had been during the chase.

A new form of organized crime has crept into the Midlands. The usually law-abiding Asian community is thought by observers to have some of the smartest players in the game. Credit cards and cheques which have been stolen in Midland cities have appeared in Liverpool and Manchester as well as in Southall within a matter of hours. Traveller's cheques stolen by one member would be cashed by a second and used by a third to buy heroin in India. There has also been a thriving trade in illegal immigrants. According to former Detective Superintendent Roy Herridge, new recruits to the Asian gangs such as the Tooti Nung and the Holy Smokes were recruited from school: 'They will start off in petty theft, graduating to burglaries at about the age of 15, moving up into bigger crimes. It appears to be an organization where any criminal talents are used to the fullest.'[11]

The same observers worry what will happen when, rather than if, some of those players put more than just a toe into the water of the drugs market.

[11] *Evening Standard*, 2 August 1989.

9

Dublin

As is the case with most police forces, the Irish Gardai
would have you believe there are no organized gangs in their
territory and never have been. 'Have a good holiday but I
can tell you you're wasting your time,' said an experienced
and long-serving Detective Sergeant. He was speaking of
professional, as opposed to political, criminals. Yes, there
had been and probably still were a few small independent
operators in the professional field such as Charlie
Ainscough, a sort of Dublin version of Fagin, who had a
few boys and prostitutes thieving for him. Poor Charlie had
been found dead by a police officer, and when his body had
been removed to the morgue it was discovered that £10,000
was sewn in the nightshirt. The Gardai who found him had
never been allowed to forget it. There was another man who
went round dressed as a policeman passing cheques and, of
course, there was the famous MacArthur murder, the
professor who killed a nurse in a park when she found
him trying to steal her car and then shot dead a man from
whom he was buying a gun. He was found at a football

match sitting next to the Attorney-General, who later resigned. And the film *The Field* was based on the murder of a man called Moore. But these were all isolated incidents. What about the man they called 'The General' who was said to wear a pig's mask? Surely he was organized crime? Well, yes, but he was probably in retirement, following years of successful hounding by the Gardai. The Dunne family? They were simply small-time criminals.

Not everyone would agree with the assessment of the situation and the bland dismissal of 'The General' and the Dunne family. What they would agree was that crime took off in a big way in the 1960s. Before then there had certainly been gangs. In the 1940s there was the Animal Gang, led by a former heavyweight professional boxer, from Sean McDermott Street, Buckingham Street and Gardiners Street in North Inner City. Like the Garvin and Moody gangs from Sheffield in the 1930s, they had been the heavy men at the Pitch-and-Toss rings and had done a bit of protection, thieving, and touting on the side. At one time they had challenged (and failed to oust) the box-man Sartini who ran a Pitch-and-Toss gang in the Greenhills wielding a short-handled dray driver's whip.[1] Their end had come after a baton charge by the Gardai at a Balldoyle race meeting. They were said to be the sons of people who had served in the British Army. Then there was the Hatchet Mob who were mainly a fighting gang, and the Red Hand gang who also dabbled in extortion. But, and on this there is a consensus, apart from these minor villains, until the

[1] It may seem strange that a man with such a name held sway in Dublin's half-world, but there had long been a strong Italian community in the city. Later the amusement arcades would be owned by other Italian families, the Senezios and their relations the Dal Rios.

1960s there was effectively no professional crime in Ireland. There were family disputes, certainly, but there was no theft or robbery. Says former Gardai, Jim Ridge, now a barrister:

> People were so poor, they had no time to go out stealing, they were simply trying to make a living. And they had nothing to steal. When I was a young officer, we dealt with gas-meter bandits. You would stop a boy in the street and sniff the coins in his pockets to try to smell the whiff of gas on them. If you wanted crime you had to go to the cinema and watch James Cagney say, 'Top of the world, Ma.'[2]

But crime did take off in the 1960s. Armed robberies jumped. In 1963 there had been none; twelve in 1969 (which netted the grand total of £7,782). By 1981 there had been 306 robberies with takings of over £1 million. Killings, which were almost invariably domestic matters in the 1960s, rose from an average of six to over twenty by the late 1970s.

In 1982 the US Embassy said that up to twenty-three replacement passports a day were being issued to their citizens who had been robbed in Grafton Street, the main tourist area. By the summer of 1993 Jury's hotel reported forty-five incidents of thefts from visitors on their premises, and representatives of the tourist industry complained that there was a group of known pickpockets operating in the St Stephen's Green – Grafton Street – Trinity Street triangle between 11 a.m. and 4 p.m. along with an organized betting ring (mainly of travellers) in the area from Trinity College to the Tourist Office. Children and young adults were being

---

[2] This was in the film *White Heat* (1949).

dropped off at various beats, and disputes over territory were sorted out by older males. The pickpocketing ring was thought to be well organized, with one woman in possession of a radio which picked up Garda messages. There were now 90,000 indictable crimes recorded annually.

The Garda Report on Crime in 1990 showed that the value of property stolen was £36,376,810, of which 8 per cent had been recovered. This compared with a total of £33,023,563 the previous year.

The reasons for the increase in crime are complex. From Independence until the 1960s the Irish economy had stagnated until with the social revolution things began to pick up. In the 1930s the old IRA had avoided commercial crime. Post offices were attacked, but only because they belonged to 'an illegitimate' state. Now the upturn in the economy coincided with the troubles in the North. In the late 1960s the IRA and Republican movement became radicalized and moved to the political left. Splinter groups such as Saor Eire (Free Ireland) rose and then waned. Political and criminal alliances were formed, so that the distinction between commercially orientated and political fund raising blurred. Some of the proceeds would go to the party and some would stay with the commercial arm of the temporary partnership.

It was also found that it was extremely easy to rob banks and this in turn coincided with the rise of the Dunne family. They were – and Christy, known as Bronco, in particular was, say admirers – the first to raise the motor-car robbery to an Irish art-form. The father Christopher, also known as Bronco, married in 1936. He came from the Liberties/ Dolphin's Barn area and worked part-time as a docker. As a young man he had served twelve months for manslaughter after hitting a youth who had struck his mother.

At the time of his marriage his bride was 15 and worked a clothing stall in Francis Street Market, and he was 22. She was to have twenty-two pregnancies and fifteen surviving children. Ten of them racked up 150 convictions between them, and eight of the eleven brothers went to industrial school for larceny. Hubert drowned whilst trying to save other boys who were in difficulties. His brother John saw the tragedy, and left Ireland to become a building contractor in England. By the time he was 18 Christy Jr, born in 1938, reckoned he had done two hundred burglaries. In 1960 he stole a judge's car. He would say of the family, 'We knew we could depend on one another with our lives. We are totally dedicated to one another.'

Henry Dunne, aged 8, and his elder brother, Larry, had caused a stir in May 1960 when they were found in London. A photograph was captioned: 'Anyone lost a son?' They were claimed by their father who had come to find work in England and told them, 'You can stay with me.' Wrong. They were packed off back to Dublin to begin a circuit of industrial schools and remand homes. In the September Larry was put on probation for theft and loitering and on 31 January the following year he was sentenced to two years' Borstal for attempted larceny. He did not last long on the outside after his release; this time it was for stealing from gas meters and he earned a year in Letterfrack.

By the time he had served the sentence his family had gone to Birmingham. One of Larry Dunne's closer friends was Eamonn Saurin, an accomplished armed robber who a decade later was wanted for questioning there for the murder on 6 November 1972 of pensioner Kenneth Adams. On 16 July 1981 Saurin was arrested over the murder of fellow armed robber Christy McAuley in an argument over a woman, an ironic situation as McAuley was a well-known homosexual. This was done in the full view of Lawrence 'Chickey' Maguire who, quite properly, refused to give evidence. The refusal did not help Saurin much; he was convicted at Birmingham in 1982 and received life imprisonment.

Larry continued to flit in and out of prison. Most years in the 1960s and 1970s there was a conviction or two. 1974, for example, was a good (or bad) year when there were eight, double the total for the previous year. In 1980 he was disqualified from driving for twenty years. By this time he had racked up ten convictions for traffic offences. Now he was chauffeured by other members of his family and friends. He said this was the best thing that could happen to him; now he could change cars at will and so confuse the Gardai. Dunne had returned to Dublin in 1969, by which time some of his brothers had begun to deal in drugs, something he seems to have avoided wherever possible. In the meantime, however, Larry Dunne concentrated on raids on banks and post offices to finance him and the rest of his family. Bank raids in which he was not involved also continued.

On 20 February 1970 seven men in a Cortina and Triumph 2000 cut all the telephone wires into the village of Rathdrum in Co. Wicklow and robbed the Hibernian Bank there of £1,500. In a particularly daring move, they stopped the local Gardai and ordered them to throw the keys of their car on to the road.

The influence of Saor Eire, which extended for only a two- or three-year period from 1967, more or less collapsed after the killing of an unarmed Gardai officer, Richard Fallon, outside the Royal Bank on Arran Quay, Dublin on 3 April 1970. No one was convicted. Previously the organization had staged a spectacular double bank raid in Newry in March 1969 when some £22,000 was taken.

The fortunes of members of the Dunne family ebbed and flowed towards the end of the 1970s, reaching a low point in 1977 when Larry was accidentally shot, and an even lower pitch when in 1980 Henry was asked to burn a garage and was trapped when it ignited prematurely. Rescued and taken to a doctor in Dun Laoghaire, he was given large doses of morphine, which was the beginning of his habit. Things picked up for him that year when he was later acquitted of a robbery at the Bank of Ireland in Finglas.

In a profile in the *Sunday Press* the Dunne family are seen as the first non-addicts who were able to organize the distribution of drugs, and as a result they prospered.[3] By 1981 Larry in particular had adopted a high profile, as did such other gangleaders as the Krays and Glasgow's Arthur Thompson. He was seen at the ringside of boxing tournaments. When the daughter of a member of the family married, an invitation to a prominent newspaper editor was only declined at the last minute; and when his sister, Colette, needed bail on a drugs charge those queueing up to stand on her behalf included a barrister, a building contractor and a company director. She ultimately received two years. When Henry Dunne went down in February 1983 for drug offences Father Michael Sweetman, a prominent Jesuit, was there to give a character reference, before the judge handed down a ten-year sentence on firearm offences. Like Arthur Thompson after him, Henry, unemployed at the time of his arrest, lived in a council house, but it was one equipped with more than the bare necessities of life. Mock Tudor woodwork had been

---

[3] 26 June 1983.

added to the porch and inside, along with a private bar there was a sauna.

Laurence Dunne did not stay around for the result of his second trial in 1983; he absconded on the second last day of the proceedings. He had been arrested not at his new house in Sandyford which had panoramic views of the city, but in his more modest establishment in Rathfarnham. When Drug Squad detectives broke in to his home in October 1980, under a pillow in a bedroom they found 70 grammes of heroin. In the living-room cocaine was discovered, and there was also cannabis in the house. Seamus Dunne, another member of the family, was in the house at the time; he had an envelope with £3,000 in it. Laurence Dunne said that he would accept responsibility for anything found in his home. The first jury disagreed.

In his absence, at the second trial the jury found Laurence guilty, and he was sentenced to fourteen years' imprisonment. He was retrieved two years later from Portugal, where he had been seen getting off the ferry at the little port of Villa Real de Santo Antonio in the Algarve. His wife, Lily, was sentenced to nine years' imprisonment. Two years later his house failed to reach its reserve of £220,000.

For a short while after Larry Dunne's conviction *in absentia* it seemed as though a small Northside operation, the Gang of Six, might take over his drugs empire. Unfortunately for the group it lacked anyone of sufficient stature to command respect, and heavies such as Harry McOwen were recruited to give the gang something of a presence. To finance a drug deal the gang embarked on the hi-jack of an ambulance, to be used in a raid on a cash consignment travelling from Belfast to the Central Bank in Dublin. But the hi-jack went hopelessly wrong when one of the ambulance drivers managed to get free and gave the alarm. The Army was invited to provide an additional escort and the raid was called off. Shortly after that McOwen, who had in the past had associations with both Saor Eire and the INLA, was shot outside the North Cumberland Street Labour Exchange.

But the consensus is that the nearest thing Dublin has had to a master criminal is the man known as 'The General'. Just as the identities of masked wrestlers have been common knowledge amongst the *cognoscenti* so, for some years before his unmasking, the name of 'The General' was well known and newspapers took to referring to him as 'the man who denies he is The General'.

Finally in October 1987 the *Sunday World* took its presses in its own hands and splashed the headline: Gardai name No 1 crime family.[4]

It told of the death of Martin Cahill's brother, Anthony, in the Curragh military jail of a drug overdose and another, Pat, in a knife fight. Two other brothers were convicted in 1979 for an armed raid on the payroll at Smurfits in Clonskeagh. John, who during the raid was shot by Gardai, was sentenced to ten years' imprisonment and brother Eddie to twelve.

In 1975 Anthony had been charged with the murder of bank official John Copeland, found dead in his basement flat on the Palmerstown Road. The case against him had been that his fingerprints were found in Copeland's flat, and the theory was that Copeland had been stabbed when he disturbed burglars. Cahill was acquitted after accounting for the presence of his fingerprints by telling the jury that he had burgled Copeland's flat a few hours before the murder.

[4] *Sunday World*, 11 October 1987.

The queue for the public gallery for the Cameo Murder Trial *(Liverpool Daily Post & Echo)*

Herbert Balmer, doyen of Liverpool Detectives
(above)
(*Liverpool Daily Post & Echo*)

**Places to cache your drugs:
in Alma Grove, Bermondsey, a stash
of heroin was found under a gnome**
(below)
(*Martin Goodwin*)

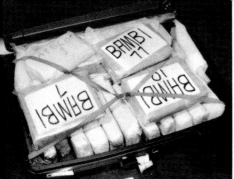

Or try a case of Bambis
(above)
(*Enterprise News*)

Floated in on a surfboard
(right)
(*Enterprise News*)

**Be careful what you eat,
these are not yet more
bread rolls**
(below)
(*Topham*)

Jimmy Nash (centre), Ronnie Kray and Christine Keeler out on the town

Viv Graham(left)
shot in Newcastle on
New Year's Eve 1993
(with his friend)
(*Newcastle Journal*)

Lee Duffy
(*North News &
Pictures*)

Joe Persico, victim of the beefburger feud
(above)
(*Leicester Mercury*)

A 'bubble' of supergrasses with their warders in Bedford Prison
(below)
(*Rex Features*)

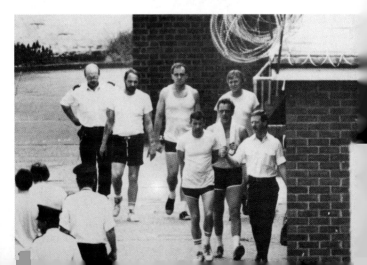

Later Anthony was convicted of participation in an armed robbery. In prison at the Curragh military camp used for difficult prisoners, he repeatedly complained of being beaten up.

Brother Pat went down in Ballyfermot, stabbed to death in the summer of 1987. Anthony Quinn, charged with his murder, was acquitted after telling the court that Patrick had stabbed his father. The Gardai said that the Cahill family had given no help in the investigation and had declined to identify the body.

Martin Cahill grew up in the Holyfield slums, at that time some of the worst in the Dublin area. At the age of 11 he was convicted of housebreaking, for which he was given probation, and in 1965 at the age of 15 he was sent to St Conleths, again for housebreaking. Discipline was harsh. He recalls there was a special strap known as the impurity strap for those caught in homosexual acts. Four years later he married Frances Lawless, whom he had met whilst working in Goodbody's making sacks. That was his last known job. He was next convicted of receiving cigarettes and a watch and was sentenced to four years' imprisonment, being released in 1973.

Now, when he was organizing the Prisoners' Rights Organization, Cahill ran up against Ned 'The Buffalo' Ryan when the latter was promoted to Detective Superintendent. According to Cahill, Ryan said he would be putting the squeeze on petty criminals who would be 'reduced to robbing grannies' handbags'. According to the *Today Tonight* programme, Cahill was responsible for the hiring of hitmen to assassinate Ryan.

Then in February 1988 it was announced that Cahill would be named in a programme by RTE. The announcement came after a £30 million dragnet the previous year when it was believed that 'The General' had got away with the Beit art robbery on 21 May 1986.[5]

The alarm went off at 2 a.m. and when Gardai officers arrived they were told by staff that everything was all right. The loss of the paintings was not discovered until 9 a.m. when the gallery opened to the public. Seven of the less valuable paintings were found discarded during the day. It is suggested that the gang had deliberately triggered off the alarm to lure the Gardai into a false sense of security.

The Beit collection had had an unhappy career. Begun by his diamond-mining uncle in South Africa, it had been brought to Russborough House in 1952 by Sir Alfred Beit, a former British MP who had retired to Co. Wicklow. On 26 April 1974 a gang of four armed men and the British heiress, Dr Rose Dugdale, had stolen nineteen paintings from the hundred-strong collection. Sir Alfred and his wife had been assaulted and tied up whilst the paintings – a Vermeer, a Goya, two Gainsboroughs and three Reubens – were removed.

Demands were made to the director of the National Gallery for £500,000 and the transfer from British prisons of the Price sisters who had been convicted of terrorist bombing offences. Eleven days later the paintings were recovered undamaged in Co. Cork. Rose Dugdale was sentenced to nine years' imprisonment for her part and was released in 1980. The raid had also been an effort to obtain the release of her husband Eddie Gallagher, sentenced for his part in the kidnapping of Dr Tiede Herrema. After the recovery of the paintings Sir Alfred donated his collection to the state under the care of the Alfred Beit

---

[5] 'The General: The world according to Martin Cahill,' Michael O'Higgins in *Magill*, March 1988.

Foundation, and Russborough House was opened to the public in 1976.

This time, under the possible supervision of 'The General', the stolen paintings included Vermeer's 'Woman Writing a Letter', which of itself was thought to be worth in excess of £5 million, and a Goya portrait.

The robbery had gone down in December 1987 and in an unconnected incident 145 files, including those relating to the highly sensitive cases of Malcolm MacArthur and Father Molloy, the priest found dead in a businessman's home, were stolen from the DPP's office in September 1987.

Five weeks later an attempt was made to steal Renoir's 'Les Parapluies' and Monet's 'Sunshine and Snow' from Dublin's Municipal Gallery. At least seven raiders entered the premises, hiding the staff and two early morning visitors at gunpoint. When they tried to remove the paintings the security alarm went off and the robbers fled. At that time it was thought that both raids were connected and they were the work of an England-based gang of international art thieves. The Gardai were strengthened in this belief because no demand was made for the return of the paintings from the Beit collection.

'The General' had first come to prominence in the £90,000 armed robbery at Rathfarnham Shopping Centre, and a decade later in July 1983 he was regarded as the prime figure in the £2 million robbery of the Thomas O'Connor and Sons' jewellery factory in Harold's Cross. It was a robbery about which the Gardai had advance information. On a number of occasions the premises had been staked out by them but no one had appeared. Now, on the night of 26 July, with only twenty-five of the 100-strong staff at work, the gang hid in a boilerhouse at the premises. As each member arrived they were locked in a lavatory, and when all had been accounted for the manager Dan Fitzgibbon was made to open the strong-room. It took thirty minutes for the gang to load their vans before they left, setting off a smoke bomb as they did so, something which led the locked-in staff to fear they would be burned alive. By the time the Gardai were notified the jewellery was in parcels all over Dublin.

A reward of £25,000 was offered for information but not a single call was made. A fraction of the stolen property was recovered, some buried in a back garden in Terenure (a suburb near the Cahill home) and some more, but not much, in Norway. There were rumours that there had been an attempted drugs-for-jewellery swap in England, but Cahill maintains he has never been involved in drug dealing. The raid broke the company, which was insured for only £900,000 of its £2 million loss; it went into receivership four years later.

It was over this raid that the story grew up that when gold from the robbery had gone missing 'The General' had a suspect nailed to the floor. In an interview he commented, 'I've heard the story. I can only say there might be some truth in it, but I wasn't there at the time.' He went on to suggest that the blame for the incident could more properly be laid on some over-enthusiastic and undisciplined gang members. The gold was the stolen property dug up from the back garden in Terenure, and Cahill is said to accept that they nailed the wrong man.[6]

Six months later on 11 March 1984 Provos kidnapped Thomas Gaffney as he left the Park Inn public house at Harold's Cross, home of the famous Irish greyhound stadium.

The next, say Gardai officers, came in December 1984 after a robbery of £90,000 from the Quinsmith branch in

[6] Neil McCormick, 'Is this Ireland's most wanted man?', *GQ Magazine*, December 1991.

Rosemount Shopping Centre in Rathfarnham. Cahill has persistently denied any involvement, but has been monitored by the Gardai from that date.

In the 1980s it was possible to lay the blame for almost every major operation at 'The General's' door, and his name was first in the frame when it was discovered that over a hundred sets of documents had been stolen from the offices of the DPP at St Stephen's Green in early September 1987. They included the files on Malcolm MacArthur, convicted of killing Bridie Gargan in 1982,[7] and the death

---

[7] On 12 January 1983 the socially well-connected Malcolm MacArthur, then aged 36 and who had just run through the money left to him by his wealthy father, was jailed for life for the killing of a 25-year-old nurse Bridie Gargan.

After he had run through his £80,000 inheritance MacArthur – who had a 9-year-old son by a girlfriend, Brenda Lyttle – planned to obtain more funds by armed robbery. His first step was to steal a car, and it was while he was attempting to steal Bridie Gargan's Renault in Phoenix Park that she surprised him. She was returning to her car after sunbathing on a warm July day. He first threatened her with a replica gun and then hit her over the head with a hammer. He then put her in the back of the vehicle and drove off. A passing ambulance driver seeing a hospital sticker on the nurse's car presumed MacArthur was a doctor with a patient and, sounding his siren, led the vehicle to St James's Hospital. MacArthur did not however stop, but drove out of the exit gates and abandoned the car two miles away. Nurse Gargan died four days later.

MacArthur was arrested in the flat of the senior law officer, the Irish Attorney-General, Patrick Connolly, whom he knew through Ms Lyttle. After MacArthur's arrest Connolly, seemingly blind to the implications of his action, went to America on holiday, but was recalled by the Prime Minister, Charles Haughey. The affair contributed to the defeat of the Haughey-led Fianna Fail party in the next general election. Another allegation of murder, that of a farmer from whom it was suggested MacArthur went to buy a shotgun, was left on the file.

of Father Niall Molloy who died at the home of Co. Offaly businessman Richard Flynn in 1985. In a sensational case Flynn had been acquitted of the manslaughter of Father Molloy, but the priest's family was taking action in the civil courts claiming £7,500 for mental distress under the Civil Liability Act.

It was, however, on the evening of 30 November 1988 that members of 'The General's' gang went too far in their escapades. Ann Gallagher, the postmistress at Kilmanagh, and her landlady were kidnapped from their home. The next morning she was made to go to Kilmanagh post office and withdraw cash and stamps worth nearly £30,000. With her was Myles Crofton, who had a radio-controlled bomb strapped to his chest. After the raid a high-profile seventy-strong surveillance unit was set up to monitor and harry the activities of 'The General', his henchmen and other target criminals.

In their turn the criminals did not make life easy for the Gardai. As they drove into housing estates they would be rammed by stolen cars. Shortly after Christmas, an informer told the Gardai that Detective Superintendent Ned Ryan, known as 'The Buffalo', was to be killed. The newspapers reported that his reaction was a characteristic laugh, but the strain of the following months told on his health.

One of the arrangements of 'The General's' gang was that associates were free to work on their own, and the surveillance on two worked well. On 23 February James 'Shavo' Hogan was found in possession of firearms and received eight years' imprisonment. Cahill was questioned and released without charge.

Four months later Eamonn Daly, one of 'The General's' most trusted lieutenants, went down for twelve years for robbery. The adopted son of a Crumlin schoolteacher, he had sixteen convictions dating back to 1973 and was already on bail for a 1985 robbery on the Equity Bank in Grafton Street (which had netted £13,000) when, on 26 March, he was arrested by Dun Laoghaire Gardai during an attempted robbery at Sandyford. Martin Cahill's brother, Michael, eventually pleaded guilty to receiving the proceeds of the Grafton Street robbery.

Daly was one of two men wearing false beards and moustaches who followed a Securicor employee into the Atlantic Homecare centre. In turn he was followed by plain-clothes detectives. When a gun was seen to be pointed at them by Daly, they jumped on him; he was found to have a loaded 9mm semi-automatic pistol in his pocket. Two other men escaped following a shoot-out.

In court, the financing of Daly's £40,000 house in Terenure was explained. He had done it with £17,000 damages from a car accident, a £5,000 government grant and a £5,000 corporation grant. After his conviction he went on a 'dirty protest' in the maximum security prison at Portlaose, complaining that he was being housed with subversive prisoners. Also protesting were the Border Fox, Dessie O'Hare, and two members of his gang, Fergal Toal and Eddie Hogan, along with Michael McHigh serving forty years for the murder of a Gardai sergeant.

The war with 'The General' has produced tales of valour from both sides. At one time when the police were surrounding the house, something they appear to have done over long periods in the 1980s and 1990s:

He wouldn't let us in; came to the door with a great big butcher's knife. One of our lads shot a dog which he thought was attacking him. Meanwhile a girl with a baby in a pram left and after that Martin came to the door and in we went, peaceful as anything. The lad said he was sorry about the dog but Martin didn't seem to mind and said he was no fucking good anyway. Of course the girl should have been stopped. Talk about Homer nodding.

Cahill maintains, 'You must never, ever look at them [the Gardai]. Their presence must never be acknowledged.' To this end, like Orphée, he had removed the reflecting glass from his wing mirrors.

Sometimes the Gardai won an engagement. Sometimes the wins were shortlived. On 13 August 1991 Cahill appeared, hooded and handcuffed, to face charges of dangerous driving, obstruction and a breach of the peace. He had been remanded in custody for a psychiatric evaluation after the arresting Garda officer Ciaran McCarthy had alleged his actions had been those of a completely irrational man. According to the officer, Cahill had stripped off on the road and again at the station.

According to the papers no report was available and Cahill was released on £100 bail. When he emerged from the District Court in Dublin, he had on a white nightshirt, and had a mask and a model of a bird's nest strapped to his forehead. 'One Flew Under the Cuckoo's Nest' was hand-written on the front and back of the nightshirt. Cahill blew a duck decoy, asked one of the many reporters whether he was a chicken and, after enquiring whether a nearby bicycle was a boat and whether the street was the River Liffey, rode off in some triumph.

As mentioned earlier, in January 1986 the theft of some £30 million paintings, including works by Vermeer and Goya, took place from the state-owned Sir Alfred Beit collection housed in Russborough House, Co. Wicklow, and sixteen months later John Patrick Naughton of Templeogue, Dublin was remanded in custody in London, charged with dishonestly handling £12.5 million of the paintings which were bound for Geneva.

In the autumn of 1987 the Gardai received what was a humiliating setback in their efforts to retrieve the paintings and arrest those responsible for their disappearance. A Dutch criminal and informant was contacted with a view to the disposal of some of the paintings. He contacted the Dutch police, and was later given a relatively small-value painting to prove the bona fides of the vendors. A 'sting' operation was set up and a Dutch detective posing as a French art dealer was shown one of the Beit paintings in a Dublin hotel. The meeting was monitored by the Gardai, and a further meeting was arranged when the detective was told to travel alone to the Kilakee Woods. Over thirty armed detectives were in the area, with about half a dozen following the buyer to his rendezvous; the remainder waited for instructions in a nearby hotel. At a crucial moment in the surveillance, the electronic state-of-the-art surveillance equipment failed and a detective had to phone a near-by bus depot for directions. The gang disappeared on their high-powered motor-bikes and no arrest was made. What apparently had happened was that two paintings were produced in the Kilakee Woods at about 2 p.m. on Sunday 27 September 1987. A series of false trails had been laid to divert the Gardai surveillance unit, and when the Gardai on the ground radioed for assistance they were unable to secure direct contact. By the time the Gardai had made their way through the boggy ground of the woods the vendors had gone. The Gardai did, however, carry out an unsuccessful search of the woods to see if any paintings had been left behind. The force had had similar troubles four years previously when in the Don Tidey kidnapping in 1983 in Ballinamore, Co. Antrim, armed men had also evaded a Garda dragnet.

'The General's' reputation soared when in February 1988 as part of the reprisals for surveillance and damage to his own car, twenty cars belonging to the Gardai were damaged at Stacksdown Golf Club, used almost exclusively by Gardai. Eleven greens were also dug up. A few days earlier a group of men had attacked a Nissan Bluebird belonging to 'The General'. The Gardai accepted that they were at the time keeping 'The General' under surveillance, but would not confirm they were in the area.

In April 1988 Cahill was bound over to keep the peace in sureties of £1,500 for a year, having been found by the court to have been threatening both neighbours and members of the Gardai. Evidence in the case was that detectives had been offered £20 notes by Cahill whilst his son stood by with a camera. This was not an altogether new technique: 'Once or twice we'd stop him and he'd pull out a tape recorder and start dictating his protest into it. Then he'd pull down his trousers and show us his Mickey Mouse underpants. Several times we left him without them.'

In court for the hearing Cahill wore a wig, a false moustache and glasses. Outside he immediately donned a ski-mask. 'There's nothing wrong in that,' says a Garda. 'He's an ugly-looking fucker.'

In *Magill* Cahill is described as bearing '. . . a close resemblance to Bob Hoskins in *The Long Good Friday* or to Del Boy in *Only Fools and Horses*'.

In June 1988, acting on a tip-off, detectives went to Cahill's house where after a search the Gardai say they found a loaded .45 Colt in the water-tank. The subsequent decision of the DPP not to prosecute angered senior officers, who believe this was a cast-iron opportunity to score even a minor triumph. The thinking may have been, however, that someone with a grudge against Cahill may have planted the gun himself and then given the tip-off.

By 1993 'The General' seemed, by all accounts, to be slowing down in the scale of his operations.

On 24 April 1993 at about 8 p.m. the Gardai received a complaint from a Mrs Sile Holmes of Swan Grove, Ranelagh, that Cahill along with his son, Christopher, and armed with sledgehammers, had forced open the front door, and smashed three television sets as well as windows and mirrors.

Shortly afterwards both 'The General' and his son, the latter noted to be sweating heavily, were stopped near by and taken to the police station. Not long after that, along came Frances Cahill together with Glen Holmes. Later Mr Holmes ordered the Gardai from his mother's house and prevented them from taking the sledgehammer for examination. The matter was dropped.

The end came for 'The General' on Thursday 19 August 1994 when he was shot dead in his Renault 5 in the Ranelagh suburb near Dublin's city centre. It seems that two men had lain in wait for him. One had sat on a black motorcycle whilst the second posed as a council worker who appeared to be checking car registration numbers. When Cahill stopped his car, the 'council worker' ran up and shot him with a .357 Magnum. The car went out of control and hit a pole. Four more shots were fired before the men escaped.

At first it was claimed that the outlawed Irish National Liberation Army had carried out the killing, but later a man using a recognised IRA codeword, told a Dublin radio station that the claim was false and that one of its volunteers had carried out the execution. The message said that '. . . his involvement with and assistance to pro-British death squads' had forced them to act.

But there are now more violent players than 'The General' even at his most tiresome, and a series of killings has all the hallmarks of gang warfare. In July 1992 it was apparent that the fragile peace which had established territorial boundaries between the six major warring gangs in the city had been fractured; fatally for Mick Travers, shot with four bullets from a pump-action shotgun outside his shop in Darndale. In December 1991 hairdresser Patrick 'Teasy Weasy' MacDonald had been executed in his salon in Fairview. Now, said the Gardai, Travers' death had the hallmarks of a gang killing – shotgun, motorcycle – as did that of MacDonald. MacDonald, armed robber and Irish National Liberation Army renegade, was believed by the Gardai to have run a one-man crime wave in a series of robberies on pubs and shops in the North Inner City. He was gunned down in front of customers in his shop; the lone gunman then stood over him and fired further shots into his body. It was the second attempt on the life of a man who had been into protection in the North City centre. Informed observers believe that his death was the result of his interference with the drugs scene controlled by Northside brothers.

They were quick to rule out four of the gangs, including that of 'The General' whom it was thought was now more devoted to tyre-slashing than other crime. A second family-based gang thought to control the heroin trade in the South of the City, and being investigated in connection with the importation of a large quantity of chemicals into Dublin that month, was ruled out on the basis that it was 'well organised, everybody knows which is their turf and they have never had to resort to serious violence.'[8]

The other Southside gang eliminated from Garda inquiries was one controlled by a Donnybrook man who specialized in protection rackets in parts of Dublin 2, as well as Ringsend and Irishtown in Dublin 4. He had been questioned over the killing of Jackie Kelly in Pearse Street in the 1980s, and was thought to have handled some of the Beit paintings as well as being a fire-raiser in the South Docks in 1990.

So far as the Northside was concerned, the position was more complicated. There were thought to be two major criminal organizations: the first operated by a man living in Swords, north of Dublin, and the second, and far the more organized and dangerous, run by a family from the North Inner City. The two units had co-operated on various projects. It was the North Inner City family who were believed to have been behind the 1990 Finglas mail-van robbery, as well as hiring the killers who shot Patrick MacDonald in Marino in December 1991.

There was, however, also the possibility that karate-expert Travers had been the subject of an independent contract as he worked in his shop in Darndale. He was not a well-liked man; he liked to hit and hurt people. According to one comment:

He hit people he knew and people he didn't. People who knew him knew better than to fight back but in a pub he would spill a drink on somebody deliberately or push somebody. When they reacted he would ask them

[8] Diarmaid Doyle quoting a Garda officer, *Sunday Tribune*, 19 July 1992.

to step outside. If they did he invariably beat them up. If they didn't he would nab them at closing time.

Another said, 'He would kick you as soon as look at you.'

After MacDonald's death the Gardai drew up a list of operators in the city whom they believed were capable of contract killings. It included two ex-paramilitaries who had, at one time, had links with the INLA and were associated with the North City gang. One was suspected of the killing of Danny McKeown outside a Dublin labour exchange in 1982 and the murder, the following year, of Gerald Horrigan in Ballymun. Horrigan, who died in a drug war raging at the time, was chased into a block of flats by a motorcycle passenger and shot in the head and chest.

June 1993 saw the temporary end of Eamonn Kelly, regarded by the Gardai as one of the most organized and intelligent of criminals in Dublin, and one who at the time of his conviction was assuming Mafia-style status. His downfall, as is the case with so many, was drugs. Born in 1949, one of nine children in the Summerhill district of Dublin, he had already been convicted four times at the age of 19. Then two of his brothers, Matt and Des, offered him the chance to get out of crime, and he became the managing director of Kelly's Carpetdrome on Dublin's North Circular Road. Des left the business to go on his own in 1976, and five years later Matt and Eamonn Kelly's company went into receivership. The brothers were held personally liable for debts approaching £2 million.

Fire-raising is a particularly Dublin activity and the Kelly business had been bedevilled by arson attacks. On 14 June 1982, the evening before the High Court liquidator was to assume control of the premises, the group's headquarters on the North Circular Road was destroyed by fire. This was by no means the only misfortune the group was to suffer. The next month up went the Fiesta club in Talbot Street, whilst a year earlier Matt Kelly's Silver Shadow Rolls-Royce was set on fire and, sadly for children, two haulage containers full of Christmas toys went up in flames whilst parked outside the Glasnevin cemetery.

Three years later Eamonn was in some difficulties, and he was sentenced to ten years for stabbing a union official. The verdict was set aside on the basis that one of the main witnesses against him had a conviction for manslaughter which had not been disclosed to the defence. On the re-trial Kelly was convicted of an assault and sentenced to three years' imprisonment. The Gardai maintain that on his release he became a major player in Dublin's underworld. Investigations into his involvement with forged currency and drug importations came to nothing until a three-month surveillance in the summer of 1992 ended in his arrest over possession of one kilo of cocaine, which would have a street value of £180 a gram. At the time, the father of nine children was unemployed and receiving £140 social security per week, but he had raised £20,000 necessary to enter the game. The drugs were smuggled by Cuban Elisabeth Yamonoha, taped in folds of fat to her stomach, and the pair were arrested in Jury's hotel. She received a sentence of four years.

At the time of his sentence in 1984, Kelly's lieutenants were brothers from another Dublin family, but by now they were breaking out on their own. In early 1987 they were suspected of involvement in the £1 million Securicor robbery in Fairview. One, a successful grocer, was investigated, to no effect, with regard to fire-bomb attacks on rival premises.

According to Patrick Hickey, who pleaded guilty to

receiving £191,000 taken in an armed raid from guards when they were loading cash-bags from the bank at Marino Mart on 27 January 1987, he had been pressured by one of the brothers into helping launder the money, making trips to Newry to pay the money into an account kept by a brother which had been opened just eight days after the robbery.

The van, which did not have a Gardai escort, had just completed thirteen collections when it was attacked outside the Bank of Ireland. Another of the receivers, Francis Sheridan, who had been found with £220,000 in a bag in the attic of his Swords home, received a sentence of twenty-one months.

The undercover Gardai exercise to nail the robbers themselves had aborted when detectives moved on Hickey as he was passing a package containing £80,000.

In November 1984 a fire destroyed the fittings and furnishings of Edward Hutch's home at Portland Place on the North Circular Road, Dublin. Three years later Mr Hutch was awarded £1,250 out of his claim for £20,000 against the Dublin Corporation. Hutch had told the court that he was an inept thief, being caught every time he pulled a job. Not so, thought Judge James Carroll who branded him as 'an idle and dishonest character'. Hutch, who produced receipts for the furnishings, had claimed he had earned his money by breeding German Shepherds and bulldogs, selling colours and hats at sporting events and from gambling.

There was success for the Gardai when John Gilligan was sentenced to four years for receiving. The Gardai believed he was leader of the so-called Warehouse Gang, operating as all good thieves should by specializing in identifying a ready market for a particular brand of stolen goods, whether it was animal drugs, videos, video games, or children's clothes. The gang, which had operated almost unchecked for ten years, would raid the target factory on a Friday night, and by the time the loss was noticed the goods would have been distributed throughout Dublin; they were then sold to small-time dealers or shops, and on occasions would be sold back to the losers.

Gilligan was trapped when he was seen unloading hardware goods from a lorry in the Walkinstown district. At a previous sentence hearing, the 38-year-old former seaman had been described in court as having no other income than from crime. In 1988 he had been living on social security of £50 a week, from which he was maintaining three ponies at livery in a local riding school. By the time of his conviction in November 1990, he had acquired a house and stables in Co. Meath.

Just as the mainland has been the scene for drug trafficking, so has the South West of Ireland where because of the particular terrain surveillance is difficult. At one time or another Howard Marks (see pp. 294–296) and James Humphreys – the porn king of Soho in the 1970s – have been alleged to have operated there along with Mark's friend James 'call me the Shamrock Pimpernel' McCann.

After the successful Operation Julie in England in 1977, which broke a ring operating out of Hampton Wick in Middlesex, said to be producing £20 million of LSD annually, the price of a microdot soared from £1 to £5. Humphreys saw a gap in the market and along with two other Londoners went to Ireland to set up operations. There in Knocklong, a small village on the Limerick-Tipperary border with the nearest local Gardai point three miles away, and with Shannon in easy reach, he posed as a greyhound breeder and dealer. Jack and Donie Ryan, who owned the local pub The Cross, were in some financial straits and agreed to store chemicals for him. At the end of the day they were the ones to suffer. Humphreys fled to Spain. Donie Ryan received three years for aiding and abetting, and Jack committed suicide by injecting himself with a humane animal killer. The other Londoners were acquitted after a re-trial.

Just as the Gardai had found it difficult to adjust to the modern car bandit, so they found difficulties in coping with the increase in drug trafficking. One man who was a shining example of humanity was Garda officer Dinny Mullins. People describe him as a true Christian who understood and wanted to help junkies, drug dealers and their problems. It is substantially due to him that there was a crackdown on the estates against drug dealers, but this did not occur before a number of families were ruined by the trade.

Prostitution has recently been more of a problem in Dublin than in cities in Great Britain. In 1983 John Cullen, a protector, was killed in a dispute over the protection of a girl, and four years later it was said that it cost £200–£300 (Irish punts) for a girl to get free of a pimp who was estimated to take 80 per cent of her wages. The cost was to hire a group to deal with the pimp and explain the facts of life. Prostitution continued to flourish around the canals, and of the approximately one hundred working around Fitzwilliam Square thirty were thought to be from Britain, remitting their earnings to that country. English girls kept such brothels as there were mainly for political and foreign clients.

Outside Dublin it seems the professional criminals kept their grip on such country sports as dog-fighting. In 1988 there was said to be a ring at Ballyfermot with thousands of punts being gambled on dogs which cost £600 plus for a male pup.

One breeder who refused to sell his dogs and threatened to report those involved was persuaded not to. He said:

> . . . these guys are deadly, they are far more dangerous than all the drug pushers and shotgun merchants around here. Everyone knows who they are but fear grips the community. The money these guys gamble each week is enormous and anyone who tries to stop them is simply asking for trouble.[9]

On perhaps a wider but less dangerous note, there has been a concerted attempt by gangs to shake down the Dublin Corporation. When one man claimed he had fallen on an uneven pavement, records showed that three out of four of his brothers and sisters and six cousins had all made claims over accidents on the particular corner where the man had fallen.

Memories fade. Within six months of his death 'The General' had been replaced in the public image by a new underworld leader, the non-smoking, non-drinking, married with a young family 'Mr Clean'. He is said to have masterminded a lightning £3 million raid on the Dublin headquarters of Brinks-Allied on 24 January 1995.

[9] *Magill*, March 1988.

10

Women

Towards the end of 1992 a conference on professional crime was organized under the auspices of the University of London. At the end of the afternoon when there was a general audience discussion, there was considerable support for the view that women were moving out from what has been seen as the traditional supporting role of their brothers, fathers and lovers and into independent operator status. Indeed, there was some admiration and support for this change. It was almost as if it was now politically incorrect to suggest that women criminals were dependent upon men for their livelihood. The feeling seemed to be that women could and should be as bad as or, preferably, worse than their male counterparts.

Yet as a general rule, certainly in Great Britain and Ireland, and even in America where criminal history is littered with such formidable women as Kate Barker and Bonnie Parker, with few exceptions the role of the little woman in professional crime has been supportive rather than pro-active. Even the position of Kate 'Ma' Barker as an organizer of crime is debatable. The official FBI version of the woman who as a child saw Jesse and Frank James and possibly died under a hail of bullets in 1935, is that she was a great organizer who planned the kidnapping of millionaires William A. Hamm Jr and Edward Bremer, and killed her lover Arthur Dunlop. The distaff version is that she was more in the traditional mould as provider for and shelterer of her certainly lawless sons. There is also an argument that, far from wielding a machine-gun in the final battle in which she and her son Freddy died, she shot herself early in the contest. Of Bonnie Parker's active participation in a series of raids in the Middle West there is no doubt. She was killed along with Clyde Barrow in a gun battle with a Texas Highway Patrol led by Captain Frank Hamer on 23 May 1934. A notable nineteenth-century American woman who played more than a subservient role in a criminal partnership was Jeanne Bonnet. She ran a gang of women – escapees from a San Francisco brothel in the 1870s – who survived on the waterfront by a series of thefts and robberies. The gang did not last long after the death of their leader who was found shot in 1876. A twentieth-century example is Barbara Graham who ran with a gang of robbers in California in the 1950s. She tortured and then killed an elderly crippled widow, Mabel Monahan, in a failed jewel snatch. Graham was executed on 2 June 1955.

Rarely have women set up shop on their own so to speak. In America, where there has been more of a tradition of a female gang, those such as the Battle Row Ladies Social and Athletic Club, better known as the Lady Gophers, were only auxiliaries of the male all-Irish Gopher gang who ran Hell's Kitchen, the district around the 8th and 9th Avenues in Manhattan, in the early years of the century. The Lady Gophers sank along with their male counterparts when railroad police put a stop to the looting of freight cars along Eleventh Avenue.[1]

Of course there have been notable exceptions where wives, girlfriends and mistresses have played an equal part, but generally their activities have been confined to hiding and caretaking the spoils, obtaining sureties and keeping the network in touch when an arrest has been made, providing comforts so far as prison regulations allowed or they could evade them, and weeping during pleas in mitigation. The girls who attached themselves to Glasgow gangs were also useful in another way, and they were probably not alone in this. They would cache the weapons of their boyfriends when they were searched on entering dance halls and later, after the inevitable fighting was quelled, during further searches by the police. They rarely were searched themselves. It was easy for a girl to cause a great deal of trouble for an officer by making a complaint of indecent assault.

From time to time women such as the prostitute Marthe Watts could be relied on to mind the shop whilst the master – in her case the vice-king Carmelo Messina – was away. She could also be relied upon to set up diversionary tactics, as when she and Blanche Costaki made allegations against the journalist Duncan Webb when he was at the height of his investigations into the Messina brothers' prostitution empire. They complained to the police that Webb had threatened that if they did not part with £50, photographs just taken of them would appear in the *People*. They had offered £7 and he had refused. The police would have

---

[1] Again, in more recent years such New York female gangs as the Dagger Debs were affiliated to the Daggers, whilst the Dragon Debs were associated with the Dragons, the Emperor Ladies with the Emperors etc. See K. Hanson, *Rebels in the Streets*, p. 15.

nothing to do with the complaint except to enter it into Webb's file.[2]

Occasionally, instead of playing the lure in the Murphy or Badger game[3] women would participate on their own

[2] Duncan Webb, the journalist, had a career during which he seems to have worn both black and white hats. So far as the white hats are concerned, he undoubtedly brought down the Messina brothers with his crusading articles. Wearing his black hat, he acquired a conviction at Plymouth Magistrates' Court for communicating the movement of His Majesty's Ships. He had telephoned the *Daily Express* and spoken so loudly he had been overheard. He was fined £50 on 26 January 1944. More peculiar was his conviction at Marlborough Street on 8 August 1946 when he was bound over under the Prosecution of Offences Act and ordered to pay 2 guineas costs. A charge of grievous bodily harm was reduced to common assault and the magistrate dismissed a charge of impersonating a police officer. According to the evidence, Webb had picked up prostitute Jean Crews and agreed to have intercourse for £2. Mrs Crews told the court they went to her flat where he 'had connections with her and then went to the bathroom to cleanse himself'. He then would not leave the flat and she said she would call the police. In the street they met Herbert Gardner Wadham, and Webb allegedly showed him a press card, masking it as a police warrant card. He seems to have arrested Wadham and then struck him in the face. As they marched along Tottenham Court Road Wadham approached a temporary reserve police officer for help. At the police station Webb denied ever having seen Wadham before. Webb later married Cynthia Hume, wife of the murderer Donald of whom he remained in fear all his life. He died of a virus.

[3] The Badger game is a variation on a confidence trick. The victim goes to a hotel with a girl who is either very young or looks it. Shortly before intercourse takes place, but when both are undressed, the 'father' or 'uncle' of the girl bursts into the room and demands compensation for the violation of his under-age daughter or niece. This compensation may enable her to be sent away to boarding-school to forget the experience, and the mark can be squeezed for a lengthy period. If an older girl is used the 'father' can be replaced by the 'husband'. The Murphy game is the simple robbery of a client during or after intercourse, often by a ligger who has remained hidden during the proceedings.

terms. In modern times one woman conducted a blackmail racket of her own devising. She would accept a lift from a male driver or force her way into a car and then threaten to cry rape if money was not handed over. On one occasion she stripped naked in the back of a taxi-cab and the driver had a heart attack. She received a sentence of three and a half years at the Old Bailey.

At the end of the last century and during the early years of this, a genuine transatlantic example of independence was May Sharpe. Born in Dublin in 1876, she spent six years in a convent school before running off to New York at the age of 13 with £60 of her father's savings. She seems to have been a genuine operator on her own account. Of course she was obliged to rely on male help but, in her late teens, she was clearly the dominant and financially successful partner. In New York she met and married Dal Churchill, 'robber, highwayman, safecracker and rustler' who rode with the Daltons and was hanged near Phoenix, Arizona in 1891. May, now 15, went to Chicago where she became queen of the Badger game. During her career she would use the names of May Wilson, May Avery, Lilian White, Rose Wilson, Mary Brown, Margaret Smith and May Latimer, by which name Eddie Guerin, the safebreaker, knew her. At the age of 17 she had accumulated the astonishing sum of $300,000. Travelling to New York she is said to have teamed up with Charlie Becker, the corrupt police officer, before she moved on to Guerin in 1901. It does seem highly likely that she was under the protection of Becker because although whilst in New York and Detroit she was convicted in fourteen cases, including dealing in revolvers and larceny as well as the more mundane prostitution and disorderly conduct, she 'seems to have escaped so lightly as to have suffered practically no punishment at all'.[4]

> Chicago May was a beautiful woman, very resourceful and courageous, what Hollywood would nowadays describe as a gunman's moll . . . [She] was no mere ornament of the alliance, but took her share of the planning and execution in many capacities. Seducing a bank-manager – to get impressions of his keys – or standing guard with a revolver while a safe was blown, or 'taking the dairy' [diverting suspicion] in a counting house, all came equal to Chicago May.[5]

It is difficult to know how Guerin and May Churchill teamed up. In her book she says it was at a thief's funeral, but there is no doubt that within weeks they were working together.

On 26 April 1901 she, Guerin and a man known as 'Dutch Gus' removed £50,000 in francs and cheques from

[4] Lieutenant Charles Becker (1869–1915) followed in the great tradition of corrupt New York policemen such as Inspector Alexander 'Clubber' Williams. After a re-trial Becker was convicted of complicity in the murder of the gambler Herman Rosenthal, who refused to pay protection money and was believed to be about to blow the story to Herbert Swope of the *New York World*. There is little doubt that the District Attorney Whitman bribed witnesses to secure the conviction. Becker was electrocuted in the most clumsy manner at Sing Sing on 7 July 1915. His wife attached a silver plate on the top of his coffin: *Charles Becker Murdered July 7 1915 by Governor Whitman.* (The District Attorney had clearly benefited from Becker's conviction.) She was persuaded to have it unscrewed when it was pointed out she might be prosecuted for criminal libel.
[5] J. Phelan, *The Underworld*, p. 111–12.

the Paris branch of the American Express Company, where they and their accomplices overpowered and gagged the attendant and blew the safe. Guerin and 'Dutch Gus' were sent to Devil's Island from which Guerin made his famous escape in 1905.[6] She and Emily Skinner, also a mistress of Guerin, had gone back to France to see what they could do to help. Both were arrested. Skinner was released after a week but Churchill received five years. As seems customary in those days, she did not serve the sentence out and was released early.

They met again in England, quarrelled at Aix-la-Chapelle – although Guerin was wanted in France he seems to have skipped across the Channel with impunity – and met up yet again this side of the water. It seems she was now blackmailing him, threatening him that if he did not look after her she would inform on him to the French authorities. It would certainly be her stock in trade. The officer in the attempted murder case which would follow, Inspector Stockley, described her as 'one of the most notorious women in London, whose chief business is to compromise and blackmail men. She has driven men to suicide by these means.'

At the committal proceedings of Churchill and Charles Smith on a charge of attempting to murder him, Guerin gave evidence that she said, 'You dirty bastard. If you don't take care of me I will send you back to Devil's Island where you will die like a dog. If I can't do you that way I will do you another.'

According to Emily Skinner, who it must be admitted may not have been a wholly disinterested witness, within ten minutes of that conversation Churchill was on her way to Tottenham Court Road police station.

[6] Ibid., p. 107 *et seq*; PRO: MEPO 3/346.

Guerin went to prison to await an extradition to France to serve the remainder of his Devil's Island sentence. It was there he met Charles Smith, also Irish, a tinsmith by trade and, wrote May, a 'good prowler' by vocation who 'reminded me of my first husband'. He had been thrown out of Cape Town the previous year. He was also known as Cubine Jackson or Clarence Coldwell, and had clearly known May Churchill at some earlier time in their lives.

He was also capable of mixing things up. According to him, Guerin had wanted him to throw vitriol over Mrs Churchill and had told him to go to Pat Sheedy, 'a well-known sporting man who lived in New York' – in fact he owned a gaming house – who would give him $200 and then he could blind her. According to Guerin it was Smith who wanted to throw the acid of his own volition. He was apparently complaining that Mrs Churchill had not done enough for him while in prison.

Sir Richard Muir, for once acting on behalf of the defence, obtained Guerin's release on Friday 14 June 1907. Guerin spent the night with Emily Skinner and next day he had to go to see his lawyers and then the newspapers in Carmelite Street who were after his story. May had clearly patched things up with Smith – if indeed they needed patching – and was living with her new companion.

There is little doubt that Guerin was a violent man and May Churchill had every reason to be afraid of him. She and Smith took matters into their own hands and went looking for him. On 16 June 1907 they went to the Hotel Provence in Leicester Square where Guerin and Emily Skinner, who may have been Churchill's maid some time earlier, had been within the hour. An acquaintance there said it was just as well Guerin had gone. May said she was afraid he might throw acid over her; Smith said that if Guerin was a bad man he could be one too. They learned that the pair had gone to Bernard Street near Russell Square tube station, and they went after them in a hansom cab.

The whole episode was a blunder from start to finish. At the corner of Marchmont Street May called out, 'There he is.' Smith got out and fired six shots at Guerin at almost point-blank range, managing to hit him once in the foot. He hadn't finished firing before a police constable arrived and arrested Churchill. Guerin said, 'When you could not succeed in sending me back to Devil's Island you stoop to murder.' 'Yes,' she replied, 'and I am sorry we did not succeed.' Smith managed to get only a short distance before he was surrounded by police and civilians. He tried to shoot again, but the gun was now empty and he merely threw it at one of the bystanders. At the trial he alleged Guerin had fired at him first and had then tried to throw vitriol over Churchill. There was absolutely no evidence to support this. Churchill, arrested by the solitary constable, was taken to the police station followed by a rough crowd, some of them kicking the officer. During the mêlée she dropped her handbag and a witness, Robert Ward, who picked it up, noticed it had an open knife sticking through the side. 'I carry it for my own protection,' she replied when questioned about it. Smith tried to do the decent thing by her; when charged he replied, 'She has done nothing wrong. I don't see how you can charge her.'

Whilst in Holloway prison awaiting trial she did her cause no good. She wrote a letter to a Mr Thompson which was intercepted by the authorities.

Dear Ted,
I wish you to retain Purcell, otherwise I am done. They
will not let me have bail everything has been kept back.
As far as you are conserned (sic), those letters of yours
would help me where you warn me of this man, will I
use them, as your name would not appear. Good bye
you might never see me again. This fellow Smith was
the one Eddy got to throw the vitriol so you see I lost
no time, turn the tables.

Yours as ever,
May

You can hear all from Arthur Newton.[7] Help me.

Smith received twenty years in the days when twenty years
meant just that, and Chicago May had fifteen for her pains.
She appears to have been a model prisoner and was released
from Aylesbury when she had served a little over ten years.
Smith served fifteen and, according to May Churchill's
book, he was released early after the efforts of Lady Astor
on his behalf. May was deported back to the United States
where she was a source of trouble to the police until her
death. She clearly held no hard feelings towards them, for
she dedicated her book *Chicago May* to the great reforming
Californian police officer August Vollmer '. . . who first
showed me a practical way to go straight'.

For part of the time May ran a small house in Philadelphia and then, before her death in 1929 in hospital there, she
announced that at long last she was going to marry Charles
Smith. She was 53 at the time. However, she may have lived

---

[7] Arthur Newton was a fashionable if dishonest lawyer of the
time. He defended the murderer Crippen and later went to prison
for fraud. See PRO Crim 1 108/2.

on. Some accounts have her arrested for soliciting in Detroit in the early 1930s, when she was said to be charging $2, and give the year of her death as 1935.[8]

Her one-time lover, Guerin, was an interesting character. He was probably born in Soho of French parents, although police reports have him as being born in Chicago in 1860. He first came to the notice of the American police at the age of 26 when he was arrested for burglary and shot an officer in an attempt to escape. The British police first arrested him in August 1887 when, under the name of George McCaull, he was given three months for possessing housebreaking implements. Next year he was back inside for burglary, and he attempted to escape from Holloway prison. On 19 May 1899 he was sentenced to ten years at Lyons for larceny from a bank; he tried to avoid extradition by endeavouring to establish that he was born in London, but failed. He cannot have served much of his sentence, for he was next arrested in Paris in 1901 for the American Express case. This was when he received a life sentence at Paris Assizes and was sent to Devil's Island in French Guiana. He escaped in either 1904 or 1905 and was arrested here on 20 April 1906, most likely on the information of Chicago May. This time he successfully pleaded that he was a British subject and was released on 14 June 1907 after thirteen and a half months in Brixton prison. There was also another technicality. In theory the French authorities had abolished Devil's Island before Guerin was sent there – it was something they did on a more or less annual basis at the time – and so he could not have escaped from there.

After the jailing of Chicago May his career was principally that of safebreaker and hotel jewel thief. According to

[8] C. Sifakis, *The Encyclopaedia of American Crime*, p. 144.

police files, January 1908 found him with Matthew Carr aka Springate, committing a heavy jewellery larceny at Starlings the pawnbroker's in Great Portland Street. He was never charged.

On 9 April 1908 Guerin was discharged at Guildhall for frequenting banks, and on 24 April of the same year he was again discharged at Westminster Police Court when a charge of throwing corrosive fluid in the face of Alice Mahoney was withdrawn. (Chicago May was clearly right to fear for her beauty.) In Glasgow in January 1912, a charge of frequenting the Central Station Hotel for the purpose of theft was found not proven. He had been loitering in the hotel on 18 October 1910 when several bags were found to have been ripped open and jewellery stolen. He was arrested with eight skeleton keys and a contrivance for obtaining wax impressions on him. The stipendiary magistrate accepted Guerin was a known and reputed thief, but despite the equipment he had with him gave him the benefit of the very little doubt. After that his career was downhill. He was convicted of being a suspected person (loitering with intent to steal) at Bow Street in September 1920, and appealed against that charge and one of assaulting a police officer. His appeal, financed by the swindler Horatio Bottomley, was dismissed. A year later, as Thomas Garen, he was accused of stealing jewellery and a dressing-case from a guest at the Hotel Metropole, Brighton. He died in a Poor House in Bury, Lancashire on 5 December 1940.

Guerin is, however, best known for that escape from Devil's Island – one of the few men to do so successfully – along with some companions. He alone was picked up by a steamer near what was then British Guiana; he was exhausted but fairly well nourished. He was brought back to

London and the French government commenced extradition proceedings. They had problems first because Devil's Island had, legally, been abolished. How then could Guerin have escaped from it? Secondly, he had a British birth certificate. The authorities refused to return him. Unfortunately, later in his criminal career Guerin let slip that on the voyage he had eaten his companions, and from then until he died he was regarded as an outcast in the Underworld. He was, according to the Home Office file, 'one of the most daring and expert criminals who has ever come under the notice of the police'.

An early British counterpart of May Sharpe was Mary Milliner, the prostitute mistress of the celebrated thief-taker and receiver of stolen property, Jonathan Wild. In 1708 he was imprisoned for debt, and when he was discharged four years later he set up house in Drury Lane with Mary whom he had met in prison. Initially he was what was called a twang, the pickpocket who would take the wallets of Milliner's clients; in those days intercourse with prostitutes was almost invariably undertaken vertically. Wild began his criminal apprenticeship proper with a Charles Hitchin, a City Marshal who taught him the trade of receiver which Wild was to perfect. For twelve years he was able to maintain such a successful double life that by 1724 he petitioned to be made a freeman of the City. His end came when he was indicted for receiving ten guineas as a reward for helping a Mrs Steham to recover stolen lace, the theft of which he had arranged. Convicted, he was hanged on 24 May 1725. He had tried to commit suicide the night before, and still drowsy was pelted by the mob on the way to Tyburn. He was survived by both Mary Milliner and Charles Hitchin. Milliner, whose ear had been sliced off by Wild in a temper, had been paid a pension by him to the date of his death.[9]

In the 1820s the Connaught circuit in Ireland had a woman hangman:

Who think you, gentle reader, officiated upon this gallows high? A female! a middle aged, stout-made, dark-eyed, swarthy-complexioned, but by no means forbidding, woman! – The celebrated Lady Betty, the finisheress of the law, the unflinching priestess for the Connaught circuit and Roscommon in particular. Few children born or reared in that county thirty or even twenty-five years ago were not occasionally frightened into being good by the cry of 'Here's Lady Betty!'

This woman (who had been previously convicted of a horrible murder) officiated, unmasked or undisguised, under the name of Lady Betty, as the hangwoman for a great many years, and she used often to flog publicly in and through the streets as part of her trade or profession, being always extremely severe, particularly on her own sex.[10]

There have been, of course, a number of women who were convicted or acquitted of murder – Florence Maybrick and

[9] Wild was born in Wolverhampton in 1683 and apprenticed to a buckle-maker. Hitchin remained a City Under-Marshal for a further three years, when he was tried for sodomy. Acquitted of the capital offence but convicted of a kindred misdemeanour, he was sentenced to a term in the pillory, as well as six months' imprisonment and a fine of £20. For a full account of Wild's life, see *The Thief Takers* by Patrick Pringle. The character MacHeath in John Gay's *The Beggar's Opera* was based on Wild.
[10] *Dublin University Magazine*, January 1850.

Adelaide Bartlett are Victorian examples of each – but these were generally poisoners of unwanted husbands rather than participants in organized crime. The sad Ruth Ellis, part Welsh-part Belgian, good-time girl, model and part-time prostitute is another, convicted of shooting her faithless lover and a passer-by in the evening of Easter Sunday, 10 April 1955, outside the Magdala public house in Hampstead. By no means was she a gangster's moll or pro-active in crime, but she belonged in the twilight world of Mayfair and South Kensington drinking clubs and the Edgware Road and Paddington abortionists. She lived at a period where a gay time in the old-fashioned slightly shrill sense of the word was had in the days after the War by slightly soiled men, often with RAF ties and moustaches, who bought and sold things cheaply and, from time to time, cashed dud cheques.

In 1946, after she had a child by a Canadian soldier, she began to work for Morris Conley, the owner of a number of clubs including the Court Club in Duke Street and the late-night Hollywood in Welbeck Street. Shortly after the Ellis shooting Duncan Webb named Conley as '. . . Britain's biggest vice boss and the chief source of the tainted money that nourishes the evils of London night life'. This was really rather going it a bit, since the Messina brothers still had part of their operations intact. Perhaps because they were Maltese this didn't count. Conley lasted another six years before the *News of the World* reported his conviction for keeping a brothel in Westbourne Terrace, Paddington. The police had seen eighty-two men go to the address over a three-day period and, best of all, there was 'the nature of various paraphernalia one associated with these types of premises'. There were four known prostitutes amongst the tenants. Conley, who initially said, 'I did not know what was going on,' had £400 in his pocket at the time of his arrest. He was fined £100 and ordered to pay 25 guineas costs.[11]

Ruth Ellis drifted from club to club and man to man, ending with racing-car driver David Blakely with whom she had a relationship for two years. She still continued her work as the manageress of the Little Bottle Club, entertaining men in her flat above the premises, and Blakely had other girlfriends. In February 1955 they began to live together in a flat in Egerton Gardens. The relationship was stormy and Blakely left shortly before Ruth Ellis had a miscarriage at the beginning of April. There is some evidence that he hit her in the stomach, which led to the miscarriage. On Good Friday, driven by a man Desmond Curren, described as her alternative lover, she went to see Blakely where he was staying with friends in Tanza Road, Hampstead, and the police were called twice to remove her. On Easter Sunday there was a party at the house; Blakely left about 9 p.m. with a friend to go to the Magdala. When he left the pub she shot at him six times. One bullet hit a Mrs Gladys Kensington Yule in the hand, one missed and the other four hit Blakely who died instantly. She was immediately arrested.

There was no real defence proffered by Melford Stevenson QC who led for the defence. She was asked only one question by Christmas Humphreys for the prosecution:

– Mrs Ellis, when you fired that revolver at close range into the body of David Blakely, what did you intend to do?

[11] *People*, 11 December 1955; *News of the World*, 10 September 1961.

– It is obvious that when I shot him I intended to kill him.

The judge, Mr Justice Havers, told the jury, 'Even if you accept every word of it [her story] it does not seem to me to establish any sort of defence to murder.' In view of the judge's ruling Melford Stevenson made no closing speech to the jury, who retired for fourteen minutes before returning a guilty verdict.

There was a very real campaign to save her from the gallows. She was an attractive woman who by now had two young children. Her mother told her story to *Woman's Sunday Mirror*, and the *Empire News* had a few words from Mrs Jackie Dyer who had been a barmaid in the Little Club. Sidney Silverman, the campaigning MP, put together a petition which carried 50,000 signatures for her reprieve. It was in sharp contrast to the recent executions of two other women, both of them ugly and with whose crimes it was impossible to sympathize. Grace Merrifield had poisoned her employer thinking she would be left money in her will, and Styllou Christofi, a Cypriot lady who spoke little English, had strangled her daughter-in-law and set fire to her body in the garden. The brilliant journalist William Connor, writing as Cassandra in the *Daily Mirror* on 30 June 1955, had this to say:

Ruth Ellis does not matter any more than her two recent female predecessors to the hangman's noose – Mrs Merrifield and Mrs Christofi.

But what we do to her – you and I – matters very much, and if we continue to do it to her sad successors then we all bear the guilt of savagery untinged with mercy.

Mrs Yule certainly didn't feel that way. She wrote to the *Evening Standard*: 'Don't let us turn Ruth Ellis into a national heroine. I stood petrified and watched her kill David Blakely in cold blood, even putting two further bullets into him as he lay bleeding to death on the ground . . .' The efforts of Silverman and the others were to no avail. The fact that a passer-by had been injured is said to have influenced the Home Secretary against granting a reprieve. Ruth Ellis had taken little interest in the efforts to save her, regarding the matter much as a life for a life. She was hanged at Holloway prison on 13 July 1955, the last woman to be hanged in this country. She was, said a prison officer to the *Daily Mirror*, '. . . the calmest woman who ever went to the gallows'.

Within two years the law was changed and the Homicide Act 1957 was passed. Now under s. 3 there was an extended defence of provocation by words as well as deeds. In 1958 Ernest Fantle, who had shot his wife's lover after verbal provocation, was sentenced to three years' imprisonment under the section. It is inconceivable that a jury would not have found the same provocation in the case of Ruth Ellis had the defence been available.

One modern example of a woman criminal who possibly killed for money other than by using poison was the admittedly unbalanced 42-year-old Margaret Allen. Formerly a bus-conductress living in Rawstensall, Lancashire, she falsely boasted that she had had a sex-change operation. On 28 August 1948 she battered a 68-year-old woman, Nancy Chadwick, to death. The elderly lady was believed to have been in the habit of carrying large sums of cash with her, and her new red purse was never recovered. Allen had thrown her bag in the river.

Since the body was found outside Allen's house at 137

Bacup Road, it was not surprising that the police wished to speak with her. At first she denied any involvement, but soon admitted battering the old lady with a hammer, putting the body in the coal cellar and then, in the early hours of the morning, dumping it in the street in the hope that it would look as though the injuries were from a motor accident rather than from nine hammer blows. Allen never admitted stealing the purse:

> I was in a funny mood and she seemed just to get on my nerves. I saw the hammer and on the spur of the moment I hit her with the hammer. I looked in her bag but there was no money. I didn't actually kill her for that. I had one of my funny moods.

At the Assizes a defence of insanity was put forward with no success. The Home Secretary ordered a special inquiry into her mental condition, but this did not save her. The one real friend she had in the town, Annie Cook, endeavoured to put together a petition for clemency but could only raise a hundred signatures. It too failed, and she was hanged on 12 January 1949. Apparently Allen kicked over the tray on which her last breakfast was brought to her, remarking that no one else was going to enjoy it. In his book[12] Edward Robey, who appeared for the Crown in the magistrates' court, wrote that of the people he had prosecuted and who had died on the scaffold she was one of three whose sentence might have been commuted to penal servitude on the grounds that she was mentally abnormal.

A female sideline was baby-farming, or angel-making as the French called it. Unwanted children would be given to

[12] E. Robey, *The Jester and the Court*, p. 131.

the baby farmer along with a lump (and possibly an additional weekly) sum. The child would not live long. On 3 February 1903, Annie Walters and Amelia Sach became the first women to be hanged at Holloway prison which had originally been built to house prisoners of the Boer War. Amelia Sach, the younger of the pair, was the one who negotiated with the mothers, and Walters killed them.[13]

Nevertheless, although women have kept – possibly because of social pressures as well as physical strengths – mainly to 'womanly trades' of prostitution, nightclub hostessing, shoplifting, passing cheques and dishonestly handling stolen goods, there have been one or two notable exceptions, but even they have generally been working in partnership with a man or in some supportive role. In the summer of 1903 a particular one, the American con-woman Sophie Beck, managed to swindle the Story Cotton Company of Philadelphia out of $2 million, after which she retired to Paris where she lived in some style.

---

[13] Another slightly earlier example was in 1896 when Amelia Elizabeth Dyer, then aged 57, was hanged at Newgate prison by James Billington. She had been convicted at the Old Bailey before Mr Justice Hawkins of the death of four-month-old Doris Marmon, after the body of another baby, Helen Fry, had been found strangled with white tape and wrapped in weighted brown paper in the Thames near Reading. Dyer was traced because the name and address on the paper was one of her aliases. It was clear she had killed a number of children but when questioned would only say, 'You'll know all mine by the tape round their necks.' She ran a defence of insanity which the jury rejected in five minutes. She had been mistress of her profession for some twenty years. The woman who had promised the babies 'mother's care' went to the scaffold praying not for herself but for her 'persecutors'. Baby-farming became less common as the twentieth century progressed.

One British woman who seems to have cracked the mould was Louisa Wright, who for eight years from 1902 was the country's top woman jewel thief. Her speciality was using her undoubted good looks to obtain jewellery on credit or on approval, and then vanishing with it. She was caught in 1905 when in a moment of weakness she went along with a plan of her current husband and tried to chloroform a jeweller. The effort failed miserably. She was arrested, charged and acquitted, possibly because she stood in the dock with a baby, rented for the day, in her arms. Defendants in those days were not permitted the luxury of a seat.

Louisa Wright was born in 1880, the only daughter of a Bedfordshire farm labourer and a cook, and came to London as a housemaid. Initially she teamed up with a small-time crook, but she had her sights on better things. By 1902 she had eradicated the traces of her upbringing and had become in all but reality a well-bred lady. Invited to country houses, she left the windows unlatched for an accomplice.

After her acquittal her position in society was gone, and so was the husband. She moved to Paris, but in 1910 was back in London where she tried another scam. This time she became Lady Campbell of Hans Crescent, SW1. A young jeweller was summoned and persuaded to leave jewellery worth some £4,000 with her, on the pretext that her aunt who was ill wanted to choose a piece for a wedding present. She had rented the house on forged references the day before. Wright was arrested at Dover as she tried to leave the country. She served seven years of a ten-year sentence, and on her release left for France where she lived on the Mediterranean coast, to all intents and purposes a thoroughly respectable and conservative woman. During her imprisonment efforts were made by members of the

Underworld to find the place where she was believed to have cached her wealth. They were unsuccessful.

In Britain the best-known individual woman criminal of the first three decades of this century was undoubtedly Lilian Goldstein, known as the Bobbed-Haired Bandit, a lower-middle-class Jewish girl from North-West London who was the driver and nurse for Charles 'Ruby' Sparks, the celebrated jewel thief who later became a smash-and-grab artist. By some accounts it is she who suggested he turn from the country house burglaries at which he had been a master to the less skilled trade of throwing bricks through jewellers' windows. She was regarded highly not only by Sparks and his friends but by the police. Detective Chief Inspector 'Nutty' Sharpe described her: 'She usually drove a big Mercedes car. Sitting at the wheel with a man's raincoat collar turned up around her close-fitting hat, there wasn't much to see of her.'

Increasing interest of the Flying Squad in the smash-and-grab raids persuaded Sparks to return to burglary, and she was caught with him at Manchester in 1927. He pleaded guilty to protect her and received three years' penal servitude. In return, she waited outside Strangeways when he escaped during the first few months of his sentence. Unfortunately he was hampered climbing the wall and she was obliged to drive off without him. Sparks went on to serve ten years' imprisonment and was involved in the Dartmoor mutiny. He escaped from the Moor on 10 January 1940, together with Alec Marsh and Dick Nolan, after serving two months of another five-year sentence; Marsh was recaptured in six days and Nolan after four months.

In the *Sunday Pictorial* of 3 March 1940, and for a number of weeks thereafter, readers were treated to the tale of the Bobbed-Haired Bandit and her renunciation of the devil in the shape of poor Ruby and all his works. She was now going straight, and to prove it she was bravely prepared to own up to what she had done – 'I can take my punishment so that I can finish with my life of degradation' – and indeed to give her correct name, Joyce Powys-Wilson. She told of smuggling money into Brixton for Sparks, of the raids and how once a fence came from Birmingham to price the stolen jewellery. She also wrote an open letter to Sparks, pictured in a prison photograph screwing his face into the shape of a gargoyle on a minor French cathedral.

I know you will be surprised to hear from me in this way. I know you will wonder how I have had the courage to do this, after all these years. But, Ruby, I have HAD to do it, because, as I told you, I want to finish for good with the past.

I want to know what it is to have a night's sleep without waking up in terror every time I hear a strange noise. I want to walk the streets in the daylight [and much more of the same until . . .] If you want to write to me for the last time you can do so at the *Sunday Pictorial*. I shall wait for that letter, because I want to know that you understand, and have forgiven me. Then I can face the future with the same courage that I showed in those nightmare days of crime together.

And so goodbye – for ever. Joy.

The cunning little vixen. It wasn't at all.

The police were puzzled. They were convinced that the Bobbed-Haired Bandit was Lilian Goldstein, not this society lady Joyce Powys-Wilson. More was revealed in the next article, in which Joy said her parents separated soon after she was born and her father (who had worked on the Stock Exchange) disappeared. She had worked in the First World War with a very select Mayfair party in a Red Cross Unit.

She had, she said, fallen in love with a peer whom she was to marry but whom she chucked because he was a snob. (His name was not mentioned 'as he is happily married and an important figure in the land'.) Then came Peter, who was a Jew.

> Now, funny as it seems now I can swear that I did not know what the word Jew meant. I thought it was some small religious point. And I was simply flabbergasted when my mother told me that my association with him was impossible.

Then she met Ruby, whom she was told was a bookmaker: 'In a few moments I decided that Ruby was just the man for me.'

Notes appear on the police file written after the publication of each article. The officer who knew her in Manchester was convinced that it was all hogwash. 'The woman known as the Bobbed-Haired Bandit is Lilian Johnson aka Lilia Goldstein or Lilian Rose Goldstein,' he wrote firmly, adding that she had convictions for shoplifting and soliciting in 1926, both at Marlborough Street.

He was able to give more details of her early life, which did not include a father on the Stock Exchange.

> Her mother's maiden name was Kendall and she was born on 4 August 1902. Her brother is Victor Kendall, with convictions for housebreaking. On 15 July 1920 Harry/Henry Goldstein was ordered to pay 10 guineas costs and 3 months' hard labour for living off her

immoral earnings at Old Street Police Court. On his release from prison on 9 October 1920, she married him and became a prostitute and saleswoman in the West End.

After the next article appeared they decided that Joy Powys-Wilson was someone who barely knew Sparks personally but had access to details of his career. Ms Powys-Wilson was an adventuress, they deduced, and they were partly correct.

On 6 June 1940 Joyce Powys-Wilson aka Jeska, a film artiste, received five months' hard labour for stealing from Harry Barley, a cardboard-box manufacturer who had befriended her after reading the *Pictorial*. Whilst at her flat at the Mount Royal off the Edgware Road, Mr Barley had gone to the lavatory and on returning he found that she, and his dressing gown, wallet and other items, were gone.

Interviewed, Ms Joyce Powys-Wilson said she had been Sparks' mistress. The police did not believe her, and again they were correct not to do so. It was all a double blind.

With help Sparks had made his way to Lilian Goldstein's home in Wembley Park where he hid out, supporting himself by doing jobs with Billy Hill. He rather touchingly describes his reunion with the Bobbed-Haired Bandit.

She looked older and tired and there was grey in her hair and the beginnings of lines down the sides of her mouth. I saw she was screwing up her eyes to see me, and I asked her: 'Lil, do you wear spectacles now?' She looked a bit uncomfortable, and said, 'Yes, sometimes – but only for reading.'[14]

[14] R. Sparks, *Burglar to the Nobility*, p. 117.

When Hill was caught after an unsuccessful raid on a jeweller's in Bond Street, Sparks found difficulty in obtaining work. To Goldstein's revulsion, he decided to set up an armed robbery. Before it was carried out Sparks was arrested by DS Ted Greeno, who had disbelieved Goldstein's protestations that she knew nothing of Sparks and had had her followed. It was not easy, she was adroit in shaking off a tail.

> Alas, it was by no means a simple assignment and she led us a merry dance. To follow her with anything like consistency you needed to be a combination of athlete and acrobat, as she knew most of the answers on how to avoid being trailed. Her normal method of losing any 'shadow' she thought might be around consisted of catching a bus and travelling a little way, jumping off when it slowed down, dashing across the road and boarding one going in the opposite direction. Often she would repeat this process in reverse. Many a seemingly discreet observer found he was strictly on his own when she had done this several times in quick succession. If he did manage to hold on and keep her in view, there were more tricks to come. She would run into an Underground station, buy a ticket and be well down the escalator before the man shadowing her could reach the barrier. Then, as he too was riding down the escalator he would quite probably see her travelling up again on the other side![15]

Goldstein was also arrested and sentenced to six months' imprisonment by Sir Gerald Dodson, the Recorder of

[15] R. Higgins, *In the Name of the Law*, p. 67.

London. She served less than three weeks because the Recorder, after a homily which would no doubt today infuriate the politically correct – but which defendants will happily endure provided it means walking into the daylight at the end of it – substituted a probation order:

> I have decided to reduce the punishment, for I think I can understand the human element in this case. He was an escaped convict to the rest of the world, but that is not how you may have viewed him. In doing what you did, although it was breaking the law, you followed a natural womanly instinct in trying to succour and protect this man with whom you had intimate relations over the years.

Sparks left behind a newspaper article which the *Sunday Pictorial* published. They had, it appears, paid over £400 for the series. Goldstein, who was, by the time of what proved to be Sparks' last escape, already involved with another man, disappeared from the scene sending a proper and traditional 'Dear John' whilst he was serving his sentence to which an additional twelve months had been added. The police were not pleased with her and a 'discreet watch' was kept on her. Some months later it was reported that she was still living in the Wembley area but was not associating with the local criminals.

Not all women have been as fortunate in their involvement in crime as the Bobbed-Haired Bandit. Eighteen-year-old Elizabeth Maud Jones, whose career lasted less than a week, was lucky to escape the hangman. She was convicted along with Karl Gustav Hulten of the murder of a taxi-driver, George Edward Heath. Hulten, then aged 22, a Swedish-American deserter from the Parachute Regiment of the US forces in Britain, met her in a café in October 1944. He was posing as Lieutenant Ricky Hulten and she as an actress. In reality she was working as a strip-tease artiste under the name of Georgina Grayson, and lived in a room in King Street, Hammersmith, near the Broadway. He fancied himself as a gangster and she as a moll. Together they set out on a nightly campaign of robbery, attacking pedestrians and cyclists. One woman, hit repeatedly with an iron bar, was then nearly strangled and thrown in the nearby Thames. Their reign of terror in West London was shortlived. On 7 October 1944, four days after their meeting, they hailed a cab driven by Heath and during the journey Hulten shot him. Jones said of the robbery: 'I knew the meaning . . . he wanted me to go with him to rob a taxi-driver . . . I saw a flash and heard a bang. I was surprised that there was not a loud bang because Ricky had told me it would make a big noise.'

The proceeds of this robbery yielded precisely nineteen shillings, a silver pencil and a cigarette case.

The pair drove on to Staines where they dumped the body in a ditch. Despite the fact that the body was found the next morning and a description of the missing Ford V8 cab circulated, Hulten and Jones continued to drive around for a further three days until on 10 October Hulten was arrested in the Fulham Palace Road with the gun and ammunition still in his pocket.

Jones did not last long on the outside. Speaking to a policeman friend who had commented that she looked pale, she said, 'If you had seen someone do what I have seen done you wouldn't be able to sleep at night.' They were both sentenced to death – with the jury recommending mercy for Jones – on 16 January 1945 after a trial lasting six days at the Central Criminal Court. Despite strong representations by the American Ambassador who visited the Home Secretary, Lord Morrison, and spent an hour arguing for a reprieve, Hulten was hanged by Albert Pierrepoint on 8 March. Jones was reprieved on the grounds of her youth – a decision apparently regretted by Sir Winston Churchill – and released from prison in May 1954. In 1992 a film was made about the case.[16] Called *Chicago Joe and the Showgirl*, it starred Kiefer Sutherland and Emily Lloyd.

The 1950s saw the rise of one of the better-known English women criminals who achieved a certain notoriety and press attention. Zoe Progl, known as Blonde Mick and, for a time, the 'Queen of the Underworld', was the first woman to escape from Holloway prison. In July 1960, during her fourth term of imprisonment when she had served one month of a two-and-a-half-year sentence for housebreaking, a rope ladder was thrown over the wall and up she went, down the 25-ft ladder on the other side and into a waiting car. She then sent her prison clothes to the *Daily Mail*, to be returned to the Governor at Holloway.

She was recaptured in Notting Hill in the October after touring the south coast with her small daughter, Tracey, her boyfriend and one of the women who helped her escape. She was traced when a police officer noticed a car number WOP 598 which he knew did not exist[17]. Inside was Progl's driving licence with her address. She was found asleep either in bed or on the kitchen floor, depending on which of the rival newspaper reports was accurate.

Whilst out, she had given an interview to the *Daily Express* and was pictured drinking gin in the Pier Hotel,

[16] The case became known as the Cleft Chin Murder, a characteristic of the taxi-driver Heath.
[17] In those days licensing authorities did not allow a car number which made 'an unfortunate word'.

Chelsea, offering to give herself up if the Home Secretary knocked a year off her sentence. Otherwise, she said, she was planning to have plastic surgery to mask a five-and-half-inch giveaway scar under her left eye.

Progl had eighteen months added to her sentence. The friends Barry Harris, her boyfriend, and Bryanna O'Malley received nine months apiece. They had financed the last few months with a series of cheque frauds. Adelaide de Boer, described as having a soft heart and eighty-three convictions for prostitution, also went down for nine months although she denied being involved in the escape. Whilst in prison Progl sued the Commissioner of Police, Sir Joseph Simpson, over a solitaire diamond ring, a gift from her former lover, the now long-dead Tommy Smithson. The police did not oppose the application; it had been confiscated on her arrest in 1960. After completion of her term of imprisonment Progl sold her story to a Sunday newspaper and announced she was going straight.

Four years later in April 1964 Progl, now aged 35, who had previously been married to US Master-Sergeant Joseph Progl, by whom she had three children, married 24-year-old salesman Roy Bowman. She had gone to the United States with Progl at the age of 16, but left after a year and returned home. When he traced her she was serving a Borstal sentence for receiving: 'Roy knows about my days as a burglar, as a rich man's mistress, as a gangster's moll. He has decided to give me a chance to become a respectable woman. I don't intend to let that chance go.'[18]

It is believed that the pair emigrated to Australia. Certainly this particular Queen of Crime has made no reappearances in the newspapers since.

[18] *Daily Mirror*, 17 April 1964.

Shoplifting has always been a woman's sport. It was from the Elephant and Castle that the female shoplifting and pickpocketing team known as the Forty Thieves originated in the 1930s. Ex-Detective Superintendent John Capstick wrote in his memoirs:[19]

> Dressed to kill, those girls would descend on a West End store like a swarm of locusts. They would roll up in taxis and chauffeur-driven limousines and practically clean the place out in an hour.
>
> London shops were not their only raiding-grounds. They worked impartially from Carlisle to Exeter, and from the coastal towns to Birmingham. Some would stay in the South while others dropped in on the Midlands or the North.

Capstick, known by the girls as Charlie Artful, went on to describe the leader of the Forty Thieves in their hey-day:

> . . . the life and soul of their parties, was a woman said to be the sister of a notorious Soho gangster king. She was one of the slickest thieves I ever tried to follow. Utterly fearless, she knew every trick in the book and she could put away three fur coats and a bolt of cloth in the time it took any of her team-mates to snitch a pair of cami-knickers.

Libel laws probably prevented him from naming her as Maggie, 'The Little Elephant', sister indeed to Soho gangster Billy Hill.

Shirley Pitts was given a great funeral when she died in

[19] J. Capstick, *Given in Evidence*, p.114.

1992. A member of the powerful South London family of Pitts, one of whom was responsible for throwing acid into the face of a man he believed had informed on him, she was a noted shoplifter in her own right.[20] She could literally strip a jeweller's shop, says a contemporary admiringly. She was a very good-looking girl, and she and a colleague would pick a good jeweller's with one male staff member. She or the colleague would take it in turns to make a play for the salesman, and the other would strip the shop. Outside her brother Aggie would be in the car acting as a minder.

Forgery is also a crime at which women can excel. Edna Dorothy Thatcher, known as 'Edna the Pen', was one who did so until she received eight years' preventive detention at the Old Bailey in October 1959. She had left school in the early 1920s, where her neat writing had led to predictions of a rosy future as a copy typist for a solicitor or accountant. Unfortunately she was soon bound over for two years for theft, and then went straight until the early 1930s when she received nine months for embezzlement. Another sentence

---

[20] The Pitts family had a long-running feud with a John Goodwin and in 1983 two members kidnapped his wife, taking her to a caravan park in Essex where she was held hostage. She was eventually released and on 22 June 1984 Charles Pitts received an eighteen-year sentence. His son-in-law, Sean McDonald, received eight years. Goodwin had long been a thorn in the side of the police and had received a seven-year sentence for jury nobbling, quashed by the Court of Appeal. Whilst on bail for a bank robbery of which he was subsequently acquitted, Goodwin had taped up his Christmas tree to record detectives receiving money. At their subsequent trial two were acquitted. The third man ran the ingenious defence that although he was taking money he would still not allow this to influence his evidence and so would not have committed perjury. He was convicted but, in turn, his conviction was quashed by the Court of Appeal.

followed in the mid-thirties and then another in 1943 when she served two years, again for forgery. In 1951 she remarried – her first husband had died on active service – and this time it was seven years for forgery. She was released in May 1956.

Edna then became the bookkeeper for a firm of gownmakers and almost immediately obtained a job with the firm's accountants so that she could cover up her fiddle. She was caught when she added a nought to the £60 personal cheque of one of the directors. Even on bail she continued 'working'. Preventive detention carried no automatic remission.

When women went on armed robberies, their role was almost always that of the driver. One such was Sheila Porritt née Tobias, daughter of a leading North Country criminal, who had married into the powerful South London Porritt family. She was convicted as the driver in a wages snatch back in her home town of Manchester. She had taken her child from a former relationship along with her on the blagging because she could not find a child-minder. Later when she did find a babysitter for an evening, she paid her £2 wage with some of the stolen money. Sheila Porritt received five years whilst others in the team drew up to fifteen. One of them, Albert Reddans from another South London family, collected ten years, but this was made consecutive to another ten-year sentence he had received the previous month.

There have been persistent rumours of women who have actually been 'on the pavement' in armed robberies. The sister of a number of Irishmen from Paddington of whom an admirer said '[she] was like a man' – presumably in courage rather than physique – was said to be one of them, as was another girl from Notting Hill. So far, however, the

best-known London female armed robber has been Linda
Calvey, who boasted she was the original of one of the
characters in the popular ITV series, *Widows*. Linda – one
of nine children in an East London family which made
dockers' hooks – became involved with Micky Calvey. A
long-time friend of Mickey Ishmael, thought by some to be
capable of being a serious contender for the top of the
league, in 1953 Calvey received eight years along with
Ishmael for robbing Marks & Spencers. Linda had married
him in 1970, when he was taken from Wandsworth prison
to a local register office. In 1977 he was acquitted of charges
of burglary brought on the evidence of supergrass Charles
Lowe.

Micky Calvey died on Saturday 9 December 1978 in a
shoot-out when he tried to rob Caters supermarket in
Eltham, South-East London. Four men had attacked
security guards as they carried a box containing £10,000.
The other three men fled after discharging a shotgun over
the heads of the crowd. On hearing of his death Linda said,
'Micky has been in trouble before, I know, but he's been
trying hard since he came out of prison a year ago.' Some
two hundred people attended his funeral at the East
London crematorium, to which Mickey Ishmael sent a
wreath in the form of the letters 'PAL'.

Linda earned her nickname of the Black Widow[21] by
shouting 'murderer' at the police officer who stood trial for

[21] An American version of the Black Widow and a very pro-active
one at that was Griselda Blanco, who headed a drugs empire
running the length of the Americas. Her three husbands, a number
of lovers and rivals have all died and she is credited with
originating the drive-by motorcycle killing. Jailed in Florida, she
is likely to serve at least twenty-five years from 1990. *Daily Star*, 5
November 1990.

the shooting. There had been some evidence that Calvey had been shot in the back, but the officer explained that this was the way he had been standing rather than that he had been shot whilst fleeing. He was acquitted and given a bravery award.

Shortly after that Linda became involved with robber Ronnie Cook, going with him on trips abroad including one to Las Vegas when it was said they spent £30,000 in just over a week. He lavished gifts on her – clothes from Harrods, jewellery, money, a car, even £4,000 for cosmetic surgery. There was, however, a down side: Cook was obsessively jealous, forbidding Linda to speak to other men, beating her savagely and, according to reports, subjecting her to sadistic sexual practices.

Three years later he was jailed for sixteen years for his part in what was described as one of the 'most spectacular and well-planned robberies in the history of crime'. Now while that is a phrase quite often used by prosecuting counsel opening the case to a jury, this did have the hallmarks of brilliance. It was in fact Billy Tobin's Dulwich raid, when a hijacked mobile crane was rammed into the back of a security vehicle containing almost £1 million near a school in Dulwich.

Calvey promised to wait for him and, as a mark of her fidelity, had 'True Love Ron Cook' tattooed on her leg. But, it seems, she could not now give up the lifestyle to which she had grown accustomed. Almost certainly Cook had had money salted away and she began to spend it, taking up with one of his friends, Brian Thorogood, whom Cook had arranged to act as a 'minder' for him whilst he was inside. Thorogood left his wife, bought a house in Harold Wood, Essex and moved in with her. Later he too was sentenced, receiving eighteen years for a post office robbery. Linda, who seems to have supplemented her income by being the armourer for various robbery teams, served three of a five-year term for conspiracy to rob. That was the end of Thorogood, but now Cook was due for release. What could she do?

Fearful that he would find out about both her infidelity and her dissipation of his money, she planned to kill him, offering a £10,000 contract. Finding no takers, she turned to Daniel Reece, a convicted rapist whose evidence had assisted the police convict David Lashley, the killer of Australian heiress Janie Shepherd. Quite apart from the money, Reece too was enamoured with Calvey and agreed to do the job.

In theory Ron Cook had a cleaning job outside the prison but, as with so many before him, he took to more agreeable days out. On 19 January 1990 Linda Calvey collected him from Maidstone Prison and drove him to London whilst Reece, whom she had already collected from another prison, waited outside her flat. Cook brought in the milk and as he stood holding it Reece followed him in and shot him in the elbow. He could not, he later told police, bring himself to kill the man: 'I could not kill him. I shot to his side and he fell backwards into the kitchen. I moved forward and stood over him. I could not kill him. I have never killed anyone.'

Linda Calvey had no such qualms. She grabbed the gun from him, ordered Cook to kneel and then shot him in the head.

Reece took a train back to the West Country to continue his thirteen year sentence for rape, buggery and false imprisonment.

At first it seemed as though Calvey had been successful. The police appeared to accept her story that an unknown gunman had burst in and shot Cook while she cowered in a corner. Then it was discovered that Reece had been with her over the weekend and had been her lover. It was curious that he had not been mentioned in the statement. Under questioning Reece cracked first, telling all.

Reece, who was not notedly popular in prison following the evidence he gave against Lashley, thought twice about squealing again and withdrew his confession in court. Linda Calvey told the jury his confession was a fabrication. 'Ron meant everything to me,' she said. This gesture of solidarity did him no good; he too received a life sentence for murder.

Just as the men in Fay Sadler's life ended up dead or in prison, so did those in the life of Linda Calvey, a classic gangster's moll turned gangster.[22]

Perhaps the delegates at the 1992 conference on professional crime were right, women were taking a more active role. They certainly had been in terrorist offences. The first traces of women as gang leaders came in August 1972 when security expert Peter Hamilton told a Council of Investigators in Brighton that, 'It is well known that there are principal leaders of guerilla organizations in Britain, Germany, and America who are women.' He went on to add, 'Women are playing a bigger part in muggings and few gangs are without them.'

In 1975 a United Nations Geneva conference was told that girl football hooligans in Britain have become as commonplace as the vicious female muggers of the States. There is little doubt that females can identify with and lead a cause, e.g. the IRA, or the Weathermen for

---

[22] Fay Sadler was the mistress of Selwyn Cooney and also Tommy Smithson, as well as Elephant and Castle villain, Jack Rosa. Cooney and Smithson were shot, Rosa died in a car accident (see J. Morton *Gangland*).

whom Bernadine Dohrn undertook a sexual as well as political revolution. But can they actually take a pro-active part in heavy career crime? The research into women criminals is, if anything, against the proposition, but it may be misleading.

The criminologist Pollak suggests that the low crime rate of women is more apparent than real, and is largely due to the masked or hidden character of female crime. He sees the crux of the sex differences in criminality as qualitative rather than quantitative, and argues that women commit crimes which by their very nature remain unreported in criminal statistics, e.g. shoplifting, domestic theft and criminal abortion. He estimated that in New York City the prosecution of abortionists and shoplifters would reduce the crime ratio man to woman from 10:1 to 4.7:1.

Other reasons are social controls. Crime amongst women is much higher in the more emancipated countries. There are genetic factors as well as physique and physiological ones. In a survey by Lombroso and Ferrero in 1892, amongst eighty women arrested for 'resistance to public officials' a high proportion were menstruating. Pollak quoted a similar survey of Parisian shoplifters in the 1890s, but a 1962 survey of London shoplifters found no such correlation.[23]

In 1991 Diana Hutchinson interviewed a girl who might almost be making the First, if not Premier, Division. Jenny had taken to cheque frauds rather than go on the game, had

[23] K. Dalton (1961), 'Menstruation and Crime', *Brit Med. J.*2. 1752–1753; T.C.N. Gibbens and J. Prince (1962), *Shoplifting*, London, Institute for the Study and Treatment of Delinquency; C. Lombroso and G. Ferrero (1894), *Das Weib als Verbrecherin und prostituierte*, Hamburg, O. Pollak (1950), *The Criminality of Women*, New York.

carried a gun, slashed people, and driven the getaway car. She had a minder and was able to write a four-figure cheque for a suit for her son rather than steal it.

> Mind you, I don't think I've heard of an all-girl gang going out to rob a bank. Girls want the quick thrill. They are not prepared to put in the months of planning, driving past the place, checking every movement like the men do. They are not so professional as the men yet. But the way women are taking to crime, that will come. It's only later women find out the hard side.[24]

Jenny had clearly not heard of the Hibbert sisters. On 10 March 1966 Eva (aged 21, with a two-year-old daughter and a pile of debts) and Christine (depressed from the death of her boyfriend and out of work) took a black air-pistol to the Barclays Bank branch in Vauxhall, South London and demanded money from the cashier. The effort was not a success; the girl simply pressed the alarm bell. They tried the same half an hour later at a sub-post office near Clapham Common with the same result. At the Old Bailey, Judge Brian Capstick (son of 'Charlie Artful' Capstick) told them, as he gave them two years apiece, 'I hope women considering offences of this sort will not think they will be treated leniently because they have small children or are pregnant.'

At least they fell into the pattern suggested by Jenny that women generally will not put in the required amount of research.

Slightly more successful was Susan Bussey, acting in cahoots with her lover Paul Byrne. She had fantasized all

[24] D. Hutchinson, 'The Godmother', *Daily Mail*, 30 May 1991.

her life over the prospect of being a bank robber and she, Byrne and three others carried out six successful raids in the summer and autumn of 1986, pulling in some £60,000. Bussey, aged 22, would be the blonde businesswoman wearing a pin-striped suit and carrying a sports bag, waiting patiently in the queue for the teller. It was she who wielded the gun and gave the orders. In a role-reversal situation, Byrne was the driver. Again the planning was not what it should have been. They used one of their own cars on the raids. The end was inevitable and came on 7 November 1986 when they raided another North London bank. This time the research was significantly wrong. They arrived late and when they returned to the getaway car they were ringed by the police. Bussey and Byrne each received a ten-year sentence.

For a time Helen Windeller was a moderately successful criminal, leaving her husband and daughter at home when she went to rob a sub-post office in Orpington, Kent. She ensured that the mothers and children had left the premises before she pulled out an air-gun and demanded and received just over £200. When her home was searched she had a stash of cannabis valued at £16,000. She was jailed for five years.[25]

One unlikely combination, in which by reason of age alone the woman must seem to have been the dominant character, was that of mother and son, Mabel Jacqueline Miller and Thomas Larvin, who in the summer of 1990 were jailed for a total of eleven years at Newcastle Crown Court. They had been caught red-handed carrying out the last of six building society armed robberies which had netted

---

[25] Lois Atkinson, 'It's a Woman's Underworld,' *Woman's World*, June 1988.

£11,500. When questioned, Mrs Miller said she knew nothing of her son's activities when out of the car; she had merely been giving him driving lessons.

There are now accounts of very young all-girl gangs dealing in cocaine and crack in South-West London. Kelly, 16, a former member of a South London female gang, said she was forced to smoke crack as an initiation test. 'Some of the girls were vicious but a lot of it was to compete with the boys. We were all armed and I carried either a machete, an army knife or a gun under my jacket.'

The report in the *Sunday Times* went on to say that:

... the female gangs were formed by women drug dealers who were tired of handing their profits to male gang leaders. Some of the women arm themselves with 'zip' guns designed in America for women and small enough to fit into a handbag.

The women's aggression has shocked even experienced police officers. One detective in Brixton, South London, said, 'These girls who work in gangs are tough because they are constantly under threat of attack from rival gangs, former employers or boyfriends. They are streetwise and they know the law inside out.'[26]

In the early 1980s Elaine Player, now lecturing at King's College, London, undertook research into groups of girls between the ages of 16 and the late twenties. She found that the black girls she interviewed had established themselves into collectives rather more than their white counterparts and, without any apparent male support, some were engaged in organized shoplifting, cheque frauds and the

[26] *Sunday Times*, 19 December, 1993.

occasional rolling of males brought back to their flats.

They have some way to go before they match the girls' gangs of California, such as the Lady Rascal gangsters who are the female equivalent of the Vietnamese and Cambodian male Tiny Rascal Gang. Where, say, ten years ago the function of the girl gang member was that of 'ho' or girlfriend, now they are starting to participate in drive-by shootings. In Chicago girls on the South Side seem to have adopted the traditional supportive role until 1992, but evidence is now emerging that they have become perpetrators. Charles Brown, the assistant director of a rehabilitation project for female gang leaders, says:

These girls feel like they have been in the dark ages for many years, just having babies, doing drugs. Now that they have the expertise, they want recognition, they want control. They want to start shooting. They feel they can control the gangland scene. Killing is now as much a girl's privilege as a boy's. There is no distinction betwen the sexes when a gun is in the hand.[27]

The latest available Home Office statistics (at 30 June 1991) show that twenty-nine women were serving sentences for robbery, not necessarily armed. This was out of an adult female prison population of 1,038. By far the highest number, 260, were serving sentences for drug-related offences, and 170 were serving sentences for violence to the person, 166 for theft or dishonest handling of property and 161 for what were called other offences. Thirty-four were serving sentences for burglary, some of which may have been aggravated burglary – which broadly means that

[27] Esther Oxford, in the *Independent*, 1 December, 1993.

violence was used whilst on the premises or weapons carried. Eleven women were serving sentences for non-payment of fines.

Statistics are not necessarily a great help. It may be that women are indeed more adroit at evading arrest or conviction, or that judges are more reluctant to send them to prison than their male counterparts. Even so, if British women criminals have started to come out from behind the washing-machine and into pro-active major league crime, it is with some hesitation.

11

This Sporting Life

So far as horse-racing, and for that matter greyhound racing, is concerned, gangland activity falls into three separate but not wholly unconnected segments. The first is concerned with the animals themselves – ringing, doping and generally fixing the races for betting purposes. The second is the control and manipulation of the bookmakers, and the third is peripheral activities such as pickpocketing and short-con tricks which are worked at the racecourse or on the trains taking punters to and from the races[1].

[1] A short con is one which requires only a few minutes or, even better, seconds of the victim's time. The rewards are limited to the amount the victim has on him when the trick is worked. A long con, of which the Big Store is the classic example, requires time and patience but the rewards are likely to be much greater. The Big Store was worked particularly in the West and Southern States of America. A complete bogus business or illegal gambling joint was set up in which the proprietors, salesmen and other customers were all part of an act designed to swindle possibly only one man. If this seems incredible, then read of an example in Philip S. Van Cise's *Fighting the Underworld*. There are two classic Big Stores operated in the films *The Sting* and *The Grifters*.

Daniel Dawson makes a convenient historical start. In 1812 he was convicted, after a second trial at the Cambridge Assizes, under an almost forgotten statute of George I making it a capital offence maliciously to destroy cattle and horses. He had poisoned a number of valuable thoroughbreds when he impregnated the drinking water at Newmarket with a solution of white arsenic. ·

There was heavy wagering in the London clubs as to whether a man could be hanged for poisoning a horse, but those who said he could be won the bets when Dawson was executed in front of Cambridge Castle on 8 August 1812. He was visited during the period between trial and hanging by a number of noblemen, but Dawson remained silent about those who had paid him.

In 1892 the Duke of Westminster's horse Orme was suspected of having been poisoned to prevent his running. If an effort had been made it was not successful, and the horse won £33,000 for his owner.

The turn of the century produced a number of scares of doping and allegations of foul riding. A number of American horses had come over along with American jockeys, the leading rider being Tod Sloan of whom, because of the regularity with which he finished in front, the phrase 'on your tod' (Tod Sloan = alone) was coined. Sloan, a man of immense talent, and a brilliant shot who won international events at Monte Carlo, was in the hands of the bookmakers. He won and then lost even more thousands and so was an easy prey. The jockey Jack Leach, when writing of him, said:

> . . . flagrant dishonesty ended the fabulous career of Tod Sloan. Tod had the ball at his feet, but kicked it the wrong way so often that he had to be got rid of.

Here was a man who had everything needed by a top jockey, but a kink in his brain unbalanced him.[2]

It was then that the allegations of doping were rife. It was suggested they were done with a mixture of cocaine and a weak solution of nitroglycerine under the mane; it was applied on the way to the start and the effect lasted five to ten minutes. This could cause a problem because if the start was delayed the effect could have worn off and the horse, reacting to the stimulant, would come home half-asleep. In one French case, where the fashionable dope of that time was strychnine and ether, the horse lay down and slept at the starting post. The other way was in the form of a pill, made of ginger or cayenne and cocaine, which took much longer to act.[3] It was also suggested that a small shot of strychnine applied between rounds could generate enough energy for a boxer being beaten on points to go for a knock-out.

There were also suggestions that mechanical aids were being employed, including a mechanical saddle which stimulated the horse by its vibrations, and an electric spur. In the forefront of these allegations was Sloan. It was said he kicked the ball into his own net once too often, and shortly afterwards was returned to America.

In 1914 the Jockey Club caused a sensation by

[2] It is said that when he died in California his coffin was put in a room at the funeral parlour next to that of a celebrated gangster. Sloan did not have too many floral tributes but when the boxers Jim Jeffries and Gentleman Jim Corbett went to pay their respects, Corbett removed most of the gangster's flowers and put them on Sloan's coffin. 'Tod always travelled first class,' he said to Jeffries. J. Leach, *Sods I Have Cut on the Turf*, p.40.
[3] *Pearson's Magazine*, 8 August 1914.

demanding that three horses had their saliva tested for drugs. In 1930, after Don Pat trained by Charles Chapman won the Bedfont High Weight Handicap at Kempton Park, it was found that the horse had been doped. There was never any suggestion that Chapman had been involved in any way, but in accordance with the severe penalties handed out by the Jockey Club in those often unenlightened days, the horse was disqualified from all further races under Rules and the unfortunate Chapman warned off Newmarket Heath. No appeal lay against the Stewards' decision, and Chapman's only remedy was an action for libel claiming that the words that he had been warned off implied he had been a party to the doping of his horse. Patrick Hastings appeared for Chapman and Norman Birkett for the Jockey Club. The jury found for Chapman and he received £13,000 damages, but the Court of Appeal overturned the verdict on the grounds that the Jockey Club's statement was privileged. The dopers were never discovered.

After the Second World War a number of trainers automatically lost their licences when their horses were found to have been doped. These included John Beary, Ernest Street – whose horse Rock Star was doped in the Clarence House stakes at Ascot in September 1950 – Morgan Scannell, Cecil Ray, Harold Isom – whose horse Compassion was doped at the meeting at Kempton Park on Boxing Day 1951. All fell foul of the rule that even if the trainer knew nothing of the doping it was his responsibility.

George Allden was one of the small trainers, who in 1949 had a yard at the fifteen-roomed Beechwood House, Newmarket. Then at Pontefract on 28 September his filly Luxuriant, trembling and sweating, won the Upton Selling Handicap by a length and a half at the price of 100–6. It does not appear that the stable had been betting heavily on the horse; the owner had had £35 each way and Allden £15 to win and £10 a place. The subsequent tests showed traces of cocaine and strychnine. In December Allden's licence was withdrawn and he was ruined. Efforts to clear his name failed and two years later, then aged 54, he was working as a production clerk in a Manchester factory.

In those days the drugs were: the stimulant cocaine; atropine, another stimulant but which in large doses could also act as a depressant, and which was found in Rock Star; strychnine; Benzedrine, which staves off fatigue, found in Woolpack, a steeplechaser which fell at Doncaster, killing its jockey, in 1948; caffeine, a stimulant, which cost Mark Collins his licence when Quizzical Miss proved positive after a saliva test, also at Doncaster, in 1950; cortisone, used for treating rheumatism, also used on greyhounds; adrenalin, a gland extract; and two stoppers – morphine, also found in Rock Star, and barbiturates, more effective with greyhounds.

The year 1952 produced another flurry of doping stories.

Dopers, their syringes charged with the costliest products of medical research, prowl British racecourses. Others lurk in roadside cafés waiting to stand coffee to the drivers of horseboxes, while they themselves step outside for a word with their charges.

Various anti-doping measures were suggested against them. Remedies offered included, 'Light chain-mail blankets to be worn on race days; horses to journey to race meetings in convoy, and proper planning for the future (the breeding of a strain of dope-immune horses)'.[4]

[4] *Daily Mail*, 16 February 1952.

It had come about because of the doping of one of Lord Rosebery's horses in training at Newmarket with Jack Jarvis. He declined to name the horse or the race, but offered £1,000 reward for information. Jarvis, protected by Lord Rosebery, was immune from the wrath which fell on the small trainers. It was the first glimmer of a relaxation of the draconian rule.

Then in 1955 ex-trainer Harry Lowe, who had sent out winners both on the Flat and under National Hunt rules from his Stockbridge yard, announced his retirement and also that he was going to tell all to the *People*.[5] 'All' meant how he had doped his horses: 'I had to do it and I am not the only one by a long chalk.'

Things had changed by 1960 when the fashionable trainer John Dunlop's horse Red Letter was to finish fourth in a field of five at Kempton Park in July. The sprinter Skymaster was also got at and beaten at Ascot. Sing Sing was got at before the July Cup at Newmarket. Getting at a favourite before a big race is more likely to be the work of a bookmaker than a punter, because the defeat of the favourite in the big race is almost invariably to the bookmaker's rather than to the punter's gain.

Charlie Mitchell, bookmaker and moneylender, was one of the great dopers of the 1950s and 1960s. He was also a member of the Krays' gang. Charlie Kray, with whom he went to Montreal in an unsuccessful visit to collect stolen bearer bonds, describes him as 'a small broad-shouldered man with a fresh face and a full set of sparkling white teeth; he was also completely bald'. He was arrested with the Kray twins and later turned Queen's Evidence, a great feather in the cap of Nipper Read and a great blow to the Krays who

[5] 13 March 1955.

had thought that Mitchell of all people would remain staunch. Mitchell told Read that there had been a contract out on him and also Leslie Payne in the sum of £50,000 each. Mitchell had, he said, been the one required to find the money and arrange for a man to come from New York to carry out the hits.

He later compounded his bad behaviour by prosecuting two men with whom he had had a row in the North End Road, Fulham, near where he had his bookmaking business. As he put his head through the car window one of the men had wound it up, and Mitchell was dragged along the road. He was later shot dead in the south of Spain; his killers were never found.

He had an even less attractive side. He was what is called a thieves' ponce (a man who couldn't do the job himself and took a cut from the men who were regarded as having the guts to do so) and one of his victims was the great con-man Charles Da Silva, who deeply feared Mitchell, to whom he would give 75 per cent of his earnings. For a time Da Silva appears to have been protected by the Kray twins, but after their arrest and conviction his luck ran out.[6]

In one of the first doping scandals of the 1960s, the police interviewed Bertie 'Bandy' Rogers at stables in Oxfordshire. He shot himself that night, and so missed the trial at Gloucester Assizes when a former jockey was found guilty of attempting to dope a horse and, despite the pleas of Sir Gordon Richards, received an eighteen months' sentence. The ringleaders received four years.

[6] According to Derek Raymond in his book *The Hidden Files*, pp. 111–12, Charlie Da Silva was killed in case he talked to the police rather than face a further prison sentence. He was one of the greatest con-men of all times, a man who once sold a fleet of ships to a Yorkshire farmer on a train between Hull and King's Cross.

Three years later in 1963, at Lewes Assizes, William Roper, as ringleader, received three years for conspiracy to dope horses. A pretty Swiss girl had toured stables on the pretext of buying a horse, and of the twenty-one stables she had visited twelve favourites had been got at. She received a sentence of twelve months' imprisonment, but her punishment was lightened because she had already taken the precaution of selling her story to a Sunday newspaper to be published on her conviction. Another defendant, Edward Smith, known as the 'Witch Doctor' because of the potions he carried with him, had unfortunately fallen to his death from a landing in Lewes prison on the eve of the trial and so missed the proceedings. Another of the gang was Joe Lowry; his convictions dated back to 1930 and he received two years. It was never made clear for whom he and the rest of his team had been working. By 1966 he was at it again; this time he tried to dope Spare Filly, a horse in Lambourn trainer Bob Read's yard, and was given five years. The police had hidden out after a tip-off.

Doping steeplechasers is tantamount to attempted murder. When Staghound was doped in a novice steeplechase in the 1960s at Birmingham with Fred Winter up, he was a red-hot favourite from hurdling. Winter knew what was in store for him at the first fence. The horse never saw it. He 'went straight on', unseating Winter as he performed a somersault, then ran blindly at the second fence at which he again fell. He never ran in a steeplechase again.

It was not as if the racecourses were not trying to protect their charges. In 1952 a secure area became mandatory at every racecourse to which no outsiders were admitted for twenty-four hours before racing. For a time 'this was so successful that no racehorse has since been got at, so far as is known, in racecourse stables', wrote Roger Longrigg.

Trainer Gavin Hunter was equally enthusiastic. 'It is virtually impossible to dope successfully, in a yard or in racecourse stables. Nowadays trainers go to the races happy in their minds that their horses will run on their merits.'[7]

Sadly the last years have shown their confidence has been misplaced. In 1957 efforts were made to get at the Derby favourite, Crepello. The owner, Sir Victor Sassoon, was followed on his visit to his trainer's stables in an effort to identify which box he visited. Crepello had been switched boxes, but the substituted animal had almost certainly been nobbled.

The next year Alcide was heavily backed for the Derby and then got at; he did not run. In 1959 Sing Sing, the undefeated champion two-year-old the previous year, was nobbled and withdrawn from the July Cup; he never ran again. In 1961 Pinturischo, favourite for the 2,000 Guineas, was given a very powerful purge thought to be used for elephants; he recovered, and the poor animal had to be doped again to ensure he did not run. Ribofilio was tailed off in the 1969 2,000 Guineas. The hot favourite 'could never raise a gallop', said Lester Piggott, his jockey.

By 1984 there were fears by the trainers that Gorytus, Forgive 'n' Forget, Gambir and Gaye Brief, all from top and different yards, had been got at. In 1988 Playschool put up a lifeless showing when favourite for the Cheltenham Gold Cup; he never won again.

The early 1990s produced another series of doping scandals. In 1990, nasal spray was used to dope two class horses, Norwich and Bravefoot, at the Doncaster St Leger meeting. They finished fourth and last in their respective races. The ITV racehorse commentator John McCrirrick

[7] Roger Longrigg, *Daily Telegraph*, 21 July 1976.

had been vociferous in pointing out the betting patterns for the races and the fact that the favourites were being opposed in the market. In Bravefoot's race the second horse was heavily backed. Speaking after the Norwich doping, the Queen's trainer Ian Balding said that he thought between six and thirty horses a year were got at.

In July 1993 a BBC television programme *On The Line* showed how easy it was to walk in and out of the 'secure stabling' of at least one racecourse. In the programme, former top jockey and later trainer Dermot Browne told how he had doped a number of horses – possibly up to eighty – with the drug acetyl-pronazine just before they ran. In 1992 he had been given a ten-year ban by the Jockey Club for telling a jockey to pull a horse and passing information to a bookmaker.

The switching of horses was for years one of the mainstays of the racetrack. As far back as 1844, Running Rein which won the Derby – the premier classic for three-year-old horses – was in fact Maccabeus, a four-year-old. At level weights a three-year-old because of its inferior physique could not be expected to defeat an older horse of reasonable quality. Maccabeus had been switched as a yearling for the foal Running Rein. Running as a two-year-old there had been doubts about his age. When he won at Newmarket one writer put it, '. . . to speak plainly, the colt is as well furnished as many of our *bona fide* three-year-olds.'

The running of that Derby was unhappy. The favourite, Ugly Buck, was the subject of deliberately foul riding; the second favourite, Tatan, was not only got at the night before but also pulled by his jockey Sam Rogers, who was warned off for his riding. Leander, who was leading at the time, was struck into by Running-Rein/Maccabeus and injured so badly that he was destroyed. An examination of his jaws showed he too was a four-year-old. His owners were warned off, and in a rage one of them announced that Leander was not four at all but six.

Switching has continued intermittently throughout this century. In the 1920s Coat of Mail was nothing if not moderate and was sold by Leech, his trainer, for export. A month later he won at Stockton by four lengths and the jockey, Billy Griggs, described him as being one of the best two-year-olds out. This was not surprising, since the horse Griggs had ridden quite innocently was Jazz, a smart four-year-old. Curiously the horses did not even look alike: Jazz was a tough little brown horse, and Coat of Mail a narrow washy bay. The coup had been organized by the notorious 'Ringer' Barry, who after his release from prison wrote in a Sunday paper how he used to paint horses to resemble one another. In his career he switched and doped horses to great effect. After his prison sentence he became a racing tipster advertising his credentials as 'The man who wrote his reminiscences in the *People*'.

One of the great switches at a racetrack occurred on 16 July 1953 when Fracasal won the Spa Selling Plate. The jockey, Billy Gilchrist, who had picked up a spare ride, reported that, '[I] picked up the stick, gave him one and he went right away to win by two lengths.' That Fracasal was unfancied in the betting was not surprising. He had been placed third in one race and unplaced in his other five. His odds of 10–1 reflected support for him on the course. What was not known at the time, however, was that there had been heavy betting on him in London, Wales, the Midlands and Scotland. Normally when this happens the money is 'blown' back on to the course and so the off-course betting on the horse is reflected in the starting price. It didn't on this occasion. The 'blower' wires had been cut at 1.30 p.m. and the bookmakers could not hedge their bets.

It all came out at the trial of Harry Kateley, Gomer Charles, Maurice Williams and Colonel Victor Dill. Fracasal was in fact Santa Amaro, a very smart French horse. Kateley, as the ringleader of the coup which should have netted at a minimum £60,000, received three years' imprisonment after a re-trial. Charles and Williams went down for two and the ex-Etonian, Victor Dill, got nine months. At one time during the case Reginald Spooner, the detective investigating the affair, was offered £20,000 if no charges were brought. Billy Gilchrist never received his riding fee.[8]

A later case of switching came in the 1980s with Flockton Grey, another three-year-old who ran as a two-year-old, again not surprisingly winning.

It has not simply been what has gone on with the horses that has caused the trouble at racecourses; it has been the peripheral 'sports' of welshing, bookmaker protection and intimidation, punter intimidation and the whole fairground of the short-con artist with the Three-Card-Trick, Crown and Anchor, Banker, Pitch-and-Toss and the Spinning Jenny or Spinner, let alone the pickpockets.[9] For a time Jack Spot ran a racecourse 'Take a Pick' contest in which the punters were invited, at sixpence a go, to pull a straw with a winning number from a cup. Even if they were successful they only received a cheap prize, whilst Spot received up to £40 a day. The Three-Card-Trick has

---

[8] There is a long account of this complicated affair in I.Adamson, *The Great Detective*, Part 4, Chapter 6.

[9] Banker was a very simple way of losing one's money. Bets were laid out in lots and it was a question of drawing a higher card than the banker whose sleight of hand would have been good enough to give him a winning edge.

flourished around the world under a variety of names and guises. Its origin lies in the Cups and Balls, one of the world's oldest conjuring tricks which manifested itself into Thimbles and Peas and the Three Shell swindle. The object of the exercise was for the punter to guess under which of three shells the operator had put a pea. There is a painting by Hieronymous Bosch of the operation of the Cups and Balls trick. To the left of the picture is a pickpocket at work.

The Three-Card-Trick, Find the Lady or Three-Card Monte are all pasteboard versions of the shell game. The three cards, usually including the Queen of Spades, are laid face down on a table or board and shuffled; the public is then invited to nominate which is the Queen. Each has the same set of devices, such as the bent corner (the pea off the board is the shell game equivalent) which can sucker the mark into believing that he has chosen the Queen of Spades.

In 1912 the Three-Card-Trick was held by the Divisional Court to be a game of skill – as of course it is by the operator.[10] If the game were a question of the sleight of hand defeating the eye then it might be so, but the operators have long taken precautions to make sure that the mark is misdirected by assistants in the crowd. If by any mischance he still picks the right card, there are still a number of options open to the operator, including the use of the assistants to claim the bet as their own, or to cry 'Police', or simply to overturn the board and rough-handle the punter. A spinner, now rarely seen, was a cross between

[10] R.v Brixton Prison Governor, ex p Sjoland (1912) 77 JP 27. Two years later it was held that where there was cheating during play this was an offence under s.17 of the Gaming Act 1845. R. v Moore (1914) 10 CAR 54.

the Three-Card-Trick and a roulette wheel. It consisted of
the punter betting on which suits of cards came up. It was,
of course, fixed by using a stick, known in the trade as a
Haley, to stop the wheel. Pitch-and-Toss was a gambling
game in which the punters laid bets on whether a number of
coins would fall head or tail up. Banker was a simple form
of *chemin de fer*, whilst Crown and Anchor was another
board game.

The police were warned to be alert for these short-con
artists. Occasional magistrates' courts were held, often in a
room behind the stands, after the last race of the day, and it
was usual for the local force to provide a 'racing book' for
any plain-clothes officer on duty. This would contain
photographs and records of all the local dips and other
rogues, so that if an officer arrested one of them the man
could be dealt with without delay.

Welshers, as Evelyn Waugh put it, the name given to
thieves on a racetrack, operated either as pairs or sometimes as a gang. In 1933 one of the great 'welshing coups'
occurred at the Derby meeting at Epsom. A fake totalisator was constructed on the course on the chassis of a
lorry hired for the day for 30 shillings. There was no sight
of the giveaway chassis itself because it was decked out in
posters, banners and flags. Set next to the site of the
St Dunstan's Derby Day Service near Tattenham Corner,
it was grandly called the St Dunstan's Tote and with 5/-,
10/- and £1 windows did big business. Once the off was
signalled the crowds rushed to the famous corner to watch
the horses come down the hill, and in their absence the
gang disappeared; it is said they cleared over £1,600. There
was a repeat effort at the Grand National meeting the next
year, this time with the grandly named 'The National
Totalisator'. This time, however, their efforts were

thwarted by racecourse security officials and the team decamped.[11]

Bookmakers have always been at risk from fraud or violence. In 1848 the Glasgow fancy used brute force to obtain a levy from the owners of stalls at Paisley Races. By the turn of the century the Glasgow fancy had metamorphosed into the Redskins, so-called because of the knife scars on their faces. They had the run of the Scottish tracks whilst the Newcastle Boys held control over those of the North East. Indeed, in the 1870s a number of small tracks were closed down in and around London because of the activities of the gangs, and in 1893 the Brums, a Midland gang, demonstrated an early version of steaming when they raided the principal enclosure at Scarborough. Together with a gang from Leeds, they rushed the turnstiles stealing what they could. This diverted the racecourse police and so a second front was able to climb over the rails which separated the paddock area. Watches and money were stolen with impunity.

Later, in the twentieth century, the Aldgate mob acted in the same fashion as the youths on the London Underground today.

Old-time bookmaker, Sam Dell, talking to Carl Chinn,[12] had this to say:

[11] W. Bebbington, in his book *Rogues Go Racing* (Chapter XXIV), has a number of stories about welshing bookmakers, including one who hired heavyweight boxers to knock down punters with winning tickets as they made their claims, and another of a Midlands bookmaker, Sam Isaacs, who decided to decamp after the Derby was run and shammed an epileptic fit. The punters on whom he was welshing assisted him to escape by calling for an ambulance. Isaacs had already given the takings on the race to his confederates.

[12] C. Chinn *Better Betting with a Decent Feller*, p.197.

They were all pickpockets, they used to walk around, a gang of pickpockets. They were led by a face amongst them called D. Right villain and he was the leader and they used to operate mostly on Bank Holidays and High Days and Holidays and they'd be twenty-handed and this new thing that goes on called steaming – when they rush in and knock you – well they did that sixty years ago. They, what they would do, they would lift a guy in the air, someone would take his money . . .

The 'D' referred to may be the great Jack 'Dodger' Mullins who was a well-known Aldgate pickpocket and hardman. Born in the 1890s, he was regarded as a tearaway and 'ignorant as hell and bloody brutal with it'. In the 1930s he served a six-year sentence for demanding money with menaces from the old villain, Arthur Harding, with whom he had worked a protection racket at one time. Harding had apparently gone straight after his marriage, but Mullins often called on him to go out to do a bit of protection work with him. When Harding finally refused, Mullins took to tapping him for money. He is reputed once to have kicked a dog to death because 'It bit me.' He served a further five after he was arrested, tooled up, going to Brighton to deal with the Sabinis on the free course there. He was later a leader of the Dartmoor mutiny.[13]

If horseracing had been more or less cleaned up during the 1920s, at least from the protection of bookmakers, the same certainly could not be said for greyhound racing.

[13] Mullins lived until his seventies, when apparently he was injured in a car crash. He was taken to hospital but died from pneumonia. There are references to Mullins in a number of books, including Raphael Samuels' *East End Underworld* and Reg Kray's *Villains We Have Known*.

Many of the racecourse bookmakers' protectors drifted over to this new and lucrative pastime. They included Alfie Solomon, released after serving his three years for the manslaughter of Buck Emden, and old 'Dodger' Mullins.

On his release Alfie Solomon went to live not all that far from Sir Edward Marshall-Hall KC in Maybury Mansions, New Cavendish Street. Life was clearly not kind to him in his efforts to find decent honest work; he was beset by villains. In February 1930 he wrote to the Director of Public Prosecutions saying that he had gone straight since his release, working on the greyhound and racetracks:

. . . A month ago I happened to go to Clapton dog races for the first time. After racing I went into the bar with a man named Bernard Dorrie, who owns and runs dogs there. A conversation was overheard while having a drink. A man named Luper took the biggest part in this, and he is a confidential friend of Superintendent Brown, who are always to be seen together. On leaving the Clapton Stadium, this particular night I was followed by a gang of men with Luper the leader under the protection of Inspector Pride. I was followed through a number of turnings, my life was threatened by a gang who is now on remand at Marlborough Street, who 'Dodger' Mullins is the head. I can't say that Inspector Pride was there then, but he was in the Stadium drinking with them until 11 o'clock at night. The words I heard used this night was, 'Let's do him,' and 'We've got the Big Five behind us now.'

The appeal I am making to you is, as this man Luper is working under the protection of Superintendent Brown, what protection have I got. If necessary to hold an inquiry into this affair I am quite willing to come and give evidence in front of you, as I have got further news to tell you, that will surprise you, and I can bring witnesses.

Hoping you will give me your protection as I don't know which way to turn.

Yours faithfully,
Alfred Solomon.

Sadly Alfie never seems to have been given that chance and so we shall never know what surprises he had in store for the Director. The letter was passed to Sir Trevor Bigham at Scotland Yard, who soon discovered that things were not quite as they appeared from Mr Solomon's letter. It was clearly intended as something in the way of a pre-emptive strike, but the Yard had already had a prior anonymous telephone call which warned that there was likely to be trouble at several dog-tracks between rival gangs run by 'Dodger' Mullins and unfortunately the 'going straight' Mr Solomon. Perhaps Solomon was unlucky in that the senior officer against whom he complained was invited to deal with the allegations.

On 7 February Solomon, Jack Burman and what Superintendent Brown (to whom the matter was passed for his attention) described as 'several other criminals' had visited Clapton Stadium and demanded money from the bookmakers. Solomon was seen in the club room with Bernard Dorrie, a bookmaker, and asked by Mr Luper, the track manager, to leave. Solomon was eventually ejected. 'I am assured by Divisional Detective Pride that although he was present at the grounds, in accordance with his duties, he saw nothing of the incident to which Solomon refers,' said Brown, who added that after Solomon was ejected he and his associates decided to take their revenge on Luper when on 18 February he and his wife went to Wembley. He was set on by Jack Burman, who attacked him with an iron bar. Burman received two months for his pains and was bound over to keep the peace for six months in the sum of £100.

Now the Gospel according to Superintendent Brown came out in a note on the file dated March 11:

Alfred Solomon is one of four brothers; the other three obtain their living, as far as I know in a legitimate manner, as Bookmakers on Race Courses, usually under the name of 'Charles Lewis', but Alfred is nothing better than a member of a gang of thieves who blackmail Bookmakers for a living. I had the conduct of the enquiries in the case referred to by Solomon when he was last sentenced to Three Years penal servitude for manslaughter, and it was generally considered at the time that he was extremely fortunate not to have been convicted of the capital charge. During the course of the proceedings in this case, and since, he has shown considerable antipathy towards me, and no doubt he has often seen me in the company of Mr Luper and upon whom he is now endeavouring to vent his spite.

Mr Luper I have known about 18 years. First as a licensed victualler at Woolwich, at Lambeth and afterwards at Hackney. He has on many occasions rendered other Police officers and myself valuable assistance by giving us information gleaned by him in his business which has led to the arrest of thieves and recovery of stolen property. Since giving up business as a licensed victualler abut three years ago, he became interested in the promotion of the Clapton Dog Racing Track, is now the manager, has heavy financial interests in the concern, and his aim is to keep the Track clean of such as Solomon and his associates, and he has legitimately sought the aid of the police to this end.

There is no truth in the suggestion that Luper is working under my protection, and I venture to express the opinion that Solomon's letter to the Home Office was written out of spite. It was brought to my knowledge that he did, in fact, broadcast amongst his undesirable acquaintances, some days before he wrote, the fact that he was writing to the Home Office.

That was about the end of the matter. A later note reads:

Alfred Solomon is a dangerous and violent person who is the last person in this world to want protection. On 27 April 1921 he was acquitted at the Central Criminal Court of shooting and wounding a man named Kimber with whom he had quarrelled, the defence being that it was an accident. On 6 July 1923 he was again acquitted of conspiracy and occasioning actual bodily harm.

It was also noted that he had the conviction for manslaughter. The note dated 14 March 1930 to the Home Office, returning their papers, reads: 'He is a dangerous rascal and his enemies are far more in need of protection than he is.'

Bernard Dorrie surfaced in July of the next year when he endeavoured to stand bail for Soloman Small, described in the police memorandum as a share pusher (also close associate of undesirable persons), who was on bail for an Aliens Act offence of not registering a change of address.

Dorras was told that the police would object if he persisted in proffering himself and he withdrew.

What was sometimes a source of worry was any other things police officers got up to during their service and after their retirement. Betting and policing very much went together. For example, Detective Superintendent Ted Greeno wrote in his autobiography that on the first day of the Ascot meeting one year he had lost almost £50 and 'the next day was just as bad'. The third day he had a further £50 on a horse which fortunately won. This was in the thirties, when his pay would amount to a few pounds a week. His superior 'Nutty' Sharpe had just retired when on 6 July 1939 an ill-written anonymous note was received by Scotland Yard complaining that pensioned policeman ex-Inspector Sharpe was in a bookmaking business in The Final public house, King William Street. Signed 'On the Beat', it alleged that he was now in partnership with bookmaker Tommy Williams and Phil Lee, the guv'nor of a pub.

The note, written in capital letters, read:

A FINE ADVERT FOR THE POLICE SHARPE A BOOK-MAKER NOW – AS BAD STILL AS EVER HE WAS WORSE WHEN IN THE POLICE HE GOT AWAY WITH IT TO THE DISGRACE OF ALL OF YOU WHO SHOULD HAVE KNOWN THE GAME HE WAS HAVING FOR YEARS ONE OF THE WICKED SCOUNDRELS IN THE POLICE FOR YEARS.

At least the poison-pen writer had his facts right. Discreet inquiries were made and it was apparent that Sharpe was associated with T. Williams & Co at 1 Thames Chambers where a *bona fide* commission agent's business was carried out and that he was an associate of Phil Lee, licensee of The

Final. There was, however, no evidence of any offences under the Betting or Licensing Acts. Sharpe was also a ring steward at Wimbledon greyhounds.

The police did see Sharpe:

Although it has been generally understood that one of his partners in the commission agent's business is the notorious Tommy Williams this is not the case. It turns out that the Thomas Williams in question is a son, said by Mr Sharpe to be of good education and reputation. When I saw him, Mr Sharpe mentioned that there had been a re-adjustment of matters and that the partnership now consists of Williams and himself only, Philip Lee of the Final Public House having ceased to be a partner on 14th July 1939.

Even as it stands at the moment, the business association with the son of Tommy Williams is not as nice as it might be. I know Mr Sharpe fairly well and whilst I am satisfied that he would not consider any business association with Tommy Williams senior, or anyone like him, I am of the opinion that having gone into partnership with the son he sees nothing wrong in it, and would be prepared to contest it if it was suggested, as well it might be, that such a connection is inclined to be unworthy of an ex-Chief Inspector of the CID of the character and principle of Mr Sharpe (Memo of 12 August 1939).

Sharpe was sent a message and the rules of the game were spelled out to him. No one could say he must not do this, but he was letting the Force down. He said he would reconsider the matter.

Next year there appears a note on the file: 'On Sunday

March 30 1940 I met Mr Sharpe and in general conversation he informed me he was no longer associated with the betting business referred to.'

A further handwritten note on the file reads:

Whilst not doubting the word of Mr Sharpe I feel it right to mention that there have been rumours that he is still connected with T. Williams & Co. and it might be as well to have the matter reviewed in say another month when flat racing is re-commenced. A Bell, Supt.

A final note suggested that things should be let lie as horseracing was likely to be suspended during the duration of the War. It was not.[14]

In any event there was dog-racing to which the ex-Chief Inspector could have turned his attention. He might have cared to cast an eye on what was the first ever dog-doping prosecution in London in 1942. The usual method of dealing with a race was employed. Generally there are six dogs in the traps (five at tracks with smaller circuits and, just to make the betting more competitive, eight in America) and the standard procedure is to dope three fancied dogs, leaving the rank outsider and the two on whom the bets are to be placed alone. The betting is then done on what is called the reversed forecast (known in betting terms as 'about'), one of the undoped dogs to win with the other undoped one to come second, and then the bet is reversed. It pays a much higher rate than a straight win, particularly if they are unfancied in the betting as is likely. Sometimes the third dog will be included in a 1–2–3 bet combination.

The standard way of getting to the dogs (apart from

---

[14] Public Record Office MEPO3/759.

through the trainer) is through the kennelmaid. All that must be avoided is a kennelmaid who develops scruples at seeing the dog for which she cares in considerable discomfort. In one early case in 1942 the girl was found a position in a kennels attached to Wembley Stadium and given the not inconsiderable sum of £50 as a retainer to dope the dogs in her care. She would be allowed to settle in for three weeks, then after she had done the first dog she would receive the sum of £400, sufficient then to buy a house. In fact the man had overplayed his hand. The girl was frightened, went to the police and was infiltrated by them into the Wembley kennels. Money was sent to her but she was not for the time required to interfere with the running of any of the dogs. Over a period of weeks she was introduced to other members of the team and finally to a woman. It was agreed she would give capsules to the animals four hours before the race and let the syndicate know she had done so. The financial arrangement was changed slightly, and now in return she would get £25 a week and then £300–£400 per race depending on the winnings.

Now an arrangement was made for her to meet a man at a West End hotel, where she was given a package and later asked to hand it back. She became cross and said she wanted to back out of the doping arrangement, but the man said that this had been a test. There was nothing in the parcel, but he wanted to see if she was being shadowed by the police.

The next time she was given the capsules it was arranged that the dog should be withdrawn from its race. The girl went to a meeting place to be paid, and as she left gave the signal that everyone was there. Three men were convicted and the woman acquitted.

Greyhounds owned by members of the public are in general sent to a trainer who is attached to a track. It is that trainer's duty to supply, fit and well, a certain number of dogs for each meeting. The owner pays the trainer for the dog's keep but receives a small sum every time the dog runs. He has no say in which races it will be placed. Unless the dog is absolutely useless there is a tacit agreement that by handicapping the various dogs – placing them in traps from which it is easier or more difficult to win – the owner can expect to see his or her dog win every few weeks. However, it does not always work that way. I remember talking to an old racehorse trainer who also raced dogs and had what amounted to a matched pair of dogs; the only difference was that one had a mole under the fur of its belly. He was not convinced that he was being given a fair crack of the whip at his local stadium, and said that unless things improved next week he was going to switch dogs as the one with the mole was a good length faster than his litter brother.

In fact switching was rife. At Southend in 1949 Red Wind won an Open puppy race (dogs came from outside tracks to compete) over 500 yards in less time than it had taken to cover 460 yards in a trial four days earlier. In greyhound racing a second is worth sixteen lengths. It had been backed to win £4,000. On a check of its details it tallied, but inquiries in Ireland showed the owner had bought a dog named Waggles. When the trainer's wife came over to England and went to see 'Red Wind', Waggles recognized her at once. The owner was convicted at the Old Bailey, when the judge said there should be a cleansing of greyhound racing stables:

That is in the interest of this recreation in which thousands of people find pleasure. It is most desirable that it should be as clean as any other form of English sport.

By 1950, only 72 of the 209 greyhound tracks in Britain were licensed; the rest were flapping tracks. On 9 June 1955 Harley Street doctor Adam Clark, together with Charles Green and Benjamin Selby, was convicted of conspiracy to cheat and defraud by doping dogs with hydrocortisone. Each received fifteen months at the Old Bailey. The doctor's mitigation was that they only operated at flapping tracks, of which there were still a high proportion.

Tote frauds were rare. In 1955 the only money known to have been obtained by fraud from the tote was less than £19 on a turnover of £25 million. There was, however, one splendid scam. It was that at certain provincial tracks there was a good view of both the tote window and the starting traps from a high point in the stands. If a particular dog trapped well, it was bound to win. The confederate went to the tote window shortly before the hare started and asked for 50 £1 tickets. By the time the race had started some thirty had been punched. The man then claimed that his wallet had been stolen and he could not pay for the tickets. What had happened was he had received a signal that the dog on which he had bet had trapped badly and could not win. Had he received the all-clear signal, he would have bought all the tickets.

On 24 June 1957, the crowd went wild at Harringay when the even money favourite Billycan Sprint bit the 10–1 outsider Ruben's Commission who was declared the winner. Protesting that they wanted the race re-run, the crowd smashed the tote board and set fire to the judge's box, starting traps and seats in the grandstand as well as stealing drinks and cigarettes worth £1,000.

An offshoot of greyhound racing was terrier racing in Ireland in the mid-1950s. As always betting was to the fore, and there were reports that a home-brew alcohol was rubbed on the dog's skin to make it run faster. According to *Everybody* in March 1958:

A dog's weight must not vary by more than 2 lbs from its registered weight. Whether you're a regular punter or only attend a dog meeting occasionally, you can rest assured that dog-racing on reputable tracks today is one of the cleanest sports in the country.

This was one of the ways the authorities could guarantee the sport would be run cleanly. It was, of course, still possible to deny the dog its walk the night before the race, give it a bowl of water or even put elastic bands on its toes. And from an outsider's point of view, quite apart from doping the animal, the traps themselves could be greased.

In December 1958 Johnny Coulon revealed all in the *People*. He maintained he smeared aniseed over the traps, which caused a dog to hesitate and not leave until it actually saw the hare. In this way, he said, in 1944 he smeared five traps at Carntyre, Glasgow, leaving Gladstone Brigadier to win handily in the Scottish Derby. In another example in 1951 in Monmouthshire, he did three dogs with hexamethomium, leaving three dogs. One, Battledore, the rank outsider, he ignored and bet on the other two in the forecast. Five dogs staggered out of the traps – a rival concern had doped his two dogs. Battledore won. Other schemes in Glasgow including trying to dye a dog black with hair dye and racing a dog over its racing weight – over the years dogs were run in weighted muzzles. He was convicted on 5 December 1958, but had sensibly left his story behind with the *People*.

Along with John Coulon, Daniel Swain, Patrick Arnold, Kenneth Collishaw and his wife Daphne, a former kennel-maid, Samuel and Charles Hoare went on trial along with other kennelmaids. Dogs had been doped at Charlton, Wandsworth and Park Royal with meatballs laced with pheno-barbitone. The tip-off had come in May when a girl at the Sunbury Kennels told the kennel manager she had been asked to dope a dog. Daphne Collishaw received a year, the other kennelmaids six months, Coulon three years, Daniel Swain two, and Kenneth Collishaw eighteen months. The girls had received between £20 and £30 a dog. Kennelmaid Barbara Baker had blown the whistle because she could not bear to think the dogs might suffer. She disappeared shortly before the trial and was thought to be in Ireland.

In the late summer of 1964 came the Dagenham Coup, following which bookmakers sued Romford Stadium as the owners of the Dagenham track. It was over an ingenious coup which partially succeeded.

The sixth race on 30 June 1964, the 4.05 p.m., was an Open over 840 yards flat. Seven tote booths and every tote window taking forecast bets was blocked. By backing eighteen out of thirty combinations the conspirators fed money into a pool by making certain losing bets. The other twelve combinations were backed to one unit on each. The odds produced were phenomenal and one punter, John Turner, claimed £987.11s. 9d. on a 2-shilling bet. It was claimed that the stadium should have refused to declare a dividend on the race. The winning odds of the second and third favourites, Buck Wheat and Handsome Lass, coming first and second were 10,000 to 1. The favourite was third, so this effectively eliminated any doping allegations. The bookmakers said the market had been rigged.

There had been examples of bookmakers involved with a market which didn't add up. On 28 June 1947 a Major 'Mac' McKenzie had laid a bet covering a three-year-old horse named Glendower to win £2,000 in the Chepstow Stakes. He expected that the horse, ridden by Gordon Richards, would cost him £4,000 if it lost. Unfortunately one of the only two rivals withdrew, and with the placing of many more bets by the blower service the odds at starting were 20 to 1 on. McKenzie lost £40,000, had to sell shares in the GRA of which he was then a director and never recovered.

The Dagenham bookmakers screamed when next day Turner told how he had masterminded the coup with 125 helpers each paid £5, and £50–£100 if it was successful. He borrowed £3,500 from a local bookmaker as a stake. The bookmakers announced they would not pay; the debts were not legally enforceable and all Turner could do would be to object to the renewal of their licences. The triumph was temporary; Mr Justice Paull's judgment was overturned by the Court of Appeal. John Turner was prosecuted for conspiracy to defraud, along with Terrence Orwell and Henry Cohen. The winnings, had they been paid out, were thought to be between £7 and £10 million.

There had been other coups. In 1963 Mrs Mary Martin had successfully objected to a bookmaker's licence after placing 25 15-shilling place-only accumulators at tote odds with William Hill. The matter went to arbitration and against Mrs Martin because accomplices had put large bets on other dogs to inflate the dividend (400-1 was the biggest ever paid out on a forecast).

On 7 November 1965 the *People* named Peter Phillip Hubbard, Ronald Maxwell and Judith Hubbard as the masterminds of greyhound doping plots. Mrs Hubbard was the owner and looked after the store of dope, and dogs were doped at what had been seen as impregnable tracks such as Harringay and White City as well as Belle Vue and Glasgow. The *People* said that dogs were being doped in such quantities that it was decided to allow them to run rather than cancel the races, or even the whole meeting, and observe betting patterns. A young boy was planted into the Northaw Kennels and Irish girls were imported. At one time Hubbard maintained that out of six kennels at Walthamstow, he had girls in four. The plan was the standard Dope Three-Bet Three.

By 2 February 1966 they were all at the Old Bailey. There was Kray-man Charles Mitchell, Peter Hubbard, Ronald Maxwell and Peter Curtis (described as a security officer, who acted as Hubbard's sidekick over the years), along with two girls Claudette Hamilton and Josephine Carroll. Girls were softened up with the bright lights of London.

The prosecution alleged that at least fifty dogs from five tracks had been doped by the ring. During the course of the first trial one witness admitted she received £390 to lie to get Charles Mitchell off. The jury was discharged from giving a verdict and, in a second trial in April 1966, Margaret Fletcher gave evidence that she was promised a dog called Monday's Ranger for her father if she doped other dogs. Mitchell and Hubbard went to prison.

In 1989 warned-off trainer Jerry Fisher was alleging he had doped dogs with cocaine, put caffeine into meat-balls and piddled in the dog's bowl to avoid detection. Dogs were being stopped at trials to lengthen their odds when they actually ran in a race, and were run at flapping tracks to regain their interest in racing, he said. In the last three months of 1993, seventy positive dope tests were recorded and nine trainers were struck off. Positive samples exceeded the total for 1992.

The old tried and tested methods still seemed to be working, even though the NGRC have recently switched from using Glasgow University for testing to the Jockey Club's sophisticated analysis centre at Newmarket.

Ex-trainer David Haywood, fined for using an illegal substance to doctor one of his dogs, said, 'A high percentage of dogs are doped to slow them down and cocaine, amphetamines and steroids have been used. Some trainers will hide a bottle of dog's urine up their sleeves so if a steward asks for a test he can bend down and pour the "clean" stuff into the sample jar.'[15]

So far as boxing is concerned, the British Boxing Board of Control has had things fairly well under control for the past sixty years. Even so things could go wrong. Nothing to do with organized crime at all, but in a contest between Steve McCarthy and Tony Wilson in September 1989 Minna Wilson, seeing her son getting a beating, climbed on to the apron of the ring and began hitting the unfortunate McCarthy with a shoe. He sustained a cut on his head, refused to fight on and was disqualified. He appealed to the Boxing Board of Control, who upheld the referee but ordered a re-match. Mrs Wilson was not at the ringside on that occasion.

More seriously, one of the Board's principal preoccupations has been the illegal prize fight which might bring the anti-boxing lobby down on its head yet again. In 1936 the fear nearly became the reality. There had been an argument between two Wandsworth labourers outside a pub over a remark passed about the wife of one of them. A blow was

[15] The *People*, 9 January 1994.

struck but not returned; instead a challenge was issued for 8 a.m. on 23 August 1936 at King George's Park, Wandsworth. An audience of between 200 and 300 turned up – one newspaper said 1,000 people were there. A bookmaker had gone to bet on the park fight, illegal bookmaking being common at fights between ordinary people settling a quarrel.

Now a local boxing promoter decided to hold a gloved contest. William Hillsley, Catch as Catch Can (29) *v* Ernest Simmonds, The Battling Dustman (36) at Wandsworth Stadium in September 1936 as a supporting contest to Maurice Strickland, the New Zealand Heavyweight Champion, and Pancho Villa. Jim Wicks, witness to the Montecolumbo killing, was now the matchmaker for the Stadium. He had said he could get the men a licence each and expected they would get between £25 and £50 nobbins.[16] He anticipated the bout would add £100 to the night's takings with these 'local sportsmen' on the bill. Proceeds were going to Battersea General Hospital.

The police sought to interfere on the grounds that it was undesirable. There was no knowledge of whether the men were evenly matched – there was a seven-year age gap – and they didn't want a promoter to unjustly enrich himself. Moreover the police were clearly sceptical as to whether all the proceeds would end up in the hospital. They thought the fight could also draw a partisan crowd, and requested the advice of the Director of Public Prosecutions as to the legality of the whole affair. When

[16] Nobbins were coins (and occasionally notes) thrown into the ring at the end of a close and well-fought contest. Traditionally they were divided evenly between the boxers, but usually the winner gave the loser all the money. The biggest sum of nobbins ever recorded was over £150.

it came to it, the promoter withdrew before a ruling could be made.

Two early prize-fight champions, Bill Stevens 'The Nailer' and Bill Darts, threw their fights in March 1761 and May 1781 respectively. Stevens was paid £50 by Jack Slack whom he had already defeated, and lost in a very quick seventeen minutes to George Meggs. Darts threw in the towel for £100 against Peter Corcoran. In this century, however, there have been few instances of fixed matches, certainly at championship level. Dai Dower and John L. Gardiner were champions who unknowingly benefited from an arrangement struck with their opponents. There are stories that Jack Spot had a hand in fixing fights and it is inconceivable that, from time to time, money has not changed hands at a number of the smaller tournaments over the years. This is more likely to have been done to promote a boy's career rather than for betting purposes. In general, however, the way of massaging a boy's reputation in this country has not, as in America, been to pay the opposition but rather to select non-punching opponents with weak chins. Nor is there any real evidence that money has been paid to referees and judges, however peculiar the scoring of some contests has been. From time to time the British Boxing Board of Control has downgraded a referee whose conduct of contests has given rise to concern, but this has more usually been because the referee has not intervened to prevent a boxer taking too much punishment rather than because he has been signalling his intention to betters at the side of the ring or deliberately favouring a contestant. This had not always been the position in the earlier days of unlicensed boxing; one sporting journalist was invited to be a judge for a bout at a promotion: 'I was told quite firmly which boy was going to win and I didn't dare do anything but score for him.'

One boxer who temporarily benefited from a fixed fight was Tony Mella, a promising heavyweight after the War. His friends bought off an opponent at the Mile End arena, but in his next contest he was matched against the Southern Area champion who would have none of it and gave Mella a bad beating. Mella went on to own a number of clubs in the West End before he was shot by his friend Alf Melvin, who immediately committed suicide.

In June 1990, however, it appears that the scales at a tournament at the Royal Albert Hall were tampered with, although it was never made clear by whom. Mark Reefer came in as a late substitute in a title match with Pedro Gutierrez. Reefer weighed in on the limit, took a bad beating and was knocked out in the last round. The promoter was later sent a letter by the managing director of the manufacturers of the scales, saying he was distressed to learn that his company had been asked to calibrate the scales short. 'Somebody asked a member of our staff to do it and he foolishly acceded to the request.' There is no evidence that the promoter knew of the matter, which was reported by the Board of Control to the police. No action was taken against anyone.

Perhaps it is looking at things through rose-tinted glasses to say that although boxing and the criminal fraternity go hand in hand, the latter – many of whom have been in the game themselves – like it too much to try to interfere with the matches on a regular basis. More often the troubles arise when boxers have to retire and have not been able to put away sufficient money during their careers. They are then recruited into the twilight world of the nightclub bouncer, and some into the even darker world of the enforcer and the robber. One prime example is the former lightweight champion Sammy McCarthy, who has served several sentences for armed robbery.

There has always been a certain amount of unlicensed boxing, in the sense that it was not under the auspices of the British Boxing Board of Control, and also some bare-knuckle fighting around. In the 1970s there was a genuine and properly organized fledging rival establishment run by Frank Warren, but when he became successful he applied for and was granted a Board licence. Since then unlicensed boxing is the place where boxers who have grown old, had poor records, or recent criminal convictions and had lost their licences, find a home along with young talent who have been persuaded against going with the Board. Boxers fight under pseudonyms – 'Tyson', 'The Duke' – and the punters like the illusion of being on the margins of the law. Unlicensed boxing has its other uses:

> This fellow's amphetamine business went down the toilet when M escaped [from prison] and set up a factory of his own. Suddenly everyone wanted to deal with M. They wanted a slice of his rep. He had to get back to basics – get back on the streets, do the rounds of the unlicensed boxing, the greyhounds to get it on its feet again.

Bare-knuckle fighting is alive and well. The old stars such as Donny 'The Bull' Adams, Lenny 'The Governor' or 'The Mean Machine' McLean[17] and Roy Shaw are now relatively old men, but their exploits on the cobbles have become legends.

In 1992 McLean served a sentence of eighteen months'

[17] *Sky*, December 1992.

imprisonment for assault after the death of Gary Humphreys who had stripped naked, urinated on the stage and played with himself at the Hippodrome nightclub in London before being hauled away by the bouncers, including McLean who was acquitted of his murder. Humphreys suffered from a hyperactive condition and had run out of tablets to control it. 'You knew he would be defenceless against you,' said Judge Richard Lowry QC, 'but you decided to teach him a lesson.' During his time on remand McLean had been seen by psychiatrists who described him as tearful and suicidal.

After the case, as often happens, he recovered his old ebullience. During his sentence he is reputed to have told his young, and nervous, cell-mate that there was to be no breaking wind. He himself immediately did so twice and then said, 'That's for both of us.' He had served a previous sentence of four years for an attack on youths in the street, a punishment he regards as unfair:

> I came out of a nightclub and there was a woman in a car with a kid and three drunks around the car going, 'Show us yer fanny' and all that. If I'd done what 90 per cent of the public would've done and walked away, those guys would've raped the woman.

McLean's most famous unlicensed fight against Brian 'The Mad Gypsy' Bradshaw was recorded on video. Mr Bradshaw was out for forty-five minutes after unwisely beginning the contest before the bell with a head-butt. McLean is said to have received £20,000 on a winner take all against the 'Old Guv'nor' Roy Shaw. He describes his technique in another contest in awesome terms: 'I broke his jaw in seven places, bit half his ear off, half his cheekbone off, half his nose off and his bottom lip and then I'm going at him like a lunatic.'

A film of McLean's life was being shot in 1993.

There is now a new generation of martial arts men who will fight for promoters in Birmingham and London, where there are three manors. The venues are parks, clubs and warehouses, where the purses are winner takes all, if he is lucky, and there is heavy betting. The rules are even more basic than in the Shaw-McLean days. A foul takes place when one of the fighters is unconscious and his opponent still damages him. The fighters are hardmen and minders who will carry out a beating as a side contract or in the guise of a contest. One warrior reported being offered £1,500 to participate in a dog-fight. This is not so bizarre as it may seem. Man *v* Dog fights have been around for many years. In Wicken, in the Fens, the first policeman sent there in Victorian times was murdered by a mob including Pitt Fletcher. Fletcher, known as 'The Fen Tiger', in one Dog *v* Man fight bit off the dog's snout, but not before he himself had lost an ear.

Football on the field, as opposed to the transfer market, has always been the subject of whispers of game fixing, often to help out friendly clubs to avoid relegation, obtain a bigger gate in a cup replay and sometimes for betting purposes. Few of the allegations and rumours have been substantiated.

In 1913 a man was imprisoned for five months for trying to bribe the English full-back Jesse Pennington to make West Bromwich lose or draw against Everton. Before the Second World War there was an attempt by the former Celtic and Scotland player Archie 'Punch' Kyle to bribe Hamilton Academicals to lose a home game against Leith Athletic, a match they should have won with some ease. He first approached the Academicals' captain Willie Moffat. Moffat contacted his Board, who called in the police.

A second approach took place with a police officer Robert Colquhoun hiding behind some curtains recording the conversation. Kyle's defence was that he was arranging the transfer of Moffat to an English club for whom he scouted. What he had meant to suggest was that if Moffat did not play to the top of his form the transfer fee might be reduced. Kyle received a short sentence. Hamilton played well that Saturday and lost.

One of the unconfirmed tales is the story of the Division Three (North) club whose players put their wages on the opposition but omitted to tell the new, young and very keen centre-forward of their bet. He equalized in the last minute.

In the 1960s, however, there was an increasing number of stories that games were being fixed for betting purposes. It began with the suspension by Bristol Rovers of two of their players, and followed with a series of stories in the *People*[18] which named players involved in bribery allegations. This was bad enough but, worse, some were household names. The black day for English football had been 1 December 1962 at a time when the players, earning £60 a week, were bribed over a First Division match. The attitude of newspaper reports of the time is curious. It seems as though a bit of skullduggery in the lower divisions was to be expected (although it could dramatically change who won the hundred thousand or so on offer by the pools companies), but that when teams reached the pinnacle of the First Division then the game must be sacrosanct. The allegation was that David 'Bronco' Layne (he was nicknamed after a popular television Western hero), Sheffield

[18] 12 April 1964.

Wednesday's star centre-forward, Peter Swan their centre-half and Tony Kay, later transferred for £55,000 to Everton from Wednesday, were guilty of backing their team to lose an away match at Ipswich, who had in fact (and unexpectedly) won 2–0. The players, said the article, had received £100 each. The man behind the fix was former Everton and Charlton player Jimmy Gauld, who had broken his leg playing for Mansfield Town at the end of his career. He had apparently met Layne in the stands at a Mansfield evening match, put the proposition to the centre-forward and in turn he had contacted Kay and Swan. According to the *People*, two other matches were fixed by Gauld on the same day. Lincoln City were to lose at home to Brentford and York City away at Oldham Athletic. Everything went well. Ipswich had won, Brentford beat Lincoln 3–1 and Oldham beat York 3–2.

Once the allegations were out in the open other reports were forthcoming. In 1962 the Oldham players had refused to accept a bribe from Gauld, who had been fined a derisory £60 for the attempt.

The financial success of such a fix would depend on the appropriately named fixed odds offered by bookmakers on single matches. The bet would be for doubles on the unfancied teams, which could pay off at odds of 10–1 or even better. To make this successful the fixer would have to involve tame bookmakers who would lay off the bets and invest some of their own money rather than by trying to spread the bet over several bookmakers, something which might attract attention. One of the two bookmakers named in the *People*, Joe Hancock (52) from Mansfield, committed suicide in a local reservoir when a police investigation seemed inevitable.

The fixing had been going on since the 1959–60 season.

According to Gauld, he received a letter saying that certain players were being paid by Tranmere Rovers to deliberately lose their next match and so help that club avoid relegation. He then arranged for Swindon, for whom he was playing in the 1959–60 season, to lose to Port Vale so there could be a 'double'.

Ten players and former players were served with summonses to appear at Mansfield. They included Gauld, Layne, Swan and Kay and Jack Fountain, once captain of York City. The case was eventually heard at Nottingham Assizes in January 1965. Matches rigged had ranged through the divisions during the years 1960–1963 and included the Scottish match of St Mirren *v* Dundee United. All were found guilty of at least one offence. On 21 January 1965 Gauld received four years and was ordered to pay £5,000 costs. Fountain received fifteen months; Layne, Kay and Swan each received four months. On the release of the players from prison, the Football Association banned some of them for life.

Rumours of attempted fixing lingered on. Arthur Ellis, the referee, disclosed he had been offered the princely sum of £35 to make sure Preston won their 1959 cup-tie with Stoke. In October 1960, amidst a flurry of reports of bribery, with players naming each other and five players from a Northern club reporting matters to the police, one former player admitted to the *Daily Mail* that he had tried to rig the Chelsea *v* Everton match and had offered another player £500. From then on allegations of match fixing died away.

Violence at sporting fixtures is as old as sport itself. Chariot drivers in Constantinople under the Emperor Justinian wore the Blue and the Green racing colours which led to clashes between their rival supporters. Racing was banned for five years after a battle between the fans of the rival charioteers.

However, the mainstream football crime has been on the terraces. Football hooliganism has long been part of the game, with English 'supporters' being at the forefront. At the end of the last century grounds were regularly closed after rival supporters had fought, but in more recent years the travelling of fans to away matches has masked a variety of crimes and has provided a legitimate explanation for criminals to be out of their home ground.

At the beginning of the 1993–4 season Superintendent Adrian Appelby of the National Anti-hooligan Unit spoke of rape, armed robbery and fraud being carried out under the cover of a hard core of some five hundred football fans as they travelled to cities where the local police did not know them.

The top tier of gangs – Chelsea, the Inter City Firm from West Ham and the Arsenal 'Gooners' – were all investigated in the late 1980s, and there had been prosecutions most of which had collapsed amidst allegations of police impropriety.

The new generation of gang members had grown up in the belief that they were untouchable and, said Appelby, the largest gang, the Chelsea Headhunters, had alliances with supporters of other teams including the seemingly unlikely ones of Colchester and Heart of Midlothian. When Hearts had played Standard Liege in Belgium, their supporters had called on Chelsea for help in the violence which was likely to ensue. The police had also found links between Chelsea supporters and the British National Party.

Professor Dick Hobbs of the University of Durham carried out research in the 1980s into members of football gangs:

I worked with a group from 1981 onwards. They were neighbourhood men of violence and several were prominent members of a group of organized football hooligans. In 1987 Ecstasy was re-discovered in Ibiza and the Acid House party scene took off. Security was needed – not from middle-aged dinosaurs but from people the same age as those who were going to the parties. The football hooligan was ideal. Some were already appearing on television on chat shows. They had become minor media stars. Their reputations had been made overnight.

Young men like them were obvious sources for security at raves and so on. The organizers turned to them for help. In turn they began to collaborate with people dealing with drugs on the premises. It was quasi-extortion. They would let people in to deal and soon in turn they cut off the middleman and sold the drugs themselves. Very quickly they made enormous sums of money.

They then began to sell the goods outside the raves and sought out importers. Ten years later they no longer operate security but have set up legitimate people to run that for them – sporting and music venues. They've on the face of it gone legitimate and they'll move about – Liverpool, Manchester, wherever. They have moved into time-share, property abroad, clubs, sweetshops, car dealerships – a wonderful front. They are constantly mutating: several have opted out, whilst others are in professional crime of a more complicated sort.

12

The Drug Trade – Soft and Hard

Writing in 1952 in *The Truth about Drug Addiction in Britain*, Kenneth Allsop was convinced, or at any rate his publishers were, that there was no problem of teenaged drug addicts in Britain:

> We are not going the way of America. But the fashion for drug-taking is on the increase, and it is a social danger that should be watched.

He cited the lack of an organized drug market ring as the haphazard price for the cost of dope. Reefers, he found, cost from 2/6d to 7/6d. Loose in paper packets, the going rate was 2/6d a gramme. A heroin taker 'once firmly addicted' will need 30–50 tablets a day at a cost of between £30 and £50 a week.

Throughout the century there has always been a drugs presence in Britain, but certainly for the first fifty years it had been a limited and relatively controlled one. Indeed, in the late nineteenth century drugs were the province of the intellectual. Opium, for example, was not made an illegal substance until 1916. A little morphine never did Sherlock Holmes any harm and, while Freud eventually destroyed his nose with cocaine, would he have been able to write quite so influentially without it?

Shortly after the First World War a five-foot Chinese, Brilliant Chang, trafficked in both women and drugs. He was almost certainly the supplier of the drugs which led to two well-publicized deaths. After the Victory Ball held at the Albert Hall, Billie Carleton, a pretty young actress, collapsed and died. The inquest showed she had died of cocaine poisoning and was addicted to opium smoking. It was common knowledge that Chang had been a close friend, but although her companion of the night before, Reggie de Veuille, was charged with manslaughter nothing was ever proved against Chang. Then in March 1922 Freda Kempton, a dancing instructress, was also found dead from an overdose of cocaine. This time Brilliant Chang did feature; he had been with Freda the night before, and faced a hostile series of questions at her inquest. 'She was a friend of mine, but I know nothing about the cocaine,' he told the coroner. 'It is all a mystery to me.'

Chang, gap-toothed with dark hair swept back, was apparently the son of a well-to-do Chinese businessman sent to England to pursue a commercial career. Instead he opened a restaurant in Regent Street and started drug trafficking on the side from his private suite. He operated more or less unchallenged until 1924 when two carriers were arrested. Letters in their possession linked them to Chang. Despite police surveillance nothing was established against him although, in the flurry of unwelcome publicity after Freda Kempton's death, he withdrew his operations to Limehouse where in 1924 the police raided his premises.

They found not only a mandarin's palace in the grimy building but more importantly, in a secret cupboard, a large quantity of cocaine. He was deported after serving a fourteen-month sentence. During his six-year reign it is estimated he made over £1 million from drugs trafficking.

When he was driven out of Soho Chang's empire there was taken over by another dope pedlar and white slaver, balding and hollow-eyed Jamaican-born Eddie Manning, who had come to Britain in 1916, worked in a munitions factory before an accident invalided him out and then played the drums in a touring company for three years. From 1919 he does not seem to have worked again and, the police thought, ran a dozen prostitutes, using them to sell cocaine at 10 shillings an injection from his flat in Lisle Street and the Berwick Street cellar café he owned with his Greek woman friend. In 1920 he had served a sentence of sixteen months for shooting at Frank Miller at Cambridge Circus. He was a trifle unfortunate; from the evidence, it does appear that on this occasion he was more sinned against than sinning. He was being pressured by Miller, known as 'American Frank', known bully and blackmailer, and his brother Charles Tunick to hand over some of his gambling winnings. When the matter came to court there was no appearance by Miller and, in a plea bargain, the attempted murder charge was whittled down.

He received three years' penal servitude for possession of opium on 19 July 1923. Efforts to deport him as an American failed. Manning claimed to have been born the son of a freed slave in 1882 in Jamaica, but inquiries there failed to substantiate his claim. Eventually the authorities abandoned their efforts and he continued to survive until he received his final sentence in 1929. By now he too had been chased out of the drug-dealing world and was into receiving. Property worth £2,000 was found at his flat. After serving his sentence, he dropped out of sight.[1]

As a rule morphine, heroin and cocaine were smuggled over from Germany in small packets. Then personal searches by the customs were the exception rather than the rule. Distribution was in the hands of the likes of Manning and also those of 'newspaper boys' who pretended to be selling the evening papers and distributed cocaine under this cover.[2]

In the middle 1950s the main area for drug dealing was the home of the musicians, 'Tin Pan Alley', Archer Street, along with Piccadilly Circus, Brixton, Westbourne Park and Aldgate. Dope was peddled at the greyhound tracks around London, and the economy showed a profit of around £200 per pound weight of marijuana.

By 1957 *The Times*, for one, was still dancing to the tune of the Black Peril. It was not our health but our morality which was at risk:

> . . . Of the people convicted, seven out of eight are coloured men, mainly West Indians. The hemp problem has been with us now for about ten years. Will it become more serious? The market in Great Britain will continue extremely tempting while it contains so many coloured people. The Home Office and police tend to lump together . . . white offenders as band leaders who specialize in the more exotic types of dance music, or even as musicians who specialize in exceptionally 'hot' music at 'modern music clubs' in

[1] There is a fairly full account of his life and death, including his pathological fear of owls, in V. Davis, *Phenomena in Crime*, Chapter 7.
[2] S. Felstead, *The Underworld of London*, VI.

the West End of London . . . White girls who become friendly with West Indians are from time to time enticed to hemp smoking . . . this is an aspect of the hemp problem – the possibilities of its spreading amongst irresponsible young white people – that causes greatest concern to the authorities. The potential moral danger is significant, since a principal motive of the coloured man in smoking hemp is to stimulate his sexual desires.[3]

Girls were being lured to smoking parties, where they were being charged 5 shillings a reefer at Swindon. On 1 July 1960 three Turkish Cypriot youths were convicted. Writing in a column for the *Empire News* in 1957, Robert Fabian, the great detective, had already warned that it was the 'easiest, newest weapon of the West End white slaver. Every pound of marijuana can make 1,000 cigarettes. They sell for 7s. 6d. each.' This appears to back up Kenneth Allsop's belief that there was no international organized ring. Either that, or the police and press did not have a clue what was really going on.

There was a bit of a home production market on which the courts were quick to stamp. In 1959 Reuben Ritchie and John Luton were convicted of unlawful possession of cannabis resin. The defence was unusual. Apparently they had bought a sixpenny packet of budgerigar seed at a pet-shop near their homes in Tiger Bay, Cardiff. Usually this was harmless, but because of an extraordinarily fine summer they were able to harvest a crop weighing six pounds – worth, said the prosecution, £2,300. They were jailed for nine months each. It all seems so innocent now but, as Tom

[3] 'Haunt of the Reefer' in *The Times*, 1957.

Lehrer sang in the nightclubs of the 1960s, 'Today's young innocent faces are tomorrow's clientele.'

Early in 1961 *The Times* was confident that headway was being made in the world battle against drug addiction. There was a decline in the use of heroin. In 1956 – the latest year for statistics, but there was no reason to suppose things had deteriorated in 1957 – only three countries manufactured heroin: Britain with 37kg, Belgium with 11kg and Hungary 12kg. Some of this was made into non-addiction forming drugs and so the net world production of heroin could be counted at 39kg.

The effect of the controls had been to reduce almost to vanishing point the possibility of drug addicts obtaining narcotics from legitimate sources, so now they had to have recourse to illicit sources. The Permanent Central Opium Board thought this was really rather a good point. The Board, which was largely concerned with the fight against illicit traffic, had advanced some conclusions from the figures:

> Traffic in opium was most active in the Far and Near East. The largest seizures in heroin were in North America, the Mediterranean basin and Hong Kong. The trade in morphine had not declined and most was seized in the Near and Far East. Traffic in cannabis was largest in Africa. The importance of cocaine as an illegal drug had considerably declined whilst synthetic drugs hardly featured. In no country or territory did the amounts of any synthetic drug seized, if at all, exceed one kilo.

Six years earlier Duncan Webb, writing in the *People*, ever worried about the dark menace, was able to have 'London's

Drug Fiends Exposed'. It was from East London that the majority of 'coloured marijuana agents' worked: 'I gained access to a Negro who was the chief market supplier to the entire East London area. He gave his name and address in Stepney, alleging that this was one of the busiest distributing points in London.' Webb also interviewed one of the man's sub-agents, who told him that most of his supplies came in through Liverpool: 'Whilst they were quite content to peddle marijuana "Negros" apparently recoiled from supplying heroin and this trade was almost wholly in the hands of white men.'[4]

Of course, organized crime was involved and there is little doubt that the Messina brothers, those Czars of London vice, were also involved in the drug trade. There is a report that in 1955 Carmelo, using the name Gino Miller, was dealing in 'silk', the trade name for heroin, in Germany. He was set up to deal in a scam with an Interpol officer, but the deal never went through because the Messinas were arrested in London over vice matters.

July 1960 had the *Sunday Graphic* speculating 'through the eyes of Ace reporter, Charles Wighton' why there was no big-scale dope traffic in London – amongst the capitals of Asia, Europe and the New World he believed this was the only city free of drugs. The answer as to why it had escaped the predations of Dope International, the worldwide criminal drug conspiracy, was not hard to explain. London was the centre of this huge undercover organization whose . . .

supply lines spread from the opium-growing lands of Turkey, right across the world. And for that reason, the higher executive of Dope International does not

[4] *People*, 13 June 1954.

want the British authorities in general – and Scotland
Yard in particular – to change their present official
attitude of, 'It doesn't happen here, it can't happen
here.'

There was, he said, considerable evidence that payments for
consignments of dope were being made through branches of
foreign banks in London, and deals were being transacted
in West End hotels by 'businessmen from the Lebanon,
Syria and Turkey and their associates from the other side of
the Atlantic'.[5]

It was not until the 1960s with a so-called swinging
London, a Conservative government pointing out that we
had 'never had it so good' and political scandals such as that
of Ivanov-Profumo-Keeler that the so-called soft drugs
market took off, to be followed by the hard market a
decade later. Yet then, Howard Marks – soon to become
a millionaire from marijuana dealing – and his kind were
regarded by the population not as criminals but more as
Robin Hoods risking their liberties to spread a little
happiness. In 1964 it was noted that drug taking was on
the increase and three years later Regional Drug Squads
were formed to combat the 'drug problem'. Now there were
signs of a moral panic and it was too late.[6]

By October 1966, despite assurances to the contrary over
the previous years that dealing was not prevalent in the city,
it was accepted that Liverpool was one of the principal
centres of trafficking. The next year nationwide saw over
3,000 convictions for drug offences. In 1973 Customs
officers had captured nine tons of cannabis, worth more

[5] *Sunday Graphic*, 10 July 1960.
[6] See *inter alia* Steve Chibnall, *Law and Order News*.

than £8 million to the pedlars, in what was recognized now to be a desperate struggle against importers. Scotland Yard arrested 700 wholesalers and middlemen in London, and with the Customs chipping in with another 500 arrests the total throughout the country rose to around 2,000 dealers as opposed to users. Cannabis was costing £500 a lb on the streets and hash oil was now a major currency. Although heroin and cocaine deals – costing £500 an ounce – were on the increase, the backbone was still in cannabis.

Fifteen years on, by the standards of the early 1970s and even by those of the previous year, seizures had become astronomical. They included 189kg of heroin and 358kg of cocaine (261 per cent increase on 1986). One seizure of 208kg in Southampton and bound for Holland was the largest ever in Europe. It was soon overtaken, however.

The smugglers were also becoming more imaginative. In his book *Snowblind*, Robert Sabbag describes the ingenious ways in which dealer Zachary Swan arranged drug shipments whilst protecting his sometimes innocent couriers. They included Aztec statues, dolls, teddy bears and rolling-pins stuffed with cocaine. On one occasion his innocent mules were given free trips to Colombia with all expenses paid. They had, however, to bring back gifts (supplied by Swan), to be photographed with them at the office of the 'tour company' through which they had won the trip. They were taken out to lunch and identical souvenirs were switched for the drug-laden ones.[7]

Sometimes things were more prosaic, as when five Colombians were found at Heathrow with £2 million (16kg) in book covers and between the two vinyl sleeves of gramophone records. At the Isleworth Crown Court,

[7] R. Sabbag, *Snowblind*, pp. 140 *et seq.*

members of the team received terms of fourteen years for the women and sixteen for their minder. The couriers had been paid £550 and their expenses.

The garagers of the drugs when they arrived here were also fairly ingenious, even if it did not always do them much good in the end. One cache was found in a collection of garden gnomes, and after another swoop caretaker Ian Berry pleaded guilty to conspiracy to supply 40kg of cocaine. He had placed it in a burial chamber. Edward Coakley, also caught in Operation Basket, was found within minutes of leaving the caretaker's lodge. He was jailed for ten years and Berry for seven at the Inner London Crown Court on 25 March 1988.

Sometimes the drugs were simply floated over from the Continent unsupervised, to be collected later. Sometimes they floated to the wrong place. On 5 June 1988 £4 million of drugs were found on the beach at Saltdean near Brighton.

That year saw the end of one of the great cannabis smugglers of all times. Howard Marks (Garw Grammar School and Balliol) went down, betrayed by the then Lord Moynihan who was under extreme pressure from the Drug Enforcement Agency because of his own nefarious activities.[8]

[8] Lord Moynihan died in 1993, leaving several claimants to the title including a son by his fifth wife Jinna, a former Manila hotel receptionist. Another claimant, Andrew, is the son of his fourth wife, Editha, a Manila massage parlour manageress. A third claimant to the title is Moynihan's half-brother, the former conservative MP and one-time Minister for Sport Colin Moynihan. In March 1994 Colin Moynihan was reported to be petitioning the Queen because his request for a writ of summons – official document necessary before a peer may take his place in the House of Lords – had been rejected by the Lord Chancellor. This aim is that the Queen will refer the matter to the Committee for Privileges. (*The Times* 12 March, 1994.)

Marks' first entry into the dealing scene was handling small amounts in Notting Hill and later in Brighton before, in 1970, taking over the smuggling route to replace a friend, Graham Plinston, another Balliol man who had been caught in Germany with 100lb of hash under the back seat and in the door panels of his car. Marks travelled to Germany to pay the fine, but he could not resist a stupid piece of small-time smuggling, a bottle of perfume on the way home. Questioned, he admitted he had been travelling on behalf of Plinston and so went down in someone's little black book.

From then on he first worked for Plinston and subsequently joined him as a partner, importing ever-increasing amounts through Shannon and into England. The first shipment was 200 lbs and the third a ton. Marks and his partners turned their attention to America. He fell out with the American authorities three years later when on 14 September 1973 he was waiting in Newport Beach for a load of hashish. He saw the bust on television and fled through New York and Montreal back to Europe. Two months later he was arrested in Amsterdam, told the Customs officers he was working for MI6 (which he just about had been after being recruited on a temporary basis by a former Balliol chum), was granted bail, was on his toes once again and was finally arrested in the Swan Hotel, Lavenham in Suffolk in May 1980.

His conduct at the ensuing trial at the Old Bailey was a masterpiece of suggestion, innuendo, and downright lies. It ran along the lines, 'Yes, he had been drug trafficking but it had all been done under the supervision of MI6.' He was even able to produce a Mexican 'secret agent' to back up his story. Against his own expectations and certainly those of his solicitor and counsel, Marks was acquitted. The defeated opposition described itself as 'astonished, disbelieving and incredulous'.

In a curious way, however, his acquittal was his undoing. Generally police and Customs officers accept losses with something approaching fatalism. The fault of a stupid jury, crooked lawyer, senile judge are some of the more common reasons trotted out for the failure of a prosecution. This time, however, they were really upset not only by the acquittal but by the book of memoirs which followed. Marks had hoped to persuade the novelist Piers Paul Read – who, ten years earlier, had written *The Train Robbers* – to write the book. Read declined the task and Marks settled on the *Observer* journalist, David Leigh, who put together a vastly entertaining romp *Howard Marks, His Life and High Times*, which first, along with many a book, did not sell as well as the authors had hoped, and second and more importantly, had infuriated the Customs officers. In particular one Drug Enforcement Officer, Craig Lovato, made the destruction of Howard Marks and his empire a prime commitment.

After his acquittal Marks, based in Majorca, was to meet his nemesis in the shape of Lord Anthony Patrick Andrew Cairnes Berkeley Moynihan, son of an English peer who had squandered a good part of the family's wealth and who died shortly before he was due to appear on a charge of gross indecency. He had been introduced by a business associate, Phil Sparrowhawk, who had interests in massage parlours in the Ermita district of Manila. Moynihan and Marks put together a scheme to improve the quality of Manila-grown marijuana. As they did so, discussing the project over the telephone, Lovato listened on a telephone tap he had been allowed by the Spanish authorities to set up.

Moynihan was an Achilles heel. He had left England in the early 1970s, closely pursued by Scotland Yard who wanted to talk to and charge him in relation to a number of commercial frauds. Over the years he had been involved with a number of disreputable schemes closely related to Filipino prostitution. Now Lovato was able to pressure him into turning against Marks. First there was the threat of an American Grand Jury indictment for conspiracy to smuggle drugs into the United States against Marks and also Moynihan; and, second, Moynihan was beginning to pine for England and his mother. Moynihan was provided with a wire, with instructions on how to turn the tape off after twenty-nine minutes so that Marks did not hear a worrying bleep. The rest, as the saying goes, is history.

Marks was arrested in his home at La Vileta in Majorca. In due course he was extradited to America and when he learned that his former partners would give evidence against him he pleaded guilty, earning himself twenty-five years.

As the end of the 1980s approached, the courts began to dish out consistently heavy sentences in an effort to deter drug traffickers.

On 9 January 1988 three Israeli army reservists and James Greenfield – a one-time member of the Angry Brigade, who once served ten years for bombing plots – were found guilty of a drugs-for-arms deal intended to provide the IRA with surface-to-air missiles. They smuggled premier quality Lebanese Gold cannabis resin worth £5 million into Britain. For their pains the sentences totalled thirty-six years.

And as they went to prison, so others came out. There was widespread belief that a gang dubbed the 'A team' and named after the actors in the popular television programme, organized the escape of drug smugglers Klass Karte and Wolfgang Oestmann who broke out of Channings Wood in

Devon in February 1988. A police spokesman said: 'We have information that there are people who will supply the plans, getaway cars, hideouts, forged passports, the lot to help top villains get free if the money is right.'

It was the third escape of major criminals in six months. Six-figure sums were on offer to teams who could organize successful break-outs.[9]

One of the problems in the drug war has long been the rivalry between police and Customs. In the past they have kept things secret from each other to reap the kudos of the capture. There has also been a long-held belief that if the police are allowed near a consignment of drugs, not all of it will be recorded. The remainder will be siphoned off for a variety of purposes, something which Customs officers would not countenance.

Now a senior police officer said, 'The battle against the drugs menace facing Britain is far too important for us to be distracted by fighting between ourselves.' This was in March 1988 on the conviction of Francis Cook at Chelmsford for importing cannabis in lorry containers. The owner of Le Fez restaurant in the Edgware Road, he had wanted to do one run a month for a year and then retire. The surveillance operation had taken two years and Cook had been on the run for four.

A senior Customs officer made a similarly laudatory statement:

If we don't work together the only people who will benefit will be the drug dealers. Operation Quest shows just what can be done. We are proud of the way Customs and police have worked together in this investigation.

[9] *Daily Star*, 19 February 1988.

It was not always the case, and one of the most spectacular busts in the history of drug trials ended in mutual Customs–police recriminations. At the beginning of 1994 there was a major disaster in the case of Joseph Kassar, a Manchester businessman, convicted of a plot to smuggle £67 million of cocaine imported amongst lead ingots from Venezuela. The shipment had gone through and had been distributed through sources in Liverpool, but the planners tried a second time. On this occasion Customs and Excise found nearly £150 million in street terms of 95 per cent pure cocaine at a warehouse in Stoke-on-Trent. They removed the drugs from the crates of thirty-two lead ingots which, this time, had come in through Felixstowe and were on their way to Liverpool. The Customs tried to prove that the £67 million had gone through Kassar's hands, but in the end they were only able to show £300,000 had passed that way.

That was bad enough, but the full story of the investigation and its repercussions was yet to come out. When it did, it showed a complete lack of co-operation between the Customs and the police. The success story which turned to ashes had begun on 26 June 1992 when the Customs were waiting as Brian Charrington landed in his private aircraft at Teesside Airport. Six months previously Customs officers had drilled into the lead ingots stored in the Stoke warehouse, and they believed Charrington was the organizer of the shipment.

At his home was £2 million in cash contaminated with traces of almost all major drugs. It is interesting that some of the notes had been passed through cash machines in the South of England in the previous fortnight; this gives an example of how quickly drug money can leave street level and end in the hands of top men. There were also details of a £4.5 million payment to a salesman known to be working with a Colombian cartel.

Charrington had been fancied as a major player since 1989. One of his runs had been to smuggle cannabis in beer crates with the aid of day-trippers to France. Drugs to the value of £500,000 were confiscated. In 1990 a Danish skipper convicted of trying to export £5 million of drugs from Denmark named Charrington as being implicated in the scheme. There was also a tale that he had been smuggling cocaine into Britain by using corrupt airport baggage-handlers to remove the bags containing the cocaine from the baggage conveyor and so thwart any investigation. It appears that members of the drug wing of the Number Two (North East) Regional Crime Squad had been working with Customs to prepare a case against him. Unfortunately, what appears not to have been mentioned is that quite apart from his being Target One, or Numero Uno as Gene Hackman playing 'Popeye' Doyle would have described him, Charrington was just about the Numero Uno police informant. The moment he was arrested the police went to his rescue; if need be they would give evidence in his defence. In fact this is not uncommon practice. For example, in January 1989 Detective Superintendent Martin Lundy was allowed to give evidence *in camera* on behalf of his protégé, supergrass Roy Garner.[10]

The Customs complained that far from producing major drug-related arrests Charrington had only implicated small-time if professional criminals. Gilbert Gray QC, the

[10] There has been considerable speculation as to the extent of Martin Lundy's involvement with his supergrasses. The extremely interesting Lundy saga is recounted from opposing points of view in A. Jennings, P. Lashmar and V. Simson, *Scotland Yard's Cocaine Connection*, and Martin Short's *Lundy*. He himself has written an article 'Bent or brilliant?' which appeared in the *News of the World*.

barrister for Charrington, asked for and was granted a meeting with Sir Nicholas Lyell, the Attorney General. Five weeks later, on 28 January 1993, all charges against Charrington were withdrawn by the Crown Prosecution Service; he and ten others were due to be committed for trial to the Crown Court. In their turn, the police complain that the bust of Charrington had pre-empted a major strike against a Colombian cartel.

In January 1994 the only person to be convicted for his part in the whole affair was Kassar, described by the trial judge, Mr Justice May, as 'not one of the principal organizers, but very much a middleman'. It is interesting to speculate on the sentences which would have been passed on the leaders. His solicitor complained that the case had been surrounded by secrecy and that the press had been deliberately gagged to prevent the truth being known. John Merry, who runs a news agency in Darlington, claims that a local Member of Parliament telephoned him urging him not to publicize the case. At the time of Kassar's trial Charrington was believed to be in Hong Kong. According to the *Observer*, one of the police officers involved in thwarting the Customs inquiry left the force in January 1993 and in the September drove to Spain with his wife, a serving police constable, in an £87,000 BMW registered to Charrington.[11]

Sometimes the Customs have to make do with just the seizure. Towards the end of 1993 friends and relations cheered as six men accused of one of the biggest drug-smuggling operations were cleared by a jury at Southwark

[11] The *Observer* was about the only newspaper to carry what would appear to be a major story. See David Rose and John Merry, 'Drugs Bust Victory Turned to Dust' in the *Observer*, 16 January 1994.

Crown Court. The allegation had been that they had smuggled 796kg cocaine worth £125 million into Britain aboard a 115-ft yacht, *Foxtrot V*, which docked at Durham Wharf, Charlton, South London in November 1992. The organization, said Anthony Glass for the prosecution, had 'taken months to plan, months of preparation, and vast expenditure'. *Foxtrot V* had been bought in the United States in 1992 and had been provisioned and fuelled before it was crewed to London, from where it sailed in October to a rendezvous off the Venezuelan coast. The cocaine, alleged Mr Glass, was air-dropped into the sea and collected by the boat which then returned to London.

At the end of a three-month trial which itself cost around £2 million, the five men who had been involved with equipping and the sixth who was said to have rented space to store the drugs were discharged. The man who had rented the space told the jury he was forced to do so at gunpoint by people who have never been caught. The other five said they did not know there were drugs on board. Three men who were named as being prime movers in the plot, including the financier, were never caught.

Sometimes they had to make do with nothing. In 1993 Customs officer Richard Holywell was jailed for nine months for breaching the Official Secrets Act by supplying information from Customs telexes which enabled a suspect to pull out of an alleged international drugs ring.

Unfortunately he had fallen in love with the suspect's 20-year-old daughter and came across a telex which said the suspected smuggler might return from Europe with drugs. The man's car number was listed. Holywell told the sister of the girl that her father was under suspicion.

The deaths of drug dealers continued to pile up. One of the earlier and more spectacular ones had been that of

Marty Johnstone, whose handless body had been found weighted and dumped in a flooded quarry at Ecclestone near Chorley, Lancashire in October 1989. Just about the only identifying mark was a charm worn around his neck with 'Good Luck' in Cantonese. He had been stabbed in the stomach and shot in the head; it took a considerable amount of talent before the police could issue an identikit of the face.

When it all came out, at a trial which at 123 days was then the second longest murder trial in Britain, the late Mr Johnstone was revealed to be a former leading member of an international drug syndicate. It had been run by New Zealander Alexander Sinclair, described unsurprisingly, in the time-honoured words of the judge, as 'ruthless and dangerous'. Johnstone had been found to have short-changed the worldwide syndicate and as a result had had to go. Mrs Justice Heilbron, who in her years at the Bar had defended, amongst many other celebrated criminals, George Kelly, the Cameo Murderer, and Jack Spot, sentenced Sinclair to life imprisonment with a recommendation that he serve not less than twenty years. It was said by the prosecution that he was worth £25 million, 'give or take a number or two'. He was also ordered to pay £1 million towards the prosecution costs, which were said to be at least £1.32 million. There were heavy sentences for other members of the organization including those who were only charged with, or convicted of, being involved with the drug side. One woman, described as the syndicate's banker, received thirteen years.

At the same time as the police were searching for the body of Gary Pettitt in Chorley there was news of two shootings in London. On Friday 28 May 1993, small-time dealer David Edwards fell foul of another dealer and was killed at his home in West Norwood, South London, with a single shot to the heart.

There were suggestions that the killing might be linked to the death of Chris 'Tuffy' Bourne, an illegal immigrant who died in a hail of fifteen bullets in a squat in Vassal Road, Brixton. He had been hit at least three times; ten bullets were found embedded in the wall behind him. His own revolver was later found by the police. Helped by the false passport racket, Mr Bourne was a frequent visitor to this country. He had been deported twice to Jamaica and was back in this country only because he had escaped from immigration officers at Birmingham airport in the February by vaulting a barrier and sprinting off towards the Bull Ring. Bourne's death was the second of the weekend.

In fact Bourne had been sentenced to two counts of life imprisonment in Jamaica. The sentence had been reduced to fifteen years on appeal, and he had been paroled in 1985. Despite his leap for freedom, the police knew where he was and had been keeping him under observation. The squat in Vassal Road was known to be a crack house, and one theory is that Bourne and colleagues met more resistance than they had anticipated when they turned up to warn the occupants off what they regarded as their turf. Bourne was a senior member of the Shower Posse and in Jamaica reprisals against their rivals the Spanglers were swift. One man was killed and dozens were injured.

One dealer from Leicester was fortunate to survive a row over crack proceeds. He was thrown fifty feet over the balcony of a block of flats in the Wessex Gardens estate off Westbourne Park Road in Paddington, but survived with multiple injuries.

Over the last five years the Yardies have established a substantial presence in the United Kingdom. Quite apart from their activities in Manchester, they have bases throughout London and every other big city, with the exception of those in the North-East of England and Scotland. 'They are ruthless killers, butchers – and in the United States they have even scared off the Mafia from their traditional trafficking grounds,' says one senior London officer.

The rewards are enormous. On every kilo of cocaine bought from Colombia there is around 800 per cent profit, something which when translated means billions of pounds a year.

The police now fear an even larger Yardie presence in the United Kingdom, and cite two grounds for this. The first is the disbandment of the specialist unit Operation Dalehouse on 'political' grounds. It is difficult to understand the reason for this move. The unit may not have smashed the Yardies, but it certainly made substantial inroads into their activities, and had almost completely disrupted the Spanish Town Posse with a total of 267 arrests. Moves were also made against other Kingston, Jamaica, gangs including the Shower Posse, the Spanglers and the Gulley men. Just as the defeat of Michael Manley's People's National Party in 1980, whom the Yardies had supported, led to their moving their operations into America, now the success of the People's National Party in March 1993 may have had the same effect. The People's National Party seems to be one of law and order, and it may try to exercise some control over the Yardies' presence in Jamaica which is discouraging tourism.

On 29 July 1993 the decomposed body of Craig Swann was found by a family mushroom-picking near Loch Tummel in Perthshire. He had been missing for over a year.

Swann had an engineering degree from Edinburgh and was studying languages at Southampton before going back to South America. He was not known for excessive drinking or going out with married women; he was, so his family said, a very ordinary bloke. On Sunday 9 August 1992, he went out for an evening in Edinburgh and never returned. A couple were later seen abandoning Swann's car in the driveway of a house in Ruchazie Road in the East End of Glasgow, scene of the Ice Cream Wars of a decade earlier. During the investigation into Swann's disappearance, the police learned that his working holidays in South America could have been covers for drug dealing. It was feared he was the subject of a contract killing by members of a South American cartel he had double-crossed.

A rather more curious killing took place in September 1993. It was that of Andrew Birchcroft, or Birjukove, who was shot in the Two Brewers at Perry Hill, Catford. Again it was a contract killing, but this time possibly with a slight difference. The style was the usual one. The killer, in black leathers, shot Birchcroft with a .22 automatic and then ran from the pub to a waiting motorcycle. The motive may have been the difference. Birchcroft had been told not to deal in drugs in the locality, and for some time it was suggested that the killing was a punishment for defying community wishes. Said one man who knew him:

This is a nice neighbourhood here – it's not North Peckham – and Andy was told not to bring cocaine into it. He ignored the warning and came back. It's not so much vigilantes as what you would call pest control. It's to keep the neighbourhood respectable.[12]

[12] Duncan Campbell in the *Guardian*, 16 September 1993.

Of course, that may be fanciful; it may just have been that another dealer wanted the territory. Seriously injured in the shooting was Bobby Campbell, the former St Mirren footballer. He had run the nearby Rutland Arms until it was temporarily closed by the brewers after complaints of drug dealing which Campbell had tried unsuccessfully to prevent.

It took some time before the traditional London criminal ventured into drugs. At one time it was regarded, along with living off immoral earnings, as something which lowered a man's status in the criminal hierarchy, but one by one the old villains turned to the more lucrative and safer – than running across a pavement towards a Securicor van where armed police might be waiting – pastime of drugs.

And down they went one by one. Joe Wilkins, nephew of the redoubtable Bert, and a prince if not King of the Soho escort trade of the 1970s; Train Robber Charlie Wilson, killed in Spain by a contract killer; Train Robber Tommy Wisbey along with his partner, fellow Train Robber James Hussey, were also sentenced to long terms of imprisonment, as was a man whom many had thought to be a potential King of the Underworld after the downfall of the Krays, Mickey Ishmael.

Others thought Ishmael didn't really have the luck necessary to go right to the top. His seemed to run in increasingly short bursts. Ishmael, who had had troubles as a bank robber, found life as a drug dealer not that much easier.[13] On 1 March 1988 he was arrested for possession of drugs. He had been planning to distribute amphetamines. There had been a round-the-clock surveillance on him and he was seen to go to a house near his home. Some sixty-five

---

[13] See J. Morton, *Gangland*, p.205.

officers were involved in the raid and Ishmael claimed he was being fitted up. He received thirteen years for conspiracy; other men in the plot received up to seven years.

Not only – as Charlie Wilson found – was the South of Spain not completely safe, nor was the South West of Ireland. It was there that English criminal Charles Brooke Pickard was abducted, either in a drug deal which went badly wrong (more popular theory) or because he was an informer (he had received a surprisingly light sentence after a eulogy by a Garda official).

He lived at Castlecove between Sneem and Caherdaniel in South Kerry. In 1988 he had been arrested by detectives in Dun Laoghaire after coming to Dublin to collect a £4,000 debt from a man named Marty, who in turn said another owed him the sum. Pickard, armed with a .22 revolver, went looking for the second man. He had served eighteen months in 1972 for drugs and firearm offences, and in 1976 five years for drug supplying.

It was thought that he might have fallen foul of a Mr Big who had masterminded a major shipment of Moroccan hashish which had landed by Derrynane. A man and woman were jailed for that operation, but the mastermind was never arrested.

On 26 April 1991 Pickard was seen being bundled into his van by balaclavaed men. On 16 May this was found burned out in the Kerry mountains. Penny Pickard, his wife, denied any involvement in drugs. Since his suspended sentence Charles had, she said, been 'born again'.

On 17 January 1994 the Customs had a spectacular seizure. Into Manchester Airport along with a consignment of flowers from Amsterdam came six boxes containing 250kg of cocaine. The drugs had come from Cali, which has replaced Medellin as the powerbase of the Colombian cartels. The Customs officers knew of this; they had been involved in an elaborate four-month-long sting operation in which two of their number had travelled to Colombia posing as wealthy buyers. At one stage in the operation they had been obliged to produce £2 million, funded by the Greater Manchester Police, to prove their *bona fides*. Two men were arrested and Pat Cadogan, an assistant chief investigator, claimed:

> We have broken an attempt by a major cocaine importer to set up a distribution network in the North West of England. We must have destroyed their credibility in the UK and a seizure of this kind must be a major setback for them.

The next day it was reported that tainted heroin had been the source of a series of deaths in and around Bristol. It transpired that the heroin was not tainted, merely 60 per cent pure and too strong for the bloodstream. Heroin is normally 'cut' with chalk or bicarbonate of soda to around 35 per cent purity, otherwise the lungs of all but the most hardened drug users are damaged. Breathing stops very quickly.

A similar problem occurred in the King's Cross area of London between the 11th and 19th of March, when seven addicts died in nine days. King's Cross, once the fiefdom of Alf White in the 1930s and 1940s, has passed through a number of controlling hands, including in the 1980s a group of Scotsmen, before becoming a dealers' paradise in the 1990s. Now King's Cross is in the hands of the Italians and the Jamaicans. The problem, as in Bristol, was not necessarily impure heroin, rather a too pure strain.

July 1993 saw a police crackdown on the area which had

been the venue for a quarter of all the crack-cocaine seizures in 1992. The crackdown had resulted in the closure of some 24-hour take-aways and mini-cab firms following under-cover surveillance and secret filming of dealers. One film showed the bizarre sight of a young man pulling (with some effort) a bag of drugs from his rectum, washing the package, storing it in his mouth and then transferring it by seeming to kiss a young girl. Until then dealers had been relying on the Police and Criminal Evidence Act 1984 which prevented officers forcing open a suspect's mouth. As a result 60-milligram balls of heroin (£10) or the rather more expensive 90-milligram balls of crack cocaine (£25) could be wrapped in clingfilm and kept in the mouth. Sentences of up to nine years were handed out. No longer, said Commander John Townsend, was it possible for a drug dealer to make £700,000 a year in the area.[14]

Dealing at street level might still be strictly small-time, with a bag of heroin going for £50 to be cut into eleven portions: one for the buyer and the rest to be sold at £10 a time. In January 1994 a take-away in the King's Cross area was doing a hot trade if not in butties at least in DIY kits of spoon, syringe and candle for £1.75. A local Salvation Army worker did not appear to think much had changed after the purge:

King's Cross is definitely a Yardie enterprise. Its organized crime and violence constantly erupts be-tween ethnic groups, to determine who's actually running the place. The Afro-Caribbeans will disap-

[14] Speaking at the Association of Police Officers' conference in Birmingham, 7 July 1993. Nick Cohen, 'Purity that kills in the darkness', in the *Independent on Sunday*, 11 April 1993.

pear for a while. And then all hell will be let loose one night and you'll find it's the Italians who are being chased through the streets by a new gang wielding everything from guns to crowbars.[15]

A habit in the area costs £150 a day which, added up, amounts to between a half and three-quarters of a million for a dealer – profit figures more or less identical to those before the purge.

Drug dealing continues at a high level in Clapham. In October, the local community officer Patrick Dunne was shot dead as he went to investigate a burglary in the neighbourhood. A number of men were arrested for the killing, but after consideration the Crown Prosecution Service decided there was not sufficient evidence to seek a committal to the Crown Court for trial.

In January 1994 the Customs and Excise released the figures for drug hauls during the previous year. Heroin seizures had risen slightly over the previous year to around 570kg, enough for five doses for every man, woman and child in the country. On the other hand cocaine seizures had fallen substantially from over 2,000kg to under 1,000kg. This was because in 1992 there had been two seizures of huge consignments of 900kg and 800kg respectively. Cannabis had risen to a record 53 tons and amphetamines had gone from rather under 20kg in 1989 to over 500kg in 1993. It was a similar story with Ecstasy. The amount seized in 1989 had been negligible; now nearly 600kg had been confiscated.

Douglas Tweddle, the Chief Investigation Officer for

[15] Trudy Culross in 'Heart of Darkness', in *Midweek*, 20/24 January 1993.

Customs, said he found the rise, particularly in synthetic drugs, very worrying. Most Ecstasy came from mainland Europe, with 90 per cent manufactured in the Netherlands which was also a major source of cocaine. For heroin, the old-fashioned overland Balkan route from the heroin-producing areas on the Afghanistan and Pakistan borders was still popular. One seizure had been of £20 million found in a lorry on the M1.

Since the Spanish authorities have tightened up the Morocco-Algeciras route for cocaine coming to Europe, direct import to the United Kingdom has become more popular. Another reason is that the Californian market has been saturated and the Colombian cartels are looking for new growth areas. Drugs have been floated and boated in to England, with the Channel Islands as a popular route. Once in, it is reasonably easy to remit consignments to the rest of Europe.

Postscript

Perhaps it would not go amiss to look at some of the theories criminologists have, and have had, about the causes and cures for crime and why people join gangs.

An immediate problem arises. Just who or what is a criminologist? Some would say that those who write true-crime books which show that Major Armstrong could not possibly have murdered his wife and tried to poison a rival solicitor are criminologists. Those who teach social science and policy courses at Universities where degrees in criminology are handed out would disagree. Their interest would be in why the Major turned to crime, and whether he was influenced by the fact that a neighbouring solicitor Mr Greenwood had been tried and acquitted of the murder of his wife a few months earlier.[1] For the purposes of this

[1] In 1922 Major Herbert Armstrong, a solicitor at Hay-on-Wye on the Welsh borders, was convicted of the murder of his wife. His practice was not doing well and there is evidence he had tried to poison another local solicitor. Nevertheless the evidence was not strong, and Sir Henry Curtis-Bennett who defended Armstrong

short essay I would adopt the attitude of the second group.

There have been theories about the causes of crime since crime itself existed but, to try to keep matters in a time frame, I propose to start with the theories from the eighteenth century onwards. Necessarily they will be in a potted version, and it may be that I shall be accused of oversimplifying, and possibly mocking, what appeared at the time to be perfectly good theories.

In defence of the over-simplification, sometimes it appears that sociologists equate incomprehensibility to all but their own inner circle with success. I hope the only time a sentence such as this appears in this book is as follows:

> With respect to the study of crime ethno-methodology, like symbolic interactionism, treats crime as a matter of definition or, more precisely, as a product of members'

cont'd

believed he would obtain a not guilty verdict. The Court of Appeal was dismissive, with Mr Justice Avory remarking, 'To find a packet of three and a half grains of arsenic in a solicitor's pocket is surely rare'. An application for a retrial, following the disclosure of the discussions by a juryman to a newspaper, was rejected. Armstrong, who continued to protest his innocence, was hanged by John Ellis who himself later committed suicide. Harold Greenwood, who had a practice a few miles away, had been acquitted in November 1920 of the murder of his wife. Greenwood, who was by no means popular with the locals, was said to have poisoned her. He was acquitted principally on the evidence of his daughter who said she had drunk from the same bottle of wine with which Greenwood was said to have tampered. Greenwood, ruined by the case, died a few years later. In an interview he commented, 'I am the victim of gossip, of village scandal and if you know Welsh village life you know what that means.' There are a number of accounts of the two cases including John Rowland's *Murder Revisited*.

methods of practical reasoning. However, unlike symbolic interactionism ethno-methodology is concerned with the situated production and use of these definitions rather than treating these as given in the fabric of local settings.[2]

Quite.

So far as the mocking is concerned, well, most of the theories proffered over the last 150 years have subsequently been discredited by a rival theorist either with cause or simply because he, or occasionally she, wished to gain fleeting attention and propagation for the theory which he held at one time and was then voluntarily or compulsorily forced to abandon. Or, from time to time, they changed their social or political stance and with it the theory.

The Italian, Cesare Beccari, can be credited with the creation of what is known as the classical school of criminology. In 1764 in the so-called Age of Enlightenment – a time which housed such thinkers as Voltaire and Jeremy Bentham and such charlatans as Casanova – at the age of 26, Beccari wrote *Of Crime and Punishment* in which he argued that a person consciously chose to adopt an unacceptable or illegal pattern of behaviour. 'Invisible' causes such as poverty had nothing to do with the exercise of the man's free will. It was a belief which held sway for a century and which still has its adherents today.

Another early theory was that of Quetelet, who argued that crime was cyclical and based on the phases of the moon. The thinking behind this was the old lunatic theory – the person who loses the ability to act rationally during phases of the moon – but I have always thought Quetelet

[2] S. Hester and P. Eglin (1992), *A Sociology of Crime*.

had something which can be applied to modern crime even if not in quite the same way. Professional crime is, and always will be, cyclical. Take a calendar year. After Christmas there is the need to earn money and pay off the debts incurred. The nights are dark; it is the time for the housebreaker. When spring comes there is a fall-off of nocturnal crime as the nights get lighter. As summer follows spring criminals, pickpockets (except those who stay behind to deal with the foreign tourists here), shoplifters and hotel thieves transfer their activities to the Continent as tourists go abroad stuffed with travellers' cheques and currency. When the summer holidays are over, the shoplifters are back in town and with dark nights coming on burglary is that much easier. November and early December is the time for lorry hi-jacking and warehouse breaking. For a start, they are full with goods for Christmas and money has to be earned for presents. By the second week in December there is a fall-off. No one wants to be in custody over the holiday and the cry becomes, 'I must have bail for Christmas to be with the kids.' It is rarely pointed out that all they will see of their father is his backside disappearing towards the pub. After Christmas, there is the need . . . Simplistic, perhaps, but probably with a grain of truth. I have to admit, however, that through a lack of statistics or willpower or both, I have never conducted anything more than what is rather grandly called empirical research, which more simply means my own experiences, to back up my modest effort to support Quetelet. However, the theory did receive some support on 30 December 1993. Firearms were carried in six separate London robberies. £1,300 went in a raid on the Leeds Building Society in Kingston, a robber was thwarted at the National Westminster Bank in Battersea and another fled empty-handed from the branch in Baker Street. Two men robbed the Leeds Building Society in the Walworth Road; a man waved a pump-action shotgun in a failed robbery at a sub-post office in the Hertford Road, Enfield, and an armed robber netted £92.75 from a betting shop in the Harrow Road.

One of the earliest members, indeed a founding father, of the so-called and rival positivist school of criminology was another Italian, Caesare Lombroso, in the 1870s. He made a study of criminal types amongst prisoners by taking skull measurements and other physical details. His theory that cranial features pointed to a criminal mentality, and that women with excessive pubic hair were more likely to become prostitutes than those less well endowed, held fashion for some years until it was discovered that the skulls of officer cadets at Sandhurst were the same as those of Lombroso's prisoners. I have never seen whether a study of undergraduates at Girton was undertaken to disprove his other theory.

Even after his basic theory was discredited, Lombroso spawned a whole series of arguments as to the causes of crime based on the human body. There were suggestions that twins were more susceptible to crime than single children, and that if one twin became a criminal his sibling was sure to follow. There were other arguments in the 1920s, that certain physical types divided into mesomorphs (strong and lean), endomorphs (short and fat) and ecto-morphs (tall and skinny) were predisposed to certain forms of crime. A parallel research produced a similar theory. A study of over 4,000 criminals produced the argument that leptosomes (long and skinny) committed petty theft and frauds, athletic types (well developed) were violence-prone, pyknics (small, round and fat) were predisposed to fraud and possibly violence, whilst dysplastics (those with mixed characteristics) favoured sex offences. Another later study by Sheldon and Eleanor Gleuck in the 1950s, of some five hundred delinquent boys matched against a similar number of non-delinquents, suggested that:

> [it] is quite apparent that physique alone does not adequately explain delinquent behaviour, it is never-theless clear that in conjunction with other forces, it does bear a relationship to delinquency.[3]

This was one of the theories which was promptly walloped by rivals. The Gleucks were said to have developed 'a new Phrenology in which the bumps of the buttocks take the place of the bumps on the skull'.

But even now the great man is not forgotten. In the 1970s came the revival of the theory, tracing directly back to Lombroso, that women are more likely to commit crime when suffering from pre-menstrual tension.

In the 1920s in Chicago, attention shifted to the relation between urban growth and urban problems. As a result a good deal of research was done by members of what became known as the Chicago School. Their findings included the confirmation that there was more crime in the inner city than in the suburbs. It was also found to be the case that this level of delinquency existed no matter how much the population shifted with an influx of immigrants. Trans-posed to London, the theory works reasonably well. Certainly in the past Soho could be deemed to be the centre and there, over the years, there has been a high level of criminal behaviour whether the English, French, Corsicans, Maltese, Cypriots or Italians have been the

---

[3] Sheldon and Eleanor Gleuck (1956), *Physique and Delinquency*.

ascendent nationality. As a general proposition, if the city is divided into circles those furthest from the centre have the least level of crime, although more crime occurs in outer circles such as Brixton, Hackney and Tottenham than in Highgate and the rest of North London. The Chicago School coined a phrase, differential association, the theory of which dated back a good seventy years. The reasoning goes along the lines that criminal behaviour is explicable not by the needs and values of the community but is learned by individuals in small groups. This often criticized argument would go a long way to dismember the next – and superficially most attractive – theory, which is that poverty breeds crime.

There is certainly evidence that when times are hard people, and women in particular, will turn to what is seen as petty crime such as shoplifting and prostitution in order to obtain food and to pay off the debt collector. There are plenty of studies which will show that poverty is an influence in criminality. But it is impossible to say that poverty is anything more than a contributing factor. One of the problems is the lack of a clear definition. Is the person truly poor or does he merely see himself as poor? If it were otherwise, why would all poor people not commit crime? There is a theory that a criminal's memoir is one of the most worthwhile studies of crime. It is here that the sociologist tends to exercise a certain amount of tunnel vision. A criminal's memoir is more likely than not to be full of self-justification. Francis Fraser, once one of London's leading criminals, wrote that his family was dirt-poor and that poverty had been the overriding reason for his career; yet Leonard Read, the police officer who was largely responsible for the downfall of the Kray empire, wrote in his memoir of his own poverty-ridden childhood:

People say the Krays had a deprived upbringing and that this could have turned them to crime, but I reckon there was more money coming into their house than into ours.[4]

It is also interesting to note that of Fraser's brother and sisters, one became a nurse and emigrated to America, where she rose high in her profession, and his brother was in work all his adult life and has no convictions.

The poverty argument supports what is called the strain theory developed by American sociologists in the 1960s. The argument runs that both individuals and whole groups find their efforts to attain desired success in society to be blocked. As a defensive mechanism these groups develop a sub-culture which has a different series of values from that of the rest of society, and it is amongst these groups that the greatest amount of crime occurs. A classic example of this is in Moss Side, Manchester today where:

More than a quarter of the population is long-term unemployed: it is not unusual to find families with three generations who have never worked. The crisis is worst amongst young blacks, up to 80% of whom are unemployed. Overall, more than half the children in Moss Side schools face the certain knowledge that they will not find work when they leave school.

'It is very difficult to appeal to young people on a moral and intellectual basis,' says Councillor Iqbar Seram, 'when they feel they have no stake in society.'

In these circumstances it is not hard to understand the attraction of joining a gang and dealing in drugs.

[4] L. Read and J. Morton, *Nipper*, p.1.

Where else can you find instant status, glamour, excitement and easy money?[5]

However, critics of the poverty variant of the strain theory suggest that 'it would be prudent to assume a low causal role for poverty specifically'.[6]

As the century went by there developed another theory, that of *anomie*, which originated in the last century with the French sociologist Emile Durkheim and was developed by the American Robert Merton. In essence it runs that a state of lawlessness in society or in an individual is caused by loss of belief and purpose. It is easy to see how it overlaps with the strain theory. According to Merton, rebellion is the last of the reactions resulting from *anomie*, and this includes the desire to substitute new goals in place of the conventional ones. The street gang, or for that matter the freedom fighter, would fit neatly into this category.

In essence it is not too different from the Marxist theory which was propagated in a slightly different form in the 1960s by the so-called radical criminologists. The Marxist theory sees the underclass as victim. The argument goes that the implementation of pure Marxism would overthrow capitalism which in turn, since there would be the reality of the promised land (to mix religions and cultures), would mean there would be no need for crime. In the meanwhile criminal activities (as defined by a capitalist society designed to keep the poor under the rich man's heel) such as theft can be related to the economic struggle, whilst prostitution is related to the weak economic and political status of women. The thoughts of the radical criminologists have shifted considerably since their heyday thirty years ago.

[5] *The Sunday Times*, 7 March 1993.
[6] Dermot Walsh in *A Dictionary of Criminology*.

After the death of the two-year-old James Bulger in Bootle in early 1993, and the conviction of two eleven-year-olds for his death later that year, there was an outcry against video violence which, the trial judge said, might have led at least one of the boys to commit the crime. It was not a new theory. Similar ones have regularly been advanced about books. 'Is this the sort of book you would wish your wife and maidservant to read?' asked Mervyn Griffiths-Jones, prosecuting in the Lady Chatterley case. The implication was clear. The book would so influence them that a number of women of hitherto impeccable morals would abandon an afternoon's tennis on a Thursday and indulge in more unseemly sport with the part-time gardener. The behaviour of the maidservants would no doubt be even more appalling.

Indeed, this has been the case whenever there has been a copying of behaviour in a book or film. The film director Stanley Kubrick withdrew *A Clockwork Orange* from distribution after reports that young men had emulated the film's anti-hero and had set fire to tramps. There were allegations that the French film *Je crache sur votre tombeau* and the video nasty *Driller Killer* had led to similar antisocial behaviour. In 1993 cuts were made to a Walt Disney production when it was found that young men had been injured and in one case killed when playing a game of chicken, lying in the road and letting lorries drive over them. The complaint was nothing new. It had been made about the 1953 James Dean film *Rebel Without a Cause*. Perhaps it is just as well that few young people read the Bible nowadays, or Scout camps might be littered with tent-peg murderers.[7]

---

[7] I cannot claim this thought is an original one. The argument was advanced by Irving Wallace in his novel *The Seven Minutes*.

Indeed, probably what can be seen from this brief review is that many of the theories have attractive aspects but no single one can satisfactorily explain why one person or group of people commits crime whilst others in a similar position do not. If they did, perhaps there would be no further need for criminologists to agonize over the causes of crime. The likelihood is that there are a number of combinations of circumstances, both physical and environmental, which will dispose a person to crime, but that not all will succumb.

But what of the punishment meted out to criminals? Surely there is some way – preferably imprisonment is today's thought – which will prevent re-offending and stop young men and women in the tracks of their chosen careers. On the other hand, do we not read in the newspapers on a weekly if not daily basis about the fact that probation costs less, that electronic tagging and custodial sentences don't work? Wasn't there a scheme in America where young criminals were taken to see men serving forty-five years who explained in simple terms and gestures what life in prison would be like for them? Can't people be made to stop committing offences? Sadly not. It is probably appropriate to quote from a handbook given to magistrates and judges:

The almost invariable conclusion of the large amount of research which has been undertaken (in various Western countries) is that it is hard to show any effect that one type of sentence is more likely than any other to reduce the likelihood of re-offending, which is high for all. Similarly, longer periods of custody or particular institutional regimes do not seem to have a significant effect. Studies comparing the reconviction rates of offenders given community service orders with

427

those given custodial sentences have shown little difference.[8]

Even in the last two years since *Gangland* was published times have changed, as indeed crimes have over the century. Gone are the days of the angler or thief who used a rod and hook to steal items from the inside ledges of windows left open by householders. Gone too are the Oysters, society women who would wear stolen jewels as advertisements for the receivers for whom they worked. Now goods are knocked out in the often less salubrious circumstances of the car boot sale where no questions are asked of the vendors and the sales themselves provide the opportunity for theft and protection racketeers who offer 'security services'. Modern technology has defeated, and a lack of willingness to serve a criminal apprenticeship has almost completely eliminated, the safebreaker. Because of social attitudes and legislation, the baby farmer has gone and the back-street abortionist has become almost obsolete. There are no great families such as the Messina brothers who control prostitutes, although there are still echoes of the white slavers in the men who run agencies for girls of little talent and less sense who wish to become members of a continental dance troupe and find it is prostitution under another name. There are, of course, still pimps and one recent, old-fashioned case was that of Kimberley Johnson-Laird and his 20-year-old pregnant and prostitute wife, Melissa, who ran a nation-wide team of prostitutes from the unlikely haven of Bury St Edmunds. He had set up a stable of fifty girls across the country from Weymouth in Dorset to Bradford, masking their activities with

[8] *The Sentence of the Court*, HMSO, p.7.

stripogram and kissogram assignments. He was jailed for eighteen months on 16 July 1993 for living off immoral earnings. Melissa received three months' youth custody. Johnson-Laird had run a similar operation out of Peterborough in 1989.

Now, as often as not, there are women running one or two of their girlfriends as prostitutes. This is not completely new. In the first case of its kind known to the Metropolitan Police on 2 June 1939, Ida Parry of 46 Old Compton Street, then aged 61, had been controlling Doris Booker who lived with her. The police arrived just as Miss Booker returned with a client who had agreed to pay her 7/6d.

The Marlborough Street magistrate, E.C.P. Boyd, sentenced her to four months' imprisonment. She had been a prostitute herself for many years and was described in reports as a 'vile and violent creature'. The women lived together at the address in the names of John and Doris Parry. 'She just lives here with me and we muck in. I pay for the food and I take her to the pictures now and again. If she wants a shilling I give it to her and if I want one she gives it to me,' said Ida Parry, but the magistrate did not believe her. The Home Office papers say it was a pity she couldn't have been deported.

The great days of the jewel thief who would wait patiently for hour after hour to steal a film star's jewels when she went on set or to a première are long over.

On the other hand, at the turn of the century there was no such thing as the motor-car theft, nor the use of the motor-car in crime. Without cars the smash-and-grab raid was unknown until the Bonnot gang in France began the practice in the early 1900s. Now we have a great increase in white collar crime – or was it always present but undetected or unremarked? Certainly there was no such thing as credit-card fraud until the 1970s, and until the chequebook became a universal prop for the handbag or inner pocket, little of that either. Credit-card frauds cost around £165 million in 1993 or, put more graphically, £5 a second. Over 1.8 million of the nation's 80 million cards went missing. But, in 1925, according to the Official Receiver, long-firm fraudsmen were getting away with between £5 and £6 million annually.[9] Nor could there have been any such thing as a British Telecom swindle. On 8 February 1994 four members of a gang, Nisar Batha, Talat Kayeni, Shoiab Mahammed and Javeid Iqbal, who had helped criminal organizations in France and the Netherlands make calls which could not be traced, were jailed for up to two years. They had rented properties in false names and then asked BT to install facilities allowing conference calls. The calls mainly went to Colombia and Pakistan. BT lost just under £448,000. It was made clear that the British end of the scam had no idea of the nature of the calls to these countries. It is an example, however, of the growth of Asian-orientated crime in Britain.

There have been other new crimes, from the one-off type run by squatters who demand £1,000 to leave a house rather than force the owner to go through the costly and time-consuming process of the civil courts.

A new form of theft which has grown up in the 1990s is that of mobile phones and the associated fraudulent use of registered users' air time. Over 12,000 mobile phones are stolen monthly. In some parts of London cars are attacked whilst standing at traffic lights or in traffic jams by youths on roller-blades. The car-jack (the forcible removal at gun

[9] Philip Knightley, 'Gang Warfare: How to thaw the freeze', in *King*, November 1956.

or knife point) of the car from its owner has flown over from across the Atlantic. On Friday 28 January 1994, the body of accountant Grant Price was found on a deserted beach at Lee-on-Solent, Hampshire. It is thought he had been abducted at a car park in Gosport on Saturday 22 January by men who wished to steal his car. Two hours earlier an electronics student had been stabbed in nearby Fareham, in another apparent attempted car-jack.

An interesting variation on an earlier type of crime has reappeared. In January 1994 a motorist stopped to assist an apparently injured man near the centre of Plymouth, having been flagged down by a youth who pointed to the motionless figure. No sooner was he out of his car than he was attacked by a gang of up to eleven youths who beat him with a stick and broke his arm when he did not hand over his money. Warning motorists to be on the look-out for this trap, the police commented that this was a 'new kind of street robbery'. But the trick is not really a new one; it has merely come round again. It was popular in France in the 1930s, and was played by Alain Delon and Jean-Paul Belmondo in the film *Borsalino*. Perhaps someone in Plymouth had hired a video of the film?

It is probable that the police in Britain and Europe did not realize the full extent of Hell's Angels involvement in drug dealing and organized crime until the beginning of the 1980s. Until then the height of the ambition of these bearded, tattooed and dirty outlaw bikers was thought to have been the public performance of oral sex with an old-age pensioner. But, even before then the British chapters of the Hell's Angels had amassed a fairly impressive record of violence, rape and killings over the twenty or so years of their existence. Now in Germany the movement, with its involvement in prostitution, arms running, drugs protection and extortion, has been declared illegal. Here they were recognized as a mini-Mafia, one of the major controllers of the soft-drug trade and, it was believed, controlling two factories manufacturing amphetamines.

The movement appears to have started in Fontana, a depressingly dull steel town fifty miles from Los Angeles, in the late 1940s. The Angels there liked to refer to themselves as the One Per Cent – something which indicated that whilst 99 per cent of motorcyclists in the States were well-mannered and well-meaning, in no way did this squeaky-clean tag refer to them.

By the late 1960s when they rode into public and press view, the London chapters of the Angels would have two or three satellite chapters in cities such as Birmingham, Manchester and Sheffield, and in October 1970 two massed and augmented gangs had met on Chelsea Bridge to determine who ran London. Ranged on one side were the Essex and Chelsea Nomads, and on the other the Road Rats whose tag team partners were the Windsor Angels and the Jokers. For over a decade the Windsor Angels saw themselves as the kings of the English chapters. Whilst others wore red and white insignia, they wore black on white death's-head patches.

It was not the only power struggle amongst rival Angels. A month later in November 1971, Kenneth Sparkes was detained for five years after being found guilty of causing an affray in which Stan Megraw, who headed the Scorpios in a battle with the Windsors, died.

Estimates of the strength of the Angels varied wildly, with Gerard Kemp reporting the next year that there were nine chapters in Britain.[10] A year earlier it had been thought that

---

[10] Gerard Kemp, 'Inside the Mind of an Angel', *Sunday Telegraph*, 9 April 1972.

there were chapters in up to forty British towns, but the press and public has long been confused over the difference between the pure Hell's Angel – if that is not an oxymoron – and the simple outlaw biker. What everyone did agree upon was that under whichever jacket they rode, they were evil, loutish, raping, pillaging monsters. This was an image the Angels of the time did their best to cultivate. When in March 1972 the allegations of an Army nurse that she had been raped by up to sixteen Hell's Angels, members of the Wessex Free Wheelers, in a candle-lit garage in Aldershot, failed to convince a jury, the Angels were reported as saying they were going to have a 'gang-bang celebration tonight'. Asked if the acquittal would stand them in good stead with other Angels, their spokesman said:

> It will certainly stand us in good class. We'll be known as a classy gang by other chapters. Our status has gone up as a result of this case because no other Hell's Angels have been to court for something like this and been cleared. We have never had any trouble finding birds. When birds hear there are Angels in town, they come flocking out of interest. But now some parents may lock up their daughters. But we'll still get birds.[11]

It was at about that time the Angels moved into the protection game here, albeit on a very small scale – a move which would be repeated ten to fifteen years later with more skill and success by the football gangs such as The Firm of West Ham. On 29 August 1972 at the Weeley Pop Festival near Clacton in Essex, the organizers paid seven Angels £4 each for 'security work'. The previous year the local Round

[11] *Guardian*, 23 March 1973.

Table which organized an annual event for charity had run a Donkey Derby. This year they had been more ambitious, but the money given to the security Angels was not well spent. Other Angels leaped on to the platform, elbowed off a pop group and announced over the microphone, 'We're in charge here.' Fighting broke out and the 130-strong group of Angels armed with knives, chains and shotguns battled with local security men who were themselves armed with sledgehammers and mallets. By the time the Angels were removed, three hundred people had to be treated for minor injuries and another twenty were in hospital.

Retribution from the local magistrates was swift. Two days later thirty-nine Angels, including a former policeman who had, it was said, become their legal adviser, appeared charged with possessing offensive weapons and using threatening behaviour. All were found guilty. Three disappeared for six months, three were remanded in custody for reports and the rest were fined between £25 and £35 each. The confiscated weapons disappeared into the Essex police museum.

In 1973 the Angels, following American tradition, gathered for an Easter Bank Holiday run from Birmingham to the West Country. Then it was feared that there would be a similar run for the August Bank Holiday. Again the spectre not only of damage to property but of mass rape was floated in the press.[12] On balance the turmoil did not materialize, although the Hell's Angels battled it out with some black youths (to whom the organization would traditionally have had some antipathy) at Ramsgate. But it was all pretty small beer and only one man was arrested.

But there were warnings that the Angels were trying to become something more than just wild men:

[12] *People*, August 1973.

The only future they see is with the club [The London Chapter]. They dream of making the big time through the club 'like in the States'. There's a scheme to organize pop concerts and make money that way, like in the States. There's a plan to move into drug dealing in a big way, like in the States. Above all else, they want a united Hell's Angels Chapter throughout the country, like in the States. Nine months ago an attempted merger failed. But they still hope that they can get together with the only other clubs they respect, the West Coasters, the Windsors, the Cotswolds and the Roadrats.[13]

Two years later the Wessex branch were again in trouble; they may not have been organizing a pop concert, rather the reverse. A group set upon the Troggs pop group who were playing at a dance at Farnborough Technical College. Two of the Angels seized the carpet on which the group was standing and 'literally pulled the rug from underneath them', said the prosecutor happily. The leader received four years' imprisonment. The same year and the next, Angels battled it out with rivals and the police at motorcycle meetings at Silverstone. Hell's Angels were again active at Silverstone in 1986, when they rioted at the Motorcycle Grand Prix meeting.

But, seemingly, the pinnacle of Angel violent activity occurred with the battle of Cookham Dean on 18 September 1983 when there was yet another so-called peace conference ostensibly to celebrate twenty years of the Angels in Britain. It seems that, at the time, the All England Hell's Angels – divided into seven chapters, each

[13] William Cran in *The Listener*, 12 July 1973.

with 10–15 members – were under pressure from chapters in the United States who thought they were not sufficiently strong and organized to deal with the drug trade. The Chapter was looking for a showdown amongst unruly minor chapters such as the Slaves, the Rats and the Mojos. There had been troubles for the Chapter over the past few years. In 1979, for example, the All England – aided by two Americans and two Dutch Angels – had dealt severely with a group of fifteen Windsors sleeping off a booze-and-drug jag in a car park near Brockenhurst, whilst in 1983 the Hell's Angels North Carolina had had a conference with the All England Chapter to discuss the difficulties they were facing. In theory, the idea of the meeting that September had been the drawing up of boundaries with the Windsor Chapter, whose President had been imprisoned for plotting the assassination of a rival, Richard Sharman – he was shot three times, once in the head, but survived. Sharman had reportedly refused to take part in the so-called peace talks. It indicated that the stronger Angel Chapters were hoping for more discipline between the chapters. With their quasi-company structure, there had never been any doubt that in an extra-curricular way there was discipline in the chapters themselves.

The troubles at the two-day meeting, which had until the Sunday been relatively well-behaved, broke out between the Rats and the Slaves when a woman was staked out and, it was said, sexually abused. Another cause of the fighting was that some Angels objected to being photographed in their colours. Now the Road Rats and Satan's Slaves from Exeter fought with axes and knives. The newspapers reported that two, Colin 'Cowboy' Hunting and Michael 'Ozzie' Harrison, were dead, and four were 'horribly wounded'. The police arrested fifty-one others.

Ozzie's funeral took place at St Agatha's Catholic Church in Kingston, attended by four hundred bikers including some from Germany. Then it was on to Kingston to bury Harrison, where girls were reported to be clawing lumps of soil out of the ground to fill the grave before six Angels took over the job. Threats of retribution was fairly swift, even if they did not materialize. The Road Rats wrote to the Slaves saying they would be making the 200-mile trip to the West Country over the Easter weekend. A week before, 100 armed police in riot gear had broken up fighting at Cheddar Gorge between the Rogues from High Wycombe, the Slough Motorcycle Club and the Griffins from Coventry on one side, and the Chosen Few from Devon and the Dark Horses from Wiltshire on the other. Again the actual cause of the problem seems to have been over women attached to the chapters rather than a territorial feud.

Retribution by the courts was a little longer in coming. In December 1984, by which time charges against two Slaves over the deaths had been dropped, John Connolly received a sentence of eight years for riot.[14] As for the allegations of sexual indecency, the girl refused to make any complaint and at the time of the trial was believed to be living with the Windsors (the chapter as opposed to the family) in Slough.

There have been continual sporadic outbreaks of violence between Angels and other outlaw bikers. In May 1988 Stephen 'the Rabbi' Brookes, a member of the Pagan Outlaw bikers from Warwickshire was shot dead.

Meanwhile, if there was any doubt that the Angels had moved into the propery market Mrs Patricia McSorley,

[14] In 1975 he had been convicted of an affray when the Road Rats were refused entry to a club in Barry, Wales. A petrol bomb had been thrown and the club manager received a fractured skull. The manager's son was set alight.

who lived in Maidenhead Road, Slough, was swiftly dis-abused of the idea. With the help of a mortgage swindle – in which two Angels Alan Kraft and Graham Geard who had posed as well-paid executives of a Watford company and who were sentenced to eighteen months' imprisonment each – the Angels now had a club-house.[15] They had put down £4,000 on the property and obtained a 95 per cent mortgage. The house now included a dormitory, juke-box and pool table. The McSorleys had the misfortune to live next door. When in December 1987 she sued Kraft and Geard for damages she claimed that the Angels subjected her to a reign of terror. Angels, she said, had had all-night drunken parties, lined up and exposed themselves to her, banged on her walls thoughout the night, called at 3 a.m. supposedly to borrow spray to drive flies from the body of a murdered Angel, and removed bricks from the wall which led into her attic. She believed that whilst she was out, Angels had got in through the unbricked attic and slept in her bed. The parties had become worse when Angel John Mikkleson died in police custody on 16 July 1985.[16]

---

[15] It was reduced on appeal to nine months, of which six months was suspended which effectively meant their immediate release.

[16] The High Court quashed a coroner's verdict on John Mikkleson, a Hell's Angel, and ordered a new inquest. LJ Watkins said he reached the decision 'with considerable reluctance'.

Mikkleson, aged 34, from Windsor, died in police custody after being involved in a fight at Bedfont, Middlesex in July 1985. He had been hit on the head with a police truncheon, put unconscious in a police van and left on the charge-room floor of the police station before being taken to hospital. He died without regaining consciousness. The jury returned a verdict of unlawful killing in March 1986. A number of officers were suspended from duty and eight of them challenged the verdict.

Lord Justice Watkins said it was unthinkable that the jury, who

Meanwhile the Council had reduced the rates on her home from £500 to a nominal £1. The club-house was sold at a profit of £30,000. They had asked £118,900 for 125 Maidenhead Road, but the price had been reduced because of dry rot, woodworm and 'extensive damage'. The Council ordered the Angels to remove their insignia from a large sign above the front door and they complied by nailing it to the front door itself.

In the witness-box Geard denied these allegations, describing the exposure as a total fabrication, and a spokesman said, 'We never wanted trouble here and we never caused anyone any problems. We just wanted to get on with our own lives and stop other people messing us about.'[17]

On 12 January the Angels were ordered to pay Ron and Pat McSorley £23,632 damages. Mr Justice Drake ruled that the Angels had made the McSorleys' home uninhabitable.

When the Guardian Building Society called in the £58,000 loan on their club-house the Angels collected the money and redeemed the mortgage. Eventually a High Court judge granted the local Council what amounted to an order for possession.

By 1993 the National Crime Intelligence Survey reckoned that although there were only two hundred active Hell's Angels in chapters of eighteen members, compared with

cont'd

added a rider to their verdict that the killing was due to manslaughter as a result of the degree of care given to the man after he was overpowered, should have been satisfied beyond reasonable doubt that a criminal offence had been committed. A new inquest was ordered before a different coroner and jury. *The Times*, 19 December 1986.

[17] *Today*, 21 November 1986.

several thousand Outlaw Bikers, nevertheless the two hundred had, it was believed, been responsible for more killings and woundings in the previous year than all of the other organized crime groups in the country put together. Over the years during which it had been believed that they were a spent force, the Angels instead had become a financially strong, self-contained unit with strong legal representation who had sued more newspapers and magazines than any other group. The NCIS members regarded the Angels as major traffickers in amphetamines, and had moved into credit-card frauds with international links to white-collar crime. They were regarded as an organized crime unit in its purest form.

Perhaps it is because we have been made more aware of it by the press, but crimes have seemed to become more violent. People are not merely robbed but are badly beaten at the same time. Take the example of a jewellery dealer and his wife who were tortured by a gang who lashed her hands together with metal strips before kicking, punching and threatening them to make him reveal the combination of his safe.[18]

In 1992 ex-paratrooper John Calton, who had already served three years for robbery, now turned to kidnap and extortion. He told his victims he was wired as a human bomb and asked one mother which of her children she would choose to die. Another family was invited to nominate which child should be drugged and locked in the boot of a car. Calton's robberies were another in the series of kidnapping by gangs up and down the country in order to extract money from supermarket managers and those with access to large amounts of their employers' money. All in all

[18] *Evening Standard*, 20 October 1992.

he pocketed some £96,000, but Calton's run came to an end when one of his associates tried to sell the radio from a stolen getaway car. His girlfriend also went to the police after finding three guns hidden in her kitchen. Calton received a sentence of twenty-five years, and his associates Sean Wain and Robert Moore twenty apiece.

But there again, is the behaviour any worse than the 1936 case of Max Mayer, a dwarf who hanged from the bedstead the fox-terrier dog of an elderly lady whose house he was burgling and whom he also killed? Edward Robey, who prosecuted the case in the magistrates' court, wrote:

> I remember when Counsel opened the case he said to the Lancashire jury something like this: 'Look at photograph No 5'. They did so; he went on, 'That was this poor old lady's only companion; when the accused was savagely hitting her with a tyre lever her faithful fox terrier tried to defend her; he kicked it and then tied a piece of string round its neck, hung it on the bedpost where it was slowly strangled to death.'
>
> I shall never forget the faces of that jury as they stared stonily in the direction of the dock. There was absolutely no defence; but whatever it was Haslam had no chance after that opening statement.[19]

In 1989 there was a particularly nasty series of robberies, rapes and murder on and around the M25 which amounted to a reign of terror. The police believe that in the second half of the year the M25 raiders committed ninety-two offences. In one raid the jury found the men had pulled a 56-year-old man out of his car, than stripped and battered him before

[19] E. Robey, *The Jester and the Court*, p.127.

dousing him with petrol. He died of a heart attack. Three men, Johnson, Davis and Rowe, were ultimately convicted although they have continued to deny their guilt. Indeed there were certain disquieting features in the evidence. For instance all the defendants were black, although one witness who gave evidence at the trial stated that one if not two of the assailants were white and that one of them had blue eyes and blond hair. The Crown in fact had called as witnesses three young men who had also been resident at the hostel where the defendants had been living. Each of these witnesses admitted to having themselves disposed of property coming from one of the robberies; fingerprints of two of them were found on the cars used in the offences, and one of them had blond hair and blue eyes. Finally, one of the defendants had an uncrackable alibi, something prosecuting counsel acknowledged in his closing speech as 'one of the mysteries of the case'.[20]

Today the stench of drugs is everywhere. In April 1992 the police formed the National Criminal Intelligence Service at a cost of £25 million to counter career or designer crime, as it is now fashionably known. The aim has been to collect and maintain intelligence back-up and to handle informants as opposed to supergrasses. The organization had something of a major hiccough in its teething years. In 1993 an officer was arrested after a television programme was shown which gave the appearance of his batting on both sides of the fence. It cannot have helped the claim being made by members of the Service that they should not merely be information gatherers but should also be allowed to be an operative squad.

[20] See Sean Enright, 'The M25 Three' in *The Criminal Lawyer*, November 1993.

In August 1993 Albert Pacey, the former Chief Constable of Gloucestershire, took over as head of NCIS. During its existence the service had, he said, identified the top 500 criminals living in Britain and a further 2,000 who needed targeting. The majority lived in the South East. It had also developed dossiers on 450 criminal operations through informants, which had led to 330 arrests, and had provided information through its drug liaison officers which had resulted in more than 760 people being arrested worldwide. In addition, it had helped in the recovery of more than £100 million in drugs. It had examined 16,000 disclosures from banks and financial houses on suspicious transactions. One in eight led to further investigations.

NCIS sees organized crime in the United Kingdom coming from the locals dealing in drugs, robbery, fraud, forgery and car theft as their staple diet. It also foresees considerably more attention being paid to this country by foreign criminals, with the Mafia interested in drug trafficking, fraud and money laundering; the Colombian cartels with cocaine and laundering; the Triads dealing almost exclusively with the Chinese community; the Asian element again interested in laundering and heroin; West African criminals dealing in fraud and drugs; the Caribbean element perhaps not as powerful because of an overall lack of structure; and from Russia and the Ukraine, criminals trafficking in firearms. At least the white-collar branch of the Yakuza from Japan, the Sokaiya, have not moved into Britain. Their speciality is extortion. Unless a fee is paid, they will appear at a company's annual general meeting and ask embarrassing questions about the potential misuse of company funds and the sexual activities of the directors. Steps have been taken to counter this, and now in order to attend a company meeting an individual investor must purchase 100 shares in that company. In 1992 1,824 companies held their annual meetings on 26 July to defeat the Sokaiya's efforts at disruption.

Guns move around at an alarming rate of knots, and they always have done. Back in the 1920s when Inspector George Cornish of the Yard was sent to Cheshire to investigate a country-house robbery – 'Brummy' Sparkes was well in the frame but was not picked out on an identification parade – a gun was found in the shrubbery, discarded by the thieves. Cornish had extensive inquiries made and it transpired that the gun, which had been made the previous year, was Spanish and had been sold to a dealer in the Argentine.

Gone in the 1990s except for the very young, the unsophisticated and the semi-amateur, is the sawn-off shotgun. In its place is the Astra .357, a Spanish gun originally designed for police work, a Walther 7.65mm PPK or a sten gun. The silencer is now being used by the hitman, and it is feared by the police that machine guns will be the next stock in trade.

The National Criminal Intelligence Service also fears that guns from the broken-down Eastern bloc will soon be on the market at bargain prices of a few hundred rather than thousand pounds for sophisticated weapons. Even in 1993 NCIS estimated that AK 47 Kalashnikov rifles were going for £100s rather than £1,000s. Weapons on offer were not all ex-Russian army surplus. In September 1993 the *Sun* purchased an Army issue Bren gun for a modest £1,400 from a dealer named Billy outside the Globe public house in Deptford, South London. The gun may have been somewhat old-fashioned, but it was still capable of blasting through a wall at 60 yards. The *Sun* reporter had suggested that he needed it because he was having some trouble with Yardies, and the vendor was most sympathetic.

You've got us on your side if you are up against the Yardies. They are only trying to tread on our patch here and we are going to show them they can't f*** us about. We've had this trade sewn up for years and we're not letting it go.[21]

In a raid on a house in Everton on 6 February 1994, a complete arsenal – including seven sub-machine guns, three Kalashnikovs, an Armalite and an Uzi along with nearly 140 rounds of ammunition – was found under a sofa bed and in a wardrobe. It was, said the police, not an IRA stack but one bound for the drug wars.

In five years' time perhaps the threat will be from Central Eastern criminals as well as Asian ones. It seems a long road has been travelled from the days of the Odessans and Bessarabians of Whitechapel at the turn of the century; perhaps the circle has turned fully. Two Armenians, Mkritch Martirossian and Gagic Ter-Ogannisyan, were charged with the February 1993 murder in London of Rusland Outsiev, the self-styled Prime Minister of Chechenia, and his brother Nazerbeck.

Outsiev had been spending money like water during his time in London – £2,000 restaurant bills, £100 tips for waiters and a string of prostitutes visiting his flat in Marylebone. The Prime Minister, who was ostensibly in London to organise the printing of stamps and currency and was also in the market for missiles, was shot in the head, as was his younger brother. He had been invited by the Armenian KGB to desist in his negotiation for Stinger missiles but had declined.

Martirossian told the police: 'The murders were planned

---

[21] *Sun*, 24 September 1993.

by the KGB. I had no choice but to obey the KGB. They would have harmed my family'. Apparently a hit-man from Los Angeles had originally been recruited but, rather prosaically, he could not get a visa. When Martirossian was searched on his arrest he was found to have snake venom hidden in a bandage. He was to use this if he was caught. Instead, after a visit by an Armenian KGB agent to Belmarsh Prison in South East London where Martirossian was on remand, he hanged himself. Ter-Ogannisyan was sentenced to life imprisonment for murder in October 1993.

The matter did not, however, end there. Ter-Ogannisyan had married Alison Ponting, a BBC World Service producer, in 1988. On April 30, 1994, Karen Reed, Alison Ponting's sister, was shot dead on the doorstep of her home in Woking, Surrey. It is thought that Mrs Reed was shot by mistake for her sister, Alison, who had been staying with her following the imprisonment of her husband. Again a professional hit-man is thought to have been used. A fortnight previously the sisters had been warned by the police that they might be the target of an attack, when a car was abandoned after a chase and a gun was found together with a map marking the area of Woking where they lived.

In the old days it was possible to count on one hand, or certainly two, the number of famous British criminals who died with their money in the bank. Billy Hill definitely, Arthur Thompson, but not the Sabinis or Billy Kimber and not, although they are still alive, either Jack Spot or Frankie Fraser. Remember how the Train Robbers lost most of their money? I recall talking to a retired bank robber from the 1960s who said that as his share he had had over £1 million through his hands. That was real money then. Even allowing for exaggeration, he must (from the number of cases on

which I defended him) have had a very substantial amount
in his pocket tax-free. 'I pissed it out the window,' he said. It
had gone on money, clothes, cars and particularly nights at
the Astor where he said you could run through £1,500 at
one sitting.

Few put their money away and when they did so, they did
not always benefit from their investments. They had never
heard of off-shore companies, tax-free havens and the like.
Cash was King. Once I introduced a thief to a solicitor,
from whom I rented an office, to buy a house. The afternoon before completion was due to take place, the client
had still not produced the balance of the purchase price and
the solicitor rang me on the intercom. 'He's coming in at
five. You'll have to tell him I'm not going to take a cheque.'
He needn't have worried. At five-past five the intercom
buzzed again. Would I come down and help count the
money? When I arrived the client was still pulling bundles
of used notes from pockets imaginable and unimaginable.

The bank robber Jackie O'Connell put some of his into
launderettes, but he was shot on the way to stand trial for
the Bank of America safe raid and his wealth did him little
good. Another man I knew invested his money in property,
and then when charged with a jewel theft could not explain
how he had come by the initial capital to set up his
development. Perhaps pissing it out of the window was
the sensible thing to do.

Now there are, say the police, around 400 'respectable'
crime lords masterminding most of the illegal activities from
drugs to gun sales on the streets of Britain. A report in the
Sunday Telegraph said that these hardened crooks had now
developed a respectable façade. The career criminal had
usually started in drugs, dabbled with guns (almost obligatory in the drug trade) and then shifted smartly into money-

laundering using a front company, possibly haulage or possibly a retail concern, to launder the illegal money.

A senior police source is quoted as saying:

> It can take just four or five handshakes to move from being a school drugs supplier to a top-level dealer. If they are violent, unscrupulous and treacherous, they can maintain their parities.

The theory is that the higher they go up the crime ladder, with more money at their disposal, the more likely it is that they can distance themselves from the chain of events. But occasionally they get close to the action and have to prove their hands-on skills. From there, the article suggests, it is difficult for them to act alone. Trusty henchmen with whom they have previously worked are recruited, but these hoped-for allies may prove to be their undoing.

Apart from the standard use of the informer, surveillance is a tool in the police armoury, but it is expensive and some of the equipment may be used only once. The designer criminal, particularly in the drug field, and even at a very low level, is furnished with counter-surveillance equipment. These are the days of the designer criminals who live behind well-manicured hedges. According to Judge Gerald Sparrow, writing in 1969 at the tail end of the Richardson-Kray era, and rather against the burden of my thesis, they have been around for a long time:

> All the trappings are acquired, the luxurious centrally heated house either in London, or in nearby Surrey or Sussex, the young and smart companion often promoted to the status of wife, the Jaguar for him and the Mini for her. Golf as a recreation with all the gadgets. a

well-stocked cellar accompanied by a passion for vodka which appears to be a status symbol.[22]

Peter Watson writing in the *Sunday Times* supported this view in July 1973. In his experience, designer criminals commuted from the Midlands and as far away as Cornwall, where when not working, they led elegant lives amongst their unsuspecting neighbours.

Perhaps both the police and Watson and Sparrow's versions are wishful thinking. I know of few relatively successful criminals' homes which match this description. Just as likely, you will have to send your clothes to the cleaners after you leave.

What is also certain is that today's career criminals are educating their children to another life. Just as a decade or two ago, in America, 'Mob' leaders sent their sons away from the waterfronts and districts where they themselves had been brought up, and to private schools and on to universities, so now are the very top criminals doing the same for their children. 'Company Director' listed against the occupation of fathers of pupils at the great public schools can cover a multitude of crimes. The interesting question to be answered is whether this and the next generation will go straight, or will they put their education to even better use? And the answer? Surely the latter. Damon Runyan wrote, 'The battle is not always to the strongest nor the race to the swiftest, but that's the way to bet.'

[22] G. Sparrow, *Gang Warfare*, p. 112.

Bibliography

Adamson, I., *The Great Detective* (1966), London, Frederick Muller
Baker, P., *Time Out of Life* (1961), London, Heinemann
Ball, J., Chester, L. and Perrott, R., *Cops and Robbers* (1979), London, Penguin Books
Bean, J. P., *Crime in Sheffield* (1978), Sheffield, Sheffield City Libraries
———— *The Sheffield Gang Wars* (1981), Sheffield, D. & D. Publications
Bebbington, W., *Rogues go Racing* (1981), London, Good & Betts
Beltrami, J., *The Defender* (1980), Edinburgh, W. & R. Chambers Ltd
———— *A Deadly Innocence* (1989), Edinburgh, Mainstream
Beveridge, P., *Inside the CID* (1957), London, Evans Brothers
Black, D., *Triad Takeover* (1991), London, Sidgwick & Jackson
Bland, J., *True Crime Diary* (1986), London, Futura
———— *True Crime Diary, Volume 2*, (1989) London, Futura
Booth, M., *The Triads* (1990), London, Grafton
Borrell, C. and Cashinella, B., *Crime in Britain Today* (1975), London, Routledge & Kegan Paul
Boyle, J., *A Sense of Freedom* (1977), London, Pan Books
Brady, C., *Guardians of the Peace* (1974), Dublin, Gill & Macmillan
Bresler, F., *Reprieve* (1965), London, Harrap
———— *Scales of Justice* (1973), London, Weidenfeld and Nicholson
———— *The Trail of the Triads* (1980), London, Weidenfeld & Nicholson
———— *An Almanac of Murder* (1987), London, Severn House
Brillett, D., *Sussex Murders* (1990), Southampton, Ensign Publications
Campbell, D., *That Was Business, This Is Personal* (1990), London, Secker & Warburg

Bibliography

————— *The Underworld* (1994), London, BBC Books

Cannon, J., *Tough Guys Don't Cry* (1983), London, Magnus Books

Cannon, E., *Gangster's Lady* (1993), London, Yellow Brick Publishers

Capstick, J., *Given in Evidence* (1960), London, John Long

Cater, F. and Tullett, T., *The Sharp End* (1988), London, The Bodley Head

Cherrill, F., *Cherrill of the Yard* (1953), London, Harrap

Cheyney, P., *Making Crime Pay* (1944), London, Faber & Faber

Chibnall, S., *Law and Order News* (1977), London, Tavistock

Chinn, C., *Better Betting with a Decent Feller* (1991), Hemel Hempstead, Harvester Wheatsheaf

Churchill, M., *Chicago May; her story* (1928), London, Samson Lowe

Cole, P. and Pringle, P., *Can You Positively Identify This Man?* (1974), London, Andre Deutsch

Colleran, G. and O'Reagan, M., *Dark Secrets* (1985), Tralee, The Kerryman

Colquhoun, R., *Life Begins at Midnight* (1962), London, John Long

Cornish, G., *Cornish of the 'Yard'* (1935), London, The Bodley Head

Cox, B., Shirley, J. and Short, M., *The Fall of Scotland Yard* (1977), Harmondsworth, Penguin

Darbyshire, N., and Hilliard, B., *The Flying Squad* (1993), London, Headline

Darling, Lord, *Lord Darling and his famous trials* (no date), London, Hutchinson & Co

Davis, V. *Phenomena of Crime* (no date), London, John Long

Dew, W., *I Caught Crippen* (1938), London, Blackie

Dickson, J., *Murder without Conviction* (1986), London, Sphere

Divall, T., *Scallywags & Scoundrels* (1929), London, Ernest Benn

Dobson, B., *Policing in Lancashire* (1989), Blackpool, Landy Publishing

Dow, P.E., *Criminology in Literature* (1980), New York, Longman

Dunne, D. and Kerrigan, G., *Round Up the Usual Suspects* (1984), Dublin, Magill

DuRose, J., *Murder Was My Business* (1971), London, W H Allen

Eddy, P. and Walden, S., *Hunting Marco Polo* (1991), London, Bantam Press

Fabian, R., *London After Dark* (1954), London, The Naldrett Press

————— *Fabian of the Yard* (1955), London, Heirloom Modern World Library

————— *The Anatomy of Crime* (1970), London, Pelham Books

Felstead, S., *The Underworld of London* (1923), New York, E P Dutton

————— *Shades of Scotland Yard* (1950), London, John Long

Finmore, R., *Immoral Earnings* (1951), London, M.H. Publications

Flynn, S., and Yeates, P., *Smack* (1985), Dublin, Gill & Macmillan

Fordham, P., *The Robbers' Tale* (1965), London, Hodder & Stoughton

————— *Inside the Underworld* (1972), London, George Allen & Unwin

451

Fraser, F. and Morton, J., *Mad Frank* (1994), London, Little, Brown

Fry, C. with Kray, C., *Doing the Business* (1993), London, Smith Gryphon

Goodman, J., *The Burning of Evelyn Foster* (1977), London, Headline

———— and Will, I., *Underworld* (1985), London, Harrap

Greeno, E., *War on the Underworld* (1960), London, John Long

Grigg, M., *The Challenor Case* (1965), London, Penguin

Guerin, E., *Crime, The Autobiography of a Criminal* (1929), London, John Murray

Hancock, R., *Ruth Ellis* (1985), London, Weidenfeld & Nicholson

Hanson, K., *Rebels in the Streets* (1964), Englewood Cliffs, New Jersey, Prentice-Hall

Hart, E.,T., *Britain's Godfather* (1993), London, True Crime Books

Hester, S. and Eglin, P., *A Sociology of Crime* (1992), London, Routledge

Herridge, R. with Hilliard, B., *Believe No One* (1993), London, Little, Brown

Higgins, R. *In the Name of the Law* (1958), London, John Long

Hill, B., *Boss of Britain's Underworld* (1955), London, The Naldrett Press

Hinds, A., *Contempt of Court* (1966), London, The Bodley Head

Hobbs D., *Doing the Business* (1988), Oxford, Oxford University Press

Hoskins, P., *No Hiding Place* (no date), Daily Express Publications

Jennings, A., Lashmar, P. and Simson, V., *Scotland Yard's Cocaine Connection* (1990), London, Jonathan Cape

Johnston, M., *Around the Banks of Pimlico* (1985), Dublin, Attic

Jones, E., *The Last Two to Hang* (1966), London, Macmillan

Kelland, G., *Crime in London* (1986), London, The Bodley Head

Kennedy, L., *A Presumption of Innocence* (1976), London, Gollancz

Knight, R., *Black Knight* (1990), London, Century

Knox, B., *Court of Murder* (1968), London, John Long

Kray, C., *Me and My Brothers* (1988), London, Grafton

Kray, Reggie, *Born Fighter* (1991), London, Arrow

———— *Villains We Have Known* (1993), Leeds, N.K. Publications

Kray, Ronnie, *My Story* (1992), London, Sidgwick & Jackson

Kray, R. and Kray, R., *Our Story* (1988), London, Pan Books

Lambrianou, T., *Inside the Firm* (1991), London, Smith Gryphon

Laurie, P., *Scotland Yard* (1970), London, The Bodley Head

Leach, J., *Sods I Have Cut on the Turf* (1961), London, Gollancz

Leeson, B., *Lost London* (1934), London, Stanley Paul & Co.

Leigh, D., *Howard Marks* (1988), London, Unwin Paperbacks

Lewis, D. and Hughman, P., *Most Unnatural* (1971), London, Penguin Books

Lucas, N., *Britain's Gangland* (1969), London, Pan Books

Mack, J.A., *The Crime Industry* (1975), Farnborough, Saxon House

Mandelkau, J., *Buttons – the Making of a President* (1971), London, Sphere

Mark, R., *In the Office of Constable* (1978), London, Collins

Bibliography

Marshall, J., *The True Story of the Ollie Murder* (1988), Lewes, Seagull Books

McConnell, B., *The Evil Firm* (1969), London, Mayflower

Meehan, P., *Innocent Villain* (1978), London, Pan Books

Merrilees, W., *The Short Arm of the Law* (1966), London, Long

Millen, E., *Specialist in Crime* (1972), London, George G. Harrap & Co.

Morris, T., *Crime and Criminal Justice Since 1945* (1989), Oxford, Basil Blackwell

Morton, J., *Gangland* (1992), London, Little, Brown

———— *Bent Coppers* (1993), London, Little, Brown

Murphy, R., *Smash and Grab* (1993), London, Faber & Faber

Napley, D., *Not Without Prejudice* (1982), London, Harrap

Narborough, F., *Murder on My Mind* (1959), London, Alan Wingate

Nott-Bower, W., *Fifty-two Years a Policeman* (1926), London, E. Arnold

Parker, R., *Rough Justice* (1981), London, Sphere

Patrick, J., *A Glasgow Gang Observed* (1973), London, Eyre Methuen

Payne, L., *The Brotherhood* (1973), London, Michael Joseph

Pearson, J., *The Profession of Violence* (1985), London, Grafton

Phelan, J., *The Underworld* (1953), London, George G. Harrap & Co.

Raymond, D., *The Hidden Files* (1992), London, Little, Brown

Read, L. and Morton, J., *Nipper* (1991), London, Macdonald

Read, P., *The Train Robbers* (1978), London, W. H. Allen

Richardson, C., *My Manor* (1991), London, Sidgwick & Jackson

Robey, E., *The Jester and the Court* (1976), London, William Kimber

Rowland, J., *Murder Revisited* (1961), London, John Long

Sabbag, R., *Snowblind* (1978), London, Picador

Samuels, R., *East End Underworld* (1981), London, Routledge & Kegan Paul

Samuels, S. with Davis, L., *Among the Soho Sinners* (1970), London, Robert Hale

Scarne, J., *Scarne's Complete Guide to Gambling* (1961), New York, Simon & Schuster

Shew, E. S., *A Companion to Murder* (1961), New York, Alfred Knopf

———— *A Second Companion to Murder* (1962), New York, Alfred Knopf

Short, M., *Lundy* (1991), London, Grafton

Sifakis, C., *The Encyclopaedia of American Crime* (1982), New York, Facts on File

Sillitoe, P., *Cloak Without Dagger* (1956), London, Pan Books

Simpson, A. W. B., *In the Highest Degree Odious* (1992), Oxford, Oxford University Press

Skelton D. and Brownlie, L., *Frightener* (1992), Edinburgh, Mainstream Publishing

Slipper, J., *Slipper of the Yard* (1981), London, Sidgwick & Jackson

Smith, P. G., *The Crime Explosion* (1970), London, Macdonald

Smithies, E., *Crime in Wartime* (1982), London, George Allen & Unwin

Sparks, R., *Burglar to the Nobility* (1961), London, Arthur Barker

Sparrow, G., *Gang Warfare* (1988), London, Feature Books

Stockman, R., *The Hangman's Diary* (1993), London, Headline

Taylor, K., *The Poisoned Tree* (1990), London, Sidgwick & Jackson

Taylor, L., *In the Underworld* (1985), London, Unwin Paperbacks

Taylor, R., *Murders of Old Sussex* (1991), Newbury, Countryside Books

Thomas, D. with Grant, R., *Seek Out the Guilty* (1969), London, John Long

Thompson, H. S., *Hell's Angels* (1966), New York, Random House

Thurlow, D., *The Essex Triangle* (1990), London, Robert Hale

Tietjen, A., *Soho* (1956), London, Allan Wingate

Tullett, T., *Murder Squad* (1981), London, Triad Grafton

Van Cise, P. S., *Fighting the Underworld* (1936), London, Eyre & Spottiswoode

Walsh, D. and Poole, A., *A Dictionary of Criminology* (1983), London, Routledge & Keegan Paul

Ward, H., *Buller* (1974), London, Hodder & Stoughton

Watts, M., *The Men In My Life* (1960), London, Christopher Johnson

Webb, D., *Deadline for Crime* (1955), London, Muller

————— *Line Up for Crime* (1956), London, Muller

Wensley, F., *Detective Days* (1931), London, Cassell & Co.

Whittington-Egan, R., *Liverpool Roundabout*

Wickstead, B., *Gangbuster* (1985), London, Futura

Wighton, C., *Dope International* (1960), London, Muller

Wilkinson, L., *Behind the Face of Crime* (1967), London, Muller

Williams, J., *Bloody Valentine*, (1994) London, Harper Collins

Woffinden, B., *Miscarriages of Justice* (1987), London, Hodder & Stoughton

Index

Index

Index